IN THE FOOTSTEPS OF PHOEBE

Dear Christine,

I thank God for you — for your faith and your friendship.

with love in Him,

Cheryl

Hebrews 12:2

IN THE FOOTSTEPS OF PHOEBE

A COMPLETE HISTORY OF THE DEACONESS MOVEMENT IN THE LUTHERAN CHURCH—MISSOURI SYNOD

CHERYL D. NAUMANN

Peer Reviewed

In loving memory of

Deaconess Clara Else Flora Strehlow:

a humble servant of the Lord,

our mentor and encourager

Peer Reviewed

Published by Concordia Publishing House

3558 S. Jefferson Ave., St. Louis, MO 63118–3968

1–800–325–3040 • www. cph.org

Manufactured in the United States of America

1 2 3 4 5 6 7 8 9 10   18 17 16 15 14 13 12 11 10 09

CONTENTS

THE DEACONESS

No regal robe of state she wears
    In service of her Lord the King;
Clad in the simplest garb, she bears
    His grace unto the suffering.

'Tis hers the troubled mind to calm,
    The fever-parched lip to cool,
Apply the mild assuasive balm
    To wounded flesh or sin-sick soul.

Self finds no room within her breast,
    Her every thought, another's needs;
With tender touch she soothes to rest,
    Whilst softly unto Heaven she pleads.

Mercy and peace upon her smile.
    The pitying Lord her prayer attends;
Hers is a holy joy, the while
    His blessing on her path descends.

Though poor of earth, a countless store
    Of wealth is hers, through Christ's own blood;
His messenger, she asks no more
    Than faithfully to serve her Lord.

Mary Weldon[1]

---

[1] "The Deaconess," *The Lutheran Deaconess* 19, no.2 (April 1942): 2.

FOREWORD

The office of deaconess is an ancient and honorable one in the Christian Church. Its roots go back to apostolic days. In Romans 16:1, the apostle Paul mentions Phoebe, a deaconess of the church at Cenchrea, a Greek city close to Corinth. Paul writes that Phoebe has been a great help to many, including himself. She was most likely the person chosen to carry the great apostle's letter to the church at Rome. Paul instructs the church at Rome to receive Phoebe "in the Lord and in a way worthy of the saints" and to give her whatever she needed to carry out her important work.

Lutheran deaconess history has its roots in the *innere mission* movement in Germany in the middle of the nineteenth century. It was a response to the need for dedicated Christian women to bring aid to the widows, orphans, the sick, and the disadvantaged in the days of the industrial revolution. This deaconess ministry was soon transplanted to the United States in the early days of what we today call The Lutheran Church—Missouri Synod.

Deaconess Naumann tells the story of the early days of deaconess ministry in North America; its connection with Missouri Synod congregations and Lutheran Hospital in Fort Wayne, Indiana; the deaconess motherhouse; Bethesda (in Watertown, Wisconsin); and other institutions. She traces the history of the Lutheran Deaconess Association and its leaders, the training of deaconesses at Valparaiso University, and the building of Deaconess Hall. The author then relates the involvement of deaconesses in the days of the doctrinal controversy in the LCMS in the 1960s and 1970s.

The author describes the Synod's relationship with the deaconess movement from the days when deaconesses were trained by a separate, independent association to the present when the LCMS has established an official deaconess training program in its schools and recognizes deaconesses as commissioned ministers of the Church. *In the Footsteps of Phoebe* tells the stirring story of how a small group of deaconesses led the LCMS to a closer relationship with the office and the dedicated women whose historic motto is "Let us not be weary in well doing."

This writer has had the privilege of knowing and working with many of these dedicated servants of the Lord and His Church. The Lutheran deaconess is an office that has been a blessing to our Synod over the years.

However, it is a resource that many have not yet come to appreciate. Whether functioning as a nurse, a social worker, a worker in the mission fields, or as a parish assistant to a pastor in a congregation, the Lutheran deaconess is a great resource for the promotion of the Gospel of our Lord Jesus Christ.

The author of this volume, Deaconess Cheryl D. Naumann, is herself an experienced and distinguished deaconess. She has served as deaconess in many roles and also as author and editor of several publications. She is a founding member of the Concordia Deaconess Conference. Her book includes much original material that is not available elsewhere. It is well documented with a rich bibliography. It is a literary work that combines interesting reading with important church history and first-class scholarship.

It is my prayer that this volume will bring about an increased realization of the potential of women to serve our Lord and His Church, even as did Phoebe in the days of the apostle Paul.

Paul A. Zimmerman

ABBREVIATIONS

Deac.	The historical (anglicized) abbreviation for Deaconess. The official stylebook of the LCMS (updated October 2007) states: "Always spell out and capitalize *deaconess* when used as a title before a person's name."
ALC	American Lutheran Church
ALCh	Associated Lutheran Charities
BHE	LCMS Board for Higher Education
BOD	LCMS Board of Directors
CDC	Concordia Deaconess Conference
CDN	Cheryl D. Naumann
CHI	Concordia Historical Institute
CPH	Concordia Publishing House
CTCR	Commission on Theology and Church Relations
CS	Concordia Seminary, St. Louis
CTS	Concordia Theological Seminary, Fort Wayne
CUC	Concordia University Chicago (was CURF)
CURF	Concordia University, River Forest
ELCA	Evangelical Lutheran Church in America
ELS	Evangelical Lutheran Synod
LCA	Lutheran Church in America
LCMS	The Lutheran Church—Missouri Synod
LDA	Lutheran Deaconess Association
LDC	Lutheran Deaconess Conference
LUA	Lutheran University Association
LWML	Lutheran Women's Missionary League
MIP	*Missouri in Perspective*
priv. col.	private collection
RF	River Forest (Illinois)
TALC	The American Lutheran Church
TLD	*The Lutheran Deaconess*
Valpo or VU	Valparaiso University

PART ONE

60 YEARS OF ASSOCIATION: 1919–1979

God used a small group of deaconesses in The Lutheran Church—Missouri Synod for a task that church leaders had repeatedly attempted to accomplish throughout the Synod's history: establishment of a deaconess training program within the LCMS.

Prior to 1979, only the Lutheran Deaconess Association, a freestanding organization, educated deaconesses for service within LCMS parishes and institutions.

Part I will explain when the Missouri Synod first recognized a need for deaconesses; what led to the formation of the LDA; the pioneer training initiated, delivered, and molded throughout the sixty years from 1919 to 1979; the definition and role of a Lutheran deaconess that developed; and why it was necessary for the LCMS to establish a synodical deaconess training program.

CHAPTER 1

GETTING STARTED

When the LCMS[1] first organized in Chicago in 1847, many of its members knew about the ministry of deaconesses in Germany and other parts of the world. But issues of identity and doctrine prevented the Synod from seriously considering a deaconess ministry for several decades.

Doctrine was important to the LCMS. The Saxons immigrated to North America seeking freedom to teach the Bible in its truth and purity and to administer the Sacraments according to Christ's institution, as expounded by the Lutheran Confessions. Accordingly, new ideas always prompted doctrinal discussions in the Synod. The existence of contemporary deaconess organizations in Europe, and later in North America, challenged the doctrine of ministry in the developing Synod. Was it possible to establish a female diaconate in the new world while retaining pure doctrine and churchly practice?

THE DIACONATE IN GERMAN LUTHERANISM

The *innere Mission* movement inspired the concept of the Lutheran deaconess in mid-nineteenth-century Germany. The industrial revolution brought social changes to Germany: population migration, the growth of cities, emergence of the industrial proletariat, prejudice, and deplorable living conditions for many among the working class. Private agencies and individuals attempted to relieve the population's physical, moral, and spiritual wretchedness, but the people needed more help.

On September 22, 1848, Johann Heinrich Wichern (1808–81) challenged all Protestants in Germany to adopt the work of the *innere Mission*.[2] Wichern defined the *innere Mission* as

> the *collective* and *not isolated* labor of love which springs from faith in Christ, and which seeks to bring about the internal and external renewal of the

---

[1] The original name for the Synod was *Die Deutsche Evangelisch-Lutherische Synode von Missouri, Ohio und andern Staaten* (The German Evangelical Lutheran Synod of Missouri, Ohio and Other States). In 1919 *Deutsche* (German) was dropped from the name. In 1947 the Synod adopted The Lutheran Church—Missouri Synod as its official title.

[2] Wichern spoke at the first *Kirchentag* of the Evangelical churches in Germany, held at the Castle Church in Wittenberg, September 21–23, 1848.

masses within Christendom who have fallen under the dominion of those evils which result directly and indirectly from sin, and who are not reached, as for their spiritual renewal they ought to be, by the established official organs of the Church. It does not overlook any external or internal need, the relief of which can be made an object of Christian love.[3]

Wichern's efforts caused the German Evangelical Church to organize the Central Committee for the Inner Mission at Berlin (January 1849). Many similar associations formed in every part of Germany, Scandinavia, and later in North America.[4] As the *innere Mission* movement grew, Pietism and Revivalism sometimes influenced it. Social action intertwined with evangelism and movement activists viewed faith as expressing itself in love toward the whole society.

Wichern began his own *innere Mission* work in 1833 by opening *Das Rauhe Haus*, a home for vagrant boys in Hamburg, Germany. Unable to place the boys with foster families, he divided them into twelve-member family groupings, each with its own housefather, or *Bruder*, who took responsibility for rehabilitating the boys. Wichern trained the housefathers for their work and founded a *Bruderhaus* to prepare men for a broad scope of Christian service. Wichern later called these men "deacons." The movement spread, and a male diaconate was born.

While Wichern concentrated on educating men for God's service, Pastor Theodore Fliedner (1800–64) played a major role in reviving the New Testament office of deaconess for Protestant women. Fliedner served a small Evangelical congregation in Kaiserswerth, Germany, but traveled far and wide to collect funds for his poverty-stricken parish. During his tours throughout England and Holland, he observed charitable institutions where women labored in love for the poor, downtrodden, and sick of the community. Mennonite deaconesses in Holland particularly impressed Fliedner. He returned to Germany full of ideas for attacking social problems with the assistance of trained female workers.

Fliedner first converted a small summerhouse on his property into a halfway home for freed female convicts. In 1836, with the help of his first wife, Friederika Muenster, he opened a hospital and a deaconess

---

[3] J. F. Ohl, *The Inner Mission* (Philadelphia: United Lutheran Publication House, 1911), 13–14. See also David Crowner and Gerald Christianson, ed. and trans., "Wichern's Explanation, Address, and Speech at the Wittenberg Kirchentag, 1848," in *The Spirituality of the German Awakening: Texts by August Tholuck, Theodor Fliedner, Johann Hinrich Wichern, and Friedrich von Bodelschwingh* (Mahwah, NJ: Paulist Press, 2003), 265–95.
[4] Ohl, *Inner Mission*, 11–12; Crowner and Christianson, "Inner Mission of the German Evangelical Church," 296–315.

motherhouse. Fliedner's charitable work quickly grew to include a Christian kindergarten, an orphanage, a girls' high school, a home for mentally ill female Protestants, a home for invalid or lonely women, a school for teachers, and a training school for deaconesses. Whenever possible, the Kaiserswerth-based Institution of Protestant Deaconesses also purchased and staffed hospitals, homes, orphanages, and schools in other parts of Germany and around the world. By the time Fliedner died in 1864, the Kaiserswerth motherhouse boasted four hundred twenty-five deaconesses and one hundred outstations on four continents. The number of deaconess motherhouses had increased to thirty-two, with a total enrollment of sixteen hundred deaconesses.[5]

TRANSPLANTED TO NORTH AMERICA

In 1846, William Alfred Passavant (1821–94), the pastor of First Lutheran Church in Pittsburgh, Pennsylvania, visited Kaiserswerth. Study of the deaconess motherhouse, the training given to deaconesses, and their work convinced Passavant that American churches should establish the same type of female diaconate. The Kaiserswerth deaconesses were primarily nurses. Passavant wanted to open a hospital in Pittsburgh, so he begged Fliedner to send some deaconess nurses to him. In July 1849, Fliedner personally delivered four young deaconesses to Passavant: Sisters Elizabeth Hupperts (1822–95), Paulina Ludewig (b. 1827), Luise Hinrichsen (b. 1820), and Maria Elizabeth Hess (1825–96).[6]

Before the four women arrived, Passavant used several pages in the April 1848 issue of *The Missionary* to promote the proposed diaconate and to recruit additional "ladies of suitable character and qualifications, who wish to devote themselves to the work of mercy and charity."[7] He wrote:

> Who . . . can yet doubt that this highly interesting institution, this Bethesda for bodies and souls, which provides with the water of life the five fields of human infirmity and misery, the field of the sick, of the

---

[5] C. Golder, *History of the Deaconess Movement* (Cincinnati: Jennings & Pye, 1903), 63; Frederick S. Weiser, *Love's Response* (Philadelphia: Board of Publication of the United Lutheran Church in America, 1962), 41.

[6] Fliedner often accompanied deaconesses to their assignments at outstations. He reported on his travels and various activities in a periodical entitled *Friend of the Poor and Sick*.

[7] Passavant began publishing *The Missionary* in Pittsburgh in January 1848 for the purpose of promoting and reporting on "the numerous and diversified interests of the church and the world . . . under the general heads of inner, home, and foreign missions." G. H. Gerberding, *The Life and Letters of W. A. Passavant, D.D.* (Greenville, PA: Young Lutheran Co., 1906), 180, 195.

poor, of the ignorant, of parentless children, and of the guilty, should have refreshed and brought from death to life many perishing souls? Who will not hope, that the humble commencement about to be made in this country, may be the beginning of a new era in the development of Evangelical life and Protestant charity? And especially, after … these deaconesses have been the instruments of seeking that which was lost, of bringing back that which was driven away, of binding up that which was broken, of strengthening that which was sick, who can doubt that it will, in particular, open a comparatively new field of usefulness and blessed occupation to female Christians in America?[8]

Passavant opened the first Protestant hospital in the United States; incorporated The Institution of Protestant Deaconesses in the state of Pennsylvania; and after a period of probationary training consecrated a member of his congregation, Catharina Louisa Marthens (1828–99), as the first American deaconess. He aspired to train Christian deaconesses for hospitals, asylums, and congregations all over the United States, but his operation and plant did not grow at the same rate that Fliedner's did in Germany. Although there was a great need for philanthropic work, the American community did not immediately embrace the transplanted deaconess motherhouse organization with its "sisters" wearing uniforms that smacked of Catholicism. Passavant's passionate appeals for more workers fell on deaf ears. In the first sixteen years (1850–66), only nineteen young ladies considered deaconess service. Only ten of the nineteen were eventually consecrated to the diaconate.[9]

Passavant experienced another bitter disappointment. Of the four deaconesses who came from Germany, only Sister Elizabeth Hupperts stayed with the motherhouse.[10] In July 1852, three years after their arrival, Sister Luise Hinrichsen resigned her post to marry Mr. Weidlich, a male nurse at the hospital. Less than six months later, on January 1, 1853, Sisters Paulina Ludewig and Maria Elizabeth Hess resigned from the diaconate for a very different reason.[11]

---

[8] Gerberding, *Life and Letters of W. A. Passavant*, 181.

[9] Herman L. Fritschel, *A Story of One Hundred Years of Deaconess Service by The Institution of Protestant Deaconesses Pennsylvania, and The Lutheran Diaconate Motherhouse at Milwaukee, Wisconsin 1849–1949* (Milwaukee, WI: Lutheran Deaconess Motherhouse, 1949), 27.

[10] Hupperts was buried on the grounds of Passavant's Orphan's Home and Farm School in Zelienople, Pa., where her tombstone can still be visited. Its beautiful inscription reads: "Here rests in Christ, Sister Elizabeth Hupperts, a Deaconess, September 8, 1822—October 27, 1895. She came with Fliedner to America and was for fifty-two years the comforter of the sick and a mother to the orphaned. She has done what she could. Mark 14:8."

[11] Resignation dates are taken from *Pioneers of God's Future: A directory of deaconesses of the Evangelical Lutheran Church in America who have served in the United States and Canada 1848–1991,*

THE LEGACY OF ELIZABETH HESS[12]

Elizabeth Hess rejoiced to perform service for her Savior. When she and three other deaconesses arrived in Pittsburgh, they declined an invitation to rest from the month-long journey. Instead, they went to live in the hospital, immediately ready for work. As they labored in new surroundings and hot temperatures (between 96 and 100 degrees), each of them contracted cholera. Miraculously, after several days of illness, each quickly and completely recovered. The women remained courageous and dedicated to their calling, thanking God that He permitted them to nurse black patients and those with cholera who had been forbidden admission to other hospitals.[13]

While employed at the hospital, Sister Elizabeth and the other deaconesses worshiped at Pastor Passavant's congregation.[14] Passavant had attended Gettysburg Seminary, where he came under the influence of Samuel Schmucker (1799–73). Passavant embraced the "New Measure Movement," with its emphasis on emotionalism and revivalist worship practices.[15] Sister Elizabeth commented in her autobiographical notes:

> Dr. Passavant was not only the director of the institution, but also the pastor of the local English Lutheran church. His congregation, however, was more Reformed than Lutheran. This fact became very noticeable when the Lord's Supper was celebrated. It was not only administered according to the Reformed ritual, but after the Sacrament had been administered to the members of the congregation, the invitation was sent out most urgently to nonmembers and strangers to receive the Sacrament. Many accepted the invitation.
>
> This practice did not offend me. On the contrary, I thought it to be great and saw no wrong in it. The differences between the Reformed and

---

comp. Frederick S. Weiser (Gladwyne, PA: Lutheran Deaconess Community, 1991), 33, 34, 45.

[12] It was common practice in German households to drop the first name given at Baptism, particularly if several members of the family held the same name.

[13] Theodore Fliedner, *Journey of Emigrants to North America for the Emigration of Four Deaconesses and for the Establishment of a Deaconess Motherhouse in Pittsburgh in Pennsylvania, in June 1849*, trans. Bertha Mueller (from the private collection of Frederick S. Weiser, New Oxford, PA), 36, 43.

[14] Although he is best remembered for founding institutions for the sick, disabled, and orphaned, Passavant was also a leading churchman. In January 1845, he was instrumental in organizing the Pittsburgh Synod, which he later served as president for six years and missionary superintendent for eight years. Ernest G. Heissenbuttel and Roy H. Johnson, *Pittsburgh Synod History: Its Auxiliaries and Institutions 1845–1962* (Warren, OH: Pittsburgh Synod of the United Lutheran Church, 1963), 139.

[15] Heissenbuttel and Johnson, *Pittsburgh Synod History*, 33.

Lutheran doctrines were immaterial to me at that time. The matter that counted with me was a living and active Christian life. The errors I had not detected, and they did not disturb me. 'Tis true, I at times received a letter from a youthful friend who was to become my husband, who had withdrawn from the Reformed (*unierte*) Church and had joined the Lutheran Church, who directed my attention to the errors of the Reformed Church and the differences [between the Lutheran and Reformed doctrines], but I could not share his views, and when he stressed the danger of holding the Reformed views, I considered his views exaggerated.[16]

Sometime in 1852, two visitors caused Sister Elizabeth to think again about church practice and doctrine.

A young girl named Franziska Harder, a member of the Lutheran congregation in Fort Wayne, Ind., paid us a visit with a view to entering the Deaconess Institute. As her escort she brought with her a Mrs. Horst, who had served five years as a deaconess in Kaiserswerth and Berlin. Great was our joy at seeing her again. We endeavored to strengthen Miss Harder in her desire to become a deaconess, and she was favorably impressed. However, after having attended the open Communion service on the following Sunday evening, her intention to remain was a thing of the past. On that very evening she vowed to return to Fort Wayne the next day, and that is what she did.

This set me a-thinking. I became restless. Frequent consultations with Dr. Passavant had no effect. Finally I arrived at the conviction to withdraw, and, after a service of four years, was peacefully dismissed from the deaconess organization together with another sister.[17]

Franziska Harder was a member of St. Paul's Evangelical Lutheran Church in Fort Wayne.[18] Mrs. Doris Horst had also been a member of St. Paul's, initially under her maiden name, Doris Haumming.[19] The pastor at St. Paul's was Rev. Wilhelm Sihler (1801–85), an uncompromising Lutheran

---

16 Elizabeth Hess Wambsganss, "Autobiographical Notes," trans. Fred Wambsganss, *Concordia Historical Institute Quarterly*, 28. 1 (Spring 1955): 42–43.
17 Wambsganss, "Autobiographical Notes," 43.
18 See *Confitienregister* (Communion Register), St. Paul's Evangelical Lutheran Church Records, vol. 1–2, 1849–53, 1126 S. Barr St., Fort Wayne, IN.
19 *Confitienregister* (Communion Register), St. Paul's Evangelical Lutheran Church Records, vol. 1, 1846–49. Page 147 records the January 18, 1849, marriage of Doris Haumming to Matthias Horst. No record explains why Doris Haumming moved from Germany to Indiana, but it is interesting to note that one of Fliedner's former Kaiserswerth deaconesses was a communicant member of St. Paul's at the time that the congregation became a charter member of the LCMS.

who reprimanded those who sympathized with Revivalism, Unionism, or Methodism. Before resigning from the Ohio Synod in 1845, Sihler had attempted and failed to remove the unionistic formula "Christ says, 'This is My body,' " from the liturgy of that synod. Sihler introduced the practice of personal announcement for Holy Communion and had always scrupulously given his parishioners thorough instruction about the Lord's Supper and other distinctive Lutheran doctrines.[20] No wonder Franziska Harder knew her doctrine concerning the Lord's Supper and considered the Pittsburgh practice unacceptable.

Paulina Ludewig was the other "sister" to whom Elizabeth Hess referred as "dismissed from the deaconess organization" with her. The two women moved to Cincinnati, Ohio, where they stayed with Pastor Theodore August Julian Wichmann (1826–94) from January 1853 until spring of that same year. When Elizabeth received news that her sister and brother-in-law had arrived from Germany and were in Fort Wayne, she and Paulina traveled to Indiana to see them there.[21]

The women stayed in Fort Wayne and soon attended St. Paul's Lutheran Church, where they gained a clearer understanding of Lutheran doctrine as derived from Holy Scripture and as explained in the Lutheran Confessions. Elizabeth expressed her thankfulness to God: "I must say that Pastor Theodore Wichmann, Dr. Sihler, and other pastors were most convincing preachers. My heart was filled with gratitude toward God for having led me into the Missouri Synod Lutheran Church, in which the Word of God is preached in its truth and purity and in which the Sacraments are administered according to Christ's institution."[22]

Indiana brought another blessing for Elizabeth in the form of a renewed acquaintance with Johannes Philipp Wambsganss (1823–1901), the young man from her hometown of Nussdorf who had written letters to her in Pittsburgh to convince her of the errors of Reformed theology. Wambsganss had immigrated a year after Elizabeth, and from 1850 to 1853 attended the Missouri Synod's "practical" seminary, which was located on property one mile east of Fort Wayne. Ordained in March 1853, he served congregations in Corunna and Fairfield Center, Indiana, approximately thirty miles north of Fort Wayne.[23]

---

[20] Walter A. Baepler, *A Century of Grace* (St. Louis: Concordia, 1947), 78–82.

[21] Wambsganss, "Autobiographical Notes," 43–44.

[22] *Ibid.*, 44.

[23] "Biographical Record for Johannes Philipp Wambsganss Sr." (St. Louis, CHI, January 29, 2004).

The two former deaconesses apparently found their future spouses at about the same time. The archives at St. Paul's show that two wedding ceremonies took place on June 19, 1853. The first recorded marriage was that of Paulina Ludewig to Pastor Friedrich Eppling, and the second, the marriage of Elisabeth Hess to Pastor Joh. Phil. Wambsganss. Seminary professor Pastor Friedrich August Crämer (1812–91) performed the ceremony for Hess and Wambsganss, and their wedding celebration was held at Pastor Sihler's parsonage.[24]

One could say that Pastor and Mrs. Wambsganss had close connections with individuals who later become key figures for the future of the LCMS. But more important, this confessional Lutheran couple spent their years laboring faithfully in the Lord's vineyard and raising devout children, all of whom became LCMS teachers and pastors or the wives of pastors.[25] Sixty-six years later, one of their pastor sons would become the first president of the Lutheran Deaconess Association.

More Deaconesses from Germany

Back in Bavaria, Pastor Johan Konrad Wilhelm Loehe (1808–1872) inaugurated Lutheran Societies of the Female Diaconate in Neuendettelsau in the 1840s to train deaconesses for professional service in Christian charity. This method of training deaconesses through societies disappointed Loehe, so in 1854 he founded a deaconess motherhouse based on Fliedner's model. He continued to mold the diaconate in light of his own confessional Lutheran understanding, requiring deaconesses to offer voluntary vows of chastity, obedience, peacefulness, and poverty. The deaconesses worshiped frequently, learned to make paraments, and worked in institutions for the sick and diseased, mentally challenged, aged, poor, delinquent, and mentally ill.[26]

Explaining the basic organization of the diaconate, Loehe wrote in 1858:

---

[24] Sihler's parsonage once stood where Heritage Hall now stands. St. Paul's Evangelical Lutheran Church Records, vol. 12, 1837–56, #9. For more information about Paulina Ludewig, see Fritschel, *Story of One Hundred Years of Deaconess Service*, 23; Wambsganss, "Autobiographical Notes," 45.

[25] Fred Wambsganss Sr., "Five Decades of Pastoral Activity," *Concordia Historical Institute Quarterly*, 30, no. 4 (Winter 1958): 146. Elizabeth and her husband, Philipp Wambsganss Sr., are buried in the cemetery of Immanuel Lutheran Church, Decatur, Indiana.

[26] See Wilhelm Loehe, *Wilhelm Loehe, Gessammelte Werke, Herausgegeben im Auftrage der Gesellschaft fur Innere und Ausere Mission im Sinne der lutherischen Kirche, IV*, ed. Klaus Ganzert, trans. Holger Sonntag (Neuendettelsau: Freimund, 1954).

We have accommodated ourselves . . . to give our deaconesses the title "sister". We have united the deaconesses who work in the same place or in the same region into chapters . . . All deaconesses are to recognize their motherhouse as their home from which they leave and to which they may return in case of illness and feebleness, from which they obtain all their needs, like children from parents, but for which they also care with deep interest. Accordingly, the motherhouse receives the salaries of all deaconesses, gives to all of them the same allowance and furnishes them all with the necessary clothing.[27]

In the decade before he began training deaconesses, Loehe's concern for the plight of German Lutherans in North America moved him to found a missionary institute to train pastors for the New World. Later, he established a practical seminary in Fort Wayne, Indiana, with Dr. Wilhelm Sihler as the first professor. Loehe also set up the Lutheran Franconian colonies in Michigan, collected and distributed large amounts of money for American mission work, and encouraged his missionaries to take an active role in organizing a confessional Lutheran synod.[28]

Many of Loehe's men helped to form The German Evangelical Lutheran Synod of Missouri, Ohio and Other States in 1847, but, sadly, a doctrinal dispute concerning the church and ministry arose between him and the new synod. In 1851, synodical president Friedrich Conrad Dietrich Wyneken (1810–76) and seminary professor Carl Ferdinand Wilhelm Walther (1811–87) journeyed to Neuendettelsau to visit Loehe in an attempt to eliminate the misgivings of their benefactor. Reconciliation seemed hopeful, but in 1853, after a subsequent visit by Johannes Andreas August Grabau (1804–79) and Heinrich Karl Georg von Rohr (1797–1874), Loehe decided to part ways with the Lutherans of "Missouri, Ohio, and Other States." Soon thereafter, in August 1854, four of Loehe's men organized The Evangelical Lutheran Synod of Iowa and Other States. The "Missouri" and "Iowa" church bodies disagreed on a number of issues. They met in colloquy in 1867 to resolve differences, but the attempt failed. In 1882, the possibility of reconciliation came to an end when Iowa charged Missouri with false doctrine.[29]

In 1857 and 1858, five of Loehe's deaconesses arrived in Dubuque, Iowa, to serve as parish deaconesses and housemothers at Wartburg Theological Seminary (Iowa Synod). By 1860 all five of the women had

---

[27] Wilhelm Loehe, *Schatzhauser der Kirche*, ed. Theodor Scober (Neuendettelsau, 1961), 22–23. For more on Loehe's important work, see Baepler, *Century of Grace*, 73–74, 143–48.
[28] Baepler, *Century of Grace*, 73–74.
[29] *Ibid.*, 143–48.

married. In 1868, Pastor Johannes Dörfler (1826–86) requested the assistance of deaconesses to establish a motherhouse for the Iowa Synod in Toledo, Ohio. Loehe promised to send two deaconesses and the equivalent of $2,500 when all was ready, but he died before completing formal arrangements.[30]

One of Loehe's Neuendettelsau deaconesses did become a member of the Missouri Synod through unusual circumstances. Around 1866, Johanna Margaretha Kamm (1844–1915) immigrated to the United States, where she expected to marry a man that Loehe had sent to the United States the previous year. When Deaconess Kamm arrived, her betrothed had already married another woman. Pastor F. A. Crämer secured a job for her at the Lutheran Orphans Home in Des Peres, Missouri, and also introduced her to Gustav Adolf Barth (1844–1917), a German glass painter who became a Missouri Synod pastor in 1869. The couple married and evidently knew C. F. W. Walther well. Walther wrote a letter of comfort to Pastor Barth, comparing him to Job, when the couple's three sons and one daughter died within a week.[31] Similar to Job and his wife, God blessed the Barths with another three sons and a daughter, plus many grandchildren, including Pastor Karl Luther Barth (b. 1924), one of the late-twentieth-century presidents of Concordia Seminary in St. Louis.[32]

CRITICISM OF THE IOWA SYNOD

Although LCMS pastors knew about deaconesses in Germany and Pittsburgh,[33] the doctrinal disputes between the Missouri and Iowa Synods formed the context in which many Missouri Synod Lutherans first

---

[30] Frederick S. Weiser, "Serving Love: Chapters in the Early History of the Diaconate in American Lutheranism" (Bachelor of Divinity thesis, Lutheran Theological Seminary, Gettysburg, PA, May 1960), 35.
[31] Carl. S. Meyer, ed., *Walther Speaks to the Church: Selected Letters* (St. Louis: Concordia, 1973), 91–93.
[32] Karl L. Barth, notes from telephone interview by Cheryl D. Naumann (CDN), June 29, 2005, private collection (priv. col.) of CDN, Pittsburgh, PA.
[33] For example, Rev. Peter Heinrich Dicke (1822–1911) worked with Fliedner in Kaiserswerth and then at the Deaconess Hospital in Dresden for several years before serving as an LCMS pastor. Peter Heinrich Dicke, Elanor Katherine Daib tran., "Autobiography of Peter Heinrich Dicke: Pastor and Pioneer Missionary," *Concordia Historical Institute Quarterly* 78. 3 (Fall 2005): 135–61.

considered the concept of the female diaconate. In 1869, the following article appeared in *Der Lutheraner*.[34]

> In the July issue of Pastor Brobst's *Monatsheften*—a circular which those of Iowa Synod now use with great diligence as a depot for the housing of their Iowa theological views—another Pastor of the Iowa Synod, Pastor J. J. Schmidt of Detroit, has eased the pressure on his heart and expressed himself on the nature of the concept of being a deaconess. He is of the opinion that the Roman Church has great hosts of kindhearted nuns. . . . Added to that, the nuns are not driven to choose this profession only through the desire or demand to earn heaven: "Must the nobler reasons of the love of Jesus, the desire to be obedient to His Holy Word" (which encourages, or which asks of them to become nuns), "the following after of the saints of all times, can all these be brushed aside?" Why then does the Lutheran church not have deaconesses? . . .
>
> What totally different notions were had in the early apostolic church regarding this issue. The apostle Paul says in I Timothy 5:9,10: "Let no widow be chosen under the age of 60 years, who has been the wife of one husband, and who has witness regarding her good works, who has raised children" etc. . . . Further, the office of deaconess in the early apostolic church was this: they were to do their service among the women of the congregation, which was actually under the office of the deacon, doing that which was not entirely seemly to the office of a deacon. They should be present at the baptism of grown women and be helpful thereby; they should visit the female sick and the poor and serve them, to comfort and to advise poor female Christians driven out by the heathen and similar such things. See Quenst. *Antiq. Bibl.* p. 95. This arrangement was a splendid one and apropos to the needs of the congregations existing at that time. The deaconess ideal of our Iowan Schmidt is, however, a totally different one. His deaconesses are to constitute a special order, which is to be arranged entirely following the analogy of the Roman order of nuns. Finally, it did not at all occur to the early apostolic church to elevate the office of deaconess so one-sidedly and to praise the order of deaconesses in such a manner as this blind adherent of Loehe does. Those first deaconesses also did not "sun" themselves in the "fame" of which Mr. Schmidt dreams; at the very least they made the church's "bridal finery" out of it.
>
> H.[35]

---

[34] Walther's St. Louis congregation began publishing *Der Lutheraner* in 1844. When the Missouri Synod was organized in 1847, *Der Lutheraner* became the property and official organ of the Synod.

Author "H" reveals at least three major issues regarding the subject of deaconesses in 1869. First, the diaconate was simply a copycat of the reprehensible Roman Catholic nunnery. Second, the nineteenth-century understanding of a deaconess promoted by Fliedner, Passavant, and Loehe contradicted the New Testament definition of a deaconess. Third, problems inevitably arise when people begin to extol the virtues of a churchly profession instead of "Christ's blood and righteousness" (for example, the implied danger of works-righteousness replacing justification by faith).

On the first two points, "H" believed that he exposed some unknown facts about Loehe and his "blind adherent." However, in 1860, in a small book entitled *About Charity*, Loehe had already explained that the Neuendettelsau deaconesses were not imitations of New Testament parish deaconesses. Instead, they were

> an evangelical copy of the Roman Catholic Sisters of Charity and can be nothing else in the conditions under which we are living. Since there are no longer any congregations like those in the early times, there can be no parish deaconesses like those at that time . . . Thus, the present diaconate, at a time of corruption in the folk churches, is the support and pillar of spiritual life; and it is not within the power of man to change that. It is just as certain that the form of brotherhood and sisterhood will come closer to perfection with the change of time. Each period of time is destined to undergo changes, and so the deaconess of the nineteenth century must happily adapt herself to changes . . .[36]

The last sentiment reflects the thinking of most of the early pioneers in deaconess ministry, namely, that the diaconate and the office of deaconess should evolve according to the needs of the Church as it strives to carry out the Great Commission commanded by Jesus in Matthew 28:18–20. This is certainly one reason why the Missouri Synod was not quick to pursue the formation of its own (synodical) diaconate.

C. F. W. Walther was president of the Missouri Synod and one of the editors of *Der Lutheraner* when the article submitted by "H" appeared in that publication.[37] Walther, Wyneken, Grabau, and Rohr had visited Loehe in

---

[35] "Wie sich ein Iowaisches Kirchenlicht uber das Diakonissenwesen anslagt" ["How a Light of the Church in Iowa Synod comments on the way of Deaconesses"], *Der Lutheraner* 26. 5 (November 1, 1869): 35–36. Translated by Rev. Arthur H. Baisch, Cabot, Pa., April 2004. The individual who wrote the article simply signed his name "H," indicating that the editor assumed the readers would know the author's identity from his initial.

[36] Wilhelm Loehe, *Von der Barmherzigkeit*, 4th ed. (Neuendettelsau: Buchhandlung der diakonissen-anstalt, 1927), 122–23.

[37] The November-Dezember 1874 issue of *Der Lutheraner* lists Walther as "Redakteur" of the magazine from 1844–1874. However, the last issue of *Der Lutheraner* to actually name

Neuendettelsau in the previous decade. They must have seen, or at least heard about, his deaconesses. As Missouri Synod leaders challenged Loehe's doctrine of the ministry and the "open questions" of the Iowa Synod,[38] they assumed a link between Loehe's doctrine of the ministry and his diaconate. Such an assumption would provide another reason to delay the use of deaconesses in the Synod. In 1865, in the context of the mission goals of his Neuendettelsau deaconess motherhouse, Loehe wrote: "We certainly would like to have a mission like Kaiserswerth has one in the Orient. For the mission is, when the deaconess matter is rightly understood, closely related to the task of the deaconesses. From the outset the deaconesshood is joined to the preaching office as Eve is to Adam, and a church which does God's work among the Gentiles without deacony [sic] seems to me like a one-legged man."[39]

The young Missouri Synod expanded rapidly after the Civil War and endeavored to establish church fellowship with any of the American Lutheran synods that espoused confessional Lutheranism. In 1872, Missouri joined together with the Ohio, Wisconsin, Minnesota, Illinois, and Norwegian Lutheran synods to create the Evangelical Lutheran Synodical Conference of North America.[40] No evidence suggests that members of the Missouri Synod expressed interest in a diaconate at this time, though other denominations around them increasingly supported their charitable work with skilled deaconesses. From 1885 to 1900, Christians founded at least one hundred forty deaconess institutions in the United States alone. By 1903, more than eighteen hundred deaconesses served in the United States, including two hundred eighteen Lutheran deaconesses working in forty fields of labor.[41]

Walther as editor was dated January 1, 1865. Subsequent issues, even as late as 1893, name the faculty of Concordia Seminary in St. Louis as the editor. Although no specific name is listed as editor after January 1865, most editorial comments were still signed with a "W." Email from Christopher Lieske, Reference and Research desk, CHI, St. Louis, to CDN, June 9, 2006.

[38] The Iowa Synod held that certain doctrines were not clear in Scripture and, therefore, were not necessary for salvation. Included among these "open questions" were subjects such as the Antichrist, the millennium, the Sabbath, and the conversion of the Jews.

[39] Wilhelm Loehe, "The Tenth Year of the Deaconess Institution Neuendettelsau, 1865," in Wilhelm Loehe, Gessammelte Werke, 4:2.

[40] See Baepler, Century of Grace, chapter 11. Walther was elected first president of the Synodical Conference.

[41] Golder, History of the Deaconess Movement, 3, 605.

ASSOCIATED LUTHERAN CHARITIES

In the early years of the LCMS, individual congregations cared for the social welfare of their members. However, as the population's physical, social, and financial needs altered with time, individual Christians and congregations saw the necessity of joining with others to address specific problems. Consequently, many banded together in geographic regions to form welfare societies and institutions. The first charitable institution associated with the Missouri Synod was Lutheran Hospital in St. Louis, Missouri, which was established in 1858. In 1868, the first Lutheran orphanage opened in Des Peres, Missouri, and in 1875, the first home for the aged opened in Brooklyn, New York.[42]

As LCMS members and congregations carried out more and more charitable activities through various agencies, charity workers in the LCMS sought opportunities to confer with one another about their work. The Lutheran Children's Friend Society of Wisconsin, organized in 1896, fostered the creation of around twelve similar agencies, which benefited from sharing experience and expertise with one another. By the turn of the century, the LCMS began calling special "city missionaries" to larger cities such as St. Louis, Buffalo, Milwaukee, and Chicago. Most of these missionaries also led the local or state "Children's Friend" work.[43]

In August 1901, three city missionaries—Pastor Frederick William Herzberger (1859–1930) of St. Louis, Pastor Frederick Ruhland (1873–1945) of Buffalo and Erie County, and Pastor August Schlechte (1868–1920) of Chicago—met in Chicago to discuss common problems in urban missions. This consultation was so helpful that the men resolved to meet together at least once a year and to encourage others to join them. Sometime in 1904, Associated Lutheran Charities[44] convened its first convention for the mutual instruction and encouragement of every type of agency engaged in Synodical Conference charity work. The first complete report of a regularly constituted ALCh convention includes the names of city missionaries, directors or representatives of Lutheran hospitals, officers and superintendents of Children's Friend societies, superintendents of orphanages, and the superintendent of an "institution for epileptics and the

---

[42] Lawrence B. Meyer, *Missouri in Motion* (New York: National Press, 1973), 78.
[43] "Historical Sketch of the Associated Lutheran Charities within the Synodical Conference," *Der Bote aus Bethesda* 17, no. 6 (November 1926): 6–7.
[44] Also known as Evangelische Lutherische Wohltütigkeitskonferenz.

feeble-minded."[45] Pastor (Johannes) Philipp Wambsganss Jr. (1857–1933), the son of Elizabeth Hess Wambsganss, was elected as first President of the association.[46]

DADDY HERZBERGER

In 1899, Pastor Herzberger had been installed in St. Louis as the first Missouri Synod city missionary.[47] A tireless worker, "Daddy" Herzberger organized a Christian day school and led St. Louis Lutherans in ministry to convicts, orphans, hospital patients, poorhouse inmates, and other outcasts of the day, including the terminally ill and insane. The work grew to an ambitious collection of charitable endeavors, always intertwined with education in the saving news of the Gospel.[48]

Herzberger noticed that other Christian denominations doing similar work had a distinct advantage because they used devoted and well-trained deaconesses. For example, ten years before Herzberger arrived in St. Louis, several pastors of the German Evangelical Synod of North America[49] organized the Evangelical Deaconess Association and established the Evangelical Deaconess Hospital and Motherhouse in St. Louis. Seeing the benefit of utilizing such consecrated workers in the Lord's vineyard, Herzberger told others about the need for female charity workers within the Synodical Conference.

In 1908, while the two men attended an annual ALCh convention in Chicago, a pivotal conversation took place between Pastors Herzberger and Wambsganss. Addressing Wambsganss, Herzberger asked: "How can we solve the problem of securing trained women workers for our institutional missions?" Wambsganss answered, "Why not begin the training of deaconesses for our work?"[50]

---

[45] "Historical Sketch of the Associated Lutheran Charities within the Synodical Conference," 7.

[46] The junior Wambsganss dropped his first name when writing "by" lines for published articles. E. H. Albers, "We Trace Our Steps: Chapter 2," *TLD* 45. 2 (Summer 1968): 5.

[47] Prior to his work in St. Louis, Herzberger served as a traveling missionary in northwest Arkansas (1882–86); was the pastor of an unnamed congregation in Carson, Kansas (1886–88); the pastor of Trinity in Hegewisch, Illinois (1888–89); and the pastor of St. Paul's, Hammond, Indiana (1889–99).

[48] Karen K. Marshall, "Lutheran Missions: Advocates of People," *St. Louis Globe-Democrat* (September 21–22, 1974): 15A.

[49] The American form of the 1817 Prussian Union, which merged with the German Reformed Church in 1934 and into the United Church of Christ in 1961.

[50] "1919–1944 Silver Anniversary of Lutheran Deaconess Service within the Synodical Conference" (Fort Wayne: LDA, 1944), brochure.

HERZBERGER'S CAMPAIGN

Between 1908 and 1911, Herzberger not only gave thought to the possible training of confessional Lutheran deaconesses, but he developed firm ideas about how and where to use their services. Significantly, he delivered his first public appeal for the use of deaconesses in a courageous memorial to the Missouri Synod's 1911 synodical convention:

The Establishing of a Lutheran Deaconess Home

To the honorable Synod of Missouri, Ohio and other states meeting as the 13th Delegate Synod out of St. Louis, May 1911.

From the 21st to the 24th of June 1910 the Conference of the Hospital, Children's Friend, and City Missions Association of Red Wing, Minnesota was held. At this Conference it was decided to establish a Deaconess Home. We emphasize that this be a Lutheran Deaconess home. The representatives and supporters of this Lutheran Deaconess Home do not want it to be from the unbiblical Deaconess existence such as found in the days among the "schwaermer" schismatics and pseudo Lutherans who would have nothing more than a Protestant nunnery.

Truly the *Lutheraner* has warned about such Deaconess existence in Issue 26, page 35. We are talking here about a Lutheran Deaconess home in which Lutheran virgins after age 20 and childless widows may enter who for the love of Christ want to learn to care for the sick (nursing) and to make this their life's profession. For such a home would want to help them for their daily sustenance. They would be taken care of during their illness and be given a Christian funeral if at the time of their death they still belong to the home.

To these virgins (young women) or widows there would be no written commitment to burden their conscience if they wanted to withdraw and enter Holy Matrimony or some other profession or if love motivates them to go back to their own family (I Tim. 5:8). For their services the deaconesses cannot ask for any remuneration. The Home takes care of its Deaconesses and all incoming finances are shared by all of the members.

What motivated the representatives of this conference to plan such a Deaconess Home is not because of business or to look for something new, but because of a crying need of the many places that desire such Deaconess ministry. Our Lutheran hospitals and boarding schools especially desire them. How greatly feminine care makes itself felt. Often it is difficult to obtain such a woman leader (head nurse) or Director in our Institutions. It takes great pains to train a nurse for three years and then have her leave the hospital for private nursing. Our hospitals lose that valuable training.

Many of our Lutheran families with sickness cannot afford a trained nurse and what one would require. How often it is among our Lutheran families with serious infectious diseases that an Evangelical or Protestant Deaconess or Catholic sister is called because they cannot afford a Lutheran nurse.

What temptations and dangers lay ahead for our believing Lutheran families becomes very clear. But, finally we think of the many nurses whose faith is threatened in their later years. In their Christian walk in life some would gladly associate themselves with a Lutheran Deaconess Home in the service of Nursing and not have to worry about their livelihood in their approaching old age.

The planned home would help to meet the above needs. The earlier mentioned Conference has therefore appointed a Committee to take the steps to make the plan a reality. We hope the Committee will have its work completed by fall. Meanwhile, our young women and childless widows who want to be a part of the planned Deaconess project can find reception in our Lutheran Hospital in Mankato or Red Wing, Minn. as well as in Fort Wayne, Indiana.[51]

Herzberger's reference to the 1869 article by "H" in *Der Lutheraner* demonstrates his full knowledge of the theological debate associated with the deaconess question for more than thirty years. However, certain that he was pursuing an important and God-pleasing course of action, he boldly outlined his definition of a deaconess, the practical function of a deaconess home, and the overwhelming need for Lutheran female nurses.

The printed proceedings of the delegate convention later reported:

Deaconess Matter

Committee No. 19 presented this statement regarding the printed Memorial found on page 131ff: "The Establishing of a Lutheran Deaconess Home."

In this petition it was announced to Synod that the Conference of the Hospital as well as the Children's Friend and City Mission Organizations of Red Wing, Minnesota decided to erect a Deaconess Home. The plans for such a home are simply stated, the assurance made that all would be done in the right spirit according to the Word of God. The reasons for establishing such a Deaconess existence in our Synod were formulated.

---

[51] F. W. Herzberger, "Errichtung eines lutherischen Diaconissenheims," *Eingaben für die Delegatensynode 1911 zu St. Louis, Mo.* (St. Louis: Concordia, 1911), 131–33. Translated by Rev. Otto A. Brillinger, Noblesville, IN, April, 2004.

As it was presented to Synod there were no comments or questions. However, the committee responded to earlier questions. Chairman Pastor Herzberger said that there would be no request on the part of the Conference to look for financial support from Synod now or later, only that Synod would speak and give its blessing to the project.

We (the committee) take the liberty of making the following recommendations.

1. That Synod may not take the Deaconess (existence) matter in their hand.

2. That Synod know the project of the brothers (committee) that are leading the undertaking of establishing this home is such that the feminine Diaconate not be against the Word of God when it is led but rather follow Apostolic examples. They would request that Synod promise this establishment in the Lutheran—that is Biblical spirit—from the beginning and while in operation. Since Deaconesses, especially in our times, would find a blessed circle of activities in the hospital, in city missions as care givers for the sick and the poor in our congregations, in our mission to the heathen, being recognized as care givers they could bear witness to the Gospel in the course of their service of mercy.

3. As experience has taught us, the Deaconess cause could get out of hand, therefore Synod should have a standing committee to oversee and look after things. The committee advice is to be heeded and followed. The leader of the Deaconess movement would need to respect the overseer, since it is easy to get out of hand. The standing committee is to supervise and to guard against things getting out of hand. Such board could be elected by the delegates of Synod who would receive the mandate and leading regulations for this work.

This committee report was tabled.[52]

The report does not clarify whether the synodical delegates ran out of time for discussion or whether they were simply too confused or undecided about the subject to act on the committee recommendations. The Synod did not reject the idea of a Lutheran Deaconess Home, but Herzberger must have been disappointed that the Synod did not give its blessing to the project.[53]

---

[52] "Diaconissensache," *Synodical Bericht, Ferhandlungern der Deutschen Evangelisch-Lutherishen Synode von Missouri, Ohio und anderen Staaten, versammelt als Driezehnte Delegatensynode Anno Domini 1911* (St. Louis: Concordia, October 8, 1911), 189–90. Translated by Rev. Otto A. Brillinger, Noblesville, IN, April, 2004.

[53] St. John's Hospital and St. John's School of Nursing were both established in 1903 in Red Wing, Minnesota, through the leadership of Pastor John R. Baumann (1872–1947), a

A DIFFERENT STRATEGY

Four months later, in August 1911, Herzberger presented a discussion paper on the female diaconate to the ALCh conference in Fort Wayne. Supporting his points with an exposition of Scripture and church history, Herzberger expounded eight theses that, for decades afterward, would form and inform the Missouri Synod's understanding of a confessional Lutheran diaconate. No extant copy of Herzberger's original presentation is known, but Herman Bernard Kohlmeier (1871–1959) made notes that summarized Herzberger's main points.

A. There is only one divinely instituted office, the holy ministry. All other offices are auxiliary offices, and may be established, changed, abrogated by the church as she deems best for her welfare.

B. The office of the female diaconate is such an office. It flourished in the early Christian church, lost its character, however, and disappeared under popery, and has been re-established in some parts of Christendom in our time. (Fliedner and Loehe)

C. The office of the Lutheran Deaconess is essentially different from the order of Roman Catholic nuns. No vow of celibacy. Marriage is a divine institution. Deaconesses must be permitted to enter marriage.

D. As the field for deaconesses Pastor H. mentions the positions of attendants, nurses, matrons of institutions in our church, teachers, parish workers, and assistants to our missionaries in the various mission fields of the church at home and abroad.

E. It is not implied that deaconesses are a special spiritual order in the church, nor serving in the ministry. Scripture bars women from the office of the ministry but they can exercise the right and obligations of the priesthood of believers. Therefore deaconesses give instruction, admonition, comfort of Scriptures as the situation requires.

F. Luther did not re-establish the female diaconate, due to conditions in his day. But he did pave the way for re-establishing such an office. Justification by faith—service in Love.

---

respected philanthropist who was active in ALCh and later became president of the Minnesota Synod. The *Red Wing Daily Republican* (June 22, 1910, page 1) reported that the Lutheran Hospital and Sanatorium Conference discussed "the fundamental principles of Lutheran deaconesses" at their June 21, 1910, meeting, but there is no subsequent historical evidence to show that a Deaconess Home was ever built in Red Wing. Emails to CDN from Char Henn, Director/CEO Goodhue County History Center, Red Wing, Minnesota, September 21, 28–29, 2004.

G. Suggested that special training be given to student nurses in one or more Lutheran hospitals in preparation for this work.[54]

Herzberger's paper generated much positive discussion. The conference earnestly considered the possibility of founding a deaconess society but took no definitive action. The conservative synods of the Synodical Conference generally acted slowly to support a new and unknown movement. Some individuals feared that training deaconesses might bring unbiblical ideas and practices to the church. President Wambsganss of the ALCh urged further study of the matter, and in the ensuing period, he actively assisted Herzberger in promoting the cause by writing letters to the presidents of Synods affiliated with the Synodical Conference and to the presidents of individual districts.[55] One of the first to reply was Missouri Synod president Johann Friedrich Pfotenhauer (1859–1939), who expressed his full support for the proposal to establish a deaconess training school.[56]

With another ALCh conference on the horizon, nearly eight years after his attempt to solicit the Missouri Synod's blessing for a deaconess home in Minnesota, Herzberger penned and distributed a tract entitled "Woman's Work in the Church." His spirited and convincing appeal is worth reading in full.

Women Workers in the Apostolic Church

It is harvest-time and Farmers A. and B. are busy gathering in the sheaves from their adjoining fertile fields. The weather has been most propitious and produced the richest kind of crops. But now black and angry storm-clouds threaten in the west, and so Farmer A. calls on his women-folks for help in his fields. With their willing help he succeeds in storing the precious grain before the storm descends and damages or destroys the golden harvest-yield. For some inexplicable reason, however, his Neighbor B. does not use the same foresight. He toils on alone in his fields with his boys, leaves his women-folks complacently at their household duties that could easily be done at some other time, and what is the consequence? While Farmer A. loses very little of his grain, Farmer B. ruefully sees the wind and rain and hail with pitiless fury ruining a great portion of his ungarnered crops. Which one of the husbandmen was wise enough and energetic enough to "redeem the time" before the stormy, evil day came upon him in his harvest fields?

---

[54] "The Deaconess Program, Lutheran Church—Missouri Synod and Affiliated Synods," typed notes, *Historical Documents, Kohlmeier 1932–41: Miscellaneous papers and letters*, LDA Archives, LDA, Valparaiso, IN.

[55] E. A. Duemling, "Beginning and Growth of Deaconess Movement," hand-written speech, Deaconess Office Archives, Concordia University, River Forest, IL.

[56] B. Poch, "Report of Deaconess Association," *Proceedings of the ALCh*, 1929, 125.

What is true in the harvest fields of nature, is true also in the extensive harvest fields of the Church. Women can and ought to be employed in them in all those capacities for which the Lord has fitted them! It is true: our Lutheran women are doing more than their "bit" in regard to providing for the material wants of the local congregation, of our charity institutions and of our numerous mission fields at home or abroad. But there is another form of woman's help that our Church needs most sorely in these days of storm and stress, and that is—to use the technical term— the FEMALE DIACONATE, meaning *trained and officially employed woman workers in the Church as assistants of the Holy ministry.*

When we turn to Romans 16:1 and 2, we read how Paul writes: "I commend unto you Phebe [*sic*] our sister which is a servant of the Church at Cenchrea that ye receive her in the Lord as becometh saints, and that ye assist her in whatever business she hath need of you; for she hath been a succorer of many, and myself also." This Phebe [*sic*] was a deaconess, as Dr. Stoeckhardt shows in his Commentary on Romans, whose official duty consisted in ministering to the sick, the poor and the strangers in the congregation at Cenchrea, the Eastern port or harbor of the metropolitan Corinth. Again we read of saintly widows, I Tim. 5:9 and 10, who performed certain duties and functions in the primitive congregations. So we learn direct from Scripture that it was customary for the congregations in times of the Apostles to employ *women workers!* They were servants of the particular congregation in which they labored and were under the jurisdiction of the local congregation and assistants of the pastor or bishop. It is of the highest importance to remember that fact that the *female diaconate is an auxiliary office of the Holy Ministry.* As the sainted Dr. Stoeckhardt sets forth in his instructive article *(Lehre U Wehre,* 1897) "Concerning the Call of Woman Teachers in the Christian Parochial School," there is but ONE divinely created office in the Church viz. the office of the Holy Ministry. The pastor is exclusively THE teacher, THE shepherd and overseer of his congregation and will have to give an account to God for his stewardship. (Acts 20:28; I Peter 5:1–3; Hebrews 13:17). Because of that fact all other offices in the Church are but human ordinances. They can and ought to be created as the exigency and the welfare of the local congregation demands. But they must all have their root in the divinely appointed Ministry and stand in vital relation to it. Thus the office of Elders (Vorsteher) is an auxiliary office of the pastorate. Elders help the pastor in overseeing the congregation, help to admonish, warn and comfort the individual members. Thus—as Dr. Stoeckhardt goes on to show—the office of Almoner (who looks after the poor), the office of nursing the sick (female diaconate) are intimately related to the ministry of the Word. Wherever these offices are well established and well conducted, there the Word of God achieves tangible power in the congregation.

We know from Church History what noble self-sacrificing service these women workers performed in the primitive Church, what a glorious host of faithful martyrs they produced in the days of persecution. Alas! with the decline of the Gospel in the fifth and sixth century and the rise of popery the female diaconate of the primitive Church also declined and unscriptural nunnery took its place. What a deadly weapon nunnery is in the hands of Rome to carry on its nefarious propaganda also in our beloved country needs no examplification [sic] here.

Why Have We Not Trained Women Workers in the Synodical Conference?

In the Protestant churches the female diaconate has been established along more or less Biblical lines in the past eighty years, especially through the labors of a Fliedner at Kaiserswerth and a Loehe in Neuendettelsau, Germany. At present there are about 20,000 trained women at work in the harvest fields of Evangelical Christendom. We meet with them in the Episcopal Church, in the Presbyterian, the Baptist, the Methodist and other Protestant denominations. The Lutheran General Council, the General Synod, the Swedish Synod also engage them and are wise in doing so. They are like Farmer A. of whose foresight we heard in our last number. But there is also a Farmer B. among the Lutheran churches who has thus far neglected to employ his womenfolk definitely and generally in his teeming harvest fields. Do you know him? It's our own Synodical Conference of which our Missouri Synod is an integral and dominant factor. Why have we Lutherans of the Synodical Conference failed so far to make a systematic use of the many gifted and pious women the Lord has given also to us for the work in the fields intrusted [sic] to our stewardship? Are we living in a different world from that in which Christians of other denominations are living—a world less afflicted by sin and want and woe than theirs? Certainly not. We meet with the same wants and afflictions they have to contend with in their church work. As they, so do we need the assistance of trained women workers in our various harvest fields. We need VISITING NURSES who can go into the hovels of the poor in our large cities or into the isolated homes in the countryside, especially when epidemics are abroad, and there nurse and comfort the sick and dying. Do not tell me the nurses from our various Lutheran Hospitals can do that sort of work. I ask: Who is to pay them for it? There must be some kind of an organization supporting them if they are to devote their time to such charity work. Again we need TEACHING NURSES for the primary classes in our parochial schools. Far be it from me to detract in any way from the splendid self-sacrificing work our parochial school-teachers are doing, but experience has long since proved in hundreds of cases that trained female help in our primary grades redound to the uplift and maintenance of our church schools.

Again, we need INSTITUTIONAL NURSES for our Orphan homes, our Home for the Feeble-minded, our Sanitarium at Denver for consumptives, our Old Folks Homes, etc. Ask the superintendents of these institutions how difficult it is to find the right kind of help for their poor and afflicted charges. We also need trained nurses for our Home and Foreign Mission Fields. How thankful we city missionaries would be for the help of a woman worker among the female patients in the hospitals and tenement districts in which we have to labor. But above all do we need PARISH NURSES to assist our over-burdened pastors in our large commercial and factory centers in looking up straying or needy members of their large flocks. Verily, we Lutherans in the Synodical Conference also stand in need of women helpers in our teeming harvest fields! Why then do we not call on them for help? We certainly cannot plead the lack of means necessary for their support. As a church we have long outgrown our pioneer age with its poverty and hardships, the struggling days when the fields first had to be cleared and the seed sown and the harvest had not yet matured. Our Lutheran Church is securely planted in this free Country of ours, her Gospel of "the faith that worketh by love" has extended and planted her acres from ocean to ocean and the fields are now white for the harvest. Her children are no longer poor hewers of wood and drawers of water but have grown well-to-do, even RICH, under the blessings of our Heavenly Father. Why then do we still fail to train and organize pious and gifted sisters for work in the Lord's harvest fields?

The chief reason for our failure to establish the female diaconate in our midst is, no doubt, the lack of understanding on [the] part of our people for this blessed institution. Or can any well-founded SCRIPTURAL argument be brought against it? We believe not. Galatians 3:26, 28 the Apostle Paul declares: "Ye are all (men and women and children) the children of God by faith in Christ Jesus. For as many of you as have been baptized into Christ, have put on Christ. There is neither Jew nor Greek, there is neither bond nor free (and now read carefully) there is neither male nor *female*, for ye are all one in Christ Jesus." What follows? That Christian women are not debarred on account of their sex from laboring in the fields of the Church, for they are one with the men in Christ and therefore have the same privileges and duties that the men have. The Apostle Peter tells us emphatically, I Peter 3:7: "that Christian women are heirs together with the men of the grace of life" and hence, they belong to that "chosen generation and royal priesthood" of which he speaks in his second chapter, "who are to show forth the praises of Him who called them out of darkness into His marvelous light." On account of their SPIRITUAL PRIESTHOOD women have the same call to labor in the Church of Christ that Christian men have. There is but one limitation— imposed by the Lord of the harvest Himself—they are not to preach the Gospel in *public worship*. When the Christian congregation is assembled, men, women, children being present, then men alone are to preach as we learn from I Cor. 14:34–35 and I Timothy 2:11–14. It is unscriptural, therefore, for women to occupy the pulpit in public worship.

What Can We Do To Secure the Much Needed Women Workers?

It is true—and pity 'tis, 'tis true—that in some branches of Evangelical Christendom the female diaconate has assumed an unbiblical form. But the wrong use of a good thing never can abolish its right usage. As long as the pure Word of God reigns supreme in our Synodical Conference we need not fear that the female diaconate in our midst will be conducted on any other but sound Biblical lines.

What, then, can we do to secure the much needed women workers of our expanding harvest fields? We can and ought to follow the example of the Christians in other Evangelical denominations and found "Deaconess Societies" in our congregations who support *our* 'General Deaconess Society" which, with God's merciful help, we purpose to organize at our coming Lutheran Charity Conference in Fort Wayne, Ind., during June or July. We will report on the plan adopted at the Conference more fully in a later number of the "American Lutheran." The main difficulty will be to secure a centrally located "Mother House" where our women workers can be trained and where they can find their home when sickness or old age incapacitates them for their duties. But that difficulty *must* and *will* be overcome.

Let no one say, if we start such Deaconess Societies and such a Mother House in our midst, that we will hurt our trained nurses in gaining their livelihood. Nevermore. Many of our trained nurses are tired of being practically "HOMELESS." They are anxious to enter such a Mother House, take the short course necessary to fit them for Church work and then go out and serve their Savior in His harvest fields. And why should they not avail themselves of the advantages such a Mother House holds out to them? The Mother House is to be their *home* and will relieve them of the great expense in providing for their own living quarters. Furthermore, they are not to work for nothing, but be paid a living wage or salary as long as they work under the direction of the Mother House, for, "The laborer is worthy of his hire." Luke 10:7. In case of sickness the Mother House looks after its faithful nurses, takes them in old age and in case of death gives them a Christian burial. If we thus make it for the interest of our trained nurses or others among our Lutheran women to come into the work, we will meet with a ready response among our women folks. Will we be wise enough and energetic enough to "redeem the time": and call on our women folks for help as Farmer A. did when the approaching storm threatened his harvest fields? That is the final, the all-important question! Our heart bleeds when we think of the many fine

Lutheran young women we have met and who have entered other denominations because their own Church would not provide them with the work they were anxious to do in the Lord's harvest fields. And our sorrow grows greater when we think of the many opportunities we miss for winning souls for Christ because of our NEGLECT in training and supporting gifted and pious women in our midst for missionary and charitable work. The World War may be over, but the sad conditions it has created in all ranks of society are not over! If ever the Church of Christ was called upon to bend every effort for the saving and uplifting of redeemed souls that time is NOW! Who has ears to hear that S.O.S. call of perishing souls? Who is ready and willing to help us Charity Workers and missionaries to establish a TRAINING SCHOOL and MOTHER HOUSE for Lutheran Women Workers in the harvest fields the Lord has intrusted [sic] to OUR stewardship? If there be any such among my readers, I ask them to send me their names so I can send them the literature we will publish for the good of the cause after our Charity convention in Ft. Wayne, Indiana.[57]

Herzberger's persistence paid off. On the first day of the July 1919 ALCh conference in Fort Wayne, the delegates agreed to initiate deaconess training and resolved to "ask the Fort Wayne Lutheran Hospital Association to give our proposed training-school for Lutheran deaconesses a temporary headquarters in its institution as well as the necessary facilities to train its members for the work."[58] Within a month, the hospital's Board of Directors responded with a yes.

On August 17, 1919, the ALCh formally organized the Lutheran Deaconess Association of the Evangelical Lutheran Synodical Conference of North America at St. Paul's Evangelical Lutheran Church in Fort Wayne.[59] Finally, members of the Missouri Synod and their partners in the Synodical Conference planned to have deaconesses working among them.

---

[57] F. W. Herzberger, "Woman's Work in the Church," tract, circa 1918–19, priv. col. of Nancy (Nicol) Nemoyer, Carlisle, PA.

[58] Wohltätigkeitskonferenz der Lutherischen Synodalkonferenz, gehalten vom 15–17 Juli 1919, in der Emmanshalle, Fort Wayne, Indiana, conference agenda, Associated Lutheran Charities Box, General Information File, CHI, St. Louis, Missouri; F. W. Herzberger, "A Historic Document," TLD 1. 2 (April 1924): 1.

[59] Letter from Arnold Krentz to Elmer E. Foelber, November 22, 1960, Historical Documents—1944; The Transition from Ft. Wayne to Valparaiso—Arnold F. Krentz, LDA Archives, LDA, Valparaiso, IN.

Illustrations for Chapter One may be viewed at www.deaconesshistory.org.

CHAPTER 2

FORT WAYNE AND BEYOND

By 1919, the Synodical Conference's "expanding harvest fields"[1] included one tuberculosis sanatorium, one home for epileptic children, one deaf institute, nine homes for older adults, nine orphan homes, thirteen children's friend societies, and fifteen hospitals.[2] Members of the ALCh were eager to get on with the task of training deaconesses for work in these institutions.

Philipp Wambsganss Jr. lived in Fort Wayne, Indiana, where he served as pastor of Emmaus Evangelical Lutheran Church. In addition to being president of ALCh, Wambsganss was president of the Fort Wayne Lutheran Hospital Association, which promised to provide temporary headquarters and facilities for the Lutheran deaconess training school. Not surprisingly, this great humanitarian became the first president of the LDA and agreed to direct the training of deaconesses until a superintendent could be found.[3]

On January 31, 1920, Rev. Philipp Wambsganss Jr., August Freese, Rev. Henry Christian Luehr (1863–1933), Rev. William E. Moll (1867–1948), August Becker, Louis Schmoe, Rev. John Reinhold Graebner (1878–1927), Rev. Jacob William Miller (1860–1933), and Charles W. Scherer signed proposed "Articles of Association" establishing the LDA as a nonprofit charitable entity in the state of Indiana for fifty years. Although the LDA intended to serve the entire Synodical Conference, these nine men, designated as the first directors of the LDA, were all members of the Missouri Synod.[4] Their leadership in the LDA reflected a strong solidarity

---

[1] F. W. Herzberger, "Woman's Work in the Church," paragraph 8.

[2] E. H. Albers, "We Trace Our Steps: Chapter 2," *TLD* 45, no. 2 (Summer 1968), 5.

[3] Wambsganss gave generously of his time to the founding and support of welfare agencies in Fort Wayne. He was president of the Lutheran Friend's Society, president of the Lutheran Children's Aid Society, director of the Fort Wayne Antituberculosis League, active in the Lutheran Social Service Bureau, and chairman of the Ministers, Teachers, and Professors Conference of Northwest Indiana. "Biographical Record for Philipp Wambsganss Jr." (St. Louis: CHI, January 29, 2004).

[4] "Articles of Association of the Lutheran Deaconess Association of the Evangelical-Lutheran Synodical Conference of North America," January 31, 1920. Recorded in the Recorder's Office of Allen County, Ind., Miscellaneous Record 54, page 198.

and support for the deacons program among Fort Wayne LCMS congregations.[5]

According to the "Articles of Association," the LDA aspired "to educate and train Lutheran deaconesses for the care of the sick and poor in the congregations of the Evangelical-Lutheran Synodical Conference, and for the administering of charity and mercy in the charitable institutions and in home and foreign mission work of said Synodical Conference; and to erect and maintain Lutheran Deaconess Schools, Motherhouses and other Institutions of like character likely to promote the purposes of the Society; and for that purpose to own, hold and sell real estate."[6]

The LDA had several immediate needs: the acquisition of funding, textbooks, teachers, female students, and, perhaps most urgent of all, a motherhouse. Neither the LCMS nor its Synodical Conference partners assumed any official role in organizing or financing the training program. Pastor F. W. Herzberger's vision progressed to reality through the tireless efforts of a voluntary association of individuals convinced that the ministrations of deaconesses would support the central mission of the Church. But where would these dedicated volunteers find the monetary, physical, and human resources necessary to ensure success in the training of deaconesses?

EVANGELISCH-LUTHERISCHES GEMEINDE-BLATT

Wambsganss wasted no time in sending communications about the LDA and its needs to the member synods of the Synodical Conference. Even before the legal registration of the "Articles of Association," he wrote an article for *Evangelisch-Lutherisches Gemeinde-Blatt*, the official publication of the Evangelical Lutheran Synod of Wisconsin, Minnesota, Michigan, and Other States. The tone of his article reflected his belief in the importance and urgency of the deaconess cause.

> I address you as the old-fashioned town crier, "Listen to what I'm saying to you!" . . . What we're dealing with is an exceedingly important subject that deserves the attention of every individual reader.

---

[5] All five pastors served LCMS congregations in Fort Wayne: Wambsganss at Emmaus; Luehr at Zion; Moll at Emmanuel; Graebner at Redeemer; Miller at St. Paul's. See *Lutheran Annual* (St. Louis: Concordia, 1920). The laymen were also members of LCMS congregations in Fort Wayne: Becker and Schmoe were members of Emmanuel; Freese was a member of Emmaus; Scherer was a charter member of Concordia.

[6] "Articles of Association," January 31, 1920.

You have all known already of Miss L. Ellermann, when she assisted our missionary in India. We call her, in the language of the Church, a deaconess, in other words, she is a female person in service to the Church. Such deaconesses—or what is the same thing, women serving the Church, of which we have many examples in the apostolic age—are in our present Church, and particularly necessary in our city missions, working for the poor, providing nursing care in larger congregations and various charities, particularly orphanages, old folks' homes, sanitariums, and the like.

The Lutheran Synodical Conference's Charity Convention in consultation this year has already seen the necessity for the female diaconate, and given their blessing for their training among us. During the final session in July, they finally came to resolve this, and it is necessary now to proceed energetically and to postpone it no further. A deaconess community should be called into life and the training of deaconesses organized in connection with an existing nursing school that has already begun among us. This decision was also immediately implemented. . . . The Board of the Ft. Wayne Lutheran Hospitals gave its consent, that those intending to serve could additionally complete a three-year nursing course. It has already occurred that a young woman has offered herself for mission service in India. The beginning is thus made, and now it follows that we go forward boldly and with confidence in God. Yet, in addition to going forward, first of all, we in our Synodical Conference must gain a large number of members willing to help put the deaconess program on a healthy financial footing.

Bear in mind and don't forget, that, for the operation of the Deaconess Program, a motherhouse is necessary, in which the deaconesses who are retained are guaranteed a haven, so that those who become ill or incapacitated have free medical care, meals, and sustenance until the end of their lives.

It is obvious that one should only apply for the diaconate in good faith and if one devoutly promises, as much as is humanly possible, to maintain her commitment. By the same token, those who pledge to establish a motherhouse, provide necessary funding, and all necessary supplies should be likewise committed to their promise.

Ask yourselves, dear readers, could not such a guarantee be obtained if we could acquire approximately 50,000 contributors, giving a minimum of a dollar each, within the congregations of our Lutheran Synodical

Conference? Certainly! Absolutely! And that is what the deaconess community has envisioned from the outset. ...[7]

THE LUTHERAN WITNESS APPEAL

The July 20, 1920 issue of *The Lutheran Witness* featured two articles designed to arouse LCMS interest and support for the work of ALCh and the LDA. In the first article, F. W. Herzberger remarked:

> . . . But the most absorbing topic engaging the Conference will be the new work started at last year's session in Fort Wayne, *viz.*, the deaconess work. May God in His mercy richly bless our Charity Convention at Chicago, and soon give us the sorely needed trained women workers for over-ripe and ever-expanding mission and charity-fields![8]

The article that followed Herzberger's was written by Pastor John R. Graebner, first secretary of the LDA and pastor of English Lutheran Church of the Redeemer, Fort Wayne. It is notable, first, that Graebner's primary emphasis was on the validity of the contemporary office of deaconess. Second, he mentions both Fliedner and Loehe in his argument for establishing the office of deaconess within the Synodical Conference.

> In the New Testament we read of deacons. They were church officers appointed to relieve the apostles by caring for the poor and otherwise assisting in church-work. A woman appointed for such work is called a deaconess. Phebe [*sic*] was one of those. We read of her [in] Rom. 16, 1. 2.
> . . .
>
> Church History tells us what noble, self-sacrificing service such women workers performed during the first centuries of the Christian Church. When by and by false doctrine and idolatrous practises [*sic*] crept into the Church, and popery became more and more established, the female diaconate gradually changed into nunnery. As a fruit of the Reformation, the office of deaconess was again established, especially through the labors of Fliedner at Kaiserswerth and Loehe at Neuendettelsau, Germany, about eighty years ago.
>
> At present there are about 20,000 deaconesses. The Episcopal, Presbyterian, Baptist, Methodist, and other churches have such trained female workers. Among Lutheran synods the General Council, the

---

[7] Philipp Wambsganss, "Lutherische Diaconissen-Gesellschaft," *Evangelisch-Lutherisches Gemeinde-Blatt* (December 7, 1919): 389–90. Translated by Rev. Dr. Jonathan C. Naumann, Pittsburgh, PA, November, 2004.

[8] F. W. Herzberger, "The Lutheran Charities Association of the Synodical Conference," *The Lutheran Witness* 39, no. 15 (July 20, 1920): 227.

General Synod, and the Augustana Synod have the help of deaconesses in their own charitable institutions and in their mission-work.

Why not our Synodical Conference? If other church-bodies have deaconess schools in which they train women for assisting pastors and missionaries in their work among the poor, the sick, the needy, the forsaken, the outcasts, both in institutions and in private homes, why should not we have the same?

There is, and has been for years, a crying need of women workers, in our city missions, our charitable institutions, and in our foreign mission-fields. After having had the matter under consideration for years, the Charities Association of the Synodical Conference at its convention in Ft. Wayne last summer resolved to organize a Deaconess Association. . . . One of the first things to be done is to provide for a motherhouse, that is, a suitable building for the deaconess school and home. . . .

May the Lord bless this new undertaking. May He make many hearts and hands willing to support this work, and may there be no lack of Christian women in our Synod also who will cheerfully serve as Lutheran deaconesses![9]

Although he cites the need for a motherhouse, Graebner makes no direct appeal for financial assistance, but simply expresses a hope that God would "make many hearts and hands willing to support this work." How encouraged he must have been when, at the first meeting of the LDA held in Fort Wayne on October 24, 1920, congratulatory messages came from LCMS President Dr. Pfotenhauer, Minnesota Synod President Rev. John R. Baumann, city missionaries Herzberger and John Henry Witte (1871–1947), and several laymen.[10] After the meeting, the LDA Board of Directors continued to receive positive correspondence, including, for example, a note from Rev. C. Buenger, president of the South-Wisconsin District of the Wisconsin Synod, who wrote, "I rejoice to hear that an Association for Deaconess work has been organized. Here is a splendid opportunity for women's work in the church. May God bless this work also."[11]

---

[9] J. R. Graebner, "Deaconesses," *The Lutheran Witness* 39, no. 15 (July 20, 1920): 227–28.
[10] F. W. Herzberger, "A Historic Document," *TLD* 1, no. 2 (April 1924): 12.
[11] "This, That, and the Other Thing. No. 3.," in Second Annual Report of the Lutheran Deaconess Association within the Ev. Luth. Synodical Conference of North America (Fort Wayne, IN: LDA, 1921), 3.

GRASSROOTS SUPPORT

The LDA did not ask the Synodical Conference or its member synods for financial support. Instead, Wambsganss led a vigorous financial campaign that urged individuals to become LDA members by donating one dollar each year to the association.[12] Along with the joy of supporting the new deaconess venture, members would have the right to select the LDA Board of Directors at an annual meeting.[13] This privilege gave members a sense of ownership in the board's activities and decisions, such as calling superintendents; placing and transferring deaconesses; and entering into agreements with institutions, congregations, or missions that desired the service of deaconesses.[14]

Shortly after the membership drive began, an ALCh convention resolved to create LDA branch societies in larger cities. These societies would assist with collection of annual dues, raise interest in deaconess work, and broadly promote deaconess ministry within the Synodical Conference.[15] Herzberger organized one of the first of these branches in St. Louis, Missouri, with a group of nineteen young women known as the Mission Circle. The objectives of the Lutheran Deaconess Association of St. Louis and Vicinity were:

> to form a branch society of the LDA of the Synodical conference, which has its headquarters and the training-school for deaconesses at Fort Wayne, Ind.; to aid the missionary and charitable endeavors of our Lutheran churches primarily in St. Louis and vicinity; to assist financially gifted but needy Lutheran girls who wish to study for the deaconess calling; to arrange for instructive lectures on deaconess and mission-work; to offer the members an opportunity to do personal work under the supervision of the Association.[16]

---

[12] The membership goal changed from fifty thousand to twenty thousand sometime between December 1919 and July 1920.

[13] "Articles of Association," Article Eight, January 31, 1920.

[14] E. H. Albers, "We Trace Our Steps: Chapter 3," *TLD* 45, no. 3 (Fall 1968): 3.

[15] "This, That, and the Other Thing. No. 3.," 3.

[16] Qualification for voting membership in the St. Louis branch was carefully monitored. Voters had to be communicant members of the LCMS and pay dues of twenty-five cents per month, plus an optional payment of one dollar each year toward the salary of a deaconess. The group also welcomed "delegates" from the ladies' aid societies of Missouri Synod congregations. Delegates brought donations from the groups they represented, and they voted but could not hold office. Other (non-LCMS) Lutherans who contributed at least one dollar per annum attended as nonvoting advisory members. By December 1937, sixteen years after its inception, the St. Louis association had 82 voting members, 20 ladies' societies represented by 27 delegates, and 226 contributing members! See page 47 of "The Lutheran

The concept of branch societies became popular. The first published list of "Branch Societies of our Lutheran Deaconess Association" (as of December 1923) included thirty-five societies, located in

Illinois: Chicago, Roselle, Nashville, New Minden, Crystal Lake, Jacksonville, Arenzville, Streator, Mount Olive, Carlinville, Kankakee, and Forest Park

Indiana: La Fayette and Logansport

Iowa: Stanwood and Davenport

Michigan: Monroe, Petoskey, and South Hadley

Minnesota: Truman

Missouri: St. Louis, Sweet Springs, and Freistatt

New York: New York, Albany, and Buffalo

Ohio: Cleveland, Cincinnati, Akron, Elyria, and Lancaster

Pennsylvania: Pittsburgh

Texas: Galveston

Wisconsin: Beaver Dam and Milwaukee[17]

Three months later, Huntington, Indiana; Waterloo, Iowa; La Grange, Texas; and Sheboygan, Wisconsin joined the list.[18]

DEACONESS MOTHERHOUSE

Herzberger reported to the LDA that the solicitation of memberships at one dollar per year was so successful that the association "could not only pay all initial expenses, but also buy our first motherhouse."[19] For many years LDA leaders recounted this fascinating story of the acquisition of the motherhouse as a demonstration of the motivating and guiding blessing of God.

> Dr. H.A. Duemling, chief surgeon at the Lutheran Hospital, had bought a property adjoining the hospital grounds. On these lots was a large dwelling. This house Dr. Duemling offered to sell to the Deaconess Association for $2,500, since he planned to build a modern clinic on his property. The Association eagerly took him up on this offer, rented sufficient grounds from the Hospital Association for the nominal sum of $5 a year and moved the house on this plot. When the Association held its

Deaconess Association," monograph, signed "The Committee" (of the LDA of St. Louis and Vicinity), 1937/38, private collection of Clara Strehlow, Deaconess Office Archives, Concordia University, River Forest, IL, 47.

[17] "Branch Societies of our Lutheran Deaconess Association," *TLD* 1, no. 1 (January 1924): 8.

[18] "Branch Societies of our Lutheran Deaconess Association," *TLD* 1, no. 2 (April 1924): 16.

[19] F. W. Herzberger, "A Historic Document," *TLD* 1, no. 2 (April 1924): 11–12.

second meeting on September 1, 1921, the treasurer could report on the cost of the Home. The purchase price of the home plus excavating for basement, moving, masonwork, repairs, furnace and plumbing brought the entire cost up to $10,252.73. Enough money had been raised through the efforts of Pastor Wambsganss so that a debt of only $2,200 remained.[20]

The deaconess motherhouse stood at 2916 Fairfield Avenue, Fort Wayne, Indiana, where it flourished as LDA headquarters until 1943. It functioned as home and classroom to the students, provided a haven of rest and encouragement for deaconesses who needed to recuperate from illness, and had a reputation for generous hospitality to all who came to visit.

CLASSES BEGIN

On April 15, 1921, five women began training together as the first class of deaconess students: Ina Kempff, Clara Dienst, Bessie Stenke, Clara Wiebke, and Muriel Watson.[21] These pioneer deaconess pupils were instructed primarily by Pastor John R. Graebner, but also by other pastors, such as Gust W. F. Doege (1875–1937), Trinity Evangelical Lutheran Church, Fort Wayne; William Moll, Emmanuel Lutheran Church, Fort Wayne; and Fred Wambsganss Sr. (1881–1957), Emmaus Evangelical Lutheran Church, Fort Wayne.[22] Since the motherhouse could not be occupied until later in 1921, the first theology lessons took place on the premises of Lutheran Hospital, at the LDA "Main Office" located at 2307 Broadway,[23] or in parsonages and other buildings associated with the teaching staff.

Director (Philipp) Wambsganss and his helpers in the Fort Wayne ministerium decided to equip the women with a solid grounding in Christian doctrine. After all, a deaconess was to have intertwining roles. While modeling the love of Christ by caring for the bodily needs of the sick,

[20] Albers, "We Trace Our Steps: Chapter 3," 5.
[21] H. B. Kohlmeier, *1919-1944 25th Anniversary of the Lutheran Deaconess Association within the Synodical Conference* (Fort Wayne, IN: Nuoffer Print, 1944), 7.
[22] In "Historic Document," Herzberger errs in naming Fred Wambsganss as "Jr." when he was in fact Fred Wambsganss "Sr." The eldest son of Philipp Wambsganss Jr., Fred Sr. was called to Emmaus Lutheran Church in 1911 to be an assistant to his father. In 1918, at the request of Philipp Jr., the two men traded positions: Fred Sr. became senior pastor and his father the assistant pastor. See Herzberger, "Historic Document," 12; "Biographical Record for Johannes Philipp Wambsganss Jr."; Fred Wambsganss Sr., "Five Decades of Pastoral Activity," *Concordia Historical Institute Quarterly* 30, no. 4 (Winter 1958): 146.
[23] The address for the LDA main office (as listed in the July 1920 article by Graebner in *The Lutheran Witness*) is identical to the parsonage address for Phillip Wambsganss Jr.; cf. *Lutheran Annual* (St. Louis: Concordia, 1920).

she also needed to declare the precious truths of God's Word to the sin-sick soul. She would be prepared for this latter task, as well as the first, with the aid of some good Lutheran textbooks: *Catechism Outlines* by W. H. T. Dau; *The Book of Books* by J. Schaller; *The Difference: A Popular Guide to Denominational History and Doctrine* by I. G. Monson; and *Life of Luther* by Gustave Just.[24]

At the LDA's request, Rev. Dr. Paul Edward Kretzmann (1883–1965) wrote *A Handbook of Outlines for the Training of Lutheran Deaconesses,* and The Young Women's Lutheran Deaconess Association of St. Louis published it without expense to the LDA.[25] Every deaconess student received a free copy of this little volume, which contained a meaty syllabus for eight "Deaconess Work" courses:

The First Year

Course I. The Great Need of Trained Women Workers and Their Field of Activity
Course II. The Office of the Lutheran Deaconess
Course III. The Qualification of a Lutheran Deaconess
Course IV. History of Missions

The Second Year

Course V. Bible Study
Course VI. The Fundamental Doctrines of Scripture
Course VII. The Distinctive Doctrines of the Lutheran Church

The Third Year

Course VIII. The Various Departments of the Deaconess's Work[26]

The LDA expected much of the women who desired to be consecrated, or set apart, for the Lord's work. During the first year of training, 38 percent of their lessons (thirty out of eighty) dealt with the spiritual, intellectual, and physical qualifications of a Lutheran deaconess! For example, a deaconess must hold "implicit belief in divinity of [the]

---

[24] William Herman Theodore Dau (1864–1944) was a professor at Concordia Seminary, St. Louis, Missouri, and Johannes Schaller (1859–1920) was president of the Wisconsin Synod Theological Seminary at Wauwatosa. See *Lutheran Cyclopedia* (St. Louis: Concordia, 1984), 222, 697. Monson's book lists him in 1915 as a pastor of the Norwegian Lutheran Synod at Williston, N. D. See Herzberger, "Historic Document," 12.
[25] Page 48 of "The Lutheran Deaconess Association," monograph, signed "The Committee" (of the LDA of St. Louis and Vicinity), 1937/38, private collection of Clara Strehlow, Deaconess Office Archives, Concordia University, River Forest, IL.
[26] Paul E. Kretzmann, *A Handbook of Outlines for the Training of Lutheran Deaconesses* (St. Louis: Young Women's Lutheran Deaconess Association), 3, 8, 18, 33, 43, 58, 73, 83.

Bible and all its doctrines" and have "personal faith in Jesus Christ as Redeemer." The fundamental principle of her life would be "faith active in love." She needed to cultivate "habits of prayer," a "spirit of service for the Master," and "a sense of fellowship with Christ" through the assurance of Scripture and "frequent partaking of the Lord's Supper." The deaconess treated her body as a "gift of God" and "an instrument to His glory," to be "preserved in health" through "mental stimulation," "cleanliness," "proper food and drink," "recreation," "exercise," "control and regulation of the passions," and "methodical living." Her Christian character embraced the biblically defined virtues of faith, hope, and love; humility, firmness, courage, and self-respect; fidelity, veracity, and sincerity; enthusiasm, diligence, affability, and neatness; individuality, patience, conscientiousness, and politeness; liberality, dignity, chastity, and self-denial; punctuality, cheerfulness, and sympathy; patience, knowledge, and interest "in every phase of church work."[27]

The books, or portions thereof, to be read for each of the *Handbook*'s 240 lessons comprised an impressive collection of titles from *Concordia Triglotta* and *Lutheran Home Missions* to *The Elements of Business Law* and *Educational Psychology*.[28] A sound and continuous grounding in God's Word is implied throughout the course outline, while one lesson makes specific suggestions for personal devotions:

Lesson 44

The private study of the deaconess:
(a) Methods of Bible reading and study: *regular* reading, either a chapter a day, or three on week-days, five on Sundays, finishing 1199 chapters of the Bible once a year; mental review, marking and memorizing of striking passages;
(b) Study of the Catechism: regular recital of text and explanation part of devotional exercise; Luther's example;
(c) Commentaries and Bible helps: Schaller, *Book of Books; Concordia Bible Class; Popular Commentary*.[29]

Given the theological discussions that accompanied the introduction of deaconesses to the Synodical Conference, it is interesting to note that Course II (The Office of the Lutheran Deaconess) addresses the role of

---

[27] Kretzmann, *Handbook*, 18, 20–25, 30–32.
[28] See Appendix 1.A.: Books listed as "References" for the 240 lessons in Kretzmann, *Handbook*.
[29] Kretzmann, *Handbook*, 24. In 1942, Kretzmann wrote a lengthy article on how the regular reading of Scripture was to be accomplished. See P. E. Kretzmann, "The Lutheran Deaconess as a Bible Student," *The Lutheran Deaconess* 19, no. 4 (October 1942): 5–6.

women in the Church. Lessons 11–15 cover "Leading women of the Old
Testament and the lessons of their lives and labors," "Prophetesses of the
Old Testament, their good and their bad qualities," "The women of the
Gospels as examples," "The women of Acts and the Epistles as examples,"
and "General passages referring to the ministry of women."[30] The outline
for Lesson 16 moves to a tighter focus:

> The status of women according to Scriptures:
>
> Question not one of superiority, but of headship; the nature of woman's
> subordination; the extent in which women may exercise functions of men;
> no essential difference in marriage and outside of marriage.
>
> Passages for study: Gen. 3,16; 1 Cor. 11,3; 1 Tim. 2,12; Eph. 5,22–31; Col.
> 3,18. 19; 1 Cor. 14,34-35.
>
> (REFERENCES: Woman in the Church, *Theol. Quart.*, 1920, Jan. and
> April.)[31]

Far from being a hot subject for debate, the role of women in the
Church appears to have been a non-issue in the Missouri Synod in 1920, at
least according to the required reading from *Theological Quarterly*[32] for Lesson
16:

> The woman in the Church, her rights and privileges, the restrictions which
> limit her activity, etc., are questions about which there has been much
> discussion, and about which the widest divergence of opinion prevails. It
> is a question, the settlement of which has, at least in our circles, been
> taken for granted, and in Lutheran literature, especially that of the
> Missouri Synod, we find only scattering paragraphs, and all of them,
> without exception, take the sole stand of absolute silence of the woman,
> not only in the divine service, but also in all the business relations of the
> Church. Our congregations have for the most part remained pretty well
> untouched by the modern suffragette movement; but with the wide-
> spread agitation of this question the related question of the standing of
> the woman in the Church may here and there become a burning one, and
> a free discussion of it in conference circles does not seem at all untimely.
>
> … In conclusion we wish to state that we personally are grateful to the
> Lord that through the mouth of the apostles he has defined the position
> of woman in the church. . . . We are happy to see that the women in the
> Lutheran Church have not yet been permeated to any great extent with
> the general modern spirit of female restlessness. They have, as true
> daughters of the Lord, always proved amenable to the instruction of the

---

[30] Kretzmann, *Handbook*, 8–10.

[31] Kretzmann, *Handbook*, 10.

[32] *Theological Quarterly* was a professional journal for pastors, published by the LCMS. The
two seminary faculties in St. Louis, Missouri, and Springfield, Illinois, served as editors for
the journal.

Word, and will in the future, no doubt, abide willingly by its precepts. We owe them much in our church work. Let us with them, in the light of the Word, with love and consideration, continue to do the Lord's work with singleness of heart.[33]

In reading this type of article, future deaconesses could take encouragement from the sentence "We owe them much in our church work," even if the words refer in general terms to female members of the Lutheran Church. Such a phrase, set in the context of this paragraph, implies that Missouri Synod women (thus Missouri Synod deaconesses) *do* have a valued role in the work of the Church *and* that they can be trusted to continue to carry out that role in harmony with the "instruction of the Word."

RAPID EXPANSION

So many things came together quickly for the LDA after it established the educational partnership with Lutheran Hospital in Fort Wayne. Wambsganss moved into the new motherhouse with his family, and without ever receiving remuneration for his work, directed every aspect of the training program until December 1, 1923, when Rev. Bruno Poch (1877–1960) became superintendent.[34] In the meantime, and indeed, until his death in 1933, Wambsganss continued in his role as president of the LDA. He shared the vision of deaconess ministry with Synodical Conference officials, wrote articles for Lutheran journals, organized financial campaigns, and often took the lead in investigating potential opportunities for the expansion of deaconess ministry. One idea that excited Wambsganss was that the LDA might own and operate its own Deaconess Hospital, which would be the central hub of the association.[35] Within a short time, this idea moved toward becoming a reality.

---

[33] Paul Lindemann, "The Woman in the Church," *Theological Quarterly* 24 (April 1920): 30, 121.

[34] Albers, "We Trace Our Steps: Chapter 3," 5; Kohlmeier, *25th Anniversary of the Lutheran Deaconess Association*, 9; F. W. Herzberger, "The Lord Hath Need of Them," *TLD* 1, no. 1 (January 1924): 1.

[35] Deaconess Clara Strehlow, interview by Deaconesses Nancy Nicol and Betty Mulholland, November 12–13, 1982, transcript, private collection of Betty (Schmidt) Mulholland, Munster, IN.

BEAVER DAM, WISCONSIN

God's Blessing With Us

Who would have thought, when in August 1919 we organized our LDA, that we would have a Deaconess home in less than two years from that time? Much less did we think that we would have our own Deaconess hospital about two years after the beginning of our Deaconess work. Such is the case, however. How was it brought about? Let me briefly tell you.

The people of Beaver Dam, Wis., a city of about 9,000 inhabitants, felt the want of a hospital in their city. A large house, built like a castle, beautifully located on the shore of Beaver Lake, within a park of three acres, could be purchased for a very reasonable price. Physicians and others declared that the building could well be used for hospital purposes, with only slight alterations. Business men of the city inquired of our local pastor, Rev. L. Kirst, whether he knew of a deaconess association that would possibly be interested in the hospital proposition in case the people of Beaver Dam would buy the place and transfer it to the association with the understanding that it would conduct the hospital. Pastor Kirst at once communicated with our LDA in this matter. After some correspondence, representatives of the Association went to Beaver Dam and conferred personally with our friends there, also inspected the building and grounds, and the agreement was reached, that our Association would undertake to conduct the hospital after the property would be purchased, made ready for the purpose intended, and transferred to the LDA. The citizens of Beaver Dam at once organized for a "drive" to raise the necessary funds to buy and equip the property and it was not long before $60,000 was subscribed. The purchase was made, the alterations now under way, including the installation of an elevator, will soon be completed, and when this report will reach our members, there will be, we hope, a Lutheran Deaconess Hospital at Beaver Dam, owned and operated by our LDA.[36]

On January 29, 1922, the Lutheran Deaconess Hospital was dedicated. The celebration started with worship at St. Stephen's Evangelical Lutheran Church (Wisconsin Synod) in Beaver Dam, followed by a formal dedication ceremony at the main entrance of the hospital building, after which the hospital was opened to the public for inspection. The order of service included congregational singing of *Lobe den Herren, den maechtigen Koenig der Ehren* ("Praise to the Lord, the Almighty, the King of Creation"). Rev. Leonard C. Kirst (1882–1975), pastor of St. Stephen's, gave an address in

---

[36] "God's Blessing with Us," in Second Annual Report of the Lutheran Deaconess Association within the Ev. Luth. Synodical Conference of North America (Fort Wayne, IN: LDA, 1921), 2.

English, and Rev. Wambsganss preached in German.[37] Three days later, on February 1, 1922, the hospital opened for business.[38]

The Lutherans in Beaver Dam formed an LDA branch society and elected a board of officers that included Pastor Kirst, president; Ernest Wegener, vicepresident; (Mrs.) A. Spars, secretary; and (Mr.) L. A. Briese, treasurer.[39] The entire membership of the LDA owned Deaconess Hospital, but since national LDA board members resided in Fort Wayne, they placed management of the hospital into the hands of the local branch society board. The national LDA board stipulated that the hospital's "Superintendent of nurses shall be a deaconess nurse."[40] The Beaver Dam board found a clever way to fulfill this requirement *and* broaden the base of deaconess training within the Synodical Conference:

> Since we have not, as yet, any graduate deaconesses, we communicated with a number of our Lutheran graduate nurses, with a view of securing their services for our new institution. We succeeded in obtaining a Lutheran Registered Nurse, who desires to become a Deaconess and eventually to aid in our foreign mission work. This Christian woman will be the head of our Beaver Dam hospital, and while there she will study Diaconics under Rev. Kirst, thus to equip herself fully for her chosen work in the mission field. Other Lutheran nurses, graduates of our Ft. Wayne hospital training school, now practicing in Wisconsin, have expressed their willingness to take positions in the Beaver Dam institution.
>
> Since according to Wisconsin laws only the large hospitals, having a greater number of beds, are permitted to have a training school for nurses, accredited by the state, our board has decided to conduct a branch school for Deaconesses in connection with our hospital at Beaver Dam. In this school, which is to be under the direction of Pastor Kirst, the pupils will be educated as Deaconesses, and also as practical nurses, so that, after three years' training at this Deaconess Hospital, they will be

[37] "Program of the Dedicational Services of Lutheran Deaconess Hospital, Beaver Dam, Wisconsin, January 29, 1922, 2:00 p.m.," private collection of Clara Strehlow, Deaconess Office Archives, Concordia University, River Forest, IL.

[38] Kohlmeier, *25th Anniversary of the Lutheran Deaconess Association*, 10.

[39] "God's Blessing with Us," 2.

[40] "Guiding Principles and Rules and Regulations for Boards and Business Manager and Superintendent of Nurses of the Lutheran Deaconess Hospital at Beaver Dam, Wis.," original typed pages, private collection of Clara Strehlow, Deaconess Office Archives, Concordia University, River Forest, IL.

prepared to pass their Deaconess examination, and to work in the various fields of labor, where Deaconesses are so sorely needed.[41]

Several Lutheran clergymen from the Beaver Dam area assisted Kirst and Superintendent Bruno Poch in teaching the deaconess students: G. Pieper, Edmund Reim, Ernst Walther, M. J. Nommensen, and H. Geiger from the Wisconsin Synod, and William Traugott Naumann (1876–1944) from the Missouri Synod.[42]

Ina Kempff, who held the distinction of being the first woman to enroll in the Fort Wayne deaconess program, graduated from the Fort Wayne Hospital Nursing School in the fall of 1922 and immediately became head matron of Lutheran Deaconess Hospital in Beaver Dam. A year later, Deaconesses Bessie Stenke and Clara Wiebke graduated and also joined the hospital staff.[43]

RECRUITMENT

Financial support and excitement for the Lutheran deaconess movement was on the rise. In addition, the number of Synodical Conference charitable institutions—representing opportunities for deaconess ministry—steadily increased. However, recruitment needed a huge boost. Women were not coming forward for training as quickly as the LDA had hoped. Whether their fathers and pastors were still skeptical about the propriety of deaconesses serving in the Church, or the idea was simply too new for conservative Germans, is difficult to determine. Whatever the reason, something had to be done to convince Lutheran women that the Church required their assistance to succeed in carrying out the biblical directive to take the Gospel of Jesus Christ to all people, including the ill and disadvantaged of society. Toward that end, Wambsganss wrote articles such as the following for several Lutheran publications.

An Appeal For Deaconesses

Deaconess work offers the young women of our church a splendid opportunity for service to their church in the ministry of mercy in caring

---

[41] E. Hildebrandt was the "Lutheran Registered Nurse" who took charge of the hospital. Cora Habighorst, a graduate of the Fort Wayne Lutheran Hospital nursing school, was her assistant. See L. C. Kirst, "Our Lutheran Deaconess Hospital at Beaver Dam, Wis.," *TLD* 1, no. 3 (July 1924): 18; "God's Blessing with Us," 2.

[42] Nommensen lived in Juneau; Walther and Geiger in Randolph; Reim in Fox Lake. Naumann lived in West Bloomfield and later in Watertown. See Kohlmeier, *25th Anniversary of the Lutheran Deaconess Association*, 11.

[43] Herzberger, "Historic Document," 12.

for the sick and the poor. Deaconess work dates back to the early history of the Christian Church, where under guidance of the Apostles, its work of mercy was performed in the service of eternal love. In the Sixteenth Chapter of Romans, we read of Phoebe, a servant of the Church, who was a Deaconess, so were also Priscilla and Mary.

There is a great need of such deaconesses in our dear Lutheran Church today. Many large congregations; our City Missions; our Charitable Institutions; Home Finding Societies; Hospitals; Hospices, and last but not least, our foreign Missions—all these are fields of labor for deaconesses.

Deaconesses must be well trained in order to be prepared for their glorious calling. . . . The course comprises a three years' training in the Fort Wayne Lutheran Hospital Training School for Nurses, and during those three years a course in diaconics, consisting of religious branches is offered. In 1921 the Lutheran Deaconess Association succeeded in gaining possession of a deaconess home on the Lutheran Hospital grounds at Fort Wayne. Last year our society also acquired its own deaconess hospital at Beaver Dam, Wisconsin, a free gift made to us by Beaver Dam Lutherans. This hospital with its deaconess school is also in a flourishing condition.

For the information of those who are thinking of becoming deaconesses I wish to say that the applicants for enrollment in our schools must be a member of a congregation belonging to the Synodical conference; they must have reached the age of 19; and above all they must be filled with a fervent love and an ardent desire to serve their Savior in his church. To enter our school at Fort Wayne one year of high school is required; the Beaver Dam school requires a good common school education.

During three years at school the pupils receive, free of charge, tuition, room and board, laundry, books, uniforms and a yearly allowance of $100 for personal expenses. In this way the association takes care of the training of its deaconesses from the beginning. After completing their course our deaconesses enjoy the following privileges:

First, an appropriate salary whenever they are engaged in the service of the association.

Second, privileges of home in the motherhouse whenever they are out of work.

Third, free medical attention in case of sickness.

Fourth, maintenance during life.

Now, my dear sisters in Christ, what do you think of the matter? Would you not like to become a deaconess and dedicate your life to this noble cause? Those of you who are not so inclined, have the opportunity of joining the Lutheran Deaconess Association by contributing one dollar per year or more to support this undertaking. . . .

May the Lord bless your societies and may He unite you all most closely with His love.[44]

THE MASTER CALLETH

While Wambsganss penned articles for journals, Herzberger continued to produce four-page tracts for different groups that he felt should be interested in the deaconess cause. Some tracts went to Synodical Conference clergy to "supply our pastors with more detailed information concerning deaconess work so as to enable them to present our cause in a more effective manner to their congregations."[45] Other tracts offered compelling reasons for young Lutheran women either to become deaconesses or to provide prayer and financial support to the LDA. "The Master is Come and Calleth for Thee" was one of Herzberger's more emotive tracts, and is a good example of the Pietism that was prevalent in the early twentieth century.

"The Master is Come and Calleth for Thee"

An Appeal to our Young Lutheran Womanhood

for Missionary Deaconess Work

The Master is Jesus, *your Jesus*, my dear young Lutheran woman. In His great Savior's love He comes to the grave of His friend Lazarus to raise him from the dead. (John 11.) There He meets Lazarus's weeping sister Martha, and at once comforts her with those ever-blessed words of imperishable divine consolation: "I am the Resurrection and the Life: he that believeth in Me, though he were dead, yet shall he live; and whosoever liveth and believeth in Me shall never die." Martha is cheered and comforted so wonderfully by these majestic words that she answers His question: "Believest thou this?" with the joyful confession: "Yea, Lord, I believe that Thou art the Christ, the Son of God, which should come into the world," and then she can contain herself no longer, but straightway hurries home where she knows her sister Mary is still in tears, and summons her to the Lord with the words: "The Master is come and calleth for thee." ..."The Master is come and calleth for thee!" Martha's

---

[44] Philip Wambsganss [Jr.], "An Appeal for Deaconesses," *Der Bote aus Bethesda* 14, no. 4 (July 1923): 11–12.

[45] F. W. Herzberger, "Some Facts About Deaconess Work (1924)," Deaconess Office Archives, Concordia University, River Forest, IL.

cheerful message [to Mary] also applies to you, my dear young Lutheran woman. Jesus is still today the same compassionate Savior that He was there at the grave of Lazarus. He alone has power to comfort and to save where grief and sorrow abide. How many homes there are in our towns and villages where grievous want or sickness abounds, and where you could bring the blessed message of Jesus and His saving love, and also relieve the dire want and distress if you were a "Missionary Deaconess," called by the Church of your Savior to look after the poor, the sick, the wayward and forlorn in your appointed field of labor! . . . Would it not be a blessed thing for you if you could help to bring the sweet Gospel-message and also bodily help to some of these afflicted, mourning, and, perhaps, perishing souls?

. . . If sacred family ties do not stand in the way and you are in good health, you can enter our "School for Missionary Deaconesses" at Fort Wayne, Ind., and there acquire, *free of charge*, the necessary training for your high and blessed calling. . . . Surely, the Lord will not let you starve if you labor for Him, will He? If you serve Him, He will provide you with "enough and to spare," and in feeble old age give you a home in the "Motherhouse" until He takes you into His everlasting home above. If you decided to serve Him as a deaconess only until you establish your own home, think of the lasting benefits your training at the school will furnish you for the better discharge of your duties at your own dear fireside.

. . . But then there is another way in which you can help this blessed work of your Lord along. You can support it by your prayers and your gifts. You can take out a membership card at one dollar a year, send in occasional contributions of thank-offerings, and persuade others to do likewise. Can't you do that for your Lord? Will you not at least do that much for Him who has done so much for you? You pledged Him your faith and love in your Baptism, and renewed the sacred pledge on the day of your Confirmation. What will you do now that you hear the master's call? How much of your heart and life will you give, are you giving, to Jesus, your blessed, blessed Jesus, my dear young Lutheran woman? Ponder the message well: "The Master is come and calleth for thee!"[46]

---

[46] F. W. Herzberger, "The Master is Come and Calleth for Thee, An Appeal to our Young Lutheran Womanhood for Missionary Deaconess Work," in Brochures & Tracts File of the Lutheran Deaconess Association Collection, CHI, St. Louis, Mo. Just four months before Herzberger's death, his tract was printed in *The Lutheran Deaconess*, without naming him as author. See "An Appeal to Our Young Lutheran Womanhood for Missionary Deaconess Work" and "Beaver Dam's Plea," *TLD* 7, no. 2 (1930): 12–13.

HOT SPRINGS, SOUTH DAKOTA

In the decade from 1915 to 1925, the number of hospitals connected with ALCh rose from twelve to nineteen.[47] Among the new affiliates was Lutheran Hospital and Sanitarium in Hot Springs, South Dakota, which came into being through the ingenuity of Rev. Elmer Eugene Foelber (1892–1987). Working as an LCMS missionary to the Southern Black Hills, Foelber knew the poverty and suffering of the local people and their need for a hospital. An opportunity presented itself when a medical quack built a hospital in Hot Springs and subsequently lost it. The building was a beautiful three-story, 106-room, castlelike edifice, situated on prime property overlooking the town. Foelber decided to acquire the building, but struggled with how to collect enough money for its purchase. He incidentally discovered that many German-American Lutherans disliked the World War I Liberty Bonds they had been induced to buy. Foelber suggested that war bonds could be donated to the hospital fund. The people responded enthusiastically, and in 1917, Hot Springs had its first hospital.[48]

Although information about the early years of the hospital is sketchy, it was closely associated with the Lutheran community in and around Hot Springs. Just before the dedication of Bethesda Lutheran Church (LCMS) in Hot Springs, the *Hot Springs Star* newspaper reported that the congregation organized on November 19, 1919, "about three years after a mission with a resident pastor had been established." The same article reported that "in the beginning" Bethesda's members worshiped in several different places, including "the large dining room of the newly opened Lutheran Hospital and Sanitarium."[49] The "resident pastor" who established this mission congregation was Pastor Foelber, who served the people of Hot Springs until October 1924, when he accepted a call to the position of institutional missionary in Fort Wayne, Indiana. Interestingly, Foelber's new responsibilities in Fort Wayne included supervision of pastoral care at

[47] F. Dean Lueking, A Century of Caring: The Welfare Ministry Among Missouri Synod Lutherans 1868–1968 (St. Louis: LCMS Board of Social Ministry, 1968), 28.
[48] The original hospital building, with "Lutheran 1917" carved in stone on the castellated roofline, still stands at 209 North 16th Street in Hot Springs. It is used by Fall River Health Services as a nursing and assisted-living facility. See Lueking, *Century of Caring*, 29–30; E. H. Albers, "We Trace Our Steps: Chapter 4," *TLD* 45, no. 4 (Winter 1968): 3.
[49] *Hot Springs Star* 39, no. 8 (June 19, 1924): 1.

Lutheran Hospital, where LDA deaconess students received their nurse's training.[50]

Before Foelber left Hot Springs in the early months of 1924, a Lutheran organization called Hot Springs Hospital and Sanitarium Association sent Pastor K. Schroeder of Chamberlain, South Dakota, to Fort Wayne to ask the LDA "to help them in their efforts to maintain an institution that would have a proper Christian atmosphere by supplying them with deaconesses."[51] The LDA responded in the affirmative. However, only five deaconesses had graduated to date, and three of those worked at Lutheran Deaconess Hospital in Beaver Dam. The association decided to send Deaconess Clara Dienst to Hot Springs to serve as superintendent of nurses and superintendent of a third deaconess training school to be established there.[52]

Deaconess Dienst arrived in Hot Springs in the middle of March 1924 and quickly assumed a leadership role in the community. The town's April 10 newspaper noted: "The ladies of the Bethesda Lutheran Church met at the Lutheran Hospital Thursday afternoon. A very interesting talk was given by Miss Clara Dienst on the missionary work done in St. Louis by the deaconesses in connection with the church. After sewing bandages and garments for the hospital the ladies were served with lunch."[53]

The following month, Superintendent Bruno Poch arrived from Fort Wayne to visit Dienst and the hospital. Poch traveled many miles each year in the course of his job, and tried to promote the deaconess cause at every possible opportunity.[54] During his trip to South Dakota, he spoke to

---

[50] In fall 1925, Foelber and pastor emeritus Wm. Diederich taught 57 of 266 lessons given to the deaconess students at the Fort Wayne training school. Foelber also led a weekly Bible study at the Nurses' Home, which all nursing students were required to attend. Foelber was an active member of the LDA Board of Directors for more than forty years. During his tenure, he served as financial secretary and vice president. See *Hot Springs Star* 39, no. 23 (October 2, 1924); "Our Deaconess Schools," *TLD* 2, no. 4 (October 1925): 26; "Our School at Fort Wayne," *TLD* 5, no. 1 (January 1928): 2; "Notes and News," *TLD* 7, no. 1 (January 1930): 7.

[51] The executive committee of the hospital included Rev. John Witt, Norfolk, Neb., chairman; Rev. Benedict Henry Julius Schwarz (1895–1954), Rapid City, S. D., secretary; and Mr. William Koch, Stanton, Neb. Rev. Jacob Holstein (1871–1944), Plainview, Neb., edited *Messenger of Health*, the official publication of the sanitarium. Witt served the Wisconsin Synod, while the other pastors were all members of the Missouri Synod. See "News From Hot Springs, S. Dak.," *TLD* 8, no. 1 (January 1931): 3.

[52] *TLD* 1, no. 2 (April 1924): 12; *TLD* 8, no. 1 (January 1931): 3.

[53] *Hot Springs Star* 38, no. 50 (April 10, 1924): 5. Dienst had been engaged in missionary work in St. Louis for two and a half months before moving to Hot Springs.

[54] In 1925, Poch recounted, "Forty-seven sermons and lectures were delivered. The mileage covered was 13,183." "Publicity Work," *TLD* 2, no. 4 (October 1925): 27.

the Lutheran pastors' conference of the Black Hills region, which included some pastors from neighboring areas of Nebraska.[55]

Another "tidbit" of information from the August 1925 issue of the *Hot Springs Star* reads: "Miss Anna Haltmann, [*sic*] principal of the training school at the Lutheran Hospital at Ft. Wayne, Indiana is spending her vacation at the Lutheran Hospital here."[56] Modern journalists may consider this brief remark to be little more than small-town gossip, but it shows deliberate contact between the training institutions.

The Hot Springs training school for deaconesses opened in fall 1924, with Dienst at its head. A year later, Poch reported to the annual LDA meeting:

> Three deaconesses were enrolled at our Hot Springs school last fall. Pastor Gerike had kindly agreed to furnish the instruction in the particular deaconess subjects, and we are informed that the newly installed chaplain of our Lutheran Sanitarium, Pastor Lewis Lang, will soon be on the teaching staff.[57] Our venerable president, Rev. Ph. Wambsganss, who visited Hot Springs a few weeks ago, assured us that the conditions under which a deaconess training school ought to be opened are ideal at Hot Springs.
>
> We are also happy to state that this institution is now on a good financial footing, and we hope that Lutherans throughout the country suffering from asthma and other chronic troubles will patronize our Hot Springs Sanitarium.[58]

TAKING STOCK

In August 1924, not long before the third deaconess training school opened in Hot Springs, a slightly different discussion took place at the ALCh conference in Indianapolis. The LDA was five years old, and the ALCh asked Herzberger to present a paper that evaluated whether the association was achieving its stated goals. The sections of Herzberger's paper that follow exemplify the thinking that continued to shape the development of the office of deaconess within the Synodical Conference for many years.

---

[55] *Hot Springs Star* 39, no. 1 (May 1, 1924).
[56] *Hot Springs Star* 40, no. 15 (August 6, 1925): 5. Elsewhere, "Haltmann" is spelled "Holtman." See "Our Deaconess Schools."
[57] The pastors referred to are Rev. John F. F. Gerike (1864–1952) and Rev. Lewis Hugo Lang (b. 1896).
[58] "Hot Springs, S. Dak.," *TLD* 2, no. 4 (October 1925): 27.

Your committee on papers has assigned me a paper with the title: "The Proper Aim of Our Deaconess Work, and How to Attain It." Before discussing it, let me raise a question, Have we a right here in the conference to speak about our deaconess work, as the paper asks us to do? Well, has a father a right to say anything to his child? If so, we have a right thoroughly to discuss the aims of our deaconess work; for it was this conference that fathered our deaconess society five years ago, and therefore it is certainly interested in the work as at present conducted and also in any improvements that can be suggested for its successful conduct.

Now, as to the first point: *the proper aim of our deaconess work.* . . . For the sake of clearness we must subdivide this declaration of purpose of our Deaconess Association into three different sections, for to my mind the declaration of purposes calls for three different kinds of deaconesses.

In the first place, it calls for such deaconesses as ought to care for the sick and poor in the congregations of the Ev. Lutheran Synodical Conference. Here the section evidently has *parish* deaconesses in mind as they were known in the primitive Christian Church, and this, as history tells us, was the original form of the female diaconate.

Secondly, the section speaks of deaconesses to be trained for the ministry of mercy in all charitable institutions; hence *institutional* deaconesses.

In the third place, Section 3a calls for such as are to be trained for the home and foreign mission work of the Synodical Conference; hence *missionary* deaconesses.

You will agree with me that the work of the parish deaconess differs materially from the work of the institutional deaconess, and both again, differ from the work of the home and foreign missionary deaconess. The three different departments of work call for three different classes of deaconesses, each possessing the peculiar spiritual and material gifts that would fit them for their chosen calling.

The chief purpose of the parish deaconess is to assist the pastor in building up the congregation which called her. The institutional deaconess has the interest of the charity institutions mainly at heart. The deaconess for home missionary work, which we had best call the Christian social worker, and the foreign missionary deaconess will specialize in the duties peculiar to their fields of labor. . . .

Now, *how to attain the proper aim of our deaconess work*,—and here comes the big rub! Section 3b in the constitution of our Deaconess Association says we should "erect and maintain Lutheran deaconess schools, motherhouses, and other institutions likely to promote the purposes of the Society."

So the constitution establishes the right to found not only one, but more institutions in which deaconess pupils can be trained for their blessed work. At present we have three hospitals in which gifted young women are trained as deaconess nurses: the hospitals at Fort Wayne, Ind., Beaver Dam, Wis., and Hot Springs, S. Dak.; and no one will deny that we need good, well-trained, and up-to-date deaconess nurses in our missionary work. However, it is a mistake to think that we ought to train only deaconess nurses and can neglect the training of institutional and missionary nurses.

Five years ago, at the request of our Charities Conference, certain brethren at Fort Wayne petitioned our Fort Wayne Hospital to open a training-school for Lutheran deaconesses in its midst. The petitioners said: "A deaconess is not a nurse in the commonly accepted sense of that term. She is rather a social worker, and if she is in the employ of a church or a churchly association, she is a religious social service worker. She can be called a nurse only in so far as she must also have practical training in nursing, since her work will make it necessary for her to care also for the sick at times. In addition, however, she must have special training for social work, as well as the ability to deal with people in a religious way."

It is an old saying that the course of true love never runs smooth, and this also holds true of the work of love done by our brethren in Fort Wayne for our deaconess cause. They were handicapped from the beginning by the firm decision taken by the hospital board that our deaconess pupils there were compelled to study as *trained nurses* and could receive instruction for their deaconess calling only in their free hours. Those among us acquainted with the situation know what dissatisfaction this has caused, not only with our deaconess pupils, but with a great number of the well-wishers and supporters of our deaconess cause in and outside of Fort Wayne. We certainly need deaconess nurses, but it cannot be denied that their training at present in the true deaconess work is most insufficient. It stands to reason that if our deaconess pupils want to study their text-books on nursing thoroughly and attend to all the medical requirements expected of them, they will not have the time nor the strength also thoroughly to follow up deaconess work. Hence I most emphatically urge an extra course of deaconess training after our deaconess nurses have absolved their training in the three above-named hospitals.

Another thing: Two years ago I sent out an appeal to establish a training-school for such of our young women as did not want to become trained nurses, and they are by far the majority of applicants. I say I sent out an appeal to establish a school for practical deaconess work in our institution at Watertown, where we find all the facilities for their training, especially as institutional deaconesses. . . .

Now, as regards the training of home and foreign missionary deaconesses, the only practical way in my mind to solve that problem is to establish and maintain a central *Woman's* [*sic*] *Missionary Institute*, where those of our deaconess nurses who wish to enter the mission-fields, or such of our consecrated and gifted young women as do not want to become nurses, but missionary deaconesses, can be suitably educated and trained for their calling. . . .

As the best way of establishing such a central Women's Missionary Institute it is evident that neither our Charities Conference nor our Deaconess Association will ever have the funds for erecting and maintaining the institute. Both societies are limited in their work, which is chiefly charity, but our synods, both the Missouri and the Wisconsin Synod, *make missionary work their main object.* . . . We want to enlist the cooperation of our Walther League and with it petition both the Missouri and the Wisconsin Synod to provide an institute for woman missionaries either conjointly or separately. Our synods consist not only of men, but to a large degree also of women, who are debarred from public preaching, but in all other respects have the same spiritual rights and duties as the men to "show forth the praises of Him who hath called them out of darkness into His marvelous light." I Peter 2:9. F. W. Herzberger.[59]

WATERTOWN, WISCONSIN

Whether ALCh further investigated a Women's Missionary Institute is unknown,[60] but Herzberger's report on the business carried out at the LDA convention in Fort Wayne the following month noted, "The most important resolution concerned the opening of a summer school next year at Watertown, Wisc., for women workers in our Lutheran Church who do not wish to become trained nurses."[61]

The facility implied as the base of operations for the proposed fourth deaconess training school was not another hospital, but Bethesda—the Evangelical Lutheran School for the Feebleminded and Epileptic Children—that opened in Watertown, Wisconsin, in 1904. Bethesda

---

[59] Herzberger presented the paper on August 7, 1924. See F. W. Herzberger, "The Proper Aim of Our Deaconess Work, and How to Attain It," *TLD* 1, no. 4 (1924): 30–32.

[60] In October 1927, Herzberger published a similar plea for a "missionary institute for the training of lay workers," where they could be "housed and instructed in the language, religion, and habits of the people in their heathen fields and also hear about dangerous Oriental diseases and how to guard against them." Again, the Missouri and Wisconsin Synods took no action on the proposal. See F. W. Herzberger, "With the Editor," *TLD* 4, no. 4 (October 1927): 25.

[61] F. W. Herzberger, "Annual Meeting of the Deaconess Association," *TLD* 1, no. 4 (October 1924): 25.

frequently published pleas for more staff. As in Hot Springs, LDA leaders thought that a deaconess training school would provide both temporary and long-term workers for Bethesda and other facilities. One of the great champions of this idea was Rev. Frederick Herman Eggers (1870–1948), pastor of St. John Lutheran Church in Watertown,[62] who also served as chaplain to Bethesda's residents. His lengthy article "We Need Deaconesses in Bethesda, at Watertown, Wis.," is a beautiful witness to the ministry of love and mercy to individuals with developmental disabilities and how he believed deaconesses "could be employed in our Home as teachers and caretakers."[63]

> The training course for "practical deaconesses" would obviously need to be structured differently than the existing one for "nursing deaconesses." The LDA appointed a committee of Rev. Philipp Wambsganss Jr., Rev. John Witte, Rev. Bruno Poch, and Rev. Frederick Eggers to address the question "How can we efficiently educate and train consecrated young Lutheran women for the work of practical deaconesses?"[64] The committee adopted a three-year plan that would include one year of on-site study at Bethesda, while the other two years would "be spent in practical training either in city missionary, parish or institutional work." For the year in Watertown, the candidates would undertake forty weeks of training: ten hours each week at lectures and twenty hours of study time, supplemented with "practical work in the Bethesda institution." The committee specified the lectures and training to include

Diaconics in General	60 hours
History of Missions	60 hours
Bible Study	60 hours
Fundamental Doctrines	30 hours
Distinctive Doctrines of the Lutheran Church	20 hours
Applied Diaconics	80 hours
Practical Pedagogica and Kindergarten Work	40 hours
Medical and Miscellaneous Practical Subjects	<u>50 hours</u>
	400 hours

> The two years to be spent in practical work are for social service work, practical missionary work, home nursing and hospital training, child's welfare work including Juvenile Court work, investigation for adoption of children, etc. The committee thought furthermore, that it would be

---

[62] St. John Lutheran Church was part of the LCMS from 1854 to 1971, when the congregation joined the Wisconsin Synod.

[63] F. H. Eggers, "We Need Deaconesses in Bethesda, at Watertown, Wis.," *TLD* 1, no. 4 (October 1924): 27–30.

[64] F. H. Eggers, "Training of Practical Deaconesses," *TLD* 3, no. 2 (April 1926): 15.

advisable to give some training in music, typewriting, stenography and business methods.[65]

A modern history of Bethesda reveals that the training of deaconess students started even earlier than the summer of 1925. In fact, a two-pronged program at Bethesda accommodated women interested in serving as Lutheran social workers or as practical deaconesses.[66]

Bethesda offered free room and board to deaconess students, while the LDA promised to provide uniforms, a small allowance for spending money, and physical care for the women throughout their lives, in sickness and old age. Eggers and Superintendent Louis M. Pingel of Bethesda worked together to teach the deaconess curriculum.[67] In August 1926, Bethesda installed its first full-time "chaplain and Pastor," Rev. William T. Naumann, who was "to have charge of the preaching and pastoral work among the inmates" and "also, teach the deaconess class and the confirmed patients."[68] Naumann had taught deaconess students in Beaver Dam and eagerly embraced his duties at the fourth LDA training school in Watertown. He wrote:

> Among the earliest and most lasting impressions the undersigned received in his childhood was that made by the quiet and unassuming working of deaconesses he had occasion to observe in the Deaconess Institute at Dresden and at Bethesda, a few miles from Dresden, among the vineyards of the Niederloessnitz. At that time, the thought never entered his mind that in later years he himself would be instructing a class of deaconess pupils in a Bethesda of the New World. . . .

---

[65] F. H. Eggers, "Training of Practical Deaconesses," *Der Bote aus Bethesda* 17, no. 2 (March 1926): 1–2.

[66] The principal of Bethesda's summer school was Pastor F. H. Eggers. He made no secret of the purpose for such a summer school: "to interest our young women in practical church-work and perchance persuade them to enter one of our deaconess training-schools." "Our Summer School at Watertown," *TLD* 2, no. 4 (October 1925): 29.

See also Marlys Taege, *Why Are They So Happy? The Story of Bethesda Lutheran Homes and Services, Inc.* (Watertown: Bethesda Lutheran Homes and Services, Inc., 1996), 54: "Thelma Mattil and Erna Heck began their training in April 1925. That July nine more women came to Watertown for a short summer course for Lutheran social welfare workers and some stayed on for the deaconess program. The regular student deaconesses attended year-round classes in religion, teaching, practical nursing, missions, and office methods during the morning hours. In the afternoon they gained practical experience by helping out in the wards, the classrooms, and wherever needed."

[67] A Pastor Stern assisted Eggers with his teaching duties when the latter became overburdened by other work. Pingel (1873–1965) was the first superintendent of Bethesda. See "School at Bethesda, Watertown," *TLD* 2, no. 4 (October 1925): 27; "Watertown," *TLD* 4 no. 1 (January 1927): 3.

[68] *Der Bote aus Bethesda* 17, no. 4 (July 1926): 15. See also Taege, *Why Are They So Happy?* 54.

On September 1 this school entered upon its second year. The superintendent of Bethesda, Mr. L. Pingel, is giving "Study and Training of the Child and Adolescent" and Music, Dr. F.T. Kosanke is instructing in "Home Nursing," and the undersigned teaches "The Distinctive Doctrines of the Lutheran Church," leads in Bible Studies, and reviews the English Catechism. Other branches will be taken up later.

Our Deaconess School here is a school for the practical training of deaconesses. From the very beginning our deaconess pupils are called upon to work in our Bethesda Home. The Home needs them, and they need the Home for their training. Going through the Home, you may see them diligently engaged in their manifold duties in the office, laundry, kitchen, dayroom, sick-room, laboratory, or sewing-room, or in the park, superintending the "hikes" and plays of the children.

We rejoice to be able to report that our call for more deaconess pupils has been heard by the Lord and His Church. We now have 15 pupils in our school. They come from all directions, from eight different States of the Union. But this does not appear in their work and studies. They all show the good training received in our dear Synodical Conference churches and schools.

Dear reader, no doubt the question has often vexed you why God, who is merciful and kind, could have willed that so many of our fellowmen should be burdened with so many bodily and mental infirmities. But when you see how Christian love is engaged in caring for these sufferers and in alleviating their burden, you can readily see that God does this also for this reason: to test our faith and to give our Christian love an opportunity to unfold and thus to grow and become stronger.

We know that you have opportunity to do this also at home; but learning of the good work our deaconess pupils are trained to do here and wherever they may be called upon to work, you will desire to share also in the blessed work that is done here. This you can do by praying for Bethesda, for our Deaconess School, and for our Deaconess Association and by taking an active part in this work as you may see fit. God will certainly show you the best way to do it, and He will bless you for it.[69]

---

[69] Wm. T. Naumann (great-grandfather of the author's husband) was born in Dresden, Germany, but his mother died when he was three years old. He and a younger brother may have been cared for by deaconesses while their father worked at the family's theological bookstore. See Wm. T. Naumann, "Deaconess School at Watertown, Wis.," *Der Bote aus Bethesda* 17, no. 6 (November 1926): 2; "Obituary of Pastor William T. Naumann," *The Bethesda Messenger* 35, no. 2 (March 1944): 1; family documents, private collection of Jonathan C. Naumann, Pittsburgh, PA.

Fort Wayne, Beaver Dam, Hot Springs, and Watertown. By mid-1925, the LDA had one motherhouse, three schools for the training of deaconess nurses, and one school to train practical deaconesses. Thirty-one students were enrolled in the four schools. Ten deaconesses served in the field: three at hospitals, three in city missions, one as matron of an orphan's home, two in the Apache Indian mission in Arizona, and one as a parish deaconess. Twelve "urgent calls" for deaconesses went unfilled because of a lack of workers, but the LDA expected to place some of its 1926 graduates in LCMS foreign missions.[70]

Was the LDA biting off more than it could chew? Or would the young organization continue to grow and thrive, despite increased financial obligations, the distances between its schools, and the distances that separated deaconesses working in the field?

---

[70] The Arizona Apache Indian mission was an undertaking of the Wisconsin Synod. See "Progress in our Deaconess Work (1925)," in the Brochures & Tracts File of the Lutheran Deaconess Association Collection, CHI, St. Louis, Mo.

Illustrations for Chapter Two may be viewed at www.deaconesshistory.org.

CHAPTER 3

SHAPING DEACONESS IDENTITY

As the work of the LDA expanded within the Synodical Conference, it was important to foster good communication among deaconesses, training institutions, LDA officials, and those who provided financial support for the deaconess cause. Director Wambsganss wrote many articles for magazines, particularly a weekly German publication called *Rundschau*, in which he explained developing deaconess ministries and called for more women to enter the diaconate. The leaders and visionaries of the LDA shared ideas at their own meetings and conferred at ALCh conventions, where official programs always included a report from the LDA. But more avenues than these were needed to get the "deaconess message" out to the Church. In September 1923, two actions helped the LDA move toward achieving this goal: the decision to call a salaried superintendent, a position filled by Rev. Bruno Poch, and the publication of a bilingual quarterly magazine to promote "auxiliary woman's service within Christ's battling Church."[1]

A SUPERINTENDENT

Wambsganss continued to serve as president of the LDA. The workload he carried was phenomenal considering his responsibilities within several charitable organizations in addition to pastoring a congregation.[2] The decision to call a full-time superintendent brought some relief to him and opened a new door to public relations and recruitment for the LDA. It also meant that from this point onward, the LDA President and the hands-on superintendent of deaconess training were different individuals, with the superintendent's role subordinate to the LDA Board of Directors.

Enthusiastic about his work, Superintendent Poch eagerly implemented any idea that would benefit the cause. As the scope of his job expanded, he would eventually teach the deaconess students at every training center and serve as liaison between all parties associated with the LDA.[3]

---

[1] F. W. Herzberger, "The Lord Hath Need of Them," *TLD* 1, no. 1 (January 1924): 1.

[2] See "Biographical Record for Philipp Wambsganss Jr." (St. Louis: CHI, 2004).

[3] "Publicity Work" and "Our Summer School at Watertown," *TLD* 2, no. 4 (October 1925): 27, 30.

Rev. Poch writes us: . . . The superintendent occupies part of the Deaconess Home. Thus far he has also discharged the duties of a secretary and has given the special deaconess instruction. Arrangements have been made for a supply teacher whenever the superintendent is on a lecture trip. The office of the superintendent is located on the first floor; it is used also as a classroom. Adjoining the classroom is the deaconess parlor, where our deaconesses may relax during their few leisure moments. The Senior class occupies two rooms on the second floor. Another room is reserved for visiting deaconesses and, in case of emergency, for deaconesses in training. When stopping at Fort Wayne, be sure to call at the Deaconess Home, where a hearty welcome awaits you."[4]

THE LUTHERAN DEACONESS

January 1924 saw the first issue of *The Lutheran Deaconess: Official Organ of the Lutheran Deaconess Association within the Ev. Lutheran Synodical Conference of North America* (*TLD*). Concordia Publishing House published the eight-page magazine in the months of January, April, July, and October, for a subscription of 25 cents per year.

Always eager to promote the female diaconate, Rev. F. W. Herzberger served as the magazine's first editor, with Rev. John Witte and Rev. Martin Ilse Sr. (1870–1955) acting as associate editors.[5] On Herzberger's death in 1930, the editor's mantle passed to Bruno Poch, who changed the journal's physical format and moved its publication to The Lutheran Press in Berne, Indiana.[6] The LDA Superintendents, or Executive Directors as they were later called, took responsibility for production of the magazine from 1930 until the last issue was published in 1971.

WHAT IS A DEACONESS?

Many rank-and-file members of the Missouri Synod remained unfamiliar with the idea of deaconess ministry unless they came into contact with deaconess nurses or lived within the precincts of city missions. In his lead article, starting on the front page of the first copy of *TLD*, Herzberger addressed the definition of a deaconess.

---

[4] F. W. Herzberger, "A Historic Document," *TLD* 1, no. 2 (April 1924): 12.
[5] Like Herzberger in St. Louis and Witte in Chicago, Ilse was an institutional missionary in Cleveland.
[6] The Lutheran Press changed its name to Economy Printing Concern, Inc., in 1945. The LDA printed the magazine in Fort Wayne or Valparaiso from 1958 onward.

Now, what is a Lutheran deaconess? Answer: A trained woman worker called by the proper authorities to do missionary, educational, or charity work within our Lutheran Church. We hold that our Lord Jesus has given our Church a most precious talent in our pious, intelligent, and willing young women, a talent we have neglected far too long to put to good use for the spread of His kingdom. Indeed, whoever knows what other denominations have accomplished through their trained workers and also knows the crying need of consecrated woman's help in our own over-ripe harvest-fields at home and abroad, in our large city congregations, in our numerous charity institutions, must admit that the Lord has need of them.

In Holy Baptism our women as well as we men were pledged to the service of our God and Savior. What is there to hinder our young women from giving their service to the Church as long as they do this in the right spirit? We need not point out to our Lutheran readers that this so-called female diaconate is no divinely appointed institution of the Lord and does not confer any special spiritual rank or dignity on its members, but that it is simply a helpful office within the Church; it is doing such work as women are best able to do. The office, as we all know, is limited in its scope by the physical nature of woman [sic] and certain limitations of Holy Writ. Within these limitations our Society purposes to carry on its deaconess work.[7]

If Herzberger's definition of a deaconess—a trained woman worker called by the proper authorities to do missionary, educational, or charity work within our Lutheran Church—seems to be over-simplified, the points of his definition are none-the-less potent. He asserts: A deaconess is female and she is properly trained. She works only in situations to which she has been called by the proper authorities. She executes missionary, educational, or charity work within the Lutheran Church, and therefore, within the proper parameters assigned to her by the Scriptures.

Note that Herzberger's brief definition does not mention nursing and does not specify to whom he is referring as "the proper authorities." Neither does he spell out exactly how deaconess work is shaped by the "limitations of Holy Writ" because he believes that his Lutheran readers "all know" and embrace these limitations. In fact, Herzberger's last sentence can be read as a pledge of assurance that the LDA intends to "carry on its deaconess work" in conformity with "these limitations."

Public relations materials about deaconess ministry in the 21st century tend to shy away from specific references to "missionary, educational, or charity work." But the reason for this is simply a change in vocabulary that

---

[7] Herzberger, "The Lord Hath Need of Them," 1–2.

has accompanied a departmentalization of types of church work within the
LCMS. Today, "missionary" work usually refers to overseas placements, the
planting of congregations, or the work of Directors of Christian Outreach
(DCO). "Educational" work might refer to jobs held by teachers or
Directors of Christian Education (DCE). "Charity" work could refer to
activities carried out by Lutheran social workers, LCMS World Relief, or the
Board for Human Care Ministries, as well as various fraternal or volunteer
organizations.[8]

It is possible that the three types of work listed in Herzberger's
definition of a deaconess—*missionary, educational, or charity work*—correspond
to the three "kinds of deaconesses" he explained were needed to fulfill the
stated aims of the LDA: missionary deaconesses to be trained for home and
foreign mission work; parish (or educational) deaconesses to care for the
poor and sick in parishes; and institutional (or charity work) deaconesses to
carry out a ministry of mercy in all charitable institutions.[9]

In early issues of *TLD*, Herzberger included articles describing the
different types of deaconesses needed by the church to fulfill her mission of
bringing the Gospel of Jesus Christ to *all* people. Several of these
fascinating pieces are printed below. Taken together, they document the
grand cumulative vision for deaconess work within the Synodical
Conference held by the LDA, members of ALCh, and other church leaders.

FOREIGN MISSIONS

The first such article in *TLD* focused on the role of deaconesses in foreign
missions. Its author, Rev. Frederick Brand (1863–1949), was vice president
of the Missouri Synod (from 1917 to 1929). Brand became Director of
Missions in 1920, and visited China and India in 1921–22. His views,

---

[8] When *TLD* first went to print, the LCMS did not have the proliferation of church worker
careers that exists today. The Synod was just beginning to recognize the need to educate
women as teachers for its Christian day schools. It had not yet granted permission for
women to attend its colleges, but "institutes for the education of women teachers" were
starting to be held on the campus located in Seward, Nebraska. See LCMS, *Proceedings*, 1926,
76–77. The first copy of *TLD* also included an article from St. John's College (High School)
in Winfield, Kansas, to recruit "co-eds" who were primarily taught to be church secretaries,
though they enrolled in religion classes, could join the college mission society, and could
participate in an adult Bible class and Sunday School teachers' training course. See A. W.
Meyer, "A Problem for St. John's to Solve," *TLD* 1, no. 1 (January 1924): 5.
[9] F. W. Herzberger, "The Proper Aim of Our Deaconess Work, and How to Attain It," *TLD*
1, no. 4 (October 1924): 30–32.

therefore, reflected first-hand knowledge of the LCMS mission fields he hoped would be served by deaconesses.[10]

The Ideal Deaconess in the Foreign Missions Field

Nowhere in the world is there greater opportunity for woman's work than in non-Christian countries. Many good and godly women have essayed the task, but have failed because they lacked the necessary equipment. It is true, they had missionary zeal, but missionary zeal alone does not fit one for foreign mission work. The work of a deaconess in the Orient differs so radically from that in the homeland that it is worthwhile to consider its requirements.

I shall speak of the ideal deaconess, conscious, however, of the fact that very few women unite all the characteristics in their person, and that in actual life many modifications will have to be allowed.

She must be physically well. It is a common misconception that the climate in Oriental countries is unhealthy. Of course, there are districts where an American could not live. We have sections of that kind on our own continent. But speaking generally, it may be truthfully said that the climate is salubrious. In the Orient there is very little sanitation, and for that reason, ordinary, common-sense precautions must be observed to conserve health. Some foreigners become acclimatized very readily. Others must pass through a period of accommodation. Wherever there are latent physical ailments, they are brought to the surface very soon during this period. This applies especially to tuberculosis and abdominal troubles, which are endemic in the Orient. But the physical and nervous strain is frequently so great that a weak system is not able to resist the constant grind. The result is an early breakdown, shattered hopes, financial loss. The missionary must be furloughed home. All because she went out with a weak body. . . . The ideal deaconess must be sound physically. She ought not to be very much younger than twenty-five and surely not older than thirty-five.

She must have a good education. In countries such as India and China we do not labor among uncivilized peoples. The culture of these countries antedates our own Western civilization by thousands of years. While these peoples are backward in many respects, they are by no means savages; frequently they are more cultured than the average American. . . . It is true that in the Orient women shared but little in this culture. Their social status was and is very low. But the Orient is awakening to the need of woman's elevation. And no one but a woman can confer it. . . .

---

[10] Brand authored *Foreign Missions in China.* See Erwin L. Lueker, ed., *Lutheran Cyclopedia*, rev. ed. (St. Louis: Concordia, 1975), 106.

She must have a good education for another and still more important reason, however. One of her duties will be to teach women and children. Christian education is one of the great missionary means in the East. Millions of children and millions of adults, but chiefly missions of girls and women, are waiting for it. Male educators, as a rule, are not permitted to instruct growing girls and women. . . . So there is no coeducation, except in isolated cases. The deaconess will have to be equipped to educate girls and women.

Furthermore, the deaconess will be expected to school girls and women to enable them to become educational and religious helpers. From the primary school through the middle school she may have only the task of general supervision and the teaching of religion. But in the college and normal grades she will have to go into active and regular instruction. Besides, there is the girls' boarding-school, the nurses' training-school, and the school for Bible women. All of this awaits the supervision, and direction, and personal effort of the deaconess. . . .

She must be equipped socially. Woman missionaries, as a rule, lead a rather abnormal life. They have no immediate home and family ties. They live together with other female missionaries in an intimacy almost unprecedented in the homeland. They must, therefore, have a special gift of accommodation. The bane of many missions and the rock on which many a missionary career shipwrecks is exaggerated individuality. Many are too temperamental. They are too self-centered. They feel that their opinion must always carry decisive weight. They easily take offense. They go to their tent and sulk. ... With a sensitiveness of this kind it is manifestly impossible for them to do teamwork. ... Oh, the injury missionaries of this kind have done in the foreign missions field to their missionary brethren, the native Christians, and the heathen world! Therefore, the ideal deaconess must be adaptable, sweetly agreeable, and pliable in the best sense of the word. She must be able to become the servant of all that in this way she may save the more.

She must not consider herself superior to the natives. She must have overcome race prejudice. She must have real love for all humankind. She must be able and willing to leave non-sinful native customs uncriticized and untouched, rather accommodate herself to them. She is not sent out to introduce Western culture, but to introduce Christianity. The native customs may be far superior to our own. All things being equal, a woman can go to heaven if she wears no shoes, sits on the floor, eats her rice with her fingers, and wears only one garment. ... In short, the ideal deaconess must have a goodly portion of Christian common sense.

She must be equipped as a nurse. From the viewpoint of health the condition of women and children in the Orient, in fact, of all natives, is pitiable beyond telling. Diseases of all kinds prevail. Sanitation and hygiene and antisepsis are unknown quantities. . . . The ideal deaconess must be fully equipped to measure up, in the greatest possible dimensions, to the ever-changing demands on her skill and must be willing and cheerful to grant it. Her ability as a nurse must help to allay native suspicion and prejudice and pave the way for her great Gospel-message.

She must be at home in the Word of God. The deaconess goes out to the foreign missions field, not first of all as an educator nor as a nurse nor as a social worker—in fact, neither does any other real missionary of whatever type—but as a witness for Christ. . . . Her Christian knowledge, then, must be more than fragmentary. It must be comprehensive. She must be more at home in her Bible than in her textbooks on physiology and in her classic on nursing. She must be familiar with the whole body of Christian doctrine. And she must be able rightly to divide it to her hearers, at the bedside as well as in the classroom. ... Nowhere will she be assailed so much by "reasonable" arguments against the truth and against the supernatural, divine origin of her message as in the Orient. She must be ready to answer, and her answer must be fit to lead the gainsayer to God.

... The Bible is to be her first and last tool. All other work of whatever character is done only for the purpose of providing an approach for the Gospel of Salvation to the minds and hearts of the heathen. . . . The deaconess must have seen her own natural depravity, must have felt the curse of God resting upon her, must have found peace in the Blood of Atonement. The faith with which she has been blessed will make her a blessing to others.

And, finally, she must have daily intercourse with God by prayer. Many missionaries are so busy that they scarcely find time for prayer. They are in a constant turmoil, rushing from distraction to distraction. They try to carry the burden of their exacting duties alone. But the Lord was busier than they, and He took time for prayer. He retired late and rose early in the morning, and communed with his Father in heaven. . . . She knows that He is able to supply her every need, that the Spirit of God is ready to strengthen her spirit. So she prays without ceasing.

This is the ideal deaconess in the foreign missions field. Is this ideal too lofty, too exalted? Let it be the ideal. "Not as though I had already attained either were already perfect, but I follow after."

Frederick Brand[11]

---

[11] Brand's last line is a quotation of Philippians 3:12 from the King James Version. Frederick Brand, "The Ideal Deaconess in the Foreign Missions Field," *TLD* 1, no. 1 (January 1924): 2–4.

HOME MISSIONS

In a second article in *TLD*, Rev. Henry Frederick Wind (1891–1966) introduced the work of deaconesses as Christian social workers in home or "city" missions. Wind was a city missionary in Buffalo, N.Y. (from 1919–1953) and an influential executive of ALCh, who would eventually become Executive Secretary of the LCMS Department of Social Welfare.[12]

Women's Work

Missionary Work Carried on by Women, through Women, among Women.

"And God created man in His own image; male and female created He them," thus the creative act of God which brought mankind into being is briefly recorded on the first page of the Bible. "Male and female created He them," first man, then woman, both springing forth out of the creative hand of their Maker. Behold them! What a miracle of the Creator's wisdom and power! Fashioned of the same flesh and blood, yet they differ from one another in every other aspect. . . . Both man and woman have thus been peculiarly fashioned and endowed that each might bear his or her peculiar gifts to the world's progress and happiness.

By the same token we may say that God gave to the Church both men-folk and women-folk, because both men and women, each endowed with particular talents and graces, are needed in the work of Christ's kingdom. The Church must employ the talents and gifts of all her members, both men and women, to do the work which God commissioned her to do.

The force of this argument was readily apparent to the members and pastors of our Lutheran churches in and about the city of Buffalo, N.Y. When the need for additional workers in the institutional missions, conducted by the churches in this section, was felt some years ago, the conviction that womankind could bring to the work certain talents and qualities more or less lacking in men moved our Buffalo Lutherans to call a woman missionary into the field. This woman missionary is locally known as the "woman worker" of the missions; and her work is styled "women's work." This "women's work" is not merely social, teaching, or secretarial work and therefore more or less indirectly mission work, but it is *real* missionary work. Thus the Buffalo "woman worker" is perhaps the first professional woman missionary in our institutional mission circles, the first real missionary deaconess, if you please, in our Missouri Lutheran Church—the first, please God, of many.

---

[12] See Lueker, *Lutheran Cyclopedia*, 818.

"Women's work,"—a peculiar title perhaps, but a very descriptive one for the work this woman missionary is doing. It is truly "women's work"; for the missionary is a woman, is supported solely by women, and works exclusively among women. The undertaking is thus in the fullest sense a beautiful testimonial to the missionary zeal of Lutheran womanhood.

The duties devolving upon the woman worker are numerous and manifold indeed. She labors, first of all, in the field of bedside missions, visiting women confined in the great wards of public hospitals and ministering to them. In these wards she may work with a freedom and a general efficiency necessarily denied to any man in such places. . . . Being herself a woman, she not only thoroughly realizes a woman's needs and understands her mental processes, but she herself possesses the woman's viewpoint, often different from that of man.

Although the woman worker is thus best fitted to do "general ward work" in women's wards, she is not to be a "woman pastor." Her work must never supplant the peculiar work of the missionary pastor whom she is assisting. Her task must remain that of an explorer and an assistant. She canvasses the ward and makes the first approach to the strange patient; but if she finds the patient to be without church connection and responsive to missionary effort, particularly if she finds that the patient will welcome the suggested visit of the pastor, she reports the case to the pastor, who then makes his pastoral calls upon the patient at convenient hours. The woman worker does not, of course, abandon the case after reporting it to the pastor, but continues her visits, bringing cheer, comfort, and sisterly love to the afflicted woman, thus supplementing the work of the pastor upon her soul.

Not only is the woman worker a valuable aid to the missionary pastor in seeking out, and ministering to, missionary prospects in women's wards of public hospitals, but she may also render valuable assistance in the work of ministering to Lutheran patients in homes for invalids, incurables, etc. . . . She will read the [Bible] text to the invalid, often to a group of invalids, or to all invalids in the ward, add a simple, pointed exposition of the text, say a prayer, recite or sing a hymn, and thus render invaluable service to souls hungry for comfort. . . .

The institutions for fallen women furnish another field of activity in which the woman worker is peculiarly fitted to labor. . . . The subjects are often hardened in their immorality; some of them are despondent, others have weak and undeveloped minds. If one of these poor social outcasts is to be won for Christ and reclaimed for society, her case must first be known and studied, a confession of her wrong-doing must then be obtained, and finally the way to salvation pointed out to her. . . . This is the most difficult and trying work, and no one but a trained woman worker, a missionary deaconess, if you prefer the term, can do such work effectively.

Women are especially talented and fitted for work among children. Now there are many tubercular or otherwise diseased children confined in large hospitals frequently over long periods of time. These are also commended to the missionary care of the institutional chaplain and must be visited, befriended, and, above all, made acquainted with the Savior. While this work can be, and is, done successfully by men, by the chaplain himself, yet the trained woman worker, endowed with a woman's natural love for, and peculiar understanding of, children, can without doubt do better and more effective work in children's wards than most men could do. . . .

As in so many other callings, proper training is the one thing that is most necessary to success. . . . And the training of a woman worker is no small matter. She must, to begin with, be a devout believer and an intelligent, well-grounded Christian woman of broad sympathies, good common sense, and good health. But she must also know how to lead others to the Savior, how to silence the blasphemers, how to answer the scoffers, how to arouse the self-righteous and to comfort the distressed. She must be taught how to approach the stranger, how to gain her confidence, how to lead the conversation over to spiritual matters. She must understand the etiquette of the sickroom and must be taught to observe many little things which may aid or, if neglected, may hinder the work. . . . While she need not be a nurse, she ought to be able to understand common medical terms, the nature of the more prevalent diseases, the common laboratory tests for certain diseases, and the principles of mental tests. No one will expect her to be a lawyer, yet she will find a rudimentary knowledge of the law a very useful thing, especially a knowledge of domestic relations, child welfare, labor, and other laws defining social relationships and social values.

A terrifying list of requirements, isn't it? And many more might be added. This, however, will suffice to show that the work of a missionary woman worker is no small task, but is worthy of the very best efforts of the very best young women of our Church.

That many such young women may be found in our Church who out of love to the loving and ministering Savior will be persuaded to enter this most difficult and exacting calling of a woman worker or missionary deaconess, that is the ardent hope and heartfelt prayer of every worker in the fields of institutional missions. We can even now see them with the eyes of our faith streaming forth from the portals of our deaconess schools in great numbers, passing out into fields ripe unto harvest, ministering to the sick, lifting up the fallen, succoring the weak, laboring as angels of the light of God's mercy in the midst of a sin-darkened and sin-corrupted world. And inspired by this vision, we pray with larger understanding and new zeal: Lord God, send forth many faithful laborers into Thy vineyard!

Buffalo, N.Y.
H. F. Wind[13]

PRACTICAL DEACONESSES—PARISH WORK

In 1925, Rev. Fred William Korbitz (b. 1898), a young Nebraska pastor who served as president of the Junior Walther League of Nebraska,[14] wrote a passionate article describing the urgent need for deaconesses and his desire to reverse the "lack of interest for deaconess work" in the congregation.

> . . . Above all, our congregations in the large industrial cities are greatly in need of parish deaconesses, who can assist the busy city pastor in caring of the needs of members who are in distress, substitute at school during the illness of the teacher, help in Sunday-school, and render great service to the young ladies of the congregation by advising them in various ways.

> Since the deaconess is merely a woman serving in God's vineyard, and since the Lord has commanded all, male and female, young and old, to labor in His vineyard, shall we then, a body of loyal Christians, merely tolerate such a noble service as that performed by the deaconess? God forbid that we remain forever lukewarm over against this blessed deaconess work! We know that it is both necessary and well-pleasing to God. O, then, let us be up and doing!

> You young women and widows of the Synodical Conference, do you wish to perform a noble service for the Lord? Come and enter the Deaconess Training School. The calling of a deaconess is not a life of seclusion, but a life for Christ. A deaconess serves the Lord in all the unfortunate people round about us. If in later years you decide to enter the state of matrimony, you can do so without breaking any vows, because no vows are required from the deaconess. Consider the calling of a deaconess conscientiously and have literature sent you, . . .[15]

Superintendent Poch often explained, "The training which our pupils receive at Bethesda qualifies them particularly for parish and institutional

---

13 H. F. Wind, "Women's Work," *TLD* 1, no. 2 (April 1924): 12–15.
14 "After graduating from Concordia Seminary, St. Louis, he (Korbitz) took up a correspondence course in diaconics." "Introduction," *TLD* 7, no. 4 (October 1930): 30–31.
15 F. W. Korbitz, "Deaconesses, Tolerated, or Necessary?" *TLD* 2, no. 4 (October 1925): 30–31.

work."[16] It took longer for parish work than for institutional work to get off the ground, primarily because the men who met together at ALCh conferences often begged for the assignment of a deaconess to the institution that they represented. When Herzberger printed a report of "Our Workers and Their Fields of Service" in January 1928, only two of 24 women served as parish deaconesses.[17] But the LDA hoped to increase this number, believing that local congregations needed deaconesses to apply practical feminine skills beyond the realm of nursing.

> If woman workers were a necessity in the early centuries, today the need is far greater, since the Gospel is being preached throughout the world. The Church today needs women to assist the ministers of the Gospel, to undertake detail work, which women can do particularly well. This does not mean that the woman worker who teaches and gives spiritual comfort can take the place of a pastor.

> In no instance can a woman worker supplant the peculiar work of a pastor. She is simply the handmaiden. She often paves the way for the pastor's visits and assists him in all his work. Examples: As *parish worker* her most important work is not pastoral work nor other routine duties in a parish, but to serve her church by winning over the unchurched and bringing back to the fold the dispersed brethren and sisters who have grown indifferent and weak in the faith.

> Bringing cheer and comfort to the shut-in members of the church is also an important part of the worker's task. These friendly visits are intended to strengthen or keep alive the spiritual life of those afflicted. Oftentimes, however, as also in Inner Mission work, the parish worker finds it necessary to render also physical aid to unfortunate fellow-members, such as providing the needy with clothing, food, fuel, securing employment for them, etc.

> . . . Our chief duty as missionary is to bring the Bread of Life to sin-sick souls. Yet, in cases of physical distress, *hunger*, can we, as workers for Christ, withhold the bread for the body or the cup of water from a poor, suffering brother or sister? To answer this, we have but to read Matt. 25, 35: "I was hungry, and ye gave Me meat; I was thirsty, and ye gave Me drink."

---

[16] B. Poch, "Watertown," *TLD* 5, no. 4 (October 1928): 27.

[17] The two parish deaconesses both worked in New York, at Immanuel Church and St. Matthew's; the latter, which was chartered in 1664, is the oldest Lutheran church in North America. "Our Workers and Their Fields of Service," *TLD* 5, no. 1 (January 1928): 4; B. Poch, "Miscellaneous," *TLD* 4, no. 1 (January 1927): 3–4.

Clara Menard, 115 Glenwood Ave., Buffalo, N.Y.[18]

Interesting and positive reports from the parish deaconesses and their pastors fuelled the goal to expand parish ministry.[19]

The "Individual" Work of Deaconesses

To visit the old and shut-ins is my delight. Many of these people have little diversion. So many things have entered into the lives of most of them that they want to share their joys and sorrows with some one. Some of them have learned to love God's Word and are always ready for further study.

I also find many who are "religious," but not Christians. There are many who are influenced by false teachings. ... One day, while visiting an old lady, a relative of hers who lives upstairs came down. I asked her if she had any church connections. "O, yes; I go to the Truth Center. It's a wonderful place." I asked her what those people teach. "They teach the truth. You know there really is no sin, and sickness is only imagination." That same day I visited another woman. I said I had never seen her in church. "But I go to all the churches; they are all good." She showed me books and tracts which were given out by the Truth Center, by Christian Scientists, Russellites, and Latter-day Saints. She did not realize the danger and was thankful when I showed it to her.

... Families have been broken up; poverty and physical and spiritual wretchedness have been the result. ... These people can be saved from the power and condemnation of sin by bringing them the Gospel. Such work is difficult because there are so very few people who realize the great need for work with individuals. So much stress is laid upon "crowds." Individual work does not seem worth while to many—except as unto Him. I often remember the ministry of our Lord to a "congregation" of only one: Nicodemus, the woman of Samaria, and Zacchaeus.

We find the same conditions at present as they were 1900 years ago. Jesus had just made a tour of the cities and villages of Galilee, "teaching in the

---

[18] Menard was a "woman missionary" in Buffalo, New York, where Pastor Wind served as city missionary. Her long article on "Missionary and Social Work" appeared in two consecutive issues of TLD. There is no record of Menard being trained by the LDA. She appears to have been trained by Wind, just as Herzberger trained a few of his own female workers in St. Louis. Clara Menard, "Missionary and Social Work," TLD 4, no. 1 (January 1927): 7.

[19] Pastor Adolph Peter Louis Wismar (1884–1977) of St. Matthew's reported: "Since she (Hulda Buegel) is with St. Matthew's the attendance at the Sunday School has increased one hundred percent, and that of the parish school twenty-five percent" (Poch, "Miscellaneous," 3–4).

synagogs [*sic*] and healing every manner of sickness and every disease among men." What He saw of the spiritual and physical wretchedness of the multitudes filled Him with compassion, and this compassion found utterance in the words: "The harvest, truly, is plenteous, but the laborers are few. Pray ye therefore the Lord of the harvest that He will send forth laborers into His harvest."

Parish Deaconess[20]

PRACTICAL DEACONESSES—INSTITUTIONAL WORK AT BETHESDA

An institution that provided a *permanent* home for individuals with developmental disabilities—in contrast to a facility that cared for people only until they recuperated from illness—provided interesting learning opportunities for the deaconesses.

Bethesda Training-School, Watertown, Wis.

When it was first proposed to begin training practical deaconesses at Bethesda, a number of arguments were advanced against the proposition. It was said that the girls would be frightened and disgusted at the work and leave in a few weeks; the work among defective people was depressing; the pupils could not be cheerful in such surroundings; Watertown was too small a place for pupils to gain experience, etc.

The school has been in existence now almost two years and has passed the experimental stage. Out of an enrollment of 17, three pupils gave up the work before completing the course, two of them on account of ill health, and the other one for good and valid reasons.

We find that the kind of girls we can get to Watertown have determination and good sense, that they do not give up because the work is disagreeable at times,—that is all the more reason for doing it. The work among our inmates is far from depressing; it is the helpers' privilege to make the children happy, so they must cultivate a cheerful disposition, and that reacts upon their own happiness. One would have to go far to find a class of girls as happy and cheerful and as willing to *serve* as our pupils.

We do not attempt to make hospital nurses out of them. The work of the deaconess is not only reading to the sick and helpless and speaking kind words to them; the deaconess should serve, that is, do the work that is to be done and make the patient comfortable and happy. . . . The work in

---

[20] "The 'Individual' Work of Deaconesses," *TLD* 5, no. 2 (April 1928): 15.

the kitchen, dining room, laundry, milk room, and laboratory gives them a chance to study how a large household can be managed economically and to know what is necessary to keep the children healthy and the conditions sanitary.

We instruct our deaconess pupils in the laws of teaching and give them practical work in the classroom. We show them how to prepare a lesson and deliver it to the class and test the results. We study the psychology of the child and the adolescent and illustrate what we have learned by examples taken from the Home.

Of course, the pupils are given intensive training in Bible study and related subjects, so that they will become firm in their faith and know how to lead others to the Scriptures, but also how to defend their faith.

Typewriting and shorthand are taught in the evening at our City High School by very capable teachers. We also try to teach them to play the organ to enable them to accompany hymns and lead a class in singing. The House physician teaches the class "first aid" and "home nursing."

This program keeps the girls quite busy. But there is some time left for recreation. The girls have a choir, which meets once a week and sings at the services in the Home and on festival days. Now and then they have a social evening among themselves in the Dormitory, which is their home. Now and then they listen in to the radio, when the music is worth while. They do not attend the movies or other worldly pleasures, but go to hear a concert here at Watertown or occasionally in Milwaukee. . . .

Eight of the pupils will finish the course this year and can then be placed in the work. We feel assured that they will be efficient workers in any position to which the Lord may call them. We shall be ready to accept members of the new class after April. Applicants should be neither too young nor too old; have received a good common school education, be in good health and of a cheerful disposition, and have the determination to give themselves to the Lord for *service* among the helpless. Application may be made to Bethesda Training-school, Watertown, Wis.

L. P.[21]

NURSING

Except for the women trained at Bethesda, deaconesses were equipped to deliver straightforward "nursing" in Lutheran hospitals, institutions, or

---

[21] L. Pingel, "Bethesda Training-school, Watertown, Wis.," *TLD* 4, no. 1 (January 1927): 5–6.

parish homes. When writing to the Board of Directors of the Fort Wayne Lutheran Hospital Association to request the training of deaconesses alongside other nursing students, LDA officials described nursing as an integral part of a much larger skill set to be employed by deaconesses, and reassured hospital officials that there should be no fear of deaconess training competing with or supplanting regular nurses' training.

> . . .The heathen do not only need the Gospel, they also need sympathetic and intelligent help in a physical way. They need medical aid. They need instruction in the ways of civilized life. Experience has taught us that spiritual and physical help must go hand in hand if we are to get the maximum results from our endeavors among the heathen. . . .

> From this, brethren, you can gather that the deaconess is not, and cannot be or become, a competitor of the professional nurse. She operates in an altogether different sphere. Yet she needs the training which a regular nurse must have. . . . There will always be a large class of young ladies who will want to take up the profession of nursing principally for a livelihood in distinction to that class of young women who will want to do religio-social work in order primarily to be of service to the Church. The call for deaconesses, therefore, will not interfere with the call for nurses and consequently not with a nurses' training-school.[22]

In October 1926, the "Silver Jubilee Convention" of the Associated Lutheran Charities within the Synodical Conference took place in St. Louis, Missouri, where a pre-convention session resulted in a historic milestone for Lutheran nurses. Pastor Herzberger reported:

> The event was ushered in on Monday, October 11, by a meeting of representative nurses from our various [18] Lutheran hospitals, which was held at Redeemer Hall, where they founded the National Lutheran Nurses' League of North America. We hail this new organization with the fervent prayer that God may further it in every way in its purposes to keep in touch with our Lutheran nurses all over the country, and especially to safeguard our isolated nurses from joining other nurses' guilds and leaving their Lutheran Church.[23]

The new National Lutheran Nurses' League of North America (NLNL) and the LDA were sister organizations, both conceived within the womb of ALCh. Understanding and cooperation between the NLNL and the LDA grew strong through the unique role of Philipp Wambsganss Jr. who, until

---

[22] Herzberger, "Historic Document," 10–11.
[23] F. W. Herzberger, "The Silver Jubilee Convention of the Associated Lutheran Charities within the Synodical Conference," TLD 3, no. 4 (October 1926): 25.

his death in 1933, served as President of the Fort Wayne Lutheran Hospital Association, President of the LDA, and President or honorary President of ALCh.[24] Anna Holtman, the Principal of nurses' training for LDA deaconesses at Lutheran Hospital in Fort Wayne, became the first president of NLNL. She publicly thanked half a dozen ALCh members, including Pastors Poch, Foelber, (Fred) Wambsganss and (Philipp) Wambsganss Jr., for their "advice and support and help" in establishing the league.[25] Concerning the nursing profession Holtman wrote in *The Lutheran Deaconess:*

Something About the Nursing Profession

Before the Civil War there was in this country not a single white-capped, white-gowned young woman hovering over the bed of a patient with her thermometer and hypodermic syringe. To-day there is hardly a large American city and town of any importance from coast to coast that does not boast its hospital and training-school for nurses. Each year large and small classes graduate to step out into the world and help alleviate human ills and suffering. The day has arrived when the world cannot get along without the nurse.

There seems to have been, for some time past, a shortage of Lutheran young women who were willing to enter our Lutheran training-schools for nurses. We have many applications, but the majority are from non-Lutherans or even unchurched young women. Why is this situation? Do Lutheran young women no longer take up nursing, or do they enter non-sectarian hospitals and training-schools? There are some Lutheran training-schools for nurses which have trouble in getting their classes filled. Permit me, if you please, to give you a better idea of what nursing really means and what wonderful benefits are derived there-from.

. . . A young woman devotes three of her best years of life to special preparation to obtain a thorough understanding of the principles of nursing. She must have love for the work, she must naturally have a longing to do something for her sick neighbor. She cannot be forced to like it. She must possess love for her Savior and humanity, must be willing to follow the example of the Good Samaritan. The spirit in which a nurse does her work makes a great difference. She should be invested with the dignity of her profession and with love for suffering humanity. If so, she can perform anything her hand may be called upon to do, and for work done in this spirit she will receive her reward. . . .

A nurse's life is a life of service to God and humanity and sacred in the eyes of both. Service is the keystone to our profession. It was the service

---

[24] "Biographical Record for Philipp Wambsganss Jr." (St. Louis: CHI, January 29, 2004).
[25] Anna M. Holtman, "Lutheran Nurses' League," *Proceedings of the ALCh*, 1926, 97.

to humanity rendered by the Good Samaritan that has made his act unforgotten since. It was the ideals visioned by Florence Nightingale that inspired her to accomplish the great work she accomplished during the Crimean War and later in establishing training-schools for nurses where others might catch those ideals and prepare themselves to render similar service.[26] If all nurses would only have within them the Spirit of our Lord and Master, . . .

There also is a great need of Lutheran deaconess nurses and social workers. The call for these women church workers is appalling. Many mission fields are asking for help. Consider how much good a young woman of our Lutheran faith may do, what a wonderful service she may render in the same spirit, how many acts of mercy and deeds of kindness she can bestow upon her fellow-men. In living such a life of service, you daily approach closer to Him who first taught men how to practise [*sic*] kindness to the sick.

May our Lutheran people support all our Lutheran hospitals and training-schools for nurses and deaconesses and see to it that our Lutheran young women who want to become nurses and choose this calling for their life's vocation enter a school of their own faith!

Anna M. Holtman

Principal, Lutheran Hospital,

Ft. Wayne, Indiana[27]

Descriptions of deaconess placements published in *TLD* show that deaconess nurses held posts as matrons or superintendents, night nurses, X-ray technicians, and operating room supervisors. However, almost nothing is recorded about the actual medical work carried out by deaconesses. The main sentiment expressed about nursing was that such a ministry of mercy formed the context in which a deaconess tended to the spiritual, as well as physical, needs of her patients. The two passages that follow, written by Minnie Hahn and another unnamed nurse, reflect how their lives as deaconess nurses focused on much more than medicine.

---

26 Florence Nightingale (1820–1910) trained in nursing at Fliedner's Institution of Protestant Deaconesses in Kaiserswerth, Germany. She later outlined the Kaiserswerth nursing principles in her writings, and in 1860 she implemented these principles in a model nursing school in London, England. C. Golder, *History of the Deaconess Movement in the Christian Church* (Cincinnati: Jennings & Pye, 1903), 173–77, 406–7; Florence Nightingale, *The Institution of Kaiserswerth on the Rhine: For the Practical Training of Deaconesses, under the Direction of the Rev. Pastor Fliedner*, 2d ed., (Düsseldorf-Kaiserswerth: Diakonissenanstalt, 1851).

27 Anna M. Holtman, "Something about the Nursing Profession," *TLD* 2, no. 3 (July 1925): 22–24.

Christmas in Lutheran Deaconess Hospital, Beaver Dam, Wis.

December 24, 1926, dawned upon us a fair day. . . .

Shortly after dinner Miss Dienst and Miss Trettin, with the help of several other R.N.'s in the hospital just then, decorated a beautiful fir in our hospital dining-room for our short, but impressive program. Then they also carried up all the gifts previously received by mail or local from the drug-room, where Miss Dienst had hid them until the time stated when they should be opened and placed them under the spreading branches of our Christmas-tree.

Enough chairs were placed in the room for possible visitors and the hospital force.

At about two o'clock our program was opened with a prayer by Rev. Kirst, and the following program was rendered: First there was a song, "O Thou Holiest," by all the nurses. Then the Christmas story as recorded in Luke 2 was read by Rev. Kirst and briefly expounded for our edification. Next we heard a duet, "O Come All Ye Faithful," by the Misses Miller and Boerger. Then there was a reading in accordance with the Christmas story by Miss Lauterbach and a solo, "Lift Up Your Heads, Ye Mighty Gates," by Miss Kleist. Finally "Silent Night, Holy Night" was sung by all present, and the Lord's Prayer was said in unison.

After every one had found a seat or a place to stand, all eyes turned toward the door, whence our Old St. Nick was to appear, whose duty it seemed to be to distribute the gifts. . . . The following moments we all were as happy as the little children present, who first of all received a little gift from his generous hands. Generously and thoughtfully indeed were we remembered by him; but we were most thankful to our heavenly Provider for all His goodness, and we were again reminded of the one "unspeakable Gift," "God manifest in the flesh," given to us.

At four o'clock everybody was busy again with duties until seven, when all those who were able, got ready to attend the children's services in St. Stephen's Church to hear the old, old story of our Savior's birth.

After the services we all assembled at the hospital again instead of going to our nurses' home, as a basketful of goodies, previously prepared, stood ready to be carried to a poor family which had lost its mother only a few months before. With our superintendent leading, we soon arrived at our destination. We lined up and sang the first verse of the hymn "Joy to the

World." When the father opened the door, the basket was given to him with our greetings, and we returned home, tired, but happy.[28]

My Experience in the Deaconess Work
By Sister Minnie Hahn

As there are different types of girls, so there are different talents. Not all are gifted for the same kind of work. Some are gifted for the care of children, others have the gift of caring for the aged, still others have a talent for surgery and nursing in the hospital, where there are wonderful opportunities to care for the soul as well as the body. Jesus, too, when he was on earth, healed the sick and afflicted, in this way drawing them to Him and then revealing Himself as the great Physician for the soul as well as for the body. The deaconess, while caring for the body, often finds greater opportunity to serve spiritually than she would at other times. Usually when people realize that our aim is to serve them, they will open up their hearts and accept such spiritual service more readily after having been ministered to bodily.

Another ready field we find when we go out into some poor family which is not able to employ the expensive services of the trained nurse. Such services will often warm the coldest hearts and get them to asking, "Why does she do it?" This will frequently suggest to them that if Christianity can do this, it must be something worth looking into. . . .[29]

USE OF THE TITLE *DEACONESS*

Miss Hahn's article in *TLD* implies that she is a deaconess, though there is no record of her graduation from a deaconess training school. It seems that LDA leaders (at least in the first ten years following the association's formation) considered several women to be deaconesses or honorary deaconesses because they carried out "real deaconess work." Pastor Herzberger may have encouraged this trend by dedicating the front page of the January 1926 publication of *TLD* to two women whom he felt had been of inestimable value in his work in St. Louis.

We take great pleasure in presenting to our readers the pictures of the two veteran woman workers who are doing real deaconess work in our teeming City Mission fields at St. Louis. Mrs. A. Vellner is a widow and the mother of our organized woman helpers in our mission work. For many years the Editor had been longing and praying for a woman

---

[28] "Christmas in Lutheran Deaconess Hospital, Beaver Dam, Wis.," *TLD* 4, no. 1 (January 1927): 6.
[29] Minnie Hahn, "My Experience in the Deaconess Work," *TLD* 2, no. 2 (April 1925): 12.

coworker who would look after the suffering women and straying girls in our big City Hospital. The exigencies of the war, when so many of the nurses went to the front, furnished the opportunity to put Mrs. Vellner to work in the City Hospital; and what blessed work she has been doing in the nine years she has been with us! . . .

Miss H. Hanser is a registered nurse, who assists Mrs. Vellner in her child-rescue work and brings the sweet Gospel and also material cheer to the women patients at the overcrowded Insane Asylum, the Koch Consumptive Hospital, and the City Infirmary. She made a trip to Germany last year to visit and study conditions at the various deaconess institutions there, and we shall publish her observations in our *Lutheran Deaconess* in this and the following numbers. May the dear Lord also bless Miss Hanser's work in his vineyard for many coming years![30]

Herzberger and other founders of the Lutheran female diaconate movement tried to recognize and praise all women engaged in "deaconess work" whether they had received formal training from the LDA or not. Whenever early issues of the LDA's magazine listed "Branch Societies of our Lutheran Deaconess Association," they also printed a list of "Woman Workers in Our Foreign Mission Fields," which included teachers, nurses and deaconesses in China and India.[31] By January 1928, a separate list called "*Deaconesses* in the Foreign Field" created a distinction between deaconesses and other female missionaries, even though a deaconess might have been working side-by-side with the other women.[32]

Somewhere along the way—perhaps in conjunction with the proliferation of deaconess schools—the idea caught hold that deaconess training could enhance the execution of mission work, wherever that work took place. Consequently, some women involved in "the deaconess work" desired to be more closely associated with the recognized diaconate of the Synodical Conference. In April 1938 the LDA reported:

It gives us great pleasure to announce to our friends that Miss Frieda Bremermann, whose picture we have above, has joined our Association as one of our deaconesses. Miss Bremermann has been doing deaconess work in the Institutional Mission in Chicago for a number of years, and God has blessed her work abundantly. She has now identified herself

---

[30] F. W. Herzberger, "The Women Workers in Our St. Louis City Mission," *TLD* 3, no. 1 (January 1926): 1.

[31] Emphasis added. "Woman Workers in Our Foreign Mission Fields," *TLD* 3, no 4 (October 1926): 32.

[32] For example, Deaconess Louise Rathke and Miss Angela Rehwinkel, R.N., both worked at Bethesda Lutheran Mission Hospital in Ambur, North Arcot District, India. *TLD* 5, no. 1 (January 1928): 8.

closely with us by being consecrated as one of our deaconesses. The consecration service was held in connection with the installation service of the Rev. Tr. Thieme as institutional missionary, on Feb. 6, in Grace Lutheran Church, Chicago. . . .[33]

Miss Bremermann received no formal deaconess training, but LDA Superintendent Kohlmeier consecrated her as a deaconess on the strength of "a course" she had formerly taken under Rev. J. H. Witte.[34] Other women, usually already busy in some sort of full-time church work, interrupted their employment in order to be educated as deaconesses. For example, in the late 1930s, after serving twelve years as an LCMS missionary in China, Gertrude Simon returned to the United States on furlough and attended the deaconess school in Fort Wayne, after which she returned to China for another 28 years.[35] Over the years until modern times, it has become increasingly common for women to become "second career" deaconesses, leaving secular employment in favor of entering professional church work.

Kretzmann's Popular Commentary

While sermons, articles, and speeches extolled the possibilities for deaconess work within Synodical Conference missions and charities, Professor P. E. Kretzmann's *Popular Commentary* on the New Testament (published by CPH in 1922) provided a quotable source for authoritative endorsement of the deaconess movement. Regarding I Timothy 3:11 Kretzmann wrote:

> The apostle has a special charge to the women deacons or deaconesses: Women likewise (to be) grave, not slanderers, soberminded, faithful in all things. This verse does not concern the wives of the deacons, but is directed to the deaconesses; for women were employed in this capacity

---

[33] "Deaconess Frieda Bremermann," *TLD* 15, no. 2 (April 1938): 2.

[34] Bremermann is the only deaconess listed under the subtitle of "Chicago" in an LDA document titled "Consecrated Deaconesses." All other deaconesses are listed under the names of cities where deaconess training programs were established. See Appendix 1E. "Consecrated Deaconesses," email attachment from E. Louise Williams to CDN, June 20, 2005; "Report Given by the Superintendent at the Annual Meeting October 23, 1938," *TLD* 16, no. 1 (January 1939): 2.

[35] Simon spent part of her furlough time at the motherhouse in Fort Wayne as early as 1932. She had undoubtedly met Clara Rodenbeck, the first LDA deaconess assigned to China in 1931. "Consecration Service," *TLD* 17, no. 3 (July 1940): 2; Henry E. Simon, "A Galatians 2:20 Missionary," in *One Cup of Water* (St. Louis: LWML, 1996), 93–113; Clara Rodenbeck, "Our Missions," *The Lutheran Witness* 51 (March 15, 1932): 106–7.

from the earliest times Cp. Rom. 16.1. These women were to exhibit the proper gravity and dignity in their deportment, which would at all times cause men to respect them and their office. With all the kindness and devotion which they were to show in their ministry they must not permit familiarity to grow into lack of respect for the dignity of their office. And since the weakest member and the greatest enemy of most women is their tongue, the apostle warns them against becoming slanderers, against indulging in sins of defamation, of evil report. The deaconesses undoubtedly often gained an insight into the sinfulness of human nature which is not vouchsafed to many; all the more it was incumbent upon them not to abuse the trust placed in them by revealing matters that should have remained secret. They should furthermore be soberminded, not merely observing a sensible moderation in all sensual enjoyments, but making use of quiet, firm common sense at all times. It is just in such situations in which the nerves of the average woman give way that the Christian deaconess should maintain the sane composure which finds the right thing to do. All other qualifications of Christian deaconesses the apostle includes in the demand that they be faithful in all things. The many apparent trifles which fell to the lot of the deaconess showed their real value. It is in the many little services, the cooling hand, the gentle word, the cheerful smile, that the real greatness of service appears; in these true faithfulness becomes evident. Fortunately, the time does not seem to be far distant when we shall have deaconesses in most of our congregations. If such consecrated women, actuated by the love of Christ, devote their lives to the service of their fellowmen, their value to the Church will be beyond calculation.[36]

Kretzmann supported the deaconess cause within the Missouri Synod and felt optimistic about the future of the LDA. He did his part to make sure that deaconesses should be both well trained and well behaved.[37]

THE TRUE DEACONESS SPIRIT

Another important item that Herzberger included in *TLD*, first in the original German and later in English, was *"The True Deaconess Spirit,"* by Wilhelm Loehe.[38]

---

[36] P. E. Kretzmann, "The Office of Deacon: I Timothy 3.8–13," in vol. 2 of *Popular Commentary: New Testament* (St. Louis: Concordia, 1922), 381.

[37] See Appendix 1.A.

[38] "Der Rechte Diakonissengeist," *TLD* 1, no. 1 (January 1924): 7. The title *Der Rechte Diakonissengeist* can be translated as "The True Deaconess Spirit." "Deaconess Motto," *TLD* 2, no. 4 (October 1925): 31.

Der rechte Diakonissengeist

Was will ich tun? Dienen will ich.
Wem will ich dienen?
Dem Herrn in seinen Elenden und
Armen.

Und was is mein Lohn?
Ich diene weder um Lohn noch um
Dank, sondern aus Dank und
Liebe.

Und wenn ich dabei unkomme?
„Konn ich um, so komme ich um",
sprach die Koenigin Esther;
und solte ich nicht dem zulieb
umkommen,
der auch für mich „umkam",
der sein Leben für mich liesz?

Und wenn ich dabei alt werde?
So wird mein Herz grünen wie ein
Palmbaum,
und der Herr wird mich sättigen
mit Gnade und Erbarmen.

Ich gehe, sitze, liege darum ganz
mit Frieden,
denn der Herr sorgt für mich.

The True Deaconess Spirit

What is my wish? I wish to serve.
Whom do I wish to serve?
The Lord in His wretched ones
and His poor.

And what is my reward?
I serve neither for reward nor
thanks, but out of gratitude and
love; my reward is that I am
permitted to serve.

And if I perish in this service?
"If I perish, I perish," said
Queen Esther.
I would perish for Him who
gave Himself for me.
But He will not let me perish!

And if I grow old in this service?
Then shall my heart be renewed
as a palm-tree,
and the Lord shall satisfy me
with grace and mercy.

I go my way in peace, casting all
my care upon Him.

This piece of prose had been adopted as a motto by deaconess motherhouses in Germany and around the world, including those connected to the Kaiserswerth Institution of Protestant Deaconesses.[39]

It seemed to be important to those who tried to germinate the deaconess cause within the Synodical Conference to establish a

---

[39] See page entitled "From Guest Books 1873" in Wilhelm Loehe, *Gesammelte Werke: Herausgegeben im Auftrage der Gesellschaft für Innere un Ausere Mission im Sinne der lutherischen Kirche*, IV, ed. Klaus Ganzert, trans. Holger Sonntag (Neuendettelsau: Freimund, 1954), no pagination.

connection—naturally in spirit rather than ecclesiastical lineage—with deaconesses who had gone before. Recruitment speeches, tracts, sermons, and official reports from the LDA often cited the example of Phoebe (Romans 16:1–2), the development of diaconates in the Early Church, and the stories of Fliedner, and Passavant.[40] When Superintendent Poch installed the first four graduates of the training school at Beaver Dam, he chose to preach the English sermon on Psalm 100:2a: "Serve the Lord with gladness."[41] He explained that this was the text Fliedner chose when he installed the first Lutheran deaconess, Gertrude Reichardt, at Kaiserswerth in 1836, and that these "same words were carved as a fitting motto over the entrance of the first deaconess motherhouse."[42]

TRUE SERVANTHOOD

The Loehe and Fliedner deaconess mottos reflected an attitude of humble servanthood that the LDA considered inherent to the true nature of the deaconess calling. Rev. Francis James Lankenau (1868–1939) portrayed a model for rendering service as a deaconess in this installation sermon he preached in 1926.[43]

> If any man minister, let him do it as of the ability which God giveth, that God in all things may be glorified through Jesus Christ, to whom be praise and dominion forever and ever! Amen—I Pet. 4,11

> My Dear Friends:

> You are about to become active workers in the service of the Lord's kingdom. . . . It is a blessed work that you are to enter upon; it is also a most arduous and responsible work to which you are commissioned in this service. It is a work that will require self-denying sacrifice, extraordinary patience, and often great courage. And if you would have your labors crowned with success, you will have to perform them in the spirit demanded in our text. According to our text

---

[40] For examples, W. Klausing, "Sermon on Rom. 16,1," *TLD* 1, no. 4 (October 1924): 26; F. W. Herzberger, "Some Facts About Deaconess Work," small tract, 1924, Deaconess Office Archives, Concordia University, River Forest, IL.; J. H. Witte, "What Others Are Doing," *TLD* 1, no. 1 (January 1924): 4.

[41] LDA installation services still featured two sermons. On this occasion, Pastor Philipp Wambsganss Jr. gave the "Address in German" on Colossians 3:12–14.

[42] B. Poch, "Quarterly Survey of our Deaconess Work. Installation at Beaver Dam," *TLD* 2, no. 2 (April 1925): 9.

[43] Lankenau went by the anglicized "Francis James" rather than his given names: Franz Friedrich Wilhelm Jakob.

THE SERVICE OF A CHRISTIAN DEACONESS

must be rendered

1. Humbly, 2. Generously, 3. To the glory of God.

1. Ever remember that your services in the hospital and in the field of Home or Foreign Missions is a channel only and not the fountain. Whatever service you are able to render is because of the ability and opportunity which God gives you. If you would be the ideal deaconesses, you must be poor in spirit. Only as you are poor, can you make others rich; only as you realize that you are the channel of God's grace and mercy, can you be true deaconesses. Only as you realize that your sufficiency is of God; only as you are convinced that your only hope is Jesus' blood and righteousness; only as you are willing to admit that you have been but unprofitable servants and at best have only done your duty; only as you despair in your own power and strength, is it that you can be a blessing to others in your work . . .

Work, then, in the strength of the Lord and ascribe any measure of success which may be granted to you wholly to that strength which God gives. Like faithful servants ascribe all success to the Lord's gifts.

In your ministrations you will be thrown in contact with the poor and lowly, with those whose earthly advantages have been few. It will be only natural that your flesh will be filled with a feeling of superiority when it compares itself with the unfortunates to whose wants you are ministering. At such times forget not that you have no advantages over them except those which God has given you. To the free benevolence of God you owe your attainments. May a recollection of the actual state of the case prevent conceit and vainglory from becoming enthroned in your hearts!

2. Your services should be given "as of the ability which God giveth." They should be given whole-heartedly. You should give the full measure of your ability. Zeal and energy should characterize your ministrations. Realizing that you are the dispensers of God's gifts which were freely given you, you should give your services without stinting and grudging. Then, too, the fervor of Christian love should impel you to benevolent activity. . . .

Like Peter you have no silver and gold to give to wretched, suffering mankind. The Church and her servants seldom have that to give. . . . Our God could easily make His Church and all its enterprises rich if He wanted to do so, for all gold and silver is His. He could supply you and all His other servants with means to relieve all physical want wherever it may show itself. But He does not do so, partly in order to exercise our faith and keep us humble, largely, however, to help us realize, as He did Peter, that the gift He has given us is far greater than all silver and gold.

As servants of the Church this precious Gospel is given you that you may freely give it to others. Let it ever be in your eyes your most precious treasure. With it you can direct the spiritually blind to safety and happiness, strengthen the weak, and lift the fallen. You will find this Gospel ever the Bread and Water of Life, able to nourish the famishing soul and quicken the faint heart. You will find it ever to be the true balm of Gilead, which can heal all the wounds of sin; ever the reliable companion when man is about to pass through the dark valley of the shadow of death.

As God gives you this gift of His, use it freely, unstintingly, faithfully, to the saving of many souls. All God's gifts are given to us we may give them to others. . . . All blessings that flow to us are to flow through us, gain force from us, and flow on in refreshing streams beyond us. If you are compelled to recognize that fact that you *could,*—you *could* give, you *could* nurse, you *could* cheer—then a solemn responsibility rests upon you. What you can do for Christ and for His brethren you are, by all holy persuasions and considerations, bound to do. Such as you have, by gracious trust from God, that you must be ever ready to *give* and to *spend* and to *use* for the service and blessings of *others.*

3. The end and purpose of all Christian service and thus also of your deaconess service shall be the glory of God. ...

The Savior said that He had glorified His Father on earth. We, His disciples, should imitate Him, learning of Him to seek the glory of God in and above all things. The love, the zeal, and the energy which true Christians exhibit to the use of the gifts given them by God show forth the glory of God; for that love and zeal can come only from His grace; weak, selfish creatures such as we are could not live holy, self-denying lives save by the help of God's gracious presence. Every act of Christian self-denial, every labor of love, is an additional proof of the reality of God's grace and power. ...

Dear friends, you in your chosen calling will have a wonderful opportunity to glorify God, since your faithful labors will be so obviously, so palpably, a manifestation of love and good will, which even the unbelieving world recognizes as divine. Where the unbelieving world sees unselfish, forbearing, helpful love, it feels the power and presence of God, and its scoffings and sneers generally cease. The atmosphere of heaven is love, and when but a breath of that heavenly love is exhaled by his servants, God will be honored and His name glorified. ...

May God be the Strength of your hearts and your Portion forever!
Oh, that each of you in the day of His coming may say:
I have fought my way through;
I have finished the work Thou didst give me to do!

Oh, that each from His Lord may receive the glad word:
Well and faithfully done!
Enter into My joy and sit down on my throne!
Amen.[44]

Consecration

The life of a deaconess was not for the squeamish. She dedicated herself to God's work and needed a genuine attitude of complete submission to His will. Therefore, parallel to servanthood, the concept of *consecration* became prominent in the training and thinking of deaconess candidates. Worship services that included the deaconess graduation rites—held separately from the "nurses' commencement exercises"—were called, interchangeably, "installation" or "consecration" services, until eventually they were only known as consecration services. A deaconess would then refer to what took place in that worship service as her "consecration."[45]

Rev. Enno August Henry Duemling (1875–1946) delivered the following sermon in Fort Wayne in 1927, just four months before he succeeded Philipp Wambsganss Jr. as president of ALCh.[46] The fact that Duemling preached this same sermon again at the 1933 graduation service for the Bethesda Home Training School showed a continued interest in promoting the concept of consecration.

> . . . The text I have chosen is recorded in the Book of Exodus, chapter 32, verse 29: "Consecrate yourselves today to the Lord." I do not intend to speak of the occasion upon which these words were spoken; I rather wish to set before you the one desirable thing here spoken of: CONSECRATION.

---

[44] F. J. Lankenau, "Installation Sermon by Rev. F. J. Lankenau," *TLD* 3, no. 3 (July 1926): 20–22. At the time that he gave this sermon, Lankenau was the honorary vice president of Valparaiso University, editor of the monthly missionary magazine *Lutheran Pioneer* (which supported Missouri Synod missions to African Americans), third vice president of the Missouri Synod [he later served as first vice president; see "Associated Lutheran Charities Meet at Fort Wayne," *TLD* 7, no. 4 (October 1930): 29], and chairman of the Advisory Committee of Synod. Lankenau also founded and served as the first president of Luther College, New Orleans, "a school to educate colored youth for the ministry and as teachers for Lutheran Colored Mission schools." See F. C. Lankenau, "Francis James Lankenau, D.D., A Biography," *Concordia Historical Institute Quarterly* 12, no. 3 (October 1939): 71, 76.

[45] B. Poch, "Installation at Fort Wayne," *TLD* 4, no. 3 (July 1927): 19.

[46] Duemling organized the mission for the deaf in Detroit in 1896. From 1902–46 he served as an institutional missionary of the Synodical Conference in Milwaukee, Wisconsin. See Lueker, *Lutheran Cyclopedia*, 248; "Associated Lutheran Charities," *TLD* 4, no. 4 (October 1927): 31.

"Consecration," my friends, is a beautiful word. What does it mean? It is the English translation of several words, one of them meaning to separate and set apart; the other, to devote or dedicate. By combining these thoughts we get the full meaning of consecration as we commonly understand it today. Thus, to consecrate a new church-building means to set it apart from every other use and dedicate or devote it solely to the worship of the Triune God. To consecrate one's life to the Lord means to separate it, to set it apart from the service of sin, of mammon, the world, and all that is of the world, and then solemnly to dedicate and devote it first, and above all else, to God and His service.

. . . Having heard the meaning of the word consecration and what it implies, let us make a few practical applications affecting the life of a Lutheran deaconess. We take it for granted that every Lutheran deaconess is true and loyal to her God and to her Church. You are to be Christ-centered, not self-centered. Your work is to be done for Christ's sake, because the love of Christ constraineth you. To be able to maintain a healthy, joyous spiritual life, you must be able to give a reason for the faith that is within you. Your spiritual life must be rooted in God, and you must know Jesus Christ from your own personal experience. Only as you are anchored to the eternal truth, can you move with freedom and glad assurance, helping your fellow-men to a saving knowledge of the truth as revealed in the Word of God and in the life and the teaching of Jesus Christ.

Your calling is a ministry of Christian love. It pre-supposes an absolutely unselfish spirit, renunciation of worldly ambitions, a desire to serve Christ whole-heartedly in whatever way His providence and Spirit may indicate. . . . Your work is not to be a work of philanthropy, but a work such as was exemplified by Christ himself, who never healed the sick, cast out the devils, helped the feeble, or took the children to His arms without having regard principally to the soul and, consequently, bestowing spiritual blessings. . . . You must live among those whom you intend to win for Christ, teaching and uplifting them as much by your example and sympathy as by the words you speak. A sincere Christian will find it more blessed to give than to receive. Christian sympathy, shown in a proper manner, will reap true friendliness and confidence.

In your dealings with the needy, the poor, the sick, and those who are most unfortunate of all, the feeble-minded and mentally diseased, three virtues should possess your minds and hearts: *friendliness, compassion, sympathy.* A sympathetic heart is to the afflicted as a warm rain to the thirsty earth. Did you ever see a pain-wrinkled brow smoothed when a kind, sympathetic hand stroked the wet hair back from the forehead? A sweet temper is a precious heritage. It lends a charm to everything. It fills the home and also our hospitals and institutions of charity with perpetual delight. The fortunate possessor of a sunny soul is God's evangel in a dark and sorrowful world. He is a living gospel, which no one will repudiate and the blessedness of which all men, especially the unfortunate, will appreciate.

. . . Enter then, dear graduates, in the name of Jesus, upon your blessed vocation under the influence of the Christian principles which you have been taught in your alma mater; enter upon it deeply sensible of your responsibilities; and you will be worthy of our good wishes and of the congratulations of your friends. Work while it is day. Spend your strength for that which is good. Always remember that what you do is performed in the presence of God, who has called you to do it. Whatever your future work may be—and each will have her own part to perform—it is required of you that it be done so that you will secure the approbation of God. Persevere, then, in your work, be devoted to it, and be steadfast in faith, and God will be with you. . . .

May the Lord be with you, dear graduates, and grant success to your self-denying service, whether done at home or abroad! We ask this in the name of Jesus. Amen.[47]

COMPENSATION

Yes, the life of a deaconess was one of consecrated servanthood to "the Lord in His wretched ones and His poor." But serving the Lord did not mean that a deaconess could have no fun, should feel sorry for herself, develop a martyr complex, or allow herself to be put on a righteous pedestal. A deaconess needed to cultivate a balanced perspective, including an appreciation for the special joys that would accompany her work. Regarding these "compensations" of the deaconess, Rev. William S. Freas wrote:

> There are indeed sacrifices and self-denials for both the minister of the Word and the minister of mercy; but what a shame that our Christianity should break down just where the test of its reality is applied! As a glorious refutation of exaggerated statements about the sacrifices of the deaconess, think of her many sweet and satisfying compensations.
>
> 1. What a blessing the true deaconess is to Christ's people and others! She soothes the distressed, wipes away tears, comforts the sorrowing, looks after poor little children, cares for orphans, guides the young, seeks the

---

[47] Enno Duemling, "Sermon on Exodus 32, 29. Delivered at the installation of the 1927 graduates of the Fort Wayne Deaconess Training-school, May 15, at Emmaus Church, Fort Wayne, Ind.," *TLD* 4, no. 3 (July 1927): 20–22; Enno Duemling, "Deaconess Graduation: Watertown, Wis., May 7, 1933," *TLD* 10, no. 3 (July 1933): 5–7.

wandering, clothes the naked, feeds the hungry, counsels with discouraged and sometimes ignorant mothers, and visits the sick and imprisoned—all for Christ's sake. Her heart is satisfied, fed with the knowledge that "her own works praise her in the gates." Her conscience approves her life. And in it all she can always hear a tender voice saying: "In as much as ye have done it unto one of the least of these My brethren, ye have done it unto Me." This alone is enough to make any good woman happy.

2. She lives in an atmosphere of spirituality and high thinking. She is not seeking her own glory, but her Master's. She has close intimacy with the best people on this earth—the workers in our churches. Her life means something worthwhile. She is the object of gratitude and love from a growing army reached by her labors. Her heart is at peace.

3. She has many warm and sweet friendships born through her unceasing ministries. The Church holds her in honor. She is associated with God's ministers in training the young for honorable life and in saving souls. Wherever she works, she leaves memories of good cheerfully done without pay, which grow sweeter and shine brighter unto the endless day.

4. She has many positive pleasures, recreations, social enjoyments, books, lectures, music, friends, vacations every summer. In the motherhouse or in the field, pleasure is mingled agreeably with labor. She is not permitted to work too hard, but given needed rest. Her associations with her fellow workers can be made very delightful.

5. She has no worldly cares. She is provided for during life, food, clothing, and necessary expenses being assured. She has a home to which she can always return for rest. When sick, she is, in turn, tenderly nursed. No expense is spared in bringing her back to health. In old age she is ministered to and held in high regard and honor. Over her grave love's immortelles keep blooming.

If on this earth there is possible happiness without care, the consecrated, lowly-minded faithful Christian woman who ministers as a deaconess comes nearest its attainment.[48]

The deaconess carried out a *ministry of mercy* that complemented the pastor's *ministry of Word and Sacraments*. Whatever situation she served in, her physical and spiritual ministration of mercy embodied God's love in action and was intended to supplement and direct individuals to the formal

---

[48] William S. Freas, "The Compensations of the Deaconess," *TLD* 1, no. 3 (July 1924): 21–22. Freas was executive secretary of the Lutheran Welfare Center for Queens, an inter-synodical inner mission society. See *Lutheran World Almanac and Encyclopedia 1934–1937* (New York: National Lutheran Council, 1937), 333–34.

administration of the means of grace. In this calling, she would find many sweet joys.[49]

---

[49] Beata Randt, "The Joy of Deaconess Work," *American Lutheran* 9, no. 3 (March 1926): 8–9. Illustrations for Chapter Three may be viewed at www.deaconesshistory.org.

CHAPTER 4

COMING OF AGE

By 1926, the LDA held interests almost as diverse as the "mission" organizations that made up the membership of ALCh.[1] Students and staff at the four training schools and the women serving in the field were spread throughout the United States, and there was demand for more deaconesses. In the few months before Pentecost Sunday (May 23, 1926), the LDA received eighteen calls for the five women scheduled to graduate from the Fort Wayne training school. The LCMS assigned two of the graduates, Alma Miller and Meta Schrader, to serve as the Synod's first missionary deaconess nurses in India. Louise Rathke, who had graduated the year before from Beaver Dam, was to join them as the first zenana worker.[2]

The grassroots response and financial commitment to the deaconess movement within the Synodical Conference had been quite remarkable for six years. However, the LDA did not achieve its target of 20,000 members, and the accumulative needs of expanding operations eventually outgrew the association's financial resources. Properties, administration, and serving deaconesses all needed to be taken into account. Another happy problem

---

[1] "Our little Charities Conference, founded twenty-five years ago in Chicago, has grown into a great and blessed organization that now includes nearly all the numerous charitable institutions within the Synodical Conference" *TLD* 3, no. 3 (July 1926): 23. The ALCh "Silver Jubilee Convention" was held at Redeemer Lutheran Church in St. Louis, Mo., on October 12–14, 1926. The convention program included one hour for LDA Superintendent Poch and Bethesda's Director Pingel to present a "Report on Our Deaconess Schools" and a "Report on Bethesda." Poch made another hour-long presentation on "The Spiritual Work of our Women Workers."

[2] The LDA later changed Miller's assignment to Lutheran Hospital in Beaver Dam and Schrader took a special course at the Chicago Lying-in Hospital before leaving for India. Hence, when Rathke arrived in India around Christmas Day 1926, she became the first deaconess in India. Almost a year later, Schrader and two other women joined her. "Zenana" is a Hindi word meaning "belonging to women." Zenanas were quarters for the seclusion of women and could be visited only by female medical or spiritual missionaries. Women who brought the Gospel of Christ to these hidden women were called zenana workers. B. Poch, "Deaconess Installation Services at Fort Wayne," *TLD* 3, no. 3 (July 1926): 19–20; B. Poch, "Miscellaneous," *TLD* 4, no. 1 (January 1927): 1, 4; "Special Services at Westcliffe, Colo.," *TLD* 4, no. 4 (October 1927): 30; "Notes and News," *TLD* 3, no. 4 (October 1926): 31; Frederick Brand, "Our Female Foreign Mission-Workers in India," *TLD* 4, no. 2 (April 1927): 13–14.

existed: "Due to the fact that our [training schools] enrollment has practically doubled within two years, we must have larger revenues to meet our expenses."[3]

In 1927, institutions making urgent requests for deaconesses received some temporary relief. At the Kinderheim in Wauwatosa and at Beaver Dam Hospital, students worked at the facilities until graduates could be placed. As the demand for deaconesses accelerated, the fundraising strategy needed to take on an additional dimension.[4]

TURNING TO SYNODS

In 1911, when Herzberger informed the Missouri Synod "that the Conference of the Hospital as well as the Children's Friend and City Mission Organizations of Red Wing, Minnesota, decided to erect a Deaconess Home," he also made the bold statement that "there would be no request on the part of the Conference to look for financial support from Synod now or later" since the Conference's wish was "only that Synod would speak and give its blessing to the project."[5] But much had changed in fifteen years, and Herzberger believed that the Lutheran Church not only needed to acknowledge the value of female church workers but also should begin to take some financial responsibility for the education and practical training of these women. He wrote:

> Our Lutheran deaconesses are *church-workers*. We repeat it most emphatically—THEY ARE CHURCH-WORKERS. They differ from the social workers in this, that they are educated and trained especially to help in bringing the saving Gospel to immortal souls. The church has no business to train social workers, but it is its business to employ and train all the talents her Lord and master has given her for the winning of blood-bought souls for His Kingdom of Grace and His Kingdom of Glory. Among those talents are the consecrated women who are willing to serve their Savior in the ever-growing harvest-fields of His Church.

> The need of such woman workers, or deaconesses, is felt by many in our midst as the roster of the societies supporting our deaconess cause, printed on the last page, will show. But in spite of their precious assistance

---

[3] B. Poch, "Thanks," *TLD* 4, no. 1 (January 1927): 4.

[4] "Beaver Dam," *TLD* 4, no. 1 (January 1927): 2; B. Poch, "Installation Services at Watertown," *TLD* 4, no. 3 (July 1927): 19.

[5] "Diaconissensache," in Synodical Bericht, Ferhandlungern der Deutschen Evangelisch-Lutherishen Synode von Missouri, Ohio und anderen Staaten, versammelt als Driezehnte Delegatensynode Anno Domini 1911 (St. Louis: Concordia, 1911), 18–90. Translated by Rev. Otto A. Brillinger, Noblesville, Ind., April, 2004.

and that of other friends, our Deaconess Society finds it impossible to make ends meet. Here the Church can help, and *in all fairness ought to help*, say, with a yearly subsidy. Our Missouri Synod sends the deaconesses our Society has educated into its Foreign Mission fields. Our Wisconsin Synod calls our deaconesses into its Indian Mission work in Arizona. Our synods annually spend hundreds of thousands of dollars for the purpose of erecting and maintaining colleges for the training of our boys for the holy ministry; they certainly can afford to give a few thousand a year for the training of our pious young women, for our deaconesses, who are doing church-work. It is to their interest to do so. The burden of maintaining our four deaconess schools—at Fort Wayne, Ind., Beaver Dam and Watertown, Wis., and Hot Springs, S. Dak.—is too heavy for our small society. "Bear ye one another's burdens!" In all fairness we ask the synods composing the Synodical Conference to put our DEACONESS CHURCH-WORK on their annual BUDGET; and we ask our big, rich, generous Missouri Synod at its thirty-third convention at St. Louis to take the lead by voting us an annual subsidy of $5,000. We ask it for the sake of Jesus and His saving Gospel.[6]

EVANGELICAL LUTHERAN SYNOD OF MISSOURI, OHIO AND OTHER STATES

The Missouri Synod habitually spent "generous" amounts of money on home and foreign missions, yet at its 1926 convention, delegates discussed options for liquidating the large debt in the Synod's budgeted treasuries. The seriousness of the Synod's financial situation surfaced in some resolutions:

> WHEREAS, Our beloved Synod for many years has been laboring under a deficit in its budgeted treasuries; and
>
> WHEREAS, The work of the Church is being seriously hampered by this continuing deficit; and
>
> WHEREAS, This deficit exerts a depressing and discouraging influence upon our congregations and their individual members, . . .[7]

The *Workbook* of memorials and overtures for the Missouri Synod's 1926 convention contained no reference or allusion to Herzberger's April 1926 appeal. And though the convention assembled in his hometown of St. Louis, there is no evidence that he attended the convention or that he lobbied committees to include deaconess church workers in the Synod's

---

[6] F. W. Herzberger, "In All Fairness," *TLD* 3, no. 2 (April 1926): 9.

[7] LCMS, *Proceedings, 1926*, 212 and 214.

annual budget.[8] In fact, it would not be until October 1931, when "the pioneer of deaconess work within the Synodical Conference" was already sainted, that the new editor of *TLD* would raise the subject of Herzberger's article for renewed consideration.[9]

Nevertheless, the 1926 Missouri Synod convention could be considered a success for the LDA. Many delegates and floor committee members had heard about deaconesses and wanted to make use of them in the mission of the Church.[10] The voting delegates adopted two resolutions stipulating the use of deaconesses in mission work within the United States—one among Jewish women and the other among Italian women.[11]

---

[8] Herzberger may have been absent from the convention because of illness. His hectic schedule caused him to suffer from exhaustion, which contributed to his death three years later. Evangelical Lutheran Synod of Missouri, Ohio, and Other States, *Eingaben für die Achtzehnte Delegatensynode versammelt zu St. Louis, Mo., von 9. bis zum 18. Juni 1926* (St. Louis: Concordia, 1926); B. Poch, "In Memorium," *TLD* 7, no. 4 (October 1930): 25.

[9] Again, though Poch renews Herzberger's plea and reprints his article word for word, no action is taken in regard to it at the delegate convention. See LCMS, *Proceedings,* 1932. "Shall We Ask?" *TLD* 8, no. 4 (October 1931): 2–3.

[10] According to the "Roster of Synod," there were several men known to be sympathetic toward deaconesses at the Missouri Synod convention. For example, Rev. G. W. F. Doege (instructor of deaconess students at Fort Wayne); Prof. P. E. Kretzmann (author of *A Handbook of Outlines for the Training of Lutheran Deaconesses*); Rev. H. B. Kohlmeier (who would become LDA superintendent in 1932); Rev. J. W. Miller, first vice president of the LCMS (one of the nine incorporating members of the LDA, thus on the first LDA Board of Directors); and Rev. F. Brand, third vice president of the LCMS (an advocate of training deaconesses for work in foreign missions). See LCMS, *Proceedings,* 1926, 8–20.

[11] The Board for Jewish Mission reported: "Jewish men and women from all parts of New York attend the services which are regularly conducted every Friday evening. On Christian as well as Jewish holidays a larger, often very gratifying audience attends. Many Jews visit the missionary privately, seeking an explanation of certain Bible-passages of the Old and New Testaments. A goodly number also request a New Testament for private study. Many return it to the missionary; still more purchase a copy of the New Testament. After receiving instruction, one Jewish young man passed a fine examination and made a splendid confession of his faith, and that in spite of bitter hostility shown by his relatives. He was baptized . . ." Thus the report concludes: "We recommend that, in the interest of more successful work among the sick and the women, Synod encourage the Board for Jewish Mission to employ a deaconess and that it appropriate $100 a month for this purpose" (LCMS, *Proceedings,* 1926, 118–19).

In the same way, the Board for Foreign-Tongue Missions reported: "Mission work among Italians is done by Rev. A. Bongarzone in West Hoboken and Englewood, N.J. The first congregation is trying very hard to raise money for a church edifice. Owing to the great expense of building, however, the time when they will begin to build is still remote. With the approval of the Hon. President of Synod, the Board approved the temporary appointment of a deaconess, Miss Tassinary [*sic*], who received her education at the Fort Wayne Deaconess Home." The committee went on to recommend, "to sanction the appointment

This was a good start. The LCMS Board for Jewish Mission would support one deaconess position at $1,200 per year, while the Board for Foreign-Tongue Missions financed another position from its annual budget. Furthermore, it was LCMS President Pfotenhauer who not only approved but also initially advised that a deaconess should be secured to work among Italian women.

Rev. Bruno Poch, LDA superintendent, attended the convention as an advisory pastor for the Central District. Poch wrote an exultant report in the July 1926 issue of *TLD*:

> While attending the Delegate Synod at St. Louis, the undersigned had ample opportunity to acquaint a good number of our people with the aims of our Deaconess Association. Those who were able to attend the convention were surprised to see the splendid exhibits in the various rooms of Holy Cross School featuring the work of Synod. The Foreign Missions exhibit proved particularly interesting to many visitors. . . . Many a visitor remarked that he had no idea as to the great extent charity work was being carried on in our circles. There were those, too, who had never realized the great importance and necessity of training deaconesses. Literature dealing with the various phases of organized charity in our circles was distributed among the visitors.[12]

EVANGELICAL LUTHERAN SYNODICAL CONFERENCE OF NORTH AMERICA

In August 1926, Rev. Wambsganss attended the Synodical Conference convention in Lockport, New York. He and LDA Secretary Rev. Walter A. Klausing (1892–1955) co-signed a letter to the delegates on behalf of "The Deaconess Community within the Synodical Conference," asking for "advice concerning possible grants from the Synods that are members of the Synodical Conference, to assist with the training of Deaconesses."[13]

A special committee appointed by the conference chairman to consider the letter reported: "The present delegates do not have authority to act in this matter. On the other hand, we are of the opinion that the many districts in the Synodical Conference can better recognize the necessity and

---

of a deaconess; that the deaconess be retained in this mission in the future" (LCMS, *Proceedings*, 1926, 115–16).

[12] B. Poch, "Notes and News," *TLD* 3, no. 3 (July 1926): 20.

[13] "Deaconess Items," in Synodical Conference, *Proceedings*, 3:41. Translated by Rev. Dr. Jonathan C. Naumann, Pittsburgh, PA, February, 2005.

importance of the items needed by the deaconesses, and the action they desire can take place through them."[14] Despite this ruling, the conference allowed Wambsganss to explain the work of the LDA. Moved by his presentation, the delegates resolved with a unanimous vote "to approve of this work and to advise the Deaconess Association to address itself to the various Districts of the synods affiliated with the Synodical Conference for financial support."[15]

Just over a year later, Superintendent Poch wrote in his "Quarterly Survey":

> Acting upon this advice, the Association addressed itself to the various Districts of the Missouri Synod. The Districts of the Wisconsin Synod and the other synods affiliated with the Synodical Conference will be appealed to in 1928. We are very grateful in being able to report that practically every District of the Missouri Synod has voted favorably in behalf of the support of our work. Wherever possible, a personal appeal was made by some member of the Deaconess Board or by his friends interested in the cause. . . . The reports which have been received thus far state that thirteen Districts have passed the resolution to urge all pastors within the respective District to present the deaconess cause to the various societies within the congregations, especially the ladies' aids, and to solicit the financial support of this very necessary work.[16]

Some LCMS district papers, such as the *Atlantic District Bulletin,* began to publish articles about deaconess work. The *Pioneer* and *Missionstaube* did likewise, and *TLD* had a circulation of around 4,500 copies.[17]

To facilitate follow-up to the important membership campaign, the LDA employed a deaconess to help the superintendent by "looking after the heavy mail."[18] In November 1927, the LDA treasurer and financial secretary, Mr. Ernst Niemeyer, confirmed that, "because of the rapid expansion of the work the revenues have not been sufficient to cover running expenses during the past year." However, the LDA still hoped to reach its goal of 10,000 members, in which case "all current expenses will be taken care of."[19]

---

[14] "Deaconess Items," 3: 41.

[15] "Notes and News," *TLD* 3, no. 4: 31.

[16] B. Poch, "Quarterly Survey," *TLD* 4, no. 4 (October 1927): 26.

[17] B. Poch, "Publicity," *TLD* 5, no. 4 (October 1928): 27.

[18] "Annual Meeting," *TLD* 5, no. 1 (January 1928): 1.

[19] Sometime between July 1920 and January 1928, the membership goal changed from 20,000 to 10,000. In April 1928, the LDA needed "six thousand more members." (See chapter 2.) Stretched resources meant the delay of some expenditures, such as painting the exterior of the deaconess home. See "Notes and News," *TLD* 5, no. 2 (April 1928): 12.

LUTHERAN EXPOSITIONS

After the ruling of the Synodical Conference, the LDA tried to have a presence at as many Lutheran Church gatherings as time, manpower, and finances allowed. This face-to-face approach gave pastors and laypeople an opportunity to ask questions and to explore the possibility of personal involvement with the deaconess movement. In fall 1926, two Lutheran Expositions provided exciting opportunities to put this strategy into practice. The first event was October 9–10 in Chicago, where a booth that displayed "pictures showing our training-schools and graduates, as well as literature explaining our work, caused many visitors to stop and make further inquiries. A new folder with illustrations and text explaining our deaconess activities had been prepared for the occasion. Nearly 5,000 copies were taken by the visitors as they passed our booth, and we hope that many of these will be induced to support our cause."[20] The following month on the Saturday after Thanksgiving, the evening program at the Milwaukee Lutheran Exposition included the president of the Milwaukee Deaconess Branch Society, Mr. Theodore Dammann. In addition, Superintendent Poch spoke on Monday Evening. The booth and the presentations gained eighty-four new members for the LDA. "Special thanks are due Miss Helen Koepke, who gained most of the new members. As in Chicago, so also in Milwaukee many visitors told the undersigned that they had never dreamt that our Church is doing such great work, especially for missions and charities, until they had seen those pictures nicely grouped together in the exposition."[21]

THE WALTHER LEAGUE

In 1893, the *Walther Liga* (Walther League) emerged as the official youth association of the Synodical Conference. The organization consisted mainly of young people's societies from within the Missouri Synod.[22] The strength of the Walther League lay in its well-organized national and international network. Walther League meetings took place on congregational, circuit, and state levels, culminating in an annual international convention.

---

[20] "Notes and News," *TLD* 3, no. 4: 31.

[21] B. Poch, "Milwaukee Lutheran Exposition Nets Eighty-Four New Members," *TLD* 4, no. 1 (January 1927): 8. Theodore Dammann was secretary of the state of Wisconsin. Helen Koepke was secretary of the Wisconsin Conservatory of Music.

[22] The Missouri Synod officially recognized the Walther League in 1920. Erwin L. Lueker, ed., *Lutheran Cyclopedia: A Concise In-Home Reference for the Christian Family* rev. ed. (St. Louis: Concordia, 1975), 836.

Activities sponsored by the League varied from worship and camping to participation in mission or hands-on service (welfare) projects. The "education" and "service" aspects of the organization's agenda often included vocational guidance, practical experience in leadership roles, and recruitment for vocations in the church.[23]

Superintendent Poch visited Walther League meetings as he toured the United States. His goal was to educate laity about the deaconess movement and recruit young women into deaconess ministry. In summer 1926, for example, Poch spoke at the first conventions of the South Dakota District of the Walther League and the North Dakota District of the Walther League. The South Dakota District resolved to give financial support to the deaconess training school in Hot Springs and requested Poch to make a four-week lecture trip around South Dakota, which resulted in 152 new memberships for the LDA.[24]

In July 1927, Poch addressed the thirty-fifth annual convention of the International Walther League assembled in St. Louis. During the lunch hour and after convention sessions, he met with individual "Leaguers" at the deaconess booth in the Exhibit Room, where he "received promises from several Leaguers that they will enroll as deaconess students."[25] The young convention delegates also unanimously passed a resolution to support the deaconess cause:

> WHEREAS, Lutheran deaconesses are performing an essential service to our Church and are materially aiding its progress, both in the home and in the mission-field abroad; and
>
> WHEREAS, Many young women of our Church and League are qualified and eligible to serve our master in a most effective way in this capacity; therefore be it
>
> *Resolved*, That this convention recommend,
>
> 1) That the deaconess service be brought to the attention of our League members at rallies, district conventions, and local meetings, and

---

23 By drawing both men and women into leadership training and activities, the Walther League assisted in effecting a change in the role of younger women within the LCMS. Ruth Fritz Meyer, *Women on a Mission: The Role of Women in the Church from Bible Times Up to and Including a History of The Lutheran Women's Missionary League during Its First Twenty-five Years* (St. Louis: Concordia, 1967), 56.
24 Poch, "Notes and News," *TLD* 3, no. 3: 20; B. Poch, "Publicity Work," *TLD* 4, no. 1 (January 1927): 3.
25 B. Poch, "Walther League Votes Support," *TLD* 4, no. 4 (October 1927): 28.

2) That local societies or groups of societies be encouraged to offer support to such young women as engage in this work.[26]

In keeping with the above resolution, Rev. Walter Arthur Maier (1893–1950), editor of *Walther League Messenger,* welcomed news and photographs of deaconess work for inclusion in the League's magazine.[27] The Walther League continued to be an important partner to the LDA for several years. When rallies or conventions received reports about the charitable endeavors of deaconesses, some type of support was likely to follow.[28]

LADIES' AIDS AND THE
LUTHERAN WOMEN'S MISSIONARY LEAGUE

As Superintendent Poch and other LDA enthusiasts gave presentations to Walther League groups or preached at mission festivals, they also made personal appeals to ladies' aid societies whenever possible. Some of these groups met with branch societies of the LDA, while most had initially come into being for purposes such as sewing and providing supplies for orphans, seminary students, deaf people, hospitals, or foreign missions. In 1925, though several pastors chose to refrain from asking their congregations to support the LDA until goals for the Missouri Synod's "Building Program" were complete, twenty new ladies' aids sent contributions to the deaconess cause.[29] Many of the women active in such ladies' aid societies believed that they could work more effectively by joining together in organized "mission circles." On March 11, 1928, this idea bore fruit at the district level with the formation of "The Lutheran Women's League of Oklahoma."[30]

Ladies' groups in the Central District of the Missouri Synod (comprising Indiana, Ohio, West Virginia, and part of Kentucky) made

---

[26] Paul G. Prokopy and Erwin Umbach, eds., Convention Year-Book of the Thirty-fifth International Convention of the Walther League, St. Louis, Missouri, Field House, Washington University, July 17–21, 1927, containing Complete Proceedings, Opening Sermon, Reports, Addresses, and Various Matters of Interest, Pertaining to the Convention in the City of Dr. Walther (St. Louis: Concordia, 1927), 106.

[27] Maier edited the *Walther League Messenger* from 1920–45. He was the first full-time executive secretary of the Walther League (1920–22); a professor at Concordia Seminary, St. Louis, (1922–44); and the first speaker of the "Lutheran Hour" (1930–31, 1935–50). See Lueker, *Lutheran Cyclopedia*, 512, 658; Poch, "Publicity," 27.

[28] E.g., the Milwaukee-Waukesha zone rally voted to give its entire collection of $86.44 to the Lutheran Deaconess Hospital at Beaver Dam. See B. Poch, "Notes and News," *TLD* 6, no. 1 (January 1929): 5.

[29] "Central District Synod," *TLD* 2, no. 3 (July 1925): 18.

[30] Meyer, *Women on a Mission,* 65.

similar efforts at the instigation of a group of women in Fort Wayne "who had the formation of a Synodwide organization of women in mind," but desired "not to form a new organization but to federate the existing organizations and coordinate their work for the benefit of missions and charity, particularly for women and children."[31] With the approval of Rev. Fred Wambsganss Sr., director of the Central District Home Mission Board, the women contacted numerous pastors and women's societies and sent a petition to the Pastoral Conference of Fort Wayne, asking for permission to organize. The Fort Wayne pastors forwarded an overture to the Central District, with the result that the following recommendations were adopted on June 27, 1928:[32]

> 1. That Synod recognize, and express gratitude for, the missionary zeal on the part of the women of the Church, particularly those of Fort Wayne . .
>
> 2. That Synod proceed to make use of the opportunity thus offered in the manner suggested by the Pastoral Conference of Fort Wayne to enlist the support of the ladies' auxiliaries within the District for the purpose of creating greater interest and financial activity regarding projects not included in the budgeted treasuries and yet necessary and desirable to complete a well-rounded-out missionary program . . . and that therefore
>
> A. The Executive Home Mission Board of our District, together with the Director of Missions, constitute a Ways and Means Committee to direct and promote these endeavors; B. This Ways and Means Committee be authorized to augment itself by adding the District representatives of the Foreign and Negro Missions boards . . . C. The ladies' auxiliaries within the District be approached for the purpose of gaining their support for this movement; . . . D. The Ways and Means Committee be authorized to print and distribute informative and inspirational literature bearing on the projects to be undertaken, enabling the pastors to present the cause of missions to their societies. . . . E. It shall be understood that this movement will in no way interfere with the regular contributions toward the Synod. F. That this movement be self-sustaining.[33]

Although the above resolution never mentioned deaconesses or the LDA, many LDA supporters facilitated the process that eventually led to the passing and implementation of the resolution. *The Lutheran Deaconess* printed the entire text of the original petition submitted to the "Easter conference of pastors and teachers of the Central District, in April 1928."[34] Following that text, an unsigned postscript explained:

---

[31] Meyer, *Women on a Mission*, 66.

[32] *Ibid.*, 66–67.

[33] "Overture No. 5," Central District LCMS, *Proceedings, June 24–29, 1928*, 78–79.

[34] "Lutheran Woman's Missionary Endeavor," *TLD* 6, no. 2 (April 1929): 9–11.

The above appeal was signed by twelve women. At the same conference a similar memorial was submitted for discussion. Pastor Fred Wambsganss (Sr.) . . . wished to enlist the support of the women in the District for missionary projects not provided for by the District budget, as, for instance, the erecting of chapels for mission-fields. The memorial was read before Synod, and a committee representing the interests of various missions was appointed to cooperate with the District Home Mission Board in devising ways and means to get the best results in the important field of missions.

According to the resolution of the Central District, the committee is to print and distribute informative and inspirational literature bearing on the projects to be undertaken, which will enable the pastors to present the cause of missions to their societies systematically and regularly. In compliance with this resolution a quarterly is being published bearing the title, *Lutheran Woman's Missionary Endeavor Quarterly.* Pastor Fred Wambsganss (Sr.), editor of the quarterly, announces in the first issue that he has been furtunate [*sic*] to receive promises from men and women with a strong missionary background to contribute regularly to the pages of this missionary periodical. The feature article in the first issue has been contributed by Pastor Frank Lankenau, who for many years served in the Colored Mission field of the South. Mrs. F. Zucker, wife of Missionary Zucker in India, has prepared most interesting articles in the first and second issues on the necessity of helping Oriental women through women.

We hope that the Lutheran Woman's Missionary Endeavor will create greater interest also in our deaconess work to help us in training young women for special service in the great harvest-fields of the Church.[35]

The author makes special mention of the possible benefits that the new Lutheran Woman's Missionary Endeavor might deliver to the deaconess movement. Furthermore, Central District "missions director" Fred Wambsganss Sr. (son of LDA President Philipp Wambsganss and a teacher of deaconess pupils) became the first editor of the *Quarterly* and embodied a key connection between the LDA and a continuum of milestones that eventually led to the formation of the national Lutheran Women's Missionary League (LWML) in 1942. Fred Wambsganss (Sr.) wrote:

Talks and discussions with other similar District women's organizations led to the authorization by Synod at its triennial convention in 1941, in Fort Wayne, of calling into existence a Synodwide women's organization. At the organizational meeting, held in St. Matthew's Church, Chicago, and

---

[35] "Lutheran Woman's Missionary Endeavor," 11.

attended by representatives of various District organizations, the objective was reached and the proposed name "Lutheran Women's Missionary League" was adopted. Together with Pastor R. H. C. Meyer of St. Louis and Mr. John Ohlis of Chicago, I was very happy to serve on the committee which presented the plan of a women's missionary organization on a Synodwide scale to the convention at the organizational meeting in Chicago.[36]

The proliferation and banding together of women's mission societies, at whatever level, would create new opportunities for recruitment and more sources of revenue for the mission work of the diaconate. In January 1929, the Fort Wayne Lutheran Ladies' Mission Society voted to give $250 toward special training for Deaconess Gertrude Oberheu, who had volunteered to serve in India.[37] This was only the beginning. In the years to come, the growing LWML provided a strong financial base for deaconess work and eventually supplied one of the largest checks ever to be received by the association, for the construction of Deaconess Hall.[38]

A HINT OF THEOLOGICAL CONCERN

The changing role of women in the United States in the early twentieth-century presented an unavoidable challenge for the theologians of the Synodical Conference. During World War I, women workers replaced men who left jobs to join the military, and after the war, they began to hold or retain jobs previously open only to men.[39] Fashion crazes during the "roaring '20s"—from clothing and hairstyles to dancing and smoking—reflected an emerging independent spirit among American women. The women's suffrage movement encouraged political activism by women as well as men. Approved by the U.S. Congress in 1919 and ratified into law in 1920, the Nineteenth Amendment to the United States Constitution gave women the right to vote, and in 1925, Texas elected the first female governor. As these events took place, the Church was forced to take a fresh

---

[36] Fred Wambsganss Sr., "Five Decades of Pastoral Activity," *Concordia Historical Institute Quarterly* 30, no. 4 (Winter 1958): 151–52. Wambsganss's wife is listed as one of twenty-eight delegates at the organizational meeting of the LWML at St. Stephen's Church, Chicago, July 7–8, 1942. See Meyer, *Women on a Mission*, 121.

[37] "Notes and News," *TLD* 6, no. 2 (April 1929): 13.

[38] Clara Strehlow, "Deaconesses Are Missionaries," *Lutheran Woman's Quarterly* 18, no. 2 (April 1960): 1, 3–4, 30.

[39] Andrew Cayton, Elisabeth Perry, Linda Reed, and Allan Winkler, "Americans on the Home Front," in *America Pathways to the Present: Modern American History* (Upper Saddle River, NJ: Prentice Hall, 2005), 432–36.

look at the role of women both in society and within its own ranks.[40] This was the context into which the LDA was born.

The evolving role of women in society prompted concern about the possible evolving role of women within the Lutheran Church. Some individuals feared that the office of deaconess, once established within the Synodical Conference, could be abused. These misgivings surfaced at the formation of the LDA in 1919 and still existed ten years later. It is not possible to pinpoint specific events that may have precipitated the assurances found in the following three passages, but the authors did perceive a need to assert that no unscriptural teaching or practice took place within the diaconate. The first quotation appeared in the October 1927 issue of *TLD*:

> We have been told that considerable apprehension was felt in various quarters of the Synodical Conference when, seven years ago, The Lutheran Deaconess Association was organized. According to its constitution the chief purpose of the Association is to train Lutheran young women as helpers in the great fields of missions and charities. There were those who feared that such a policy of training women for special service in the Church might eventually lead us into sectarian channels. There is, however, no reason for entertaining such thoughts. We are in full accord with the Scriptures when appealing to our young women to help us in the missionary, educational, and charitable endeavors of our dear Lutheran Church. St. Paul, the greatest missionary among the apostles, has much to say in praise of woman helpers in the Church. Deaconess work, which is comparatively new in our circles, was carried on by the early Christians. . . .[41]

The second quotation is part of the beginning of a sermon by Rev. Kohlmeier, delivered at the May 1928 installation service for deaconess graduates in Fort Wayne:

> Three years ago you entered our school with the object of preparing yourselves for deaconess work in the Lutheran Church. You were prompted to do this, I take it, by sincere love for the Savior, in order to equip yourselves so much better to serve Him in serving your fellow-men and especially to be helpful in saving souls.

> It is not God's will that women should serve in the pastoral office as ministers of the Gospel. This service of the public ministry God has

---

[40] See for example, Louis J. Sieck, "Attitude Lutherans Should Take Towards Woman's Suffrage," *Lutheran Witness* 38, nos. 10–12 (May 13, 1919; May 27, 1919; June 10, 1919): 149–50, 162, 179–80; "The Future," *American Lutheran* 5, no. 4 (April 1922): 35–36.
[41] "The Spiritual Work of Our Woman Workers," *TLD* 4, no. 4 (October 1927): 28.

restricted to men. But women can and should be of help in the Gospel-service. Trained deaconesses especially can be of great service in the Church.

In our own particular church-body this branch of service has but recently been established; but it is by no means a new institution in the Church. In fact, we know from Scripture that there were deaconesses in the days of the apostles and that they rendered very valuable and blessed service to the cause of Christ. It is the example of those early deaconesses that you wish to follow.

Today you publicly, before God and this assembled congregation, promise to serve the Savior in this office as long as it shall please Him to use your gifts, your talents, for this special work. In a solemn service you are being installed into the office of deaconesses, and the prayers of your fellow-Christians ascend to the throne of God asking Him to grant you fervent love and zeal to do your work, faithfulness in performing your duties, courage and strength in all difficulties, and richly to bless your labors for the salvation of many and unto the praise of His glorious name. . . .[42]

Kohlmeier's statement that it is not God's will for women to serve in the pastoral office served several purposes: it instructed the congregation, reminded deaconess graduates to keep their proper station, and provided a declaration of theological intent to all who might be wondering about the position of the LDA on the subject.

A year later, in 1929, Rev. William Naumann began his sermon at the installation of deaconess graduates in Watertown in a similar but slightly more emphatic manner:

The Christians of the Synodical Conference have only recently made a beginning of training and employing deaconesses. The name matters very little but the need of Christian women trained to assist in parish work, in mission fields, in hospitals and in institutions of charity has always been present and has often been felt very keenly. Those who promoted this comparatively new enterprise in our circles have been well aware of the fact that the employment of women workers in the church has its limitations and that a breaking down of such limitations would mar the Christian character of such institution. But at the same time they were fully convinced, that the eventual abuse of such an institution does not abolish its rightful use, and that with the help of God the work of

---

[42] H. B. Kohlmeier, "Sermon Delivered at Installation Service," *TLD* 6, no. 1 (January 1929): 1. Kohlmeier would become Superintendent of the deaconess training program four years after delivering this sermon.

Christian trained women in their proper sphere would materially increase the efficiency of our work in the Christian Church.

Whenever in the course of centuries the deaconess cause has been misused it was when the bishops and pastors have slept and when the people have ceased to watch and to pray and to let the Word of God be a lamp unto their feet and a light unto their path. We, the Christians of the Lutheran Church, pastors and hearers, today anew make a solemn promise to God that also in this deaconess cause as in all our work we will be guided not by mere consideration of opportunity, but first and last by the Word of God. And we do not doubt that God will bless our efforts in this direction and that the Deaconess Cause will prove a valuable aid in the upbuilding of our dear Lutheran Zion in this country. It is impossible that we should fail having the Word of God as a lamp unto our feet and a light unto our path.

This truth holds good also in respect to our deaconesses themselves, to them that are in the field already and to them that are about to enter into the field: That they will only become and be a success and blessing, when they make the Word of God a lamp unto their feet and a light unto their path.

When we speak of the Word of God, we mean the whole Word of God as it is found in the writings of the holy prophets in the Old Testament and of the holy apostles and evangelists in the New Testament. "Whatsoever things were written aforetimes were written for our learning," Paul says, Rom. 15,4. And we are to learn not only from the statements of doctrine or from the precepts found in the Scriptures, but also from the examples of the lives of the children of God described by the holy writers.[43]

Pastor Naumann did not justify the office of deaconess on the basis of New Testament practice, but he argued that whatever they may be called, women are needed to work in the Church "in their proper sphere." He revealed the heartfelt deliberation that took place among the founders of the training schools. These individuals had considered the likely "eventual abuse" of the institution of deaconesses. Naumann did not imply that such abuse existed in relation to the LDA but that it occurred "in the course of centuries" whenever members of the Church, both clergy and laity, ceased to look to God's Word for illumination.

---

[43] Wm. T. Naumann "Sermon Preached at the Installation of Lutheran Deaconesses at Watertown, Wis. May 5, 1929," *Der Bote aus Bethesda* 20, no. 3 (May 1929): 4. Naumann's sermon also appeared in *TLD*, heavily edited and retaining only a short paraphrase of its original introduction; see "At Watertown," *TLD* 6, no. 3 (July 1929): 20–21. At this time, Naumann taught deaconess students at both Beaver Dam and Watertown.

The most stunning part of Naumann's sermon introduction was his "solemn promise"—a promise made not to any man but to God alone—spoken on behalf of all members of the Lutheran Church, to be guided "first and last by the Word of God." Over and over again Naumann referred his listeners back to the Word of God as a "lamp unto their feet and a light unto their path," and then made sure that they understood what he meant by the "Word of God." Why he felt the need to clarify these points is unknown, but it can be assumed that some sort of problem had surfaced and was being laid to rest by these remarks. Moreover, if Naumann's sermon represented the thinking of the LDA leadership, these men sincerely desired to build and nurture the diaconate on God's Word as set forth in the Lutheran Symbols. Deaconesses were to be faithful to Scripture in their teaching, leadership, and service.

Almost a Decade

At the ALCh convention held in Watertown, Wisconsin, in September 1929, Superintendent Poch gave a brief summary of the history of the LDA, its current progress, and his hopes for the future:

> . . . This year there was a total of fifteen graduates from our three training schools. We were not able, however, to supply in full the demand for workers. We expect to see our Deaconess Hospital at Beaver Dam enlarged in the very near future. Thirty-two deaconesses are in the service and twenty-seven are in training. Twelve deaconesses are stationed in institutions. Eleven are employed at three different hospitals. Three are engaged in parish work; two are serving the foreign mission field in India, and four are stationed in the American Indian Missions at Gresham, Wisconsin, and Whiteriver, Arizona. . . . Although the financial situation has improved compared with former years, we are still a long ways off from the coveted goal of a membership of 10,000.

> An increased revenue would enable us to provide special courses for positions calling for special qualifications. We stand sorely in need of trained executives for the various responsible positions in our charitable and semi-charitable institutions. Urgent calls for Lutheran executives to serve as matrons in hospitals or children's homes, calls for superintendents of nurses and similar positions come to us time and again, and I hope that the 28th Convention of our Associated Lutheran Charities will be able to suggest a plan that will prove a solution to the serious problem just stated.[44]

---

[44] B. Poch, "Report of Deaconess Association," in *Proceedings of the ALCh*, 1929, 125–27.

Poch concluded his remarks on a positive note, with words of appreciation for "the invaluable services rendered the deaconess cause by Dr. P. E. Kretzmann."[45] After becoming acquainted with the Lutheran Social Service League that had been organized by Fort Wayne Lutherans, the LDA added a course in "religious social work" to the curriculum for deaconess training.[46] Kretzmann wrote a textbook for the course, titled *The Christian Woman as Social Worker*, which would be used by pupils for decades to come.[47]

In support of the deaconess cause, ALCh passed a resolution "to permit the soliciting of memberships during sessions of Conference."[48] At its next convention in 1930, the ALCh took a closer look at how to provide Lutheran executives for Lutheran institutions. At that time, "a committee was elected which drew up a recommendation to the effect that the hospitals provide such training for Lutheran nurses who would qualify for such positions and, if necessary, supply financial aid."[49]

Up to this point, the majority of deaconesses working in hospitals or other institutions acquired leadership roles at the time of their consecrations or soon thereafter. The LDA practice of assigning deaconess nurses to positions such as superintendent of nurses or asking practical deaconesses to be head matrons at orphanages and homes for the elderly developed out of the urgency to fill vacant positions. This practice continued as long as the number of charitable organizations within the Synodical Conference continued to increase.

TENTH ANNIVERSARY CELEBRATIONS

The following information appeared on the back of the worship bulletin for the service commemorating the tenth anniversary of the LDA:

SOME HISTORICAL DATA

"Hitherto the Lord hath helped us."

Organization meeting at St. Paul's Hall, Fort Wayne, August 20, 1919.

---

[45] Poch, "Report of Deaconess Association," 127.

[46] The committee that designed the content of the course consisted of Rev. (Professor) Paul Frederick Bente (1886–1957), Rev. E. Foelber, Miss Anna Holtman, Miss Emma Jensen, Rev. B. Poch, and Professor George Schmidt. See "Additional Course at Fort Wayne," *TLD* 4, no. 3 (July 1927): 23.

[47] Poch worked closely with Kretzmann on behalf of the LDA, but the two men were also related by marriage. Poch's wife, Elizabeth, was the sister of P. E. (and M. F.) Kretzmann. See "Book Review," *TLD* 7, no. 4 (October 1930): 32.

[48] "Tuesday, September 17th," in *Proceedings of the ALCh*, 1929, 8.

[49] "Associated Lutheran Charities Meet at Fort Wayne," *TLD* 7, no. 4 (October 1930): 29.

Motto of Association: "For Missions and Charities"

President since organization: Pastor Ph. Wambsganss.

First Deaconess graduated in 1922: Miss Ina Kempff.

Deaconess graduates in 1929, fifteen.

Deaconesses in the service, thirty.

Deaconesses sent to India, five. Three more have been asked for.[50]

The *TLD* announced: "November 10, 1929, will go down in the history of our Deaconess Association as a red-letter day because on that day we celebrated the tenth anniversary of our society."[51] And what a joyous celebration it was! The association's annual meeting took place at the parish house of Emmaus Lutheran Church in Fort Wayne, where LDA officials and representatives from the various local branch societies and ladies' auxiliaries gathered in a celebratory mood. President Wambsganss gave a keynote address based on the words "Not unto us, O Lord, not unto us, but alone to Thy name belongs all honor and glory." Superintendent Poch prefaced his normal report with a long historical sketch of the female diaconate, and those present agreed that the Lord had much more for the organization to do in the future.[52] As a prelude to the evening worship service held at Emmaus, Mr. C. Rupprecht, a well-known Lutheran musician from Chicago, entertained the congregation with an organ recital.[53] It is likely that several clergymen took part in the service, but the bulletin only noted the preacher: Pastor L. Kirst, director of the training program at Lutheran Hospital in Beaver Dam. He expounded on "The Struggle of the Church of God Against All Her Enemies and Her Victory over Them," using Revelation 20:7–9 as his text.[54]

There were a number of unavoidable absences from the anniversary celebrations, including that of Mr. Theodore Dammann, president of the large Milwaukee branch society; Pastor E. A. Duemling, LCMS city

---

[50] "Tenth Anniversary of the Lutheran Deaconess Association within the Synodical Conference," Worship Service Bulletin, Services held November 10, 1929, Emmaus Lutheran Church, Fort Wayne, Indiana, 3. CHI, LDA file: 1929.

[51] "Tenth Anniversary and Annual Meeting of Deaconess Association," *TLD* 7, no. 1 (January 1930): 1.

[52] "Tenth Anniversary and Annual Meeting of Deaconess Association," 1–4.

[53] The worship folder lists "Prof. Hahn" as giving the organ recital, but the official report of the event, printed after the fact, lists Mr. Rupprecht. See "Organ Recital and Jubilee Service," *TLD* 7, no. 1 (January 1930): 4.

[54] *TLD* printed the sermon in two parts: L. Kirst, "Sermon on Rev. 20,7–9: 1," *TLD* 7, no. 2 (April 1930): 9–11; L. Kirst, "Sermon on Rev. 20,7–9: 2," *TLD* 7, no. 3 (July 1930): 17–18.

missionary in Milwaukee; and most notably, Pastor Herzberger, who sent a rousing letter to the assembly:[55]

> I very much regret to say that circumstances here, my dear friends, will not permit me to be present with you at the tenth anniversary of our beloved Deaconess Association. But I shall be with you in spirit, see your happy faces, and hear your resounding hymns praising our Lord and Savior, who has so wonderfully blessed our deaconess work.
>
> When I consider how much effort it cost, for years indeed, to awaken even a little interest for this most needed female diaconate; when I consider how meager and precarious its beginning was, what little funds we had, how hard it was to find and salary a competent superintendent, and how the dear Lord has signally prospered our efforts and endowed our executive at Fort Wayne, especially our beloved president, Pastor Ph. Wambsganss, to carry on the work and never say die,—then I can only fold my hands and in joyous gratitude of my heart exclaim with the psalmist: 'This is the Lord's doing; it is marvelous in our eyes.' Yes, 'the Lord hath done great things for us, whereof we are glad,' and we raise this Ebenezer to His glory.
>
> But, dear friends, let this memorable day not be merely a day of praise and thanksgiving and rejoicing, but let it be a day on which we all consecrate ourselves anew to carry on this work of the Lord, which provides faithful, believing, and trained women workers for our charitable institutions, our mission-fields, and our large city congregations.
>
> Thank God we have pious young women who have entered the work and are making good, and I, for one, know of no other deaconess society, either in Europe or in America, that can tell the world how in ten short years it has succeeded in establishing three deaconess training-schools, put thirty-one women workers in the field, and is instructing twenty-eight pupils in its training-schools.
>
> Verily, in view of the great success the Lord has granted our work, we have all reason to carry it on with courageous and joyous hearts, knowing that our labors also in the years to come will not be in vain in the Lord.[56]

A GREAT LOSS

Poor health kept Herzberger from the anniversary celebration and other important meetings. In April 1930, Superintendent Poch visited Herzberger at the Lutheran Hospital in St. Louis, where he had been "confined to his

[55] "Tenth Anniversary and Annual Meeting of Deaconess Association," 4.
[56] F. W. Herzberger, "Pastor Herzberger's Letter," *TLD* 7, no. 1 (January 1930): 4–5.

bed for several weeks with pleurisy."[57] On August 26, 1930, he died, exhausted from a lifetime of selfless work, in which he was driven—determined and single-minded—to accomplish all that he could for his Savior and those whom the Savior came to save.

"Daddy" Herzberger was never an officer of ALCh, never held an elected position in the LDA, and never taught or trained deaconess pupils, yet his ideas and writings, especially as editor of *TLD,* had a huge influence on the formation and perpetuation of the deaconess movement within the Synodical Conference. Herzberger spent eighteen years as the pastor of LCMS parishes in Arkansas, Kansas, and Indiana, and then just over thirty years as city missionary in St. Louis. During all his service in the pastoral office, he was a zealous visionary, whose personal commitment to "kingdom work" inspired others to grasp his vision and join him in mutual service to the Lord.[58] The LDA Board of Directors "voted a memorial wreath" to their friend and acknowledged that he would have an effect on his fellow workers for years to come. The last sentence of a front-page tribute to him read: "May the example of Pastor Herzberger stimulate us in the work which he loved so dearly that we may also work while it is day, before the night cometh, when no man can work!"[59]

Using Different Types of Media

In the 1930s, the LDA made efforts to facilitate better organization and communication with members of the Synodical Conference. Because of an "ever-increasing volume of correspondence," Poch found it impossible to leave his office for very long to comply with requests for lectures on the deaconess cause.[60] The solution was to call a Field Secretary, Rev. Fred W. Korbitz, who would lead a nationwide membership campaign and solicit contributions for building a sorely needed annex at Lutheran Deaconess Hospital in Beaver Dam.[61] Korbitz devised a "key-man" system to assist the

---

[57] "Notes and News," *TLD* 7, no. 2 (April 1930): 14.
[58] ALCh President Duemling paid tribute to Herzberger; see E. A Duemling, "Opening Address," in *Proceedings of the ALCh,* 1929, 12–13.
[59] B. Poch, "In Memoriam," *TLD* 7, no. 4 (October 1930): 25. Another loving tribute to Herzberger as parish pastor can be read in *Saint Paulus Evangelische Lutherische Kirche UAC, Hammond, Indiana 1882–1907.* This twenty-fifth anniversary book, published by the congregation, was translated by Betty Mulholland, Munster, Ind., February 2004. Herzberger was buried in Concordia Cemetery, 4209 Bates St., St. Louis. His grave can be located on the left side of the road, about twenty yards beyond the Concordia Cemetery monument dedicated in 1845 by C. F. W. Walther.
[60] B. Poch, "Quarterly Survey," *TLD* 6, no. 2 (April 1929): 9.
[61] "An Introduction," *TLD* 7, no. 4 (October 1930): 30–31.

campaign. Starting in Wisconsin, he recruited pastors within the Wisconsin and Missouri Synods to serve as key-men who assumed responsibility for soliciting memberships and providing information on deaconess work within their own geographical areas. Most key-men also had "captains" to help them with the job.[62] Korbitz used this network to disseminate information to grass roots LDA supporters, even providing articles for publication in church newsletters.

Superintendent Poch remained busy with correspondence, teaching, and the general oversight of the deaconess training schools. As they went about their work, both Poch and Korbitz explored the use of new media to further the deaconess cause. On a January 1931 road trip, Poch spoke about deaconess work on radio station KFUO in St. Louis.[63] In spring 1931, with support from the Walther League Slide Bureau, Korbitz compiled a "Lantern Slide Lecture" that showed "the various phases of deaconess activity."[64] He used the pictures to illustrate his speaking engagements. Copies of the slides, including lecture notes, could be borrowed by key-men or church groups from the office of Rev. Julius Herman Gockel (1896–1965) at the Walther League Headquarters in Chicago.[65]

CHANGES IN THE MOTHERHOUSE

From the time of its dedication in 1923, the director or superintendent of the LDA occupied part of the Fort Wayne deaconess motherhouse. In 1931, the Board of Directors determined that the superintendent should find other quarters so that the motherhouse could accommodate deaconesses in the field who wished to spend some time at the home. In light of the diaconate's expansion, the LDA felt that not only deaconess students but also deaconess graduates—regardless of the training school they attended—should be able to retreat to the motherhouse when they were ill, desired short visits or vacations, or eventually needed a place to live

---

[62] There is no evidence that the LDA carried out its intended 1928 financial campaign among the districts of the Wisconsin Synod or other synods affiliated with the Synodical Conference. This is the first mention of membership solicitation within the Wisconsin Synod. Lists of key-men and captains may be found in several 1931 issues of *TLD*. See F. W. Korbitz, "Quarterly Report of the Field Secretary," *TLD* 8, no. 1 (January 1931): 1.

[63] "Notes and News," *TLD* 8, no. 2 (April 1931): 5.

[64] F. W. Korbitz, "D—Lectures, with Slides," *TLD* 9, no. 1 (January 1932): 5.

[65] F. W. Korbitz, "Quarterly Report of the Field Secretary," *TLD* 8, no. 3 (July 1931): 5–6; see also Korbitz, "Deaconess Work—Analyzed!" *American Lutheran* 14, no. 5 (May 1931), 16–17 (1284–85).

in old age.[66] The LDA financial statement for 1930 reflected this caring attitude toward deaconesses—including disbursements for items such as dentists and doctors, uniforms and coats, and even funeral expenses for one of the women.[67]

The changes in the use of the motherhouse occurred after Field Secretary Korbitz visited Sister Superior Ingeborg Sponland and Field Worker Mabel Thorstensen, who gave him a tour of Norwegian Lutheran Deaconess Hospital and the brand new $200,000 Norwegian Lutheran Deaconess Motherhouse on North Leavitt Street in Chicago. Korbitz described the well-appointed building in a 1931 quarterly report and concluded:

> We do not fear that our deaconess will ask for a building such as was described above, but we are certain that all of them will go about their work more enthusiastically after the Board's resolution has gone into effect. Our Motherhouse is but a modest home. Let us all do our part that our deaconesses are happy in it. If you, dear reader, wish to assist in some way kindly write to our Office. The Norwegian Deaconess Motherhouse is entirely a gift of the friends of the deaconess cause.[68]

In 1930, the Deaconess Ladies' Aid of Fort Wayne gave a Christmas gift of ten dollars to two institutions run by deaconesses in other parts of the world, namely, the Lutheran orphanage at Jerusalem and the Institute for Epileptics in Bielefeld, Germany.[69] These gifts and the field secretary's visit to deaconesses of the American Lutheran Conference indicate the desire of the LDA for communication and interaction with deaconesses outside of the Synodical Conference.[70]

---

[66] "Change of Residence," *TLD* 8, no. 4 (October 1931): 7; "Annual Report by Superintendent," *TLD* 9, no. 1 (January 1932): 2.

[67] "Financial Statement of the Lutheran Deaconess Association," *TLD* 8, no. 1 (January 1931): 8.

[68] F. W. Korbitz, "Quarterly Report of Field Secretary," *TLD* 8, no. 4 (October 1931): 3–4.

[69] "Notes and News," *TLD* 8, no. 1 (January 1931): 4.

[70] The federation known as American Lutheran Conference included the American Lutheran Church, the Augustana Synod, the Norwegian Lutheran Church, the Lutheran Free Church, and the United Danish Church. All these synods, along with the United Lutheran Church in America, had deaconess motherhouses that banded together in 1896 to form "The Conference of Evangelical Lutheran Deaconess Motherhouses in America." See *Lutheran World Almanac and Encyclopedia 1934–1937* (New York: National Lutheran Council, 1937), 68.

THE END OF AN ERA

In April 1933, the deaconess community suffered another deep loss at the unexpected death of the beloved Pastor Philipp Wambsganss Jr.:

> On April 21, the venerable president of our Association was called to his eternal rest, after an illness of three weeks' duration. Our Association suffers a great loss through the death of Pastor Wambsganss. He was not only one of the early supporters of deaconess work in our circles, but took an active part in the organization of our Association, in fact, he was the leading spirit in bringing our Association into being. For the first years he served also as superintendent and he was the first and only president of our organization, serving as such until the time of his death.

> Pastor Wambsganss was a man of rare abilities and he put his gifts into the service of the Master. He did this as a pastor of the Church and in taking a leading part in all charitable activities within the Church, serving the Savior in his brethren and inspiring others to join him in such work. His name became known for such service not only in the Synodical Conference and in our county but also in Germany and other countries. Many looked to him for advice and help, and they were not disappointed. Looking back upon his life of active service we thank God for what He has done through Pastor Wambsganss and pray God to give us such trusting, child-like faith, such zealous love, and such ever-joyful, buoyant spirit as were given to this, our departed leader in Israel. . . .[71]

The LDA members, deaconess students and deaconesses who knew and loved Pastor Wambsganss were not alone in their bereavement. A local newspaper reported:

> Beloved Pastor Buried Monday - 2,500 Persons Attend Wambsganss Rites

> Final tribute to Rev. Philipp Wambsganss, pastor of the Emmaus Lutheran church, was paid by over 2,500 persons at funeral services yesterday afternoon at 2:15 o'clock at Emmaus church. Both the church and parish hall, which was equipped with sound system, were filled.

> It is estimated that over 6,000 persons passed the casket as Rev. Wambsganss lay in state at the church and at the home of the son of the deceased, Rev. Fred Wambsganss. By count, 4,300 persons filed past the bier Sunday, and it is estimated that 1,000 persons viewed the remains at home. Over 700 persons viewed the body Monday before the services.

> Rev. William Moss, pastor of Emmanuel Lutheran church, delivered the German sermon at the church services and Rev. H.A. Klein, president of

---

[71] "Pastor Philipp Wambsganss," *TLD* 10, no. 3 (July 1933): 2.

Concordia seminary at Springfield, Ill., delivered the English sermon. Rev. Walter Klausing, pastor of Concordia Lutheran church, read the German scripture and Enno Duemling of Milwaukee, Wis., chairman of the Lutheran Charities' conference, spoke during the services in behalf of the Missouri Synod charity organization.

Rev. Paul F. Miller, pastor of St. Paul's Lutheran church, officiated at the short service in the home at 2 o'clock. A group of policemen escorted the funeral cortege from the church to Concordia cemetery, where Rev. Paul L. Dannenfeldt, pastor of Zion Lutheran church officiated at the graveside service. The faculty of Concordia college attended the home, church and cemetery service in a body.[72]

The board and faculty of Concordia college passed the following resolutions at a special meeting Monday morning:

"The board and faculty of Concordia college regret exceedingly the passing of the Rev. Philipp Wambsganss. He has always taken a cordial interest in the institution. It was chiefly through his influence that students received free service at the Lutheran hospital since its beginning. Having been blessed with the gift of retaining a youthful and optimistic spirit, he enjoyed mingling with the students and was an ardent fan at the athletic games of his alma mater. To honor the memory of Pastor Wambsganss, the board and faculty decided to drop lessons on Monday afternoon, so that the faculty and students may attend the funeral. The board, faculty and students of Concordia college extend to the family their cordial sympathy.

(Signed) "Ernest C. Lewerenz, Secretary to the Faculty."[73]

As the wider Lutheran community of Fort Wayne mourned the loss of a great Christian leader, it also took inspiration from the memory of Wambsganss's love-filled service to Christ in His wretched ones and His poor. Indeed, for decades to come, Wambsganss's admirers, including many deaconesses, would carry on the important work that he had initiated in charitable organizations.[74]

---

[72] Visitors to the "old" Concordia Lutheran Cemetery, located at the corner of Anthony Boulevard and Maumee Avenue in Fort Wayne, can view the graves of Philipp (Jr.) and Fred Wambsganss (father and son), Walter Klausing, Paul L. Dannenfeldt, and Bruno Poch, all buried only yards apart in a pastors' section of the cemetery.

[73] "Beloved Pastor Buried Monday," newspaper article (no indication of newspaper name), CHI, Wambsganss File.

[74] For a sample of the inspirational addresses often given by Wambsganss to encourage others in their charitable endeavors, see "President's Address," *Der Bote aus Bethesda* 17, no. 6 (November 1926): 5–6.

Illustrations for Chapter Four may be viewed at www.deaconesshistory.org.

CHAPTER 5

CHANGE AND CONSOLIDATION

The LDA staff changed significantly during the short time between the deaths of Herzberger and Wambsganss. Korbitz resigned his post as Field Worker after fifteen months of service, citing his primary reason as "the present economic situation which has entirely delayed the solicitation of funds for expansion work at the Beaver Dam Hospital and also greatly retarded the expected quota of memberships for the Association."[1]

In October 1932, Rev. Herman Bernard Kohlmeier, the pastor of Emanuel Lutheran Church in New Haven, Indiana, succeeded Poch as Superintendent. Kohlmeier had served as Vice-President of the LDA for many years and understood the huge task in front of him.[2] Kohlmeier's call document obligated him:

> To discharge all the duties pertaining to an office of this kind with all faithfulness in accordance with the canonical writings of the Old and the New Testament as professed in the confessional writings of the Lutheran church;
>
> To supervise the Deaconess Motherhouse at Fort Wayne, Indiana;
>
> To supervise our Deaconess Training Schools at Beaver Dam and Watertown, Wisconsin, and at Fort Wayne, Indiana;
>
> To represent the Motherhouse and Schools as well as the Organization in all internal and external matters pertaining to his administration in accordance with the present rules of the Association and its Board of Directors;
>
> To further the interest of the Association before the Church and the world, in the religious press and otherwise;
>
> To serve as an example by his Christian conduct, and by the Grace of God to do all that is possible for him to do within the limits of his calling,

---

[1] Korbitz, "Field Worker's Farewell," *TLD* 9, no. 1 (January 1932): 8.
[2] The first published record (1926) of "Officials of Our Deaconess Society" lists Kohlmeier as Vice-President. *TLD* 3, no. 1 (January 1926): 8.

for the building up of our work and for the general advancement of the kingdom of Christ."[3]

Superintendent Kohlmeier approached his new responsibilities with humility and optimism. He wrote:

> ". . . I am glad that God has deemed me worthy to be called into this office of unlimited opportunities for service. On the other hand, I am weighed down with the feeling of my inexperience in the work and of the lack of ability to do proper justice to the duties of my office. For that reason I ask for the sincere prayers of all friends of the cause, that God may give me the necessary wisdom for my important duties and guide me by His Holy Spirit in all my labors. . . ."[4]

Kohlmeier was relying on God's guidance. What strategy would he and the LDA be led to use, in order to do "proper justice" to such an array of responsibilities and concerns, spread across a good portion of the United States?

ONE LESS TRAINING SCHOOL

Kohlmeier's call document did not mention the deaconess school in Hot Springs, South Dakota. In 1927, Esther Larsen and Lulu Noess were the first *and last* women to graduate from the Hot Springs training school. Within months of their graduation, Pastors Gerike and Lang, instructors for the deaconess courses, "accepted calls in different fields."[5] Near the end of 1928 Poch reported:

> There were no deaconess pupils enrolled at Hot Springs last year. A number of "Western" young ladies preferred to take their training either at Fort Wayne or at Watertown. Deaconess Lulu Noess served as superintendent of nurses after her graduation from the Hot Springs Deaconess training school last summer. As soon as a larger number of Lutheran young ladies elect to take the deaconess course at Hot Springs, plans will be made to organize deaconess classes.[6]

The anticipated larger number of young ladies never materialized, and other problems developed at Lutheran Hospital and Sanitarium due to "a

---

[3] "Diploma of Vocation," signed by Rev. Ph. Wambsganss, July 12, 1932, priv. col. of Rev. Ted W. Kohlmeier, Las Cruces, New Mexico.

[4] H. B. Kohlmeier, "A Word of Greeting," *TLD* 9, no. 4 (October 1932): 4.

[5] "Hot Springs," *TLD* 5, no. 1 (January 1928): 3.

[6] B. Poch, "Hot Springs, S. Dak.," *TLD* 5, no. 4 (October 1928): 27.

lack of cooperation among the doctors" that resulted in "severe financial reverses."[7] In January 1931, the LDA Board of Directors announced:

> . . . Because of the difficulty to secure regular instruction in deaconess subjects, it was decided to discontinue the Deaconess training school until conditions would warrant its reopening. . . . The Hot Springs Sanitarium deserves whole-hearted support not only of the Lutherans of South Dakota and Nebraska, but of all Lutherans affiliated with the Synodical Conference. A great deal of charity work is being done by the institution. . . . Anyone suffering from asthma, gout, rheumatism, and kindred ills ought to go to our sanitarium, which allows special rates for Lutheran pastors, teachers, and brethren in the faith who cannot very well pay the regular fees.[8]

The LDA maintained a cordial relationship with Lutheran Hospital and Sanitarium, but the deaconess school never re-opened in Hot Springs.

COMPLICATIONS IN BEAVER DAM

Once Kohlmeier was installed as Superintendent, he moved to Beaver Dam, Wisconsin, where the Board of Directors had resolved he should live on a trial basis.[9]

The Beaver Dam Lutheran Hospital and deaconess training school rejoiced in many blessings from God. In 1931, during a period when the depression caused several congregations and institutions to postpone calling deaconesses, Beaver Dam had a record nine students plus two Lutheran nurses enrolled in the deaconess classes.[10] Furthermore, in 1932, Rev. Kirst reported that during the ten years that the LDA had operated Lutheran Hospital, the association had never needed to appeal to the general public to provide funds for operating costs.[11]

However, the hospital was overcrowded. Korbitz tried to initiate fund-raising for the construction of an annex to the institution, but his efforts were hampered by a different problem. Though the LDA assumed management of the hospital in 1922, the citizens of Beaver Dam had never legally transferred the property rights to the LDA, and as early as 1930,

---

7 B. Poch, "Hot Springs, S. Dak.," *TLD* 7, no. 4 (October 1930): 27.
8 "News from Hot Springs, S. Dak.," *TLD* 8, no. 1 (January 1931): 3.
9 Letter from Philipp Wambsganss to H. B. Kohlmeier, July 12, 1932, priv. col. of Rev. Ted W. Kohlmeier, Las Cruces, New Mexico.
10 "Report of Superintendent," *TLD* 8, no. 4 (October 1931): 7.
11 L. C. Kirst, "Historical Sketch," *TLD* 9, no. 2 (April 1932): 5.

Beaver Dam Lutherans reported "influences at work . . . that would like to interfere with our plans (to gain clear title to the property)."[12]

Before the title issue could be resolved, another serious problem arose with the state of Wisconsin. The LDA responded with significant actions that ultimately eliminated both problems. Kohlmeier explained:

> On June 16, 1934, the Board of the Deaconess Association resolved to discontinue the training school. The hospital was not large enough for accreditation by the State Board, and the result was that the students at Beaver Dam were not eligible for the State Board examination and so could not become registered nurses. Not being registered nurses, they were not accepted as fully recognized nurses in many hospitals and other institutions. The graduates often later on thought it unfair to have spent three years in training and yet not be recognized nurses after finishing the course.

> A local hospital Board with the Rev. L. C. Kirst as president had charge of the immediate management of the hospital, being responsible, though, to the Board of the Deaconess Association. In the fall of 1934 a drastic change was made in respect to ownership and management of the hospital. The Deaconess Association transferred the hospital entirely to the newly organized Lutheran Deaconess Hospital Association of Beaver Dam. . . . It had always proved difficult to govern the hospital and direct its affairs by the Board of the Association through a local Board at Beaver Dam. The Superintendent, who had located in Beaver Dam for the purpose of giving more attention to the deaconess training course at the hospital, realized during the three years of his residence there the difficulties in the management of the hospital according to the existing set-up and suggested the transfer of the property to the brethren of Beaver Dam and vicinity.[13]

Thus the LDA relinquished the only charitable institution that it owned (and has ever owned) as an organization.[14]

---

12 "Annual Meeting of Beaver Dam Branch Society," *TLD* 6, no. 4 (October 1929): 28-29; "A Splendid Offer," *TLD* 7, no. 3 (July 1930): 18; B. Poch, "The Beaver Dam Project," *TLD* 7, no. 4 (October 1930): 27.

13 Kohlmeier refers to himself as "the Superintendent." H. B. Kohlmeier, *1919-1944 25th Anniversary of the Lutheran Deaconess Association within the Synodical Conference* (Fort Wayne: Nuoffer Print, 1944), 11, 13.

14 The hospital in Beaver Dam was known as "Lutheran Deaconess Hospital" into the early 1970s. Around 1972-73, it combined with St. Joseph's (Catholic) Hospital, with the result that hospital patients were thereafter taken to St. Joe's (now called Beaver Dam Community Hospital) and the old deaconess hospital became a nursing home. The Lutheran Deaconess Hospital building sustained several changes over the years, so that by the time the author visited it in August 2005, only the original sunroom remained as part of the edifice. In 2005,

A RECIPE FOR PROBLEMS?

Long before the LDA resolved to discontinue training in Beaver Dam, Kohlmeier had become uncomfortable with the idea of maintaining three separate deaconess schools. His reservations had nothing to do with the *quality* of education being received by the women. Former Superintendent Poch taught the students at the motherhouse in Fort Wayne and Kohlmeier met with them once a month when he attended LDA Board meetings there. At Bethesda in Watertown, the same men who trained practical deaconesses for many years continued to do so, with Kohlmeier also teaching once a week. In Beaver Dam, about 23 miles north of Watertown, the Superintendent took full responsibility for the deaconess courses and "had the unrestricted opportunity to teach as much as his time permitted."[15] No, Kohlmeier had other reasons—three of them—for his dissatisfaction with the arrangement he inherited. Referring to himself as "the superintendent," he wrote some years later:

> . . . We had sufficient opportunity for teaching our deaconess classes. And yet, the arrangement did not satisfy the superintendent. It was an unavoidable result of having three different training schools that we were training three different groups of deaconesses, and thereby we were creating a situation that could easily lead to the rise of factions among our deaconesses and so endanger the unity that is so necessary in an organization of this kind. The superintendent also felt that the students in Ft. Wayne could not receive sufficient instruction in deaconess subjects while taking the course in nurses' training. The theoretical and practical course in nursing as given in a hospital of high standards, such as our hospital in Ft. Wayne is, requires all the time the students can give to it. It was inevitable that the students at this school could not apply themselves so fully to the deaconess course as was desirable. The deaconess course had to sink in their estimation to a level of lesser importance. . . .

> And there was a third reason which influenced the superintendent to propose a change in the system of training. The superintendent should be well acquainted with the deaconesses and the deaconesses should know the superintendent well. If that is not the case there can hardly be a thorough understanding of each other and that will make it difficult to have that mutual confidence so necessary for full cooperation. With the old arrangement there could be but a very superficial acquaintance of the

---

a Dr. Kann purchased the building, intending to tear it down in 2006. Jeanette Diels, LPN (resident of Madison, Wisconsin), notes from interview by CDN, August 10, 2005, at Beaver Dam, Wisconsin, priv. col. of CDN, Pittsburgh, Pa.

[15] Kohlmeier, *25th Anniversary of the Lutheran Deaconess Association*, 13-14.

superintendent and some of the students and graduates. This hindered the superintendent in placing graduates wisely and it kept the graduates from seeking advice and guidance in their difficulties from the superintendent.[16]

The LDA Board agreed with the Superintendent's suggestion to discontinue the three deaconess schools and open a new Central School for Deaconess Training, where women would attend one year of "deaconess work" classes *after* having already acquired some type of professional education or experience. With only one deaconess school, all students would receive their training under the direct supervision of the superintendent irrespective of the prior certification they received in nursing, teaching, or other disciplines.[17]

Separating deaconess training from nurses' training insured that there would be no more competition or conflict between nursing classes and deaconess classes, since deaconess students could concentrate on one discipline at a time without the temptation to allow the requirements of one course to take precedence over the other. The new educational plan would also provide much more flexibility for the LDA and its prospective students. For example, a Synodical Conference R.N. could attend the central deaconess school regardless of where she acquired her nursing degree, and teachers or social workers could enroll in the deaconess program without being obliged to take nurses' training.[18]

REORGANIZATION

At the 1934 annual meeting of the LDA, four months after the Board had actually resolved to close the Beaver Dam operation, Kohlmeier mentioned the proposed "consolidated" deaconess school in his formal report:

> . . . We have a class of eight students at the Lutheran Hospital in Fort Wayne; a class of five in Beaver Dam; and three are taking the pre-deaconess course at Watertown. In the Junior and Freshman classes at the Ft. Wayne Training School for Nurses we have five and two respectively who have the intention to take the Deaconess Course after graduating as nurses. We hope the Association will at this meeting fully endorse our

[16] Kohlmeier, *25th Anniversary of the Lutheran Deaconess Association*, 14.
[17] *Ibid.*
[18] H. B. Kohlmeier, "Reasons for Establishing the Deaconess Training School and the Proposed Course," *TLD* 12, no. 4 (October 1935): 2-3.

plan of establishing the proposed school for Deaconess Training, so that we may open the same next fall.[19]

The LDA ratified the proposal to reorganize the training of deaconesses, however, the association did not determine a permanent location for the school. Some individuals wanted the school to be at the Bethesda campus; others thought it should be in Fort Wayne; still others believed there would be an advantage to placing it in St. Louis.[20] It was finally determined "that the School be opened temporarily for the first year beginning next fall in the Deaconess Home at Fort Wayne and that the question of the permanent location of the School be postponed until our next annual meeting."[21] Kohlmeier moved to Fort Wayne and the school opened in the *Deaconess Home*—for some reason no longer referred to as the *motherhouse*—on October 1, 1935. As anticipated, at its next meeting the LDA ruled that the school should be located permanently in Fort Wayne.[22]

THE AFTERMATH OF CONSOLIDATION

What effect, if any, did these changes have on Lutheran Hospital in Fort Wayne, Lutheran Hospital in Beaver Dam, and Bethesda Lutheran Home in Watertown, where these institutions had worked with the LDA to train 45, 34, and 30 women respectively?[23]

The deaconess training school in Fort Wayne had been closely connected to the Fort Wayne Lutheran Hospital Training School for Nurses since 1919. It was deemed desirable for deaconesses to be nurses and the arrangement was mutually satisfying to both parties. But it is curious that, in 1935, no consecrated deaconess had ever been employed as a deaconess nurse at Lutheran Hospital in Fort Wayne. The two training organizations no longer had the link that they once enjoyed in the person of

---

[19] H. B. Kohlmeier, "Superintendent's Annual Report, October 28," *TLD* 12, no. 1 (January 1935): 3.
[20] Kohlmeier spoke openly about the proposal for a single school already at the "Deaconess Group meeting" held at the July 1934 ALCh conference. At that time, Pastor Henry Holls, representative of the St. Louis Deaconess Society, "showed the advantage of having the central school at St. Louis, Missouri." Clara E. Strehlow, "Minutes of Deaconess Group Meeting," hand-written notes on Morrison Hotel stationery, *Reports of Officers and Committees* file, *Associated Lutheran Charities* Box 1, Concordia Historical Institute (CHI), St. Louis, Missouri, 2.
[21] "Our Annual Meeting," *TLD* 12, no. 1 (January 1935): 2.
[22] "Echoes From The Annual Meeting," *TLD* 13, no. 1 (January 1936): 2; "The Superintendent's Annual Report, October 27, 1935," *TLD* 13, no. 1 (January 1936): 5.
[23] See Appendix 1.E.

Pastor Wambsganss, who served as President of both the LDA and the Lutheran Hospital Association until his death. From this time forward, it seems that no formal connection existed between the LDA and Lutheran Hospital, except that the Deaconess Home sat on Hospital property.[24]

As stated above, the Lutheran Hospital in Beaver Dam had a problem with accreditation that rendered the facility undesirable for further nurses' training. Of course, since the LDA no longer included nursing as a possible component of deaconess education, the Central School for Deaconess Training could have been established in Beaver Dam, or in Watertown for that matter. Regarding the former, Kohlmeier wrote, "The hospital at Beaver Dam has been given to a Lutheran Deaconess Hospital Association of Beaver Dam. The agreement is, that the hospital Board will also in the future engage our deaconess nurses whenever they need such and suitable deaconess nurses are available."[25] This "agreement" was honored. The last complete directory of deaconesses printed in *TLD* in 1953 still listed two women, Frieda Poetter and Bertha Pohlmann, as stationed at Beaver Dam.[26]

Though Mr. Pingel thought it deplorable for the deaconess training school to be discontinued in Watertown, Bethesda has actually never been without the service of deaconesses, deaconess field workers, or deaconess interns from 1925 to the present day.[27] In April 1931 *TLD* noted regarding Bethesda, "God's blessing has been resting visibly upon this largest charitable institution within the Synodical Conference."[28] As Bethesda Lutheran Home, and later the "Bethesda Group" continued to expand over the years, this charitable endeavor has seen the service of more deaconess students and deaconess graduates than any other parish or institution in the

---

[24] *The Lutheran World Almanac* listed The Lutheran Hospital, located at Fairfield and Wildwood Avenues, Fort Wayne, as an institution of the Synodical Conference. Ralph H. Long, chairman ed. committee, *The Lutheran World Almanac and Encyclopedia 1934-37* (New York: The National Lutheran Council, 1937), 221.

[25] "The Superintendent's Annual Report, October 27, 1935," 5.

[26] "Roster of Deaconesses—1953," *TLD* 30, no. 4 (October 1953): 8.

[27] Louis Pingel, "Child Welfare in the Past Fifty Years," mimeographed pages, Watertown, Wisconsin, August 26, 1948, priv. col. of Clara Strehlow, Deaconess Office Archives, Concordia University, RF, Illinois, 4; Pastor Frederick Adolf Stiemke, D.D., notes from telephone interview by CDN, June 30, 2005, priv. col. of CDN, Pittsburgh, Pa. Stiemke (b. 1929) was the Corporate Chaplain for Bethesda from 1974-1994; in 1991 he wrote "A History of the Ministry of the LCMS with People who have Mental Retardation," later edited and reprinted by Thomas Heuer, Manager of Outreach Services, and Timothy Dittloff, Director/Lutheran Liaison, National Christian Resource Center, Bethesda Lutheran Homes and Services, Inc., 1997.

[28] "Notes and News," *TLD* 8, no. 2 (April 1931): 6.

synods that made up the Synodical Conference.[29] Today, the 25 voting members of Bethesda's Board of Directors are still pastors and laymen from both the Missouri and Wisconsin Synods,[30] and as this book goes to print, six Missouri Synod women—four deaconesses and two deaconess interns—are serving their Lord through Bethesda.[31]

THE REVISED EDUCATION PLAN

Soon after the LDA decided to restructure deaconess training, Superintendent Kohlmeier used *TLD* to publicize 25 helpful questions and answers about the LDA and the changes to its educational program.

. . . (Question) 9. How long will the course of training at this school be?

ANSWER: One year.

10: What are the entrance requirements?

ANSWER: To be eligible for enrollment applicants must be graduate nurses, teachers, social welfare workers, or have other special training in some phase of work which they later would do as deaconesses. Applicants must have the recommendation of their pastor[32] and certificate of health by physician.

11. What are some of the main courses to be given at the Deaconess Training School?

ANSWER: Bible Study, Comparative Religion, History of Missions, Personal Mission Work, Qualifications of a Lutheran Deaconess,

---

[29] Norma D. Neuhart, in her thesis submitted for a Master of Arts degree, lists over 100 deaconesses or deaconess students who have served at Bethesda. Norma D. Neuhart, "Appendix A—Deaconesses with a Ministry to People with Mental Retardation," *The Work of the Lutheran Church—Missouri Synod with People who are Mentally Retarded—Past, Present, and Future* (River Forest: Concordia University, 2002), 64-67.

[30] The synods are represented on the Board of Directors in approximate proportion to their size: 18 from the LCMS, five from the Wisconsin Synod, one from the Evangelical Lutheran Synod, and one from "other" Lutheran synods.

[31] "Three graduate deaconesses are Parish Ministry Consultants in Florida, Illinois, and Minnesota. The other three are Chaplaincy Representatives: two on the Watertown campus (one intern and one graduate) and the third (an intern) in the Dominican Republic, where Bethesda is partnering with LCMS World Missions." Deaconess Jeanne Dicke, notes from telephone interview by CDN, June 30, 2005, priv. col. of CDN, Pittsburgh, Pa. For more on Bethesda's history, see "A Century of Service," DVD, Bethesda Lutheran Homes and Services, Inc., 2005.

[32] The LDA often printed the stipulation, "Only such applicants will be enrolled as are members of a church whose pastor is affiliated with the Synodical Conference." "Beaver Dam Training-School," *TLD* 7, no. 2 (April 1930): 13.

Sociology, and other courses tending to educate and train the students for efficient work in their future positions.

12. Will any opportunity be offered for practical training?

ANSWER: Every opportunity will be utilized to gather experience in parish work, Sunday School teaching, Institutional mission work, etc.

13. How much will it cost the student for tuition, board, etc?

ANSWER: There is no tuition fee nor any charge for board and lodging. Students will pledge themselves, however, to serve as deaconesses at least until the Association is reimbursed by salary earned above allowance given the deaconess, or to repay whatever the Association has expended in their case.

14. To whom is the salary earned by the deaconess paid?

ANSWER: It is paid to the treasurer of the Association.

15: What provision is made for the deaconesses?

ANSWER: Deaconesses receive a monthly allowance while in active service. At present the regular allowance is $35.00. Besides this, deaconesses are assured free maintenance (board and lodging), free medical care in case of illness, the use of the Deaconess Home and free maintenance when not in active service (when out of employment temporarily, or in case of illness or old age).

16: Do the deaconesses wear a special garb?

ANSWER: They are required to wear the deaconess garb while in service, while at the Home, and when appearing at any public function. The Association offers to furnish three uniforms a year to every deaconess.

17. Do the deaconesses make any vow when entering service?

ANSWER: They promise to be faithful in the performance of their duties and to lead an exemplary Christian life. They also agree to submit to rules and regulations as set forth in the Deaconess Agreement. Otherwise they make no special vows.[33]

Pastor Kohlmeier obviously wanted applicants to the school to understand what they could expect in their training and in their lives as deaconesses, and on the other hand, what the LDA would expect from them as students and deaconesses in the field. Hence, subjects like the

[33] "Twenty-five Questions with their Answers on The Lutheran Deaconess Association and its Work," *TLD* 12, no. 3 (July 1935): 2-3.

"deaconess garb" and "vows" were addressed in print in this article for the first time.

THE DEACONESS AGREEMENT

At the end of the "Twenty-five Questions" article, the "Deaconess Agreement" (referred to in the answer to question seventeen) appeared, with no further explanation.

> Our deaconesses do not form a sisterhood in the sense of the Roman orders of nun[s], yet they have a common interest in the welfare of the Association and are to be united with each other by the bond of Christian sisterly love. This spirit should govern their behavior towards each other at all times and prove itself by peaceful co-operation [in the household duties] and in Christian courtesy towards and consideration of each other [while in the Home]. During the stay at the Home each one will cheerfully submit to the rules drawn up by the Board and will assist in maintaining a truly Christian atmosphere.

> The deaconess agrees to submit to the decisions of the Board excepting in matters of conscience, and to abide by assignment of position made by the superintendent. It is understood that the superintendent will take into consideration the wishes and inclinations of the respective deaconess.

> The net earnings of the deaconesses flow into the Deaconess Permanent Maintenance Fund, and salary received for the service of a deaconess shall therefore be paid to the treasurer of the Association, unless special exception to this rule shall have been agreed upon as in the case of our deaconesses in the foreign mission field. If a deaconess severs her connection with the Association, she thereby also relinquishes the position she has filled. The Association pays the deaconess a monthly allowance, guarantees her free medical care when sick, and offers her the use of the Home when not in active service or when incapacitated through illness or old age. The Association also agrees to furnish three uniforms a year[,] and the deaconess promises to wear the deaconess uniform while on duty and when appearing as a deaconess at a church service or any public function.

> I hereby sign the above declaration statement, declaring myself in full agreement with the principles and rules expressed therein.[34]

---

[34] The personal papers of Clara Strehlow (consecrated in 1927) include an unsigned copy of this agreement. Brackets in the text printed here indicate words, letters, or punctuation that appear in Strehlow's copy that do not appear in the article printed in *TLD*. "Deaconess

An "Understood" Commitment

A closer look at the answers to questions thirteen and seventeen, together with the "Deaconess Agreement," give some insight into the nature of the commitment that women made when they joined the diaconate. The deaconess took no "special vows," which would certainly have been read as a euphemism for not taking a vow of celibacy. Nor was she in any way "married" to the "sisterhood," in the same way that would be true of the "Roman order of nuns." However, the deaconess also understood that she would either delay entering the estate of matrimony or face the penalty of having to reimburse the LDA for all expenses incurred by the association during her training. The oral legends that the author has heard about this understanding are varied—with claims that anywhere from three to seven years of active deaconess work were expected—which makes sense since the number of years of training altered throughout the decades, and the lengthier the training, the more a deaconess would need to give back in return.

In light of this understanding, the assertion that "there is no tuition fee nor any charge for board and lodging"[35] did not ring entirely true. Deaconess salaries were paid directly to the LDA, out of which, almost like indentured servants, deaconesses repaid the association for their tuition, board, and room. A few years after publication of the "Twenty-Five Questions," *TLD* put it more plainly:

> Our deaconesses make a real contribution to the work of the Church, not only by serving at the least possible cost but especially by rendering efficient service in the Christian spirit. They do their work, whatever it may be, with the purpose in mind to assist in soul-saving and are educated and trained for this very purpose.

> Any Christian lady who is in a position to *dedicate her life* to this work is urged to write the superintendent for information and application blank for enrollment. The cost of training is very low. The students pay only for their personal expense and for a few textbooks. There is no charge for board, lodging, or tuition. The students pledge themselves to serve as deaconesses after graduation and so to reimburse the Association by salary earned above their allowance."[36]

Agreement," single typed page, priv. col. of Clara Strehlow, Deaconess Office Archives, Concordia University, RF, Illinois; "Deaconess Agreement," *TLD* 12, no. 3 (July 1935): 2-3.
[35] See answer to question thirteen.
[36] "Our Deaconess Training School," *TLD* 14, no. 3 (July 1937): 2. Italics added by author.

There is no record of women refusing to pay the balance of the cost of their training if they stopped working before covering their personal obligation. Nor is there anything in writing to indicate that the LDA dissuaded consecrated deaconesses from leaving the diaconate, although in the memory of one woman, "the LDA frowned upon deaconesses getting married until they had given at least seven years of service."[37] It is unlikely that a woman of the early 1930s would have any thought of continuing to be a deaconess after she married. In fact, this question would be left untouched for approximately three more decades.

Kohlmeier's approach to the "Twenty-Five Questions" may have been influenced by his personal disappointment at having seen several deaconesses marry soon after the completion of their training. In a paper addressed to the ALCh Convention in September of 1935, he mentioned this phenomenon in relation to the Fort Wayne school as one of the reasons for establishing a new Central Training School.

> . . . We found also that the interest of the students was centered more on the course in nursing than on the course in deaconess subjects. Many lost the interest and enthusiasm so necessary for a proper preparation for the future work of deaconesses. Some also formed attachments during the three years of training which resulted in this, that they probably entered the service of the Deaconess Association, but with the intention to serve only for a very limited time. They were not in the service wholeheartedly. Now we do not censure our deaconesses for entertaining matrimony, but naturally these students would not have entered deaconess training and have been consecrated as deaconesses, if they had known that God would lead them so soon into marriage. . . .[38]

MOVING FORWARD

A year later, again at the ALCh convention, Kohlmeier gave a positive, albeit cautious, progress report titled "New Developments in Deaconess Work."

> . . . We need all the encouragement and assistance you can give us. Our task of training Lutheran deaconesses as our Church needs them is a big task. We have not by any means attained the ideal. But we have made progress. . . . We now have a Training School. Our students come to us after finishing their course in nursing or other preparatory work. This

---

[37] Notes taken by CDN during conversation with Dolores Jean Hackwelder, May 20, 2005, priv. col. of CDN, Pittsburgh, Pa.
[38] H. B. Kohlmeier, "Outlines of Course for the Deaconess School," in *Proceedings of the ALCh*, 1935, 87.

enables us to take more mature students and also others besides graduate nurses, as for instance, former teachers, social workers, and others who have had some professional training and experience. . . . Classes are conducted every forenoon, and the afternoon and evening hours are reserved for study periods and for practical work in assisting in parish and city mission work. The principal course is that of Bible study, supplemented by a thorough review of the Catechism, a course in Comparative Religion and Distinctive Doctrines, and Personal Evangelism. Other courses include one on the Qualifications of a Lutheran Deaconess, the History of the Female Diaconate and of Christian Missions. Emphasis is also placed on a brief course in Sociology and Social Pathology. The class work is supplemented by private reading and book reports, using these reports at the same time for practical experience in public speaking. One hour a week is used for preparation for the Sunday School lesson. Our students are regular teachers in the Sunday School of one or the other of our churches in the city and teach classes at the TB Sanitorium [*sic*].

. . . We welcome constructive suggestions. But above all, we need your wholehearted cooperation. And by that I mean, that you will not only support us by your prayers and financial aid, but that you will also try to have a sympathetic understanding of our difficulties. Do not expect the impossible of us. Think of the task we have in training deaconesses for such a large field of different types of work, and do not clamor too impatiently for professionally trained workers in your specific field. Tell us what you need. Your suggestions will receive due consideration. In the present status of our work we can and do lay the foundation for real deaconess service, but in certain professional or semi-professional positions this must be supplemented by coaching the new worker in that specific work.

How rapid our further development will be depends upon God's blessing and your cooperation. I shall not speak of the hopes and the plans, or, if you please, the dreams I have as to the future, but they are for an ever higher standard of efficiency of our deaconesses and so in them and through them for an ever greater contribution of useful service in the Master's kingdom.[39]

Several months before his speech to the ALCh brethren, Kohlmeier used an article in *TLD* to explain the type of difficulties he referred to when appealing for a "sympathetic understanding of our difficulties."

---

[39] H. B. Kohlmeier, "New Developments in Deaconess Work," in *Proceedings of the ALCh*, 1936, 85-86.

. . . We are not discouraged, nor do we doubt the worth and necessity of the service we render to our Church, but we are not satisfied with the progress made. . . . I am referring to the progress made in gaining ground for our cause and getting support for our work. And I have in mind especially the moral support. I know the financial support will follow, if we gain the moral support.

What is the situation? I find that it is very difficult to gain the interest of our people in the work we are doing. There is a certain apathy toward it. We meet little opposition, but also little enthusiastic support. Very many show the attitude of indifferent neutrality. And that does not help us. Others assure us that they value the services of our deaconesses highly, but they do not really help us to carry on. Still others make demands on us as to the training and qualifications deaconesses should have, but we miss the active support and whole-hearted cooperation, which is so essential for success.

What may be the reason why it is so difficult to gain better support for our cause? One reason, undoubtedly, is the attitude of many of our people towards all work in the Church. They have given way to a feeling of depression, of being discouraged. They lack enthusiasm, and it is difficult to gain their interest for any kind of church-work. . . .

Another reason why our Deaconess cause finds such difficulty in gaining ground is, in my opinion, the fact that it is something comparatively new to our people. Our Church has always been very conservative. And that is good in many respects. Besides the strictly Biblical position which our Church holds in matters of doctrine and practice, the policy of being conservative guards against the introduction of fads and fancies of enthusiasts into our methods of church-work. Our Church can not be taken by storm for anything that is new. Also our deaconess work must prove its worth before it can hope to find general support. Since, however, it is work that does not come to the attention of many, we must continue to tell others about it. The fact is that most of our people do not know why we are training deaconesses and what our deaconesses are doing. Even at the danger of being censured we must tell people about our work. This is not done in a spirit of boasting or of seeking honor, but simply for the purpose of acquainting people with our work.[40]

The frustration expressed by Kohlmeier has been repeated time and again, up to the present day. In addition, a glance at the challenges presented to the Lutheran diaconate over the years reveals a cycle of problems related to the constant need for education about the deaconess

---

[40] H. B. Kohlmeier, "Is Our Deaconess Work Worth Support?" *TLD* 12, no. 2 (April 1935): 2.

"cause." When enthusiasm about the diaconate was high and money plentiful, the number of deaconess candidates fell short of the requests for workers. During times when student enrollment peaked, the economy was often in trouble, making it difficult to place those who were trained and waiting to serve.[41] Furthermore, as long as no synod of the Synodical Conference took direct responsibility for deaconess training, there continued to be issues relating to deaconess identity and the future role of deaconesses within the church.[42] Kohlmeier seemed to be aware of this latter point and inclined toward bringing the LDA into a closer relationship with the church. In 1937 he wrote:

> It is proper that we should be asked by the Church to make a report on our work. It is true, it is not a work done officially by Synod or by a district of Synod, yet it is carried on under the auspices of the Church, and the moral and financial support of the members of the Church is solicited for it. The Church, therefore, has a responsibility for the work and should supervise it in some way.[43]

After championing so much change in regard to the training of deaconesses, Kohlmeier never actually defined how he thought the church might supervise and take responsibility for the work of the LDA. It would have been a complex business, taking into account the whole of the Synodical Conference.[44] But Kohlmeier was already busy with other irons in the fire.

---

[41] For examples of these cyclical concerns, see "Beaver Dam's Plea," *TLD* 7, no. 2 (April 1930): 13; "Report of Superintendent," *TLD* 8, no. 4 (October 1931): 7; "Notes and News," *TLD* 9, no. 2 (April 1932): 5; "Superintendent's Report at Annual Meeting," *TLD* 11, no. 1 (January 1934): 2; "The Superintendent's Annual Report, October 27, 1935," 5.

[42] See for examples: P.E. Kretzmann, "Nurse, Deaconess, Social Worker," *Concordia Theological Monthly* 8, no.12 (December 1937): 932; "Requirements for a Parish Deaconess," *TLD* 13, no. 1 (January 1936): 6.

[43] "Report on the Work of the Lutheran Deaconess Association," *TLD* 14, no. 3 (July 1937): 2.

[44] In a report to the Central District of the Missouri Synod Kohlmeier commented, "Although our Association is really an organization within the Synodical Conference and composed of members of congregations of all synods united in the Synodical Conference, yet we feel especially close to this district of the Synod of Missouri because our headquarters are here in Ft. Wayne. This body assembled here is also the only one that asks for regular reports on our work." H. B. Kohlmeier, "Report of Deaconess Work Given at the Convention of the Central District of the Synod of Missouri, Ohio, and Other States, Assembled at Ft. Wayne, Indiana, June 19-23, 1939," *TLD* 16, no. 3 (July 1939): 3.

THE DEACONESS CONFERENCE

In 1933, when the LDA still trained deaconesses in three locations, Superintendent Kohlmeier initiated the formation of a "conference" for consecrated deaconesses. Kohlmeier and Mr. L. Pingel (Superintendent of Bethesda) met with nine deaconesses during the annual LDA meeting in Fort Wayne to plan the new organization.[45] After Kohlmeier opened the meeting with prayer and a reading from Colossians 3:1-17, the group transacted an amazing amount of business.

> Rev. Kohlmeier was elected Chairman pro-tem. Ida Trinklein was elected Secretary pro-tem. Letters and telegrams of greetings and wishes of God's blessings were received from Deaconesses Lydia Lutz, Anna Schrader, Margaret Spencer R.N.

> Rev. Kohlmeier then read his suggestions on the following topics:

> 1. How can our deaconesses help to advance the deaconess cause?

> 2. What obligation has the Association to the deaconess, and what obligation has the deaconess to the Association?

> 3. Reasons why our deaconesses should habitually wear the deaconess uniform.

> 4. How can we help our deaconesses retain the spirit of consecration?

> The discussions of the above mentioned topics had great educational value for the deaconesses. It was moved and supported that the Superintendent request the Association at the annual meeting on October 15, 1933 to allow him to call an Advisory Committee of five deaconesses into existence for the purpose of bringing matters of interest to the General Board of the Association through the Superintendent. Motion was further made and supported that the Superintendent appoint the Committee of five for the first year until the time of the next conference.

> It was moved and supported that the Superintendent write a brief manual on ethics, or, in other words, "What is expected of the deaconess with reference to their attitude to the Association and their conduct as deaconesses and what obligations the deaconess has to the Association." It was further agreed upon that this manual be studied by the Advisory Committee and, if approved, that it be brought up for consideration at the next annual meeting of the Association.

---

[45] Amelia Erdelbrock, Erna Heck, Alverda Johnson, Cora Leader, Louise Moehlenbrock, Henrietta Nanke, Martha Schmidt, Clara Strehlow, and Ida Trinklein.

It was agreed upon that the deaconess conference be held annually some time during the summer; that the Advisory Committee take this matter in hand and arrange for the summer conference, deciding upon the places where the conferences are to be held and at which times. Upon request, the Superintendent read the Constitution of the Association (LDA). The rules for the Deaconess Home were also read by the Superintendent. The Conference adjourned with the Lord's Prayer.[46]

The LDA did grant the request for an Advisory Committee of five deaconesses to be formed so that "matters of interest" could be presented to the LDA Board of Directors through the Superintendent. Kohlmeier immediately began to draft the manual on ethics, which was read at the first official gathering of the new Deaconess Conference held at Bethesda Home in Watertown on July 2-3, 1934.[47]

The thirty-four deaconesses and guests at the first Conference enjoyed a variety of presentations, from Rev. Enno Duemling on "Duty," Rev. Otto William Christopher Boettcher (1885-1963) on "Mission Work Among the Indians," Deaconess Martha Theilmann on "Work with the Children at our Institute for the Deaf at Detroit," Rev. Wm. T. Naumann on "Doing Mission Work," Deaconesses Clara Strehlow and Henrietta Nanke on "Work at the Lutheran Industrial School at Addison," Deaconess Louise Moehlenbrock on "Work at the Deaconess Home in Fort Wayne," Rev. Theodore Albert John Eggers (1894-1969) on "Lutheran Chorales," and Superintendent Kohlmeier on "his experiences and impressions received at other Lutheran Deaconess Motherhouses in our country."[48]

During the afternoon session on the first day of the Conference, Deaconesses Louise Moehlenbrock, Martha Schmidt, and Margaret Spencer were elected by acclamation to draw up a Constitution for the new organization.[49] The three women must have worked hard and fast, because the following afternoon saw the adoption of the constitution, with the proviso that it would be ratified the following year.[50]

---

[46] Ida Trinklein, "Extract from the Minutes of the First Deaconess Conference Held at the Deaconess Home in Fort Wayne, Indiana Oct. 14, 1933, at 3:00 p.m.," TLD 11, no. 1 (January 1934): 5-6.

[47] "The Deaconess Conference," TLD 11, no. 3 (July 1934): 3-4.

[48] Alice Dey, "Minutes of the Meeting of the Deaconess Conference at Bethesda Home, Watertown, Wisconsin," July 2, 1934, priv. col. of Clara Strehlow, Deaconess Office Archives, RF, Illinois; Cora Leader, "Minutes of the Meeting of the Deaconess Conference at Bethesda Home, Watertown, Wisconsin," July 3, 1934, priv. col. of Clara Strehlow, Deaconess Office Archives, RF, Illinois; "The Deaconess Conference," 4.

[49] Alice Dey, "Minutes of the Meeting of the Deaconess Conference ...," July 2, 1934.

[50] Cora Leader, "Minutes of the Meeting of the Deaconess Conference...," July 3, 1934, 4.

I. Name

The name of this Conference shall be: Conference of Deaconesses within the Ev. Lutheran Synodical Conference of North America.

II. Purpose

The purpose of this Conference shall be to discuss matters of interest to deaconess work, to keep alive and deepen the spirit of consecration, and to strengthen the bond of sisterly love among the deaconesses.

III. Officers

The officers of the Conference shall be: a president, a vice-president, and a secretary-treasurer. These officers and two additional members shall constitute the Advisory Committee.

IV. Term of Office and Duties of Officers

All officers shall serve for a term of two years or until their successors are elected, provided that the president, vice-president, and secretary-treasurer elected at this first meeting shall serve for a full two year term of office and the two additional members of the Advisory Committee elected this year for a term of one year. In case a vacancy shall occur, the other officers shall choose a member to fill this vacancy until the time of the next conference. The duties of these officers shall be those commonly assigned to such officers in their respective capacities.

V. Membership

Only deaconesses of the Ev. Lutheran Deaconess Association within the Synodical Conference may be members of the Conference. The superintendent of the Association shall be an ex officio member of the Conference and of its Committees.

VI. Changes and Additions

Changes of the Constitution or additions to the same may be made at any regular meeting of the Conference by a two-thirds majority vote of all members of the Conference.[51]

The first five members of the Advisory Committee elected by the Conference were: Clara Strehlow, president; Margaret Spencer, vice-president; Alice Dey, secretary-treasurer; Erna Heck and Martha Theilmann, members at large. The Conference declared the election ballots

---

[51] The Conference ratified the constitution, without any changes, on July 2, 1935. "Minutes of the Meeting of the Deaconess Conference, at Concordia College, Fort Wayne, Ind. Tuesday July 2nd 1935 (Morning Session)," priv. col. of Clara Strehlow, Deaconess Office Archives, RF, Illinois; "The Deaconess Conference," 4-5.

unanimous and also decided that, "All deaconesses of the Deaconess Association are to be charter members of the Conference."[52] Interestingly, Clara Strehlow, who would serve the Deaconess Conference as president from 1934-38 and vice-president from 1940-42, would 46 years later become a founding member of the Concordia Deaconess Conference - Lutheran Church-Missouri Synod!

A Blessing for All Parties

In executing his idea for an annual Deaconess Conference, Kohlmeier gave the diaconate a forum that not only addressed the felt needs of deaconesses, but also had the potential to foster better communication and cooperation between deaconesses and the LDA. As a case in point, the manual on ethics, or *Deaconess Manual* as it was later referred to, was favorably reviewed by the Advisory Committee and Kohlmeier presented it to the annual meeting of the LDA in October 1934 (at the same time that he submitted his plan for a Central Deaconess Training School).[53] The Board of Directors assigned a committee to study the manual, after which it would be published and given to every deaconess.[54]

The deaconesses themselves were delighted with their new organization. President Strehlow's opening address to the 1937 conference held at the Institute for the Deaf in Detroit echoes how important the women believed the Deaconess Conference to be, both for their personal well-being and for encouragement in the mutual work of the diaconate within the church.

> As Chairman of this conference I greet and welcome you one and all, members and friends. We are happy to see so many present who were with us at previous meetings. Yes, dear sisters, conference needs you and you need the conference.
>
> It is here that we may find fresh inspiration for the work to which the Lord has called us. Here we may bring our problems and discuss them in order to find a solution by comparing them with similar problems or taking the advice of those who have had the same experience. Above all,

---

[52] This meant that every consecrated deaconess trained by the LDA, who was still a deaconess, was to be a charter member of the Deaconess Conference. Although 101 women had been consecrated by 1934 (See Appendix 1.D), only 59 were listed as deaconesses in the July 1934 issue of *TLD*. Cora Leader, "Minutes of the Meeting of the Deaconess Conference…," July 3, 1934.

[53] "Annual Meeting of the Association," *TLD* 11, no. 4 (October 1934): 2.

[54] "Our Annual Meeting," *TLD* 12, no. 1 (January 1935): 2.

we need the comfort of Christian fellowship which a meeting of this kind affords. ...

Our Conference is rather small but if we have faith we will grow. It was just a hundred years ago last October that Pastor Theodore Fliedner, of Kaiserswerth, Germany, began his first school for deaconesses with one student. In a comparatively short time the work developed so that before Fliedner's death 425 deaconesses had been trained in the motherhouse at Kaiserswerth. Besides the school at Kaiserswerth other schools were begun in other places, patterned after Pastor Fliedner's institution. Today there are deaconesses in practically all Protestant church bodies. ...

Business men often use the slogan: A satisfied customer is the best advertisement. Let us therefore in all meekness and humility, yet firmly and bravely, carry on in our chosen calling, so that our cause may be brought to the attention of those seeking better trained and efficient church workers. Yes, dear sisters, let us work, not as men-pleasers, but as serving the Lord. And if the task seems greater than we can manage, may we say with St. Paul, "I can do all things through Christ who strengthens me."[55]

The Deaconess Conference Advisory Committee invited seminary and college professors, pastors, foreign and city missionaries, individuals representing charitable institutions associated with ALCh, and of course, the Superintendent, to address the Deaconess Conference each year. In return, deaconesses often spoke at Ladies' Aids or Auxiliaries, Deaconess Branch Societies, Walther League gatherings, and the like.

THE CONNECTION WITH ASSOCIATED LUTHERAN CHARITIES

In addition to attending their own Deaconess Conference, Superintendent Kohlmeier encouraged the women to attend ALCh conventions whenever possible. Here they would be exposed to the particulars of ministries that they were likely to be involved in one day. And here they would be noticed, encouraged, and listened to by people that might one day be their supervisors and co-workers.

In 1939, with ten deaconesses in attendance, the ALCh proposed that the Deaconess Conference should hold its annual meeting in connection

---

[55] Clara Strehlow, "Opening Address by the President of Conference, Deaconess Clara Strehlow, at Deaconess Conference held at the Institute for the Deaf, Detroit, July 15-17, 1937," *TLD* 14, no. 4 (October 1937): 2-3.

with the annual meeting of the ALCh. At their next Conference, the deaconesses politely rejected this offer, reasoning:

> Much inspiration is gained and a closer bond of fellowship developed among the deaconesses, and it is of advantage to become better acquainted with the women in the various places where our conference is held and, we fear that much of this would be lost to us if we accept the kind offer of the Charities Conference.[56]

The invitation from ALCh to the Deaconess Conference to hold their annual meetings together was not surprising given that the ALCh was instrumental in the formation of the LDA and the interests of the two organizations were entirely intertwined. While these two organizations shared a common president in Philipp Wambsganss Jr. for fourteen years, for twelve of those years both organizations also shared the same treasurer in Mr. August Freese, who habitually encouraged ALCh convention attendees to become LDA members.[57] The obvious result was an overlap of membership in the two associations. The LDA held membership as an association in ALCh, and delegates to the ALCh conventions, from the whole range of charitable societies and institutions, held personal membership in the LDA.

Between 1935 and 1941, beyond the customary report from the LDA Superintendent, agendas for the four-day ALCh meetings included several presentations relating to the work of deaconesses.[58] For example, the 1937 annual convention featured lectures on "History of the Female Diaconate in the Early Christian Church" by Kohlmeier, "The Field for Trained Deaconesses in our Church Work" by Deaconess Clara Strehlow, "The Parish Deaconess" by Deaconess Martha Eber, and "Deaconess Work in City Missions" by Deaconess Esther Haeger.[59]

---

[56] "Resolutions Passed at Conference," *TLD* 16, no. 4 (October 1939): 3-4.

[57] Freese also served as treasurer of the Fort Wayne Lutheran Hospital Association from 1919-1930.

[58] "Topical Index: proceedings of Associated Lutheran Charities 1925-1955 (File)," Associated Lutheran Charities Conventions 1926-1961 (Archive Box), CHI, St. Louis, Mo.

[59] "Program of Convention," *Thirty-Sixth Annual Convention Associated Lutheran Charities*, Hotel Anthony, Fort Wayne, Ind. Aug. 31—Sept. 3, 1937 (Watertown: Jansky Printing Co., 1937), 3. For text of three of these speeches see *Thirty-Sixth Annual Convention Associated Lutheran Charities*, Hotel Anthony, Fort Wayne, Ind. Aug. 31—Sept. 3, 1937 (Watertown: Jansky Printing Co., 1937), 120-133.

ASSOCIATED LUTHERAN CHARITIES AND THEOLOGY

Given the close relationship between the LDA and ALCh, it is appropriate to provide an example here, of the sort of theological statements made by the Charities Conference leadership within the hearing of deaconesses and many LDA members. The following quotation contains the introductory paragraphs of the "Report of the Executive Board," delivered by First Vice-President H.F. Wind at the 1937 ALCh convention.

> The character of a church is determined not only by the truth and purity of the doctrine which it upholds and confesses, but also by the manner in which it endeavors to apply this doctrine to the problems of individual and social living. This is true particularly of that type of doctrine which presumes to establish the principles governing both the sanctification of life in the individual and the individual's relationship to society at large. Specifically, the new commandment of Jesus that we love one another, which the church is divinely obligated to teach and proclaim, must be obeyed both by the individual in his group relationships and by the church in her relationships to the community and to society at large. For it is just as possible and just as reprehensible for the church to love "in word" and "in tongue," neglecting to live "in deed and in truth" as it is for an individual to be guilty of such conduct. And just as the character of the individual Christian is determined both by his profession and by his practice of the truth in life, so the church is judged by God and by man both by its doctrine and by its exemplification of this doctrine in relationships to society. We may know both the individual and the group "by their fruits".

> The realization of this fact has prompted your Executive Board and the individual members of the Board to view the task entrusted to them in the light of a real challenge.

> For we believe that the Associated Lutheran Charities, though not constituted and recognized as a part of the official machinery of the church, is in fact the chief visible expression of our church's active, living faith, the chief among the "fruits" by which men may know and judge our doctrine. If this be true, it follows that it is incumbent upon the Associated Lutheran Charities, its member agencies and its delegates, its officers and its Executive Board, to exert every effort and to labor and strive with all diligence that the fruits of our church's faith as expressed in works of charity may not fall short of our high and noble profession of the truth, but that the ever progressing and always progressive character of our Work of Love may truly reflect our church's growing faith and her increasing devotion to our Savior's cause. . . .

To the mind of your Executive Board, a local charitable agency is the visible expression of the saving faith and the glorious hope engendered in God's children within a congregation or group of congregations by the preaching of the gospel of the Savior; the Associated Lutheran Charities is the ever active, ever planning, ever progressing manifestation of the love of the church, of the faith-filled heart and mind of the church at large, the merciful hand of the church, if you please, through which the church lifts up the fallen, assists the feeble, strengthens the weak. And the Executive Board, as we conceive of it, is solemnly charged with the duty of exercising the necessary and inevitable leadership in the Association's program of active, progressive service to the church and humanity. To their fulfillment of this duty, your Executive Board and its individual members have pledged their energies and efforts. . . .[60]

Indeed, to cite Wind's own words, he and his colleagues on the Executive Board revealed themselves to be radically "progressive" in the assertion that the work of ALCh—though not constituted by or officially part of any synods associated with the Synodical Conference—"is in fact the chief visible expression of our church's active, living faith, the chief among the 'fruits' by which men may know and judge our doctrine." This statement was certainly contrary to what was historically assumed in the Missouri Synod: that orthodox confession of God's Word and correct use of the Sacraments constituted the chief visible expression of the church's living faith and sound doctrine.[61]

As the type of thinking expounded by Wind continued to develop into the early 1940s, and the discussion of church fellowship issues escalated within Synodical Conference circles, several LCMS members who attended ALCh meetings became involved in doctrinal disputes. As a case in point, Wind and eight other men who attended the 1937 ALCh convention eventually signed the Chicago "Statement of the 44" in 1945.[62] Three of

---

[60] "Report of the Executive Board," *Thirty-Sixth Annual Convention Associated Lutheran Charities*, Hotel Anthony, Fort Wayne, Ind. Aug. 31—Sept. 3, 1937 (Watertown: Jansky Printing Co., 1937), 12-13.

[61] See for example, Walther, C. F. W., "Dr. Walther's First Presidential Address," trans. Paul F. Koehneke, *Concordia Historical Institute Quarterly*, 33, no. 1, April 1960, 12-20; Walther, C. F. W., *The Proper Form of an Evangelical Lutheran Congregation Independent of the State*, translated by Th. Engelder, Concordia Publishing House, 1938.

[62] "On 7 Sept. 1945 a group of 44 Missouri Synod clergymen signed 'A Statement' in which they called for a greater measure of evangelical practice within the Synod, a definition of prayer fellowship that was at variance with some of the traditionally held views within Synod, and a greater readiness to reach agreement with other Lutherans. Twelve propositions with comments made up the document." Meyer, Carl S., ed., *Moving Frontiers: Readings in the History of The Lutheran Church-Missouri Synod, 1847-1962*. St. Louis: Concordia, 1964, 422-25.

those signatories served on the ALCh Executive Board; six delivered major lectures at the conference, one preached the conference sermon, and one sat on the Nominating Committee.[63] The following year, a seminary professor who would also sign the "Statement of the 44" provided significant theological instruction to the ALCh conference.

> Richard Caemmerer, of the Department of Practical Theology of Concordia Seminary, St. Louis, presented the first of numerous essays to the Lutheran Charities Conference of 1938. He provided the most penetrating and sustained formal theological contribution to the Charities conferences both before and after World War II. In his paper on Lutheran social action, Caemmerer called for a fresh appreciation of justifying grace that always motivates the individual to a new life expressed in a love for the next man, Christian and non-Christian alike. Neither the New Testament itself nor the Reformation era provides the contemporary church with a blueprint for social action. But Caemmerer discerned the need for a revamping and revitalizing of the training of ministers and teachers in the Lutheran church who will see the proclamation of the Gospel in the context of modern human need, and will hold forth that Gospel as the power which sways men in the church to live as Christ lived in the world. He outlined the necessity to recognize and recruit the full resources of the laity to march in unity upon the plight of human need, and through pertinent literature, patient parish study and guidance, and through the example of sacrifice on the part of the church's workers, to awaken a lethargic church body to the vocation of loving other people, now that Christ had died for all. Eight years later he was heard again by the Charities convention on the application of Christian ethics to current social problems. Here he expanded upon and greatly enlarged the Biblical basis relating the traditional Lutheran emphasis upon justification by grace through faith to the newness of life lived outward toward others in the power of divine love, and coupled it with an incisive

---

[63] C. A. Behnke presented "Psychological Implications in Pastoral Therapy;" E. J. Friedrich presented "The Church and the Working Man;" E. B. Glabe (Second Vice-President) presented "The Family Crisis" and "The Worker in Child Care;" A. R. Kretzmann presented "Must Youth Mark Time?;" O. P. Kretzmann was on the Nominating Committee; Werner Kuntz preached the convention sermon; Paul Miller (son of former LDA Board member, Jacob Miller) was registered as a guest; Edmund Weber (Convention Committee Chairman and Executive Board member at large) presented "Practical Plan for Lutheran Hospital Chaplaincy;" and H. F. Wind (First Vice-President) presented "The Disorganization of the Family." *Thirty-Sixth Annual Convention Associated Lutheran Charities*, Hotel Anthony, Fort Wayne, Ind. Aug. 31—Sept. 3, 1937 (Watertown: Jansky Printing Co., 1937), 2-11.

analysis of the social problems evident in the family, industrial civilization, racial tensions, and government.[64]

Despite the LDA membership in ALCh, there is no indication that Superintendent Kohlmeier or members of the LDA Board of Directors considered themselves to be trailblazers in the application of theology to social ministry. These individuals focused on preparing women for service, and simply desired to succeed in the many facets of their work in order to perpetuate the deaconess movement within the Synodical Conference.

The reality remains, however, that the LDA and its deaconesses were supported and encouraged in their work by Missouri Synod clergymen who skirted the edge of what was considered to be mainstream Lutheran theology. Perhaps the significance of this connection can be better understood by examining some numbers in relation to the above example. In 1945, there were 4,388 ordained ministers rostered in the LCMS; 44 of those clergymen signed the "Statement of the 44;" and at least 15 of those 44 signatories were known to be associates or active allies of the deaconess movement within the Synodical Conference. At the same time, it must be remembered that many orthodox Lutheran clergymen also encouraged deaconesses in their work. One example was Dr. P.E. Kretzmann, a great friend of deaconesses and one of the most ardent supporters of the LDA training program from its inception, who also lectured and wrote against the "Statement of the 44."[65]

MORE TRANSITION

In 1939 Kohlmeier's health problems necessitated some changes at the Training School. Deaconess Henrietta Thorsness, office secretary for the LDA since September 1938, relieved Kohlmeier of teaching certain subjects and undertook the teaching of new courses in Child Psychology and Hymnology. Other deaconesses and pastors also assisted Kohlmeier by

---

[64] F. Dean Lueking, *A Century of Caring: The Welfare Ministry Among Missouri Synod Lutherans 1868-1968* (St. Louis, Missouri: Board of Social Ministry of The Lutheran Church—Missouri Synod, 1968), 56. For texts see Richard R. Caemmerer, "Lutheran Social Action," *The Thirty-Seventh Annual Convention of the Associated Lutheran Charities* (Watertown: Jansky Printing Co., 1938), 48-54; Richard R. Caemmerer, "The Application of Christian Ethics to Current Social Problems," *The 43rd Annual Convention of the Associated Lutheran Charities* University Campus Valparaiso, September 8 to 13 (Watertown: Jansky Printing Co., 1946), 28-58.

[65] Kretzmann resigned from teaching at Concordia Seminary, St. Louis, effective 20 May 1946, and in 1951 left the LCMS to help form the Orthodox Lutheran Conference. P. E. Kretzmann, "Sowing the Wind—Reaping the Whirlwind," Kretzmann file, CHI, St. Louis, Mo.

conducting lecture tours in his stead.[66] Unfortunately, the Superintendent's health did not improve. Heeding the advice of his doctor, Kohlmeier resigned his position effective July 1, 1941. Sadly, on that same day, Deaconess Thorsness died after three weeks of suffering subsequent to the removal of her gall bladder.[67]

The LDA moved quickly to find a new Superintendent, issuing a call to Rev. Arnold Fred Krentz (1896-1961) on July 18. Krentz was a seasoned pastor of twenty-one years, most recently at St. Paul's Lutheran Church near St. Clemens, Michigan, where he also taught school for eleven years. Though a newcomer to LDA circles, Krentz was "highly esteemed by the brethren with whom he has worked and by his former parishioners," and had a broad range of experiences that qualified him for the job.[68]

About three weeks before his formal induction as Superintendent, Krentz addressed the ALCh convention on the topic of "Integration of the Lutheran Deaconess Movement with the Work of the Associated Charities."

> I feel particularly happy to have the privilege of discussing with you the Lutheran Deaconess movement and its integration and interrelation with the blessed work of the Associated Lutheran Charities. You know, many of our deaconesses are rendering consecrated and efficient service within your organization. . . .

> Friends, I take it that all of you are interested in the growth of this service of mercy. You need workers, consecrated, efficient, resourceful, intelligent women workers in our charities. . . . You are the consumer, we the producer. . . .

> One of the problems of our deaconess work is the fact that we place our women workers into so many different fields of labor. Complex and varied is the work of the deaconess in 1941. Our deaconess in Nigeria has a different day's work mapped out for her than the deaconess at Bethesda. We do want to integrate our deaconess movement with the work of our Lutheran Charities and yet we feel our limitations in this direction. Our Deaconess Association can train its workers only in a general way. To use a parallel, at our seminary in St. Louis we do not train specialists. Certain students are not selected and trained as city missionaries, foreign missionaries, superintendents of children's friend societies. After graduation from the seminary certain pastors show ability and capacity to

---

[66] H. B. Kohlmeier, "Annual Report—October 22, 1939," *TLD* 17, no. 1 (January 1940): 3.

[67] H. B. Kohlmeier, "A Word of Farewell," *TLD* 18, no. 3 (July 1941): 2; H. B. Kohlmeier, "In Memoriam," *TLD* 18 no. 4 (October 1941): 4.

[68] H. B. Kohlmeier, "Our New Superintendent," *TLD* 18, no. 4 (October 1941): 2.

qualify as college professors, city missionaries, district presidents. So with our deaconesses; in the field certain aptitudes in them come to the fore.

. . . In order to integrate the training of our Lutheran Deaconesses yet better with the glorious work you men and women are carrying on in the field, in order that our deaconesses may cope more efficiently with a world strangely out of joint and topsy-turvy socially, in order to make our school a high potential, we are constantly looking for a better method of training our deaconesses. And so I am happy to inform you of the important fact that the Board of the Lutheran Deaconess Association at Ft. Wayne—God bless this fine group of men—has on September 19 resolved that beginning with this new school year the course of instruction shall be extended to two full years. . . .

Evidently the matter of integrating the Deaconess Movement with the Associated Lutheran Charities calls for reciprocity of relationship. You can help us tremendously in making this integration even better. We are endeavoring to visualize and understand your problems. One of our pressing problems is to secure students of high mentality, of outstanding spirituality, and physical fitness. Won't you help us find such students? Another problem is the financial problem. We need larger sums of money for equipment, for building, for field work. You can help us solve these problems. We need publicity, much publicity, favorable to our cause. You as influential leaders in the Associated Lutheran Charities can promote such publicity. We need more members of our Deaconess Association; need more women's organizations in the larger cities to support our work. Will you be our promoter?

Brethren, the Lutheran Deaconess Association is a service station. We mean to serve you better, both quantitatively and qualitatively. . . . I like to think that in the plan of Christ to uplift suffering humanity, he does employ in measure, that quiet but consecrated Christian, the Lutheran Deaconess.[69]

Krentz continued to attend ALCh meetings for many years; however, he never again addressed the conference with a special appeal for assistance. Instead, Krentz proceeded to experiment with other ideas for publicity within the church.

---

[69] Arnold F. Krentz, "Integration of the Lutheran Deaconess Movement with the Work of the Associated Charities," *Fortieth Annual Convention Associated Lutheran Charities*, Hotel Lincoln, Indianapolis, Indiana, Oct. 7-10, 1941 (Watertown: Jansky Printing Co., 1941), 32-35.

USING LUTHERAN NETWORKS

When he lived in Michigan, Superintendent Krentz was actively involved in youth work, editing the *Michigan Leaguer* and providing high profile leadership to the Walther League. He also served as chairman of the Mt. Clemens District of the Lutheran University Association for the support of Valparaiso University.[70] The network of contacts Krentz developed in these circles would prove to be beneficial to his new work.

Rev. Otto Paul Kretzmann (1901–1975)—Associate Secretary of the Walther League, President of Valparaiso University, and Secretary of the LCMS Board for Higher Education (BHE)—liked Krentz and wrote favorably about "deaconess work" in his regular column in *The Walther League Messenger* in September 1942 and April 1943.[71]

> A word or two about the Lutheran Deaconess Association. We believe that Lutheran Deaconess work is one of the great fields of the future in our church. They are needed not only in charitable institutions but in hundreds of urban parishes. Few vocations, we believe, can offer more lasting and continuing satisfaction than Deaconess work. It should be admitted that we Lutherans have not been very efficient in providing avenues of service for women in the church. We hope that the day will come when thousands of Lutheran young women will go into training for this work. . . . By the way, we are proud of the fact that the University nurse on the campus at Valparaiso, Miss Clara M. Dienst, is president of the association.[72]

> On a hurried journey over to Detroit we were reminded of something that we have wanted to say for a long time. . . . The most impressive event of the day was Pastor Arnold Krentz's appeal before the assembled brethren for more deaconesses. He's really got something there. More deaconesses in the Church will be an answer to many of our problems—social work in the Lutheran way, help for crowded pastors, work with children and old folks, charity in Lutheran sense. Our Church has never used the latent power of our consecrated womanhood. Personally we believe that there are great possibilities here. We suspect that there are hundreds of secretaries, stenographers and clerks in our church who are tired of the

---

[70] Kohlmeier, "Our New Superintendent," 2.

[71] Kretzmann's Valparaiso University presidency ran from 1940 to 1968 and he was secretary of the LCMS BHE from 1938 to 1953. Therefore, he held both positions for the 13 years from 1940 to 1953.

[72] Deaconess Dienst was president of the Deaconess Conference. O. P. Kretzmann, "By the Way," *The Walther League Messenger* (September 1942): 23.

routine of "Yours of the 8th instant received and contents noted"[73] and accounting and filing. They would be glad, we feel, to transform their lives and glorify them by serving as deaconesses—a service which only they can give. Here surely is another frontier of our Church, and pioneer women are needed. Of course, there will be no large salaries, no rows of buttons to push, and no office parties; but it will be a living where life pulsates to the tempo of our time—the answering love of little children, the gratitude of the poor and downtrodden whom the Galilean knew so well, the lasting satisfaction of casting bread on far waters. Pastor Krentz tells us that all he needs to make a deaconess is a high school graduate of sound body and good mind. With our own ears we hear a number of Detroit pastors, among the busiest in the land, rise to their feet and say that they would employ a deaconess tomorrow if one were available. . . . A good deaconess can double and triple the service rendered by a congregation to its members and its immediate environment. A good deaconess can put the pastor back into the study and the pulpit where his major work lies. The whole matter really looks tremendous to us. Perhaps we can use the period of the war, when men are busy with other things, to build women's place in the Church.[74]

Kretzmann does not specify the occasion at which Krentz spoke in Detroit, but the superintendent's CPH appointment diary contains the words "Detroit Pastoral Conference" for Monday, February 22, 1943, and a note that he preached in Detroit on the following Sunday.[75] In general, Krentz's diaries from 1941 onward show that he did extensive traveling and speaking on behalf of the deaconess program. The names of pastors and churches in both the Missouri and Wisconsin Synods, ladies' aids, Walther League conventions, deaconess consecrations, deaconess conferences, and groups such as the Lutheran Nurses' Club appear frequently in his calendars. The fact that "Free Sunday" is written on the space for April 11, 1943, indicates that it may have been rare for him to pass the Sabbath without some sort of preaching or speaking engagement.[76]

Several entries in the Superintendent's appointment calendars read "send deaconess to," followed by a name and address, indicating the involvement of deaconesses in various public relations endeavors. Indeed, from the time that Superintendent Kohlmeier became ill, consecrated

---

[73] Quotation indicates a typical response that would be sent to acknowledge receipt of a letter. The vernacular means "Your letter dated the 8th of this month has been received and the contents have been noted or considered."

[74] O. P. Kretzmann, "By the Way," *The Walther League Messenger* (April 1943): 432.

[75] Arnold F. Krentz, diary entry for February 22, 1943, CPH Calendar Diaries 1918-1960, Arnold Krentz, Box 200 KRE, CHI, St. Louis, Mo.

[76] Arnold F. Krentz, diary entry for April 11, 1943.

deaconesses began to have a higher public profile in advocating the deaconess cause to potential candidates, pastors, and churches. For example, on four consecutive Sunday evenings in the autumn of 1941, Deaconess Margaret Spencer delivered live broadcasts about deaconess work from radio station KFUO in St. Louis.[77]

While making the most of contacts from his parish days, Krentz pursued opportunities to build new networks of support for the LDA. In spring 1942, Carl Mundiger, president of Concordia College in Winfield, Kansas, announced that his faculty would offer a "pre-Deaconess Training Course" and that he intended to "co-operate in every way to help train more deaconesses."[78] This decision to prepare women for deaconess training on a Missouri Synod campus gave a huge boost to the perceived integrity of the deaconess movement within LCMS circles, and may even explain why the LDA eventually concentrated on working with the LCMS almost to the exclusion of other members of the Synodical Conference. *The Lutheran Deaconess* chronicled a growing interest in the deaconess movement among LCMS professors and pastors.

> Pastor Andrew Schulze, that tireless worker in Negro Mission Work, called together a small group of pastors for a meeting on Saturday afternoon, March 14, at Concordia Seminary, St. Louis, to discuss the future of the Lutheran Deaconess. As is often the case in a small group, each one present contributed heavily to the discussion. Prof. Rehwinkel,[79] who for years has been interested in developing women workers for the Church—at our Concordia College, Winfield, Kansas, he introduced the pre-Deaconess Course—was the leading speaker ably assisted by Pastors Lange, Roschke, Torgler and others. Discussions centered about the training of a deaconess, the service of a deaconess in the congregation, wider publicity of the deaconess movement and other points.
>
> So convinced was your superintendent of the helpfulness of these brethren in St. Louis to our cause that he invited Prof. Rehwinkel to come to Ft. Wayne to think through with our Board in a special meeting the various phases of the Deaconess Movement as we find it today. More yet. Prof. Rehwinkel has consented to come. So we hope to have the pleasure of having our esteemed professor and eminent man of vision with us some time in May.

---

[77] "News Items," *TLD* 18, no. 4 (October 1941): 5. Spencer was matron at the Lutheran Altenheim in St. Louis.

[78] "Seeing Stars," *TLD* 19, no. 2 (April 1942): 6.

[79] Alfred Martin Rehwinkel (1887-1979) taught at Concordia Seminary in St. Louis (1936-65), and had served as president of Concordia College, Winfield, Kansas (1928-36).

Upon suggestion of City Missionary M. Ilse, Sr., of Cleveland we presented our plans and pleas on Deaconess Work to the Cleveland City Pastoral Conference in January. Here also we found a ready response on the part of the brethren to study the possibility of widening out the influence of the fulltime women worker in the local congregation.

One of the signs of a bigger and better Deaconess Service is the thoughtful interest leading pastors scattered throughout our far-flung Synod are taking in our work.[80]

While Krentz courted "leading pastors," he also realized the importance of introducing the female diaconate to seminary students.

History was made for Concordia Seminary and for the Lutheran Deaconess Association on March 16. On that evening at 6:30 p.m. members of the Mission Society of Concordia Seminary, St. Louis, gathered to hear a discussion on the Lutheran Deaconess.[81]

The writer [Pastor Krentz] sketched the history of the Deaconess movement from the early church when full-time women workers in the Church were quite common to Pastor Fliedner who is rightly regarded as the Father of the Modern Deaconess Movement and then traced the course of the Deaconess movement in our Synod. To these future leaders of our Churches he pointed out what a potential power these trained women workers are and that every larger congregation would do well to engage such specially trained workers for work in their midst. He ended with this challenging thought: The Lutheran Deaconess as a Parish Worker—the One Talent Buried in our Synod.

The second speaker was Deaconess Florence Storck who with her bell-like voice told in a winning way of several actual conversations in her work at Koch Sanatorium. . .

The third speaker who riveted the attention of the students was another of our faithful workers, Miss Margaret Spencer, R.N., Deaconess, who in

---

[80] "St. Louis and Cleveland Pastors Evince Interest in Deaconess Work," *TLD* 19, no. 2 (April 1942): 7-8.
[81] The seminary's 1941-42 catalogue included the following paragraph: "THE MISSIONARY SOCIETY is an important student organization supported and operated by the [Students'] Association under the general supervision of the Dean. Each student is required to be a member and financial supporter of this organization. It operates mission stations, assists congregations in missionary endeavors, and carries on work in hospitals and other public institutions under the direction of the Lutheran City Mission. A program of special instruction and guidance for workers in the various fields of mission work is being introduced under the charge of members of the Faculty." "The Students' Association," *Concordia Theological Seminary: Evangelical Lutheran Synod of Missouri, Ohio and Other States, One Hundred and Third Year 1941-1942* (St. Louis: Concordia, 1941), 10.

a way which suggested the executive, showed the various places where deaconesses may well function. . . .

. . . Rev. Guerecke [sic],[82] city missionary of St. Louis, gave a warm testimonial to the efficiency and the blessing of our Lutheran Deaconesses as he knew them. He pointed out that our ministers can help much to enlist the best type of students and that the Seminary students as future pastors of our Church would do well to plan even now some day to employ a deaconess. . . .

We carry with us the deep conviction that once our PASTORS get the vision of the need and the blessing of the parish deaconess a new day will have dawned in this movement which has such tremendous possibilities. . . . We hope that a similar meeting can be arranged at Concordia Seminary, Springfield, so that our future pastors will support our work and let our work support them. We feel that many such meetings are one of the "MUSTS" for effective publicity in our noble cause."[83]

SHARING THE TEACHING RESPONSIBILITIES

The LDA implemented several changes in deaconess training when Pastor Krentz became Superintendent. As of fall 1941, deaconess students attended 12 credit hours of classes in Sociology and Psychology at the Indiana University Extension Center in Fort Wayne (and Krentz took the classes along with his students).[84] The entire Deaconess Training Course was lengthened to two full years, making it possible for the students to have "Two semesters (36 weeks) academic Work at the Deaconess Home and the Indiana Extension Division; One semester (18 weeks) practical experience in institutional work; One semester (18 weeks) academic work at

---

[82] Henry F. Gerecke (1893-1961) was a St. Louis city missionary (1935-43), and then a Chaplain with the 98th General Hospital in England, France, and Germany and the 6850th Internal Security Detachment, Nuernberg, Germany (1943-46). During his service abroad, Gerecke served as a chaplain to the Lutheran German prisoners tried at the War Crime Tribunal, Nuernberg, Germany 1945-46. CHI, "Biographical Record for Henry F. Gerecke," May 13, 1998.

[83] "Concordia Seminary Students Think Deaconess Work," TLD 19, no. 2 (April 1942): 3.

[84] The LDA Board reserved the right to assign substitute courses to those women who already had the equivalent courses in Sociology and Psychology. "The Training School," TLD 18, no. 4 (October 1941): 3; Arnold F. Krentz, "The Transition from Ft. Wayne to Valparaiso," partially typed and partially hand written notes, Krentz file, LDA Archives, LDA, Valparaiso, Indiana; "Seeing Stars," TLD 19, no. 1 (January 1942): 5-6; "Deaconess Training Course," TLD 20, no. 1 (January 1943): 4.

the Home; and supervised social service work under a recognized agency."[85] The LDA paid all of the tuition fees for the additional courses, and continued to provide the women with room and board at the Deaconess Home during the lengthened training time.

The first hitch to the updated curriculum occurred when Indiana University failed to offer one of the required Sociology classes during the second semester. Rev. Dr. Walter G. Herrling (1896-1958), Head of the Department of Social Sciences at Concordia College in Fort Wayne, came to the rescue by offering to teach the class in his home. Around the same time, P.E. Kretzmann, professor at Concordia Seminary in St. Louis, promised to assist Krentz in a study of the deaconess school curriculum, with a view toward further possible improvement.[86]

When Krentz's first year came to a close, O. P. Kretzmann expressed his conviction that Valparaiso University could offer several courses to deaconess students that would better prepare them for their future work. About 110 miles separated Valparaiso University and the Fort Wayne Deaconess Home. The superintendent judged President Kretzmann's offer to be "reasonable and applicable," but took no action on it.[87]

Regarding his second year of teaching, which started in September 1942, Krentz wrote:

> Our staff of teachers was now augmented and included the following: Dr. Engle (Indiana University Extension) 3 hours; Dr. Herrling (Concordia College) 3 hours; Miss Marie Zucker (Social Service) 1 hour; Personal Mission Work (alternated Pastors Hofius and Wambsganss) 1 hour. Thus my teaching load was lightened considerably. I taught Isagogics, N. T. 3 hours; catechism teaching mostly labortary [sic] work, 1 hour; mission history, 1 hour; Church History, 2 hours; Personality, 1 hour; Sunday School, 1 hour. Total 9 hours. Total 17 hours. The second semester . . . I taught Isagogics, Prophets 1 hour; 2 hours Symbolics; Institutional Work, 1 hr., Pedagogy 1 hr. Speech 2 hours, verse speaking choir. Rev. Koehler gave a series on working in China Mission.[88]

---

[85] "Deaconess Training Course: Lutheran Deaconess Association within the Synodical Conference, Deaconess Home and Training School," mimeographed sheet, Misc. 1941 Convention file, Associated Lutheran Charities Box 2, CHI, St. Louis, Mo.

[86] "Seeing Stars," *TLD* 19, no. 1 (January 1942): 5.

[87] "Seeing Stars," *TLD* 19, no. 3 (July 1942): 8.

[88] "In Personality we discuss ways to improve our personality so that we may be a credit to Christ's Church on earth." Thelburn Engle, Ph.D., lectured on Elementary Psychology. Marie Zucker was Executive Secretary of the Lutheran Social Service League of Fort Wayne and President of the Allen County Association of Social Workers. Wambsganss refers to Fred Wambsganss (Sr.). William Louis Hofius (1896-1955) was the LCMS city missionary in

THE UNEXPECTED TWIST

Superintendent Krentz obviously desired to broaden all public relations avenues for the diaconate. Whether deliberately or coincidentally, he succeeded in securing positions for deaconesses that often increased their visibility to the church. For example, when the 1942-43 academic year began, *TLD* announced that deaconesses served three LCMS colleges: Deaconess Matilda Pfund as nurse at Concordia College in Milwaukee; Deaconess Lulu Noess as the new supervisor for women at Concordia Teachers College, River Forest; and Deaconess Johanna Schmidt as campus nurse for Concordia in Fort Wayne.[89] As noted above, Deaconess Clara Dienst also held the post of university nurse on the Valparaiso campus. This exposure of active deaconesses to so many youth within the Synodical Conference could only be good for the deaconess cause.

And yet the LDA still needed more deaconess students. In 1943, the Central School for Deaconess Training in Fort Wayne was seven years old. Its five graduating classes from 1936 to 1940 could boast a total of 18 consecrated deaconesses, but the school had no graduates in 1941, only three in 1942, and none in 1943. In addition, in spring 1943 a different problem became more pressing than enrollment figures—a problem that had the potential to either strengthen or destroy the deaconess movement within the Synodical Conference.

> In 1943 the Lutheran Hospital Board gave notice to our Association that they considered the Deaconess Home necessary for their own use and that in accordance with the agreement made when the Home was placed on the grounds of the hospital, they now wished to buy the Home.[90]

LDA Board members must have been stunned when they heard the news that they must immediately sell the Deaconess Home to the hospital. Herzberger and Wambsganss had considered the motherhouse an essential part of the equation for a successful diaconate, so much so that their first publicized goal was to acquire one. Indeed, the Deaconess Home, as it was now called, brought together every aspect of the work of the LDA. It was

---

Fort Wayne. Adolph Theodore Koehler (1904-1969) taught "Chinese Language Study" in the Missions Department at Concordia Seminary in St. Louis. "Courses of the Graduate School," *Concordia Theological Seminary: Evangelical Lutheran synod of Missouri, Ohio and Other States, One Hundred and Third Year 1941-1942* (St. Louis: Concordia, 1941), 29; Krentz, "The Transition from Ft. Wayne to Valparaiso," 2; Nettye Kimberley, "Miss Nettye Kimberley Reports on Valparaiso Deaconess Training," *TLD* 21, no. 2 (April 1944): 7.

[89] "Two Concordias Engage Deaconesses," *TLD* 19, no. 4 (October 1942): 7.

[90] Kohlmeier, *25th Anniversary of the Lutheran Deaconess Association*, 16.

the main classroom for instruction in deaconess work; a place of joyful fellowship for women on vacation or furlough; a nursing home for recuperation from illness; and expected to serve as long-term residence for retired deaconesses who had spent their lives in the service of Christ.

Where and how would the LDA acquire a new Deaconess Home? It certainly was an inopportune time to purchase a replacement, and building a new motherhouse was out of the question because of war-time restrictions. With his usual determination, Krentz prepared to take up the challenge. In personal notes, he later wrote: "Must sell. Not disappointed. Felt the Lord was ruling and overruling our entire Deaconess Schooling."[91]

[91] Arnold F. Krentz, "The Transition from Ft. Wayne to Valparaiso," 2.
Illustrations for Chapter Five may be viewed at www.deaconesshistory.org.

CHAPTER 6

THE MOVE TO VALPARAISO

Decisions needed to be made quickly with regard to a new Deaconess Home. Neither Pastor Krentz's personal notes nor any of his published articles mention the different options discussed by the LDA Board of Directors. It could be that the Board considered properties near Lutheran Hospital or in close proximity to Concordia College as possible sites for a Home. Certainly the Board would not have thought long about purchasing property outside of Fort Wayne, since all LDA Board members resided in that city and the base of practical support for the Central Training School was situated there.

In the midst of turmoil and prayer, an alternative idea was presented. Former Superintendent Kohlmeier explained, "Valparaiso University heard about the predicament of the Deaconess Association and sent representatives to the Deaconess Board to propose the transfer of the School to Valparaiso."[1] President O. P. Kretzmann, Walter Friedrich, Albert Scribner, and W. Charles Dickmeyer met with the LDA Board of Directors, and after several meetings the Board resolved to "transfer Deaconess Education to Valparaiso, Indiana."[2]

What a leap of faith! For the first time in the history of diaconal training in the United States, and perhaps even in the world, student deaconesses would live and learn within the context of a university campus instead of a motherhouse. The whole concept was so radically different that it would take a great deal of thought and planning to execute.

---

[1] Valparaiso University received its name from the small town of Valparaiso, Indiana, where the university is still located today. H. B. Kohlmeier, *1919-1944 25th Anniversary of the Lutheran Deaconess Association within the Synodical Conference* (Fort Wayne: Nuoffer Print, 1944), 16.

[2] Friedrich was dean of the faculty and served as acting president of Valparaiso University before Kretzmann took office. Scribner was the university's business manager; Dickmeyer the Chairman of the Valparaiso University Board of Directors. Arnold F. Krentz, "The Transition from Ft. Wayne to Valparaiso," partially typed and partially hand written notes, Krentz file, LDA Archives, LDA, Valparaiso, Indiana, 2.

IRONING OUT THE DETAILS

One of the first issues that needed to be addressed was the relationship between Valparaiso University and the training program. Pastor Krentz noted:

> These points were especially agreed upon June 8, 1943. 1) That the educational (program) was on an experimental basis, 2) That the Deaconess Association was to retain full control of deaconess training, 3) That deaconess training is a distinct entity, not just a department of Valparaiso. This implies that the secular studies are taken at the university and that religious education is in my hands.[3]

Krentz announced the impending move to Valparaiso right away in the July 1943 issue of *TLD.*

> We believe our readers will be happy to be informed that beginning with the school year 1943-1944 the LUTHERAN DEACONESS TRAINING SCHOOL will be located in VALPARAISO, IND., instead of Ft. Wayne as heretofore. The new location of our School at Valparaiso is definitely experimental.
>
> In the Deaconess Training School in Valparaiso the students will receive a course in religious subjects such as Isagogics (Introduction to the Bible), Comparative Symbolics (Doctrine), Church History, etc. In addition to these religious subjects, the students will take regular college subjects such as Education, English, Psychology, sociology [*sic*], etc. at Valparaiso University.
>
> It goes without saying that Lutheran deaconesses in the education-conscious age should receive the best possible training, just as our pastors and parish school teachers receive the ultimate in higher education. This raising of educational standards becomes imperative in the face of the numerous requests for parish deaconesses. Our pastors in this war era are gaining the perspective of the parish deaconess in taking off part of the load from the pastor's shoulders. Naturally such parish deaconesses will need to be equipped as well as possible.
>
> It needs to be emphasized that the Lutheran Deaconess Training School at Valparaiso is to remain a separate entity, will not become another department of Valparaiso University, but will retain its peculiar identity. This is the wish of both the Board of the Lutheran Deaconess Association and the Board of Valparaiso University. The Deaconess School will continue its distinct existence for the purpose of doing a distinct work, that of training Lutheran deaconesses. . . .

---

[3] Krentz, "Transition from Ft. Wayne to Valparaiso," 2-3.

To achieve this high objective we need students for our School at Valparaiso. We firmly believe that Deaconess Work offers one of the great opportunities for young Lutheran women who are desirous of serving their Savior and His Church. Any young women of fine personality, and high spiritual and mental and social traits, whom our readers may induce to enter our Deaconess School with this new educational set-up, will be a contribution on their part to the glorious cause of trained women church workers, whose services are so sorely needed in church work today.

The HEADQUARTERS for DEACONESS WORK will remain in FORT WAYNE, INDIANA. Address all correspondence from now on to: 2808 Hoagland Avenue, Fort Wayne, Ind.[4]

Superintendent Krentz needed to make personal sacrifices to accommodate the new training plan. He would continue working in Ft. Wayne—with the LDA headquarters based at his home residence—and travel to Valparaiso each week to teach the special deaconess courses. Notes like "Fare to Valpo $1.93" in his diary indicate that Krentz made the journeys by train.[5] In his own words, he retained the "same spirit of adventure, of consecration, of joy in serving the Lord."[6]

STUDENT ACCOMMODATION

When the 1943-44 academic year began, five new students entered the Deaconess School and one resumed her studies after spending a "probationary period" in a Detroit congregation. When three other women returned to Valparaiso for the second semester after full-time fieldwork experiences in Fort Wayne, Cleveland, and New York, the Deaconess School enjoyed the largest enrollment that it had seen for several years.[7]

Though the idea of a central motherhouse had been abandoned, the LDA wanted to find a place for the students to live together in Valparaiso, preferably in a private residence with space for deaconess classes and a place for the women to gather for devotions or activities. The LDA rented a large house, initially known as the Deaconess School, which by April 1944 was called the Deaconess Chapter House. According to the frequently published list of "Deaconesses According to their Stations," one or two

---

[4] "Deaconess School Moves to Valparaiso," *TLD* 20, no. 3 (July 1943): 2.
[5] Arnold F. Krentz, diary entry for August 23, 1943, CPH Calendar Diaries 1918-1960, Arnold Krentz, Box 200 KRE, CHI, St. Louis, Mo.
[6] Krentz, "Transition from Ft. Wayne to Valparaiso," 3.
[7] "Our Students," *TLD* 20, no. 4 (October 1943), 6.

deaconesses lived in the Chapter House, presumably caring for the students and the home. In 1946, the house acquired a permanent matron in the person of Mrs. Sylvia Trautmann.[8] The LDA furnished the student bedrooms "college-dormitory style" and the entire house was reputed to be comfortable and inviting, just like the Deaconess Home before it.[9]

> When we speak in America of high standards of living we invariably mean a life of economic security with physical needs adequately met.
>
> Physically, the group of deaconess students at the Deaconess Chapter House, 605 Chicago Street, Valparaiso, Ind., live on a high standard. The meals there and at Altruria Hall[10] are very satisfying. The fireplace gives a home-like feeling to the Chapter House. Economic worries are absent.
>
> Further, the deaconess students live on a high standard socially. Their fellow deaconess students are young women of the highest type whose inner urge to serve Christ makes them agreeable companions to associate with. An air of calm and composure pervades the Chapter House. Then, too, the deaconess students mingle with hundreds of fine Lutheran young men and women on the University campus—all of which is important in the socializing process.
>
> Moreover, deaconess students live on a high standard mentally. They come into direct contact in the classroom with instructors who are authorities in sociology, psychology, English, music, etc. What a privilege to read books that build up, to be stimulated by noble minds and hearts in the classroom!
>
> Above all, our deaconess students live on a high level spiritually. Their pastor, the Rev. Armin Oldsen,[11] Sunday after Sunday energizes their faith and life by timely sermons based on God's infallible Word. From Monday through Friday chapel exercises at the University lift our students up

---

[8] Page 8 of *TLD* often featured "Deaconesses According to their Stations." Sylvia (nee Stork) Trautmann was the widow of Rev. Robert Godfrey Michael Trautmann (1897-1945). Mrs. Trautmann's dog, Ginger, also lived at the Chapter House and the deaconess students adopted her as their mascot. There is no indication that deaconesses who were ill, on vacation, or taking an extended period of rest spent time at the Deaconess Chapter House. In June of 1944 Kohlmeier announced, "Deaconesses may, whenever they wish to do so, come to the home of Rev. and Mrs. Kohlmeier where a room is reserved for their use by arrangement with the Deaconess Board." This is the only mention of such an arrangement. Kohlmeier, *25th Anniversary of the Lutheran Deaconess Association*, 9.

[9] A Visitor, "A Glimpse at 605 E. Chicago," *TLD* 22, no. 3 (July 1945): 6.

[10] A women's dormitory on the university campus, where deaconess students often ate meals.

[11] Armin Charles Oldsen (1910-1994) served as pastor of Immanuel Lutheran Church in Valparaiso from 1940-50.

spiritually. In addition, a distinctive feature at the Chapter House is the evening devotion which focuses attention upon our Beautiful Savior and the future service the students will render Him and suffering humanity. Often the students themselves contribute to these stimulating evening moments with God.

Most emphatically, in the best sense of the expression, deaconess students at Valparaiso LIVE ON A HIGH STANDARD.[12]

The entire situation at Valparaiso sounded wonderful for *students*. But what did removing the motherhouse infrastructure from the diaconate actually mean to those women who were already serving as deaconesses?

ADJUSTMENTS FOR CONSECRATED DEACONESSES

The conscious and subconscious idea of community in the diaconate was, at least in part, disrupted by the lack of a motherhouse. After all, the Deaconess Home had been a place where the women gathered for meetings, billeted during furloughs, or gravitated toward for a quiet visit with another sister in the faith. The Deaconess Conference went a long way toward providing fellowship and camaraderie for the women. But they no longer had a home base that they could always look forward to returning to one day. The Deaconess Home—functioning, as a haven for times of rest, recuperation, and retirement—was gone, forever. From now on Synodical Conference deaconesses would be forced to look after their own interests in these areas, without much assistance from the LDA or the Superintendent.

If there were private misgivings among some of the seasoned deaconesses, there is no trace of those sentiments now. The women could do nothing about the LDA breaking its pledge to provide them with the convenience and security of a motherhouse. They promised in the *Deaconess Agreement* to "submit to the decisions of the Board,"[13] and would adjust their expectations accordingly. Of course, in a very short time, the new system would bring increased material wealth to the individual women.

The economic system under which the deaconess, who enters service after January 1, 1946, lives, is similar to that of our female Christian Day School teachers. She is paid by the mission, institution, or congregation which she serves. Deaconesses who were consecrated prior to January 1, 1946, have the right to come under the system also.

---

[12] "High Living Standards," *TLD* 23, no. 2 (April 1946): 6.
[13] See discussion of the *Deaconess Agreement* in chapter five.

Upon entering service the deaconesses who are consecrated from now on come automatically under the Synod's Pension Plan. The mission, institution, or congregation pays 4% of the salary paid the deaconess into the Pension Fund; this 4% is over and above the salary paid the deaconess. In addition, the deaconess pays 4% of her salary into the Pension Fund. Upon retirement from service at the age of 65, if she so desires, the deaconess will receive $50.00 monthly.

This new system of remunerating deaconesses being introduced at the present time within the Synodical Conference is unique among the Lutheran Church bodies in America. For the first time a deaconess will draw her full salary herself and yet have security for her old age. This would appear to be a highly significant step in Deaconess Work within the Lutheran Church.[14]

Until this point, the net earnings of LDA deaconesses were paid into the Deaconess Permanent Maintenance Fund, from which each deaconess received the "nominal wage of $30 a month plus care."[15] Now the women would be given their entire salary and a guaranteed pension of $50 a month—a 66 percent increase above what they were accustomed to receiving. By 1953, the pension figure would double to $100 per month.[16] The LDA had broken new ground, and was very pleased about it.

Valparaiso University and the Synodical Conference

To fully appreciate the unique setting into which the LDA placed its training school in autumn 1943, it is helpful to understand the relationship between Valparaiso University and the Synodical Conference.

Valparaiso University—known affectionately as Valparaiso, VU, or Valpo—was, at the outset of its purchase by The Lutheran University Association (LUA) in 1925, established as an independent Lutheran University.[17] In other words, Valparaiso was not one of the 26 colleges or seminaries owned jointly by the Synodical Conference or operated

---

14 "Remuneration of the Deaconess," *TLD* 23, no. 4 (October 1946): 4.

15 E. H. Albers, "Lutheran Deaconess Association History," December 1967, Krentz file, LDA Archives, LDA, Valparaiso, Indiana, 3.

16 "Deaconess Salaries," *TLD* 25, no. 4 (October, 1948): 4; "Station LDA Tune In," *TLD* 30, no. 3 (July 1953): 6.

17 Before its purchase by the LUA the Valparaiso campus housed (Methodist) Valparaiso Male and Female College (1859-1871) and Northern Indiana Normal School, later called Valparaiso College and then Valparaiso University (1871-1925).

separately by the Norwegian, Wisconsin, or Missouri Synods.[18] The premise that Valparaiso University focused on the education of laity also differed from the primary purpose of synodically-owned schools: to train professional workers for the church.

However, the LUA did have strong connections to the Missouri Synod in the same way that other organizations—ALCh, The Fort Wayne Lutheran Hospital Association, and the LDA itself—had, namely, that the majority of their founders were Missouri Synod clergy and laity, many of whom hailed from Fort Wayne, Indiana. The overlap of leadership and membership in the Fort Wayne Lutheran Hospital Association, the ALCh, and the LDA has already been demonstrated in chapters three and five. What should also be noted here is that many of the men who were active in those organizations were the same individuals who worked together to establish and develop Valparaiso. A September 2000 press release from Valparaiso University highlights some of these names:

> VALPARAISO—Because of the Fort Wayne community's significant role in the formation and history of Valparaiso University as a Lutheran school for the past 75 years, VU's president will preach at the 8:45 a.m. Oct. 8 service at St. Paul's Lutheran Church. . . . Many of the early figures in the sale and organization of the new Lutheran school were from Fort Wayne including Dr. Jacob Miller, pastor of St. Paul's Lutheran Church, and his son the Rev. Paul Miller, co-pastor of St. Paul's; Dr. Herman Duemling, W. Charles Dickmeyer, Charles Scheimann, the Rev. John Baur, Professor H.D. Mensing and Martin Luecke.[19]

It is no coincidence that Valparaiso chose St. Paul's Lutheran Church as the center of its 75th anniversary celebrations in Fort Wayne. At a meeting of the American Luther League (ALL),[20] held at St. Paul's in 1925, Rev. George Freimund Wolfgang Schutes (b.1874), pastor of Immanuel

---

[18] The Synodical Conference owned Immanuel Lutheran College, Greensboro, North Carolina and Alabama Lutheran Academy, Selma, Alabama. Institutions belonging to the individual synods are listed in *The Lutheran Annual* (St. Louis: Concordia, 1943), 49-51.

[19] John C. Baur (1885-1984); (Rev.) Heinrich Dietrich Mensing (1880-1940); (Rev.) Martin H. Luecke (1859-1926). Office of University Relations, "Fort Wayne Lutherans played major role in forming VU," www.valpo.edu, Valparaiso University: News and Press Releases, September 21, 2000.

[20] The American Luther League came into being as a lay organization in the early 1920s through the efforts of Fort Wayne businessman, H.D. Holtermann. Its purpose was to safeguard the rights of Lutheran schools, with particular reference to constitutional liberties. A similar association called the National Lutheran Education Association, founded in 1918, focused on promoting higher education for Lutheran laity. Individuals from these two organizations formed the independent Lutheran University Association that purchased the campus in Valparaiso, Ind.

Lutheran Church in Valparaiso, presented the idea of purchasing the Valparaiso college campus to create a Lutheran university. Pastor Jacob Miller, a vice-president of the Missouri Synod and founding member of the LDA, became a major advocate for the proposal. Dr. Herman Duemling, chief surgeon at Fort Wayne Lutheran Hospital and president of ALL, became the first Chairman of the Valparaiso University Board of Directors.[21] Incidentally, this was the same Dr. Duemling from whom the LDA acquired its deaconess motherhouse in 1921.

THE VALPARAISO MOVEMENT

The need for a Lutheran university and the support thereof was explained to members of the Missouri Synod via a publication called "Valparaiso University: A God-given Opportunity for Our Lutheran People." A portrait of C. F. W. Walther graced the front cover of this 12-page booklet, with inside pages featuring pictures of the VU buildings and group photos of the 60 men credited with the decision to move forward with purchasing the campus. A sample of text from several pages reveals the sense of urgency felt by the leaders of this new endeavor.

> Today thousands of the young men and women of our churches are given the opportunity of a higher education. Parents are eager even to the point of personal sacrifice to give their children a better chance in the struggle of life through a higher education.

> Some day these young men and women are going to occupy positions of influence among friends and associates. Their ideas will help fashion the lives of others. What is being done to conserve their loyalty to the Church, their trained minds and powers for the service of the kingdom of God? In the matter of education practically nothing at all.[22]

> . . . Fully 4,000 of our Church's youth are today studying in secular and sectarian institutions. The number is steadily increasing.

> What happens to their faith, to their loyalty to the church in which they were baptized and confirmed? Large numbers lose their faith and come to look down upon their Church. Instead of becoming a power for good, their powers are thrown in with the scoffer and the agnostic. ... One

---

[21] For a comprehensive history of the purchase of Valparaiso University, see Richard Baepler, *Flame of Faith, Lamp of Learning: A History of Valparaiso University* (St. Louis: Concordia, 2001), 131-150.
[22] "Valparaiso University: A God-given Opportunity for Our Lutheran People," 12 page brochure, Valparaiso, IN Box 6, Valparaiso University File, LCMS Indiana District Archives, Fort Wayne, Ind., 3.

pastor says that in his time of service fully fifty young people from his church went to college and university. Only one today is an active church member. Three are indifferent members. The rest are lost.

Everyone knows these conditions and deplores them. Is it right to let them continue? Can we afford year after year to lose the pick of our youth? Is it wise to spend thousands for expansion and do nothing to stay the drain of this life blood? . . .[23]

Apart from and, perhaps, just as important as the provision for the Christian training of our youth is the meaning of this step for the ideals of conservative Lutheranism for which we stand.

We know the influence exerted by Catholic schools on public thought. We meet the many non-Catholics whose mind was fashioned by Catholic instruction and who have become tolerant and sympathetic toward that Church.

Here is OUR chance to put our light on a hill that its rays may radiate far and wide. Thousands of students from non-Lutheran homes in the years to come will receive their training at Valparaiso. Not a few will be won to active membership in our Church. Many more will come to think with sympathy of our ideals, grateful of the chance of an education which we have given them.

An educated man or woman touches, sways, influences the lives of hundreds. A teacher in the years of her service moulds [sic] the character of countless young folks. Every dollar that we place into Valparaiso promises to become a missionary force of untold power.[24]

Despite an initial groundswell of support for the new Lutheran University, several prominent individuals, including men such as Missouri Synod President Frederick Pfotenhauer and Professor Theodore Conrad Graebner (1876-1950), expressed strong reservations about the enterprise. At one point, the "powerful clergy" of the LCMS Western District "closed ranks around a refusal to participate in the Valparaiso drive."[25] Later, as William Dau considered an invitation to be the first Lutheran president of Valparaiso, he encountered opposition from his colleagues on the Concordia Seminary faculty. "Dau argued in response that leading a university would better prepare laity to help the clergy," and he eventually accepted the presidency, "interpreting it as a divine call that he could not

---

[23] "Valparaiso University: A God-given Opportunity for Our Lutheran People," 4-5.
[24] Ibid., 7.
[25] Baepler, *Flame of Faith, Lamp of Learning*, 149.

refuse."[26] Richard Baepler's popular history of Valparaiso provides an explanation for the tension that existed between those individuals who supported the concept of a church-sponsored university for laity and those who did not.

> The Lutherans who purchased Valparaiso University that summer of 1925 were members of a German immigrant church commonly known today as The Lutheran Church—Missouri Synod. The Lutheran University Association they had organized was a self-styled "progressive" group of clergy and laity who had often found themselves at odds with the leadership of the Synod on many matters related to the Americanization of their immigrant religious tradition and its Christian mission in a new land. The creation of the modern Valparaiso University involved not only the founding of a school, but it represented the centerpiece of a movement for social and intellectual change within this large subculture that constituted about one-third of American Lutheranism.

> Throughout the nineteenth century, and well into the twentieth, the Missouri Synod was a cohesive, largely German-speaking immigrant community, a highly distinctive conservative subculture of American life. For much of its history, the reborn Valparaiso University represented a kind of counterculture within that subculture, with its student body, faculty, and supporters drawn from the people of the Synod who supported what was known as the "Valparaiso movement." The movement's institutional manifestation was The Lutheran University Association, but it had widespread connections and implications that reached considerably beyond simply running a college. It was a prime carrier of a new view of what American Lutheranism was and what it should become.[27]

VALPO AND THE LDA

Pastor Krentz and the LDA Board of Directors knew that they took an unusual step in transferring the Central Training School to a university environment. It seems unlikely, however, that these individuals would have thought consciously about how such a move would place deaconess students, and hence the diaconate, in closer proximity to a "counterculture" that struggled with traditional Missouri Synod thinking. They certainly could

---

[26] Baepler, *Flame of Faith, Lamp of Learning*, 152.
[27] Richard Baepler (b. 1930) began teaching at Valparaiso University in 1961. He was head of the Department of Theology from 1963-66; became the first Dean of Christ College in 1966; and the Vice President for Academic Affairs in 1979. Baepler, *Flame of Faith, Lamp of Learning*, 131-32.

not have guessed that W. C. Dickmeyer, Chairman of the Valparaiso University Board of Directors, would raise funds for O. P. Kretzmann and other like-minded clergymen to meet in Chicago, where they would sign the controversial "Statement of the 44" in September 1945.[28] Nor could they know that Kretzmann, in his efforts to champion social and intellectual change at the university level and beyond, would stoke conflict between members of the Missouri Synod and Valparaiso's faculty and supporters for years to come.[29]

At the time the LDA moved its deaconess training to Valparaiso in 1943, the university had enjoyed 14 years of full accreditation and appeared to be gaining respect within the LCMS.[30] The training school's new location had been announced as "definitely experimental" and Superintendent Krentz was responsible for all "religious" education. President O. P. Kretzmann already mentioned his admiration for Krentz and the work carried out by deaconesses in parishes, institutions, and missions in *The Walther League Messenger*. Kretzmann's Aunt Elizabeth was married to former LDA Superintendent Bruno Poch; his Uncle Paul wrote the handbook for training Lutheran deaconesses. Yes, Valpo's President would

---

[28] O. P. Kretzmann, Otto A. Geiseman, and E.J. Friedrich organized the Chicago meeting. Mark E. Braun, *A Tale of Two Synods: Events that Led to the Split between Wisconsin and Missouri* (Milwaukee: Northwestern Publishing House, 2003), 179; Baepler, *Flame of Faith, Lamp of Learning*, 211.

[29] Kretzmann had only recently resolved the difficult issue of "social dancing on campus" that caused concern within LCMS circles during the previous decade. From 1945 onward he would be frequently criticized for his leadership in "A Statement" and the promotion of Lutheran unity and ecumenism that was evident in his speeches and in activities hosted by the university. "Memorandum" from O. P. Kretzmann to the Board of Directors, April 15, 1942, with attached explanation of "the discussion which followed," Box 1 #6 Valpo, CHI, St. Louis, Missouri. See for example, Letter from W. E. Bauer and 45 faculty members to the Members of the Praesidium [sic] and of the Board of Directors of the Lutheran Church—Missouri Synod, June 6, 1953, Box 1 #1 Valpo, CHI, St. Louis, Missouri; Baepler, *Flame of Faith, Lamp of Learning*, 211-12.

[30] In 1932, Missouri Synod convention delegates defeated Memorial 207 B to grant an annual subsidy of $100,000 to Valparaiso, but instructed Synod's Board of Directors to appoint a standing Advisory Committee for the university. The first Advisory Committee consisted of Martin Frederick Kretzmann (1878-1963), O. P. Kretzmann's uncle, pastor of St. John Lutheran Church in Kendallville, Indiana and a former member of Valparaiso's Board of Directors; Oscar Fedder (1880-1972), pastor of St. Stephen's Lutheran Church in Chicago, who later served as a member of the LDA Board of Directors for many years; and a layman named Ed. Tatge. In 1935 the Synod commended Valpo. In 1938 and 1941 the possibility of combining Valparaiso with other synodical colleges was considered (to no avail). In 1941, a synodical resolution directed the BHE to include VU in a survey of all synodical educational institutions. LCMS, *Proceedings*, 1932, 75-76; LCMS, *Proceedings*, 1935, 113-14; LCMS, *Proceedings*, 1938, 62, 94-96, 268; LCMS, *Proceedings*, 1941, 109-112.

be keen for this experiment to succeed, for the sake of the diaconate, and for the sake of the university, which needed female students to compensate for the young men who were off at war.

1944: SILVER ANNIVERSARY CELEBRATIONS

Less than a year after moving the deaconess training school to Valparaiso, the LDA celebrated its 25th anniversary in conjunction with the Conference of Deaconesses held at Concordia College in Fort Wayne.

> Our Lutheran women of Fort Wayne, under the direction of Mrs. Paul Bente and Mrs. Fred Wambsganss, proved themselves to be perfect hostesses when they entertained the Deaconess Conference, June 15–17 at Concordia College. Mrs. Ottomar Krueger, in charge of registration, reported: 21 deaconesses present, 5 deaconess students, more than 24 guests. Fourteen of these guests were from Cleveland and represented the fine spirit and interest which our Cleveland ladies maintain for our Deaconess Cause.
>
> Deaconess Johanna Schmidt, nurse at Concordia College, arranged for sleeping quarters in the Hospital and Sihler Hall for all deaconesses and guests. Sessions were held in the Martha Room, where the Display Committee had arranged a display of pictures illustrating the work of the deaconesses in their various positions. . . .[31]

The conference agenda listed the names of several prominent LCMS clergymen. LDA President Walter Klausing gave the "Address of Welcome." Rev. Fred Henry Heidbrink (b.1901), Rev. Erwin Louis William Tepker (1908-1989), Rev. Paul Frederick Miller (1887–1958), and Concordia College President Ottomar George William Krueger (1892–1976) led "inspirational devotions." Along with the usual presentations by deaconesses about their work, session topics included "Educational Step to Valparaiso University" by E.E. Foelber; "Beginning and Growth of Deaconess Movement" by Enno Duemling; "Deaconess Work During the Next Decade" by B. Poch; "Mission Work in the Orient" by Rev. Otto Henry Schmidt (1886–1971); "The Deaconess School Consolidated and Other Developments" by H. B. Kohlmeier; "Liturgics" by Rev. Erwin William Emil Kurth (1898–1989); "The Transition to Valparaiso" by A. Krentz; and "The Deaconess of Tomorrow" by O. P. Kretzmann.[32]

---

[31] "Silver Anniversary Deaconess Conference," *TLD* 21, no. 3 (July 1944): 3.
[32] Schmidt was Executive Secretary of Foreign Missions for the Missouri Synod.
"Conference of Deaconess [*sic*]: Silver Anniversary," *TLD* 21, no. 2 (April 1944): 4.

About 300 persons enjoyed a festive anniversary banquet in the college's dining hall. Concordia's string quartet provided dinner music. LDA Vice-president Foelber was Master of Ceremonies and Dr. P.E. Kretzmann of Concordia Seminary, St. Louis, delivered the principal banquet speech. The celebration culminated in a silver anniversary service held in the "beautiful Concordia (College) Chapel."[33]

CONFORMING TO THE EDUCATIONAL SET-UP

Pastor Krentz believed that the whole "Transition to Valparaiso" boded well for the deaconess school and its students. In handwritten notes, very likely used to prepare his silver anniversary speech, Krentz wrote:

> In conclusion, rich three years. Things have moved rapidly in our Deaconess Work. As you know, our Education has changed from semester to semester. In a constant state of flux. A good sign. Static education in a changing world society will definitely lag behind. Last semester, some work in psychiatry, mental cases more prevalent. There will be more changes in our course of study as time goes on. We must grow and not become stratified in our thinking or teaching. World conditions are a challenge to deaconess training as never before. Feel my responsibility very keenly . . .

> We peer painstakingly into the future. What will the coming years bring for Lutheran Deaconess Work? My firm conviction is that the best is yet to come, that the second quarter century will see our work expanded. I believe that our connection to the University will give much needed prestige to our work. I believe we shall attract more young women for this work. I believe that Lutheran Waves, Wacs and Marines will be one of the sources of supply for students when the war is over. I believe we should extend our work in institutional work, especially on the administrative basis. I believe that parish work will expand in the coming years. Signs on the horizon point to this.

> Let us commend our work of the future to Almighty God. Let Him renew our vision and give us the proper perspective. Let Him be our guide and guardian. Let Him bless our workers. I will. Let Jesus' words still ring in our ears, motivate us to renewed vigor: ('Let her alone; she hath wrought a good work in me.') Woman, great is they faith.[34]

---

[33] "Silver Anniversary Banquet," TLD 21, no. 4 (October 1944): 2; "Silver Anniversary Deaconess Conference," 4.

[34] Krentz, "Transition from Ft. Wayne to Valparaiso," 3-4.

In the fall of 1944, a few months into the deaconess school's second academic year in Valparaiso, the LDA took a close look at itself and its training program and began to make some of those adjustments anticipated by Krentz.

> The Association passed several resolutions. 1. The Association acted upon the suggestion of Pastor [Paul] Miller[35] and lowered the entrance age to "upon graduation from high school." 2. The Association voted to authorize the Board to enlarge itself from nine to fifteen members. 3. The Board was asked to rethink and restudy the objectives of the Association and to formulate plans in accordance with them and the times in which we are now living.[36]

The first resolution made the entrance requirements for the deaconess school essentially identical to the entrance requirements for Valparaiso University. After the LDA consolidated its three training schools into one central school in 1935, students came to the deaconess program as graduate nurses, teachers, social welfare workers, or in possession of other professional training. From this point forward, women only needed a high school diploma to apply. The LDA believed that deaconess students could learn everything they needed within the contexts of the university campus and fieldwork sites. The latter, of course, included specialized instruction at the Deaconess Chapter House.

A PERMANENT SOLUTION

The decisions made at the 1944 LDA meeting indicate that a major shift in thinking had occurred regarding the deaconess training school, though this change was never officially articulated or announced. Stated simply, the location of the training school at Valparaiso was no longer experimental, but permanent. The confidence in this idea probably developed quickly for two reasons: Krentz's outspoken enthusiasm about the university setting and, just as importantly, the earnest attention that university president O. P. Kretzmann gave to the LDA and the work of the diaconate.

---

[35] Paul Miller served as secretary of the Lutheran University Association in 1935; a member of the Valparaiso University Board of Directors from 1925-1951; the pastor of St. Paul's Lutheran Church, Fort Wayne, first as assistant to his father and then as senior pastor, from 1910 until his retirement in 1950.

[36] The "times in which we are now living" was an allusion to World War II and everything that being at war meant to life within the United States and other countries where the diaconate hoped to serve. The war already affected deaconess placements and travel plans for women working in foreign missions. "The Annual Meeting," TLD 22, no. 1 (January 1945): 2.

Kretzmann's interest in involving his university with deaconess training became evident even before the LDA was forced to sell its motherhouse in Fort Wayne.[37] Once the move to Valparaiso had taken place, his name was immediately associated with the school. In January 1944, regarding the annual LDA meeting held in October 1943, *TLD* reported:

> . . . The major step in Deaconess Work during the past year was in the sale of the Deaconess Home in Ft. Wayne to the Lutheran Hospital Association and the transfer of Deaconess Training to Valparaiso, Ind. Here an educational set-up has been reached with Valparaiso University so that our deaconess students receive a part of their deaconess training at the University. This *new experiment*[38] in Deaconess Training is, we have been informed, being watched with interest not only within our Synod, but within other Lutheran Church bodies. President O. P. Kretzmann of Valparaiso University spoke at the meeting about this new venture in deaconess education at Valparaiso, and the superintendent dwelt on this phase of this work in his annual report. . . .[39]

The next issue of *TLD* (April 1944) contained the proposed program for the silver anniversary Conference of Deaconesses that listed President Kretzmann as speaking on "The Deaconess of Tomorrow." Page three of the following magazine (July 1944) featured a photo of Kretzmann, vested in cassock and surplice in front of an altar, with the caption: "President Kretzmann opened the door of Valparaiso University to deaconess students." An article on page seven of the same magazine paid tribute to all previous and present members of the LDA Board of Directors, with the rather surprising closing sentence: "Dr. O. P. Kretzmann, Valparaiso University, is advisory member of the Board."[40] Kretzmann held this position for the entire time that he was president of the university.[41] The

---

[37] "Seeing Stars," *TLD* 19, no. 3 (July 1942): 8.

[38] Emphasis added by author. This is the last time that the "educational set-up" at Valparaiso is called an "experiment" in *TLD*.

[39] "Annual Meeting of the Lutheran Deaconess Association," *TLD* 21, no. 1 (January 1944), 2.

[40] H. B. Kohlmeier, no title, *TLD* 21, no. 3 (July 1944), 3,7.

[41] O. P. Kretzmann's name appears on every list of individuals on the LDA Board of Directors published in *TLD*, up through the last list printed in the July 1960 magazine. The minutes of Board meetings after that period show that he personally attended meetings (and even special committee meetings) whenever possible. On his retirement from the Presidency of Valparaiso in 1968, the LDA presented Kretzmann with a "special plaque of recognition of these 25 years of association in deaconess education and for his more than 25 years of personal interest, support, and promotion of deaconess ministry." "Board of Directors," *TLD* 37, no. 3 (July 1960): 4; "O. P. Kretzmann Honored," *TLD* 45, no. 2 (Summer 1968), 7; Dorothy Liebmann, "Lutheran Deaconess Association Plenary Board Meeting April 19,

fact that Kretzmann was also Secretary of the LCMS BHE (from 1938–1953) made him an important ally for the Deaconess Cause.

LENGTHENING THE DEACONESS COURSE

As the LDA Board of Directors reviewed the organization's objectives, it came to the conclusion that the academic part of deaconess training should be somewhat longer. In April 1945 *TLD* announced:

> Progressive Deaconess Education. The course of study has again been lengthened, this time to two years; in 1941 it had been lengthened to a year and a half. The length of the internship remains at six months. Thus deaconesses receive two and a half years of preparation for their work.[42]

One year later, convinced that a college degree would better prepare deaconesses for their work in the modern world, the Board of Directors brought the LDA into a closer educational partnership with the university.

> On April 26, 1946, the Board of Directors of the Lutheran Deaconess Association assembled in St. Paul's School, Ft. Wayne, Ind., passed the resolution to extend the Deaconess Training Course at Valparaiso University to a four-year college course. This is undoubtedly the greatest academic step taken during the twenty-seven years of deaconess history within the Synodical Conference.

> Prior to this a momentous meeting had been held in Dr. O. P. Kretzmann's office at Valparaiso University—see picture on front cover. The purpose of this historic meeting was to plan the future of deaconess education at Valparaiso University. Representatives of the University were President O. P. Kretzmann, Dean Walter G. Friedrich and from the Department of Religion Dean H. H. Kumnick and Rev. Luther Koepke— Rev. Armin Oldson was unable to be present. Representing the Deaconess Association were President Walter Klausing, Vice-President E.E. Foelber, and Arnold Krentz.

> After considering the education of our deaconesses it was readily agreed upon by all representatives present that the education of our deaconesses should be a full four-year course leading to the A.B. degree.[43] Valparaiso University will extend its course of study in Religion so that a major will be offered in this department. . . . Doubtless the clergy and the laity

---

1968, Box: Board for Professional Education Services Box 5: Deaconess Materials and BHE Materials, found loose at front of box, CHI, St. Louis, Mo.

[42] "Station LDA," *TLD* 22, no. 2 (April 1945): 8.

[43] The A.B. degree was a Bachelor of Arts degree, eventually called the "B.A." instead.

throughout our Church will heartily approve this very progressive step of putting Deaconess education on a full-college basis.

The new plan will be put into operation this coming fall semester.[44]

VALPARAISO IMPLEMENTS CHANGES

A Bachelor of Arts degree with a major in Religion was an exciting step for the LDA and also for the university. A Department of Religion had been established at Valparaiso in 1928, combined with Philosophy in 1929, and then re-established as a separate department again in 1941. However, Valpo only offered a major in Religion from 1928–32, and since it took four years to earn a Bachelor of Arts, degrees with a major in Religion could only have been conferred in 1932.[45] No wonder Krentz acclaimed the major in Religion, reinstated for deaconess students, to be an "academic victory."[46]

During the 1945–46 academic year, Valparaiso's Department of Religion offered a meager six courses: *The Bible* and *Jesus and His Teachings*, taught by "The Staff" and required of all students; *The Church and Her Work* and *History of Early Christianity* instructed by Rev. Henry Herman Kumnick (1891–1965); *Christian Ethics* taught by President O. P. Kretzmann; *Christianity and Modern Problems* taken by both Kretzmann and Rev. Adolph Theodore Esais Haentzschel (1881–1971).[47] In 1946–47 the university bolstered the number of Religion courses to thirteen, including *Principles of Religious Education* taught by Superintendent Krentz.[48] The requirements for a major or minor in Religion were also printed in the course catalog for that year:

---

[44] "Full College Course for Deaconess Students," *TLD* 23, no. 3 (July 1946): 2.

[45] Email to CDN from Mel Doering, Archivist, Valparaiso University, Valparaiso, Indiana, October 13, 2005, priv. col. of CDN, Pittsburgh, Pa.

[46] "Station LDA," *TLD* 23, no. 3 (July 1946): 6.

[47] Pastors Oldsen and Krentz are also listed as members of the Department of Religion, though there is nothing written to indicate which courses they taught. *1945-1946 Course Catalog for Valparaiso University College of Arts and Sciences*, 98-99, Archives, Valparaiso University Christopher Center, Valparaiso, Ind.

[48] By 1950, twenty-one different Religion classes appeared in the catalog. The number of teachers for the Department of Religion also increased. New names up through 1950 included Adolph Peter Louis Wismar (1884-1977), Luther Paul Koepke (1917-2000), Ernest Benjamin Koenker (b.1920), Carl Albert Gieseler (1888-1965), Robert Walter Bertram (1921-2003), Richard Henry Luecke (b.1923), and Ross Paul Scherer (1922-1999). *1946-1947 Course Catalog for Valparaiso University College of Arts and Sciences*, 109-110; *1948-1949 Course Catalog for Valparaiso University College of Arts and Sciences*, 114-115; *1950-1951 Course Catalog for Valparaiso University College of Arts and Sciences*, 126-27.

This department offers instruction in the sources, history, and teaching of Christianity. Its aim is not only to lay a solid foundation for Christian thinking, but also to stimulate the translation of Christian thought into life and conduct. The distinctive doctrines of the Christian Church receive special emphasis.

MAJOR—Twenty-four credit hours of religion are required of students taking a major in this department.

MINOR—Twelve credit hours of religion are required of students taking a minor in this department.[49]

The *1947–48 Course Catalog* amended the definition of a major to "twenty-four credit hours *beyond Religion 51 (Introduction to the Bible)*" and updated the objectives for the Department of Religion to accommodate the university's agreement with the LDA:

The aims of this department are (1) to acquaint the student with the sources, development, and teachings of Christianity, (2) to set forth the relevance of Christianity for the present age, (3) to prepare students for greater lay service in the church, and (4) to provide the courses in religion required by the deaconess training program offered by Valparaiso University.[50]

The wording of the fourth point in the above paragraph is worth noting. It indicates that at the outset of this new venture with the LDA, the university administration viewed—or at least wished to portray—the deaconess training program as being "offered by Valparaiso University," just like other programs that might be offered by the university. No mention is made of the LDA. The "courses in religion required" for deaconess training are obviously all offered by the university. This change became made more apparent in the *1948–49 Course Catalog,* which listed *The Field of Deaconess Work* as a credited university course, though open "only to seniors in the deaconess training program." For several years Krentz team-taught this course with Rev. Luther Koepke, Valparaiso's academic advisor for deaconess students, who displayed a keen interest in working out the best possible curriculum for them.[51]

Building the deaconess training program on university classes brought new structure, prestige, and educational opportunities unknown to the training program in former decades. It also meant that the LDA would no

---

49 1946-1947 Course Catalog for Valparaiso University College of Arts and Sciences, 109.
50 1947-1948 Course Catalog for Valparaiso University College of Arts and Sciences, 114.
51 1948-1949 Course Catalog for Valparaiso University College of Arts and Sciences, 115. Photo and information about Koepke is located in TLD 24, no. 2 (April 1947): 3.

longer have full supervision over the "religion" taught to deaconess students. Indeed, the set-up had evolved far beyond the original intention for religious education to remain in the hands of the Superintendent. Furthermore, Valparaiso was, from this point forward, in a position to make various demands of the women in order for them to acquire a Bachelor of Arts degrees. None of this appeared to be problematic to Krentz. He thrilled to watch the program blossom with each new semester, enjoying his teaching of the deaconess students and also the non-deaconess students who registered for his lectures in *Principles of Religious Education*.[52]

PUBLIC AFFIRMATION

Recorded reactions to the progressive changes in deaconess education, like the following article that appeared in *The St. Louis Lutheran*, were overwhelmingly positive in nature.

> Expansion of the Deaconess Training course at Valparaiso University into a full four-year college course, as announced in this issue of the St. Louis Lutheran, is another indication that those who have been entrusted with the guidance of the deaconess cause are determined to place it on a high level of usefulness. That usefulness has been somewhat impaired by a number of obsolete aspects, such as the lack of adequate renumeration [*sic*] for the deaconesses, the employment of deaconesses in services which might have been performed by persons without special training, the awkward provisions for security for deaconesses in their old age, and a training that did not measure up to the potentialities of deaconess work. Our young women in general were not attracted to a service that was patterned after concepts that belonged to another age and required sacrifices that were not required of any other group in the Church.
>
> Now that the deaconess calling has been largely divested of these aspects, the young women of our Church need no longer hesitate to enter upon the calling of deaconesses, for it is church work, spiritual work, blessed work.
>
> The American point of view is accustomed to the feminine approach in social, educational, and religious services. This sympathetic attitude should be exploited for the sake of the Gospel. Also in foreign mission work the services of deaconesses are not only desirable, but practically indispensable, owing to Oriental customs. May, then, the young women

---

[52] Krentz, "Transition from Ft. Wayne to Valparaiso," 3-4.

of our Church be motivated to enter upon deaconess work in large numbers.[53]

TUITION SCHOLARSHIPS

In October 1943, the first issue of *TLD* to be published after the training school moved to Valparaiso featured an article proposing student scholarships.

> A friend of the Deaconess Cause recently made the suggestion to us that we should work for student scholarships. The idea appeals to us. The suggestion has much in its favor in view of the fact that the Deaconess Association now pays the tuition fees of its students at Valparaiso University where they receive the major part of their training. Such scholarships would enable the Association to meet its larger financial obligations.
>
> Perhaps some ladies' aid society may favor us with a scholarship for one of our students. Or some individual Christian may feel the urge to give us this needed assistance.
>
> Who will make history by establishing the first scholarship? Wouldn't it be encouraging if several scholarships would be established, perhaps one from Indiana, a second from Michigan, a third from Wisconsin, a fourth from Illinois, a fifth from California! Who will lead the way?[54]

A swift answer to the challenge was announced in the January 1944 magazine:

> Miss Clara E. Strodel, of La Grange, Ill., has helped make Deaconess History. She has established the first scholarship for a deaconess-student in our new set-up at Valparaiso, Ind.
>
> We quote from her letter: "I should like to establish the scholarship in memory of my sainted parents, Mr. and Mrs. William (Carolena) Strodel, and am enclosing a check of $100.00 for the cause of the 'woman in blue,' as you refer to it."
>
> Our conviction is that there are other friends of this noble work who will follow Miss Strodel's lead. . . . Scholarships may be established in amounts of fifty, one hundred, or two hundred dollars.[55]

---

[53] Article in *The St. Louis Lutheran* (no date given), as reprinted in *TLD* 23, no. 3 (July 1946): 4.
[54] "Deaconess Scholarships," *TLD* 20, no. 4 (October 1943): 2.
[55] "First Scholarship Established," *TLD* 21, no. 1 (January 1944): 4.

Whoever "our" was, their conviction was correct. Subsequent issues of *TLD* continued to report the receipt of more gifts to establish scholarships: a second from an anonymous couple referred to as Mr. and Mrs. N. N. (Fort Wayne); a third from Miss Leona Schroeder (Detroit, Mich.); and then four at once, from Mr. E.O. Kucher (New Haven, Ind.), Mr. G.N. Kucher (Pittsburgh, Pa.), Mrs. Martha Seifrid (Pittsburgh, Pa.), and Mrs. G.N. Mueller (Pitcairn, Pa.). In January 1945, Mr. Charles Goetting (Sturgis, Mich.) and the first congregation (Trinity Lutheran of Sturgis, Mich.) joined the list of scholarship contributors, while Miss Strodel renewed her initial gift for another year.[56] Over the next several years, deaconess auxiliaries, Sunday Schools, LWML districts, local ladies' guilds and other Lutheran fellowship groups established more scholarships.[57] By the time the 1949-1950 academic year rolled around, each of the 34 deaconess students enrolled at Valparaiso would receive a scholarship of $150 from the LDA—the exact amount needed to cover 100 percent of their university tuition bills.[58]

OTHER FINANCIAL STRATEGIES

Soliciting scholarships for women to be educated within a university setting made good sense for fund raising. Plus, the ability to promise scholarships to prospective students proved an effective recruitment tool. A similar idea took shape in the formation of a "Library Fund" for the purchase of library books and textbooks. Again, contribution amounts and contributors were regularly publicized in *TLD*.[59]

One of the keys to the LDA Board's overall fund raising strategy was for Krentz to maintain a high personal profile with new and old donors. His calendar diaries and the accounts of his activities published in *TLD* indicate that he often traveled around the country when not teaching at Valparaiso.[60] Sometimes Krentz spoke at mission festivals, where the LDA would receive a portion of the offering along with other mission endeavors,

---

[56] "Second Scholarship Established," *TLD* 21, no. 2 (April 1944): 8; "Third Scholarship Established," *TLD* 21, no. 3 (July 1944): 2; "Four Scholarships Established," *TLD* 21, no. 4 (October 1944): 7; "New Scholarships," *TLD* 22, no. 1 (January 1945): 7.

[57] "Two Scholarships Established," *TLD* 22, no. 3 (July 1945): 2; "Two Scholarships Given," *TLD* 23, no. 2 (April 1946): 3; "Scholarship Specials," *TLD* 23, no. 3 (July 1946): 3; "Scholarship Specials," *TLD* 24, no. 4 (October 1947): 2.

[58] "Scholarship Specials," *TLD* 26, no. 3 (July 1949): 4.

[59] "Our Library Fund: Watch it Grow," *TLD* 20, no. 4 (October 1943): 8.

[60] Arnold F. Krentz, diaries from 1941-60.

but just as frequently, he preached at Sunday services, emphasizing the church's great need for deaconess work.[61]

> St. Peter's Lutheran congregation at Fuelling's Settlement, near Decatur, Ind., the Rev. Karl Hoffmann, Pastor, has set aside one Sunday in the year in the interest of Woman's Work in the Church. The writer preaches in the congregation, and the congregation raises an offering for the work.
>
> Brethren, we need more congregations to establish a Deaconess Sunday. Which congregation will follow in setting this new custom? In the Augustana Synod much stress is laid upon Deaconess Sunday. It would seem as though our Synod will give such a Sunday wider observance in the future.[62]

Krentz knew that to secure the future of the diaconate in the Synodical Conference, and in particular, within the Missouri Synod, he needed the cooperation of parish pastors. Two months after the training school moved to Valpo, Krentz made a visit to both LCMS seminaries, speaking to the entire student body at "our Springfield Seminary" and the Mission Society at "our St. Louis Seminary."[63] When the LDA observed its 25th anniversary, all 5,300 pastors of the Synodical Conference received a "beautiful Silver Anniversary pamphlet on Lutheran Deaconess Service," along with an attractive "memorial folder."[64] In 1946, desiring to augment this line of communication, the LDA began sending copies of *TLD* to all Synodical Conference pastors. Ten years later, the magazines went out in bulk to LCMS schools, so that every one of Synod's parish teachers could have a copy.[65]

THE HOUSING CRUNCH

Once the four-year degree program was in place and the LDA could almost guarantee scholarships to deaconess students, enrollment began to increase quickly. Krentz freely shared his dream to have 1000 deaconess students, even printing his hopes in *TLD*.[66] Of course, an increased number of students brought certain logistical problems, the most immediate being the

---

[61] For examples, see "Financial Favors," *TLD* 20, no. 3 (July 1943): 7; "Preaching on our Work," *TLD* 21, no. 1 (January 1944): 8.

[62] "Deaconess Sunday," *TLD* 20, no 4 (October 1943): 8.

[63] "Seminarians Hear About Deaconess Work," *TLD* 21, no. 1 (January 1944): 3.

[64] "Station LDA Fourth Broadcast," *TLD* 21, no. 4 (October 1944): 6.

[65] "5,900 Copies of the Lutheran Deaconess," *TLD* 23, no. 4 (October 1946): 4; "The Lutheran Deaconess Sent to all Parish School Teachers," *TLD* 33, no. 2 (April 1956): 2.

[66] "Station LDA," *TLD* 24, no. 1 (January 1947): 6.

provision of suitable accommodation. In April 1948, student Elaine Davis wrote:

> We are faced with a staggering housing problem at the Deaconess Chapter House. Fourteen girls sleep in three bedrooms. Double bunks in each room make it possible to place four girls in the smallest room which ordinarily would barely hold a double bed and bedroom suite. Here four girls are expected to sleep and study. Six girls sleep in the largest bedroom. All are not able to study at desks in their room at the same time.
>
> Although sleeping accommodations and proper studying arrangements are major problems, the worst result of such close uncomfortable conditions is the necessary atmosphere of restrained expression if consideration for others is to be observed. All are in such close association with each other that the various duties and activities of one person are likely to interfere seriously with the study and concentration of another.[67]

The LDA continued to rent the Deaconess Chapter House for its students. But before the next academic year started, the association purchased the home next to the Chapter House for $7,000 and spent another $5,000 renovating it. The new residence was christened "Chapter House Annex" and designated as living quarters for the upperclass women.[68] The Annex was only a stopgap measure, however. In November 1946, at its annual meeting held at St. Paul's Lutheran Church in Fort Wayne, the LDA had anticipated this situation and committed itself to a long-term solution.

> The following resolution was adopted by the Association:
>
> Whereas our deaconess student enrollment is steadily increasing, and
>
> Whereas it is difficult to rent adequate quarters for our purposes,
>
> Therefore:
>
> Be it resolved that we start a Building Fund for the purpose of ultimately erecting our own building to house Lutheran deaconess students.[69]

Krentz began using *TLD* to request donations to the Building Fund while still encouraging gifts to the scholarship fund, library fund, and general deaconess work.[70] By January 1949 the Building Fund held over five

---

[67] Elaine Davis, "Deaconess Chapter House," *TLD* 25, no. 2 (April 1948): 5.

[68] "Chapter House Annex," *TLD* 25, no. 4 (October 1948): 8.

[69] H. H. Backs, "Annual Meeting," *TLD* 24, no. 1 (January 1947): 8.

[70] "Building Fund: The First Thousand Dollars," *TLD* 24, no. 2 (April 1947): 4; "The Financial Picture," *TLD* 26, no. 1 (January 1949): 7.

thousand dollars, which was not as high as the LDA had hoped. At that point, a rather desperate letter was sent to all known LDA benefactors and magazine subscribers.

AN URGENT PLEA

The Lutheran Deaconess Association houses its deaconess students in the Deaconess Chapter House and its Annex.

In the Deaconess Chapter House the study desks are next to the doubledecker beds. In the Annex about ten students study in one room. Such conditions are not conducive to the best study habits.

But our major problem continues to be: More housing space, a large building for the mounting number of our students.

The estimated cost of a new building to house sixty students is $150,000.00—probably the estimate is too low. To date $5,416.00 have [*sic*] been contributed for the new Chapter House.

Here is an opportunity for you to contribute either a large or a small sum to this needed undertaking.

Are you in favor of providing a new building for deaconess students, future workers in our Church? Of course you are.

Will you send in a contribution for this proposed new building? We trust you will.[71]

At no time did the LDA refer to the desired new building as a future motherhouse or even as a Deaconess Home. With all of the changes put into place for consecrated deaconesses serving in the field, the concepts associated with such titles were too out of vogue to be resurrected again. The sole reason given for needing a new Chapter House was to provide lodging for deaconess students while they studied at Valparaiso University. The residence hall would certainly need to have space for the women to gather together for devotions and a place to prepare and eat meals, but these details would not actually be developed for several years.

PRESSING FINANCIAL NEEDS

As the Deaconess Training Program moved into the 1950s, the Superintendent spent an increasing amount of time on financial concerns.

---

[71] Arnold F. Krentz, "An Urgent Plea," mimeographed page, tucked inside January 1949 copy of *TLD*, priv. col. of Clara Strehlow, Deaconess Office Archives, Concordia University, RF, Illinois.

TLD reflected this reality. The focus of the magazine shifted somewhat, so that fewer articles featured the dedicated work of consecrated deaconesses, while more reported the needs of students and the training program. Sometimes entire pages were devoted to lists of donors. Krentz tried to add variety to the presentation of statistics. For example, alongside a "Register of Student Deaconesses According to States," he included a tally of quarterly contributions to the LDA, not mentioning the benefactors, but listing the total amount of money received from any U.S. state, Canadian province, or LWML district.[72]

Despite what seemed like a preoccupation with money matters, annual financial reports from the LDA treasurer "showed that the Association was operating on a very sound financial basis."[73] The housing issue now needed to be resolved. In the fall of 1952, twenty-six women lived in the Chapter House and Annex, with another twenty-three students in private residents one to three blocks away![74] Small and moderate gifts were already arriving. The most pressing challenge was to generate gifts of substantially larger sums of money for the Building Fund, or the new Chapter House might never be built.

FINALLY SOME BIG BREAKS

While soliciting funds from within congregations, Krentz had been wary of upsetting pastors who were already encouraging their parishioners to contribute to special LCMS synodical appeals. The LDA often said, and widely publicized that, "no synodical funds are allotted to Deaconess work, and this budget is raised wholly through gifts and donations."[75] Thus the association went to the Missouri Synod administration to secure official permission to solicit funds from within its ranks.

On March 13, 1953, at a meeting of the LCMS Board of Directors (BOD), the board's Committee two recommended to Committee three, "after examining the entire Lutheran Deaconess Association program, that the association be granted permission to solicit $250,000 for a building at

---

[72] "Register of Student Deaconesses According to States 1950-1951," and "Favorable Finances," *TLD* 28, no. 2 (April 1951): 3.
[73] "Deaconess Association Annual Meeting," *TLD* 30, no. 1 (January 1953): 8.
[74] "A Most Pressing Problem: Adequate Housing for our Students," *TLD* 29, no. 4 (October 1952): 2.
[75] "Help *diakonia*," 16 in. x 18 in. poster, (Fort Wayne: LDA), LCMS Indiana District Archives, Fort Wayne, Ind.

Valparaiso University."[76] Committee three concurred, and the BOD adopted the recommendation after amending it "to limit this (solicitation of funds) to the central area of Synod."[77] A second big break came in July 1953, at the Fifth Biennial Convention of the Lutheran Women's Missionary League held in Portland, Oregon. The league's "ballot for Projects" listed five possible mission endeavors:

1. Home for Deaconess Students, Valparaiso
2. School for Deaf, Mill Neck Manor, Long Island
3. Chapel for Mexican Missions, Los Angeles
4. Retreat Homes for Missionaries, South America, Japan, Philippine Islands
5. Churches and schools, equipment for hospital, Calabar Region, Eket, Africa

Convention delegates chose three projects, including the "Home for Deaconess Students," and pledged $60,000 to the LDA Building Fund in the coming biennium.[78]

TWO STEPS FORWARD, ONE STEP BACK

In fall 1953, congregations began to request "envelopes for the Deaconess cause" to be added to the annual envelope packets they ordered from CPH.[79] This sort of in-house contribution method had obvious advantages, including the assumed support of the local pastor and district president. Krentz worked hard to move the financial campaign forward in several districts. In January 1954 he wrote:

> District Boards of Directors have expressed themselves in favor of allowing the Deaconess Association permission to collect within their districts almost without exception. It was a pleasure to address the following district boards in the interest of our building program: Michigan, Central (president and Stewardship comm.), Northern Illinois,

---

[76] "Seventeenth Meeting of the Bd. of Dir. 3/13/53," 530313-B: Report of Committee 2, *Board of Directors Missouri Synod July 1950 to May 1953*, 305, CHI, St. Louis, Mo.

[77] "Seventeenth Meeting of the Bd. of Dir. 3/13/53," 530313-D: Report of Committee 3, 308, CHI, St. Louis, Mo.

[78] When the new "Home for Deaconess Students" was complete, a plaque in the main lounge read: "In Grateful Appreciation to the Lutheran Women's Missionary League for the $60,000 Project Grant Toward the Erection of Deaconess Hall." Mrs. E.A. Eggert, "Proceedings of the LWML," 1953, mimeograph pages, 1, 4-5, 18, 23, LWML Minutes, CHI, St. Louis, Mo. Clara Strehlow, "Deaconesses Are Missionaries," *Lutheran Woman's Quarterly* 18, no. 2 (April 1960): 3-4, 30.

[79] "For Your Envelope Packet," *TLD* 30, no. 4 (October 1953): 4.

Central Illinois, Southern Illinois, North Wisconsin, South Wisconsin, Western, Southern Nebraska, Northern Nebraska, Kansas, and Minnesota. Other districts in the central section of Synod have not yet held district board meetings since our campaign has been set into motion.

Reactions such as these were received from district boards. The Deaconess Association may set $50,000 as its goal in our district; or—the collection for these funds is heartily approved and a district committee of a pastor, layman and woman will be appointed by our district president. Another district resolved to give its mailing list to the Association for contacting individual families. We are grateful for all such encouraging reactions.[80]

The architectural firm engaged for the new Deaconess Chapter House was Forese, Maack and Becker, the same company that designed the LCMS synodical building located at 210 North Broadway in St. Louis.[81]

Everything seemed to be moving forward for the deaconess cause within the Synodical Conference, and particularly within the Missouri Synod—at least until some un-named individuals began to question the wisdom of a single-project financial campaign when other special interest groups also needed funds. Krentz explained a change of plans:

The Board of Directors of the Lutheran Deaconess Association set the machinery into motion to conduct this campaign for capital expansion. Mr. W.C. Dickmeyer, Fort Wayne, Ind., declared his willingness to serve as General Chairman of the campaign.[82] The Rev. Arthur Hanser, Baldwin, N.Y., became the Campaign Consultant, who laid out a very workable campaign for our Association.[83] District Boards of Directors granted us permission to collect within their districts. District Committees were set up and Field Men appointed.

However, the Board of Directors of Synod, the Survey and Findings Committee of Synod established at the Houston Convention, and the Council of Lutheran Agencies, of which the LDA is a member,[84] feel that

[80] "Building Fund Campaign $250,000," *TLD* 31, no. 1 (January 1954): 2.
[81] "Station LDA Tune In," *TLD* 30, no. 3 (July 1953): 6.
[82] Layman Dickmeyer was president of Wayne Candies, Inc., Fort Wayne. He was president of the Lutheran University Association for many years and continued to be an active member of the VU Board of Directors until 1966.
[83] Arthur Robert Gottlob Hanser (1880-1955).
[84] In 1950 delegates at the LCMS convention in Milwaukee resolved to set up a coordinating council of the various auxiliary agencies associated with the Synod. The Council of Lutheran Agencies organized in Chicago, with the LDA as one of its twelve members. At the 1953 LCMS convention in Houston, delegates voted "that the LCMS recognize the Council of Lutheran Agencies and approve its organization and purposes" and that Synod "officially

it would be better for the Deaconess Association to participate in a unified campaign which will presumably be conducted in 1955. The Board of Directors of the Lutheran Deaconess Association resolved to follow the directive of the Board of Directors of Synod to channel its campaign into this larger effort which will include several agencies. No doubt our pastors and congregations prefer a campaign of a larger dimension to a series of campaigns.[85]

"BUILDING FOR CHRIST" COLLECTION

The subsequent "Building for Christ" campaign sanctioned by the Missouri Synod expected to benefit five non-synodical agencies through the collection of five million dollars: $250,000 for the LDA; $150,000 for Mill Neck School for the Deaf; $400,000 for World Relief and Refugee Service; $1,700,000 for Bethesda Lutheran Home; and $2,500,000 for Valparaiso University.[86]

The "Building for Christ" collection was largely successful, bringing $223,168 into the LDA Building Fund![87]

Tonn and Blank, Inc. won the contract to erect the new LDA structure after offering the lowest of six bids ($408,916). Of course, the contract fee did not include architect's costs or furnishings for the Chapter House, so the real anticipated cost was $481,000. Combining the "Building for Christ"

---

commend these intra-Synodical agencies to its Districts, Circuits and congregations and urge them to give these agencies liberal and continued financial support, also remember them in their prayers so that they may continue to serve our Lord and master, Jesus Christ, to their fullest potential." "Report and Recommendations on Non-Budget Items," in LCMS, *Proceedings*, 1950, 767-768; "Overtures of the Council of Lutheran Agencies: Overture 1 and Overture 2," in LCMS, *Proceedings*, 1953, 749.

[85] "The Deaconess Campaign to Raise $250,000 for a new Deaconess Chapter House," *TLD* 31, no. 2 (April 1954): 2.

[86] The same LWML Biennial Convention that voted to give $60,000 to the LDA resolved to decline any allocation of money for building a church on the campus of Valparaiso University. Mill Neck Manor School was on the ballot but not chosen as one of the three national projects for the biennium. The unified campaign gave these organizations an opportunity to work together, rather than compete for funds. Eggert, "Proceedings of the LWML," 5; "'Building for Christ' Five Appeals But One Collection," *TLD* 31, no. 4 (October 1954): 5; "The Meeting of the College of Presidents, The Lutheran Building, Saint Louis, Missouri, May 4-6, 1954," *Minutes 1951-1969 Council of Presidents*, no pagination, but reference should be made to the third and fourth page of the document, CHI, St. Louis, Mo.

[87] Moneys given to the other agencies also indirectly aided deaconesses or the deaconess cause: deaconess training was located at Valparaiso; one deaconess taught at Mill Neck School; four deaconesses worked at Bethesda; and foreign deaconesses were aided in their work by World Relief. "Moneys Available for Deaconess Hall," *TLD* 34, no. 1 (January 1957): 2.

collection, LWML grant, and $23,000 from individuals and societies, the LDA had just over $306,000 at its disposal. To make up the shortfall, the LCMS BOD granted permission to the LDA to borrow up to $175,000.[88] By July 1955, the association had moved forward with the purchase of some prime property.

> The Lutheran Deaconess Association has purchased 4.4 acres of land in Valparaiso from Messrs. Clarence Barnes and James Ketterman. Purchase price was $5,000 an acre. . . . This will be the site of the new Deaconess Chapter House. Sufficient land was purchased to insure future expansion of buildings if and when that becomes necessary.

> This piece of land now owned by the Deaconess Association is bounded on the east, west, and south by the new Valparaiso University campus and on the north by property owned by Messrs. Barnes and Ketterman. It is ideally located for our new Deaconess Chapter House. According to the master plan of Valparaiso University the new library will be erected to the east of our property.[89]

The LDA broke ground on May 13, 1956, the same day that the largest jet Hydrogen bomb was to be detonated somewhere in the Pacific. Rev. Eugene Rudolph "Rudy" Bertermann (1914–1983), director of the "Building for Christ" campaign, delivered the main address for the ceremony. Bertermann assured those assembled "that in the Lord and under His guidance, the Deaconess Chapter House can have more 'power' in the world through those deaconesses whom it shelters as they prepare to serve, than the hydrogen bomb."[90] Rev. Edgar Henry Albers (1911–1996), President of the LDA, and Superintendent Krentz served as liturgists for the occasion. Others who participated in the "Rite of Groundbreaking" included President O. P. Kretzmann and Dean Luther Koepke representing the university; Mrs. Arthur Preisinger, President of the LWML; Deaconess Shirley Groh, LDA Field Secretary; and LDA Board members: Rev. Herman H. Backs (1905–2000), vice-president; Mrs. Paul F. Bente,

---

[88] G. R. Eckhardt (a partner of Yates, Heitner and Wood, St. Louis, Mo.) granted the desired loan of $175,000 at 4.5% interest for ten years. "Loan," *Deaconess Hall Adds Dimensions to Your Deaconess Program, The Annual Meeting November 8, 1957 Holy Cross Church, Fort Wayne, Indiana,* mimeograph, no pagination. "Contract Let for Deaconess Hall," *TLD* 34, no. 1 (January 1957): 2; "Moneys Available for Deaconess Hall," 2.

[89] "Land Purchased for Site of New Deaconess Chapter House," *TLD* 32, no. 3 (July 1955): 2.

[90] Bertermann was Executive Director of the *Lutheran Hour* for the Lutheran Laymen's League. "Ground Breaking for Deaconess Chapter House," *TLD* 33, no. 3 (July 1956): 8.

Secretary; Professor Paul F. Bente; Oscar Salzbrenner; Oscar Lehrmann; Hugo Boerger; and Pauline Krudop.[91]

Sometime between May and October the name of the new deaconess students' residence changed from Deaconess Chapter House to Deaconess Hall. The architect's drawings of the building also changed considerably from the first one that appeared in July 1953, showing a traditional plan with a pitched and gabled roof, to the final drawing published in October 1956 with a modern flat-roofed design.[92]

LAYING THE CORNERSTONE

The laying of the cornerstone of Deaconess Hall took place on June 2, 1957. O. P. Kretzmann served as liturgist and Adolph Haentzschel, recently retired as head of the VU philosophy department, gave an address in which he stressed Christ's love and the love of deaconesses expressed in service to Christ and their fellowmen. LDA Board member Oscar Salzbrenner enumerated and described the items placed into the cornerstone. Deaconess students sang a hymn of praise and Mr. John Graebner played the trumpet. Pastor Krentz laid the beautiful Indiana limestone cornerstone, which bore the inscription: "Lutheran Deaconess Hall, 1957, Let us not be weary in well doing.—Gal. 6:9."[93]

The following month it was announced that Mrs. Trautmann felt constrained to retire as director of the Deaconess House due to a heart ailment. How the deaconess students were supervised in their housing during the fall of 1957 is not clear, but when the new Hall finally opened in January 1958, Deaconess Clara Strehlow began serving as the first House Director of Deaconess Hall.[94]

---

[91] "Groundbreaking Service for the New Deaconess Chapter House Sunday May 13, 1956," printed service sheet, priv. col. of Clara Strehlow, Deaconess Office Archives, Concordia University, RF, Illinois.

[92] Drawings are on the front cover of *TLD* 30, no. 3 (July 1953) and on page 7 in *TLD* 33, no. 4 (October 1956).

[93] "Corner-Stone Laying of Lutheran Deaconess Hall," *TLD* 34, no. 3 (July 1957): 2.

[94] "Mrs. Sylvia Trautmann Resigns Because of Sickness," *TLD* 34, no. 3 (July 1957): 5; Deaconess Clara Strehlow, interview by Deaconesses Betty Mulholland and Nancy Nicol, transcript, Oshkosh, Wisconsin, November 12 and 13, 1982, priv. col. of Betty (Schmidt) Mulholland, Munster, Indiana, 8-9.

DEACONESS HALL OPENS

At last! Eleven years after resolving to raise money to build its own student lodgings, the LDA celebrated the completion of Deaconess Hall on January 12, 1958. The day resonated with ceremony—The Giving of the Key; The Opening of the Door; The Procession; The Dedication of the Building; The Placing of the Service Books; and the Lighting of the Candles—all within a larger "Service of Dedication" attended by about 350 people.[95] Guests of honor included presidents of the LWML and the Deaconess Conference; Rev. Walter Emil Bauer (1897–1987), Valpo's Dean of Faculty and Dean of the College of Arts and Sciences; and Rev. Walter Frederick William Lichtsinn (1889–1982), Third Vice-president of the Missouri Synod.[96]

The three floors and 236,000 cubic feet of Deaconess Hall contained bedrooms for 74 women, prayer nooks, dining room, kitchen, lounges, consultation room, recreation room, parlor library, house director's suite, office, piano practice rooms, laundry room, and a chapel which was considered to be the most beautiful feature of the building.[97]

> The chapel in Deaconess Hall has a seating capacity for 100 worshippers. The focal point of the chapel is the simple altar, set in recess, flanked by carved wooden screens. The screen on the left side depicts women of the Bible, Phoebe, Priscilla, Mary Magdalene, and Mary of Bethany. The other screen pictures modern deaconesses helping the handicapped in Institutions for the Mentally Retarded, Schools for the Deaf, Child Welfare Agencies or Homes for the Aged, or serving in parishes and in foreign missions. Stained glass windows depict the words of Christ, "I am the Vine, Ye are the Branches." The brick walls, lined with oak benches and lighted by candles, the lectern and kneeling benches combine to insure a churchly atmosphere.[98]

Protruding from the front of Deaconess Hall, the architect deliberately designed the exterior of the Chapel as the focal point of a frontal view of the building.

---

[95] "The Dedication of Lutheran Deaconess Hall, Valparaiso, Indiana: First Sunday after Epiphany, January 12, 1958, 3 p.m.," 13 page service folder, priv. col. of Clara Strehlow, Deaconess Office Archives, Concordia University, RF, Illinois.

[96] Although the service folder names President O. P. Kretzmann as a guest of honor, Bauer evidently took his place on the day. The photo caption mistakenly lists Bauer's middle initial as A. Photo caption, *TLD* 35, no. 2 (April 1958): 8.

[97] "New Chapter House of the Lutheran Deaconess Association to be built on the Campus of Valparaiso University," extra page tucked between pages 2 and 3 of *TLD* 31, no. 4 (October 1954).

[98] "The Chapel," *TLD* 35, no. 2 (April 1958): 2.

Unique will be the frontage of the chapel of Deaconess Hall, inasmuch as the figure of a young woman done in stone will meet the eyes of everyone who approaches the Hall.

This stone figure of the woman will be separate from the building proper to signify that young women will go forth from the Hall to serve their fellowmen. The idea of service will be indicated by having the woman's open hands turned downward. Before the statue of the woman, a rock will be placed to denote the trials and difficulties the deaconess will remove for mankind through her testimony of the redemption in Christ, the Savior.

Attached to and part of the wall will be a cross signifying that the Christ is the center of Deaconess Hall. Here resides the Savior, whom deaconess students worship privately in prayer chapels, and corporately each day at 6:30 p.m., in the chapel of the Hall. The stone figure, looking at the cross, shows that only the supreme sacrifice of Christ shall motivate and give the deaconess strength to serve others.

The whole idea of the carved stone figure of a woman looking at the cross is tied up with the motto of Deaconess Hall: Pi—*pistis*, faith; Delta—*diakonia*, service; Chi—*Christos*, Christ: Faith and Service in Christ. ... The cost of this beautiful statue will be borne by Deaconess Martha Eber.[99]

Indeed, the Chi Rho cross (about 18 feet tall) and the limestone statue (about 9 feet tall) formed an imposing witness. Sculptor William C. Severson (1924–1999) said of his work, "I should like to call my statue the 'Spirit of Love Eternal'—and hope that through the medium of my art to have expressed my respect and admiration for the Deaconess."[100] With due respect for the artist's sentiments, deaconess students fondly dubbed the statue "Phoebe," a nickname still used two decades later when this author lived in Deaconess Hall.[101]

---

[99] Eber gave $1,720 for the statue, in memory of her sainted mother. Other deaconesses raised $3,600 over two years, to provide items needed for the interior of the Chapel. "Statue of a Woman Symbolizing a Deaconess," *TLD* 35, no. 2 (April, 1958): 5; "Deaconesses Pledge for Chapel and Stone Figure," *TLD* 34, no. 1 (January 1957): 2.
[100] "The Dedication of Lutheran Deaconess Hall," 13 page service folder, 6.
[101] The specialized *Field of Deaconess Work* class included assigned readings from authors such as L.B. Buchheimer, who wrote: "There can be no doubt that the office of the diaconate of women is mentioned in Romans 16:1-2. The verses read: 'I commend unto you Phoebe, our sister . . .'" L.B. Buchheimer, "Highlights in the History of the Female Diaconate," *Concordia Theological Monthly* 21, no.4 (April 1950): 276.

TRANSFER STUDENTS

After the four-year training program was in place at Valparaiso, women began transferring to the university from other colleges in order to become deaconesses. Sometimes these students came from secular colleges and sometimes from Synodical Conference schools.[102] Women also began to ask permission to take their first two years of deaconess or "pre-deaconess" training on a campus closer to their own homes. The LDA developed informal understandings with various institutions in order to comply with these requests.

Interestingly, the Evangelical Lutheran Synod (ELS)—one of the Norwegian Lutheran synods that was part of the Synodical Conference—established a "Pre-Nursing or Pre-Deaconess" program at Bethany College in Mankato, Minnesota, in 1944 as part of a new "Four Year Junior College Plan."[103] In 1947, Krentz met with Dr. Sigurd C. Ylvisaker (1884–1959), president of Bethany and chairman of its Religion Department, who was "desirous of correlating the deaconess course at Bethany with the deaconess course at Valparaiso."[104] According to official ELS archives, the training program at Bethany lasted for twenty years and participants went on to Valparaiso University or other schools of their choice for further training. No evidence has been found, however, to show that a deaconess ever served within the ELS.[105]

In July 1955, *TLD* featured a map of the United States marked with eight numbered dots and accompanied by the text:

Two Year Pre-Deaconess Course now Offered at These Colleges:

Concordia College, Bronxville, N.Y.

Concordia College, Ft. Wayne, Indiana

Concordia College, St. Paul, Minn.

---

[102] Before the four-year training program was established, women with some college experience came to receive deaconess training, but they did not transfer to VU. For example, of the first five deaconess students at the Valparaiso site in 1943, one student studied for a semester at Concordia College in Bronxville, New York, and another studied for two years at the Teachers' College in River Forest, Illinois. "Our Students," *TLD* 20, no 4 (October 1943): 6.

[103] *1944 Bethany College Bulletin*, printed locally, 12-13, Department of Archives and History, Evangelical Lutheran Synod, Mankato, Minnesota.

[104] "Minnesota Memories," *TLD* 24, no. 3 (July 1947): 8.

[105] Letters from Paul G. Madison, Archivist, Department of Archives and History, Evangelical Lutheran Synod, Mankato, Minnesota, to CDN, October 24, 2005 and October 26, 2005, priv. col. of CDN, Pittsburgh, Pa.

Bethany College, Mankato, Minn.

Concordia College, Seward, Neb.

St. Johns College, Winfield, Kan.

Concordia College, Oakland, Calif.

Concordia College, Portland, Oregon

For information write to the "Entrance Counselor" at these colleges.

Students wishing to become deaconesses who cannot take all 4 years of college at Valparaiso University may now take the first 2 years of their University work at the above-mentioned schools as pre-deaconess students. They may then transfer to Valparaiso University as student deaconesses for the final 2 years of work toward the A.B. degree with concentration on the religion major.[106]

Six of the forty-six deaconess students at VU during the 1955-56 academic year transferred from other institutions—one from Bethany, one from a state college, and two from each of the colleges in St. Paul and Bronxville.[107] Previous classes had already received transfers from Winfield and Oakland, and possibly other Concordia campuses.[108]

PRE-DEACONESS CURRICULUM

The pre-deaconess program at Bethany College offered a four-year course, starting with the junior year of high school and finishing with the sophomore year of college. Prescribed subject areas included Religion (16 credit hours), English (18), Math (6), Latin (12), Typing (2), Shorthand (6), Health (1), Sociology (4), Humanities (6), History (12), Biology (16), Chemistry (8), and Psychology (6).

Students took one required Religion class each semester, with the same topic studied for the duration of the year:

High School grade 11—Religion 101 & 102: Old Testament
High School grade 12—Religion 103 & 104: Church History
College Freshmen—Religion 107 & 108: The Augsburg Confession
College Sophomores—Religion 109 & 110: Lutheran Church History.[109]

---

[106] "Two Year Pre-Deaconess Course now Offered at These Colleges," *TLD* 32, no. 3 (July 1955): 7.
[107] Photo caption, *TLD* 33, no. 1 (January 1956): 7.
[108] "Station LDA Tune In," *TLD* 27, no. 4 (October 1950): 6.
[109] Letters from Paul G. Madison to CDN.

St. Johns College, Winfield, had been the first LCMS institution to implement a pre-deaconess program in the early 1940s.[110] Designed for high school graduates, the curriculum there consisted of three Religion classes—Introduction to the Bible (4 credit hours), Christian Doctrine (4), and Survey of Church History (4)—plus English (8), Foreign Language (12), Sociology (3), Humanities (5), History (6), Biology (6), and Psychology (9). An addendum to the curriculum outlined further expectations for pre-deaconess students:

> All students in programs preparing for religious service are also encouraged to acquire the ability to play piano or pipe organ, and are expected to belong to a choral organization, the local Walther League, and the Sunday School.[111]

All of the other pre-deaconess programs advertised by the LDA as available at LCMS colleges were more loosely defined, and sometimes piggybacked a veteran Associate of Arts degree curriculum. The program available at Bronxville, for example, was a "Transfer Program in Liberal Arts" for "Parish Teaching and Deaconess work." As implied by the title, Bronxville provided identical classes for both vocations, including eight credit hours in Religion (Christian Doctrine and Confessions I & II).[112] Other LCMS colleges simply advised students to put together their own list of courses in line with what would be expected at Valparaiso. For example, the 1956-57 catalog for Portland simply stated:

> Deaconess students will arrange their programs individually with the registrar. Their program is designed to enable these students to continue and complete the four year deaconess program at Valparaiso University.[113]

It is interesting to note that, for the 1958–59 school year, three years after the list of colleges with pre-deaconess programs was printed, 29 out of 49 upperclassmen (excluding only freshmen), "transferred from Lutheran colleges and state schools to the Deaconess program at Valpo." These figures included one woman from St. Olaf's College, six from schools of

---

[110] See chapter five.

[111] "The Pre-Deaconess Program," *St. John's College Academic Information* 33, no. 8 (June-July 1955): 24.

[112] "Programs of Study," and "Courses of Instruction," Concordia Junior College Bronxville, New York, Announcements for 1956-57, 32-33, 38.

[113] Concordia College, Portland, Oregon, Catalog 1956-57, 26.

nursing, five from state colleges, four from other programs at Valparaiso University, and 13 from LCMS synodical schools.[114]

On the surface it seems that this transfer system appealed to LCMS colleges. After all, supporting the deaconess movement in this way meant that a college could have more local Lutheran women on its campus for two years, rather than losing them to Valparaiso straight away.[115] In promoting these educational arrangements, the LDA indicated that general "core curriculum" subjects for the bachelor's degree could be acquired at the other colleges, while all deaconess-specific classes would be taken at Valparaiso.[116]

There were distinct advantages to the LDA in partnering with pre-deaconess courses on other campuses. The resulting "feeder system" encouraged Lutheran women from all over the country to begin deaconess training and then transfer to Valpo to complete the course. The housing situation in Valparaiso eased too when students studied elsewhere for two years. Furthermore, only Valparaiso students received LDA scholarships, which meant a slower depletion of the scholarship fund.

LCMS BOARD FOR HIGHER EDUCATION

When the Missouri Synod established its Board for Higher Education in 1938, one of the several directives given to the Board in a "Brief Digest of Powers and Duties" was to "establish and maintain educational and amicable relationships with Valparaiso University."[117] Minutes of the Board show that its members were conscientious in fulfilling this duty. For example, the Board investigated different ideas over the years, such as

---

[114] "Studies in Deaconess Education at Valparaiso University, 1958-1959 and in Internship," *Twenty-Fifth Annual Lutheran Deaconess Conference June 30—July 3, 1959*, mimeographed sheets, 6, priv. col. of Clara Strehlow, Deaconess Office Archives, Concordia University, RF, Illinois.

[115] Some colleges even reported the number of deaconess students studying at their campus in their official report to LCMS synodical conventions. See for example: "Seminaries and Colleges: Report from Concordia College, Portland," in LCMS, *Reports and Memorials*, 1959, 75.

[116] A comparison between standard freshman and sophomore courses at Valparaiso and other colleges, e.g. St. John's, shows almost no difference between the core curriculums in the different Lutheran schools. "Curriculum for Student Deaconesses," *TLD* 27, no. 2 (April 1950): 2.

[117] "Brief Digest of Powers and Duties of the BHE," *Minutes, BHE*, February 9 and 10, 1939, item 9, page 3 of a five-page document bound between pages 5 and 6 of the minutes, CHI, St. Louis, Mo.

merging the LCMS Senior College with Valparaiso and placing an emergency synodical teacher-training program on the VU campus.[118]

Regarding the deaconess program, three entries in the BHE minutes from 1956 to 1959 are helpful for understanding the unique relationship that developed between the LDA, Valparaiso University, and The Lutheran Church—Missouri Synod. The first entry from March 1956 notes:

> The Board reviewed a variety of correspondence relating to the existence and introduction of the pre-deaconess training course on the junior college and teachers college campuses. The Board thereupon resolved to send a circular letter to the presidents of the institutions informing them that the status quo be maintained for the new academic year with no new introductions of this program to be made until such a time as the Board has had an opportunity to review and evaluate the entire program. Meanwhile, the Deaconess Association representatives are to be invited to prepare a brief for study by the Board with possible later appearance before the Board so that the issues involved may receive full consideration.[119]

The correspondence reviewed by the BHE obviously reflected concerns relating to the uniformity, and perhaps legitimacy, of practice among LCMS institutions. The next reference to deaconess training was recorded in September 1957.

> The Puget Sound Pastoral Conference has requested the [LCMS] Board for Higher Education to assume direct jurisdiction over the Lutheran Deaconess Association and its training program. The executive secretary is to respond fully to the conference pointing out that the Board has no authority or jurisdiction over this extra-synodical program but that the executive secretary is by special appointment serving on a committee of the president of Synod and the Board of Directors to review this program.[120]

The pastoral conference raised a difficult issue. It was now possible for women to fulfill pre-requisite educational requirements for an "extra-synodical" training program by attending synodical colleges. If the women

---

[118] "Valparaiso and the Senior College," *Minutes, BHE,* October 15, 1951, CHI, St. Louis, Missouri; *Minutes, BHE,* October 23 and 24, 1953, CHI, St. Louis, Missouri, 45; "Proposal of Valparaiso University for the Teacher-Training of Women," *Minutes, BHE,* January 8 and 9, 1954, CHI, St. Louis, Missouri, 1-5, 64; *Minutes, BHE,* February 12 and 13, 1954, CHI, St. Louis, Missouri, 65.

[119] *Minutes, BHE,* March 1-2, 1956, item 20, 186, CHI, St. Louis, Mo.

[120] Members of the Puget Sound Pastoral Conference lived west of the Cascade Mountains in Washington State, ranging from the Canadian border on the north to the Oregon border on the south. *Minutes, BHE,* September 11, 1957, item 21, 270-271, CHI, St. Louis, Mo.

in the pre-requisite classes were being trained for work in the Missouri Synod, was it right to transfer the women and the baton of jurisdiction over to an auxiliary association not answerable to the Missouri Synod? The Pastoral conference thought not, and asked the BHE to work out some way to assume jurisdiction over the LDA.

The BHE did not appear to be concerned about obtaining jurisdiction over the LDA, but seemed satisfied that a special committee of the president, which included BHE executive secretary Rev. Walter Frederick Wolbrecht (1915-1990), was already reviewing the "program."[121] The result of the committee investigation can be surmised by the subsequent conclusion of the BHE, recorded in the Board's minutes from March 1959:

> 18. In the light of the report that the Lutheran Deaconess Association is asking the Synod to open the junior college level of training in our schools to students for the diaconate, who after the successful completion of two years would thereupon transfer to Valparaiso for the junior and senior years of training, the Board reached the consensus that this arrangement would be acceptable subject to the following conditions: that the curriculum would make no unique demands; that additional staffing would be minimal; that priority of admission would continue to be given to women teacher training students; and that the deaconesses be subject to regular Synodical placement.[122]

MOVING FROM PRACTICE TO POLICY

Eager for synodical ratification of existing practice, the LDA Board of Directors resolved to present a memorial to the 1959 LCMS Synodical convention in San Francisco.[123] As Missouri Synod clergymen, LDA President Albers and Krentz (whose title had changed from Superintendent to Executive Director in 1957) submitted the following memorial.

> WHEREAS, There is a growing need for more professionally trained women workers in our church, which is evident from the fact that the

---

[121] Minutes for a September 11, 1958 meeting of the College of Presidents show that President Behnken "touched on the topics of . . . training and assignment of deaconess and parish workers." "Meeting of the College of Presidents, Concordia Seminary, Saint Louis, Missouri, September 11, 1958," Box 7 College of Presidents: J.W. Behnken Suppl. I, From Letters re Seminary (St. Louis), '47-59 to Min. and Reports 1947 Convention, File: College of Presidents Minutes, 1948-60, CHI, St. Louis, Missouri, 1.

[122] Minutes, BHE, March 14 and 15, 1959, item 18, 359, CHI, St. Louis, Mo.

[123] "IV. Memorial to be Presented to the San Francisco Convention in June 1959," Annual Meeting Lutheran Deaconess Association Zion Parish Hall Fort Wayne, Indiana, November 9, 1958, mimeographed stapled booklet, no pagination, File titled Ft. Wayne, Indiana: Lutheran Deaconess Association 1948-1960, Indiana LCMS District Archives, Fort Wayne, Ind.

number of requests for deaconesses far exceeds the number of graduates available; and

WHEREAS, Deaconesses serve professionally in parishes, institutional and foreign missions, and in the institutions of mercy within our Synod; and

WHEREAS, Pastors and student prospects frequently request the Deaconess Association to give student prospects the privilege to attend college near home, preferably the junior colleges of The Lutheran Church—Missouri Synod; and

WHEREAS, The courses offered at our junior colleges are general, and students preparing for deaconess service are required to take such courses during their first two years of training, no curriculum change or addition would be necessary, since specialization for students preparing for deaconess service begins at Valparaiso University in the Junior year; and

WHEREAS, The admittance of students preparing for deaconess service to our junior colleges would greatly increase their number and hold out the hope of a larger number of deaconess graduates; and

WHEREAS, Our junior colleges, with a single exception, are already accepting women students who are preparing for the teaching profession in our church; and

WHEREAS, Some of our students who are preparing for deaconess service have already transferred to our synodical colleges to prepare for the teaching ministry and synodical college students have already transferred to our deaconess program at Valparaiso University; and

WHEREAS, Deaconess Hall at Valparaiso was built to accommodate only 74 resident students and more students preparing for deaconess service would receive their professional training at Valparaiso if some could get their first two years in general education at our junior colleges; therefore be it

RESOLVED, That the LC-MS open the doors of its junior colleges to students who desire to prepare for the diaconate and on the same terms as women students who have the teaching ministry in our church in view.[124]

Another two memorials submitted for the 1959 convention revealed the conviction of some Missouri Synod members that the work of the church would be better facilitated if the Synod established direct supervision and/or jurisdiction over the LDA.

---

[124] Memorial 161. "Seminaries and Colleges," in LCMS, *Reports and Memorials*, 1959, 216.

[1013] Synod to Take Over Lutheran Deaconess Association

WHEREAS, Because of increased enrollment in the deaconess-training program the Lutheran Deaconess Association is experiencing increasing financial difficulties; and

WHEREAS, Graduates of the deaconess-training program are becoming a growing force in the work of Synod and its member congregations; therefore be it

RESOLVED, That Synod offer to take the work of the Lutheran Deaconess Association into Synod's budget and jurisdiction.

Emmanuel Lutheran Church, Milbank, SD

Earl Bohlen, Secretary C.J. Schleicher, Pastor

[1014] Synod to Supervise Program of Lutheran Deaconess Association

WHEREAS, The Lutheran Deaconess Association has proved the need and value of deaconess service to the church; and

WHEREAS, The work of the deaconess is closely associated with the ministry of the Word; and

WHEREAS, It seems apparent that many of our congregations would avail themselves of the opportunity to employ a deaconess in Kingdom work were more deaconesses available, and it is highly probably that there is also a field of service for them in the foreign field; and

WHEREAS, It would seem highly desirable that the training of the deaconess be under the direct supervision of the church; therefore be it

RESOLVED, That we memorialize Synod to institute, when feasible, a training program for deaconesses under the direct supervision of the church, using our present preparatory schools for preparatory training, giving such students equal status with those preparing for the ministry and the teaching profession, and that Synod make further arrangements for the terminal training of students for the deaconess profession either at one of the present institutions or by arrangement with Valparaiso University.

Northwest District

Victor A. Schulze, Secretary[125]

Memorial 1013 may have been initiated in response to a letter sent from the LDA office to every congregation in the Missouri Synod in

---

[125] Memorials 1013 and 1014. "Miscellaneous Matters," in LCMS, *Reports and Memorials*, 1959, 710.

October 1958, "requesting that they place the Deaconess program in the annual budget of their congregation."[126] On a slightly different track, Memorial 1014 lacked reference to financial difficulties, but implied that every phase of deaconess training should be under the direct supervision of the Missouri Synod, simply due to the nature of deaconess work in the Synod's congregations and missions. In the end, Convention Committee 1 decided to word Resolution 35 in a way that reversed the intention of these two memorials.

Deaconess Training Program – Resolution 35, Committee 1

Resolved, That the Synod decline to take over the deaconess program, but include a study of the diaconate in the general study on theological issues currently affecting synodical higher education; and be it further

Resolved, To permit the synodical institutions to admit qualified deaconess students to the junior college level of training in accord with campus space limitations and in accord with synodical curricular, instructional personnel, and placement policies.

Action: This resolution was adopted.[127]

The adoption of Resolution 35 was an important milestone for the LDA. Eighteen months after the doors of Deaconess Hall opened, the Missouri Synod officially endorsed the educational partnership between its junior colleges and the LDA and Valparaiso University. The deaconess cause was racing forward, and from the time of the dedication of Deaconess Hall onward, instead of "The Lutheran Deaconess Association within the Synodical Conference," the association only referred to itself as "The Lutheran Deaconess Association within The Lutheran Church— Missouri Synod and Affiliated Synods."[128]

---

[126] On Nov. 9, 1958, Krentz reported: "To date we have 135 replies. The response is encouraging. Some have placed us in their budgets, some promised to do so, some promised to take it up with their congregations." "V. Finances," *Annual Meeting Lutheran Deaconess Association Zion Parish Hall Fort Wayne, Indiana, November 9, 1958.*
[127] LCMS, *Proceedings,* 1959, 143.
[128] The masthead of *TLD* first carried the designation: "official organ of the Lutheran Deaconess Association within the Ev. Lutheran Synodical Conference of North America." When Arnold Krentz became editor of the magazine (19, no. 1), he altered the front cover design and reduced the phrase to "official organ of the Lutheran Deaconess Association within the Synodical Conference." The service bulletin for the dedication of Deaconess Hall included the following sentence: "With the erection of Deaconess Hall a new era is beginning for the Deaconess program within the Lutheran Church-Missouri Synod and affiliated Synods." When the next issue of *TLD* came out after the dedication (35, no. 2), it contained the words "Official Quarterly of the Lutheran Deaconess Association, Inc., within

PLACEMENT OF DEACONESS GRADUATES

By far the most significant result of Resolution 35–couched in the words "in accord with synodical...placement policies"–was that deaconesses, just like teachers and pastors, would henceforth be placed in their first positions by the LCMS College of Presidents acting as the Board of Assignments.[129] This part of the resolution reflected the BHE desire that deaconesses should "be subject to regular Synodical placement," implying that such placement would include the appropriate screening of candidates.[130]

From 1922–1949, the Director or Superintendent of deaconess training assigned deaconess graduates to their first field of service. In 1950, the LDA Board of Directors created a "committee on placement" to assume this responsibility, and named Walter Klausing and Edgar Albers (LDA president and vice-president), O. P. Kretzmann (still president of VU), Luther Koepke, Sylvia Trautmann, and Arnold Krentz as committee members.[131] The committee functioned independently for ten years, and then continued as an advisory board when Resolution 35 came into effect for the 1960 graduating class.[132]   A new edition of *The Deaconess Quiz* explained:

46. How is the graduate deaconess placed?

The Board of Directors of the LDA receives applications for deaconesses from various missions, congregations and agencies. These are matched

---

the Lutheran Church-Missouri Synod and Affiliated Synods." This designation continued to be used through the last issue of the magazine, printed in 1971 (49, no. 2).

[129] "The College of Presidents in the LCMS dates its origin to 1854, when it was known as the 'Praesidium.' In the course of time, the synodical president, together with the vice-presidents, was referred to as the 'Praeses Kollegium.' Just when the two terms shifted in meaning is difficult to say. It is, however, noticeable that by 1917 the term 'Praesidium' referred to the synodical president and vice-presidents, while the Council of Presidents was identified as the 'Kollegium der Distrikts Praesides' from which emerged the English 'College of Presidents,' which was renamed by official synodical resolution (LCMS *Proceedings*, 1965, 117) "Council of Presidents."' J.A.O. Preus, "The Council of Presidents, the Synodical President, and the District Presidents, with reference to the duties under the Constitution and Bylaws of the Synod," Minutes Insert C, binder: Official Copy Council of Presidents Minutes of 9/16-19/1974 Meeting 1) Agenda 2) Minutes 3) Inserts, Box: Council of Presidents Minutes 1951—April 1977 Box #9, archive location: 111.1C.17, CHI, St. Louis, Missouri, 1.

[130] *Minutes, BHE*, March 14 and 15, 1959, item 18.

[131] "Deaconess Board Appoints Committee on Placement," *TLD* 27, no. 1 (January 1950): 3.

[132] The members of this committee changed over the years as new individuals were elected or appointed to the various offices and positions represented on the committee. For example, see "Want a Deaconess Graduate?" *TLD* 36, no. 4 (October 1959): 6.

with the graduates' abilities and aptitudes, and discussed with them. They are then assigned by the Committee on Placement according to I Cor. 12:4-5. The placements of deaconess graduates by the Committee on Placements are then submitted to the College of Presidents of The Lutheran Church—Missouri Synod for final approval. After the initial placement, transfers are made through the LDA Board.[133]

While the authors of Resolution 35 may have only thought about the placing of deaconess *candidates*, the assignment of deaconess *interns* also immediately fell to the College of Presidents. The LDA Board of Directors decided in February of 1958, "All students in the Deaconess program in the spring of 1960 will be required to complete one full year of vicarage or internship between their junior and senior year at Valparaiso University."[134] Thus when LDA President Edgar Albers appeared before the LCMS Board of Assignments for the first time in May 1960, he presented "the proposed assignments of the nine graduate deaconesses and two students," after which the presidents resolved, "To receive them for placement in the work of the church," and, "To adopt the assignments of deaconesses *and* students (interns) as presented."[135]

Before 1960, deaconesses received placements for only one year at a time.[136] This practice disappeared once the LCMS became involved in the placement process. However, another arrangement between the LDA and consecrated deaconesses remained intact. The "Deaconess Agreement," refined over the years but still signed by all graduates, acknowledged that the Executive Director of the LDA would "assist deaconesses to be transferred to another field of service if such a change is desired."[137] In essence, then, initial placement of consecrated deaconesses by the College of Presidents meant that the women were recognized as legitimate workers within the Synod, but once in the field, subsequent placements (also called transfers) were under the supervision and jurisdiction of the LDA rather than any Missouri Synod officials or committee. When explaining this system about eight years later, LDA President Albers wrote, "Thus the

---

[133] *The Deaconess Quiz* 5th Edition (Fort Wayne: LDA, 1960), printed brochure, File LDA General, "Brochures and Tracts," CHI, St. Louis, Missouri, 10.

[134] "New Trends in Deaconess Education," *TLD* 35, no. 2 (April 1958): 4.

[135] "Meeting of the College of Presidents, The Lutheran Building, Saint Louis, Missouri, May 3-5, 1960," Box 7 College of Presidents: J.W. Behnken Suppl. I, From Letters re Seminary (St. Louis), '47-59 to Min. and Reports 1947 Convention, File: College of Presidents Minutes, 1948-60, CHI, St. Louis, Missouri, 5.

[136] "Your Questions Answered," *TLD* 32, no. 4 (October 1955): 8.

[137] *The Deaconess Quiz* 5th Edition, 11.

[LDA] Executive Director and/or Director of Education fill a similar roll as that of circuit counselor or district president."[138]

As noted above, in 1959 Missouri Synod convention delegates voted to "decline to take over the deaconess program, but include a study of the diaconate in the general study on theological issues currently affecting synodical higher education."[139] During the next two decades it would became clear how this decision impacted the LCMS, the LDA, Valparaiso University, and the triangle of partnerships between them.

---

[138] Edgar H Albers, "Definitive Statements and Statistics, Prepared for The Board of Directors The Lutheran Church - Missouri Synod and its Board of Higher Education," mimeographed pages (Fort Wayne: LDA, March 12, 1968), 46.

[139] LCMS, *Proceedings*, 1959, 143.

Illustrations for Chapter Six may be viewed at www.deaconesshistory.org.

CHAPTER 7

STILL SHAPING DEACONESS IDENTITY

By the time that the doors of Deaconess Hall opened to students, many changes had taken place in the Synodical Conference diaconate and the training program. These changes dealt with practical matters, but they also played a role in the formation of deaconess identity.

To start with, deaconesses were increasingly better educated and some did post-graduate studies in areas like social work or education.[1] The LDA valued on-the-job training. Summer fieldwork jobs had been popular since the late 1920s, especially at Bethesda in Watertown. In 1950, summer fieldwork sites included churches in Wisconsin, Ohio, and South Dakota; campgrounds in New York and Michigan; a children's home in Illinois; a Spanish mission in Texas; a retirement home in Wisconsin; and St. Louis city (institutional) missions.[2] In other years students worked at the orphanage for Apaches in Arizona; Institute for the Deaf in New York; LCMS district missions; Concordia Historical Institute in St. Louis; and parishes in several states, including Florida, California, and Hawaii.[3] After 1960, summer fieldwork became optional and all students were required to serve a yearlong internship between their junior and senior years at the university.

ENTRANCE REQUIREMENTS

Once the deaconess program was situated at Valparaiso, a woman was only admitted to deaconess training if it was clear that she could cope with university work. The LDA also applied certain *non-academic* criteria in the screening of applicants:

---

[1] "Campus Connings," *TLD* 21, no. 4 (October 1944): 3; "Station LDA Tune In," *TLD* 29, no. 3 (July 1952): 6; "Placements," *TLD* 31, no. 3 (July 1954): 3.

[2] "Summer Field Workers," *TLD* 27, no. 4 (October 1950): 8.

[3] "I Spent a Summer Among the Apaches," *TLD* 27, no. 1 (January 1950): 2; "Write for Summer Help Now," *TLD* 31, no. 1 (January 1954): 2-3; "Summer Field Work," *TLD* 33, no. 3 (July 1956): 7.

The following are the pre-requisites for entering deaconess training: 1). Age limits up to 35, with rare exceptions made; 2). Graduation from a recognized high school; 3). Sound physical health—a certificate of health is required from the applicant's physician; 4). The sincere desire to serve Christ and His Church; 5). The recommendation of her pastor; 6). The student need be no nurse, as is often thought, nor need she give the vow to remain unmarried.[4]

Starting in the late 1950s, Professor Lawrence Hess, a Vocational Guidance Counselor who served as Personnel Consultant to the LDA Board of Directors, administered a "Battery of Tests and Inventories" to applicants.[5] As the LDA employed these layers of selective recruiting tools over a period of years, they appear to have produced a more similar set of students—women who were bright and assertive; aware of their own strengths and weaknesses; able to articulate personal needs and desires; dedicated to the values of the deaconess movement; and very trainable.

Community Life

The third edition of *A Deaconess Quiz*, printed in 1958, explained that the training of a deaconess had three main components: first, the bachelor's degree from VU with a major in religion; second, supervised field work in a church or institution; and third . . .

> Benefits from *group living at the Deaconess Chapter House* at Valpo such as special speakers from various fields of church work, group worship and growth, service projects in the Valparaiso and Gary churches, and campus extracurricular work helping to prepare the student deaconesses for church work.[6]

Morning and evening devotions became a cherished part of community living in the Deaconess Chapter House and later in the slightly more formal chapel at Deaconess Hall. Such times brought the women back to the

---

[4] "Entrance Requirements for Students," *TLD* 23, no. 2 (April 1946): 5.
[5] "The Battery of Vocational Guidance Tests and Inventories which each girl takes includes: 1) Science Research Associates—Primary Mental Abilities Test. 2) Science Research Associates—Reading Test. 3) Interest Inventory: Kuder Preference Interest Test. 4) California Personality Inventory: Profile of Self-Adjustment and Social Adjustment. 5) Person-Social (Aptitude) (Everyday Psychology). 6) Study-habits Inventory by Dr. C. Gilbert Wrenn." *The Deaconess Quiz* 5th Edition (Fort Wayne: LDA, 1960), printed brochure, File LDA General, "Brochures and Tracts," CHI, St. Louis, Mo., 4.
[6] Bold print is part of the original publication. *A Deaconess Quiz: Over 50 Answers to Your Questions About the Deaconess Program*, 3rd Edition, (Fort Wayne: LDA, 1958), printed brochure, no pagination, File LDA General, "Brochures and Tracts," CHI, St. Louis, Mo.

reason that they were in Valparaiso, and strengthened the bond of faith that would be an important component of diaconal service. Student Marlene Birkholz wrote:

> Living in Deaconess Hall is a living together in unity. We are set apart to strengthen our unity of purpose: faith and service in Christ.
>
> In preparation for work in His kingdom we feel the need of well-disciplined lives in worship. Together we all take an active part in our devotions. We begin our group worship by keeping in mind the necessary inward preparation and recognizing that God is present.
>
> We come together each morning at 6:45 to sing praises to God, thank Him for His protection through the night, and ask for His guidance during the new day.
>
> Each evening at 6:30 the candles are lit in our beautiful Chapel. Devotions are led by one of the deaconess students.
>
> Yes, the family at Deaconess Hall does pray together and in so doing we hope to preserve unity. Our group worship is an important part of our spiritual life, strengthening our own and the faith of fellow students.[7]

Outside of the deaconess residence, teams of deaconess students carried out a broad range of service projects. In 1954, the students took it upon themselves to revive a Sunday School that the University Youth Council had dropped due to a lack of workers. Students enthusiastically canvassed for prospective children in the town of Valparaiso and the Sunday School re-opened with twenty-two children.[8] In 1958, groups of deaconess students visited Lake County Jail to sing hymns; attended worship at the Lake County Old Peoples Home, where they also provided one-on-one devotions for women who were unable to attend services; and made calls on the sick and shut-in members of Immanuel Lutheran Church in Valparaiso.[9]

CAMPUS LIFE

Living together in off-campus housing and studying for the same degree in order to become deaconesses gave the students a unique identity within the larger university environment. At the same time, they could be involved in whatever campus activities interested them. Some of the women played in

---

[7] Marlene Birkholz, "Devotions at Deaconess Hall," *TLD* 36, no. 2 (April 1959): 8.

[8] Ilene Behlmaier, "U.Y.C. Sunday School," *TLD* 31, no. 2 (April 1954): 8.

[9] Gladys Noreen, "Field Work at School," *TLD* 35, no. 1 (January 1958): 7.

the university band or sang in the choir. Several worked on the *Valparaiso Torch,* a newspaper published by the student council. For the 1948–49 school year, one student served as business manager for Valpo's yearbook, *The Beacon,* while another bowled the top score at a "W.A.A. bowling tournament" hosted at the university.[10] The "Gown and Gavel" frequently invited deaconess students to join their organization, which honored female students on the basis of leadership, scholarship and character.[11]

In January 1950, *TLD* featured a photograph of the "Student Deaconess Volley Ball Team" which was having a good season, already winning eight of the first nine games played against Valpo's campus sororities.[12] This broader participation in sports and other university activities really opened up for the women through the formation of their own student organization. Helen Eliopoulos explained,

> At the beginning of the 1947–1948 school year the girls at 605 Chicago Street unanimously agreed to give their House a Greek letter name. This was sanctioned by the Board of Directors of the Lutheran Deaconess Association.
>
> The name chosen was PI DELTA CHI, which stands for "Faith and Service in Christ." Indeed a fitting motto for us deaconess students.
>
> It is not the purpose of the girls to be known as a college sorority, but this was done for the purpose of being known and accepted as a campus organization.[13]

Athletic teams played a large role in student life at the Pi Delta Chi House. In addition to volleyball, Pi Delta Chi competed against sororities and other organized campus groups in ping-pong, badminton, tennis, and basketball. Additional favorite pastimes included roller-skating, ice-skating, and swimming parties.[14]

---

[10] Photo caption, *TLD* 24, no. 1 (January 1947): 8; "Serving on the Torch Staff," *TLD* 24, no. 3 (July 1947): 8; "Kathleen Rubow, Beacon Business Manager," *TLD* 26, no. 2 (April 1949): 3; "Grace Braeger—Bowler Preeminent," *TLD* 26, no. 2 (April 1949): 5.

[11] "The Dream of Every College Girl," *TLD* 27, no. 3 (July 1950): 7.

[12] Photo and caption, *TLD* 27, no. 1 (January 1950): 3.

[13] A large Pi Delta Chi sign was erected on the Deaconess Chapter House. See photo on front of April 1952 issue of *TLD;* Helen Eliopoulos, "Pi Delta Chi," *TLD* 25, no. 2 (April 1948): 2.

[14] Lois Roepke, "Sports Review," *TLD* 25, no. 2 (April 1948): 3.

A PROFESSIONAL SOCIETY

Not long after they named their house Pi Delta Chi, the women determined that they wanted a professional organization for student deaconesses by the same name. They adopted a constitution in spring 1948, officers were elected, and Pi Delta Chi meetings held regularly at the Chapter House. The objectives of the organization were, in brief:

1. To build a feeling of oneness among the students in the organization; to build motivation for service and consecration to Christ.

2. To foster closer fellowship among the deaconess and pre-deaconess students.

3. To provide for participating in and leading worshipful devotions . . .

4. To provide opportunities for gaining experience in the various areas of deaconess work . . .

5. To maintain the bond of friendship between the deaconess and pre-deaconess students and those deaconesses serving in the field . . .

6. To provide a link between Pi Delta Chi and the Deaconess Conference for preparation for membership in the latter.[15]

Pi Delta Chi differed from other female societies at the university in its emphasis on professional development and building lasting relationships between the women who expected to share a common mission in life. In some regard, the organization provided a type of sisterhood that replaced, at least in part, the deaconess culture that had been lost with the passing of the deaconess motherhouse. The esprit de corps enjoyed in Pi Delta Chi would later carry over into the Deaconess Conference.[16]

The Greek letters—Pi, Delta, and Chi—were carved in stone on the outside of Deaconess Hall next to the Chi Rho cross and statue of Phoebe. At some point between 1947 and 1957 the student deaconess sorority motto, "Faith and Service in Christ," superseded the original LDA motto: "For Missions and Charities." Interestingly, the change of words also

---

[15] "Pi Delta Chi," *TLD* 41, no. 4 (Fall 1964): 5.

[16] Speaking about her student days at Valparaiso, Rhoda (nee Rasmusson) Pfotenhauer explained, "When I was president of Pi Delta Chi during my senior year (1962-63) I helped to make the decision that the girls could be in another sorority on the campus. After that, some of the gals lived two years on campus and then would come into the program. We were a professional sorority and sometimes it didn't mesh that well with what the life of the campus was." Rhoda (nee Rasmusson) Pfotenhauer, notes from telephone interview by CDN, February 17, 2006, priv. col. of CDN, Pittsburgh, Pa.

reflected a subtle shift of direction that had been taking place within the LDA and the diaconate for some time, that is, a move away from the corporate work of deaconesses in inner missions and charitable institutions to a sharper focus on personal faith and personal service to Christ in one's neighbor.

PRE-EDUCATED STUDENTS

In the 1950s, women who already held bachelor's degrees in non-theological disciplines began to inquire about becoming deaconesses. The LDA saw these mature women as a new source of recruits for the diaconate.

> The new trend is this: Young women who already have a college degree are entering our Deaconess Program. Thus Miss Marilyn Meier, a graduate of our River Forest normal, has applied for admission into our Deaconess Service Program and has successfully passed her colloquium. Another instance, Miss Julia Hennig who received her Master's degree in Music from the University of Michigan last January is now taking our Deaconess Course at Valparaiso. Another example, Miss Ruth Broermann who has her bachelor's degree and has taught several years at our Bronxville Concordia is another student in our deaconess program. Before me lies the application of Miss Hertha Fischer who has her degree in chemistry from Hunter College and desires to take the deaconess course at Valparaiso University this fall.
>
> Young women who already hold college degrees may enter deaconess service after only one year at Valparaiso University under the deaconess program where they take courses in the religion department.[17]

The "colloquium" passed by Meier consisted of a personal interview conducted by Krentz and one other member of the LDA Board of Directors. On that occasion, and in the case of a second colloquy in 1959, both candidates graduated from Concordia Teachers College in River Forest, but no representatives of that college or officials of the Missouri Synod were involved in the colloquy process.[18]

It should be noted too that serving God as a deaconess was still considered to be an attractive option for nurses. In January 1959, Krentz

---

[17] The student deaconess roster listed these women as "unclassified" students, that is, they had no designation as juniors or seniors and only received a Deaconess Diploma at the end of their training. "A New Trend in Deaconess Work," *TLD* 31, no. 3 (July 1954): 7; "Student Deaconess Roster," *TLD* 31, no. 4 (October 1954): 3.

[18] "Colloquy Given Miss Lorraine Behling," *TLD* 36, no. 4 (October 1959): 2.

was pleased to report that six nurses would be among the fourteen women who were expected to complete their deaconess training that year.[19]

NEW ROLES FOR DEACONESSES

In harmony with the changing role of women during the war and post-war years, the LDA encouraged deaconesses to view themselves as ambassadors for the deaconess movement. One of the pioneers in this endeavor was a remarkable young woman named Florence Storck who, in 1943, became one of the first two women to be elected to the Executive Board of Associated Lutheran Charities.[20]

At the time of her consecration in 1937, the LDA assigned Storck to the Orphans Home at Des Peres, Missouri, and in 1940 she transferred to the St. Louis Lutheran City Mission. Enlisting local assistance for City Mission work was important to its success, so she worked closely with the Lutheran Deaconess Association of St. Louis, encouraging Lutheran women to give financial support to the deaconess cause and "to do personal work in the various missionary and charitable undertakings in St. Louis."[21]

Storck was a prolific writer and a gifted public speaker. For six years she regularly delivered her own talks for a KFUO radio show called "Adventures in Faith." She loved to record the little sayings of her orphan children or the moving stories of the women she ministered to at the TB Sanitarium. Many of these real-life anecdotes later found their way into her radio programs and public speeches.[22] The following radio manuscript, dated September 30, 1943, gives some insight into how Storck understood and promoted the role of deaconesses in the church.

---

[19] "Applications for Graduates," *TLD* 36, no.1 (January 1959): 2.

[20] The other woman was Miss Marie Zucker, Executive Secretary of Lutheran Social Services, Fort Wayne, who had taught social work at the Central Deaconess Training School in Fort Wayne. "Station LDA Initial Broadcast," *TLD* 21, no. 1 (January 1944): 5.

[21] Florence Storck, "Lutheran Deaconess Association St. Louis, Missouri," small tract, *Deaconess Historical Materials* box, Deaconess Office Archives, Concordia University, RF, Illinois; "Consecration Service," *TLD* 14, no. 3 (July 1937): 5; "Deaconesses According to Their Stations," *TLD* 17, no. 2 (April 1949): 8.

[22] Several extant radio manuscripts, as well as other writings, are owned by Storck's daughter, Gloria Zimmerman, Seattle, Wa. Radio manuscripts seen by the author were dated as early as January 1941 and as late as December 1946. Gloria Zimmerman, notes from interview by CDN, Seattle, Wa., October 15, 2005, priv. col. of CDN, Pittsburgh, Pa.

Dear Friends of Station KFUO,

Since it is the general opinion of the people that the work of a deaconess is something quite new, I should like to speak to you this morning on the work of a Deaconess. Shortly after the church at Jerusalem was founded, its membership increased to such an extent that it became impossible for the apostles to attend to all the affairs of business which were growing in magnitude. There were widows to be provided for, poor to be visited, the sick to be ministered to, and there was much other work to be done. It soon became evident that the powers of the apostles were not sufficient for this great work; the complaint was publicly made that widows were being neglected in the daily ministrations. The apostles then set aside and ordained seven godfearing men to assist them in the work. But even this arrangement did not fully satisfy the need, for there was much work to be done for which the deacons were not apt, and which did not seem in good taste to allow them to do and particularly was this true in congregations composed mostly of converted heathen. Take the women of the congregation at Corinth; when they were ill and needed care, the deacons could not well look after them. Again advice and assistance of a kind which deacons were not qualified to give was needed. Here circumstances were constantly arising where only women would be in a place to render the needed assistance if no offense were to be given.

When we further recall the crimes and vices which were popular in those cities, and how Paul himself admonished the congregation at Corinth, the necessity for deaconesses as well as deacons in the congregation becomes obvious. There were manifold duties which devolved upon Christian women at the beginning of the Church's history. Although there were many willing hands, constrained by the love of Christ who offered themselves for this service, Phoebe was the only regularly appointed woman servant in the early Church of whom we have any knowledge and who was the only one called by the particular title of deaconess. She was the first person mentioned, who by particular appointment of the Church performed the works of mercy and love so abundantly illustrated in the New Testament. Phoebe was not simply a member of the congregation, one of those faithful, willing, sacrificing workers; but she was a servant employed by her congregation and bore the title of deaconess. She assisted the apostle Paul in looking up and encouraging such women in the faith as had heard the Word preached. She ministered to many in mercy and love, but besides the performance of these duties she is especially distinguished by her mission to the congregation at Rome at which she delivered Paul's epistle. In Phoebe we see the first bearer of this noble office which the Lord has given to His church.

Today the same conditions and circumstances are to be found in our churches. Elders, deacons, and others who are to assist the pastor in his work are not always the proper persons. Services are often required, for example at the sick bed of a widow, or in a poor family, where both father and mother lie ill. At no other time do people seek comfort, sympathy, kindness and love more than in the hours of sickness. It is then that the deaconess can be of great assistance. What a privilege it is to call upon the many sick and shut-ins, to bring cheer and sunshine to saddened hearts, to watch by the bedside of the dying, and above all to strengthen them with God's Word and prayer.

Under the direction of the pastor the deaconess visits the sick and the suffering, the unfortunate and the dying, ever pointing them to Christ our Savior. She also visits the families, not only to supply their material wants, but to bring words of comfort and encouragement and hope. She invites the parents to the services of the Church and the children to the Sunday School, for she believes that the soul of charity is charity to the soul. As the pastor's assistant she greets and welcomes the strangers who attend the services of the church; she calls upon prospective members; she visits the new members of the congregation, inviting them to become active in the various organizations; and under the pastor's directions she follows up on delinquent members. Manifold are the duties of a deaconess and may our pastors ever realize the importance and better acquaint themselves with this work. . . .

This service, if it is to be performed properly, must become a life task. And Deaconesses, in order to be efficient helpers, must be educated and trained for this work and hindered by no other duty, give their entire time, powers, and gifts to the service of the Lord Jesus. No matter what field of work a deaconess may serve, she should have a good knowledge of Bible truths and should know how to apply it. . . . There is one great motto which all Christians should keep before their eyes at all times, namely, "The love of Christ constraineth us," and it is the constraining force of Christ's love which impels Christian young women to follow in His footsteps to minister to others. It is the great desire to serve Christ by serving "one of the least of these." It is Christ who stands before us in the widow and orphans, and in those needing comfort, advice and help, it is Christ who stands before us in those who reach up for the friendly, helping and uplifting hand. No hands are so tender as the hands of women when they are guided by the love of Christ.

Some months ago Mary was brought to the hospital. She informed us that she had never been baptized. Each week we tried to bring cheer to her bedside, ever pointing her to the cross on Calvary. We continued to encourage her to be baptized and stressed the importance of it for our salvation quoting passages such as "He that believeth and is baptized shall be saved.—Baptism doth also now save us, etc." She was never quite ready. One week realizing that she was getting weaker we began pleading with her to take instruction. She said, "I want you to instruct me, I want you to come back tomorrow." After studying the law and also the sweet Gospel message she asked one day, "How soon may I be baptized?" How happy she was on that great day. She stated to one of the other patients, "If I had never gotten sick perhaps I would have never known my Savior and been baptized." Several weeks later standing at her bedside together with her husband and several nurses she fell asleep. In that little hospital room, Mary's breathing had ceased. We knew that now she was standing before the throne of God. At her bedside where we had often spoken to Mary we prayed. The husband and nurses bowing their heads and trying to hide the tears which trickled down their cheeks.

"I was sick and ye visited me," the Lord will say to those who have willingly chosen this service out of love for Him.[23]

Not surprisingly, on January 1, 1947, Deaconess Storck became the first female Field Secretary for the LDA. She traveled extensively across North America, speaking about the joys of deaconess ministry to church groups, LWML societies, and Ladies' Aids.[24] On June 1, 1947, only five months after starting her new job, Storck married a pastor whom she had met on one of her lecture tours in the state of Washington. Krentz announced the marriage in the association's magazine, noting that Storck "served faithfully and efficiently as a deaconess for ten years;" finishing his article with the sentence, "We wish her the Lord's richest blessings in her new capacity as a pastor's wife."[25]

PUBLIC RELATIONS OPPORTUNITIES

Deaconesses were often asked to speak about diaconal ministry in their own congregation or circuit, and even further afield. This practice was promoted in *TLD*.

> Many of our church members have never seen a deaconess and it will be a thrill for them to meet one of our deaconesses. Often meeting a deaconess removes misconceptions. More yet, having heard a deaconess, members of our churches become loyal supporters of our deaconess program.
>
> To find which deaconess might be available to lecture in your area, consult page 167 of the 1951 Lutheran Annual, which lists the names and

---

[23] Florence Storck, "Dear Friends of KFUO," typed manuscript, Sept. 30, 1943, priv. col. of Gloria Zimmerman, Seattle, Wa.

[24] "Deaconess Florence Storck to Lecture," *TLD* 24, no. 1 (January 1947): 2.

[25] "Deaconess Storck Married," *TLD* 24, no. 3 (July 1947): 4.

addresses of our deaconesses. Also, if you write to Fort Wayne, we shall consider it a privilege to mention deaconess lecturers to you.[26]

As Krentz attended Lutheran gatherings on behalf of the LDA he sought opportunities for women to speak to pastors about the deaconess cause. In June 1949, for example, two student deaconesses accompanied the Superintendent to the Eastern District LCMS Convention at Camp Pioneer, where they addressed the convention. It was later reported that the brethren liked it so much that "the girls got a rousing hand of applause."[27] More importantly, the convention delegates approved the use of district Student Aid funds for the training of deaconesses, with one stipulation:

> . . . Resolved, that applicants for such support agree to serve the Church in a full-time capacity for a period of five years. In case they cease serving as deaconesses in a shorter period of time, they shall consider themselves honor-bound to refund pro rata the amount the District has invested in their education.[28]

In July 1950, an article in *TLD* stated, "The first woman to address the convention of The Lutheran Church—Missouri Synod at Milwaukee, Wisconsin, was Deaconess Lois Jank, parish worker in Faith Lutheran Church, Milwaukee, Wisconsin."[29] In subsequent years the magazine infers that Krentz took other deaconesses to district conventions to speak on subjects like recruitment, financial aid and placement.[30]

"I think that the Deaconess is a beckoning star—or a constellation—on the church's service horizon."

Rev. Arnold Krentz *(Note written on a blank page of his 1958 CPH diary, CHI, St. Louis.)*

THE HEART OF DEACONESS WORK

A deaconess was (and is) a woman who believed in Jesus Christ as her personal Savior, and the Savior of all mankind. No matter what type of work she did, a deaconess spent much time, either formally or informally, in

---

[26] "Deaconess Lecturers," *TLD* 28, no. 4 (October 1951): 4.

[27] "Station LDA Tune In," *TLD* 26, no. 3 (July 1949): 6.

[28] Eastern District LCMS, *Proceedings*, 1949, 91.

[29] "Convention Connings," *TLD* 27, no. 3 (July 1950): 8.

[30] Photo caption, *TLD* 28, no 3 (July 1951): 5.

teaching and building the faith of the women and children in her charge. At the same time, every deaconess involved herself in the task of spreading the Gospel of Jesus Christ to those who did not yet know Him as their Lord and Savior. LDA Board member E. E. Foelber witnessed to the joy of this task:

> If we were asked to rank our joys, we should place the joy that comes from soul-winning immediately after the joy number one, the joy which springs from the certainty of having a Savior for one's own soul and body. Surely all other joys, based on the successes of lesser worth, such as achievements in the realm of economics, physical power and suppleness, art and philosophy, legitimate though they be, are by comparison inferior.

> Our deaconesses, being first of all soul-winners and soul-conservators, experience joys number one and two with unusual frequency. Like pastors and Christian teachers, they give their full time, with no other end or purpose in view, to holding up before all whom they serve the adorable Redeemer Jesus. As they, day after day, minister to the thousands entrusted to their care and speak the Word that is spirit and that is life, they draw from their fruitful labors a sweetness that pervades their entire being. Theirs is an extraordinarily rich life. They are, in truth, a happy people.[31]

So as a deaconess lived this rich life, punctuated with the joys of knowing salvation and bringing others to Christ, how did her working role relate to pastors and teachers who also spent their lives in service to the Redeemer? In 1946, Krentz wrote briefly,

> A Lutheran deaconess occupies an important position in church work. Hers is an auxiliary office to the Christian ministry. The diaconate was originally established (Acts 6) to relieve the apostles of certain responsibilities, the serving of tables. Today the deaconess still serves the same purpose, to relieve the pastors of certain details in their work. It should be emphasized that the need of specially (trained) women workers, to whom certain spheres of church work can be delegated, is strongly felt in our complex and multilateral church work today.[32]

When Krentz stated that deaconesses were to "relieve pastors of certain details in their work" he was not implying that such details were mundane jobs that pastors preferred to do without. On the contrary, he understood that the normal pastor was overworked—especially in larger congregations or institutions—and a great amount of very important work could be

---

[31] E. E. Foelber, "The Joy of the Deaconess," *TLD* 19, no. 3 (July 1942): 6.
[32] "Status of the Deaconess," *TLD* 23, no. 2 (April 1946): 8.

delegated to deaconesses without blurring the lines between the pastoral ministry (with its focus on Word and Sacraments) and diaconal ministry (with its focus on acts of Mercy).

PARISH MINISTRY

The area of service that really opened up under Krentz's leadership (1941–61) was parish ministry. However, Krentz's predecessor, Superintendent Kohlmeier, set the stage for progression in this field of service in a paper on "Requirements for a Parish Deaconess" presented to the annual ALCh convention in 1935.

> A parish deaconess is the assistant to the pastor. That states briefly the character and field of her work. That determines also the requirements for a parish deaconess. One difficulty that presents itself to me is this, however, that I find a difference of opinion among pastors as to the work they would wish a deaconess to do. . . .
>
> To be of real assistance to the pastor, it is absolutely necessary that she be well informed in matters of Christian doctrine and Christian ethics. Her work will bring her into contact just with such people who need to be guided and advised in spiritual matters. That requires a thorough knowledge of Christian doctrine. And her work is of the nature of pastoral work. That demands that she be discreet and tactful. She must be able to gain and to hold the confidence of people with whom she deals. In addition to this, she should be of a pleasing personality, have refined manners, and know how to approach people. And of course she must have the disposition and ability to cooperate fully with the pastor and to work under his direction.
>
> She is not primarily a social worker, but a church-worker. Yet she should have some knowledge of sociology, so as to understand the social angle involved in the problems which she meets in her work, and to be able to co-operate intelligently with social workers who may be dealing with the same people that are in her charge as parish deaconess.
>
> These, I think, are the main requirements for a parish deaconess.[33]

A consecrated Christian with a thorough knowledge in doctrine and ethics; personable and winsome; possessing the ability to work in tandem with the pastor, under his direction; understanding the basics of sociology.

---

[33] H. B. Kohlmeier, "Requirements for a Parish Deaconess," *Thirty-fourth Annual Convention Associated Lutheran Charities*, Hotel Lowry, St. Paul, Minnesota, Sept. 10-13, 1935 (Watertown: Jansky Printing Co., 1935).

These things Pastor Krentz later worked toward securing in deaconess education, particularly when the training program moved to Valparaiso.

Most congregations employing deaconesses could do so because they were large and had the financial resources to support more than one fulltime worker. Furthermore, it was the overworked pastors of these larger parishes who felt the need for assistance with the day-to-day running of their congregation, and sometimes their Lutheran school. The following quotations from 1944 and 1945 give some idea of the variety of activities that occupied a parish deaconess.

Parish Deaconess Work at St. John's Church, Cleveland

> The duties of the parish deaconess here are manifold. But first and foremost is the work of teaching the four R's in the primary grades.[34] That, of course, takes up most of the time. The deaconess is in the class room from 8 a.m. until 3:30 p.m.

> What time is left after school is spent on doing such work as recording communion announcements, making changes of addresses and helping with general office work. Friday evening and Saturday morning the bulletin for the Sunday service must be gotten out and envelopes addressed and bulletins sent to shut-ins.

> In the evenings there are meetings—Sunday School Teachers, Ladies' Aid, Missionary Society, Walther League, Choir and various committee meetings. Occasionally a lesson must be prepared and presented to the Sunday School teachers, a topic for the Walther League, or perhaps a topic for the Ladies' Aid.

> On Sunday morning the deaconess is in charge of the primary department of the Sunday School. She conducts the opening, reviews the lesson, teaches new songs, and has charge of the closing exercises. The deaconess has organized the 6, 7, and 8 grade girls into a Girls' Club. . . . Then there are a number of extra curricular activities which the deaconess provides for the children such as trips to the museum, etc., a spring operetta and a school victory garden. Occasionally the deaconess is invited to other churches to speak on deaconess service in a group of ladies or young people, to give a topic for the Sunday School Convention, or to do work for the Cleveland Teachers' Conference.

> One of the most important activities of the parish deaconess is to visit the sick and shut-ins. What a privilege to bring cheer and comfort to those who day after day lie enclosed by four walls alone and in pain. . . . There is happiness and much gratification in my work here as parish deaconess.

---

[34] A reference to "reading, 'riting, 'rithmetic, and religion."

True, at times one is overwhelmed with the amount of work to be done in the building of the Kingdom of our Lord, and I feel so humble, and I thank God for His grace that permits me to help in this work.[35]

∗ ∗ ∗

Deaconess Service in a Metropolitan Area

Miss Eber's many duties as a parish deaconess at Immanuel Church, New York City, included teaching in Sunday School, Vacation Bible School, and Saturday School. She helped in the mission work among the Spanish. She ministered to the poor and needy. In those homes in the heart of this great metropolis she was often confronted with distressing problems of illness and suffering. She was able to reach these people spiritually by first giving them material aid in the way of food, clothing, medication, and nursing. She also took sick children to clinics, arranged to have thirty or forty children go to camps or farms for two weeks each summer, and assisted in finding homes for orphans.[36]

What a broad spectrum of work! Just as a Lutheran pastor needed to be capable of shepherding different kinds of congregations with the ministry of Word and Sacrament, so a deaconess also needed to be prepared to carry out a ministry of mercy in whatever type of parish she served. Of course, the same principle held true for those women who served in institutions.

INSTITUTIONAL MINISTRY

Institutional missions focused on caring for people who lived outside of a normal home environment. Some of these people temporarily occupied schools, hospitals, orphanages, or jails, while others lived for longer periods in homes equipped to care for residents with similar needs. The LDA expressed its intention to continue training institutional workers in a brief statement in *TLD*.

> Academically, the student deaconesses at Valparaiso may take a double major, one in Religion and the other in Social Work. This is an almost ideal academic set-up for our future deaconesses. It helps equip our graduates to serve effectively as institutional workers in child welfare, homes for the aged, and other charitable institutions.[37]

---

[35] Rose Ziemke, "Parish Deaconess Work at St. John's Church, Cleveland," *TLD* 22, no. 3 (July 1945): 4-6.

[36] "Deaconess Service in a Metropolitan Area," *TLD* 21, no. 1 (January 1944): 7.

[37] "Institutional Service of the Deaconess Program?" *TLD* 27, no. 1 (January 1950): 3.

Deaconesses who worked in institutions sometimes had special training as nurses, teachers, or social workers, but many learned the necessary skills for their work through on-the-job training. A remarkable example of loving service in institutional settings is recorded in the following article written by Martha Theilmann.

Interesting Chapters in My Diaconate

Chapter 1. After I was consecrated as a deaconess in 1927 [sic],[38] I was asked to serve as nurse at our Concordia Teachers College in Seward, Nebraska. I wondered how I could take care of so many boys. At that time I was a little timid and didn't know boys as well as I know them now. I liked the little "foxes" especially well, that would come to me with every little scratch, still craving a mother's love and attention. During sports there were sprained ankles, broken noses, a misplaced shoulder blade, a broken collarbone, not to mention the many bruises. No doubt those boys have responsible teaching positions now and are leading precious souls to their Savior.

Chapter 2. During the last two years of its existence I was privileged to serve at our Indian mission School, Red Springs, Wisconsin. Of the 132 Indian children coming from all parts of the country I had charge of the boys. It was not uncommon to hear of an Indian brawl, with fighting and sometimes killing. Also immorality was very prevalent. So we had our problems with the children. In spite of all of the difficulties—scabies and delousing included—when it was announced that the mission Board School would be closed, it made our hearts ache to think that these children would have to go back to their old environment.

Chapter 3. Next I served as matron at the Lutheran Institute for the Deaf, Detroit, Michigan. Rev. Scheibert[39] gave me a few instructions in the sign language, so I learned to understand the deaf children fairly well. At that time it was hard to get the children to understand such concepts as sin, grace, God, the Savior from sin, the Holy Spirit, heaven, hell and the like. I still hear from some of the girls occasionally. One of the girls has a government position in Washington D.C.

Chapter 4. For eleven years I was matron at our Bethesda Lutheran Home, Watertown, Wisconsin. To look after 350 to 370 residents is a big responsibility. . . . Naturally, the most important aim of the Home is that all residents learn to know their Savior. These children learn to love their Jesus, to sing hymns to the Savior's praise. When I first saw these

---

[38] This date contains a typographical error. Theilmann graduated from the deaconess training school in Watertown in 1929 and was consecrated the same year.
[39] Ernest John Eduard Scheibert (1898-1977).

unfortunate people enter chapel for service, each with an affliction, I thought I could never "take it." As I learned to know them, however, each became to me an individual with a soul. After all, they too are God's children, with blood-bought souls. The gratefulness of these children has always been a compensation to me.

Chapter 5. During the past year I have been with the Lutheran Child Welfare Association, Indianapolis, serving as a nurse and doing relief work as time permits. With few exceptions the children have come from broken homes, quite pathetic, since they have had little training, much less have enjoyed the Christian atmosphere of a happy home. . . . We members of the staff need to have an understanding heart . . . to lead these children to their Savior.

Looking back over these eventful years I feel a deep sense of gratitude to my Savior for the privilege of serving Him.[40]

In larger cities like Chicago and St. Louis, city mission societies employed deaconesses to work in several health facilities at the same time. The following summary of Frieda Bremermann's typical workweek shows how she organized her service to the needy in multiple institutions.

Sunday: Sunday morning I conduct a Sunday School in the Children's Orthopedic Ward of a large General hospital. Class begins at 9:30 a.m. and lasts one-half hour. Ages of children are 2 to 8 years. Lessons are taught with flannelgraph aids. On the last Sunday of the month I attend our service at the Juvenile Detention Home and assist in interviewing girls who are detained there.

Monday: Visit the County Hospital and make bedside calls in the women's wards. Home calls on special cases or follow-up calls on former patients.

Tuesday: Visit a large Mental Hospital about 35 miles from Chicago and make calls in two women's infirmaries.

Wednesday: Visit a large Mental Hospital in Chicago and call on women in all women's wards. From there to County Hospital for a short period to check any information or referrals at the Social Service Department. In the evening assist our chaplain in a State Hospital by going to the wards to assist patients who want to attend the service.

Thursday: Visit the County General Hospital and make calls in the women's wards. Also assist our chaplain by assisting the patients who want to attend the service.

---

[40] "Interesting Chapters in My Diaconate," *TLD* 29, no. 1 (January 1952): 3.

Friday: Visit a Chicago Mental hospital to make calls in the women's wards and diagnostic section.

Saturday: Some mornings are devoted to home visits, telephone calls and correspondence. Prepare the Sunday School lesson.[41]

Institutional deaconesses usually kept good records of their work and the fruit of their labor: to provide regular reports to their supervisors and supporters; to make sure that no one "fell through the net;" and to recall the great things that God has done and is still doing for His people.[42]

NEIGHBORHOOD MINISTRY

Meeting people in the neighborhoods where they lived provided different opportunities for service to *the Lord in His wretched ones and His poor.* Here— bringing relief and respite to the poverty stricken, the lonely, the ill, the outcast, the weary—a deaconess would match her charitable work with an explanation of the Lord of love.

A Unique Missionary Endeavor

In Cleveland, Ohio, the Central District of the Missouri Synod operates the Gospel Center. This Center represents the efforts of our church to reach the under-privileged, the relief-clients, the infirm, the shut-in, and those who for reasons of culture, race, nationality, poverty, and even mentality are not easily attracted to the established churches. In this field works Deaconess Boss, R.N. . . .

The religious portion of our deaconess' work is varied. She has full charge of all records connected with the Sunday School. The majority of the mission and follow-up calls connected with the Sunday School are left to her. Besides, she has her regular class on Sunday morning. During the week a children's Bible class is conducted after School with Miss Boss taking care of the children ages 9-11. Present plans are to develop this afternoon class into a Boys' and Girls' Club, with Miss Boss taking charge of the girls. In midsummer there is a Vacation Bible School for which our deaconess must do most of the planning, besides taking charge of one of the groups. As far as the regular church services at the Center are concerned, Miss Boss plays the piano, secures the services of other musicians for Sunday evenings and special occasions, and, if necessary, takes complete charge of the Ladies' Bible Class. Christmas and Easter

---

[41] Frieda Bremermann, "A Week with a Deaconess," *TLD* 30, no. 2 (April 1953): 3, 5.
[42] See for example, Florence Storck, handwritten journal entries, January and February 1946, priv. col. of Gloria Zimmerman, Seattle, Wa.

mean that our deaconess has charge of the rehearsals for plays and pageants.

It is important at the Gospel Center that the pastor and the deaconess work together as a team. Very often it is the deaconess who must prepare the way for the coming of the pastor. Especially among the widows, the aged women, in large buildings where introductions must be made over the house phone, and in certain other situations, the deaconess has ready entrance where a man would find difficulty in even seeing his prospect. When once the deaconess has made the initial opening, the pastor can carry on his work with much greater chances of success. Likewise the deaconess is sometimes made the confidant in matters of a personal nature.

Since the Gospel Center caters to those whom it pleases to call the "lower classes," there is much Social Service work—or let us say Christian Charity—to be carried on. Our deaconess can never tell what service she may be called upon to perform. There may be a sick person to be introduced to one of the clinics, or a relief client who is desperately in need of food, or a drunk who wants to make a nuisance of himself, or a needy person for whom a coat and shoes might be sought from the clothing department. . . .

Miscellaneous duties are unlimited. The Volunteer Group, ladies recruited from Cleveland Lutheran Churches, work together with Miss Boss, and she sees to it that work is laid out for the Volunteer when she comes in during the morning. Mimeographing, typing, mailing, filing, indexing, and similar duties frequently fall upon Deaconess Boss. Young People's meetings mean that the deaconess plans games, provides for refreshments, and also directs much of the activity. Frequently one of the Ladies' Societies of the many Lutheran churches in Cleveland desires a speaker. Our deaconess is always ready to address these groups and can vary her lecture so as to emphasize deaconess work, Gospel Center, or some other topic. For Gospel Center's deaconess it's never a question of "What shall I do?" but "Where shall I start?"

Gospel Center is indebted to its deaconess. Any expansion in our work, a greater degree of thoroughness in our work, and plans which we have been able to make for the future are due to the fact that we were able to secure the services of a combination social worker, nurse, religious instructor, secretary, and general assistant in the person of Deaconess Martha Boss.

(Rev.) Robert Weller, Cleveland, Ohio[43]

---

[43] Robert Edward Frederick Weller (1914-1978). Robert Weller, "A Unique Missionary Endeavor," *TLD* 20, no. 1 (January 1943): 3-4.

The above article is a wonderful tribute to the deaconess, as well as an example of how pastors and deaconesses could work together in team ministry. Of course, this type of partnership was not limited to home missions, but was expected to be the norm in every field of service.

MINISTRY IN FOREIGN NATIONS

The LDA took an active interest in foreign missions. When serving as first editor of *TLD*, Pastor Herzberger used the magazine to solicit contributions for a medical mission student, and for three years he listed "Women Workers in Our Foreign Mission Fields" on the back page of each publication.[44]

The first roster of women working in foreign lands included four women in China and four in India.[45] In 1926, a graduate of the Beaver Dam Deaconess School became the first deaconess nurse to join the LCMS mission team in India, and three additional deaconess missionaries joined her the following year.[46] In 1931, a graduate of the Deaconess Training School at Fort Wayne became the first deaconess to join the established mission efforts in China.[47] Several years after World War II, deaconesses also worked with LCMS missions in Hong Kong (1950) and Japan (1951).[48]

Starting in 1877, supported largely by members of the Missouri Synod, the Synodical Conference began to "initiate work among the heathen or at least religiously neglected and forsaken Negroes of this country."[49] Half a century later, the African Americans who benefited from these mission efforts challenged the Synodical Conference to take up a new mission field.

---

[44] The Missouri Synod commissioned its first two foreign missionaries in 1894, to serve in India. One missionary nurse was sent to India in 1913 and another in 1921, when the Synod established a hospital at Ambur, India. In 1917, the Missouri Synod took over the mission work started by one of its pastors in China, and again, female nurses and teachers were sent to that mission field. Meyer, Carl S., ed., *Moving Frontiers, Readings in the History of The Lutheran Church-Missouri Synod, 1847-1962.* St. Louis: Concordia, 1964, 302, 306-308, 337.

[45] F. W. Herzberger, "The Only Solution for our Medical Mission Work," *TLD* 1, no. 3 (July 1924): 22; "Women Workers in our Foreign Mission Fields," *TLD* 2, no. 4 (October 1952): 32.

[46] See Chapter four.

[47] Clara Rodenbeck, "Our Missions," *The Lutheran Witness* 51 (March 15, 1932): 106-107.

[48] Marian Epp, "First Impressions of Japan," *TLD* 28, no. 4 (October 1951): 7; Martha Boss, "Mission Work in Hong Kong," *TLD* 30, no. 3 (July 1953): 5.

[49] Synodical Conference, *Proceedings,* 1878, Trans. Richard Drews, 58-60. As printed in Meyer, ed., *Moving Frontiers,* 317.

Our Negro Christians have donated a chapel to each of our mission fields in China and India. They, too, have a warm heart for the missions among the blind heathen. At their second general conference, held last August [1925] in Concord, N.C., the representatives of our Negro congregations resolved unanimously and with great enthusiasm to ask their mission board to place before the Synodical Conference their request that they be permitted to begin a mission in Africa. . . . To show the earnestness of their desires they also gathered an offering for the mission in Africa."[50]

In April 1936, Dr. Henry Nau (1881–1956), President of Immanuel Lutheran College in Greensboro, N.C., went to Nigeria for several months to lay the groundwork for Synodical Conference missions there.[51] Rev. Vernon William Koeper (1912–1974), Rev. William H. Schweppe and Deaconess Helen Kluck followed as missionaries in March 1937. Koeper was an LCMS candidate straight from seminary, ordained and commissioned at a service somewhere in Chicago. Schweppe had been serving as a Wisconsin Synod pastor in Osceola, Wis., and Kluck as surgical supervisor at the Beaver Dam Deaconess Hospital. Not surprisingly then, the farewell service for the latter two missionaries was held at a Wisconsin Synod congregation in Milwaukee; the sermon was preached by Professor J. Meyer of the WELS Lutheran Theological Seminary in Thiensville; while LCMS pastor Rev. Louis Adam Wisler (1876–1945), Executive Secretary of Colored Missions for the Synodical Conference, performed the commissioning rite.[52]

A decade after the African missions were underway, Rev. O.H. Schmidt, Executive Secretary of the LCMS Board for Missions in Foreign Countries, was doing his best to recruit deaconesses to serve in the Synod's mission fields. His arguments were compelling.

It does not take a great deal of reflection to understand that there ought to be a definite place for deaconesses in the foreign mission endeavor of the Christian Church. . . .

---

[50] Synodical Conference, *Proceedings*, 1926, 27. Meyer, ed., *Moving Frontiers*, 320.

[51] *Ibid.*, 321.

[52] A later report about the service states that Wisconsin Synod pastor, Rev. Im. Albrecht of Minnesota preached the sermon in Milwaukee, but the service bulletin names Meyer as the preacher. "Farewell Service in Honor of The Rev. Wm. H. Schweppe and Miss Helen Kluck, R.N., Deaconess, to be Commissioned by the Ev. Luth. Synodical Conference to work among the Ibesikpos in Nigeria, Africa," Sexagesima Sunday, January 31, 1937, St. John's Lutheran Church, Milwaukee, Wis., service bulletin, "Deaconess Historical Archives" box, Deaconess Office Archives, Concordia University, RF; "Our First Deaconess in the African Mission Field," *TLD* 4, no. 1 (January 1937): 7.

There are reasons stemming from the conditions on the foreign mission field which eloquently plead the cause of using deaconesses over there. Our foreign mission work carries us into countries where the separation of the sexes is much more pronounced than in this country and where it is, therefore, exceedingly difficult for a male missionary to move about as freely and to carry on his missionary work in as general a fashion as that would be possible in this country. It is well known that in many of these foreign countries women are kept in a secluded position and that it would be impossible for a missionary to penetrate into these interiors and to have the opportunity of speaking to all the members of the family and inviting them to accept Christ as their Savior. We, therefore, need women mission workers who can approach women on the foreign fields, gain their confidence and discuss with them the needs of their soul and tell them the story of salvation through Christ and his blood. . . .

And there is another reason why women workers are so necessary. Heathenism is dreadfully hard for womankind. It keeps women in a very humiliated position. And yet women are the most fanatic devotees of those heathen religions. Ignorance and superstition have such a hold on them that it is extremely difficult for them to break that hold and, therefore, also extremely difficult for a missionary to win them away from their heathen views and practices. Since a missionary would hardly have a chance to say much or do much about these things by reason of the Oriental seclusion of the women, it is necessary to have women mission workers try to break down this fanatic adherence to heathen views and superstitions. Only if it is possible to gain the women in greater number for the Christian church can we hope to build up a well balanced indigenous church. If we can reach only the men, and if the women, and that usually means the whole household remain shut away from Christianity, then our missionary efforts will be badly handicapped. . . . Let us repeat it: If the church in the foreign country is really to grow, then we need the family units in the church, and that will mean that also the women must be won for Christianity. And here the work of a Christian deaconess should prove extremely valuable. . . .

From all that has been said, it will be seen that the work of a deaconess on the foreign mission fields calls for specialized training and for a combination of Christian qualities that may be rare. There must be, to begin with, a great deal of consecration and earnest zeal for the Lord and His work. There must also then be a more than ordinary amount of intelligence and sympathy of courage and patience. With all this there must go a constitution of very good health and a winning and pleasing personality so that the confidence of shy and fanatic women and girls may be gained. But we feel sure that the Lord will give this combination of qualities to women who may be trained for the specialized field of endeavor of a deaconess in the foreign mission field.[53]

CONCORDIA SEMINARY—ST. LOUIS

The specialized training referred to by Schmidt consisted of one year of study at Concordia Seminary in St. Louis. The School of Foreign Missions, opened at the seminary in September 1941, operated in conjunction with the LCMS Board for Foreign Missions to educate "St. Louis and Springfield graduates, nurses, deaconesses, and missionaries' wives for foreign duty."[54] Just before Schmidt's article appeared in print, Deaconess Martha Boss finished a year of study at the Mission School and left for service in China.[55] During the 1946–47 academic year, thirteen future missionaries, including five women, studied at the Mission School. Among the women was Deaconess Rose Ziemke, preparing to serve in India.[56] Five years later, Deaconess Adeline Rink also studied at the seminary and Dr. Schmidt himself commissioned her for work in India.[57]

The above examples refer to deaconesses who were already consecrated and had worked before attending the Mission School. In October 1951, Superintendent Krentz announced another track for women who wanted to be missionaries in foreign lands.

> The question is frequently asked: How long is the Deaconess Course of Study? Frequently we receive inquiries about the possibility of taking a short course to become a deaconess. Others ask: may I take a correspondence course to prepare for the diaconate? The answer is: Our regular course of study for student deaconesses is a full four-year college course . . .

> However there are two exceptions to taking this full college course at Valparaiso University. Exception 1: If some lady has professional training, such as a graduate nurse, she may take a one-year course largely in the

---

[53] O. H. Schmidt, "The Place of the Deaconess in the Foreign Mission Enterprise of the Church," *TLD* 23, no. 1 (January 1946): 6-7.

[54] "Mission School," *The 1947 Vicar*, Concordia Seminary, St. Louis, Mo., student yearbook, no pagination, Archives, Concordia Seminary Library, St. Louis, Mo.; "The Graduate School," *Concordia Theological Seminary: Evangelical Lutheran Synod of Missouri, Ohio and Other States, One Hundred and Third Year 1941-1942* (St. Louis: Concordia, 1941), 20.

[55] Walter Gerhard Boss, "With China in View," *TLD* 23, no. 1 (January 1946.): 2.

[56] "Campus Women are Interesting, Active," *The Seminarian* 38, no. 8 (March 12, 1947): 9. See also "Rose Ziemke," *Concordia Historical Institute Quarterly* (Winter 2001): 196.

[57] "Dr. O. H. Schmidt Commissions Deaconess Rink for Service in India," *TLD* 29, no. 4 (October 1952): 5; "Deaconess Adeline Rink Accepts Call to India," *TLD* 29, no. 2 (April 1952): 3.

field of Religion. . . . Exception 2: If the Board of Foreign Missions, Dr. O.H. Schmidt, Executive Secretary, approves some woman for service in the foreign field, she may take a one-year course in the Mission School of Concordia Seminary to become a deaconess in our overseas missions.[58]

The logistics of what Krentz described above are vague. Did he mean that the LDA would consecrate as a deaconess any woman who was approved by Schmidt and had studied for one year at the Mission School? If he did, it was certainly a departure from all precedent. There appears to have been no mention of this alternate plan in other publications, and LDA records list no deaconesses as graduating in St. Louis. On the strength of these facts it seems plausible that potential missionaries never explored this option.

There were other deaconesses who entered mission work, however. In 1956, Schmidt appointed Deaconess Dorothy Folkers a missionary teacher in New Guinea, where she organized a school for the natives, and Deaconess Candidate Ruth Mueller, R.N., to carry out mission work among the Mohammedans in India. The Mission Board of the Synodical Conference also called Deaconess Elaine Yoreo to teach in Nigeria that same year.[59] In later years, others went to New Guinea, Venezuela, and Japan.[60]

HEALTH ISSUES

In the concluding paragraph of his article, Schmidt asserted that any deaconess desiring to serve in foreign missions needed "a constitution of very good health." From the time that Herzberger began writing public pleas to young women to consider deaconess work, he assumed that only those who had good health should enter the diaconate. Hence for many years a doctor's certificate was required as part of the application process for deaconess training. In spite of this precaution, in the early decades of the diaconate, issue after issue of *TLD* reported the illness of deaconesses (and sometimes deaconess students) as a matter for remembrance in prayer. The following quotation provides a typical example of such reports.

> Miss Rosa Bremer was compelled by illness to leave her position at the hospital at Alamosa, Colo. She is at home in Ocheydan, Iowa at present. The last reports from her are encouraging. May the Lord restore her to

---

[58] "Length of the Deaconess Course," *TLD* 28, no. 4 (October 1951): 7.

[59] "Station LDA Tune In," *TLD* 33, no. 2 (April 1956); 5.

[60] "Station LDA," *TLD* 36, no. 4 (October 1959): 5; "News From Foreign Fields," *TLD* 39, no. 4 (October 1962): 6.

complete health! . . . Miss Louise Gieschen has been at the Deaconess Home for a rest. She spent the holidays with her folks in Milwaukee.

The superintendent (Kohlmeier) received a welcome letter from our deaconess in China, Miss Clara Rodenbeck. We are sorry to note, however, that she is compelled to take a rest cure. The physicians assure her that she will be fully restored to health, and she writes that she is making rapid improvement. For this we are truly thankful. She is at the seminary in Hankow at present, taking care of the medical needs of the students and continuing her language studies.[61]

When Krentz became Superintendent he recognized that many of the health problems the women experienced were related to their work, or more accurately, their workload. In 1942, he wrote, "Students taking this course must be physically sound, since working in an orphanage, an old folks' home, or in the foreign mission field, over a term of years saps the vitality of our women workers, as experience clearly shows."[62] One example of this experience, by no means unique, can be found in Dr. Frederick Stiemke's *A History of the Ministry of the LCMS with People who have Mental Retardation:*

In 1925, Bethesda became the fourth site in the Missouri Synod to train deaconesses. . . . Some chose to remain at Bethesda. These faithful—now, by our standards, abused—sisters in Christ willingly worked 12–18 hour shifts, often with days off only for sickness or family emergencies, such as the death of a loved one. Hearing the stories of veterans like the now sainted Deaconess Christine Seckel, I marvel at their commitment and why so many served for so many, many years.[63]

As mentioned in chapter six, the LDA placed deaconesses in fields of service for only one year at a time until 1959. A survey of reports on the travels of deaconesses before that time shows that the women often visited their families or other members of the diaconate en route to their next assignment.[64] This appears to be the closest thing to a regular vacation that any deaconess expected to receive. Indeed, the word vacation or holiday never appears in any LDA materials regarding the life and work of a deaconess, and formal arrangements for such were never in place until after 1960.

---

[61] "News Items," *TLD* 10, no. 1 (January 1933): 4.

[62] "You Want to Know About the Lutheran Deaconess," *TLD* 19, no. 4 (October 1942): 6.

[63] Frederick Adolf Stiemke, ed. Thomas Heuer and Timothy Dittloff, *A History of the Ministry of the Lutheran Church—Missouri Synod with People who have Mental Retardation* (Watertown: National Christian Resource Center, Bethesda Lutheran Homes and Services, Inc., 1997), 7.

[64] "News Items," *TLD* 15, no. 1 (January 1938): 3.

Of course, if a deaconess needed complete rest before 1943, it was common for her to retreat to the soothing environment of the deaconess motherhouse in Fort Wayne. Many issues of *TLD* listed the women staying at the motherhouse, as well as the women "on leave of absence" in other locations.[65] After the LDA training program moved to Valparaiso, a sick or exhausted deaconess needed to recuperate with relatives or perhaps at a Lutheran Hospital where another member of the diaconate could look her after.

Unfortunately, the deaconesses did not have good role models for taking care of their health. Many of the leaders of the deaconess movement, from Herzberger through Krentz, worked too hard for their own physical good. For some it was a reflection of their pietism—for others just a strong work ethic. Either way, there does not seem to have been any serious attempt to instruct the women on how to care for their own person. If a deaconess wanted to continue in her vocation, she needed to have a strong body as well as a strong faith, a strong mind, and a strong spirit of service!

THE MARRIAGE QUESTION

One of the most frequently asked questions with regard to deaconess ministry in the Synodical Conference and later in the Missouri Synod was: *May deaconesses get married?* In 1982, when asked to discuss this question in relation to the early years of the LDA, Deaconess Emeritus Clara Strehlow answered:

> It was never forbidden. From the very beginning Pastor Wambsganss said, "We do not ask our deaconesses to remain single because that's contrary to God's Word." During Pastor Kohlmeier's time, he never discouraged marriage. But I think every once in a while we got some girls, deaconesses themselves, who felt that you ought to promise to remain single.[66]

Strehlow never mentioned whether the Superintendent corrected these deaconesses, but it is easy to see that LDA officials consistently contradicted their ideas in print. In fact, the answer to the marriage question was always a resounding yes, with the assurance that no vows were required of deaconesses, except the promise to be faithful in the performance of

---

65 "Deaconesses According to Their Stations," *TLD* 14, no. 4 (October 1937): 8.
66 Deaconess Clara Strehlow, interview by Deaconesses Betty Mulholland and Nancy Nicol, transcript, Oshkosh, Wisconsin, November 12 and 13, 1982, priv. col. of Betty (Schmidt) Mulholland, Munster, Indiana, 13.

their duties, to lead an exemplary Christian life, and to submit to the Deaconess Agreement.[67]

That is not to say, however, that the LDA encouraged marriage. Why? Because when a deaconess married, the LDA viewed her as lost to the diaconate. In his 1937 report to the LDA, Superintendent Kohlmeier mentioned the recent effect of matrimony.

> Numerically we have lost during the last year. Since the last annual meeting nine deaconesses have resigned, six of these on account of getting married. Naturally we feel the loss of so many active deaconesses. To our organization this made the problem of supplying adequate help to the respective fields quite acute. Yet the loss of service to the Church is not as large as it may appear when hearing these figures. Most of the former deaconesses still continue to serve the Church, as much as their time permits. This will be understood, if I add that five of the six deaconesses who entered holy matrimony were married to pastors and missionaries in their respective field of service.[68]

Note that Kohlmeier referred to the married women as *former* deaconesses, even though he recognized that most of them still served the Church. This actually makes sense if considered in light of the Deaconess Agreement. After all, a woman could no longer be expected to keep her promise to submit to the decisions of the LDA Board or agree to transfers of position assigned by the superintendent when she was, by definition of Christian marriage, required to submit to her husband and see to the needs of her family.

The real key to understanding why adherence to the Deaconess Agreement defined who was or was not a deaconess is found in Kohlmeier's lament that matrimony is a problem for the *organization* (as opposed to being a problem for the Church). The LDA functioned separately from the Church. It assigned deaconesses trained *by the organization*, to fields of service chosen *by the organization*, and considered the women to be deaconesses as long as they were working under the auspices of (or in obedience to) the *deaconess association*. Therefore, when the nine deaconesses mentioned by Kohlmeier *resigned from the LDA*, they were no longer considered to be deaconesses, even though some continued to work for the Church in the same positions that they had held before marriage.

---

[67] See Chapter five. "Twenty-five Questions with their Answers on The Lutheran Deaconess Association and its Work," *TLD* 12, no. 3 (July 1935): 2-3.

[68] "Annual Report of the Superintendent at Annual Meeting of the Association, October 31, 1937," *TLD* 15, no. 1 (January 1938): 4.

That this was Kohlmeier's thinking is clearly illustrated in an article written by him in January 1938.

> Deaconesses Oneida Witte and Clara Hilken resigned their positions at the hospital at Yuma, Colo., leaving there the first days of December. Before returning they paid a visit to the Indian Mission at Whiteriver, Arizona, and our former deaconesses, Mrs. Otto, Mrs. Riess, and Mrs. Sorgatz. . . .
>
> . . . The following extract from a letter recently received from Mrs. Stelter of India (formerly deaconess Gertrude Oberheu) will be of interest to our readers.. . . [Last year] I took care of over 900 children on dispensary, weekly sewing classes, and classes with women. A few Sundays ago there were six women baptized in this compound congregation. The first to make this step. They were women who attended classes that I started, and then we got them going to instruction classes. How good it makes one feel to see that! . . . We like the work and ask you to pray for us to do our part for what you all sent us out here. In fact, we are only your representatives. It is your work as much as ours. Give us your prayers, as we pray for you all, too."
>
> We see from this letter that our former deaconesses in the Foreign Mission still have an active part in the work. We may add that also our former deaconesses in the Indian mission in Arizona continue to assist the missionaries by teaching classes of women and children.[69]

Four months after publishing the above article, Kohlmeier presented a paper on the use of deaconesses in "follow-up work" to a conference of institutional missionaries meeting in Fort Wayne. Interestingly, he prefaced his paper by defining a deaconess.

> What is a deaconess? A deaconess is a trained woman church-worker, a trained woman assistant to the pastor or missionary. I say, a **trained** woman church-worker. . . . Here I would like to say just a few words on what I have in mind, when I use the title "deaconess." In some localities where institutional mission work is carried on, the missionary has a group of volunteer workers, ladies who devote some time to this work, or he has some one especially engaged by the mission society to assist him in his work. And these ladies are often referred to as their deaconesses. And this custom of calling these ladies "deaconesses" can probably be defended.

---

[69] Deaconess Gertrude Oberheu (Mrs. Stelter) transferred from the Beaver Dam Hospital to India in the fall of 1929. The LDA placed or transferred Deaconess Irma Gallmeyer (Mrs. Sorgatz), Deaconess Edna Stuebs (Mrs. Otto), and Deaconess Gladys Connolly (Mrs. Riess), into positions at the Lutheran Apache Indian Mission in Whiteriver, Arizona in 1934, 1935, and 1936 respectively. "News Items," *TLD*, 15, no. 1 (January 1938): 3.

Yet you will understand that it somewhat beclouds the minds of our people as to the value and need of the work of the Lutheran Deaconess Association and of the deaconesses trained by us. Since we have this Association and are training deaconesses and trying to place them in the various fields of church-work, where trained women workers are needed, it would help us to have our people associate the name "deaconess" with those have taken our course and are in the service of our Association. In this essay I shall use the name "deaconess" as applied to a woman worker, trained for assistance in church-work, making this her profession and devoting her entire time to the work assigned to her.[70]

A decade later, the idea that a deaconess was someone who had taken the LDA training course *and* served through the association (*and* devoted her time exclusively to the work assigned her) was starting to be questioned, especially by women who had either continued to work after marriage or returned to some type of church work after having children.[71] Krentz addressed the topic in a *TLD* article in 1951.

Frequently questions have been asked us about the marriage of deaconesses. It seems a few lines on this topic may be welcome.

On the one hand, now and then we meet with the thought that deaconesses are not allowed to get married. The Deaconess Association has never placed a barrier before deaconesses who wanted to enter marriage. After all, God instituted marriage. Some of our deaconesses marry after a few years of service, some serve a decade or two, before they get married.

However, before a student prospect is accepted as a student deaconess, she agrees in writing to serve as a deaconess for a minimum of three years. It seems altogether fair that after a girl has received four years of college work at Valparaiso University under the auspices of the Deaconess Association in collaboration with Valparaiso University, she should feel in duty bound to serve the church for at least three years. After all, getting a college education with a major in Religion, is not an end in itself, but a means to an end, namely, to serve our Church and suffering humanity.

Then again the thought has been expressed that the education of young women for the diaconate is quite futile since so many of them render short-lived service. So we checked our records. We found that of the 150 deaconesses consecrated to date, 70 have been married. This goes to show

---

[70] "The Deaconess in Follow-Up Work: A paper read before the Conference of Institutional Missionaries, Fort Wayne, Indiana, May 10-11, 1938," *TLD* 15, no. 3 (July 1938): 4.
[71] "Station LDA Tune In," *TLD* 26, no. 4 (October 1949). 8 is printed in error; the actual page number is 6.

that a large percent of these women consider Deaconess Service a career. So the record is quite good, about seven years of service on the average.

> Then it should be emphasized that after marriage many of the former deaconesses have been quite active in church work. Thus a married deaconess is serving in our child welfare work, Addison, Ill. And in overseas missions, deaconesses who have married missionaries are a great help in our mission endeavors, especially among the women.[72]

It is interesting that *before* a woman was accepted for deaconess training she signed a contract with the LDA. Such a requirement may not have seemed unusual during a decade when young people enlisting for military service would have signed similar documents. In the article above Krentz used the phrase "duty bound to serve the church for at least three years." However, since students promised to render their service *as deaconesses*, his words clearly meant "duty bound to serve the church for at least three years under the auspices of the LDA." What the Superintendent did not write above, was that a student would be required to repay scholarship monies to the LDA if she reneged on the signed work agreement.

Krentz hoped to recruit women who would consider Deaconess Service as a career, to the exclusion of marriage or other obligations that might distract them from their duties. And yet, when enquiries came to his office from prospective students or their families, the truncated question, "May a deaconess get married?" was increasingly being asked in a longer form: "May deaconesses get married *and* continue to be deaconesses?"

In April 1952, *TLD* included a roster of student deaconesses for the 1951–52 school year. Three of the 48 names on the list had a double asterisk after them, indicating the simple explanation: "Has withdrawn."[73] Two of these women had the same reason for withdrawing.

> I was in my junior year when I withdrew. I fell in love with a young man, and Mrs. Trautmann, who was our contact from the LDA, came to me and strongly suggested that I withdraw. She said, you probably ought to drop out because you won't be able to fulfill your three years of obligation to work for the LDA after you graduate, and then you would have to pay back all that the LDA gave you in scholarship money. The LDA had paid for half of our tuition and Valpo paid the other half. All that we deaconess students paid was our room and board.[74]

---

[72] "Do Deaconesses Get Married?" *TLD* 28, no. 2 (April 1951): 8.

[73] "Roster of Student Deaconesses According to States, 1951-1952," *TLD* 29, no. 2 (April 1952): 2.

[74] Joanne (nee Gilmore) Kerkhof, notes from telephone interview by CDN, February 1, 2006, priv. col. of CDN, Pittsburgh, Pa.

I had already met the man that I would marry at the end of my freshman year. When I was a junior, I was asked what my intentions were—and I really didn't know at that point—but it was put to me that if I intended to marry the boy and not fulfill my obligations to the LDA then I should withdraw. I don't think Krentz was aware of how many of us, or who, were dating, but Mrs. Trautmann knew. I think she was the one who mentioned it to him. Rev. Krentz came to Valparaiso every Monday to visit us and have devotions with us, and on that particular Monday he and the housemother spoke to me together.[75]

Both of these women earned bachelor's degrees with a double major in Religion and Education from Valparaiso University. One married an electrical engineer and had a long career as a Lutheran schoolteacher, while the other married a US Navy man and worked extensively in the education program of churches all over the world. While they were finishing their college education outside of the deaconess program, the women knew deaconess students who planned to marry Lutheran pastors or teachers, but had not been asked to withdraw from the program.[76]

One of my good friends married a pastor. She finished the training and worked for one year as a deaconess and then they got married. It didn't bother me at the time that women who were going to marry pastors could stay in the training. It was presumed that they would be more of an assistant to their husbands in the deaconess type positions even if they weren't paid.[77]

At the time it didn't really sink in to me. But it was obvious that if you were marrying a Lutheran schoolteacher or a minister you could stay in the deaconess program but if you were marrying a layman you could not. That was never officially said to me, but it worked out that way. There were several instances of women who were marrying Lutheran schoolteachers and pastors who were allowed to finish.[78]

For the first time, in October 1951, the list of "Deaconesses According to Their Stations" included the names of two active deaconesses married to pastors.[79] Answering questions from an Iowa pastor, Krentz wrote in 1953,

[75] Marilyn (nee Heather) Wessel, notes from telephone interview by CDN, February 1, 2006, priv. col. of CDN, Pittsburgh, Pa.

[76] Kerkhof, telephone interview by CDN.; Wessel, telephone interview by CDN.

[77] Joanne (nee Gilmore) Kerkhof, notes from second telephone interview by CDN, March 9, 2006, priv. col. of CDN, Pittsburgh, Pa.

[78] Wessel, telephone interview by CDN.

[79] Kathleen (nee Rubow) Gaudian and Marian (nee Speckhard) Epp, who both graduated in 1950. "Deaconesses According to Their Stations," TLD 28, no. 4 (October 1951): 8.

"Our problem today is to get the deaconess to defer marriage until she has given a minimum of three years to service as a deaconess."[80]

In 1959, the LDA sponsored a display on diaconal ministry at the LCMS Synodical Convention in San Francisco. The presence of a young deaconess assisting Krentz at the display became a public relations triumph for the LDA when the convention press team wrote a *News Release* about her.

Wedding Bells Must Wait While Deaconess Works

Wedding bells must wait for attractive Mertice Spaude, 23, because she has pledged three years of deaconess service to her church. The deaconess order of the Lutheran Church—Missouri Synod does not forbid her to marry. But since she has pledged this service, she feels that she can best carry it out prior to her marriage. But with a diamond sparkling on her finger and a glow in her eye, she says, "I'm going to marry a minister."

As parish worker for Trinity Lutheran Church, Great Bend, Kansas, Mertice speaks with enthusiasm as she relates her joy in serving the congregation as organist, music director, youth counselor, and educator. A graduate of the Lutheran Deaconess School at Valparaiso University in Indiana in 1958, she has served the Kansas congregation for just one year.

Mertice is one of 78 deaconesses presently serving in the Missouri Synod. Not all of her colleagues are serving as parish workers in congregations. Some have specialized for work in hospitals and institutions; some serve in social welfare agencies working in orphanages, homes for the deaf, or for the mentally retarded; still others have gone into foreign mission work.

While attending the triennial convention of The Lutheran Church—Missouri Synod in San Francisco as a representative of the LDA she was in charge of the Deaconess Display. She hopes to encourage other girls to consider deaconess work as a life's career. "More and more young women who learn how they can serve their Lord through deaconess work are considering it as a field of service in Christ's kingdom," she said. "Even if wedding bells must wait!"[81]

Almost as an Army recruiter might do, Spaude was encouraging other women to consider deaconess work *as a life's career*, and yet planned to finish

---

[80] "Question Department," *TLD* 30, no. 1 (January 1953): 8.
[81] "Wedding Bells Must Wait While Deaconess Works," *The Lutheran Church—Missouri Synod 44th Synodical Convention,* Department of Public Relations, LCMS—CN #38—Feature, Immediate Release, June 19, 1959, printed page, priv. col. of Clara Strehlow, Deaconess Office Archives, Concordia University, RF, Illinois.

her own *field of service* before marriage. She evidently never mentioned the possibility of serving as a deaconess again later in life.

In the early 1960s a variety of circumstances existed among married deaconesses. Some women held "Deaconess-Pastor's Wife" positions; some worked for only one or two years before marrying a pastor or layman; a few served as deaconesses for many years and made the choice to continue serving when they married.[82] The one thing that these women had in common was that they had been deaconesses *before* they married. So the answer to the question, "May deaconesses get married *and* continue to be deaconesses?" was a definite yes. At the same time, the marriage question would now need to be turned around. In other words: *May married women become deaconesses?* Of course it was always assumed, according to the example of the New Testament, that widows could be deaconesses. But what about women who were living with a spouse or raising children? As expected, the evolving marriage question would continue to be answered in the affirmative, starting in 1963, when for the first time, a deaconess student married before she was consecrated.

> I was engaged in December of 1961 while on internship. The LDA knew it when I came back to Valparaiso for my senior year of college. I graduated on June 10 and married on June 21. We moved right away to Ottawa, Canada, where my husband had been assigned to his first church as a pastor. I was consecrated in December of 1963. Pastor John Korcok, the circuit counselor for Ottawa, did the consecration at Our Savior's Lutheran Church in Ottawa.[83] The consecration service was a procedure that took place to finalize your training, almost like a graduation ceremony, so that you were ready to serve whenever you were called. I always worked in the same congregation with my husband, doing the music and a women's ministry and things like VBS. The church tried to give us more money to cover my work, but I never had a call.[84]

Two years later, in 1965, the Director of Training dedicated several paragraphs of his annual report to his understanding of the marriage question.

> Most people probably know that the diaconate of the Lutheran Church - Missouri Synod, in contrast to that of other Lutheran diaconates, permits a woman to retain her status as a deaconess after marriage. This development has been accepted as normal, and even applauded by many.

---

[82] "Deaconess-Pastor's Wife Works in Inner City Church," *TLD* 38, no. 2 (April 1961): 4; "Staff Thoughts," *TLD* 40, no. 2 (Spring, 1963): 2.

[83] Rev. John Korcok (1925-1994).

[84] Pfotenhauer, telephone interview by CDN.

On the other hand, there are others who feel that this is an unfortunate development. They base their feelings on the question of the meaning of the deaconess consecration service under these conditions.

There are good arguments on both sides. The fact is, however, that the typical student in the program at present time has no intention of spending her life as a deaconess. She hopes eventually to be married and to have a family. Furthermore, we are finding that congregations are entirely willing to retain the services of a deaconess even after marriage. In spite of what has been said above, we are careful to inform our students that: 1. We cannot have a student marry prior to graduation and remain in the program, and 2. If she has definite plans for marriage immediately or soon after graduation, then placement at the time of graduation will be complicated.

Although we are in favor of personal freedom regarding marriage, we are nevertheless of the opinion that there should be stronger emphasis upon, and encouragement for, life-time commitment to service in the diaconate. We are beginning to think of ways in which this can be accomplished, including new structural forms for alternative types of commitment to the diaconate.[85]

What a fascinating final sentence! What were these "new structural forms" and "alternative types of commitment"? Unfortunately the answer is unknown, since LDA publications never again mentioned or even alluded to these concepts.

There is an abundance of oral history to support the fact that deaconesses who married laymen in the '50s and '60s were—just like those who had married pastors—very interested in using their deaconess training to serve within the church. These former deaconesses often gave untold and unsung hours of volunteer service to congregations and institutions. By 1968, the LDA began giving permission for deaconesses who had married and raised families to re-enter deaconess service.

After we got married in 1955 I couldn't continue to serve as a deaconess. My husband insisted that we honor the written agreement, so we paid back all of my scholarship money to the LDA, even though I always thought that I would be able to go back to being a deaconess some day. When we were students the idea was already being put into our heads, once a deaconess always a deaconess. In 1968 I told my pastor that I was thinking of going back to work and would appreciate it if he could inform me of any deaconess positions that might be open. Right away he suggested that it might be possible to have a position at my home

[85] Arne Kristo, "From the Director of Training," *TLD* 42, no. 4 (Winter 1965): 11.

congregation. Pastor spoke to the deacons and invited the LDA Executive Director to meet with us at the church, and the two of them agreed that I could serve as a deaconess.[86]

It is interesting to note here, that even though the LCMS College of Presidents placed deaconess interns and graduates, the LDA (independent of the Missouri Synod) still assumed responsibility for *authorizing* placements for women after a leave of absence. After all, the training of deaconesses was solely in the hands of the LDA, and the association still held to the tenet that women were deaconesses only if they served under the auspices of the LDA and were recognized by the association as members of the diaconate.[87] Approving work sites and authorizing deaconess service did not imply, however, that the LDA accepted responsibility for *finding* placements for women who wished to begin working again.

Though the LDA allowed married women to rejoin the diaconate in the late 1960s, students in the training program at Valparaiso continued to struggle with engagement issues.

I remember you could not be engaged and get a call from the LDA. That was 1968. I was engaged on call night. That was common. If you were going to get a diamond, you got it on call night after the calls were given. And some people got pearls so that it wasn't so obvious. I don't remember who told us that we couldn't be engaged and receive a call. It was common knowledge, but I don't know if it was written anywhere.[88]

Whether or not the Executive Director knew about the students' way of coping with the engagement issue is unknown—but by the turn of the decade the LDA recognized that some changes needed to be implemented. In 1970 the total number of active deaconesses had declined from the previous year. A new category of "part-time deaconess" was created, and the LDA Board of Directors decided to make the training program more attractive to women who planned to marry! One of the ways that the Board accomplished this was to give students the option of serving their internships after, rather than before, their senior year. This meant that they could graduate from VU, get married, and then go on internship. Or, if a

---

[86] Betty (nee Schmidt) Mulholland, notes from telephone interview by CDN, April 1, 2005, priv. col. of CDN, Pittsburgh, Pa.

[87] In 1966 the Board resolved that consecration services for deaconesses would only be authorized if the graduate accepted a position recognized by the LDA as a deaconess position. Arne Kristo, "From the Director of Education," *TLD* 43, nos. 3 and 4 (Winter 1966): 6-7.

[88] Janet (nee Thompson) Tindall, notes from telephone interview by CDN, April 6, 2005, priv. col. of CDN, Pittsburgh, Pa.

woman had already fulfilled the requirement of two years of community living in Deaconess Hall, she could marry after her junior year, serve her internship, and then complete her senior year at Valparaiso. Another significant change came in 1971, when the Board decided that deaconesses who had worked less than the minimum three years no longer needed to repay scholarship money received from the LDA.[89]

The author remembers conversing with a student in the Deaconess Hall lounge (in the fall of 1974) who claimed to be the first woman to be married *before* she entered deaconess training. Her case was an unusual one, but from the early 1970s onward, the marriage question faded and was replaced by other questions that sought to define a progressive diaconate in a modern society.

---

[89] Peter Zadeik, "Minutes of the Annual Meeting," *TLD* 47, no. 1 (Spring 1970): 7; Wilma S. Kucharek, *A History of the Lutheran Deaconess Association*, research paper written for Theology 180A at Valparaiso University, mimeographed pages, 1976, 32-34.

Illustrations for Chapter Seven may be viewed at www.deaconesshistory.org.

CHAPTER 8

THE MARKS OF A DIACONATE

Chapters three and seven of this book examine topics that informed the shaping of an identity for individual deaconesses. This chapter now turns to what could be collectively referred to as external marks of the Synodical Conference diaconate, that is, tangible items and experiences held in common by all of the deaconesses and that contributed to the understanding and ownership of a group identity. Though these marks or characteristics changed and evolved over the years, they still played a role in defining the diaconate as a whole.

WEARING THE DEACONESS GARB

Early photographs of graduates from the deaconess training schools housed at Lutheran hospitals in Fort Wayne, Beaver Dam, and Hot Springs show women in smart nursing uniforms, complete with the different nursing caps worn at each school.[1] The graduates from the Watertown school were also pictured in uniforms unique to the Bethesda home, but with no head covering.[2]

Desiring a unity of practice in order to promote the deaconess cause, the LDA postulated that a single garb should be chosen for all consecrated deaconess. In October 1930, Superintendent Poch reported, "The question as to what kind of uniforms our deaconesses are to wear has been definitely settled by a committee of the Fort Wayne Deaconess Auxiliary. Every deaconess will receive a copy of the regulations."[3]

Deaconesses in the field disliked the uniform mandate and discussed the matter at length. The minutes of the 1934 Deaconess Conference noted,

---

[1] Photos with caption: "Deaconess Graduates of 1923," *TLD* 1, no. 1 (January 1924): 1; Photos with caption: "Beaver Dam Graduates," *TLD* 2, no. 2 (April 1925): 1; Photos in section titled: "Our First Deaconesses from Hot Springs, S. Dak.," *TLD* 4, no. 4 (October 1927): 27.

[2] Photos with caption: "Watertown Deaconess Graduates. Class 1927," *TLD* 4, no. 3 (July 1927): 18.

[3] "Notes and News," *TLD* 7, no. 4 (October 1930): 31.

"The matter of a uniformity of uniform was tabled until next year."[4] One week after the Deaconess Conference, a "Deaconess Group Meeting" took place during the ALCh Conference in Chicago. Minutes from this meeting make it clear that the discussion did not center on whether or not deaconesses should wear a uniform, but rather, what *kind* of a uniform they should wear.

> The question of a distinctive uniform was discussed, as girls wearing the present uniform are often mistaken for district visiting nurses. It was therefore moved and supported to recommend to the Board of the L.D.A. to take up the question of finding a more distinctive uniform for the deaconesses.[5]

About a year later, Superintendent Kohlmeier wrote a circular letter, informing all deaconesses about the 1935 Deaconess Conference and inviting them to the installation of the Fort Wayne graduating class to be held on the Sunday prior to their conference. His letter also included the plea: "All deaconesses will wear the deaconess uniform for the attendance on Sunday and for the Conference. Please! We deem this very important, that all appear in the regular uniform!"[6] Not surprisingly, Kohlmeier included "the Uniform Question" under "Unfinished Business" on the conference agenda.[7] The conference minutes noted:

> ...After much discussion, a motion was made and carried that all deaconesses should wear the Deaconess Uniform. Deaconess Bender presented drawings and patterns of a garb which might be considered for adoption.

> Two questions arose: "Should we make a complete change of garb, or should the present uniforms (plural) be kept, with only minor changes?" Motion was made to leave details of minor changes with the Advisory Committee and when agreed to get in touch with the Board for final decision.

> Motion made and carried that the Advisory Committee take into consideration the choosing of a coat or cape and head gear for proper

4 Cora Leader, "Minutes of the Meeting of the Deaconess Conference at Bethesda Home, Watertown, Wisconsin," July 3, 1934, priv. col. of Clara Strehlow, Deaconess Office Archives, RF, Illinois.
5 Clara E. Strehlow, "Minutes of Deaconess Group Meeting," (July 1934), hand-written notes on Morrison Hotel stationery, *Reports of Officers and Committees* file, *Associated Lutheran Charities Box 1,* CHI, St. Louis, Mo.
6 H. B. Kohlmeier, no heading, typed mimeographed letter, hand written date: 1935, priv. col. of Clara Strehlow, Deaconess Office Archives, RF, Illinois.
7 Kohlmeier, no heading, typed mimeographed letter, hand written date: 1935.

distinction. A rising vote of thanks was given Deaconess Bender for her splendid paper.[8]

The Advisory Committee and Board evidently settled on a "complete change of garb" and the LDA offered to furnish every deaconess with three uniforms per year.[9] From 1936 to 1942, graduates from the Central Deaconess Training School in Fort Wayne were photographed in identical dark blue dresses with large white collars. No hats, coats, or capes appeared in the pictures.[10] During the same period, some of the older deaconesses who trained as nurses still wore their nursing uniforms and caps.[11]

NEW GARB FOR A NEW ERA

With the move to Valparaiso in 1943, Superintendent Krentz "determined that the association would have a uniform that the young deaconesses would want to wear."[12] Taking their cue from Krentz, women began to follow their own preferences as to which garb they wore, and whether or not they wore it. In 1944, the *Fort Wayne News-Sentinel* ran an article on the twenty-fifth anniversary of the LDA, along with a photograph of Pastors Poch, Kohlmeier and Krentz with the first three women to graduate from the Valparaiso training school. Though this was an historic occasion, none of the women wore uniform for the picture.[13] In the summer of 1946, amid

---

[8] Alice Dey, "Minutes of the Meeting of the Deaconess Conference at Concordia College, Fort Wayne, Indiana," July 2, 1935, priv. col. of Clara Strehlow, Deaconess Office Archives, RF, Illinois.

[9] "Twenty-five Questions with their Answers on The LDA and its Work," *TLD* 12, no. 3 (July 1935): 3.

[10] The exact shade of blue used for the uniform cannot be determined from the black-and-white photographs. In January 1938, Miss Mary Sauer of Fort Wayne was identified as "the seamstress who makes our deaconess uniforms." "News Items," *TLD* 15, no. 1 (January 1938): 3; Photo with caption: "Our deaconess graduates," *TLD* 16, no. 3 (July 1939): 2.

[11] Photo with caption: "Deaconess Clara Dienst R.N." and Photo with caption: "Deaconess Lulu M. Noess, R.N., holding a Mexican baby," *TLD* 17, no. 1 (January 1940): 5, 6.

[12] Paul John Kirsch, Conversation between Arnold F. Krentz and Paul John Kirsch, September 5, 1960, Deaconesses in the United States Since 1918: A Study of the Deaconess Work of the United Lutheran Church in America in comparison with the Corresponding Programs of the Other Lutheran Churches and of the Evangelical and Reformed, Mennonite, Episcopal, and Methodist Churches, PhD Thesis for New York University, 1961, 286.

[13] The *Fort Wayne News-Sentinel* photograph was reprinted in *TLD* in October 1951. That magazine also included, in a question and answer section, "Why do deaconesses wear uniforms? The uniform marks the deaconess as a servant of the church. It also promotes a feeling of equality and fellowship among the deaconesses." Photo and "Information Please," *TLD* 21, no. 4 (October 1944): 5, 6.

excitement about the new four-year college course at Valparaiso, the Deaconess Conference made another attempt to resolve the issue.

> At the closed meeting on Friday evening several items were informally discussed. The committee on uniforms, Frieda Bremermann chairman, reported on the possibility of having suits for street wear. Two styles were modeled: a regulation suit in grey, by Florence Storck, and a summer suit-dress, navy, by Frieda Bremermann. . . .
>
> Special meeting Saturday P.M.
>
> The following resolutions were presented and duly carried:
>
> 1. That the present blue uniform remain the official uniform until suitable materials are available, and that the uniform committee continue its research.[14]

Deaconess Conference minutes never mention the uniform again until 1956. However, in 1948, the young deaconess students at Valparaiso University apparently took the bull by the horns and helped to sort everything out for the diaconate. Retired deaconess, Dolores Hackwelder, recounts how it all happened:

> To the best of my recollection, the whole deaconess student body, seniors all the way down to freshman, met together in our living room there in Pi Delta Chi and decided that they would like to have a uniform. I guess the girls had talked to Mrs. Trautmann about it at various times. So we decided that this would be a good idea, something we should do.
>
> There was a group of us—I can't remember who all was in this group, except that Mrs. Trautmann was with us—and we went up to Chicago to what was called the garment district and talked to the people there. They indicated that they could help us and we got a few ideas. We took the information back to the whole group and then they selected myself and another girl—I think she was a senior—to go back to choose the material and the design of the uniform according to what the store could make.
>
> The girls thought that the uniform should be navy blue, and other than that there were no instructions except that it was to be nothing fancy. So we went back to that garment district and they custom made the uniform to our specifications. It was a skirt and jacket and you could wear any type of blouse you wanted. No one really said that the blouse had to be white but I usually wore white. The women needed to be measured because the uniform was tailored. We definitely wanted a cross somewhere on the

---

[14] Clara Strehlow, "Minutes of the Deaconess Conference, Concordia Seminary, St. Louis, Missouri, June 27-29, 1946," priv. col. of Clara Strehlow, Deaconess Office Archives, Concordia University, RF, Illinois, 4, 6.

uniform to make it distinctive, so the arm insignia was part of the uniform from the start.[15]

In 1950, Superintendent Krentz noted that the deaconesses took pride in their uniforms and also mentioned Deaconess Bremermann of Chicago as deserving a "barrel of credit" (presumably because she served as chairman of the uniform committee).[16] For many years the use and value of the deaconess uniform was described in *The Deaconess Quiz*, a popular little catechism-type brochure that listed questions and answers about the "Lutheran Deaconess Profession."[17] In 1958, the third edition of the *"Quiz"* read:

50. Does the deaconess wear a uniform?

The deaconess uniform of the Synodical Conference is a distinctive two piece navy blue suit with a gold cross emblem on the left arm and the gold lapel cross. She wears this on her consecration day for the first time and may wear it thereafter. Though wearing the uniform is optional, the deaconess finds that her uniform gives her recognition as a professional church worker and usually makes it easier for her to enter public hospitals and institutions in an official capacity.[18]

Further editions of the *Quiz* contained the above entry, but with small changes. For example, in 1960 the words "Synodical Conference" were altered to "The Lutheran Church Missouri Synod and Affiliated Synods" and in 1962 it was explained that a deaconess intern could also wear the uniform, but without the "gold Deaconess cross." In the second half of the 1960s an intriguing sentence was added: "The uniform lends itself well to current style changes."[19]

---

[15] Hackwelder ordered two uniforms that she believes were the first to be made by the garment store in Chicago. In 2005 she gifted one of these uniforms to Concordia Historical Institute in St. Louis. Dolores Jean Hackwelder, interview by CDN, transcript, Oakmont, Pa, February 11, 2004, priv. col. of CDN, Pittsburgh, Pa.

[16] "Station LDA Tune In," *TLD* 27, no. 4 (October 1950): 6.

[17] Several editions of *The Deaconess Quiz* were printed by the LDA between 1956 and 1969.

[18] *A Deaconess Quiz: Over 50 Answers to Your Questions About the Deaconess Program*, 3rd Edition, (1958), printed brochure, no pagination, File LDA General, "Brochures and Tracts," CHI, St. Louis, Mo.

[19] *The Deaconess Quiz: 61 Answers to Your Questions About the Deaconess Program*, 5th Edition, (1960), 12; *The Deaconess Quiz: 66 Answers to Your Questions About the Deaconess Program*, 7th Edition, (1962), 5; *The Deaconess Quiz: A Catalog of Information* (undated), 6. All printed brochures, File LDA General, "Brochures and Tracts," CHI, St. Louis, Missouri, 6.

The Deaconess Cross

The Deaconess Cross appears to have been cherished by all deaconesses, whatever uniform they wore it on. Every deaconess received this emblem of service to the Lord "in His wretched ones and His poor" at a ceremonial pinning that took place during the consecration of her graduating class. Initially, the Superintendent of Nurses' Training at Fort Wayne Lutheran Hospital or the deaconess motherhouse Supervisor affixed the cross to each deaconess.[20] Starting in the 1940s, this honor was often given to benefactors of the deaconess cause, for example, the president of the Fort Wayne Deaconess Auxiliary, the president of the Deaconess Conference, or a female member of the LDA Board of Directors.[21]

In 1951, the deaconess graduation class requested and received permission for each woman to be consecrated in her home congregation. As these consecration services continued to take place all over the United States and Canada, it became fashionable to ask district presidents of the LWML to perform the pinning-on of the Deaconess Cross.[22] The LDA Field Secretary, presidents of local ladies' aid societies, and veteran deaconesses also carried out this solemn privilege.[23]

The idea of a Deaconess Cross was nothing new to Pastors F. W. Herzberger or Philipp Wambsganss Jr., who certainly saw various types of crosses on the uniforms of deaconesses from other denominations. Whether or not Elizabeth (Hess) Wambsganss had a Deaconess Cross is not known. But it is easy to see that her son liked the concept. A photograph of Wambsganss as a mature man, on display at Emmaus Lutheran Church, Fort Wayne, shows a Deaconess Cross boldly pinned to the knot of his tie.[24]

Director Wambsganss may have been the one to commission Ernest Wegener to create the Deaconess Cross—a task which he was still cheerfully performing thirty-seven years later. In July 1956, the diaconate

---

[20] "Annual Meeting of the Deaconess Association," *TLD* 1, no. 4 (October 1924): 26; "Consecration Service," *TLD* 14, no. 3 (July, 1937): 4.

[21] "Deaconess Consecration: Redeemer Lutheran Church, Ft. Wayne," *TLD* 19, no. 2 (April, 1942): 5; "Consecration of Deaconess Kluge," *TLD* 25, no. 4 (October 1948): 2; "Consecration of Deaconess Betty Gallion," *TLD* 26, no. 4 (October 1949): 5.

[22] Krentz did a large amount of public relations work with the LWML, which produced long-term fruit for the LDA. See for example, Arnold F. Krentz, "Deaconess Endeavors," *Lutheran Woman's Quarterly* (April 1945). "Consecrated, Lord, to Thee," *TLD* 28, no. 3 (July 1951): 4.

[23] "Deaconess Consecrations," *TLD* 31, no. 4 (October 1954): 7.

[24] In 2006, Emmaus Evangelical Lutheran Church moved to 8626 Covington Road, Fort Wayne, Ind.

expressed appreciation for Wegener's many years of dedication to the deaconess cause.

Deaconess-Cross-Maker

When Ernst [*sic*] Wegener celebrated 50 years as a jeweler, engraver and watch maker in 1951, he said about his work: "Throughout my life I've had an INTEREST in the things I do. It was just plain interest, not the kind with a percent sign on it." Maybe that's why he is still making the official Deaconess Cross today as he was 37 years ago when the LDA began training deaconesses! He has an "interest" in this!

Mr. Wegener of Beaver Dam, Wis., is an artisan of first rank. His 55 years as jeweler, and his hobbies of building miniature cameras and violins, only sharpen his senses for precision work.

The gold cross seen on the lapel of every deaconess is the work of his hands. It is a simple, wide, gold cross with a beveled edge.

A tribute to Mr. Wegener from the deaconesses for his skilled workmanship in making the outward mark of the deaconess' calling, her gold lapel cross![25]

The lovely little gold crosses made by Wegener continued to be pinned on the left lapel of new deaconess uniforms for another thirteen years. In 1969, a new symbol would be adopted in conjunction with the fiftieth anniversary of the LDA.

THE RITE OF CONSECRATION

Consecration services took place at a time other than the regular Divine Service and were usually followed by a reception. The pinning-on of the deaconess cross, albeit significant, was only a small part of the service. The following quotation provides other details common to reports of consecrations printed in *TLD*.

Sunday, July 6, 1952, was an important mile-stone in the life of Miss Anita Rentz, Decatur, Ind. For on the evening of that day she was consecrated in Zion Lutheran Church of Decatur as a Deaconess, set apart for service to Christ and her fellowmen.

The service began with a beautiful processional. Pastor Edgar Schmidt of Zion Church served as the liturgist. Assisting in the rite of consecration were the Pastors Edgar Schmidt, Otto Busse, Walter G. Schwehn, and Albert Fenner. These pastors with the laying on of hands quoted

---

[25] "Deaconess-Cross-Maker," *TLD* 33, no. 3 (July 1956): 2.

appropriate verses of Scripture for comfort, strength, and admonition. Miss Rentz was given the deaconess cross to wear as a symbol of the office of the diaconate, which was pinned on the lapel of her deaconess uniform by Miss Pauline Krudop, President of the Fort Wayne Deaconess Auxiliary. This cross is to remind the deaconess not to be ashamed to confess her faith in the Crucified Christ and ever to bear in her heart the remembrance of His love Who died on the cross for her. The choir sang an appropriate hymn and the Rev. Arnold Krentz preached the sermon and led in the rite of consecration.[26]

The front cover of the January 1953 issue of *TLD* depicts Rentz kneeling at an altar rail, with Krentz and the other four pastors each holding a hand over her head. The original "Form of Installation of Deaconesses," written by P.E. Kretzmann (and included as an appendix to his *Handbook of Outlines for The Training of Lutheran Deaconesses*) did not include the laying on of hands.[27] In that rite, designed to be used with several candidates at the same service, Kretzmann suggested that the installing clergyman should take each of the probationers *by the hand* and say:

> May God, our dear and faithful heavenly Father, grant you strength, and with His grace fulfil [*sic*] what we are unable to do. May He richly bless you according to His infinite grace. Amen.[28]

At some point, presumably when Kretzmann's *Handbook* was no longer the primary textbook for deaconess education, the LDA (or perhaps Krentz himself) introduced the laying on of hands in consecration services. Copies of essays presented at the annual Deaconess Conferences in 1948 and 1949 reveal that the LDA deaconesses heard lectures about how the laying on of hands occurred in "the diaconate in the American Lutheran Church" and "in the early Christian era."[29] Krentz also mentions this practice in the opening paragraphs of an article announcing consecration services for the 1954 graduates.

---

[26] "Anita Rentz Consecrated as a Lutheran Deaconess," *TLD* 30, no. 1 (January 1953): 2. See also: "Consecration Rite for a Deaconess," *TLD* 40, no. 3 (Summer 1963): 9.

[27] See Appendix 1.B. The terms *Installation Service* and *Consecration Service* were used interchangeably.

[28] Paul E. Kretzmann, *A Handbook of Outlines for The Training of Lutheran Deaconesses*, Published by The Young Women's Lutheran Deaconess Association of St. Louis, Mo., St. Louis, 124.

[29] Magdelene Krebs, "The Aim and Purpose of the Diaconate in the American Lutheran Church," four mimeographed pages, no pagination, August 27, 1948, priv. col. of Clara Strehlow, Deaconess Office Archives, Concordia University, RF, Illinois; Muriel James, "History of the Diaconate," three mimeographed pages, 1949, priv. col. of Clara Strehlow, Deaconess Office Archives, Concordia University, RF, Illinois, 1.

It seems right and proper that our deaconesses who are called for such a very special work in our church should be set apart by some special religious service so that the new deaconesses and the congregations may be suitably impressed with the importance and solemnity of the office with which the deaconess candidate is invested.

In the early centuries of the new Testament Church, two significant acts were incorporated into the rite of consecrations. 1. A simple, stole-like cloth was placed about the neck of the candidate with the exhortation to take on the yoke of Christ. 2. The laying on of hands was practiced not as though this act gave any specific spiritual power but symbolic of the help given the ordained deaconess by the Holy Spirit.

Also the prayer spoken at the consecration of a deaconess, which dates back to the fourth century, is quite beautiful and touching. It begins; "O eternal God, Father of our Lord Jesus Christ, Creator of man and woman, who didst fill with thy Spirit Miriam and Deborah and Hannah and Hulda; who didst not disdain to cause thine only-begotten son to be born of a woman . . . do thou look now also upon this thy servant to be ordained to the office of a deaconess and grant her Thy Holy Spirit."[30]

Although Krentz appears to have liked the practice of laying hands on the deaconess candidates, there is no record of him ever laying a "stole-like cloth" on the women. Furthermore, this is apparently the only place where he ever used the designation, "ordained deaconess."

IDENTIFYING AN HISTORICAL MODEL

When references are made to earlier centuries of the Christian church, they beg the question: Did the LDA, or those who directed the association's deaconess training program, deliberately adopt particular diaconate models or philosophies employed by antecedent deaconess organizations and their leaders?

The answer to this question is both a weak yes and a resounding no, for reasons that can be only briefly outlined in this book.

WILHELM LOEHE

The LDA readily perpetuated Loehe's deaconess motto because it stimulated a desirable attitude of servanthood.[31] Beyond the motto, little

---

[30] "Deaconess Consecrations," *TLD* 31, no. 4 (October 1954): 7.

[31] Indeed, the motto inspired and supported the ideals of servanthood in organizations outside of the LDA. For example, Rev. Enno Duemling quoted it in his 1943 speech to the annual ALCh convention. E.A. Duemling, "Institutional Missions—Then and Now," hand

238 In the Footsteps of Phoebe

was taught about Loehe and the diaconate at Neuendettelsau, a fact substantiated by a short article in the April 1947 issue of *TLD*.

> During this Centennial Year of our Beloved Synod, Pastor Wm. Loehe will be repeatedly mentioned as a man of remarkable missionary vision and zeal who educated pastors for the great American mission field. . . .
>
> A fact that merits consideration, but is less known, is that Pastor Loehe trained deaconesses for church work. He organized a Deaconess Society in Bavaria in 1854, and in that year he also dedicated the Deaconess home in Neuendettelsau. Academically, in his deaconess training, he demanded a high degree of intellectual cultivation.
>
> The Deaconess Motto which hangs in every Deaconess Motherhouse and School comes from the pen of Loehe.[32]

In 1949, Deaconess Muriel James prepared a lengthy "History of the Diaconate" to present at the annual Deaconess Conference. James spoke about Theodore Fliedner, Florence Nightingale, William Passavant; the motherhouse at Philadelphia, and the Norwegian and Swedish Lutheran diaconates in America, but never mentioned Loehe.[33] Six years later, in 1955, Field Secretary Shirley Groh wrote a paper on "The Role of Deaconess Through The Ages" which she mimeographed and distributed to interested parties from the LDA office in Fort Wayne.[34] Groh's essay did mention Loehe, but only to the extent of a brief introduction, followed by the quotation of Loehe's intriguing "*steps* for the deaconess vocation" and his deaconess motto.[35]

Of course it is possible that earlier LDA leaders knew about Loehe but chose not to speak about him. The founders of the LDA were closer to the controversy between Loehe and the Missouri Synod and may have desired to distance the new world deaconess movement from Loehe's name.

---

written speech, *1943 Convention Minutes, Reports* folder, *Associated Lutheran Charities Box 2*, CHI, St. Louis, Missouri, 11.

[32] "Wm. Loehe Trained Deaconesses," *TLD* 24, no. 2 (April 1947): 5.

[33] Muriel James, "History of the Diaconate," three mimeographed pages, 1949, priv. col. of Clara Strehlow, Deaconess Office Archives, Concordia University, River Forest, IL.

[34] Shirley A. Groh, "The Role of Deaconess Through the Ages," mimeographed pages, (Fort Wayne: LDA, 1955).

[35] Groh refers to Loehe's *steps* as "steps to the calling of [a] parish deaconess." She provides a Bibliography for the 15-page paper, but there are no footnotes and no indication as to from which resource the Loehe quotations were taken. This is significant only in that the translation of Loehe used by Groh is different from more recent renderings. See for example: Wilhelm Loehe, ed. Klaus Ganzert, trans. Holger Sonntag, "On the Deaconesses 1858," *Wilhelm Loehe, Gessammelte Werke, Herausgegeben im Aufrage der Gesellschaft fur Innere un Ausere Mission im Sinne der lutherischen Kirche,* IV (Neuendettelsau, Freimund Verlage, 1954).

Alternatively, those men who knew Loehe's views on the diaconate may have deliberately ignored him, either because they disagreed with his theology or did not believe that the Neuendettelsau model would work in modern America.

Krentz never publicly stated that he disagreed with Loehe, yet during his Superintendency he made statements that were contrary to Loehe's teaching about the diaconate. The laying on of hands is one case in point. Both men had obviously read the liturgy of the eighth book of *The Apostolic Constitutions* (commonly called the Clementine liturgy), which makes reference to the ancient prayer for deaconesses and the laying on of hands. As noted above, Krentz interpreted the laying on of hands as practiced in the early church as "*symbolic* of the help given the ordained deaconess by the Holy Spirit," rather than an act that gave any specific spiritual power to the deaconess.[36] In Loehe's 1858 writings "On the Deaconess," he attached more significance to the rite, asserting that "through the laying on of the Episcopal hands as well as the prayers of the church . . . the deaconess not only gained the publicly recognized position in the congregation, she also received her particular divine blessing of office."[37]

Aside from the short article cited above, Loehe is only mentioned one other time in *TLD*, in an article by a pastor who visited Neuendettelsau. His remarks end by highlighting differences between the German and American diaconates.

> As one wanders about in this little village of Bavaria, one may wonder about the wisdom of having such young women make the vow of life-long celibacy and devotion to church work, one may wonder at the severity of their garb and the seriousness of their mien, about the great emphasis on liturgy, and about other things, but there is no doubt about the consecration, the wonderful spiritual motivation, and the blessed services rendered by these women in black, the deaconesses of Neuendettelsau.[38]

> *I commend to you our sister Phoebe, a servant of the church in Cenchrea. I ask you to receive her in the Lord in a way worthy of the saints and to give her any help she may need from you, for she has been a great help to many people, including me.*   Romans 16:1–2

---

[36] "Deaconess Consecrations," *TLD* 31, no. 4 (October 1954): 7.

[37] Loehe, ed. Ganzert, trans. Sonntag, "On the Deaconesses," 1858.

[38] E.L. Roschke, "Deaconesses of Neuendettelsau," *TLD* 28, no. 4 (October 1951): 2-3.

PHOEBE AND THE NEW TESTAMENT CHURCH

The foremost historical reference held up to Synodical Conference deaconesses was Phoebe and the New Testament office of deaconess. Whether it was in Herzberger's tract on *Woman's Work in the Church,* Kretzmann's *Popular Commentary,* numerous consecration sermons, class lectures, recruitment materials, or presentations to ALCh conferences and LWML meetings—the example of Phoebe in Romans 16:1–2 was unanimously cited as setting the precedent for female lives dedicated wholly to the service of the Lord.

Other examples of pious Bible women sometimes mentioned in conjunction with Phoebe included Miriam, Deborah, Hannah, and Huldah from the Old Testament, and Mary, Martha, Dorcas, and Lydia from the New Testament. Occasionally a speaker or writer might also make reference to Macrina and Olympias, two well-known deaconesses of the fourth century.[39]

If one were to go back to examining the contents of *TLD* as done above—that is, as a sort of litmus test as to the LDA's possible interest in modeling its diaconate after the pattern of others—a number of names should be considered.

FRIEDRICH VON BODELSCHWINGH

The first article to ever appear in *TLD* (1925) concerning other diaconates featured Friedrich von Bodelschwingh (1831–1910) and the courageous ministry of mercy he established through a colony of deaconess institutions near Bielefeld in Westphalia.[40] During the last quarter of the nineteenth century, Bodelschwingh trained and sent more than one thousand deacons and deaconesses "into the service of suffering humanity" and was acknowledged as the national leader of deaconess work in Germany.[41] LDA leaders hoped to perpetuate Bodelschwingh's high level of industry and his endless love for suffering humanity in their own organization. In 1939, Deaconess Annchen Vierck wrote a series of articles

---

[39] H. B. Kohlmeier, "History of the Female Diaconate in the Early Christian Church," *TLD* 14, no. 4 (October 1937): 5-7.

[40] "Friedrich von Bodelschwingh," and "Bethel," *TLD* 2, no. 2 (April 1925): 15-16.

[41] In the early 1890s Bodelschwingh even sent two deaconesses to an interdenominational Protestant Deaconess Home in Dayton, Ohio. Gerald Christianson and David Crowner, *The Spirituality of the German Awakening: Texts by August Tholuck, Theodor Fliedner, Johann Hinrich Wichern, Friedrich von Bodelschwingh* (Mahwah, N.J.: Paulist Press, 2003); C. Golder, *History of the Deaconess Movement in the Christian Church* (Cincinnati: Jennings and Pye, 1903), 84-91; Jeannine E. Olson, *One Ministry Many Roles: Deacons and Deaconesses through the Centuries,* CPH, St. Louis, 1992, 266.

about her holiday in Germany, in which she described a visit to Bielefeld; the 1944 Deaconess Conference included a paper about Bodelschwingh; and in 1946 *TLD* mentioned the charity work among epileptics, the mentally sick, and alcoholics carried out by Bodelschwingh's son, who became his successor in the "City of Mercy."[42]

JOHANN WICHERN AND THEODORE FLIEDNER

Between 1930 and 1938, *TLD* contained four meaty articles on the life of Johann Wichern and the story of *Das Rauhe Haus*, as well as seven articles touching on the work of Theodore Fliedner. Another three articles mentioned Fliedner in 1947, 1957, and 1959.[43] While articles viewed Wichern as the pioneer of deacon ministry, Fliedner was always recognized as the father of the modern deaconess movement.

In 1937, *TLD* reported that Deaconess Lydia Lutz visited Kaiserswerth. Fliedner's work at Kaiserswerth was revered, again not with regard to the specifics of his organizational model, but in the fact that enormous amounts of good were accomplished, with prayer and unwavering dedication. Of course it is true that the LDA sustained a motherhouse infrastructure for twenty years, and for a time maintained conditions for admission to deaconess training similar to those used by Fliedner, but when circumstances dictated, the association moved away from that model, and the diaconate changed accordingly.

WILLIAM PASSAVANT

The front cover of the July 1949 issue of *TLD* featured a large photograph of Passavant with the caption, "Dr. William A. Passavant, Founder of the American Female Diaconate in 1849."[44] *TLD* mentioned Passavant and/or his pioneering work in Pittsburgh, along with the four deaconesses from Germany, in four magazine articles between 1934 and 1949. Viewed as particularly inspirational for diaconates of the New World, Passavant was portrayed as a man who persisted in doing whatever it took to provide care for the sick, poor, and orphans.[45] In 1952, as part of his "Station LDA Tune In," Krentz reported, "Recently we stepped into the

---

[42] "Lutheran Deaconess Conference Meets in Chicago," *TLD* 21, no. 1 (January 1944): 6; "Station LDA," *TLD* 23, no. 4 (October 1946): 6.

[43] *TLD*: 7, no. 1; 8, no. 1; 8, no. 2; 10, no. 2; 10, no. 4; 11, no. 1; 11, no. 2; 11, no. 4; 14, no. 1; 15, no. 1; 24, no. 3; 34, no 3; 36, no. 3.

[44] *TLD* 26, no. 3 (July 1949).

[45] The LDA also frequently noted, either in writing or in speeches, that Director Philipp Wambsganss Jr. was directly descended from one of Passavant's deaconesses. *TLD* 11, no. 1; 14, no. 1; 26, no. 3; 26, no. 4.

Passavant Hospital in Pittsburgh, Pa., the first Protestant hospital in America. . . . Today this hospital serves quite a few colored people who live in this area."[46]

THE WEAK YES AND RESOUNDING NO

A thorough reading of all LDA materials indicates a desire to copy attitudes from history that would ensure successful diaconates—attitudes of love and charity, dedication and servanthood, and a genuine desire to administer care to poor and wretched people. This goal is voiced extremely well in the following article, published on the occasion of the laying of the cornerstone at Deaconess Hall.

Let Us Not Be Weary In Well Doing

The words above from Paul's epistle to the Galatians are chiseled into the cornerstone of Deaconess Hall. Fitting words indeed.

Of Phoebe, the first deaconess mentioned in the New Testament, Paul writes in Rom. 16:1: "She is a helper of many and of myself as well." She probably did Christian social work in the maritime city of Cenchrea. Certainly, she did "not grow weary in well doing."

When Pastor Theodore Fliedner revived the modern Protestant diaconate in Kaiserswerth, Germany, in 1836, he had as his objective to train deaconesses to serve children, the helpless, the sick, and the underprivileged. The 121 years of the history of that glorious institution show that the thousands of deaconesses prepared for service there did "not grow weary in well doing."

When four deaconess nurses came over from Kaiserswerth, Germany, in 1849, to staff the first Protestant hospital in America in Pittsburgh, Pa., among whom was Elizabeth Hess, who later married Pastor Philip [sic] Wambsganss, Sr., they served gladly under very trying and primitive conditions. Once again we hear the refrain, "Let us not grow weary in well doing."

And those two stalwart pioneers of the diaconate within the Synodical Conference, pastors F. W. Herzberger and Philip Wambsganss Sr., [sic] exemplified in their own services as city missionary and promoter of charitable institutions that their motto might well have been, "Let us not be weary in well doing."

---

[46] "Station LDA Tune In," *TLD* 29, no. 1 (January 1952): 6.

And now may the aim of each and every deaconess of the Lutheran Church—Missouri Synod and affiliated Synods, continue to be in the future as it has been in the past: "Let us not be weary in well doing."[47]

Beyond the Christian virtues desired in members of the diaconate, there is no evidence that the LDA, at any point in its history, made deliberate attempts to copy a model of the physical makeup and running of another diaconate. Furthermore, when the four early training schools opened and closed, consolidated and moved, the LDA made no attempts to protect the educational set-up from further change. When the motherhouse had to be sold and new areas of ministry opened up for deaconesses, adjustments were made quickly, with the attitude that everything transpired according to God's will and timing. In fact, it can be stated with certainty that the LDA was proud of being flexible and progressive, and pleased that other US diaconates recognized and emulated the association's "advanced steps in the training of Deaconesses."[48]

One curiosity in this mix is the fact that on September 7, 1955, the United States Internal Revenue Service (IRS) "determined that deaconesses of the Lutheran Deaconess Association are members of a religious order"[49]—an amazing designation given that no *order* was mentioned in LDA literature; and consecration services, though they might mention the *office* of deaconess, included no reference to entering an *order*. Furthermore, the LDA no longer had a central motherhouse and deaconesses lived across the United States and in foreign lands. Looking again to the context in which the LDA received this ruling from the IRS, one can see that a flurry of financial appeals was in motion: for the scholarship fund, the library fund, and the building fund. In fact, a month after the ruling arrived, the LDA announced that it had just purchased property and intended to go forward with plans to build a new Chapter House. Given this context, it is reasonable to assume that the status of *members of a religious order* provided some sort of financial benefit to the women and the congregations or other agencies that employed them.[50]

---

[47] "Let Us Not Be Weary In Well Doing," *TLD* 34, no. 3 (July 1957): 2.

[48] "Conference Committee Studies Deaconess Education and Service within the Synodical Conference," 24, no. 2 (April 1947): 4; "Deaconess Training in Australia," *TLD* 22, no. 4 (October 1945): 6; "Station LDA," *TLD* 24, no. 2 (April 1947): 6.

[49] Letter from Philip E. Draheim (Draheim & Pranschke, Attorneys at Law) to Deaconess Nancy E. Nicol (Director of Deaconess Program, Concordia College), October 1, 1985, Deaconess Office Archives, Concordia University, RF, Illinois.

[50] The result of being *members of a religious order* was that LDA deaconesses, pursuant to IRS Code Sections 3401(a)(9) and 3121(b)(8), were not to have income tax withheld from their compensation, were not subject to FICA, and participated in Social Security by paying the

Provisions for Deaconess Students

Due to the illness of Executive Director Krentz, the LDA Board of Directors arranged for replacement instructors to teach the specialized deaconess courses in the fall of 1958. Mr. Milton Marten, Principal of Immanuel Lutheran School in Valparaiso and visiting instructor in the VU Department of Education, taught "The Principles of Religious Education." Rev. Kenneth Fredrick Korby (1924–2006), a new professor in the university's Religion Department, agreed to teach "The Field of Deaconess Work" and to act as Resident Counselor for the deaconess students.[51]

During the few years that Korby worked on behalf of the LDA, he introduced some thoughtful concepts to the process of deaconess education. Speaking to the annual Concordia Deaconess Conference[52] meeting forty years later, Korby explained:

> In 1958–59 I started my tenure as professor at Valparaiso University. During that time, Pastor Krentz, who was officed in Ft. Wayne at the Lutheran Deaconess Association office . . . would come to Valparaiso to teach the deaconess courses. He became ill, and because I was new on the faculty—young and strong at that time, and had just been a pastor—I was asked to teach those courses. . . . I was a single-minded simpleton and knew nothing else than to be a pastoral theologian, so that what happened was, for the first time in the history of the LDA there was a pastor in their residence who was beginning to shape the prayer life, the worship life, the study life under a pastoral regiment. I didn't know what I was doing, but that's what happened.[53]

Professor Korby is probably most frequently remembered for writing "A Litany for Deaconesses." Deaconess students prayed the litany regularly in the corporate devotions at Deaconess Hall, and Korby stipulated that it should also be used "wherever any deaconess was, anywhere in the world ... in an attempt to keep some sense of bonding with all of the sisterhood."[54] The full text of Korby's *Litany* can be found in Appendix 1.K.

After his official work for the LDA was finished, Korby continued to be fascinated by diaconal ministry and engaged in an earnest study of Loehe

---

self-employment tax. Letter from Philip E. Draheim to Deaconess Nancy E. Nicol, October 1, 1985.

[51] *TLD* 36, no. 1 (January 1959): 7.

[52] See Chapters 14 and 15 for a full explanation of the Concordia Deaconess Conference—Lutheran Church-Missouri Synod.

[53] Kenneth F. Korby, "Concordia Deaconess Conference 1998: Lectures by Rev. Dr. Kenneth Korby," Video Tape 1 of 4, Session 1 of 4, transcribed by CDN, 2005.

[54] Korby, "Concordia Deaconess Conference 1998," Video Tape 1, Session 1.

and his diaconate, spending the summer of 1969 working in the Archives at Neuendettelsau.[55] Interestingly, Korby asserted that it was in Neuendettelsau that he learned that the prayer life of deaconesses under the supervision of Loehe included the development of litanies—a fact that he did not know at the time that he wrote the litany for the Synodical Conference diaconate.[56]

RELATIONSHIPS WITH *OTHER* DEACONESSES

Serving as a deaconess often carried women to destinations many miles from other members of the diaconate. An awareness of this reality existed in *A Litany for Deaconesses* in the petition: "satisfy with Your own gracious gifts those of our sisters who work in isolated places." However, deaconesses from other denominations sometimes lived in close proximity to the women, so that friendships would be built with women from other diaconates.

LDA officials, starting with Field Secretary Korbitz, took it upon themselves to develop good relations with the heads of other diaconates. In 1938 and 1939, Sister Flora Moe of the Norwegian Lutheran Motherhouse in Chicago attended the consecration of graduates from the LDA Central Training School in Fort Wayne.[57] As mentioned in chapter four, Korbitz also spent some time at the Norwegian Lutheran Deaconess Hospital and Motherhouse in Chicago in 1939.[58] Two years later, reporting on a 4,000-mile journey he took on behalf of the deaconess cause, Superintendent Kohlmeier wrote:

> I had the opportunity to visit our deaconesses in the far West, to get acquainted with some of our workers whom I had not met before, to study their problems and get a better understanding of what is required of us. ... I visited many of our institutions of mercy and the Deaconess Motherhouses of other Lutheran church-bodies and gained much knowledge that I hope will be beneficial to us. . . . The Danish Lutheran Church has a Deaconess Institute at Brush (Colorado). They call it Eben

---

[55] Korby directed Valparaiso's overseas study center in Reutlingen, Germany, for the 1968-69 academic year, and then spent the summer of 1969 in Neuendettelsau engaged in research for his ThD dissertation. Korby received his doctorate from SEMINEX in 1975. Jeanne (nee Lindberg) Korby, notes from telephone interview by CDN, April 8, 2006, priv. col. of CDN, Pittsburgh, Pa.

[56] Korby, "Concordia Deaconess Conference 1998," Video Tape 2, Session 2.

[57] "The Deaconess Consecration Service," *TLD* 15, no. 3 (July 1938): 2; "Consecration Service," *TLD* 16, no. 3 (July 1939): 2.

[58] F. W. Korbitz, "Quarterly Report of Field Secretary," *TLD* 8, no. 4 (October 1931): 3.

Ezer. They gave me an opportunity to study their institution and to learn much that is of value. . . . Besides our own institutions, there was a special attraction for me in Omaha in the Swedish Lutheran Immanuel Deaconess Home and its institutions. The fine General Hospital, the Children's Home, the Hospital for Invalids, the Old Folk's Home, the entire Institute is a monument to the work of these deaconesses and their unselfish labors.[59]

When Krentz became Superintendent he maintained the cordial relationships with other Lutheran diaconates and followed Kohlmeier's example of visiting their establishments when possible.[60] Krentz's frequent contact with other Lutheran diaconates resulted in a proliferation of information about them in *TLD*. Some articles came from the official journals of other diaconates, some included correspondence from non-Synodical Conference deaconesses, and many simply reported the workings of deaconess schools, building programs, or any news related to deaconess ministry.[61] Krentz enjoyed this exchange of information and for several years reported on what he called a "friendly rivalry" between the LDA and other Lutheran diaconates, "in recruiting a large number of students for their Deaconess Programs."[62] Though the majority of articles about other diaconates related to other Lutherans, some also included snippets of correspondence from or information about the diaconates in Episcopal, Methodist Episcopal, Methodist, Baptist, Waldensian, and Mennonite Churches.[63]

---

[59] Kohlmeier also mentioned visiting orphanages in Des Peres (Mo.) and Freemont (Ia.); a church in Kansas City; the Wheat Ridge Sanitarium in Denver (Col.); hospitals at Alamosa and Yuma (Col.), Norfolk (Neb.), Sioux City (Ia.), and Omaha (Neb.); the Lutheran Sanitarium in Hot Springs (S.D.); the Old Folks' Home and Walther League Hospice in Omaha (Neb.); and the College at Seward (Neb). "The Superintendent Makes a Trip," *TLD* 11, no. 2 (April 1934): 2-3.

[60] For example, Krentz visited the Deaconess Motherhouse of the United Lutheran Church in Philadelphia in 1947. "Station LDA," *TLD* 24, no. 3 (July 1947): 6.

[61] A few photographs were also included—the most notable one showing seven Augustana Synod deaconesses at their consecration, with four clergymen, including the President of the Augustana Synod. The photo caption begins: "It pays to observe what others are doing." *TLD* 24, no. 4 (October 1947): 7. For examples of articles see: *TLD* 5, no. 4; 7, no. 1; 11, no. 1; 12, no. 1; 13, no. 4; 18, no. 3; 19, no. 2; 20, no. 3; 21, no. 3; 22, no. 4; 23, no 2 and 4; 24, no. 2; 27, no. 1; 29, no. 1; 30, no. 2; 31, no. 3; 33, no. 2; 34, no. 3; 35, no. 4; 36, no. 3.

[62] "Student Statistics," *TLD* 26, no. 2 (April 1949): 4; "Station LDA Tune In," *TLD* 27, no. 4 (October 1950): 6; "Student Deaconess Enrollment," *TLD* 29, no.1 (January 1952): 4.

[63] For examples see: *TLD* 6, no. 1; 24, no. 2; 27, no. 1; 34, no. 1 and 2; 35, no. 1.

THE DEACONESS CONFERENCE AND OTHER DIACONATES

Deaconesses from other Lutheran bodies visited the annual Deaconess Conference on a regular basis, starting in 1935 when Sister Theodora of the Baltimore Deaconess Motherhouse gave the women "a few pointers on her work as a parish deaconess."[64] Other notable speakers included Sister Ingeborg Sponland speaking on Norwegian Deaconess Work in 1936 and Deaconess Magdalene Krebs from the Milwaukee Motherhouse, who addressed the women on "The Aim of the Deaconess Movement in the American Lutheran Church" in 1948.[65]

In 1949, Deaconess Martha Seitz of the Stuttgart Motherhouse in Germany spoke about her work in China, after which the Conference voted to give her a Synodical Conference Deaconess Cross! The same 1949 meeting resolved to empower its president to select one of its members to represent the Conference at all meetings of the General Conference of Deaconesses in America. The minutes from the 1950 Deaconess Conference—where those in attendance heard a paper on "Avenues of Service for the Lutheran Diaconate during the Second Century," presented by Sister Nanca Schoen—noted: "it would be well if there were a closer relationship between the diaconates for mutual solutions of the deaconess problems."[66]

Feeling an empathy with others who carried out the same type of work, the idea of drawing closer to other diaconates to resolve "deaconess problems" seemed natural to the Synodical Conference women, especially since LDA Superintendents exampled the same attitude. Of course the process had already begun in several small ways. For example, in 1944, a

---

[64] "Minutes of the Meeting of the Deaconess Conference, at Concordia College Fort Wayne, Ind. July 1st, 1935," priv. col. of Clara Strehlow, Deaconess Office Archives, Concordia University, RF, Illinois.

[65] "The Program of the Lutheran Deaconess Conference July 21-23, 1936, at Concordia Teachers College, River Forest, Ill." and Magdelene Krebs, "The Aim and Purpose of the Diaconate in the American Lutheran Church," four mimeographed pages, no pagination, August 27, 1948. Both documents from priv. col. of Clara Strehlow, Deaconess Office Archives, Concordia University, RF, Illinois.

[66] Lulu Noess, "Minutes of the Meeting of the Lutheran Deaconess Conference Held at Lake Geneva, Wisconsin, August 18-20, 1949"; "Resolutions of Deaconess Conference Held at lake Geneva, Wisconsin. August 18-20, 1949"; Lulu Noess, "Minutes of the Lutheran Deaconess Conference August 7 to 9, 1950 Camp Augustana, Wisconsin." All three documents from priv. col. of Clara Strehlow, Deaconess Office Archives, RF, Illinois.

special feature of the Deaconess Conference in River Forest was a visit to the Norwegian Deaconess Home in Chicago.[67]

But the LDA diaconate also gave tutelage to other church groups. In 1954, Rev. Ernst Harder, head of the Deaconess Program of the Mennonite Church at Newton, Kansas, attended the Deaconess Conference at Camp Arcadia, to explore the possibility of reviving the Mennonite diaconate using the LDA model.[68] At the 1956 Deaconess Conference in St. Louis, a Miss Barnwell, Executive Secretary of the Methodist Deaconess Program was in attendance, as well as fourteen observers from the Mennonite Conference.[69]

Outside of Deaconess Conference meetings, the LDA diaconate sent representatives to two significant meetings in 1955 and 1956:

All-Lutheran Diaconate Conference Held

The chart below gives statistics for all Lutheran Diaconates in America as presented at their 32nd Conference in Axtell, Nebraska June 6-8. As guests at the Conference, Deac. Evelyn Middelstadt, president of our Synodical Conference Deaconess group, and I experienced **over and over** the warm glow of the common bond uniting us to all of the sixty delegates attending—namely, our united goal, to serve Christ, as embodied in our very title, Deaconess, from the Greek **diakonos** meaning servant. Whether we wore a garb with a crisp white bonnet or a tailored navy blue with a gold cross insignia, we were all deaconesses—and the tie that bound us was no small one. . . .[70]

+ + +

A FIRST meeting of all Deaconess Programs in America was held in St. Louis, Mo., at the Evangelical and Reformed (E & R) Deaconess Home in February. Under the motto "Joining Hands in Service," representatives of the E & R, Methodist, Mennonite, Salvation Army and these Lutheran bodies—ULCA, ELC, ALC, Norwegian, Augustana, and Synodical Conference met. The Danish Lutheran and Episcopal Diaconates were not present.

---

[67] Such visits seem to have taken place at various times over the years, whenever circumstances would allow. E.g., in 1964, when the LDC was meeting in Milwaukee, the conference paid a visit to the American Lutheran Church Motherhouse in that city. Ruth Beach, "Lutheran Deaconess Conference Meets in Chicago," *TLD* 21, no. 1 (January 1944): 6; "30th Anniversary Celebrated," *TLD* 41, no. 3 (Summer 1964): 8.

[68] "Station LDA Tune In," *TLD* 31, no. 3 (July 1954): 5.

[69] Mary Arbeiter, "Minutes of the Lutheran Deaconess Conference, held at the Lutheran Building, 210 North Broadway, St. Louis, Missouri, July 9-11, 1956," priv. col. of Clara Strehlow, Deaconess Office Archives, Concordia University, RF, Illinois.

[70] Shirley Groh, "All-Lutheran Diaconate Conference Held," *TLD* 32, no. 3 (July 1955): 6.

Hats off to the sisters of the E & R Diaconate who arranged this meeting. Once again our sites for service were lifted and focused as we looked about and saw Christian women confess Christ and happiness in His service.[71]

1955 Statistics of Lutheran Deaconess Programs in America[72]

Education headquarter	Synod	Year organized	Consecrated			Students	
			Active; Studying	Leaves	Retired	In School; Field Work	Total
Philadelphia, Pennsylvania	ULCA	1884	82	2	13	13	110
Baltimore, Maryland	ULCA	1895	52	2	10	22	86
Chicago, Illinois	ELC	1897	22	2	7	3	34
Brooklyn, New York	ELC	1893	3	-	2	-	5
Milwaukee, Wisconsin	ALC	1893	33	-	15	3	51
Axtell, Nebraska	Estr-Synod	1913	13	-	3	-	15
Brush, Colorado	Int	1904	1	1	3	1	6
Omaha, Nebraska	Aug.	1887	43	1	24	18	87
Minneapolis, Minnesota	Luth. Free	1888	6	-	4	-	10
Valparaiso, Indiana	Synod. Conf.	1919	77	4	1	55	137
TOTAL			333	12	82	115	541

Active Lutheran Deaconesses in 1955: 333

Deaconess Students in 1955: 115

[71] Shirley Groh, "In the Fields," *TLD* 33, no. 2 (April 1956): 6.
[72] Information taken from *TLD* 32, no. 3 (July 1955): 6.

The LDA leadership and the Deaconess Conference attempted to maintain relationships with the deaconesses of other Lutheran synods for many years. Of course, the synods that belonged to the Synodical Conference were not in fellowship with the synods to which these other Lutheran deaconesses belonged, but some of the Lutheran bodies, including the Missouri Synod, were making great efforts to seek agreement and fellowship among the different Lutheran bodies in America.

FROM SYNODICAL CONFERENCE TO MISSOURI SYNOD

As mentioned in chapter six, after the dedication of Deaconess Hall, The Lutheran Deaconess Association within the Synodical Conference marked itself as The Lutheran Deaconess Association within the Lutheran Church—Missouri Synod and Affiliated Synods.

The decision for the name change was primarily related to the Building for Christ campaign, but troubles within the Synodical Conference itself may have contributed to a closer alignment with the Missouri Synod. As early as 1946, attendees at Synodical Conference conventions acknowledged that problems existed between the member synods. The Evangelical Lutheran Synod resolved to break fellowship with the LCMS in 1955. In 1952 the Wisconsin Synod delegates at the Synodical Conference convention declared themselves to be in "a state of protesting fellowship" with the Missouri Synod; in 1961 their synod broke fellowship with the LCMS while remaining in the Synodical Conference; and in 1963, Wisconsin pulled out of the Synodical Conference altogether. By that time, only the Slovak and Missouri Synods were left in the Synodical Conference.[73]

When the LCMS held its Centennial Synod at the Palmer House, Chicago, in July 1947, the LDA provided a colorful Deaconess Display in the exhibition area.[74] A commemorative booklet called *See His Banner Forward Go*, produced for the Synod's anniversary convention, recognized the work of deaconesses within the Missouri Synod:

> Of ever-growing importance in our Church is also the work done by our *deaconesses*. Parish deaconesses are in charge of various charitable endeavors of a local congregation. Deaconess nurses are trained to have charge of a full nurse's work in connection with the charitable undertakings of the entire Church. Some deaconesses serve as social

---

[73] Mark E. Braun, *A Tale of Two Synods: Events That Led to the Split Between Wisconsin and Missouri* (Milwaukee: Northwestern Publishing House, 2003).

[74] Photo and caption, *TLD* 24, no. 4 (October 1947): 8.

workers, being active in general Inner Mission work. Other deaconesses minister as Bible women, especially in Foreign Mission work, where they bring the Gospel of Jesus Christ to women who are not permitted to take part in public worship and must be served in private or zenana mission endeavors.[75]

After the special synodical convention, a telling article appeared in *TLD* titled "Report Prepared for the Centennial Synod," which looks like a speech that Superintendent Krentz delivered to the convention. Whether he spoke to "the brethren" or only wrote his remarks, it should be noted that the author consistently refers to the LCMS as "our synod" or "our Church."

Report Prepared for the Centennial Synod

During the first half of our Synod's history, from 1847 to 1897, three major Lutheran church bodies in America, the United Lutheran Church, the Augustana Synod, and the American Lutheran Church had already established Deaconess Service in their midst.

Not until 1919, or approximately during the last quarter of Synod's first hundred years, did our Church begin training deaconesses for parish, missionary, and institutional services.

If there is **one unfinished task** in the work of our Synod in the past, it is definitely the education of deaconesses. During the past century 140 young women were consecrated for the diaconate.

We dare not be satisfied to educate 140 or 240 or 340 young women for deaconess service during the next hundred years. Rather let our aim be the education of 1040 deaconesses during the coming century.

Synod's entrance into the second century, if it means anything, means a more intensive and extensive missionary program. ...

Brethren, we are in need of your financial help to promote the Deaconess Cause. May we plead with you to motivate your Sunday school, your Walther League, your ladies' aid, your Lutheran Women's Missionary league to help us financially.

Remember, our education program for deaconesses is not allowed one cent of Synod's money. Yet we furnish you with qualified women workers. Just last month we commissioned a deaconess for service in India.

---

[75] See chapter four for definition of zenana missions. See His Banner Forward Go: This book is published by the Evangelical Lutheran Synod of Missouri, Ohio and Other States in commemoration of its Centennial (St. Louis: Concordia, 1947).

When Miss Olive Gruen, long-time mission worker in China, heard that we had established a full college course for deaconess students at Valparaiso University, she wrote us an enthusiastic letter, in which she emphasized the great improvement this education at Valparaiso is over the education she received in preparation for her service in China. When she was informed that we sorely needed a new Deaconess Chapter House at Valparaiso, she promised us a $1,000 check for this purpose.

Brethren, your greater support of the Deaconess Cause will make the second century of our Synod differ from the past century in this respect. During the first century Deaconess Work was in the budding stage; during the second century it will reach full-bloom.[76]

To say that the deaconess program "is not allowed one cent of Synod's money" was technically correct, and yet LCMS members and districts indirectly supported the LDA by awarding scholarships. In 1948–49, the Colorado, South Dakota, and Central districts all voted to open the use of district financial aid funds to deaconess students.[77] By the time that pre-deaconess programs were officially established on LCMS college campuses, any college or district funds available to students studying for full-time church careers could be used for deaconess education.

Missouri Synod President Rev. John William Behnken (1884–1968) cooperated in promoting the Deaconess Movement within the Missouri Synod following the Centennial celebrations. In a letter to Krentz dated March 25, 1949, the president wrote:

Dear Brother Krentz:

As per your request I am herewith giving you a testimonial which you may use as you deem fit:

The training of Lutheran Deaconesses, still rather new in our church, deserves earnest and wholehearted emphasis. As time advances the need for consecrated deaconesses will increase. May God's blessings rest upon the work which you are conducting[78]

---

[76] "Report Prepared for the Centennial Synod," TLD 24, no. 4 (October 1947): 3.

[77] "Student Aid For Deaconesses," TLD 25, no. 3 (July 1948): 2; "Colorado District Extends Aid to Student Deaconesses," TLD 26, no. 2 (April 1949): 8; "Central District Adopts Student Aid Resolution," TLD 26, no. 3 (July 1949): 8.

[78] Behnken was president of the LCMS from 1935-1962. His testimonial appeared in TLD in April 1949. Letter from J.W. Behnken to Arnold F. Krentz, March 25, 1949, Historical Documents—Krentz 1941-60s, Miscellaneous Lecture Notes and Correspondence, LDA Archives, LDA, Valparaiso, Ind.

Interestingly, in 1948, the word *Lutheran* began to be used in front of *Deaconess Conference*, and from 1949 onward, the minutes of the conferences referred to the organization as *Lutheran Deaconess Conference* or LDC. President Behnken greeted the LDC at its meeting in St. Louis in 1957, "and encouraged the women to continue to give faithful service in the Lord's kingdom."[79] When Deaconess Gertrude Simon and another missionary completed thirty years of foreign mission service, President Behnken preached at a special anniversary service held at Hong Kong College, Howloon, Hong Kong.[80]

. . . AND AFFILIATED SYNODS

In the early days of the deaconess movement within the Synodical Conference, the LDA trained several young women who came from the affiliated synods. In 1957, the LDC voted to send its annual conference mission offering to the Wisconsin Synod medical mission in Rhodesia in memory of Deaconess Martha Herzberg who had been a member of the Wisconsin Synod.[81] Stations for deaconess service in Wisconsin Synod missions or ministries included the Indian Mission at San Carlos, Arizona; the Orphanage and Schools at the Apache Indian Missions in Whiteriver, East Fork, and Peridot, Arizona; Fountain City Home for the Aged in Fountain City, Wisconsin; Lutheran Home for the Aged in Belle Plaine, Minnesota; and the Lutheran Hospital in Beaver Dam.[82] A Missouri Synod woman could be assigned to a Wisconsin Synod mission, or vice versa, and while those two church bodies remained in altar and pulpit fellowship, a deaconess could transfer her congregational membership between the Missouri and Wisconsin Synods as needed. Krentz had no qualms about preaching from the pulpit of an affiliated synod, especially when a congregation raised large collections for charity work.[83]

In 1949, *Lutheran Annual* listed deaconesses for the first time, along with the names and workers of other auxiliary groups related to the Missouri Synod. After 1961, when the Wisconsin Synod broke fellowship

---

[79] "Deaconess Conference," *TLD* 33, no. 4 (October 1956): 8.

[80] "Thirty Years of Service in Foreign Missions," *TLD* 34, no. 1 (January 1957): 8.

[81] Mary Arbeiter Finau, "Minutes of the Lutheran Deaconess Conference, Island Camp, Minnesota," July 2, 1957, priv. col. of Clara Strehlow, Deaconess Office Archives, RF, Illinois.

[82] "Our Pictures," *TLD* 9, no. 3 (July 1932): 5; "Indian Mission Work: Deaconess Leaves for Arizona," *TLD* 20, no. 2 (April 1943): 2; "From Apacheland in Arizona," *TLD* 28, no. 3 (July 1951): 6; "Martha Herzberg 1893-1957 In Memoriam," *TLD* 34, no. 2 (April 1957): 8.

[83] "Preaching at West Bend, Wisconsin," *TLD* 20, no. 3 (July 1943): 6.

with the LCMS, Wisconsin Synod pastors and missions were no longer listed in the *Annual*, but entries that listed deaconesses of the LDA were still included.

Two Wisconsin Synod men, Bethesda's Louis Pingel and Beaver Dam's Pastor Kirst, served as members of the LDA Board of Directors from the mid-1920s to October 1932. Both men were so highly regarded that when their elected terms finished, the LDA declared them to be honorary members of the Board of Directors. They continued to attend meetings and carry out duties on behalf of the LDA, even when the Central Training School was established in Fort Wayne and later moved to Valparaiso. Hence, starting in January of 1933, every issue of *TLD* through January of 1959 (twenty-six years!) included Pingel and Kirst in the published list of LDA Board members. This is noteworthy, given the fact that the Wisconsin Synod declared itself to be in a state of protesting fellowship with the Missouri Synod already in 1952. Both men lived until 1965, but in April of 1959 their names disappeared from the roster of Board Members, even though O. P. Kretzmann continued to be listed as an advisory member of the Board.[84] Interestingly, the LDA Treasurer's report of "Receipts by Districts 1960–1961" includes $197.50 from "Wisconsin Synod."[85]

DEACONESS ETHICS

The fortieth anniversary of the LDA and the twenty-fifth anniversary of the LDC were simultaneously observed at a deaconess conference held at the Fort Wayne Senior College from June 30 to July 3, 1959. Executive Director Krentz produced a long and meaty report for the occasion, with fourteen sections that included LDA milestones, various types of statistics, an outline for a deaconess manual, guidelines for those employing deaconesses, and a document on ethics.[86] While every aspect of Krentz's report touched on the past, present or future of the diaconate, the ethics document was clear on how each deaconess was expected to behave as part of the diaconate.

---

[84] "Pastors Who Have Served the Congregation," *St. Stephen's Centennial History 1875-1975*, mimeographed pages (Beaver Dam: St. Stephen's Lutheran Church, 1975), no pagination; "Louis M. Pingel," *Watertown Daily Times*, obituary, January 1965; "Mrs. Louis Pingel," *Watertown Daily Times*, obituary, December 1970; "Officials of LDA," *TLD* 36, no. 2 (April 1959): 4.

[85] "Receipts by Districts 1960-1961," *TLD* 38, no. 4 (October 1961): 4.

[86] "Index," *Twenty-Fifth Annual Lutheran Deaconess Conference June 30—July 3, 1959*, priv. col. of Clara Strehlow, Deaconess Office Archives, RF, Illinois.

Deaconess Ethics

The professional worker of our Church, the Deaconess, strives for a high code of ethics. Other professional people, such as doctors, lawyers, clergymen have high codes of ethics. To help maintain a high standard of service to Christ and her fellowmen, the following code of ethics is suggested for our Deaconesses within the Synodical Conference.

1. The Deaconess recognizes from Holy Scriptures that she is born in sin, that she therefore is under the wrath of God by nature, and cannot by her own spiritual strength right herself with God.

2. She knows that the Lord Jesus Christ has redeemed her from all her sins by His substitutive death on Calvary's cross.

3. She has become Christ's own by faith since He has bought her with a price and she is grateful to Him for this great love shown her.

4. She feels constrained to serve Him in return for His love and can do this by serving her suffering fellowmen. "Inasmuch as ye have done it unto one of the least of these my brethren, ye have done it unto me." Matt. 25:40.

5. This service to her fellowmen in congregations, missions, and charitable endeavors is motivated by her love to Christ and her fellowmen and not by self-love and selfish interests. "We love Him because He first loved us." I John 4:19. "By love serve one another." Gal. 5:13.

6. There is only one divine office, namely, the holy ministry. All other offices in the Church are auxiliary offices to the holy ministry, as is the office of the Deaconess.

7. In her office the Deaconess will serve faithfully and diligently according to the ability which God giveth, as she vowed on the day of her consecration.

8. In her office she will give a good example by word and deed, as she vowed on the day of her consecration as a Deaconess.

9. She will mold her official life according to the directive given in I Tim: 3:11. "Must be serious; no slanderers, but temperate, faithful in all things."

10. In her relationship to the pastor or other church executive, she will serve faithfully and work in close harmony and cooperation with him.

11. In her dealings with her pastor, board, or fellow-christians [sic], she will keep confidential matters to herself.

12. As a title to designate the deaconess, "Sister" may be used since this title is used Rom. 16:1, although this title has not been widely used in our

branch of the Lutheran Church. She may be addressed by the formal "Miss" or by her given name, as local conditions will determine.

13. As to dress, the Deaconess realizes that good grooming is an asset to any professional church worker. Extremes in dress had best be avoided. The attractive uniform may be worn, but there is no "must." Deaconesses find that their uniforms give them easier access to hospitals and other institutions. More important than the uniform or title of a deaconess is the acquisition and retention of the love and respect of the people she serves.

14. In the matter of placement after graduation, she will abide by the decision of the Placement Committee which places the Deaconess Candidates according to the needs of the Church, the special abilities and talents of the graduates, and the field of service towards which they show an inclination.

15. All agreements for the placements or transfers of Deaconesses are made by the LDA and the employers of the Deaconesses be they congregation, institutions, or missions.

16. In the matter of a transfer the Deaconess will first confer with the Fort Wayne Office before the change takes place. She will not terminate her service in a given field but make known her desire for a change to the LDA. Likewise, she will confer with her employer, that is, congregation, institution, or mission board far enough in advance so that a satisfactory replacement can be made when her services are terminated.

17. If the Deaconess leaves church work to enter a secular vocation, she had best send in her formal resignation to the LDA. If she has served fewer than three years, she will return the amount of scholarship money due the LDA. Should she later desire to return to full-time service in the Church, she may be reinstated as a Deaconess in the LDA.

18. It is optional for the Deaconess to enter the pension plan of Synod. If she does enter the pension system of Synod, she should remit her pension money regularly to the Pension Board, 210 N. Broadway, St. Louis 2, Mo. If she enrolls in the Blue Cross—Blue Shield Insurance Plan she should send in her payments promptly. She may also enter social security, if she so desires, on a self-employment basis.

19. The Deaconess will aim to grow professionally year after year so that the quality of her service will improve by private study of books and journals that apply to her field, by attendance at the Deaconess Conference and other Conferences, and by further study at educational institutions if this is desirable and feasible.

20. In short the Deaconess will be controlled by a functional love to Christ, His Church, the people whom she serves, and the LDA under

whose sponsorship she has been educated for Deaconess Service and now serves.[87]

The code of ethics presented by Krentz summarized the more invisible marks of the diaconate that he had worked so hard to shape and define for nearly two decades. Krentz was aware that it was time for him to sum things up. In October of 1958 he suffered a heart attack that kept him in the hospital for four weeks.[88] On March 15, 1961, less than two years after the anniversary conference and only a month after his sixty-fifth birthday, the LDA and its deaconesses received the sad news of his death.

Early on the morning of Wednesday March 15 it pleased the Lord to call a halt to the labors of our Executive Director for almost twenty years, the Rev. Arnold F. Krentz. He had been ill for some time and in spite of that still tried to keep up in his enthusiastic energy with the program as it developed.

His enthusiasm and dedication to the cause is well known to those of us associated with the LDA, so much so that he was often referred to as "Mr. Deaconess." Under the blessings of God, it was during his administration that the training of Deaconesses developed and grew into the expanded program which it now enjoys with training headquarters at Valparaiso University and auxiliary training available at our Junior Colleges in the United States and Canada.

Only eternity will reveal all that has been accomplished during his administration to the Glory of God and the welfare of countless numbers of souls. It behooves us to continue with the same dedication and zeal the work so definitely advanced by him and so blessed under the Hand of God.

Funeral services were conducted at Redeemer Lutheran Church, Fort Wayne, where Pastor Krentz held membership with the Pastor, the Rev. Herbert Lindemann, conducting the service. Pastor George Maassel, First Vice-President of the Central District, represented President Ottomar Krueger and expressed the sympathy of the District. The Lutheran Deaconess Association was represented by the Rev. Edgar H. Albers, President of the Association, and Valparaiso University was represented

---

[87] "Deaconess Ethics," *Twenty-Fifth Annual Lutheran Deaconess Conference June 30—July 3, 1959*, priv. col. of Clara Strehlow, Deaconess Office Archives, RF, Illinois.

[88] "Deaconess News," single mimeographed sheet, Dec. 1958, File titled Ft. Wayne, Indiana: Lutheran Deaconess Association 1948-1960, Indiana LCMS District Archives, Fort Wayne, Ind.

by Prof. Kenneth F. Korby. The honors of a Christian burial at the new Concordia Cemetery were given by Pastor Lindemann.[89]

The fact that Krentz directed the deaconess training program for twenty out of the forty-two years that the LDA had been in operation reflected his never-ending zeal for the deaconess cause. He would be missed by the LDA, by the Valparaiso and Fort Wayne communities, and by the Missouri Synod.

---

[89] "Director Krentz," *TLD* 38, no. 2 (April 1961): 2.
  Illustrations for Chapter Eight may be viewed at www.deaconesshistory.org.

CHAPTER 9

NEW DIRECTIONS

When it became obvious that Executive Director Krentz would never be able to resume all of his duties due to prolonged illness, the LDA made several staffing decisions to prepare the organization for moving forward in the new decade.

In April 1960, Rev. Walter Carl Gerken (1912–1991) accepted a call to serve as Assistant Executive Director of the LDA. Gerken had been a member of the LDA Board of Directors since 1955 and came to this new position with a record of distinguished and varied pastoral experiences.[1] Pastor Gerken assisted Krentz by taking over all public relations work such as preaching, producing *TLD,* and addressing conferences or conventions.[2]

At about the same time that Gerken joined the staff, the LDA hired its first full-time office manager in the person of Mrs. Paul (Dorothy) Liebmann. Like Krentz and Gerken, Liebmann lived in Fort Wayne, and worked from the LDA office at 3417 S. Hanna Street. She provided valuable help with "typing, mimeographing, filing and the myriad duties that accrue in an office."[3]

In addition to the three individuals mentioned above, other LDA staff included Deaconess Marilyn Brammeier, Field Secretary (working from the Fort Wayne office); Deaconess Clara Strehlow, House Director at

---

[1] Over a period of twenty-three years, Gerken served parishes in Thawville, Ill., and Oxford and Rochester, Michigan; was an Army Chaplain (1941–46); and worked in the Lutheran Hour office. He was also counselor of the Pontiac Circuit of the Michigan District; chairman of the Michigan District College of Counselors; member of the General Committee on Educational Television, representing Lutheran Schools in Michigan; member of the Working Committee on Educational Television for the State of Michigan; and a member of the Executive Committee of the Religious Assistance Program of churches of Oakland County under the Auspices of the Youth Protection Division of the Juvenile Court, Pontiac, Michigan. An accomplished musician, he also gave organ concerts in St. Louis for radio station KFUO. "Pastor Gerken Accepts Call to Become Assistant," *TLD* 37, no. 2 (April 1960): 5; Herbert Martin Gerken (son of Walter C. Gerken), notes from telephone interview by CDN, April 30, 2006, priv. col. of CDN, Pittsburgh, Pa.

[2] "The Annual Meeting," *TLD* 37, no. 4 (October 1960): 4.

[3] "Increased Expenses," *TLD* 37, no. 2 (April 1960): 4.

Deaconess Hall; and Mr. Edward Anderson, custodian at Deaconess Hall.[4]
When Krentz became seriously ill again in January of 1961, Gerken became
Acting Executive Director, and when Krentz died two months later, he
stepped into the position of Executive Director.

One More Staff Member

Though there was more work than one man could reasonably handle, the
LDA had no intention of calling another *Assistant* Executive Director.
Instead, the association had also been trying to secure a Director of
Training to be based in Valparaiso. This person would "be a member of the
(Valparaiso University) faculty, teach special courses for Deaconess
students, and be in charge of the new one-year internship program for
Deaconess students."[5] Indeed, the Director of Training—in later years also
referred to as the Director of Education—would "coordinate the training
of our Deaconess students at our Valparaiso University as well as at our
Junior Colleges" and "serve as advisor to the students training on the
campus of the University."[6] The initial call for this new position was
extended in 1960 and subsequently declined.[7]

In 1961, a second call was issued and accepted by Rev. Arne Pellervo
Kristo (b. 1920), a pastor in Port Credit, Ontario, who was also the Vice-
President of The Lutheran Church—Canada. Kristo was a new name in
LDA circles, but again, he was a seasoned pastor with the type of
experience and connections deemed necessary for a director of the
deaconess education program.[8] The LDA deliberately designed the working
relationship between pastor and deaconess—that is, between the Director
of Training and the Deaconess in Residence (House Director)—to give

---

[4] The term *Housemother* had been dropped in favor of *House Director*, which in later years
would be changed to *Deaconess in Residence.* "Progress and Expansion," *TLD* 37, no. 4
(October 1960): 4.
[5] "Progress and Expansion," 4.
[6] "Report From the Lutheran Deaconess Association," one page mimeographed letter to
potential financial supporters, 1961, priv. col. of CDN, Pittsburgh, Pa.
[7] This first call went to Rev. Ronald Charles Starenko (b.1930). The "call not accepted"
announcement appeared in the October 1960 issue of *TLD.*
[8] Kristo served congregations in both California and Canada; had been speaker on the
Southern California Lutheran Hour for three years; Chairman of the Public Relations
Committee of the Lutheran Church—Canada; a member of the National Religious Advisory
Council of the Canadian Broadcasting Company; a member of the Toronto Chapter of the
National Religious Publicity Council; Chairman of the Canadian Council of the English
District (LCMS); and Pastoral Advisor to the English District LWML. "The Office of
Director of Training Becomes a Reality," *TLD* 38, no. 2 (April 1961): 5.

student deaconesses "a visible demonstration of the kind of partnership in which they will later function as deaconesses."[9]

RAPID GROWTH AND FINANCIAL CRISIS

When Pastor Kristo took up his duties on June 15, 1961, the LDA Board of Directors felt that it had enough manpower in place to cover the growing needs of the organization. Indeed, the increase in staff turned out to be vitally important for the period of unprecedented expansion that would follow. LDA President E. H. Albers explained:

> In this short span of four years (1960–64), the greatest expansion in the history of the Association took place. The staff now consisted of an Executive Director, a Director of Education, a Field Secretary, a House Director, and an Office Manager. The student body had grown to 114 students. By 1963 the enrollment reached 149, and by 1964 it stood at 174.[10] In 1958 the annual budget of the Association was $59,000. By 1961, due to rising education costs, increased enrollments and additions to the staff the budget had risen to $93,000.

> Yet for half this time the Association did not have the full services of its Executive Director. The hoped-for growth in financial support did not materialize. Consequently the Association ran into heavy indebtedness.

> In the matter of financial support the Association now entered upon the most critical period in its history. Resources were not sufficient to meet the large mortgage payments on Deaconess Hall. In addition, after 8 years of capacity use Deaconess Hall needed extensive rehabilitation and refurbishing. After the Board had exhausted all avenues for funds it approached the Board of Directors of Synod for permission to make a special appeal to the congregations of the Synod.[11] However, before the Association could take action, Synod itself launched the Ebenezer Thankoffering and included the Association for a 1% share. The

---

[9] "Deaconess in Residence Position Filled," *TLD* 40, no. 3 (Summer 1963): 3.

[10] These figures represent the total number of students enrolled in deaconess training at VU and the LCMS Junior Colleges.

[11] At the Annual LDA Meeting held on November 8, 1957, the Association increased its membership fee from one to two dollars per year. In April 1962, the LDA Board published that it was operating on "reserves" and, in May 1962, the Board authorized its treasurer to sell the Association's Series J. Bonds and borrow up to $20,000 to pay current operating costs. Two years later the Board announced a substantial increase in room rent charges at Deaconess Hall. "Highlights of the Annual Meeting," *TLD* 35, no. 1 (January 1958): 8; "Deficit? How Much?" *TLD* 39, no. 2 (April 1962): 4; "Plenary Board Meeting," *TLD* 39, no. 3 (July 1962): 5; "Room Rent Raised," *TLD* 41, no. 3 (Summer 1964): 11.

Association received enough to pay the mortgage and to do some necessary work at Deaconess Hall.[12]

In January 1964 the LDA Board of Directors resolved, "to appoint a planning committee constituted for the purposes of liquidating our debt, considering the expansion of our present plant and considering the manner in which the Association may be regionally organized."[13] What an amazing combination of tasks for this committee! In spite of serious money problems, the LDA evidently believed that it was time to look into the possibility of enlarging Deaconess Hall. A year later the association's financial report still showed an "operating deficit of $33,500."[14]

The LCMS finally approved the Ebenezer Offering mentioned by Albers at its 1965 convention in Detroit and collected the monies primarily in 1966 and 1967. The Synod designated four areas of ministry with "capital needs" to share the offerings: missions and church extension (50 percent); higher education (46.5 percent); Valparaiso University (2.5 percent); and the LDA (1 percent).[15] This initiative was a real lifesaver for the LDA, even though the collection brought less than anticipated.[16] After receiving its portion of the Offering, the LDA still needed to raise funds to liquidate over $36,000 in "notes at the bank," but in the meantime, the association paid off the Deaconess Hall mortgage without having to take any more money from the operating fund.[17] In addition, the LDA painted the exterior of Deaconess Hall, paved the driveway and parking lot, and fitted the House lounge with new furniture, drapes, and carpet.[18]

---

[12] E.H. Albers, "We Trace Our Steps: Chapter 8," *TLD* 46, no. 4 (Winter 1969): 9.

[13] "LDA Financial Conditions Basis of Discussion," *TLD* 41, no. 1 (Winter 1964): 9.

[14] "From the Executive Director," *TLD* 42, no. 4 (Winter 1965): 2.

[15] Resolution 15-18, in LCMS, *Proceedings,* 1965, 192-193.

[16] "One of the reasons why the forty million dollar Ebenezer fund drive is falling behind so seriously is that many members, congregations, and even districts are withholding contributions as means of protesting the theory of evolution as taught at Valparaiso University. Such protests are consistently ignored by the official Missouri Synod press. For example, Associated Press on June 9, 1966, reported from London, Ontario that the Ontario District presented a resolution that Valpo's teaching regarding creation and evolution be brought into line with the Word of God and doctrinal teaching of the church, or that the university be removed as a beneficiary of the Ebenezer offering. (The Kansas City Star, June 9, 1966) Nothing appeared in The Lutheran Witness or Reporter on this resolution." Marcus R. Braun, "A Layman's Concern About His Church," an Address before the LLL Zone Rally at St. John's Evangelical Lutheran Church, Clinton, Iowa, May 7, 1967. See also: "Finances," *TLD* 44, no. 3 and 4 (Winter 1967): 6.

[17] Edgar H. Albers, *Newsletter* (Fort Wayne: LDA, June 1968), 2.

[18] "Thanks to Ebenezer," *TLD* 44, no. 3 and 4 (Winter 1967): 4.

A New Decade

Before taking a look at more new directions that the LDA and LDC explored in the 1960s and 1970s, it is worthwhile to review how the deaconess association viewed itself at the threshold of this new era. At first it may seem strange to examine the organization's understanding of itself, but group perception and identification of the association's relationship to other groups—from students and deaconesses to the university and various Lutheran synods—had been particularly important to the LDA from its inception. The degree to which LDA leaders repeatedly rehearsed the history and status of the association gives the impression that they felt it was necessary to do so in order to safeguard the LDA against misunderstanding and against change—especially if that change would in any way challenge the association's autonomy. The 1960-61 "Handbook for Deaconess Students" provides a prime example of how such information was regularly imparted to students.

The Handbook for Deaconess Students

History

The Lutheran Deaconess Association was organized in Fort Wayne, Indiana . . . In 40 years, 235 young women have been consecrated as deaconesses within the Lutheran Church—Missouri Synod and affiliated Synods. There are 80 students now in training. ...

Relationship of the LDA to Synod

Deaconess Work is not sponsored nor financed by The Lutheran Church—Missouri Synod. The Deaconess Association belongs to the Council of Lutheran Agencies, a voluntary association of Auxiliary Agencies operating within Synod. Synod does not control nor guide Deaconess work through a committee or board. It has passed resolutions commending the work of the Association and urges support of the Deaconess program. A Memorial was recently passed at the Synodical Convention in San Francisco to officially open the doors of Synod's junior colleges to pre-deaconess students on an equal basis with teacher-training and ministerial students. In regard to placements, after the placement committee of the LDA has made the assignments of the various graduates, these assignments will be brought to the attention of the College of Presidents of the Lutheran Church—Missouri Synod for final approval.

Relationship of the LDA to Valparaiso University

The Association and the University cooperate in providing qualified young women a college education that prepares them for service as deaconesses. The Deaconess program is not an integral part of the University. The Deaconess Association retains its autonomy in administering the Deaconess program in all its phases, including its Deaconess Hall. It may suggest courses of study to the University administration. It has its own staff of workers, consisting of . . .

Relationship of Deaconess Students to the LDA

1. The LDA accepts students into its program who have been academically approved by the University. Student applicants must take a battery of six tests and inventories. The results of these tests and inventories are used in counseling a student during her college years. To be accepted as a student deaconess, the applicant must be in the upper two-thirds of her high school graduating class, be physically and emotionally fit, and recommended by her pastor.

2. Students must maintain an average of C or better to remain in good academic standing in the Deaconess college program . . .

3. Students who contemplate withdrawing from the Deaconess program should consult with the executive director and secure his approval before they take any steps toward withdrawing. . . .

4. Student deaconesses may be classified in these groups: A) Regular students who enter as Freshmen or transfer students from some other college or university; B) Students professionally trained with a B.A., B.S., R.N., or other degree who are enrolled as unclassified students; C) Special students.

5. In order to qualify the deaconess for better service, students enrolled in the Deaconess program in the spring of 1960 will do one full year of field work under the supervision of a pastor or director respectively of the parish, mission, or institution where they will serve. This "vicarage" year will be taken after the junior year at Valparaiso University.[19]

Thus it can be seen that the first three pages of the "Handbook for Deaconess Students" primarily defined the nature of the relationships between the LDA and other entities. The contents of the remaining ten pages of the booklet addressed practical matters important to students, for example, information on scholarships; the Deaconess Agreement; tuition,

---

[19] *Pi Delta Chi Guidelines: The Handbook for Deaconess Students,* Fort Wayne: LDA, 1960-1961, 13-page mimeographed booklet, priv. col. of Clara Strehlow, Deaconess Office Archives, Concordia University, RF, Illinois, 1-3.

room rent and piano room rental costs; set times for House devotions; the sixteen House regulations; curfew hours for each night according to class; how to obtain permission for overnight, vacation or out-of-town trips; assigned hours of study and rest; rules for social activities; "Men's Calling Hours" by day and time according to class; Pi Delta Chi songs; and a list of all current students.[20]

Whoever wrote the student handbook painted a curious picture of the LDA's relationship to the Missouri Synod. The association trained women to work in the parishes, institutions, and missions of the Synod, but the LDA placement committee assigned placements to its own deaconess candidates, which were then in effect rubber-stamped by the LCMS Council of Presidents. The LCMS officially sanctioned the first two years of this training at its own colleges, but did not control or even guide deaconess work, and by implication, any of the affairs of the LDA. The LDA asserted that the deaconess program was not an integral part of the university, and yet required its trainees to acquire a bachelor's degree with a major in Religion specifically from Valparaiso University, an independent Lutheran university with no official ties to the Missouri Synod. Furthermore, the LDA only accepted women into the deaconess program if they received approval from Valparaiso, did above-average work in high school, were in good health, and had been recommended by their pastors. It is interesting to note the absence of any requirement for applicants to be members of the Missouri Synod or affiliated synods, particularly since previous guidelines stipulated that prospective deaconesses (and their recommending pastors) needed to hold membership in one of the Synodical Conference churches. Of course, as had always been the case, no mention is made of any synodical body having the opportunity to provide input into the process of choosing or training deaconess students.[21] In actual fact, even if a woman had successfully completed two years of pre-deaconess training at one of

---

[20] Pi Delta Chi Guidelines: The Handbook for Deaconess Students, 4-13.

[21] In 1958, the LDA appointed an *Advisory Council* of leaders in the fields of Higher Education, Home and Foreign Missions, and Social Services, along with two parish pastors. The purpose of the council was to "advise the Association on all phases of its work and to help provide the Church with the best and most acceptable deaconess service." This Advisory Council only met one time, in February of 1959. "Deaconess News," single mimeographed sheet, Dec. 1958, File titled Ft. Wayne, Indiana: Lutheran Deaconess Association 1948-1960, Indiana LCMS District Archives, Fort Wayne, Indiana; "Advisory Council of Church Leaders Formed" and "Functions of the Advisory Council," *TLD* 36, no. 1 (January 1959): 6; Albers, "We Trace Our Steps: Chapter 8," 8.

the Missouri Synod colleges, there was no guarantee that she would be accepted into the Valparaiso-based program.[22]

CHANGES FOR 1961–62

Dealing with the realities of limited financial resources, Executive Director Gerken reluctantly announced that less money would be available for students who began their deaconess studies at Valparaiso in the fall of 1961.

> In the interest of good stewardship of time, talent, and treasure on the part of all concerned, financial aid in the form of tuition remission by Valparaiso University to students in deaconess training at the University will no longer be granted (this does not pertain to those students now enrolled in deaconess training at Valparaiso). Neither will the LDA **automatically** give financial aid to any student in deaconess training. Financial aid, however, will be available, God willing, for those who require it; requests for aid are to be made to the school involved and to the LDA. Scholarship and need, objectively determined, will be the chief evaluating factors.[23]

Although the above announcement seems to imply that new deaconess students would receive no special tuition rates from Valpo for the duration of their five years of training, Gerken later explained that this decision only affected the freshman and sophomore years.[24] The last paragraph of the article added:

> Another change in the interest of good order is that application for enrollment in the Deaconess training program is no longer to be made to the LDA and the school involved, but is to be made only to the school, whether Valparaiso (Freshman year) or one of our Junior colleges.[25]

This last change made sense from the point of view that, beyond providing information as to what classes and credit hours should be transferred to Valpo, neither the Executive Director nor the Director of

---

[22] Krentz, Gerken, and Kristo all encountered women, parents, or LCMS colleges that complained about applicants not being accepted into the Valpo training program. Arnold F. Krentz, CPH Calendar Diaries 1918-1960, Arnold Krentz, Box 200 KRE, CHI, St. Louis, Missouri, 1960 Diary; Walter C. Gerken, "Staff Thoughts," *TLD* 41, no. 4 (Fall 1964): 3; Arne P. Kristo, interview by CDN, transcript, Norfolk, Virginia, November 7, 2005, priv. col. of CDN, Pittsburgh, Pa.

[23] "Changes! Changes!" *TLD* 38, no. 2 (April 1961): 4.

[24] Jan Orluske, "Minutes of the Lutheran Deaconess Conference, Bronxville, N.Y., July 3-5, 1961," priv. col. of Clara Strehlow, Deaconess Office Archives, Concordia University, RF, Illinois, 1.

[25] "Changes! Changes!" 4.

Training needed to be involved with the first two years of pre-deaconess education at any of the college campuses.

ANOTHER TRAINING SCHOOL?

The minutes of the 1961 annual meeting of the LDC reveal a surprising element in Gerken's report to the deaconesses. The secretary recorded:

> Pastor Gerken gave his report. He urged all Deaconesses to write for materials and to make themselves available at all District conferences of our church. Pastor Kristo was introduced and his work explained. Pastor Gerken announced that enrollment at our Junior colleges is growing. He stated that in the future a terminal training school at one of the colleges might be a reality.[26]

By a *terminal* training school Gerken meant a school where women finished the last three years of their training. It is obvious that the Executive Director had considered the possibility that, in time, one terminal training site might not be enough to accommodate the steadily increasing numbers of women enrolled in pre-deaconess training. Of course, the interesting point here, is that Gerken contemplated the idea of a second LDA training program *on the campus of an LCMS college*. How such a step would alter the relationship between the LDA and the LCMS was a big question, and an issue that may have ultimately contributed to the fact that this plan never materialized.

A MEMORIAL TO THE LCMS

Delegates to the 1962 LCMS Synodical Convention received many "Unprinted Memorials," including the following submitted by the LDA Board of Directors.

> Whereas, The increasing need for professional workers in the church has led not only to the training of pastors and teachers, but also to the establishment of programs for the training of deaconesses and other church workers by auxiliary organizations of the church, as well as by the Synod itself; and
>
> Whereas, There is need for the clear definition of the purposes and functions of each of the training programs in the Synod for deaconesses and other church workers other than pastors and teachers, as well as the

---

[26] Orluske, "Minutes of the Lutheran Deaconess Conference, July 3-5, 1961," 1.

interrelationships of these auxiliary training programs and fields of service; therefore be it

Resolved, That the convention of The Lutheran Church—Missouri Synod convening in Cleveland 20 to 30 June 1962, request the Board for Higher Education to initiate a study of the interrelationships of the various training programs and fields of service in the Synod for deaconesses and other church workers other than pastors and teachers, with the view toward clearly defining their purposes and functions as well as their interrelationships and recommending ways and means to avoid as much as possible the duplication of purposes and efforts.

The Board of Directors

Lutheran Deaconess Association

Robert V. Schnabel, *Secretary*[27]

In some ways the above Memorial was a cry for help in the oft-repeated task of establishing deaconess identity in the context of a growing number of church worker vocations. The first two paragraphs give the impression that the LDA Board considered the pre-deaconess programs at LCMS colleges to be part of the LDA's own operation, even though women no longer applied to the association to gain entrance to them. No wonder the Board desired some sort of clarification! The Synodical delegates complied with Resolution 1-42:

Unprinted Memorial 179, pp. 44, 45, *Today's Business*

Whereas, The Synod has been petitioned to request the Board for Higher Education to initiate a study of interrelationships of various programs and fields of service in the Synod; therefore be it

Resolved, That this petition be referred to the Board for Higher Education.

Action: This resolution was *adopted*.[28]

Eight months after Resolution 1-42 passed, Pastor Kristo attended a plenary meeting of the LCMS BHE where he and fifteen other individuals provided information related to the *various programs and fields of service in the Synod*.[29] Exactly how the Plenary Board later used the collected information

---

[27] "To Request BHE to Initiate a Study of Interrelationships of the Various Training Programs, etc.," in LCMS, Unprinted memorials, *Reports and Memorials*, 1962, 172.

[28] "BHE to Study Interrelationship of Various Programs, etc." in LCMS, *Proceedings*, 1962, 88.

[29] The BHE plenary agenda included: Report of the Curriculum Commission, Stimulating Literary Production and Scholarly Research, Retention and Direction of Ministerial Students,

is difficult to determine, since the BHE was only asked to initiate a study, without receiving a request to report back to Synod.

LDA Secretary Rev. Robert Victor Schnabel (b. 1922), first elected to the LDA Board of Directors in 1957, signed Memorial 179 on behalf of the LDA. The convention *Workbook* also listed Schnabel as a member of the Curriculum Commission appointed by the BHE in the previous triennium. This Commission had been working with the instructional staffs at Synod's schools, to assist the BHE in providing "a full report of the curricular changes necessitated by the newly established senior college (opened in 1957)."[30]

THE 1962 BHE REPORT

In 1950, the LCMS directed its BHE to develop a curriculum for Concordia Senior College, and thereafter to provide for the integration of the entire curriculum of all LCMS colleges and seminaries.[31] The following quotations taken from the "Report of the Board for Higher Education," given to delegates of the 1962 LCMS Synodical Convention, show that in the course of carrying out this directive, the BHE already gave thought to the role of deaconesses and the deaconess training program within the Missouri Synod.

[123] B. REPORT OF THE BOARD FOR HIGHER EDUCATION

... II. Review and Preview

A. Basic Assumptions

... 9. Major ecclesiastical alignment shifts by merger or in division of existing Lutheran bodies in the United States are more likely to increase

---

Accelerated Study Programs in the Synodical System, Role of Future Conference of College and Seminary Professors, Faith Forward, Staff Size and Teaching Loads, Inter-School Relations and Recruitment, Synodical Legal Service, The Two-year Parish Work Program, The Lutheran Lay Training Institute, The Deaconess Program, Proposed Program for Social Workers, Programs of Sacred Music, Directors of Christian Education Program, and Preparing Workers for Foreign Mission Assignments. *BHE Minutes,* February 16, 1963, item 33, 329, CHI, St. Louis, Mo.

[30] Schnabel was a professor at the new Senior College in Fort Wayne (1957-71); president of Concordia College, Bronxville, N.Y. (1971-76); vice president for academic affairs and dean of the faculty at the American Lutheran Church Wartburg College, Waverly, Iowa (1976-78); and president of Valparaiso University (from 1978-88). He was a member of the LDA Board of Directors from 1957-65 and 1967-68. "Curriculum Development," in LCMS, *Reports and Memorials,* 1962, 49.

[31] LCMS, *Proceedings,* 1950, 231 and 241.

rather than diminish the synodical demand for pastors, teachers, and deaconesses in the period of the long-range forecast.

. . . 12. The congregations in the synodical fellowship are both the source of recruits for pastors, teachers, and deaconesses here and abroad and also the first and prime user of these recruits after completing their program of training. . . .

15. An adequate forecast will include an estimate of the number of students who should be graduated from the Synod's theological seminaries and colleges, so that the estimated needs for pastors, teachers and deaconesses can be met. . . .

Planning Propositions

. . . *Proposition One.* An intensified and continuing enlistment program is a prerequisite for the steady growth in numbers of pastors, teachers, deaconesses, and parish workers which will be needed throughout this planning period to provide the necessary constituted leadership for the members of the Synod.

III. Pastors and Teachers at Home

and Abroad with Professors,

Deaconesses, and Parish Workers. . .

B. Long-range Programed [*sic*] Development and Reorganization Proposal

At the end of this developmental program the Synod might be expected to have in use the following integrated system of colleges and seminaries providing professional and lay church workers in quantity sufficient to meet the anticipated demand and in proficiency and dedication suitable to the demands of the Lord of the church and the opportunities which His Holy Spirit continues to present:

1. Southern California. The establishment of a junior college ... 2. San Leandro (Lake Chabot, Calif.). The establishment of the third theological seminary ... 3. Oakland. Retention of the present campus ... 4. . . . establishment of a preparatory school in the southeast. 5. The establishment of a senior college unit of pre-theological education in the western states . . . 6. . . . The acquisition of a suitable site in the Middle Atlantic Seaboard region . . . 7. Concordia, Ann Arbor, Mich., . . . 8. Concordia, Austin, Tex., . . . 9. Concordia, Bronxville, N.Y., . . . 10. St. Paul's, Concordia, Mo., . . . 11. Concordia, Edmonton, Alta, . . . 12. Concordia, Milwaukee, Wis., . . . 13. Concordia, Portland, Oreg., . . . 14. Concordia, St. Paul, Minn., . . . 15. St. John's, Winfield, Kans., in substantially its present pattern of organization and offerings with appropriate increase in capacity and with formal approval for the two-year

women parish worker program and with emphasis on St. John's College as the center for the first two years of deaconess training. 16. Concordia Senior College, Fort Wayne, Ind., . . . 17. Concordia Teachers College, River Forest, Ill., . . . 18. Concordia Teachers College, Seward, Nebr., . . . 19. Concordia Theological Seminary, Springfield, Ill., . . . 20. Concordia Seminary, St. Louis, Mo., . . . [32]

LDA members must have been encouraged to see such natural use of the phrase "pastors, teachers, and deaconesses" in the BHE report. On the other hand, the "Long-range Program Development and Reorganization Proposal" might have puzzled them. Twenty colleges and seminaries were projected to be part of the Missouri Synod's future educational system. The summary for every junior college already in business (like number 15 above) included the descriptive phrase: *in substantially its present pattern of organization and offerings with appropriate increase in capacity.* Thus it could be assumed that the BHE expected to continue offering the pre-deaconess program on all of these college campuses. However, only the description of St. John's College in Winfield, Kansas contained a specific reference to deaconess training. It had to be wondered, if the BHE designated St. John's College as *the center* for the initial two years of deaconess training, did that imply that eventually St. John's would be the *only* college designated to have such a program? Could it be that the BHE, and perhaps Gerken too, felt that such an arrangement might be a helpful precursor to someday establishing a second deaconess program on a Missouri Synod campus?

Reports to the Convention from the LCMS junior colleges provided encouragement with regard to the continuation of pre-deaconess programs on their campuses. A breakdown of student personnel provided by the schools in Winfield and Portland included statistics for deaconess students as well as pre-seminary, teachers, and parish workers.[33] The report from Concordia Lutheran Junior College, Ann Arbor, which was scheduled to open in the fall of 1963, would also certainly have been viewed as being very supportive of the deaconess movement within the Missouri Synod.

. . . Accreditation

Concordia, Ann Arbor, will provide the first two years of college training for Lutheran pastors, teachers, and deaconesses. Its graduates will transfer to Concordia Senior College, Fort Wayne, Ind.; Concordia Teachers College, River Forest, Ill.; Concordia Teachers College, Seward, Nebr.;

---

[32] "Report of the BHE," in LCMS, *Reports and Memorials,* 1962, 43, 49, 52-54, 57-58.
[33] "St. John's College, Winfield, Kans." and "Concordia College, Portland, Oreg." in LCMS, *Reports and Memorials,* 1962, 30, 33.

and Valparaiso University, Valparaiso, Ind. These institutions will accept its credits without question. . . . [34]

Of course the Report from the BHE made no mention of Valparaiso University—but from reports such as the one from Ann Arbor, delegates could deduce that LCMS institutions and Valparaiso University continued to work together for the purpose of training deaconesses.

PROJECTING THE DESIRED CONCEPT OF DEACONESS MINISTRY

Once the 1960s were underway, LDA leaders saw the need to bring the church up to speed in its understanding of deaconess ministry. The Missouri Synod, too, seemed to acknowledge that the roles of its professional church workers, though guided and bound by certain Scriptural principles, were not necessarily static. In the introductory section of its 1962 report on "Curriculum Development," the BHE wrote:

> Two general factors seemed to the commission and the board to be beyond debate. Our curriculum first arose in a time when social change did not seem to be a permanent and accelerating characteristic of the setting in which the work of the church was placed. In contrast, social change seems to be the abiding characteristic of our society.[35]

In 1962, the LDA Board of Directors asked its Admissions Committee to prepare "a concise and precise statement of the modern concept of the deaconess and her responsibilities."[36] When the committee gave its report on May 4, 1962, the Board tabled the matter for restudy and presentation at a future meeting.

Creating a concise and helpful document on the desired understanding of deaconess ministry to present to the church was not an easy task at a time in which American society was in a state of continuous change. So many undulating issues—the population explosion; urbanization and poverty; the struggle for civil rights, women's rights, and student rights; the trauma of political assassinations, and Vietnam—somehow seemed to work together to encourage a mindset of social action and reaction.[37] But perhaps

---

[34] "Concordia College, Ann Arbor, Mich.," in LCMS, *Reports and Memorials*, 1962, 20.

[35] "Curriculum Development," in LCMS, *Reports and Memorials*, 1962, 50.

[36] "Plenary Board Meeting," *TLD* 39, no. 3 (July 1962): 5.

[37] In his "review of the second decade of the postwar period," Albert George Huegli (1913-1998), Valparaiso's Vice-President for Academic Affairs (1961-68) who would be elected President of VU in December 1968, wrote: "If anything stands out in the period 1955-1965, it is that the dynamic and revolutionary thrusts of our time have accelerated change. They

more than the current events and trends of society, the LDA was forced to consider problems within the church, including the growing tension between some members of the Missouri Synod and the Valparaiso community. Richard Baepler, who served as Head of the Department of Theology[38] at Valpo from 1963 to 1966, wrote:

> Within the church, too, politics heated up during the 1960s. In 1961, conservative dissidents against the increasingly "moderate" Synodical leadership mounted a major "State of the Church" conference in Milwaukee. One of their prime targets was Valparaiso University. Some VU leaders were worried by the long list of complaints: the teaching of evolution, the dialogues with Notre Dame, "liturgical excess," and a variety of theological positions taken by members of the theology department that seemed to depart from conventional Missouri themes.

> In a speech to the board, W.C. Dickmeyer saw opportunity rather than threat in these developments. The Missouri Synod was in the process of splintering, he declared, and this was the time for Valparaiso to take a leadership role. It should begin by publishing a statement of the University's general position, and individuals should tone down approaches that might suggest freelancing to the contrary. Such a document was widely distributed. The Ten-Year Plan had emphasized that one of Valparaiso University's goals was to give intellectual leadership to its major constituency. Many of Kretzmann's policies and statements, backed by other leaders such as Dickmeyer, were designed to give VU a key role in remaking the Missouri Synod into a church body worthy of its "high destiny" as a progressive, confessional voice in American Lutheranism and American Christianity.

> The next several years seemed to move toward that promise. In 1962, the Reverend Oliver Harms, a strong friend of Valparaiso, was elected president of the Synod.[39] Within a few years, members of the VU faculty—such as Robert Bertram, Edward Schroeder, Richard Baepler, Paul G. Bretscher, and John Strietelmeier—were appointed to important Synodical committees.[40] In 1963, Concordia Seminary bestowed an

---

seem to create for us and our children what might be called a permanent state of fluidity. We had better recognize now that many of the old familiar landmarks are going or have gone. We had better accustom ourselves to a social setting in which nothing very much is enduring except that which bears the stamp of divine durability." A. G. Huegli, "The Church in the Great Society," *The Cresset* 28, no. 9 (September 1965): 8; See also: "Violence Hits Schools, Colleges," *U.S. News & World Report* (May 20, 1968), 36-44.

[38] In 1963 Valpo's Department of *Religion* was changed to the Department of *Theology*.

[39] Oliver Raymond Harms (1901-1980).

[40] Robert Walter Bertram; Edward Henry Schroeder (b. 1930); Paul Gerhardt Bretscher (b.1921). These clergymen later left (or were removed from) the Missouri Synod, in the wake

honorary doctorate on Strietelmeier.[41] There were suggestions that the Synod might subsidize VU for educating church professionals— deaconesses, youth leaders, parochial school teachers, social workers—but these plans were wisely discarded with the realization that control inevitably would follow subsidy, which would be inimical to the University.[42]

FURTHER ATTEMPTS

About a year after Gerken became editor of *TLD,* he started publishing a column called "Staff Thoughts," written either by the Field Secretary, the Deaconess in Residence, the Director of Training, or the Executive Director. Two of these pieces, published in the summer and fall 1963, demonstrated a consistent burden to help the church understand her need for the diaconate. First, from the Director of Training . . .

> By now it is axiomatic that the church had better be prepared for a much larger membership, and thus a much larger service corps in the form of professional workers. In order to minister to people who are the church out in the community, other people are needed in the background. Perhaps you never thought of your pastor, and other professionals as being in the background of the church's battle, but that's the picture we get from the New Testament!
>
> Part of the growth in service personnel will come, we are confident, from growth in the diaconate. This means at least three things.
>
> First, it means that the concept of a division of responsibility in the one ministry of the church will need to be more widely accepted. From our point of view this means that the church will need to recognize the old but seemingly new idea that women, too, can develop their God-given talents for special ministries in the church.
>
> Secondly, it means that the specific professional role of today's diaconate in our church will need to be understood. The investment we make in

---

of doctrinal disagreements. See Chapter 6 footnotes for biographical information on Baepler.

[41] Layman John Henry Strietelmeier (1920-2004) taught geography at Valpo; was managing editor of *The Cresset* ("A Review of Literature, the Arts, and Public Affairs" published by the President's office); and served as Vice President for Academic Affairs. Richard Baepler, "John Strietelmeier: Called to the 'Holy Laity,'" *Concordia Historical Institute Quarterly* 78, no. 4 (Winter 2005): 219-244.

[42] Richard Baepler, *Flame of Faith, Lamp of Learning: A History of Valparaiso University* (St. Louis: Concordia, 2001), 265-66.

preparing these women is too heavy to warrant using them in ways that are not sufficiently relevant to that training.

Thirdly, congregations and institutions of our church should know that our women are volunteering for service in the diaconate in greatly increasing numbers. We will need a significant increase in the number of applications for deaconesses and deaconess internes[43] already this year.

Our women are saying, "Here I am. Send me." Will we as a church speak and act for God by putting these women to work in the Vineyard? AK[44]

. . . and later from the Executive Director:

Confucius said: "Men must have mothers, and so women are a necessary evil." According to the Talmud, "A man should never walk behind a woman along a road, even his own wife. A man should walk behind a lion rather than behind a woman."

Christianity, however, elevated woman and placed her on a pedestal as a symbol of beauty, purity, honesty, kindness, and all the fine things in life, a creation of God to be admired, respected and protected. Incidentally, when woman steps down from that pedestal and competes with man she loses as a woman.

According to the Order of Redemption it is true that "there is neither male nor female," that all are on the same level and there is no distinction between sexes. However, according to the Order of Creation, there are two areas in which God has established an order He wants observed between sexes and these areas are the home and the church.

"The husband is the head of the wife even as Christ is the Head of the Church" is the order for the family; woman is "not to usurp authority over the man" is the order for the church. This is not a comparison between man and woman involving intelligence and abilities but simply an order God wants observed.

We feel that the church has leaned over backwards to keep from violating this order in the church and consequently has failed to make as full a use as possible of the gifts and talents God has given the women of the church. That's why we are so happy to observe the growth, under God, of the Lutheran Women's Missionary League program, as well as the training programs for women in special ministries. We, of course, are partial to the Deaconess program and happily report that, God willing, we will have

---

[43] Until the summer of 1966, the LDA included the letter e when writing the words *interne* and *internes,* and occasionally included it in the words *interneship* and *interneships.*
[44] Arne Kristo, "Staff Thoughts," *TLD* 40, no. 3 (Summer 1963): 2.

forty four [*sic*] (graduates and internes) available for placement in June 1964. WCG[45]

Looking at the above two articles one after the other is an interesting exercise. Kristo asserted that the professional role of the diaconate in the church needs to be understood. Gerken took care to inform his readers that that professional role had been inadvertently limited in an effort to maintain churchly practice in accord with doctrine. Aside from Gerken's inference that deaconesses are not to usurp authority over men, neither of the men actually articulated how the diaconate should be understood. Both authors touched on the general role of women in the church, but for the moment, this was as close as the LDA needed (and probably wanted) to get to a public discussion of the subject. That issue would come to the fore again later in the decade.

INTERNSHIPS

The practice of sending student deaconesses out into the field for one-year internships began during the 1960–61 school year. Until that time, it was normal for all students to have at least one, and sometimes two or three, summer internships at Bethesda in Watertown or at any number of other locations. As noted in chapter six, the LCMS College of Presidents initially assigned intern candidates to their field of service. However, in 1964, this procedure changed when the Placement Committee for Deaconesses advised the Presidents that the interns would be better served if the LDA negotiated and supervised their placements.[46] The following article, which appeared a few months later, contained a good summary of the philosophy behind the internship program.

> To become a deaconess, a woman must successfully fulfill one year of interneship, ordinarily the year between her Junior and Senior years at

---

45 Walter C. Gerken, "Staff Thoughts, *TLD* 40, no. 4 (Fall 1963): 3.
46 "Since the year of internship is an important phase of the training program, it would be desirable to be selective in choosing the most desirable program as well as supervisor judged on the basis of goals to be reached during the internship years as scheduled in the training program. Under the present system the training program must often be adjusted to the requests and locations over which there is no direct control. It is felt that by direct negotiations with congregations and institutions throughout the year a better meeting of minds can be established regarding the desired program best suited for the development of the individual student. The aim is also to develop the proposed program especially within a reasonable radius of Valparaiso University to enable the Director of Training more efficiently to supervise this year of training." Minutes of the College of Presidents, The Lutheran Building, Saint Louis, Missouri, April 21-23, 1964, pages 4-5, CHI, St. Louis, Mo.

Valparaiso University, to experience the tasks and responsibilities of a deaconess for one year in order to determine her capabilities.

The interneship year offers a congregation or an institution an opportunity to become acquainted with the services of a deaconess, to enlarge its ministry, and to share in the preparation of future workers for the church. The interneship year may, for example, be the answer for congregations who have been considering the idea of adding to their permanent staff, but who do not feel ready to commit themselves. A deaconess interne is ready, willing and able to perform important Christian work and thus to add to the effectiveness of a congregation's or institution's program. Finally, the congregation that secures the services of a Deaconess interne has the opportunity to give of itself—in the form of the time and energy of its pastor and the willing interest of its membership—toward the growth of another worker for Christ's Church.[47]

The pattern of specialized education for deaconess students paralleled that of men studying to be pastors at LCMS seminaries, in that, just as the men went on a year of vicarage before their last academic year, so also the women went to a year of internship before their last academic year. The LDA believed that this model benefited the women by giving them ample time during their final year at university to discuss experiences and assimilate skills obtained during the internship year.

CELEBRATING TWENTY YEARS AT VALPO

President O. P. Kretzmann suggested a colloquium to mark the twentieth anniversary of the partnership between Valparaiso and the LDA in educating deaconess students. The LDA took up the idea and acquired a $5,600 fraternal benevolence grant from Aid Association for Lutherans to fund the celebration. Christened "The Diakonia of the Church in a New Age," the colloquium sessions took place in Valpo's Wesemann Hall[48] over the weekend of May 1–3, 1964. [49]

"The end goal of the colloquium," according to the Rev. Walter C. Gerken, "was to structure the Deaconess program toward an ever wider, more purposeful and fruitful service of the female diaconate to the church

[47] "Interne Placements," *TLD* 41, no. 3 (Summer 1964): 6.
[48] Wesemann Hall was the newly dedicated Law Building on the Valparaiso University campus.
[49] "Colloquium Plans Announced," *TLD* 41, no. 1 (Winter 1964): 7; "Twenty Years of Partnership Celebrated," *TLD* 41, no. 2 (Spring 1964): 6-7.

in this generation and the next," and also "to explore the area of the male diaconate."[50]

A *Forward* [*sic*] printed in the spiral-bound collection of essays produced for the anniversary observance explained the make-up of the colloquium participants.

> . . . The planning committee has determined that this colloquium should have at least two characteristics: it should be made up of a relatively small group of persons who would be invited to come together to share their common interest in the total ministry of the church, and it should offer an opportunity for the diaconate of The Lutheran Church—Missouri Synod to engage in fruitful conversation with representatives of other diaconates and churchmen from other church bodies. It was felt, to put it another way, that the discussions should be enriched by persons from other professions and occupations and that the thinking of Christians in other groups would strengthen the dialogue.
>
> This is an open-ended colloquium. We are fortunate to have competent and stimulating essayists and participants in this project. The interaction of essayists, panelists, and participants should lead us all into a deeper understanding of the "Diakonia of the church in a new age." We are confident that from our discussions there will proceed new insights and understandings so that those of us involved in the deaconess movement will be able to chart our course for the next two decades, and beyond![51] . . .

The most remarkable point in the above *Foreword* is that the planning committee looked outside of the LCMS, and those synods affiliated with the LCMS, to receive stimulation and insight for the best way to move forward in the development of the diaconate. *TLD* reported:

> Five essayists and fifty-four participants from all areas of the country and representing all the Lutheran diaconates and also the Methodist and Episcopal diaconates contributed toward producing "new insights and

---

50 "Twenty Years of Partnership Celebrated," 8.

51 The *Forward* [*sic*] is not signed, but was almost certainly written by Director of Training Arne Kristo, who made identical remarks from the Colloquium podium. Pastor Kristo and his wife received credit for spending many hours in preparation for the anniversary observance. See photo caption, *TLD* 41, no. 2 (Spring 1964): 6; "Forward," *The Diakonia of the Church in a New Age: a colloquium to celebrate 20 years of partnership between Valparaiso University and the Lutheran Deaconess Association in the education of deaconesses for The Lutheran Church – Missouri Synod*, May 1-3, 1964, Wesemann Hall, Valparaiso University, spiral-bound book containing colloquium program, names of participants, essays, and *A Litany for Deaconesses*, no pagination for "Forward."

understandings" for charting the course of the Deaconess movement for the next two decades.[52]

Thirty-one of the fifty-four colloquium participants were from the LCMS;[53] nine were from the Lutheran Church in America (LCA);[54] nine from The American Lutheran Church (TALC);[55] three from the Episcopal Church; and one each from the Methodist and Roman Catholic churches.[56] Dr. Donald Charles Mundinger, Assistant Dean of Valparaiso's College of Arts and Sciences, who had become a member of the LDA Board of Directors in 1962, chaired the gathering.[57] The colloquium's general format consisted of five essays followed by panel discussions with audience participation.[58]

---

[52] "Twenty Years of Partnership Celebrated," 8.

[53] Clergymen Edgar Albers, Walter R. Bouman (1929-2005), Walter Gerken, Samuel I. Goltermann (1925-2004), Edwin Theodore Heyne (b.1921), Wilbur Clarence Koester (1912-1980), O. P. Kretzmann, Arne Kristo, Donald H. Larsen (1925-1990), Erwin Louis John Lueker (1914-2000), F. Dean Lueking (b.1928), Karl Ernst Lutze (b.1920), Donald Edward Schedler (b.1929), Reuben J. Schmidt (b.1918), Robert Schnabel, David Simon Schuller (1926-2002), Raymond Carl Schulze (b.1932), and Normand John Widiger (1921-1996); Deaconesses Helen Beckman, Martha Boss, Jacqueline Haug, Jean Hoover, Edith Hovey, Patricia Martin, Evelyn Middelstadt, Jan Orluske, and Lucille Wiese; Laymen Jack Ansett, Mahela Hays, Robert Mickelson, and Donald C. Mundinger.

[54] Clergymen E. Theodore Bachmann, John Reumann, John Wagner Jr., and Frederick Weiser; Deaconesses Marion Anderson, Louise Burroughs, Anna Ebert, Anna Melville, and Catherine Neuhardt. The Lutheran Church in America came into being in 1962 through the combination of four synods: the United Lutheran Church in America (a merger of the General Council, General Synod, and United South Synod), the Swedish Synod, the Danish Synod, and the Finnish Synod. Patsy A. Leppien and J. Kincaid Smith, *What's Going on Among the Lutherans?* (Milwaukee: Northwestern Publishing House, 1992), 301, 330-31.

[55] Clergymen LeRoy Aden, H. A. Flessner, and Arthur J. Seegers; Deaconesses Mildred Christensen, Elinor Falk, Olive Hanson, and Hulda Simenson; Laymen Donald Imsland and Norman Madson. The American Lutheran Church was the result of the merger of four synods in 1960: both the large Norwegian Synod and the smaller Norwegian Lutheran Free Church, the German (American Lutheran Church) and the Danish (Inner Mission) Synod. Leppien and Smith, *What's Going on Among the Lutherans?*, 301, 330.

[56] From the Episcopal Church: Rev. Forrest B. Clark; Deaconesses Edith Booth and Amelia Brereton. From the Methodist Church: Deaconess Betsy Ewing. From the Roman Catholic Church: Father Aloysius O'Dell.

[57] In September 1965, Gerken refers to Mundinger as Dean of the College of Arts and Sciences at Valparaiso University and Chairman of the Committee on Deaconess Training. Letter written by Walter Gerken to All Voting Members of the Lutheran Deaconess Association, September 24, 1965, File titled Ft. Wayne, Indiana: Lutheran Deaconess Auxiliary, Indiana LCMS District Archives, Fort Wayne, Ind.

[58] Following the printed lists of participants, Chairman, and Chaplains, colloquium "Guests" are named as "Plenary Board of the Lutheran Deaconess Association; Department of Theology, Valparaiso University; Deaconess and Pre-Deaconess Students at Valparaiso

Essayists, their topics, and the discussants for the colloquium were:

Dr. John Reumann (LCA), Lutheran Theological Seminary, Philadelphia, Pennsylvania. "Diakonia: Scriptural Foundations." Discussants: Mr. Donald Imsland (TALC), Dr. Erwin Lueker (LCMS), Deaconess Pat Martin (LCMS).

Dr. David Schuller (LCMS), Concordia Seminary, St. Louis, Missouri. "Diakonia: Twentieth Century Implications." Discussants: Dr. E. Theodore Bachmann (LCA), Sister Elinor Falk (TALC), Mr. Norman T. Madson (TALC).

The Rev. John Wagner (LCA), National Council of Churches, New York. "New Forms of Parish Life." Discussants: the Rev. Donald Larsen (LCMS), the Rev. Prof. Karl Lutze (LCMS), the Rev. Raymond Schulze (LCMS).

Dr. Walter Bouman (LCMS), Concordia Teachers College, River Forest, Illinois. "Communal Ministries for American Lutheranism." Discussants: Sister Anna Ebert (LCA), Father Aloysius O'Dell (RC), the Rev. Frederick Weiser (LCA).

Dr. LeRoy Aden (TALC), University of Chicago Divinity School, Chicago, Illinois. "Dynamic Psychology and the Church's Ministry of Service." Discussants: Deaconess Evelyn Middelstadt (LCMS), Dr. Arthur Seegers (TALC), the Rev. Prof. Normand Widiger (LCMS).

A banquet was held Saturday evening in the Great Hall of the Student Union. Dr. O. P. Kretzmann, President of Valparaiso University, was the speaker. Deaconess Lucille Wiese, Field Secretary of the Lutheran Deaconess Association, acted as toastmistress.[59]

Despite the diverse denominations represented by participants—none of which were in altar and pulpit fellowship with one another—the colloquium finished with a service of Holy Communion in the University Chapel. Rev. Roland Paul Wiederaenders (1908–1995), First Vice-President of the LCMS, preached for the service, while O. P. Kretzmann served as the celebrant.[60] The printed Communion statement read:

The ministry of Word and Sacrament in the Memorial Chapel is sponsored by Valparaiso University and conducted in accordance with the

University; Father Richard, Seven Dolors Shrine, Valparaiso, Indiana; Dr. Roland Wiederaenders, First Vice-President, The Lutheran Church—Missouri Synod." "Program" and "Participants," *The Diakonia of the Church in a New Age: a colloquium*, 102-105.
[59] "Twenty Years of Partnership Celebrated," 8-9.
[60] "Program," The Diakonia of the Church in a New Age: a colloquium, no pagination for "Program."

theology of the Lutheran Confessions. The sacrament of Holy Communion is intended for all Lutheran students and for such others as shall be served by this sacramental ministry after sufficient pastoral consultation. Parents, relatives, and friends who are communicant members of the Lutheran Church are invited to join with student members in the sacrament of Holy Communion.[61]

It must be noted that, though the LDA trained deaconesses specifically for service within the Missouri Synod and affiliated synods, the planning committee deliberately ignored official LCMS policy by providing an opportunity for all Lutherans at the colloquium to partake of the Lord's Supper under the auspices of Valparaiso University. This was normal practice at the University. For even though the University drew its largest base of financial support from the Missouri Synod, the pan-Lutheran association that owned Valpo felt obligated to provide for the joint spiritual care of all Lutheran students.[62]

Did the anniversary colloquium succeed in drawing out new insights and understandings that would be used to chart the course of the deaconess movement within the Missouri Synod for the next two decades? The answer must be yes, if even in very subtle ways. For example, twelve years later, during the 1976–77 academic year when this author took the "Deaconess Work" course at Valparaiso, the first colloquium lecture by LCA Professor John Reumann was still required reading for that course.

MEETINGS WITH THE MISSOURI SYNOD

By 1965 (and perhaps even earlier), Pastor Gerken engaged in a campaign to sort out what he felt would be a more appropriate and more productive relationship between the deaconess program and the Missouri Synod. In his "Staff Notes" column in the summer 1966 issue of *TLD,* he wrote:

For the past year the Executive Director has had several meetings with Synod's Board of Directors, the President of Valparaiso University as well as the Vice-president in Charge of Academic affairs, the Executive Secretary of the Board of Higher Education and others to discuss the Deaconess program in the Church with special emphasis on the relationship to Synod and the University as the program is now

---

[61] *Ibid.*
[62] See Chapter 6.

constituted. Future direction and/or developments will largely depend upon the results of studies now in progress.[63]

From his perspective as Executive Director, Gerken was convinced that the Missouri Synod should take over the deaconess program, either at one of the seminaries or at the teachers' college in River Forest. He believed that it was important for Synod to have more control of the training of its deaconesses, thereby also securing a better knowledge of every aspect of the program and the diaconate as it functioned in LCMS congregations and institutions.[64] Minutes from the September 1966 meeting of the Synod's BHE noted:

> Doctor Huegli and the executive secretary (Mr. Arthur M. Ahlschwede) attended the plenary board meeting of the Lutheran Deaconess Association at Valparaiso University on September 16. It is interesting to note that the Lutheran Deaconess Association is an autonomous organization. It is a part of the university program at Valparaiso, but is under a completely separate administration. Valparaiso University subsidizes the organization to the extent of approximately $16,000 annually by providing one-half tuition rates to deaconess students. Most of the deaconess students enrolled in the program at the freshman and sophomore college level attend Synodical junior colleges. They do not pay the Synodical tuition, since the first two years of the deaconess program are recognized as Synodical programs.[65] . . .

> The relation of the Lutheran Deaconess Association to the Board for Higher Education is to be studied further; additional consideration is to be given and reports made. The Reverend Walter C. Gerken, Executive Director of the Lutheran Deaconess Association, will be a participant of the October 14–15 plenary meeting of the Board for Higher Education.[66]

Gerken spoke for thirty minutes before the plenary board, which in addition to the eight members and four permanent staff of the BHE included the Presidents of all sixteen LCMS institutions of higher learning.[67]

---

[63] Words in the quotation have been capitalized or not capitalized according to how they appear in the original quotation. "Staff Notes," *TLD* 43, no. 1 and 2 (Summer 1966): 7.

[64] Herbert Martin Gerken (son of Walter C. Gerken), notes from telephone interview by CDN.

[65] To "not pay the Synodical tuition" meant that pre-deaconess students *did* receive the tuition discount automatically given to students who were registered in church work programs at LCMS colleges.

[66] *BHE Minutes,* September 23-24, 1966, item 8, CHI, St. Louis, Mo.

[67] BHE, *The Lutheran Church—Missouri Synod Plenary Meeting, Saint Paul's College, Concordia, Missouri, October 14-15, 1966,* file: Participants and Schedule, folder: LCMS—Bd. For Higher

Nine days later he announced the outcome of his endeavors to the annual meeting of the LDA held at Gethsemane Lutheran Church in Fort Wayne.

> . . . After discussion at the Plenary meeting of Synod's Board for Higher Education, the question of more control by Synod was considered creation of a problem where none exists. Lutheran Deaconess Association will continue as a Synodically approved agency operating in affiliation with Valparaiso University and Synod.[68]

This was a blow for Gerken, a conservative pastor who loved the LCMS and expressed his hope that the diaconate would always walk with the Synod in both doctrine and practice. The Executive Director did not ever print his reasons for caution in this area, but it is obvious that certain trends and decisions in the LDA and its diaconate might have given him cause for concern. For example, at the same LDA meeting where Gerken gave the above report, a representative of the LDC announced that the deaconess conference had decided to join an "inter-synodical group" called the Lutheran Deaconess Conference of America—an organization "presently composed of Deaconesses belonging to National Lutheran Council churches."[69]

EXECUTIVE DIRECTOR ACCEPTS PARISH CALL

Gerken submitted to the decision of the BHE plenary meeting, but soon realized that God was calling him to a different field of service. The minutes of the LDA Plenary Board meeting held at Concordia Senior College, Fort Wayne on January 6, 1967 recorded:

> Pastor Gerken commented on the four calls he had received—Decatur, Ind; El Paso, Tex.; Pasadena, Cal.; Orchard Park, N.Y. and said that he had returned the first two and was holding the latter two. He stated that he felt that the Lord wanted him back in the parish ministry as evidenced by these four calls received within a four-week period. His desire to reenter the parish ministry, he stated, was not to be construed that the LDA ministry is not important, but that he felt more adequate in the parish ministry.

Education Plenary Meeting 14-15 Oct 1966, Box: LCMS BHE Plenary Meetings 1966-1968 Box 8C, CHI, St. Louis, Mo.
[68] Peter A. Zadeik, Jr., "Minutes: Fort Wayne, Indiana, October 23, 1966," *TLD* 43, no. 3 and 4 (Winter 1966), 13.
[69] Zadeik, "Minutes: Fort Wayne, Indiana, October 23, 1966," 13; Evelyn Middelstadt, "From the Conference President," *TLD* 43, no. 3 and 4 (Winter 1966): 10-11.

RESOLVED that recognizing the distinct contribution he made to the LDA program through an awkward and critical part of LDA history, he be released to accept a call into the parish ministry.

At this point Pastor Gerken committed himself to accept the Pasadena, California, call.

RESOLVED that the above resolution be amended to state that the LDA releases him to accept the call from First Lutheran Church of Pasadena, Calif.[70]

A farewell dinner and reception were held for Pastor and Mrs. Gerken at Deaconess Hall on February 26, 1967, where the LDA, LDC, and Valparaiso deaconess students presented them with "gifts of remembrance."[71] While the LDA proceeded to find a new Executive Director, LDA President Albers and Director of Training Kristo shared the duties belonging to the vacant post.[72]

THE MISSOURI SYNOD BOARD OF DIRECTORS

Almost exactly a year after Gerken attended the plenary meeting of the BHE, a letter from the LCMS Board of Directors to the LDA and the BHE made it clear that the Synod's BOD still wished to discuss the future of the deaconess program in relation to the Synod.[73]

In a letter dated October 10, 1967, Doctor Wolbrecht addressed the Lutheran Deaconess Association and the Board for Higher Education stating the following:

---

[70] Dorothy Liebmann, "Lutheran Deaconess Association Plenary Board Meeting January 6, 1967," Box: Board for Professional Education Services Box 5: Deaconess Materials and BHE Materials, found loose at front of box, CHI, St. Louis, Mo.

[71] Edgar H. Albers, "We are at Present without an Executive Director of the Association," *TLD* 44, no. 1 (Spring 1967): 2.

[72] In the winter of 1966, a retired businessman named Paul Nieter agreed "to assume the title of Executive Assistant to the Director" for one year. Nieter had served the LDA Board in an advisory capacity for 18 months before that, and continued to assist the association for some time after the Executive Director accepted a call. E. H. Albers, "From the President," *TLD* 43, no. 3 and 4 (Winter 1966): 4.

[73] In addition to LCMS President Oliver Harms (as ex officio member of the BHE), three other members of the LCMS Board of Directors were present at the Plenary Meeting of the BHE in October 1966. "Participants," *BHE, The Lutheran Church—Missouri Synod Plenary Meeting, Saint Paul's College, Concordia, Missouri, October 14-15, 1966,* file: Participants and Schedule, folder: LCMS—Bd. For Higher Education Plenary Meeting 14-15 Oct 1966, Box: LCMS BHE Plenary Meetings 1966-1968 Box 8C, CHI, St. Louis, Mo.

"In its latest meeting the synodical Board of Directors came to adopt the following resolution:

WHEREAS, The Lutheran Deaconess Association has for many years been having major financial problems; and

WHEREAS, Placement of deaconesses is under the direction of Synod's Council of Presidents; and

WHEREAS, There needs to be close liaison between the Deaconess program, curriculum, and graduate utilization involving both the Association and the Synod; therefore be it

RESOLVED, That the Lutheran Deaconess Association be strongly urged to consider having its curriculum administration assumed by Synod's Board for Higher Education; and be it further

RESOLVED, That the Association and the Board for Higher Education consider this recommendation and report to the Board of Directors at the January, 1968, meeting."[74]

On the evening of December 14, 1967, BHE and LDA subcommittees met together for an initial sharing of information and discussion of particular points in the BOD resolution. Those present at the meeting were: Edgar Albers, Arne Kristo, Hartwig Schwehn, and Peter Zadeik (LDA);[75] Adolph Rittmueller, Elmer Pflieger, and Richard Engebrecht (BHE); Arthur Ahlschwede (Executive Secretary of the BHE) and Albert Huegli (Chairman of the BHE *and* Valparaiso University Vice-President for Academic Affairs). After considering its own subcommittee report given on the following day, the BHE outlined a strategy for moving forward on the BOD resolution.

The Board for Higher Education recommended the following: That the Board of Directors request the Lutheran Deaconess Association to conduct a thorough study of the entire deaconess program and operation. It is suggested that the Lutheran Deaconess Association employ a competent professional person to conduct this study with the assistance of a Board for Higher education staff member. A report of this study should be available by April 1968.

The suggested study should incorporate at least all of the following:

A. A definitive statement of the present Lutheran Deaconess Association operations:

---

[74] *BHE Minutes,* December 15, 1967, item 5; CHI, St. Louis, Mo.
[75] Rev. Hartwig Schwehn (1916-1968); Rev. Peter A. Zadeik (b. 1933).

a) Administration

b) Review of current curriculum offerings and requirements

c) Review of financial status and current operational budget

d) Relationship with Valparaiso University

e) Relationship with Synodical junior colleges

f) Relationship with Synodical placement practice

g) Statistical analysis of student population, graduates in the field and other related items

h) Public relations and development program

B. A statement comparing:

a) The diaconate with other church ministries

b) The diaconate training program of the Lutheran Deaconess Association with the current Synodical training program for other ministries

C. A full exploration of possible new areas of service for the deaconess program

D. A full exploration of a pan-Lutheran deaconess program

The Board for Higher Education strongly urges the Synodical Board of Directors to ask the Lutheran Deaconess Association to refrain from calling an Executive Director.[76]

The BHE obviously took this resolution from the BOD very seriously since it requested the BOD to ask the LDA to delay electing an Executive Director to replace Gerken. After all, if the BHE took over administration of the deaconess program curriculum, the Board would want to have a hand in choosing the new Executive Director, particularly if the training program ended up being transplanted to one of the LCMS campuses.

At its meeting in January 1968, the BOD approved the study of the deaconess program as outlined by the BHE, with one change. Under point D, where the BHE recommended "A full exploration of *a pan-Lutheran* deaconess program," the BOD wrote in its place "A full exploration of *other-Lutheran* deaconess programs."[77]

---

[76] *BHE Minutes,* December 15, 1967, item 5; CHI, St. Louis, Mo.
[77] "Minutes of Meeting of the Board of Directors, January 18-19, 1968, St. Louis, Missouri," Committee 4: item 191, pages 29-30, unbound, Box: BD Minutes Only (copy 2), 1965-1983, archive 2.5.4.2., CHI, St. Louis, Mo.

STATEMENT ON SPECIAL MINISTRIES

Immediately after creating the outline for a study of the workings of the LDA and the diaconate, the BHE requested its staff to "prepare a summary statement on the entire matter of special ministries within the church for the board's consideration in its deliberations regarding the LDA as requested by the Synod's Board of Directors."[78] When finished in January 1968, the four-page "summary statement" included a section on "The Diaconate." Excerpts from the document's introduction and the section on the diaconate provide insight into general attitudes and presuppositions held by the staff, while reflecting some of the Missouri Synod's internal conflicts about "ministry."

Special Ministries

The members of the board will understand that any exhaustive study of the so-called "auxiliary ministries" will not only involve substantial educational and institutional issues, but will also plunge us into a veritable morass of theological and ecclesiastical concerns. If not insuperable, they are at least formidable. Included are such items as the relationship of "the ministries" to "the ministry" (and the very legitimacy of the former term), of church to ministry, of the "public ministry" to the "priesthood of all believers," of "professional ministry" to "lay ministry," and the perpetually difficult matter of the implications of ordination. . . .

What follows, therefore, can be at best a very cursory review—not so much of the distinctly theological and ecclesiastical aspects as the more organizational (if you will, "practical") considerations involved. They are discussed on an implicit assumption of a sort of pragmatic rubric, that the church is free at any point in its history to define new "forms" of ministry and to provide and prescribe programs of preparation for them. The intricate ramifications of that rubric we will have to let slide for the moment.

One detail which we can point out, however, is that the provision in the Synodical constitution that one of the objectives of the Synod is "the training of ministers and teachers for service in the Evangelical Lutheran Church," must certainly be seen in its historical context and does not prevent the church from authorizing a somewhat broader program of professional preparation than the strict meaning of the terms used would seem to call for.

It is apparent that for some years we in The Lutheran Church—Missouri Synod have been working with greater or lesser accuracy of expression

---

[78] *BHE Minutes,* December 15, 1967, item 6.

with such "auxiliary ministries" (it should be remembered that for many, many years the teaching ministry was referred to as an "auxiliary ministry") as the female diaconate, the positions of the parish worker (etc.) . . .

It may be gratuitous to point out—but perhaps also helpful—that one of the factors which has undoubtedly contributed to the viability of each of these offices is the simple fact that most employing agencies (congregations and institutions) do not employ with a particularly strict concern for the precise elements of the individual's preparation. In other words, many agencies need and "hire" what employment agencies call a "girl Friday," that is, a person versatile enough to be helpful in many aspects of congregational or institutional activity, without particular reference to genuinely professional skills or qualifications.

The Diaconate

The board is presently active through a subcommittee in studying the present advantages and difficulties inherent in the tripartite arrangement for the education of deaconesses in The Lutheran Church—Missouri Synod. The three parties are, of course, the Lutheran Deaconess Association, Valparaiso University, and the Synodical colleges, represented by the Board for Higher Education.

While the precipitating factor for the present discussion seems to be the persistent financial crisis facing the Lutheran Deaconess Association, there are larger issues, involving mostly the professional identification of the deaconess. ...

The fact of the matter is that deaconesses are not nuns, they are not nurses, they are not teachers, they are not social workers, and it is understandable that they do not want to be considered secretaries. One answer, of course, is that they are none of these—because they are deaconesses! Their major is theology, and the central function of their office is that sort of activity which we consider to be very close to the literal communication of law and Gospel—the teaching of religion, ministering to shut-ins, making mission calls, providing religious leadership to parish and other voluntary groups.

The precise, or effective, demand for these services is naturally hard to measure. Fortunately, supply and demand have been in remarkable balance—and both have been small, numerically considered.

What seriously complicates every attempt to solve immediate, pressing issues is the haunting realization that there may not be a really pressing need to maintain the diaconate as a separate office, that more might be gained by transforming the curriculum into one with a basic teacher education or social work education framework, and that the Synodical involvement could be greatly simplified by absorbing the individuals involved into the programs of our existing junior colleges and four-year teachers' colleges.[79]

How interesting it is that once again the topic has come full circle to the issue of deaconess identity. Certainly the LDA and consecrated deaconesses continually worked toward the goal of helping the church understand what a deaconess was and how she might fit into institutional or congregational life. But the combination of factors such as increased professionalism, internships, and the variety of different (and sometimes new) positions being filled by deaconesses, somehow served to blur the understanding of the uniqueness of deaconess work that was centered in the *Ministry of Mercy* to both body and soul.

DEACONESS DISCUSSION MEETING

On January 24, 1968, a special Deaconess Discussion Meeting took place in Chicago. Five of the men who attended the December meeting of the LDA and BHE subcommittees were present (Albers, Kristo, Schwehn, Rittmueller, and Huegli), plus LDA board member Mr. Harold Hollman, LCMS President Oliver Harms, VU President O. P. Kretzmann, and BHE Assistant Executive Secretary Samuel Goltermann. Such a collection of top leadership from the LCMS, LDA, and Valparaiso University showed a serious and intense desire by all three organizations to bring the "deaconess question" to a satisfactory conclusion.

Significantly, the meeting did not address the recommendation of the LCMS Board of Directors "that the Lutheran Deaconess Association be strongly urged to consider having its curriculum administration assumed by Synod's Board for Higher Education."[80] Instead, LDA President Albers, who served as Chairman for the summit, began by reading "A Statement and a Proposal," which was followed by an exchange of ideas, questions, and comments related to the "Background Discussion Guide" that had been received by all participants before the meeting.[81] The "Background"

---

[79] "Special Ministries," a report written by BHE staff, *BHE Minutes,* January 11, 1968, CHI, St. Louis, Mo.

[80] *BHE Minutes,* December 15, 1967, item 5.

[81] The author of the "Background Discussion Guide" is unknown, though it seems likely that Albers wrote it. No copies of the document called "A Statement and a Proposal" were found with the "Background Discussion Guide" or with Kristo's report on the meeting. Arne Kristo, "Deaconess Discussion Meeting, January 24, 1968, Chicago, Illinois," Box: Board for Professional Education Services Box 5: Deaconess Materials and BHE Materials, found loose at front of box, CHI, St. Louis, Mo.

document included eight possible alternatives for the future development of the deaconess program, a statement about "The Theology of Deaconess Work," and a note about the need to "engage an outsider to conduct a study of the program."[82] In short, the alternatives for the future included:

A. Leave the program unchanged . . .

B. Leave the program unchanged except for returning to direct placement of deaconesses by the LDA instead of Synodical placement . . .

C. Turn the program over entirely to the Lutheran Deaconess Association . . .

D. Turn the program over entirely to Valparaiso University . . .

E. Turn the program over entirely to the Synod . . .

F. Change the Deaconess Association to an Association of persons concerned with promoting deaconess ministry but without involvement on the student level . . .

G. We could make the deaconess program Pan-Lutheran . . .

H. Finally, another option (which is not inconsistent with the preceding options) is to establish a separate college for deaconesses at Valparaiso University . . . [83]

Seeing the presence of so many other less plausible alternatives listed in the "Background Document," it is difficult to comprehend why the option proposed by the BOD—namely, that the LDA would continue as it always had, but with its curriculum administered by the BHE—was not at least included for consideration.

Appendices 1.G and 1.H of this book provide the entire text of the "Background Discussion Guide" and Pastor Kristo's report on the Deaconess Discussion Meeting. Here it will simply be noted that those who attended the meeting reached a general consensus on four items: that the deaconess program will continue unchanged (as described in alternative A); that an "outside researcher" should be hired to conduct a study and offer suggestions to the LDA; that LCMS President Harms should make a public statement of support for the deaconess program; and that a Synodical Advisory Committee was needed. After receiving a report on what transpired at the Deaconess Discussion Meeting, the BHE resolved to

---

[82] "Background Discussion Guide: Deaconess Program," Box: Board for Professional Education Services Box 5: Deaconess Materials and BHE Materials, found loose at front of box, CHI, St. Louis, Missouri, 1-4.
[83] *Ibid.*

abide by its recommendations of December 1967, that the LDA "conduct a thorough study of the entire deaconess program and operation" and "refrain from calling an executive director."[84]

MEMO FROM THE PRESIDENT

About three months after the Deaconess Discussion Meeting took place, LCMS President Oliver Harms carried out the suggestion that he "make a public statement of support for the deaconess program." In a memo to all Missouri Synod pastors, professors, and male teachers, Harms addressed nine different topics, one of which was titled "Deaconess Workers." President Harms wrote:

> The two previous subjects lead me to comment briefly about the work of our deaconesses. Trends have been changing recently. For a number of years most deaconesses worked in welfare and educational institutions. Now a growing number of deaconesses serve in parish work. In part this change reflects the changing nature of much parish work. I[t] also reflects a greater willingness to use a wider range of workers for full-time service in the church. At the present time 80 deaconesses are serving in the Synod in various capacities while 180 are in training either at Valparaiso University or at various Synodical institutions. I have been impressed by the announcement that the average length of service among all deaconesses who have been placed into service since 1922 is 5.5 years.
>
> Voluntary groups like the Lutheran Deaconess Association have always faced an uphill struggle for survival. The Synod is constantly and sympathetically reviewing the relationships and support which the church as such owes to institutions of this kind. We recognize that there is also an ongoing need for popular support. I mention this item here to encourage you to keep this valuable agency of the church on your list of worthy projects for continued and generous support.[85]

COMMENCING THE STUDY

In response to the January 1968 statement from the BOD, which suggested that the LDA "employ a competent professional person to conduct a study with the assistance of a Board of Higher Education staff member," LDA President Albers compiled a 48-page document titled "Definitive

---

[84] See earlier section in this chapter titled "The Missouri Synod Board of Directors." *BHE Minutes*, February 22-24, 1968, item 12, CHI, St. Louis, Mo.
[85] Oliver R. Harms, "Memo to My Brethren," Letter to all Pastors, Professors, and Male Teachers of the Lutheran Church—Missouri Synod, April 1968, CHI, St. Louis, Mo.

Statements and Statistics, Prepared for The Board of Directors The Lutheran Church—Missouri Synod and its Board of Higher Education."[86] This document made a start toward describing LDA operations and recounted the LDA's understanding of its relationship with Valparaiso University, LCMS junior colleges, and the Synodical placement practice.[87] Albers gave copies of the paper to the BHE, and explained that it would provide needed background material for the "professional" study consultant.[88]

The Executive Committee of the LDA Board of Directors engaged the services of Rev. Frederick Sheely Weiser (b. 1935) to carry out the study.[89] An LCA pastor, professor, and archivist for Lutheran Theological Seminary at Gettysburg, Pa., Weiser had written some fairly well-known histories of the work of deaconesses in the United States.[90] Weiser also attended the 1964 Colloquium and was already familiar with the LDA and the diaconate of the LCMS and affiliated synods. Minutes for the April 19, 1968 LDA Board of Directors mention that Weiser was a guest at the meeting and

---

[86] Albers announced at the annual LDA meeting in October 1967 that he had agreed to be interim Executive Director for the LDA on a part-time basis. He also edited TLD for four issues, beginning with Spring 1968. He was first elected to the LDA Board of Directors in 1947; was Vice-President from 1948-55; President from 1955-69; and then continued to serve on the Board into the 1970s. Like Wambsganss and Klausing before him, Albers was a parish pastor during the years he served the LDA: at Peace Lutheran Church, Fort Wayne (1946-55); Calvary Lutheran Church, Indianapolis (1955-65); and Immanuel Lutheran Church, Mokena, Illinois (1968-1980). During four of his years as LDA President, Albers served as the Associate Director of Public Relations for the LCMS (1965-68). "Peter Zadeik, "Lutheran Deaconess Association Annual Meeting October 19, 1967," TLD 44, no. 3 and 4 (Winter 1967): 10; Edgar H Albers, "Definitive Statements and Statistics, Prepared for The Board of Directors The Lutheran Church—Missouri Synod and its Board of Higher Education," mimeographed pages (Fort Wayne: LDA, March 12, 1968), Introduction, no pagination.

[87] Albers, "Definitive Statements and Statistics."

[88] BHE Minutes, March 29-30, 1968, item 10; CHI, St. Louis, Mo.

[89] The LDA Board of Directors endorsed the Executive Committee's action on April 19, 1968. The cost of the investigation was set at "$750.00 plus expenses incurred," with a "total estimated cost of $1,500.00." Dorothy Liebmann, "Lutheran Deaconess Association Plenary Board Meeting April 19, 1968," Box: Board for Professional Education Services Box 5: Deaconess Materials and BHE Materials, found loose at front of box, CHI, St. Louis, Mo.

[90] Books authored by Weiser include: Serving Love: Chapters in the Early History of the Diaconate in American Lutheranism, A Thesis submitted to the faculty in partial fulfillment of the Requirements for the degree of Bachelor of Divinity, Department of Church History, Lutheran Theological Seminary, Gettysburg, Pa., May 1960; Love's Response: A Story of Lutheran Deaconesses in America, with an Introduction by F. Eppling Reinartz, The Board of Publication of the United Lutheran Church in America, Philadelphia, 1962; United to Serve, with a Foreword by Sister Anna Ebert, The Board of College Education and Church Vocations, Philadelphia, 1966.

promised to give exclusive time to the study for the next several weeks. The LDA would receive Weiser's report and forward it to the Synod's Board of Directors with appropriate recommendations.[91]

BUSINESS AS USUAL, BUT ONLY IN VALPARAISO

After Albers reported the BOD recommendations at the LDA Board of Directors meeting in April 1968, "Pastor Schwehn turned the meeting over to Pastor Ziegler who chairmanned [sic] the calling of an executive director."[92] No reason was given as to why the LDA decided to go forward with replacing its Executive Director after both the BHE and the BOD "strongly urged" the LDA "to refrain from calling an executive director." After the interview of four candidates, a call was extended in June, and subsequently declined.[93] A few months later, the Fall 1968 issue of *TLD* announced:

> We are most happy to announce that Pastor Arne Kristo, our Director of Education, has accepted the call of the Lutheran Deaconess Association to become the Executive Director of the Association.
>
> . . . Pastor Kristo, for the time being, will retain his duties as Director of Education. However, the Board of Directors is engaged in providing him with the necessary assistance for the heavy responsibility that he has assumed.[94]

The same magazine that printed the above quotation also reported:

> We are very happy to announce that Mrs. Arne (Ethelyne) Kristo has consented to serve as house director for Deaconess Hall during this school year. Our former house director, Mrs. Gehrke, had to retire because of illness. Mrs. Kristo is eminently qualified for this important post.[95]

Since the Executive Director lived in Valparaiso and worked from an office in Deaconess Hall, it no longer made sense for the LDA to maintain an office in Fort Wayne. On June 15, 1969, the LDA completed removal of all its business affairs from Fort Wayne to Valparaiso, at which point the

---

[91] Liebmann, "Lutheran Deaconess Association Plenary Board Meeting April 19, 1968."
[92] Rev. Arthur Henry Ziegler (1911-2001). Liebmann "Lutheran Deaconess Association Plenary Board Meeting April 19, 1968."
[93] This first call was to Rev. Clifford Harold Peterson (b.1927), Dean of Students at Concordia College, Bronxville, New York.
[94] "Executive Director," *TLD* 45, no. 3 (Fall 1968): 7.
[95] "Our New House Director," *TLD* 45, no. 3 (Fall 1968): 6.

services of Mrs. Paul Liebmann, Office Manager for the LDA, came to a close.[96] The property on Hannah Street, Fort Wayne, sold for $13,500, and helped to reduce the association's debt.[97] After almost fifty years of work in Fort Wayne, the LDA was now solely based in Valparaiso!

An Experiment in Community

Between 1966 and 1968, Pastor Kristo and other members of the LDA expressed an interest in experimenting with deaconess ministry in the context of cell communities. In spring 1968, Kristo brought a specific proposal to the LDA Board.

> This year three members of the graduating class have expressed a serious interest in the possibility for service in a communal form.. . .
>
> First of all, we would like to make a brief statement of the philosophy behind this approach to ministry. The three deaconesses would serve in three separate parishes. However, those parishes are all located within a five-mile area within the inner city on the east side of Detroit. The deaconesses would serve these three separate parishes but would live together.
>
> We visualize several benefits coming from communal living. First of all, the deaconesses would be able to encourage one another in their work. Secondly, they would be able to develop a program of worship and study in their home. One of the important features of the community would be that the three deaconesses would operate out of a common budget. In other words, their finances would be unified in the same way that the finances of a family are unified. The income would be to a common treasury, and each deaconess would draw from the common budget a personal living allowance. Other expenses would be planned according to an agreed budget.
>
> The three members of the community would commit themselves to life together for a period of two years. There would be provision made for either a continuation of the association, or the departure of one or more members of the community after the initial period of two years. There would also be provision for introducing new members to the community as such need arose. . . .
>
> Finally, we propose that for the sake of future development of communities as "outposts" of the deaconess program, the financing of this project be handled through the Lutheran Deaconess Association.

---

[96] "Fort Wayne Office Closes," *TLD* 46, no. 2 (Summer 1969): 13.
[97] Peter Zadeik, "Minutes of the Annual Meeting," *TLD* 45, no. 4 (Winter 1968): 11.

This means that we would urge the three congregations involved to remit their finances to the Deaconess Association instead of making payment directly to the individual deaconess. The Association would then, in turn, remit a monthly check to the community in Detroit where the monies would be distributed according to the agreed budget.

Some of the hoped-for values of the communal type ministry have already been mentioned. We see this as a vehicle for challenging deaconesses to minister in more radical ways than we have done in the recent past. Furthermore, we see the effect of the community being one of multiplying the effectiveness of the ministry in a way that would be superior to that of several isolated deaconesses in the same community. We also see this arrangement providing a stability for ministry which could have serious implications for the future of our program.[98]

The minutes of the April 1968 LDA Plenary Board meeting note the outcome of Kristo's presentation on the experiment in deaconess community.

Pastor Kristo stated that he had discussed this matter with The Rev. E. C. Weber,[99] Michigan District President, and with the Circuit Counselor of the Detroit Area. All were in agreement that this plan should be tried. This would mean that one of our Deaconesses would be on loan to Grace congregation, an American Lutheran Church, and the three Deaconesses would be in the employ of The Lutheran Deaconess Association.

RESOLVED that we demonstrate leadership in this experimental project for two years with the accompanying budget, details to be worked out. Adopted.[100]

Albers announced the experimental community project to the grass roots LDA membership in a feature article in the association's summer 1968 magazine. The third paragraph of the article explained the details of the placements for the three "community" members.

At the annual placements in St. Louis, three deaconesses were assigned to serve three parishes close to each other on the east side of Detroit. Miss Marlys Abley will work at Concordia Church. Miss Miriam Rueger will

---

[98] Arne Kristo, "Proposal to the Plenary Board for an Experimental Deaconess Ministry in Communal Form," Exhibit O, attached to minutes of "Lutheran Deaconess Association Plenary Board Meeting April 19, 1968," Box: Board for Professional Education Services Box 5: Deaconess Materials and BHE Materials, found loose at front of box, CHI, St. Louis, Mo.
[99] Edwin Carl Weber (1910-1988).
[100] Dorothy Liebmann, "Lutheran Deaconess Association Plenary Board Meeting April 19, 1968," 2.

serve as deaconess-nurse in the program of Riverside Congregation, and Miss Anne Marie Sargent will be located at Grace Church (ALC).

The new, yet old, feature of the arrangement is that the three deaconesses will establish a community of living under the auspices of the Deaconess Association. They will work at their respective parish locations under the direction of the respective pastors.[101]

How is it possible that "at the annual placements in St. Louis" a deaconess candidate was placed by the LCMS Council of Presidents in a congregation of the ALC, at a time when the Missouri Synod and the American Lutheran Church *were not yet in fellowship* with one another? Kristo identified this aspect of the arrangement as one of "two special problems connected with this proposal,"[102] and came up with a clever solution to get around the difficulty. The Missouri Synod recognized the LDA to be an auxiliary organization affiliated with the Synod. Therefore, the LDA itself could issue a call to the deaconess candidate and then deploy her to work in the ALC congregation. This strategy also solved the other "special problem"—that one of the LCMS congregations involved with the experimental community did not feel right about issuing a call on the basis of the minimal salary that it could offer.[103]

The LCMS College of Presidents workbook listing the 1968 deaconess placements included the three experimental community placements as follows:

Call	District	Candidates
DETROIT, MICHIGAN	MICHIGAN	Miriam Reuger
Riverside Church		Buffalo, New York
Pastor David Eberhard		(Manual, p. 327)
(Manual, No. 4) . . .		
FORT WAYNE, INDIANA	INDIANA	Marlys Abley
Lutheran Deaconess Association		Fall Creek, Wisconsin
Pastor E.H. Albers		(Manual, p. 318)
For Concordia Church		
Detroit		
Pastor A. Kebschull		
(Manual Supplement, No. 17)		

---

[101] "Something New in Detroit," *TLD* 45, no. 2 (Summer 1968): 12.
[102] Kristo, "Proposal to the Plenary Board for an Experimental Deaconess Ministry in Communal Form."
[103] *Ibid.*

FORT WAYNE, INDIANA   INDIANA
Lutheran Deaconess Association
Pastor E.H. Albers
For Grace Church (ALC)
Detroit, Michigan
Pastor L. Gotts
(Manual Supplement, No. 18)[104]

Anne Marie Sargent
Jackson, Michigan
(Manual, p. 328)

Although the minutes of the April LDA Board meeting state that all three deaconesses were to be "in the employ of The Lutheran Deaconess Association"—with the arrangement that each parish remit funds to the LDA, which in turn sent money to the women—the above quotation shows that the LDA extended calls to only two of the three women participating in the experimental community.

It is also interesting to note that, of the five requests for deaconess candidates that went *unfilled*, one was located in Detroit, at Lutheran School for the Deaf.[105] There is no indication as to why the LDA went to such lengths to secure a placement in an ALC congregation when another field of service was available in Detroit. A further curiosity is Kristo's statement that communal deaconess ministry would be "a vehicle for challenging deaconesses to minister in more radical ways than we have done in the recent past." Although the experiment was highly acclaimed when it started, there appear to be no published reports about the progress or evolution of the community, or whether or not the LDA ever repeated the experiment.[106]

---

[104] "Assignments, Spring—1968, Deaconesses," mimeographed sheets, pages 1, 3; filed under LCMS College of Presidents, together with placement manuals called *Part III Deaconesses* and *Supplement—Part III Deaconesses*, Box: 111.1C.09 Assignment of Calls 1968, CHI, St. Louis, Mo.

[105] "Assignments, Spring—1968, Deaconesses," mimeographed sheets, page 1.

[106] Anne Marie Sargent wrote a 29-page paper on "The Diaconate and the Concept of Community," for an independent study course at Valparaiso University. In the paper's introduction she wrote, " This independent project has included not only the writing of this paper, but also discussions with Pastor Frederick Weiser, correspondence with Sister Anna Ebert, attendance at the Conference on Communal Ministries at Valparaiso June 17-19 [1968], visiting the Lutheran Deaconess Motherhouse in Milwaukee, visiting the Dominican motherhouse (Convent of St. Catherine) in Racine, Wisconsin, and living for three weeks in the Dominican convent at Nativity Church in Detroit, Michigan, and participating in an inter-community urban orientation program involving sisters from several orders who worked in Detroit for the summer." Sargent includes no mention of the special LDA Community project in her paper. Anne Marie Sargent, "The Diaconate and the Concept of Community," Independent Project, Theology 390, Valparaiso University, September, 1968, LDA Archives, LDA, Valparaiso, Ind.

THE AMPLIFIED ROLE OF THE LDC

The Lutheran Deaconess Conference met for three days every year during the summer months. The women normally convened in the Midwest (Fort Wayne, Watertown, River Forest, Detroit, St. Louis, Cleveland, Milwaukee, Lake Geneva, Valparaiso, Arcadia, Fairview Park, Henning, and Winfield), but occasionally went further afield (Pittsburgh, Angola, Bronxville, and Waterloo in Ontario, Canada). In addition to consecrated deaconesses, whether active or inactive, the deaconess conferences welcomed guests interested in the work of the diaconate.[107]

As the number of deaconesses and interns in the field grew from year to year, more of the women found themselves in closer proximity to other members of the diaconate, with the result that small clusters of women began to meet once or twice a month for mutual support in their life and work. In 1961, the LDC recognized the benefit of such meetings, decided to establish Area Conferences, and also adopted "Guidelines for Area Conferences."[108] Just a year later, the President's Address to the annual LDC conference included some positive observations about both the national and local area conferences.

> . . . Let us look more closely at this Lutheran Deaconess Conference inner-mission. First of all, we have the opportunity to grow intellectually and spiritually through the Bible study and program topics which have been arranged. We need to grow in these areas. We need to grow also emotionally to face the very difficult tasks which lie before us.
>
> As I was beginning to put these thoughts together, my thoughts were caught up by the opening article in the last NEXUS.[109] I quote, "As the graduates and interns anticipate their Deaconess role with thoughts of happiness as well as some anxiety, they are looking to the fellowship of the diaconate to be a resource for the opportunities to share their joys and sorrows." I would like to follow this up with the statement something to

---

[107] The LDC occasionally voted to extend honorary membership to certain women who were not deaconesses, e.g., the beloved widows, Sylvia Trautmann (housemother) and Magdalene Krentz (wife of former Executive Director Arnold Krentz).

[108] "Constrained by Love," *TLD* 38, no. 3 (July 1961): 8.

[109] Deaconess students produced the magazine called *Nexus* on behalf of the LDC. "Nexus arose out of a desire to create a publication which would allow conversation between graduate deaconesses in the Synodical Conference churches, institutions, and missions all over the world, and the young student deaconesses at Valparaiso University, who are still in stages of preparation to serve full time in the Church." *Nexus* 1, no. 1 (January 1961): 1; "Nexus Report," typed pages, no pagination, *Nexus* file: LDA Archives, LDA, Valparaiso, Ind.

the effect that this can be found in the Deaconess Conference and area conferences.

I am sure that all of us have attempted to verbalize the reasons that we like the area conferences so much, we have found that we are trying to describe intangibles. Let's listen to the NEXUS article again, "As we analyze our people's weaknesses, feelings and forms of sinfulness, we should never forget that our analysis must not be for judgment but must be for deeper service and greater understanding of their needs. As we look to our pastor or fellow-Deaconesses to fill our needs we must not fail to be at work serving them in their needs."

. . . Finally, to set our goal, "if our sisterhood seeks to keep alive this concept of His service in the hearts of the Deaconesses and seeks to enrich this service by being an effective resource of edification for the sisters, then we have a very vital and revelent [sic] diaconate, vital to the church, vital to the Deaconesses."[110]

The concept of the diaconate as a sisterhood had always been present in the LDC but began to be more clearly articulated in the early 1960s. As the decade progressed and moved into the 1970s, many LDC resolutions and actions would be influenced, and sometimes even driven, by the mandate of loyalty to the sisterhood.[111]

In 1964, an optional two-day intensive seminar followed the annual LDC conference. VU Professor Paul Bretscher, and Miss Dorothy Mundt from the Lutheran Social Welfare Agency of River Forest, presented sessions on the gospel of Matthew and facilitated discussion on the subject of "Understanding and Accepting Ourselves."[112] For the next several years, post-conference seminars explored topics such as "The Role of Women in the Twentieth Century;" "Finding Fulfillment;" "Reflections on Romans; Justification by Faith—Jargon or Jewel;" and in the later 1960s, featured

---

[110] Evelyn Middelstadt, "The President's Address, Minutes of the Lutheran Deaconess Conference Winfield, Kansas, July 9-11, 1962," priv. col. of Clara Strehlow, Deaconess Office Archives, Concordia University, RF, Illinois.

[111] For example, in 1964, the Thirtieth Anniversary LDC conference voted to raise an offering of $2,500 to purchase a station wagon for use by the Deaconess Hall residents who needed to drive to field work assignments at churches and institutions in the area around Valparaiso. In 1962, Kristo made field work a required part of the student deaconess curriculum for one semester of each academic year. Jean Hoover, "From the Conference President," TLD 42, no. 4 (Winter 1965): 16; "Wanted: A Station Wagon," TLD 40, no. 1 (January 1963): 6.

[112] "30th Anniversary Celebrated," TLD 41, no. 3 (Summer 1964): 9-10.

experimental group dynamics and a "sensitivity lab."[113] In 1970, the LDC decided to try something different again.

> A new format was attempted at the Deaconess Conference held in early August at Valpo. It was a "happening." What is that? Well, it was an opportunity to confront important issues in living today. Resource persons shared information and stimulated expression of ideas which were sometimes vigorously batted back and forth. The issues included poverty, hunger, relevance of the church's mission, the role and image of women, and racism.

> Here are some comments from deaconesses who attended:

> "The Conference exposed us quickly to some new ideas and patterns."

> "The speakers were catalysts whom I remember not so much for what they said, but for what they encouraged me to say."

> "For women who profess to be Christian, we certainly showed a lot of insensitivity toward one another."

> "The speakers made me feel involved in a part of life, not just someone listening to a lecture of facts."

> "With increasing clarity, the participants came to see how deeply they were divided in their points of view and in basic life-styles."

> From these comments it is obvious that this type of Conference was regarded with mixed feelings. When confrontation and openness occur, pain is involved, and there were some difficult moments. The healing of the closing Eucharist was perhaps the more appreciated and meaningful. The Eucharist, in a variety of styles, was celebrated each day of the Conference.[114]

In the mid 1960s, members of the LDC rejoiced when their president became an advisory member of the LDA Board of Directors, because they believed that such a move would increase communication between the groups *and* give deaconesses more of a say in the future direction of the diaconate.[115] The "happening" that took place in 1970 produced several resolutions designed to affect the future of the diaconate by requesting the LDA to take action in certain directions. For example, one resolution asked

---

[113] "Deaconess Hall—Site for 1965 Conference-Seminar," *TLD* 42, no. 2 (Spring 1965): 11; "Tomorrow's Ministry Today," *TLD* 42, no. 3 (Summer 1965): 11; "From the Conference President," *TLD* 43, no.3 and 4 (Winter 1966): 10; "Deaconess Conference," *TLD* 44, no. 1 (Spring 1967): 3; "Minutes of the Annual Meeting," *TLD* 45, no. 4 (Winter 1968): 11.
[114] "Minutes of the Annual Meeting," *TLD* 47, no. 1 (Spring 1970): 7.
[115] Hoover, "From the Conference President," 16.

the members of the Board of Directors to reconsider the "limitations" placed on the office of deaconess, so that they "add to our ministry new forms and new frontiers such as non-organizational church positions, secular situations, and agencies."[116] Another resolution requested the LDA Board to "investigate all areas of working together with the LCA Deaconess Program." This was an unusual request given the fact that the LCMS was not in fellowship with the Lutheran Church in America.[117]

Hot topics within the diaconate throughout the 1960s and 1970s included communication and the processes of the art of communication. Mutual respect of all people, a social conscience, responsibility toward all, and a great deal of "talk"—not only between peers, but between the levels of any organizational hierarchy—were almost militantly called for during this era.

MORE PUBLICATIONS

Executive Director Kristo used newsletters designed for different audiences to increase communication between various segments of the association. For deaconess students, he wrote *"Communi Key:* Christ—Key to Community and Communication," and for consecrated deaconesses he wrote *Dominus:* News and Ideas for Deaconesses. These mimeographed publications provided an avenue for dissemination of information, but also served as vehicles for guiding and directing the readers in certain activities and attitudes.[118]

---

[116] The second part of the Resolved included the names of four 1970 graduates that the LDC wanted the LDA to recognize "as fulfilling the Office of Deaconess" even though the women worked "in one of these new forms." "1. 1970—New Forms and Ministries," *Lutheran Deaconess Conference Major Resolutions from 1970ff Printed in Chronological Order*, 15 mimeographed pages, priv. col. of Ruth (nee Broermann) Stallmann, St. Louis, Missouri, 1.

[117] No reason is given as to why the Deaconess Conference stipulated the Lutheran Church in America, rather than the American Lutheran Church. The Missouri Synod had declared altar and pulpit fellowship with the ALC the previous year. "4. 1970—Association With Other Church Bodies," *Lutheran Deaconess Conference Major Resolutions from 1970ff Printed in Chronological Order*, 1.

[118] For example, Kristo used these newsletters to encourage all students and deaconesses to become voting members of the LDA, so that the program could be strengthened through the women participating in "the basic matter of helping to elect members of the Plenary Board, and in other ways to influence the (LDA) policy." Arne Kristo, *Dominus* (LDA: Valparaiso, June 1969), 4-5; Arne Kristo, *Communi Key* (LDA: Valparaiso, May 1969), 4, from priv. col. of Helen (nee Haase) Tesch, Blue Earth, Minn.

Kristo also encouraged production of a monthly *Intern Letter*. This was a collection of short updates from every deaconess intern, compiled by one intern (on a rotating basis) and circulated to all of her classmates in the field. These letters are now helpful for documenting common attitudes, trends, or issues that were important to the interns, and hence to the LDA and the diaconate as a whole. When reading the monthly circulars for the 1967–68 intern class, for example, at least two major areas of discussion can be traced throughout the letters, which prove valuable to an historical understanding of how the diaconate moved toward new directions in the late 1960s. One of these subject threads could be described as an exploration and re-thinking of the proper leadership role of deaconesses within any given field of service, and the other, a desire to participate in a progression toward pan-Lutheran and ecumenical ministry enterprises in the Missouri Synod.[119]

ON THE CUTTING EDGE

It was not until 1969 that delegates at the LCMS convention in Denver voted—with 522 yeas and 438 nays—to establish altar and pulpit fellowship with the ALC.[120] Discussion and opinions about this matter had been polarized for many years within the Synod, and continued to be so even after the resolution was passed.[121] Looking at events like the 1964 anniversary colloquium and the LDA's placement of a deaconess candidate in an ALC congregation (both mentioned above), there is no doubt that many church leaders who promoted the deaconess cause also favored church fellowship with the ALC, and some saw no problem with implementing the pan-Lutheran or ecumenical practice that they felt certain would eventually be endorsed by the Synod. This type of thinking—and the desire to just *do* what one believed to be correct—was also reflected in the 1967–68 *Intern Letters*.

> "The second high point of our life here was reached when we were invited to participate in an ecumenical retreat. ... Most of the people there were representative of Roman Catholic orders. Our chief speaker was a Roman Catholic Luther-scholar. Peggy and I both agree that his

[119] *Intern Letters*, compilations of mimeographed letters, collected by month for the 1967-68 academic year, priv. col. of Helen (nee Haase) Tesch, Blue Earth, Minn.

[120] "Resolution 3-15," in LCMS, *Proceedings*, 1969, 96-99.

[121] For background information on this subject, see: Suelflow, August R., ed., *Heritage in Motion: Readings in the History of the Lutheran Church--Missouri Synod, 1962-1995*, St. Louis: Concordia, 1998, chapter 2.

understanding of Lutheran theology and his hopes for greater church unity were strengthening and certainly provided lots of food for thought." (*Shirley*, October, 1967)

"Yesterday our parish participated with fifteen other Lutheran parishes— including such heretical groups as the ALC and LCA—in a Reformation worship. It was really great." (*Karen*, November, 1967)

"Another part of the Reformation celebrations was the coffee house for Lutheran and Catholic youth. We had the privilege of having with us two girls who participated in the eight week session of dialogue among 6 Lutheran and Catholic youth in 1966." (*Kaylyn*, Advent, 1967)

"We hosted our second area deaconess conference here . . . We were privileged and pleased to have Sister Anne (a Roman Catholic nun from Trinity College here in D.C.) speak to us on community life and how this could relate to our own diaconate in the future and how it relates to us at the present." (*Peggy*, Advent, 1967)

"My work in the hospital brings me into contact with much 'sick' religion—Lutherans no exception. It has forced me to sort out what it really means to be a Christian; as opposed to what it means to be religious. I do not feel that our commitment should be <u>to</u> a particular 'order' or 'denomination'. It is—as it is for all Christians—a commitment of service to Christ. The failing of the institutional church today is shown through the commitment to <u>one's</u> church or <u>one's</u> professional ties (i.e. clergy) . . . Now, I do not want to abolish the organized church or our sisterhood. Just want us to keep our commitment in proper perspective." (*Caroline*, February 1968)

"Last night without one dissenting vote the proposals for revising the S.S. which the superintendents and I had worked on were passed by the Church Council. A divine call for teachers, LCA curriculum, no openings and closings were some of the main points." (*Karen*, April 1968)

"My weekday school class of fifth and sixth graders had a very successful field trip visiting three area churches in connection with their study on worship. This was excellent for the students themselves, for the parents who went along, and also for inter-church relationships. Janesville now has two deaconesses serving its people. An LCA (or is it ALC?) church has recently acquired an older deaconess. She is quite a jolly woman and just as human as Missouri Synod girls! We will get together to compare notes and it should be a good experience." (*Phyllis*, April 1968)[122]

---

[122] *Intern Letters*, compilations of mimeographed letters, 1967-68.

In spite of a monthly correspondence among the interns, none of the women ever challenged or questioned one another—at least not in these letters—regarding their activities that went beyond official Missouri Synod practice. Furthermore, even though it would be more than a year before the resolution for fellowship with the ALC was passed, there is no indication that Kristo or anyone else from the LDA dissuaded students from participating in pan-Lutheran or ecumenical events.

Deaconess Helen Haase, one of the women in the 1967–68 intern class, graduated in January 1969 and became the first LDA Staff Deaconess in Valparaiso.[123] Haase's primary areas of responsibility were public relations and student recruitment, though she also assisted the Executive Director with securing and supervising internship placements. Reminiscing about her work with the LDA, Haase (now Tesch) recalled:

> I noticed when I was working with Pastor Kristo at Deaconess Hall that there was a different type of mentality developing, both at the university and among the deaconess students. A lot of the girls, myself included, had an idea in our minds of what deaconess ministry was all about. There were things that we were not allowed to do. For example, we didn't preach. But there were many things that needed to be done in the church. And it was that serving, and that helping role, that I envisioned as the role of the deaconess. Well, this was changing. At that time more jobs were opening up to women and there was quite a discussion going on about the role of deaconesses in the church. In many ways it was an exciting time, because by being a part of the diaconate, it was like you were helping to open some doors that may have been shut before.

> When I came onto the staff Pastor Kristo had already been involved in training for many years, but then, as Executive Director, he really began to set a more progressive course right away in a lot of what he was saying and doing. He certainly was influential in the women's movement. Many of us girls were young and naïve, and were able to be molded. Pastor Kristo never forced us into a role of any kind—but he was certainly planting some ideas about deaconess ministry. Part of the idea was that there was some power involved in the diaconate and the whole deaconess structure, and the challenge was in front of you—what are you going to do with the power? Where are you going to take it?

> Some of the momentum of the women's movement may have been due to the influence of Valpo, because it was a more liberal, progressive type

---

123 Deaconesses already served the LDA in the capacity of *Field Secretary* (based in Fort Wayne) and *Deaconess in Residence* (as a live-in Housemother at Deaconess Hall), but Haase was the first deaconess to work with the Executive Director as a *Staff Deaconess*. "Staff Deaconess," *TLD* 46, no. 1 (Spring 1969): 3.

of place—probably quite different from the Concordias. However, there were still those of us with another whole mindset that said, "I don't think we better go there," and the new ideas gave many of us pause for thought, though we still wanted to serve as deaconesses. Girls kept quiet because there was an unspoken rule that those who were in line with Pastor Kristo's thinking would get the good jobs. We knew that jobs were scarce, and the girls thought that if you didn't go along with this new kind of thinking, you were in danger of not getting a job. So ten years later, even though I was out of the loop and raising my children, I wasn't really surprised to hear that a new deaconess conference was being formed in the Missouri Synod. I could see the split coming.[124]

These recollections of Deaconess (nee Haase) Tesch describe an awareness of increasing tension and uncertainty, right in the bosom of the deaconess movement. Of course, the basic issues addressed within the diaconate were the same ones that plagued the Missouri Synod as a whole. The September 1969 *Concordia Theological Monthly* defined the areas of concern:

In this journal we intend to concentrate on the theological issues which trouble the Synod. It seems to us that the Denver convention underlined at least three key issues: the doctrine of the Word, the nature of the mission of the people of God, and the quest for fellowship.[125]

As the LDA and LDC moved into the next decade, some members of the LCMS began to ask pointed questions. Was the LDA taking an official stand on certain issues coming to a head in the Missouri Synod? Were any LDA leaders or Valparaiso University professors (as co-educators with the LDA) compromising deaconess education by teaching the women to embrace questionable doctrine or bad churchly practice? The answers to these questions would eventually have implications for the future partnership between the LDA and the Missouri Synod.

---

[124] In 1969, Helen Haase married Richard Meyers. She became a widow in 1999 and married Armand Tesch in 2000. Helen (nee Haase) Tesch, interview by CDN, transcript, Coon Rapids, Minnesota, March 25, 2006, priv. col. of CDN, Pittsburgh, Pa.

[125] Herbert T. Mayer, "Editorial: The Task Ahead," *Concordia Theological Monthly* 40, no. 8 (September 1969): 527.

Illustrations for Chapter Nine may be viewed at www.deaconesshistory.org.

CHAPTER 10

KEEPING THE CAKE

In June 1968, President Albers presented a "preliminary draft of Pastor Weiser's report, pages 49-80" to the LDA Board of Directors, with instructions that comments or suggestions for revision should be directed to him.[1] By August, the Missouri Synod's BHE and BOD received Weiser's report. The BOD resolved:

> . . . that the Board for Higher Education should study the report and the entire operations of the present deaconess training program and make recommendations to the Board of Directors for further consideration as soon as possible, preferably in the September meeting or certainly in the November meeting.[2]

The BOD wanted to resolve the deaconess education question in a timely manner. Would the professional examination and analysis of the LDA provide some clear-cut direction for the BHE, so that the Board could in turn make definitive recommendations to the BOD?

---

[1] The "Definitive Statements and Statistics" compiled by Albers ended on page 48, so Weiser's document continued on page 49. See Chapter 9 regarding the former document. Looking at the two identical extant copies of Weiser's report, located at Concordia Historical Institute and in the LDA archives, it appears that fifteen pages were added to the draft document, which can be accounted for by the additions of a contents page and a 14-page appendix that described "Church Vocations Standards Established by the ALC and LCA." Dorothy Liebmann, "Lutheran Deaconess Association Plenary Board Meeting June 13, 1968," Box: Board for Professional Education Services Box 5: Deaconess Materials and BHE Materials, found loose at front of box, CHI, St. Louis; Frederick S. Weiser, "Study of the Lutheran Deaconess Association Made for the Board of Directors The Lutheran Church—Missouri Synod and its Board for Higher Education," June 29, 1968, Box: Board for Professional Education Services Box 5: Deaconess Materials and BHE Materials, 111.1.0.09 Supp X, CHI, St. Louis, Mo. The same document may be found in the LDA Archives in Valparaiso, Ind.

[2] "Minutes of the Meeting of the Board of Directors, St. Louis, August 1-2, 1968, item 361, unbound, folder: Minutes 9/67-8/68, Box: BD—Minutes Only (copy 2) 1965-83, archive: 2.3.4.2., CHI, St. Louis, Mo. *BHE Minutes,* August 15-17, 1968, item 9; CHI, St. Louis, Mo.

CONTENT OF THE WEISER PAPER

Pastor Weiser focused his research on the four areas outlined for study, supplementing the facts and statistics already provided by Albers.[3] In addition, Weiser also added three sections of material that he thought would be beneficial for a better understanding of the LDA and its mission within the church: an historical analysis of "how Lutheranism in particular and Protestantism generally came to have deaconesses" (five pages); a summary of the work of the LDA (two pages); and an explanation of the problems facing the LDA (seven pages). These sections contained some astute observations.

Weiser demonstrated how the LDA diaconate was similar or dissimilar to other world diaconates, and how the emphasis of ministry shifted from institutional and hospital service to the parish. In explanation of the recurring identity crisis faced by the diaconate, he explained,

> . . . The diaconate in early Christianity and in 19th century Germany was an attempt to create an office around a theological virtue or disposition, that is, a gift of the Holy Spirit. The New Testament, especially Paul, can use the word <u>Diakonia</u> to describe any service in the church—the "ministry of reconciliation", for instance, is the broadest expression he reaches; at the same time the term is used to designate a certain attitude toward fellowman unique to Christianity, arising in the freedom of the Gospel, <u>a predisposition to serve rather than be served</u>: Mark 10:45. . .

> However, in American life and in American church life, such a broad designation encounters a challenge. The fact is that Americans begin with a function and define a job in terms of it. It is generally easier for us to conceptualize 'parish worker,' 'social worker,' 'matron,' ' nurse,' than it is 'deaconess.' The broad tent of the diaconate is challenged by the other specific occupations available.

> This predicament, common to all American church life, is heightened in the Missouri Synod which has created or is creating specific church occupations called: parish worker, lay worker, teacher, and director of Christian education. Deaconesses have been all of these things and more, of course, but if no one area of ministry is reserved to the diaconate exclusively and there is no overwhelmingly unique feature to it otherwise,

---

[3] See the study outline in Chapter 9. During an initial discussion of the paper, BHE members noted three specific concerns that they felt had not been addressed in the report. "a) It was indicated that no one could produce a job description of the work of the deaconess. b) There was no attempt to enter into the discussion of the adequacy of the curriculum. c) There was no description of what the Lutheran Deaconess Association actually did." *BHE Minutes*, August 15-17, 1968, item 9; CHI, St. Louis, Mo.

as our investigation seems to suggest, the diaconate has a problem of identity.[4]

In his summary of the work of the LDA, Pastor Weiser noted that the association raises funds, carries out publicity and promotional work, recruits and admits students to the educational program, counsels students and deaconesses, and admits candidates to the ministry of deaconess. He also observed that, due to the educational arrangement with LCMS colleges and Valparaiso University, the LDA "no longer actually trains or educates deaconesses in the fullest sense of those words (as its charter empowers it to do), nor has it its own school (as the charter envisions)."[5] Weiser concluded the section by stating:

> It is perhaps unique in American Protestantism to find an independent association fostering a church occupation such as the diaconate. Certainly no other diaconate—among Methodists, Episcopalians, Presbyterians in Canada, and all Lutheran Church bodies—has such a structure, except the small deaconess house (ALC) at Milwaukee, Wisconsin. Generally American Protestants have placed responsibility for training and/or admission to church occupations into the hands of an ecclesiastically selected body.[6]

Weiser identified four types of problems that faced the LDA: finances; jurisdiction (ecclesiastical and educational); retention (trainees and workers); and uniqueness (in terms of training, life arrangements, service, and gender). His conclusions regarding jurisdiction were particularly germane to the root of what really needed to be sorted out between the Missouri Synod and the LDA.

> Although the initial problem which gave rise to this study was the financial one, there is, in fact, an imposing set of problems facing the LDA and these may not all be readily apparent from the statistical material before us. . . .
>
> 2. Jurisdiction. Somewhat related to the first problem [finances] is the jurisdictional anomaly in which the LDA finds itself. This occurs at several levels:
>
> a) Ecclesiastical. Deaconesses are recognized in the LCMS as members of one of the auxiliary ministries in the Church. The initial placement of deaconesses is made by the Synod's placement procedure for all church occupations candidates—implying Synod's jurisdiction over the diaconate

---

[4] Weiser, "Study of the Lutheran Deaconess Association," 12-13.

[5] *Ibid.*, 7.

[6] *Ibid.*, 7.

at that point. They are listed in the Annual. The LDA functions within the Council of Lutheran Ministries. What occurs, however, is an independent association within the Church training persons for a church occupation. The LDA relationship to the graduate deaconess is largely undefined and certainly most deaconesses would not feel under its discipline, for instance!

This may be innocuous depending upon the point-of-view of the inquirer. But it is an anomaly, because in the LCMS, training those who hold church occupations, admitting them to their vocation, and disciplining them in it is a responsibility exercised directly by the Church itself. In a word, the uncertainty of this policy is bound to be a recurring point of confusion and conflict.

b) Educational. Whereas the other holders of church [vocations][7] in LCMS are trained in Synodical colleges, deaconess candidates are trained by the Association. . . . The liberal arts training at Valparaiso doubtless has distinct benefits, and at this point there is no four-year synodical college offering a program for deaconesses. But there is, as one observer put it, an "interesting awkwardness" because the education of deaconesses is partly a synodical matter, partly the concern of Valparaiso University, partly, but ultimately, the concern of the LDA. In this connection, it should be pointed out that there is machinery for keeping this tri-headed system functioning well in the Synodical Relations Committee described on pages 6 and 7 of the Statements and Statistics. This committee, to date, has not functioned officially.[8] Problems that would be its concern have been met informally.

The ultimate answer to the question of who should train and discipline [those who work in] church occupation[s] is not in the province of this writer, but the general position of the LCMS and the existence of a separate organization to train deaconesses seems to be at least juridically at odds—and such things pose problems sooner or later.[9]

As Weiser noted, a relationship existed between the financial and jurisdictional concerns. His report implied that, if the whole matter of jurisdiction—over education, authorization, placement, and discipline—were settled, prevention (and solution) of confusion and conflict would

---

[7] The original word, "ovations," was obviously a typographical error.
[8] The Synodical Relations Committee consisted of six individuals: The President and Executive Director of the LDA; Valparaiso University's President and Vice President of Academic Affairs; the LCMS BHE Chairman and Executive Secretary. "1968 Officers and Committees," TLD 45, no. 1 (Spring, 1968): 2.
[9] Weiser, "Study of the Lutheran Deaconess Association," 8-10.

more easily fall into place. Discussing his study with the author, Pastor Weiser expounded:

I went to St. Louis and spent an afternoon with Executive Secretary Wolbrecht and the head of the Board for Higher Education, and there were many conversations with Rev. Albers in Fort Wayne and Valparaiso, and on the telephone. They were all very helpful and very frank. I felt that there was less than a total embracing of the LDA within the Missouri Synod. But coming from a pretty tightly organized church, I didn't understand the existence of separate vocational programs, like the one for parish workers that I examined at St. John's College. On the other hand, I felt that the LDA wanted to be good members of the Missouri Synod. I didn't think there was any reluctance on their part, but they coveted, they enjoyed their independence. And I sensed that that was going to prove to be fatal to them. That wasn't the way to go. What I was really saying to them, was that it would be better for the diaconate and better for the church if the two were tied up together instead of going their separate ways; it would be better if the diaconate was a part of the Synod, rather than peripheral.[10]

MORE DISCUSSION

On October 23 and November 14, 1968, representatives of the LCMS Board of Directors and BHE, the LDA, and Valparaiso University, came together for "deaconess discussion" meetings.[11] Between these two discussion meetings, the annual LDA meeting also took place at Concordia Lutheran High School in Fort Wayne. At this meeting, open to all voting members of the LDA, Pastor Albers began his last report as President of the LDA by describing his "feeling of renewed hope and spirit for the future of the diaconate."[12] Likewise, after mentioning financial and staffing concerns, Executive Director Kristo finished his report with upbeat words:

---

[10] Frederick S. Weiser, interview by CDN and Nancy Nemoyer, transcript, New Oxford, Pa, March 21, 2004, priv. col. of CDN, Pittsburgh, Pa.; Frederick S. Weiser, notes from telephone interview by CDN, May 5, 2006, priv. col. of CDN, Pittsburgh, Pa.

[11] BHE Minutes, November 15-16, 1968, item 19; CHI, St. Louis, Missouri, 12.

[12] Albers served as Vice-President of the LDA from 1948 to 1955; as LDA President from 1956 to 1969; and continued to serve on the Plenary Board after retiring from the president's post. At the January 1969 meeting of the LDA Plenary Board, Rev. Arthur Ziegler, pastor of Trinity Lutheran Church, Cleveland, Ohio, was elected President of the LDA. Ziegler was also on the Board of Parish Education of the LCMS; Counselor for the Ohio District LWML; Ohio District representative to Project Equality; the Ohio District representative to Lutheran Metropolitan Ministry in Cleveland; and Chairman of the Cleveland Lutheran Pastoral Conference. "The Gavel Changes Hands," TLD 46, no. 1 (Spring 1969): 8; "The

. . . We must keep faith with the founders of the deaconess program. They were pioneers in their day. They spoke to a church unaware of the potential of women for the church's public ministry and insisted that there was need for the woman's point of view in such ministry. The ministry of deaconesses, and of the Association, may need to take new directions, so there must be a continuing openness to the Spirit's leading in today's world. Just as our predecessors responded to the needs of their time, we must be sensitive to the needs of our day. We face the future with confidence.[13]

Kristo did not extrapolate on how he thought the "ministry of deaconesses . . . may need to take new directions," but his statement was a curious one, given that the LDA was in the middle of negotiations with Valparaiso University and two high-level LCMS boards. Before long it became obvious that, rather than facilitating a mutual understanding or conclusion among all parties, the two deaconess discussion meetings resulted in an even greater divergence of opinion regarding the best course of action for both the diaconate and the Missouri Synod.

The LDA Request

The minutes of the November 1968 BHE meeting recorded the receipt of a somewhat surprising request from the LDA, which was to be transmitted to the LCMS Board of Directors through the BHE. The LDA request read:

a) That the Board of Directors continue to recognize the diaconate as an approved ministry of The Lutheran Church—Missouri Synod

b) That the Lutheran Deaconess Association wishes to remain an autonomous and independent organization

c) Because of its current financial difficulties, the Lutheran Deaconess Association requests that the Synod provide financial assistance in the form of a direct subsidy over the next five-year period on the following schedule:

1968–1969	$30,000
1969–1970	$25,000
1970–1971	$15,000
1971–1972	$10,000
1972–1973	None

President's Annual Report to the Lutheran Deaconess Association November 1968," *TLD* 45, no. 4 (Winter 1968): 6.
[13] "The Executive Director's Annual Report," *TLD* 45, no. 4 (Winter 1968): 10.

The above schedule is premised on the assumption that the existing tuition remission arrangement with Valparaiso University remains unchanged. Recognizing that its program would be subject to any review under such a subsidy arrangement, the Lutheran Deaconess Association agrees to cooperate fully with the Synod by submitting required reports and by seeking the counsel and advice of the Synod and Valparaiso University.[14]

The BHE formulated an immediate response to the LDA. The Board minutes continued:

The Board for Higher Education suggests that it is to be recognized that the tuition remission arrangement of the Lutheran Deaconess Association with Valparaiso University could change at any time in future years.

The Board for Higher Education cannot concur with the request of the Lutheran Deaconess Association as made to the synodical Board of Directors. Also, the Board for Higher Education concludes that the program as presently conceived and constituted, cannot continue. It is the opinion of the Board for Higher Education that the synodical colleges and seminaries can supply an educational program which will prepare individuals to do the church work currently done by graduates of the Lutheran Deaconess [Association] educational program.[15]

The LDA may have anticipated the rejection of its request for financial support, but the rest of the response was probably unexpected. How were these words to be understood or applied? The BHE knew that the LDA's declaration to "remain an autonomous and independent organization" meant that the jurisdiction issue was not resolved. Unless the LDA willingly allowed its curriculum administration to be assumed by Synod's BHE, as suggested by the LCMS Board of Directors in October 1967,[16] there was no way that the BHE could just take over the LDA training program. If the BHE was truly convinced that "the program as presently conceived and constituted, cannot continue," what type of action, if any, would the Board take to make that statement a reality? And perhaps the most interesting question of all—what type of an educational program did the BHE have in mind, that could be supplied by "the synodical colleges and seminaries?" Either the BHE assumed that individuals in other church worker vocations should be taught to do the work that deaconesses do (or were needed to

---

[14] *BHE Minutes*, November 15-16, 1968, item 19; CHI, St. Louis, Missouri, 13.
[15] *Ibid.*
[16] See section titled "The Missouri Synod Board of Directors" in Chapter 9.

do) in their various fields of service, or, this was the first inference that the LCMS might create its own synodical deaconess program.

Although Valparaiso University is mentioned in the above request and response, there is no evidence to suggest that the BHE held a bias against VU. On the contrary, the members of this BHE had already concurred with the Study Commission on Lutheran Lay Higher Education, that the Board's report to the LCMS Synodical Convention in 1969 would include the recommendation that the Synod "support Valparaiso University wholeheartedly and cooperate with Valparaiso in her concern for Lutheran lay higher education."[17] Furthermore, close connections existed between the BHE and Valparaiso. BHE Chairman Albert Huegli, who served for seven years as Valpo's Vice President for Academic Affairs, became Acting President of Valparaiso University on the retirement of O. P. Kretzmann in summer 1968. So at this point, Huegli was both Chairman of the BHE *and* Acting President of Valparaiso. Interestingly, Huegli continued as BHE Chairman until the end of his term in October 1969, even though he was elected President of Valparaiso University in December 1968.[18]

A New Deaconess Cross

Sometime during the first half of the 1967–68 academic year, the LDA launched a competition for the creation of a new "Deaconess Symbol." The competition generated nineteen entries by the March 1 deadline—from pastors, laity, deaconesses, deaconess students and Senior College students. In order to see how the designs would "stand up under prolonged viewing," they were displayed in Deaconess Hall during the spring semester and exhibited at the LDC Conference that summer. The LDA Board of Directors reviewed the designs in April, but according to an article in the association's magazine, the Valparaiso artist, Rev. Richard Caemmerer, would make final recommendations on the design.[19]

Miss Lisette Bruss, of Milwaukee, Wisconsin, drew the winning design and the new deaconess symbol appeared on the front cover of the fiftieth anniversary edition of *TLD* in July 1969. The following description of Miss Bruss' design was included in the magazine.

---

[17] *BHE Minutes,* August 15-17, 1968, item 8; CHI, St. Louis, Mo.

[18] *BHE Minutes,* August 15-17, 1968, item 5; CHI, St. Louis, Mo.; *BHE Minutes,* October 3-4, 1969, item 1; CHI, St. Louis, Mo.

[19] Richard Rudolph Caemmerer Jr. (b.1933). "19 Designs Submitted in Competition for New Deaconess Symbol," *TLD* 45, no. 1 (Spring 1968): 10.

The central portion of the symbol is a stylized shield to represent the shield of faith. The four corner images are set into oval versions of the shield. The Chi Rho, symbol for Christ, is set into the middle of the central shield, with the basin of service resting on one arm.

"Faith and Service in Christ," the motto of the deaconess corps, is set into the shield. The ministry of deaconesses, centered in the church but taking place wherever God calls in the contemporary world, is suggested by the figures in the four corners.[20]

The LDA used the new Deaconess Symbol on its letterhead and printed it on all Deaconess Diplomas. Silver-colored "Deaconess Cross" pins were also made from the new design, utilizing the shield as a backdrop for the *chi rho* and basin. From this time onward, like the gold crosses before them, the new Deaconess Symbols were "pinned" on to all deaconesses at their consecration services. In 1971, when "anonymous friends" gave a new chalice to the Deaconess Hall Chapel, the donors had the new Deaconess Symbol engraved on its base.[21]

MARKING 50 YEARS

The LDA Board of Directors resolved to begin an observance of the association's fiftieth anniversary in July 1969, to coincide with the LCMS convention in Denver, where "appropriate memorials" could be presented to convention delegates.[22] Many issues regarding women would be in front of the 1969 convention, including women's suffrage. In one overture, the LDA requested the LCMS to "remember with thanksgiving the ministry of women to the church as exemplified in the deaconess program."[23] In his capacity as editor of *TLD,* Kristo wrote:

---

[20] "The Cover," *TLD* 46, no. 2 (Summer 1969): 18.

[21] See photograph on front cover of *TLD* 49, no. 1 (Spring 1971).

[22] The Board's resolution contains the date "July, 1968," but that 1969 was actually intended is shown from an announcement in the association's Summer 1968 magazine. The 50th anniversary committee consisted of Rev. Herbert Steinbauer of Detroit; Mr. Edwin Benz of Fort Wayne; Dr. Elmer Foelber of St. Louis; Mr. Truman Hey of Fort Wayne; Mr. Hugo Boerger of Fort Wayne; and Deaconess Evelyn Middelstadt of Wichita, Kansas. "Anniversary Plans" and 50th Anniversary Committee Elected," *TLD* 45, no. 2 (Summer 1968): 7, 15; Dorothy Liebmann, "Lutheran Deaconess Association Plenary Board Meeting April 19, 1968," Box: Board for Professional Education Services Box 5: Deaconess Materials and BHE Materials, found loose at front of box, CHI, St. Louis, Missouri, 3.

[23] The words "remember with thanksgiving the ministry of women to the church as exemplified in the deaconess program" were also printed on the front cover of *TLD* 46, no. 1 (Spring 1969). "Overture 11-13," in LCMS, *Convention Workbook (Reports and Overtures),* 1969, 441.

... the church is confronted by a massive revolution in the roles and life styles of women. The church has responded in a variety of ways, and still is uncertain of its position, as indicated by debates regarding women suffrage in recent conventions.

Through its overture, the Lutheran Deaconess Association is doing more than asking the church to commemorate the services of deaconesses. It is calling the church to engage in an open and vigorous study and discussion regarding the role of women in the church. In doing so, the Association considers itself as ministering to the church and offers its resources to the ongoing discussion.[24]

Kristo was saying that the LDA had a mission to be a catalyst in the women's movement within the Missouri Synod. But before the overture came to convention, the floor committee altered the wording of the resolution to remove the general reference to "the ministry of women." Kristo presented a report to the convention and introduced eight deaconesses to the delegates.[25] The convention responded by adopting Resolution 11-01:

Whereas, The Lutheran Deaconess Association this year observes its 50th anniversary of service to the church; and

Whereas, The church has received many blessings from the association and the services of the more than 300 deaconesses during these 50 years; therefore be it

Resolved, That this convention encourage all congregations of the Synod to remember with thanks to God the service to the church by the association and its deaconesses by observing the association's golden anniversary on Sept. 21, 1969, or on another Sunday of their own choosing; and be it further

Resolved, That this convention encourage all the congregations of the Synod to consider whether their programs might be strengthened by the inclusion of a deaconess in their ministry; and be it finally

Resolved, That this convention receive with thanks the report of the Lutheran Deaconess Association.[26]

---

[24] "Deaconess Association Asks Synod to Consider Ministry of Women," *TLD* 46, no. 1 (Spring 1969): 3.

[25] "Special Ministries and Sundry Matters," in LCMS, *Proceedings,* 1969, 21.

[26] "11. Special Ministries and Sundry Matters: To Remember Lutheran Deaconess Association Resolution 11-01," in LCMS, *Proceedings,* 1969, 153.

THE MINISTRY OF WOMEN

After Resolution 11-01 passed at the 1969 LCMS convention in Denver, the topic of the role of women in the church continued to surface in LDA publications. Concerning the first edition of *TLD* that came out after the Denver convention, editor Kristo explained:

> The theme of this issue is the ministry of women. The Denver Convention of the Missouri Synod referred to the Commission on Mission and Ministry in the Church the task of making a study of the role of women in church and society. Since we were the ones who submitted the memorial to which this resolution was a response, we feel a special concern for the discussion. You will find several statements in the following pages by and about women.

> First, Dr. Edward Schroeder, Chairman of the Department of Theology, Valparaiso University, and member of the LDA Board, makes a theological statement regarding the professional ministry of women in the church. . . .[27]

Hence, the purpose of *TLD* appears to have changed—from disseminating news, recruiting students and placement sites, soliciting speaking engagements and funds, and providing encouragement to students and deaconesses in their fields of service—to an organ whose primary purpose was to provide a forum for the discussion of cutting-edge issues in the church. Again, the issues centered on "the doctrine of the Word, the nature of the mission of the people of God, and the quest for fellowship."[28] The "theological statement" by Schroeder, which Kristo mentioned in his editor's column above, is one case in point. Schroeder wrote,

> In considering the public professional ministry of women in the church, it seems to me that the issue is a three-fold one. First, how to use the Scriptures—and especially St. Paul's statements about women in the public work of the church—in understanding the place of women in the

---

[27] Articles in this edition included "The Public Professional Ministry of Women in the Church of Jesus Christ" by Edward Schroeder, Chairman of the Department of Theology and member of the LDA Board; "A Woman on 28th Street," by Norma Everist; "Woman Suffrage in the Church: A Reaction" by Ruth Newquist; and "Women in the Church" by LDA Executive Director Arne Kristo. The front cover of the magazine had in large letters, "Woman in the larger context of life;" and in smaller letters in an artistic design, "woman. warmth. woman. witness. woman. willing. woman. watchful. woman. worship. woman. welcome. woman. world. woman. work. woman. wife. woman. wh." [*sic*] The Editor (Arne Kristo), "Fiftieth Anniversary—II," *TLD* 46, no. 3 (Fall 1969): 2.

[28] See section titled "On the Cutting Edge" in Chapter 9. Herbert T. Mayer, "Editorial: The Task Ahead," *Concordia Theological Monthly* 40, no. 8 (September 1969): 527.

church. Second, what are the "orders of creation" which ostensibly underlie Paul's reasoning behind his statements? And third, what is the church in terms of its one central ministry and the variety of ministries?[29]

As Schroeder went on to answer the three questions, the text of his article represented what most individuals in the Missouri Synod would have considered to be a liberal viewpoint on the nature and interpretation of Holy Scripture.[30] Interestingly, this pattern of expressing opinions that challenged traditional Missouri Synod belief and practice became increasingly consistent in *TLD*. In the Editor's column for Spring 1970, Kristo wrote:

> . . . It is self-evident to say that the church is ambivalent about the role of women. After all, the current feminist movement is saying a great deal on the subject, even within the church. But the point is that we in the deaconess program have a peculiar interest in, and hopefully, a peculiar sensitivity to this question.

> We see the annual procession of students equipping themselves for service. We observe the earnestness with which they apply themselves to their tasks. We share with them in the agony of developing understanding of themselves as women and as functionaries. . . .

> We want to predict, as we conclude our fiftieth anniversary emphasis, that within the next fifty years we will need to work at bringing together into a

---

[29] Edward H. Schroeder, "The Public Professional Ministry of Women in the Church of Jesus Christ," *TLD* 46, no. 3 (Fall 1969): 3.

[30] Sample passages from Schroeder's article in *TLD*: "Hopefully it is clear now that we cannot find a satisfactory answer by looking to Scripture as a legislative handbook which will give a clear-cut answer as to where and when and how women are to serve specifically in the church professions. Scripture does not do this. Nor do we find an answer by recognizing an order of creation which arranges people in boxes that cannot be rearranged, . . . The issue then is: to which of the varieties of ministries may women be ordained? The Gospel itself makes no prohibition. Instead it urges churchmen to use the gifts (the people) that God has given to be His church. But how can this "urging" be put into practice? When churchmen ask how the Gospel is to be practiced in any given age, they must take into consideration the specific shape of that age or as stated in Luther's perspective, the unique shape of God's ordering activity at this time in its psychological, sociological, political, economic and other dimensions. This is the important issue when considering the public professional ministry of women in the church of Jesus Christ. Therefore, practices may differ in different segments of the church. But the questions of practice are resolved for the church by listening to the Gospel (not the legislation) of the New Testament and doing so in the light of the contemporary church's own God-given responsibilities and effectiveness." Schroeder, "The Public Professional Ministry of Women in the Church of Jesus Christ," 4.

closer harmony our image of women's role and the actuality to which that image refers. And this is a task for all of us, not just for the women."[31]

Looking at Kristo's text, the questions abound: To what was the Executive Director referring exactly, when he highlighted the deaconess students' "agony of developing understanding of themselves as women and as functionaries?" And what specific image or vision did Kristo and other LDA leaders hold with regard to the role of women—the vision that still needed to be actualized? Did Kristo intend to predict that "we will need to *work* at . . . harmony," or did he really mean to predict that in the next 50 years "our image of women's role" would be achieved?

The answers to many of these types of questions were vague, or subtle at best. But there were unmistakable hints in LDA practice. It cannot be a coincidence, for example, that the leading article for the summer 1970 issue of *TLD*, located on the page opposite to Kristo's above remarks, was a piece titled "From the Chapel: Matthew 16:21-28." This article consisted of the "Homily given" by a deaconess student in the Valparaiso University Chapel, on February 16, 1970. The homily started with a full reading of the designated words from the Gospel of Matthew, and followed what would be recognized as a normal sermon pattern, starting with the words, "In the text for this first Monday in Lent, we read about Jesus. . ."[32]

Deaconess students had certainly been giving homilies—a fancy name for small sermons—in the Deaconess Hall chapel for quite some time, within the context of dormitory worship led by and for women alone (unless the odd boyfriend happened to join in on occasion). To preach a homily—which was in fact, to preach a sermon—in the large university Chapel of the Resurrection, during one of the weekday worship services attended by a co-ed congregation, constituted a completely new activity that had opened up to deaconess students sometime during the 1969-70 school year.[33] There is no evidence to suggest that any LDA leader tried to dissuade deaconess students from preaching in the University Chapel. On the contrary, the fact that "From the Chapel" appeared in *TLD* implies that the LDA leadership condoned the practice, while knowing that Missouri Synod doctrine reserved preaching only for the pastoral office.[34]

---

[31] The Editor (Arne Kristo), "Fiftieth Anniversary—IV," *TLD* 47, no. 1 (Spring 1970): 2.

[32] "From the Chapel: Matthew 16:21-28," *TLD* 47, no. 1 (Spring 1970): 3-4.

[33] Helen (nee Haase) Meyers Tesch, interview by CDN, transcript, Coon Rapids, Minnesota, March 25, 2006, priv. col. of CDN, Pittsburgh, Pa.

[34] Pastor Kristo confirmed for the author that he would have been in favor of a woman giving a Homily in the university Chapel. Arne P. Kristo, interview by CDN, transcript, Norfolk, Virginia, November 7, 2005, priv. col. of CDN, Pittsburgh, Pa., 24.

Again, it should be remembered that, in addition to students from the LCMS, Valparaiso University educated young adults from the American Lutheran Church and the Lutheran Church in America (as well as non-Lutheran church bodies). Chapel services included men and women from the whole array of denominations; open Communion was practiced; and to hear a sermon given by a woman may have seemed quite natural in the context of a progressive university environment, in an age that demanded equal rights for women. For those from the LCA, Valpo's liberal worship practice appeared to be in tune with their own church body, which would authorize the ordination of women in 1970.[35]

SHORTAGE OF PLACEMENT SITES

When it came time to place deaconess candidates in the spring of 1970, the LDA had a big problem. The number of requests received for deaconesses equaled "only about one-half of the people available."[36] Kristo mused about the "discernable causes" of the predicament in *TLD*, and then went on to make several points he referred to as "affirmation."

> . . . Of course, we know that God caused it to happen—but what were the discernable causes? Was it a financial problem? That is the most consistently repeated theory we have heard expressed. . . . Is it one aspect of the Lutheran Church's inability to see the potential role of women? At least one deaconess thinks so. She wrote and said, "Let's face it; the church isn't ready for us." Is it because pastors do not understand what deaconesses can do? Alas, we have reason to believe that this is too often true.

---

[35] Regarding the impact of this decision on the LCA diaconate, Frederick Weiser wrote: "Ordination of women, authorized by the Lutheran Church in America in 1970, also worked an effect on the diaconate. Some women had become deaconesses because this was the only form of ministry open to them. Consequently, a number have resigned over the years and been ordained. Some would have liked to continue in the fellowship of the sisterhood, but the ministry of the Word and the ministry of serving love are themselves disparate gifts. Wisely, the Lutheran church [LCA] insisted that they not be mixed. Former deaconesses now in the clergy have often maintained close ties to the community; the community of deaconesses has been among the most enthusiastic supporters of ordaining women. At the same time deaconesses have welcomed the clear distinction of what their task is." Frederick S. Weiser, *To Serve the Lord and His People: Celebrating the Heritage of a Century of Lutheran Deaconesses in America 1884-1984*, with an introduction by Sister Frieda Gatzke, The Deaconess Community of the Lutheran Church in America, Gladwyne, 1984, 27.
[36] The Editor (Arne Kristo), "Workers Idle in the Market Place," *TLD* 47, no. 2 (Summer 1970): 3.

... But enough of questions. On to affirmation. We affirm, first of all, that deaconess students are a great gift of God to the church and that the church will make a mistake if it does not utilize their potential. . . . We affirm, secondly, that deaconesses are equipped to share in important ministries. . . . Above all, God's people need to have their lives centered in their Baptism and in the Celebration of the Eucharist—*and to relate people to the Word and Sacraments is the central thrust of deaconess ministry.*

... But, the deaconess, we have felt, is by vocation someone committed to the public ministry of the church. If positions do not come from within the structures, can one blame the deaconess for thinking that perhaps she must go elsewhere? Is that what even God is saying? There are those who feel this way. We do not share that view. But who knows?

We affirm, finally, that the question is not whether we in the Association should continue our ministry (and we do not say this boastfully, but in faith), but under what circumstances, with what techniques, and to what goals. The Plenary Board of the Association has been studying our educational program and made important changes at its last meeting. There is no guarantee that even more radical changes might not be made. We ask you, our brethren in the church, again—as we have in the past— to help us determine our course. ...[37]

Certainly all good Lutherans would (or should) agree with the editor's assertion, "God's people need to have their lives centered in their Baptism and in the Celebration of the Eucharist." And it sounds very Lutheran to contend that, "to relate people to the Word and Sacraments is the central thrust of deaconess ministry." However, interpreting the role of a deaconess in this manner was really a new development. The ministry of Word and Sacraments—"relating" people to the means of Grace—had always been cited as the chief responsibility of the pastoral office, while the traditional central thrust of the diaconate was to carry out a *ministry of mercy* complementary to the ministry of Word and Sacraments. So wherever a deaconess served, the combined physical and spiritual ministrations of mercy she performed were a manifestation of God's love in action *and* an evangelistic tool to point individuals toward the formal administration of the means of Grace.[38]

Kristo's plea to "our brethren in the church" was curious for two reasons. First, both the BHE and BOD of the Missouri Synod had spent a good deal of time trying to help the LDA "determine our course," but the

---

[37] Italics in second paragraph added by author for emphasis. "Workers Idle in the Market Place," 3-4.
[38] See also Chapter 3.

advice of both bodies had been, in effect, rejected by the association.[39] Second, *TLD* had "a circulation of over 40,000 copies per issue mailed both to individuals and in bulk to groups within the Church,"[40] however; the editor addressed his entreaty only to "the brethren," which implies that he was speaking pointedly to the clergy among the readership. All members of the LDA who paid the prescribed annual membership dues were voting members, so what was it that Kristo desired from the clergy that could not be collectively provided by all LDA members? The logical answer is, that the phrase "to help us determine our course," meant *to help us achieve that which we have already determined to do*, or, in other words, *help us find placements for the deaconess candidates so that the LDA can continue its ministry.*

FINANCIAL INCENTIVES

In its determination to find placements for all fourteen of the women that completed their training, the LDA Board finally resolved to offer some financial incentives to prospective deaconess employers, even though the association struggled with increasing monetary problems. The following announcement appeared in *TLD*, on the page following Kristo's editorial.

> In response to the shortage of calls for deaconesses this year, the Plenary Board at its May meeting committed the Association to provide up to $10,000.00 for the first twelve months to assist in setting up deaconess ministries. In addition, $2,000.00 was set aside for special situations. This $10,000.00 is intended to be used in four places, providing a salary subsidy of $2,500.00 to each. Pastors wishing to discuss the possibilities of this in their circumstances should immediately phone the Association at: (219) 462 4197.[41]

In fall 1970, Pastor Albers joyfully announced that the "emergency" was over. Interestingly, the turnaround happened in "just a few weeks" and the LDA received more than enough requests for deaconesses.[42]

---

[39] See above in Chapter 10 and also Chapter 9, starting with section titled "The Missouri Synod Board of Directors."

[40] "Statement," *TLD* 47, no. 1 (Spring 1970): 2.

[41] This phone number was for the office at Deaconess Hall. "Plenary Board Takes Action on Behalf of Graduates," *TLD* 47, no. 2 (Summer 1970): 5.

[42] While Executive Director Kristo trained in Clinical Pastoral Education during the summer of 1970, Albers, though no longer President of the LDA, took on many of Kristo's duties and served as editor for the fall 1970 edition of *TLD*. E. H. Albers, "No Longer Idle," *TLD* 48, no. 3 (Fall 1970): 2.

OPEN CRITICISM OF THE MISSOURI SYNOD

Eighteen months after the LCMS Convention in Denver, LDA leaders engaged in intensive discussions about issues related to women in the church. The winter 1970 edition of *TLD* featured a four-page article titled "Women . . . God's Creation: Some Thoughts on the 1969 Denver Convention Statement, 'Woman Suffrage in the Church.'" A few editorial notes preceded the article:

> In recent months the Plenary Board of the Association has devoted time to discussion of various aspects of the larger problem of women in the church. At a recent meeting, one of our Board Members, Dr. Lucille Wassman,[43] led the discussion. The Board felt her remarks should be shared with the readers of our magazine. . . .[44]

Wassman's "Thoughts" were not complimentary to the LCMS. She accused members of the Synod's Commission on Theology and Church Relations (CTCR) of using clever, slippery, and emotive language in their report to the Denver Convention; claimed that "Missouri Synod women have never been more than second-class citizens;" and devoted one and a half pages to examples of these alleged abuses of both language and women.[45]

The last two and a half pages of Wassman's article consisted of a diatribe in support of her declaration that "Part III of the Denver Statement titled *Exegetical Evaluation* is a big disappointment because of its limited exegesis."[46] Wassman quoted and paraphrased Russell Prohl (author of *Women in the Church*), W. Arndt, and Luther; and then laid out six "Theological Principles Determining the Role of Christian Women in Church and Society," which had been presented by Julius Bodensiek at a Lutheran Social Ethics Seminar hosted by Valparaiso University in December 1955.[47] The CTCR's rejection of advice or guidance from these men, asserted Wassman, "prevents the laity and clergy of the Missouri

---

[43] Lucille Emily Wassman (1920-2007) became a member of the LDA Board of Directors in 1969. At that time she was Assistant Professor in Education at the University of Wisconsin Milwaukee School of Education, where she was head of the Department of Curriculum and Instruction, and chair of the Early Childhood Education Area. "Introducing Dr. Lucille Wassman," *TLD* 48, no. 3 (Fall 1970): 4.

[44] Arne Kristo, Editor's note on Wassman, "Women . . . God's Creation: Some Thoughts on the 1969 Denver Convention Statement, 'Woman Suffrage in the Church,'" *TLD* 48, no. 4 (Winter 1970): 3.

[45] Lucille Wassman, "Women . . . God's Creation: Some Thoughts on the 1969 Denver Convention Statement, 'Woman Suffrage in the Church,'" *TLD* 48, no. 4 (Winter 1970): 3-4.

[46] Wassman, "Women . . . God's Creation," 4.

[47] *Ibid.*, 4-6.

Synod from getting a broader perspective of Christ's ministry and of the almost unfathomable responsibility each individual has who calls himself a member of God's kingdom." The article finished with strong words: "NOW is the time for males to stop their bickering about, and their distorting of, the status and role of women in the church!"[48]

It is interesting that Wassman laid the blame solely at the feet of males, when there were plenty of women in the Missouri Synod—including many deaconesses—who held to the Synod's traditional understanding of the role of women in the church. Even more intriguing is the fact that the LDA Board revered Wassman's remarks and requested them to be published, even though she had absolutely no formal training in Theology.

Serious Financial Difficulty

In April 1971, Executive Director Kristo wrote to "approximately three thousand individuals plus congregations and groups," to inform them of how the LDA hoped to be kept from the financial ruin that threatened the organization.

> Throughout the past decade, there has never been a year in which the Deaconess Association has met its annual budget needs. Ordinarily one simply reduces expenditures and hopefully secures additional income through extra efforts, and the problem is solved or tolerated. This is what has happened to us for the last few years.

> More recently, however, the pressure has become greater. During this current fiscal year, for example, we are receiving only about one-half of our budget needs. Even allowing for reduced expenditures, we have already spent $23,000 more than we have received during the first six months of the current fiscal year. . . .

> The Executive Committee of the Association is recommending to the Plenary Board at its meeting on April 23, 1971, that the Association sell its real estate (Deaconess Hall and grounds). The purchaser would be Valparaiso University. The reason for disposing of the property is that the Association would thereby be enabled to continue its ministry with a smaller annual budget. . . .

> First it is the determination of the Board that the cash received from any transaction be set aside as an Endowment Fund. The income from the Endowment would serve as basic annual income for the continued ministry of the Association. The income, it must be emphasized, would

---

[48] Wassman, "Women . . . God's Creation," 6.

not be enough to carry the entire program. In other words—to make the point very clear—your support will continue to be necessary!

Secondly, the transaction, if consummated, will include provision for scholarship assistance for deaconess students. Thirdly, President Huegli has stated that if it is our wish, and the wish of the students, the University will provide common living facilities for deaconess students in some existing University dormitory. Finally, the agreement with the University will also include space for offices for the Association and a place for student and Board meetings.

It is clear, therefore that the Plenary Board of the Association, if it goes ahead with the proposed step, will do so on the grounds that this is the way to <u>continue</u> the ministry of the Association. ... we feel it important for you, as supporters of the Association, to know that our action is not a <u>disregard</u> <u>for</u>, and a <u>dissipation</u> <u>of</u>, past offerings made by many in the church, but quite the opposite: a means for keeping those gifts at work for the cause of Christ! We feel certain that it would be remiss of us to allow the property to lead us into possible disaster. We are confident that our brothers and sisters in the church will recognize that the Board has a responsibility to act on the basis of today's circumstances, just as the original decision to build Deaconess Hall was legitimate for the situation at that time. . . .[49]

The above information—that the beloved Deaconess Hall might need to be sacrificed in order to keep the LDA in business—would have been very disappointing news to the association's supporters. After all, the building was only thirteen years old, and it had taken eleven years of planning and intense fundraising to see the project come to fruition. Not only had monies been received from the Ebenezer Offering and from the LWML at local, district, and national levels, but nearly a quarter of a million dollars had been secured through the Missouri Synod's "Building for Christ" Collection, and countless people and societies had subsequently given more funds for everything from furniture to mortgage payments.[50]

A CHANGE OF LEADERSHIP

Kristo's letter to LDA supporters did not finish where the above quotation ends. The next paragraph of the letter continued:

---

[49] Arne Kristo, "Newsletter To: Supporters of the Lutheran Deaconess Association," April, 1971, File titled Ft. Wayne, Indiana: Lutheran Deaconess Auxiliary General Correspondence, Indiana LCMS District Archives, Fort Wayne, Indiana, 1-2.
[50] See Chapter 6.

There is another item of business for this newsletter. After a decade of service with the deaconess program, I will be making a change. I have accepted another appointment to a year of internship in the Department of Pastoral Care at Lutheran General Hospital, Park Ridge, Illinois. Our Staff Deaconess, Miss Jacqueline Haug, will also leave after fulfilling two years with the Association.[51]

The Executive Committee of the Association has engaged in discussions concerning filling the office of Executive Director. The Executive Committee is recommending that the next Executive Director be a woman. More specifically, they are submitting two names to the Plenary Board: Miss Evelyn Middelstadt, M.S.W.,[52] and Miss Lucille Wassman, Ph.D. Deaconess Middelstadt is Supervisor of Social Work for Lutheran Social Service in Wichita, Kansas. Dr. Wassman is Assistant Professor in Education at the University of Wisconsin, Milwaukee. . . .[53]

When the next issue of *TLD* came out in summer 1971, it contained a brief notice of Kristo's leaving and an equally short article revealing the new Executive Director as Dr. Lucille Wassman.[54] Concerning the choice of Wassman, the article explained:

In choosing her, the LDA has made a deliberate break with a practice going back over the more than fifty years of its existence: choosing a male and a pastor as the executive officer. The Board felt that this decision was consistent with the concern of the deaconess program for the ministry of women. . . . She will assume her new responsibilities on July 1 (1971).[55]

A new era was underway for the LDA! The director of the association's deaconess program would now be female instead of male and trained in Education rather than in Theology. The LDA leadership felt that such changes boded well for the association, and certainly for the ministry of women in the church.

The LDA had several problems that needed to be addressed. The same issue of *TLD* that announced Wassman's appointment also spoke about

---

[51] Haug graduated from the Valparaiso deaconess training program in 1961; served St. Paul Lutheran Church, Royal Oak, Michigan, from 1961-63; served as Dean of Women at Concordia Lutheran College Ann Arbor, Michigan, from 1963-67; and took over as LDA Staff Deaconess in 1969 when Haase left the post to be married. "Deaconess Jacqueline Haug Joins LDA Staff," *TLD* 46, no. 2 (Summer 1969): 6.

[52] Middelstadt was a member of the LDA Board of Directors. She graduated from the Valparaiso training program in 1952.

[53] Kristo, "Newsletter To: Supporters of the Lutheran Deaconess Association," 2-3.

[54] "Pastor Kristo Leaves Deaconess Program," and "Cover Photo: Our New Executive Director," *TLD* 49, no. 2 (Summer 1971): 2, 5.

[55] "Cover Photo: Our New Executive Director," *TLD* 49, no. 2 (Summer 1971): 2.

"inadequate financial support, insufficient requests for graduates, and declining freshmen enrollments" that had "forced the Board to self-analysis" during the previous six months.[56] The Board of Directors also informed readers that it "was *not* convinced that it should dispose of Deaconess Hall at this time," and that Wassman and the LDA Executive Committee were to continue to analyze the situation and bring recommendations to the September Board meeting.[57]

Dr. Wassman was ready for the challenge, though she knew it would be a difficult job. Speaking to the author about her thoughts before and at the time of her appointment as Executive Director, Wassman said,

> When I was on the board for the deaconess association, I began to realize that the deaconess program was in a lot of trouble. There were considerable problems, and as I worked on the board I became more acquainted with the deaconess students and the problems as they saw them. There was the problem of not being able to attract young women to come into the deaconess program. I thought that I could make a contribution because—how shall I put this—my experience was such that I thought I could contribute to a change in the program itself, and that I would be able to just simply work well with the students because of the educational background that I had.
>
> The LDA was greatly in debt. The number of students was very low. The number of places available in the LCMS for deaconesses was very low. The students talked to me because I was listening to what they were saying. They fussed about the content of the program itself, and I saw my role at that time, while I was on the board, as a listener. When Arne Kristo resigned, the Board members turned to me. I wasn't sure that this position was for me. My background was in teacher education, but I felt strongly that if someone didn't take hold of the LDA they would go under. They were in debt up to $40,000. If you go back to those days, that was a lot of money.
>
> I was sure I would have to spend a considerable amount of time going to the LCMS colleges to see what women I could draw to our program. And

---

[56] "Plenary Board Considers Issues," *TLD* 49, no. 2 (Summer 1971): 3.
[57] Fifteen years later, the LDA sold Deaconess Hall to VU, receiving over half of the purchase price at the time of closing (May 30, 1986) and the balance over five years (with interest). The LDA relocated its base of operation in the former home of the VU Dean of Chapel. The LDA moved several items from Deaconess Hall to its new *Center for Diaconal Ministry*, including the Deaconess Hall cornerstone, "Phoebe," and the chapel's carved doors, altar boards, and candles. Letter from Diane Greve, Director of Diaconal Services to "sisters," January 13, 1986, priv. col. Luella Mickley, Chicago, Ill.; Louise Williams, in letter to LDA members from the Executive Director, *Lutheran Deaconess Association*, Spring, 1986, mimeographed newsletter; "Plenary Board Considers Issues," 3.

I did. I traveled widely—to New York, Michigan, Minnesota, Portland, Austin, and probably others that I am not mentioning. I had contacts everywhere, and none of them were very willing to let go of their students. Many times I also ran into the factions of conservatism and moderatism, and what some of them saw was that their students were going to go to a liberal university. But I didn't really get tangled in any of that stuff.

I was controversial, there's no doubt about that. There were many difficult and unpleasant decisions. I was going to have to get a different treasurer on the Board and also a younger person to deal with the money matters—a person who was well versed in investments. The LDA had assets, but they were not invested wisely. I've read articles about people who have had to step into a position where they had to deal with big challenges, and when they straighten it out, they either succeed or fail, and then they move on. I didn't go into that position because I was going to do it for the rest of my life. I was concerned with indebtedness, lack of students, and lack of places to do deaconess ministry. I felt that if I could get a handle on all of that, then I wanted to see a very good deaconess get into that job.[58]

One of the first difficult decisions that Wassman made in her conscientious effort to cut expenditure was to cease publication of *TLD*. Hence, the summer 1971 magazine that carried the news of her succession as Executive Director was the last issue to be printed.[59]

Other adjustments also needed to be made. Once the academic year started, Wassman periodically called all of the deaconess students who lived in Deaconess Hall together to give them little pep talks. The LDA could no longer afford a housekeeper, she explained, and the third floor of the building would need to be rented out to as many traveling choir groups, and others, as possible. The students would need to do the housekeeping chores and make the beds for the guests that rented the third floor. One deaconess who lived in the dorm at that time remembers that there was a great spirit of camaraderie among the students as they worked together for the common cause of the survival of the program.[60]

---

[58] Lucille E. Wassman, notes from telephone interview by CDN, July 20, 2005, and July 27, 2005, priv. col. of CDN, Pittsburgh, Pa.
[59] Wassman, notes from telephone interview by CDN; Letter from Dr. Lucille Wassman to "Our Contributors and Supporters of Deaconess Ministry," Spring 1972, priv. col. of Nancy (nee Brandt) Lingenfelter, Morrisdale, Pa.
[60] Joyce A. Ostermann, notes from telephone interview by CDN, June 10, 2006, priv. col. of CDN, Pittsburgh, Pa.

When Wassman addressed the LDC for the first time as Executive Director, she used the words "Woman-Courage-Onward" as the theme for her remarks. She told the deaconesses, "to be a woman in church, in American society, in the world, and in the Missouri Synod requires a great deal of mature thinking, wisdom, knowledge, faith and love."[61] After presenting a "full and detailed explanation of issues which confront gifted women," Wassman recommended books and articles "about women" for further reading.[62]

TWO OVERTURES

Two and a half years had elapsed since the Missouri Synod BHE denied the LDA's request for financial support and stated that the deaconess training program "as presently conceived and constituted, cannot continue." The LDA was still an autonomous and independent organization, with no intention of offering (or allowing) its curriculum administration to be taken over by the BHE. On the other hand, the BHE took no measures to encourage the deaconess students on LCMS campuses to enter other church work vocations; nor did the BHE take any steps toward creating a Synodical deaconess program. In a nutshell, the LDA and the LCMS seemed to be at an impasse regarding any change in the formal relationship between the two entities. Furthermore, it appears that the BHE neglected to communicate its decision (that the deaconess training program "cannot continue") to the LCMS Council of Presidents, since that body continued to place deaconess candidates just as it had since 1960.[63]

---

[61] Wassman actually addressed the LDC on the morning of Saturday, June 26, 1971, and was installed into her office in the Gloria Christi Chapel (part of the Valparaiso University Chapel) in the afternoon of Sunday, June 27, 1971. Carol Sokofski, "Minutes of the Lutheran Deaconess Conference June 25-28, 1971, Deaconess Hall, Valparaiso, Indiana," priv. col. of Betty Mulholland, Munster, Indiana, 2,4.

[62] Two of the books Wassman recommended were "Developing Women's Potentials" by Lewis (first name or initial unknown) and "The Natural Superiority of Women" by Ashley Montague. Carol Sokofski, "Minutes of the Lutheran Deaconess Conference June 25-28, 1971," 2.

[63] See Chapter 6 to understand why the Council of Presidents made assignments to deaconess candidates. "LC-MS Placements 7% Ahead of Last Year," News: The Lutheran Church—Missouri Synod, Immediate Release, 5/9/69-014, news release on letterhead from LCMS Department of Public Relations, Rev. Kenneth M. Lindsay, St. Louis, Missouri, Director, Box: Assignment of Calls, 1969, archive location: 111.1C.09, CHI, St. Louis, Mo. Minutes of spring meetings of the Council of Presidents also verify this continued action. The minutes may be found in: Box: Council of Presidents Minutes 1951- April 1977 Box #9 and Box: Council of Presidents Minutes Box #7 May 1977—April 1981, archive location 111.1C.17, CHI, St. Louis, Mo.

Within this context, as the time for the 1971 LCMS Convention approached, LDA leaders decided to press the LCMS once again for greater recognition and more rights for deaconesses within the Synod. The last issue of *TLD* reported:

Women and Ministry

We were tempted to entitle this item, "Women's Ministry", as a kind of parallel to "women's lib." But we restrained ourselves. For one thing, we didn't want to antagonize those who are uptight about women's lib.[64]

All of this is really tangential to the subject. But there is a connection. The connection is that whether we like it or not, the question of the role and status of women in the church is very much on the minds of people in the church, as the question of the role and status of women in society is on the minds of people in the nation and world.

For practical purposes, and with reference to the Milwaukee Convention of the Lutheran Church—Missouri Synod, the LDA has confined itself to questions relating to the public, professional ministry of deaconesses. We felt that for now, and in terms of our direct calling, we should say something about deaconesses.

The result was that we submitted two overtures which we hope will reach the delegates at Milwaukee through a floor committee. (We apparently no longer have the right to submit overtures directly.) Both of those overtures speak to the status of the deaconess in the church. We felt that by challenging the Synod to consider them, important issues would be faced and the role of deaconess/woman in the church would be furthered.[65]

It is interesting to note how the LDA chose to confine itself "to questions relating to the public, professional ministry of deaconesses." The LCMS had far more female teachers than deaconesses, but the association

---

[64] "Women's Lib" was a generic term that referred to the Women's Liberation Movement, also called feminism. This movement gained momentum in the 1960s with the aid of several influential books, most notably *The Feminine Mystique* by Betty Friedan, co-founder and first president of the National Organization of Women. The most prominent feminist spokesperson for Women's Lib was Gloria Steinem, the founder and first editor of *Ms* magazine. Women's Lib was openly discussed and written about on the VU campus, e.g., Don A. Affeldt, "Comment on Current Issues: Amen to Women's Liberation," In Luce Tua, *The Cresset* 35, no. 3 (January 1972): 3-5. For further reading related to the Women's Liberation Movement see books such as Bee Jepsen, *Women Beyond Equal Rights*, Waco, Word Books, 1984; Beth Impson, *Called to Womanhood*, Wheaton, Crossway Books, 2001.
[65] "Women and Ministry," *TLD* 49, no. 2 (Summer 1971): 8,11.

obviously judged, and probably rightly so, that it would be best to stick with the concern of deaconesses, and hope that further headway could be made for women in the church at a future convention.[66]

The two overtures referred to in the above article were titled "To Designate Deaconesses As Ministers of Religion" and "To Include Deaconesses in the Synodical Constitution and By-Laws." The final paragraph of the latter overture resolved that "The LDA shall be represented at Synodical Conventions by one deaconess for each twenty deaconesses in active service within the LCMS as advisory delegates to the Synodical Convention. Fractional groupings shall be disregarded, except that there shall be at least one advisory deaconess delegate."[67] This overture shows that the LDA indeed hoped to raise both the profile of deaconesses *and* the voice of women at LCMS Synodical conventions, since advisory delegates could speak on the convention floor even though they could not vote.

THE 1971 MILWAUKEE CONVENTION

When Executive Director Kristo stood before the Missouri Synod convention delegates on behalf of the LDA for the very last time, his report mentioned the association's financial difficulties, the need for more places for graduates, and the consistent decrease in freshman enrollment during the previous four years. As could be expected, he plugged the two overtures submitted by the LDA, and then, before naming the members of the Board of Directors and other "more institutional concerns," spent a considerable amount of time explaining three areas of "feelings," one of which touched again on the topic of women.[68]

Perhaps the Synod would be interested in a statement of needs felt within the deaconess program. Here, then, are some of our feelings:

1. We feel that there should be, on the part of the Synod, the conscious cultivation of an office and sense of the diaconate. . . .

2. The voice of women needs to be heard more clearly in the Synod. Steps were taken in that direction at Denver with the granting of woman

[66] Indeed, at the following convention held in New Orleans in 1973, LCMS delegates resolved "that all teachers, male *or female,* who have met all requirements for inclusion in the official roster of the Synod be considered eligible for membership under the terms of Article V and VI of the Constitution." Resolution 7-05, in LCMS, *Proceedings,* 1973, 190.

[67] "Women and Ministry," *TLD* 49, no. 2 (Summer 1971): 11.

[68] Arne Kristo, "Report on Lutheran Deaconess Association," X-06, in LCMS, *Convention Workbook,* 1971, 486-87.

suffrage. Yet the implementation of that decision is moving forward in an uneven manner. In the meantime, many women feel that they have just grievances, not only within the nation, but also in the church. Whether we like it or not, they feel "unequal." They feel that granting the vote was only the beginning. If the deaconess program is to thrive—and if the Synod is to be enriched through the efforts of women—then we must turn our attention to the question of the status of women. . . .[69]

The Convention minutes recorded, "The report of the LDA was received, congregations were encouraged to consider engaging a deaconess on their staff, and the convention expressed its wish for the Lord's blessing on Dr. Lucille Wassmann [sic] as she begins her work as executive director of the program."[70] The single resolution that LCMS convention delegates finally adopted regarding deaconesses differed from the two suggested by the LDA, but the final "resolved" incorporated a study of those two overtures. The resolution read:

> Whereas, There are questions concerning the relationship of deaconesses to the Synod, therefore be it
>
> Resolved, That the President of the Synod appoint a committee of representatives from the Lutheran Deaconess Association, Valparaiso University, the Board for Higher Education, and the Council of Presidents to study this matter and make appropriate recommendations to the next convention; and be it also
>
> Resolved, That the two overtures printed on pages 8 and 11 of *TLD*, Vol. 49, be given full consideration by the committee herewith established.
>
> **Action:** *Adopted as amended (17).*
>
> (Amendment: second resolved.)[71]

In carrying out the resolution, LCMS President Jacob Aall Otteson Preus II (1920–1994) appointed five individuals to the committee: Dr. Roland P. Wiederaenders, Dr. Arthur H. Ahlschwede, Rev. Wilbert Elfred Griesse (1917-2002), Rev. Herbert L. Steinbauer, and Dr. Donald C. Mundinger. He also appointed Dr. Lucille Wassman to serve as a consultant to the group. The committee met in St. Louis on January 22, 1973, but without Pastor Steinbauer, who decided that since his term as President of

---

[69] Kristo, "Report on Lutheran Deaconess Association," X-06, 486.

[70] Session 5, in LCMS, *Proceedings*, 1971, 27.

[71] "To Study the Relationship of Deaconesses to the Synod," in LCMS, *Proceedings*, 1971, 210.

the LDA had finished at the end of 1972, he should decline to be part of the committee.[72]

Wassman sent a letter to all deaconesses summarizing the five-hour meeting and explaining the three options that would need to be considered by the diaconate and the LDA Board of Directors. She wrote:

A personal comment: I think it is important that each of us try to identify the pluses and minuses of each option, to consider the price to be paid in each, and whether that price will benefit the ministry of Christ and you as workers within it.

Option 1—To continue as we are with no directives from Synod about our program, no financial support from Synod. Placements of Graduates would continue to be made through Synod's Board of Assignments based on recommendations by the LDA Executive Director. Problems pertaining to our identity and status, to housing allowances, Internal Revenue, recognition and inclusion in Synodical Handbook, etc., would be ours to struggle with and ours to try to solve. We are not Synod's program. We are independent and have considerable freedom. What price are we willing to pay for this independence? Does it bring about the greatest benefits for the ministry of Christ and for you as its workers?

Option 2—To bring the total Deaconess Educational Program and its Ministry under Synod's direction. Move the program to the campus of a Synodical College such as Senior College in Fort Wayne, Concordia in St. Paul or to Ann Arbor. The problems listed above would become Synod's problems to solve and we would work with Synod's officials and committees to bring about the needed changes. The changes made may or may not coincide with our preferences and recommendations. Our educational program and our forms of ministry would be determined to a large measure by Synod. What price would we pay under this total support and direction by the LCMS? Would it bring about the greatest benefits for the ministry of Christ and for you as its workers?

---

[72] Wiederaenders served as first Vice-President of the LCMS, advisory member of the BOD, Chairman of the Division of Theology and Church Relations, and Chairman of the Colloquy Board. He was familiar with the diaconate, having preached for the closing service of the 1964 Colloquium held at Valparaiso. (See chapter 9). Ahlschwede was Chairman of the Division of Higher Education in the LCMS, and Executive Secretary of the BHE. Griesse was Chairman of the Council of District Presidents, President of the Mid-South District, and Pastor of First Lutheran Church in Fort Smith, Arkansas. Steinbauer had been Vice-President of the LDA from 1969 to 1971; President from 1971 to the end of 1972; and was pastor of Peace Lutheran Church in Detroit. Mundinger was a professor of Government and Vice-President for Academic Affairs at Valparaiso University. "Letter from Lucille Wassman and LDA Plenary Board to All Deaconesses," February 1973, priv. col. of CDN, Pittsburgh, Pa., 2.

Option 3—To combine Options 1 and 2, that is, to give up <u>some</u> of our independence and to receive <u>some</u> of our directives from Synod, such as follows: The educational program would remain at Valparaiso University. We would have direct discussions with Synod's BHE or its representative about our entire educational program and file with BHE a detailed philosophical statement in curricular terms of our standards and requirements. The BHE, acting on directive from Synod, would review this program, react to it, and assist in determining the thrust of the program and the specific areas in which Deaconess Ministry is needed as seen by Synod. Synod would pick up Valparaiso University's current financial subsidy and maintain, increase or decrease the amount currently provided by Valparaiso University. The LDA Executive Director and a BHE representative would cooperatively certify and issue the list of Deaconess graduates to Synod's Board of Assignments for the graduates' initial placements. A committee comprised of representatives from the Council of Presidents, the BHE and Valparaiso University would meet annually with representatives from the LDA Plenary Board to be appraised of all facets of Deaconess Ministry and to determine jointly new objectives as needed for the development of the full potential and use of Deaconess Ministry within the LCMS. Changes in the Constitution and By-Laws of the LDA would seem to be inevitable and would result after adequate study. Problems identified in Option 1 would see solutions arrived at jointly by the LDA and Synodical representatives. What price would we pay under this option? Would it bring about the greatest benefits for the ministry of Christ and for you as its workers?

. . .As an administrator, as the Director of the Deaconess Association, I stand ready to move the Deaconess Program and Ministry in the direction of any one of the three options OR an alternative which someone may wish to develop and propose.[73]

Wassman asked the deaconesses to inform her of their "reaction" to the options by February 20. When the Synod's Ad Hoc Committee met again on March 12, she went armed with a resolution that had been hammered out by the LDA Executive Committee and Plenary Board. The resolution was four pages long—with thirteen "Whereas" paragraphs and eleven different "Resolved" statements—in support of option number one, to maintain the status quo.[74]

---

[73] "Letter from Lucille Wassman and LDA Plenary Board to All Deaconesses," February 1973, 3-4.
[74] Evelyn Middelstadt, "Concerning the Relationship of Deaconesses to the Synod Resolution 11-17," attached to the "Minutes of the Lutheran Deaconess Association Plenary Board Meeting, March 9, 1973, Deaconess Hall, Valparaiso, Indiana," Box: Board for

SUCCESS AND DISAPPOINTMENT

The discussion at the second meeting in St. Louis went well for Wassman. She persuaded the Ad Hoc Committee to accept the option preferred by the majority of deaconesses. The Committee condensed the resolution prepared by the LDA Board of Directors to one page, with only three "Whereas" and six "Resolved" paragraphs, and sent it to the Synod's Committee on Sundry Matters, to be considered for inclusion at the 1973 synodical convention in New Orleans.[75]

As it happened, so many other pressing issues needed to be studied by the Committee on Sundry Matters that the resolution never came out of that committee to the New Orleans convention.[76] In 1975, however, the resolution appeared in the Anaheim *Convention Workbook* as Resolution 5-19, identical to the resolution submitted by the committee appointed by President Preus, with the exception that one "Resolved" had been dropped. The remaining "Resolved" paragraphs read:

> *Resolved,* That the Synod continue to recognize the efforts and work of the Lutheran Deaconess Association in providing an educational program for women who are seeking opportunities to serve in the ministry of the church; and be it further
>
> *Resolved,* That the administrators of the Synod and the presidents of synodical Districts include information about deaconess ministry in their recruitment efforts for church workers and that they recommend the consideration of deaconesses to serve on boards, commissions, and committees at local, circuit, District, and synodical levels; and be it further
>
> *Resolved,* That a representative from the Synod's Board for Higher Education continue to serve as an advisory member on the Board of Directors of the Lutheran Deaconess Association; and be it further
>
> *Resolved,* That a successor ad hoc committee be appointed by the President of the Synod to serve until the next synodical convention to explore further the questions concerning the relationship of deaconesses to the

---

Professional Education Services Box 5: Deaconess Materials and BHE Materials, found loose at front of box, CHI, St. Louis, Mo.

[75] "Concerning the Relationship of Deaconesses to the Synod: Resolution 11-17," Report submitted by the Ad Hoc Committee appointed by President J.A.O. Preus to study the relationship of Deaconesses to the Synod, March 23, 1973, Box: Board for Professional Education Services Box 5: Deaconess Materials and BHE Materials, found loose at front of box, CHI, St. Louis, Mo.

[76] Letter from Norma Everist to LDA Board and LDC, July 1973, Box: Board for Professional Education Services Box 5: Deaconess Materials and BHE Materials, found loose at front of box, CHI, St. Louis, Mo.

Synod and the expansion of women's ministry in the church; and be it finally

Resolved, that congregations and institutions blessed with deaconesses on their staff give greater recognition to women serving in their midst, with special reference to ministry and compensation.[77]

After four years of waiting to acquire an official synodical mandate to maintain the status quo for deaconess training, LDA leaders expressed disappointed when Resolution 5-19 "died since it failed to receive action before adjournment."[78]

CHANGES IN LDA LEADERSHIP

In February 1973, Wassman wrote a letter to all deaconesses. She announced: "It is another new venture for the LDA! The Plenary Board has elected its FIRST WOMAN for President! Congratulations, Norma Jean! and God's blessings."[79] Norma Jean Everist was not only female, but also a deaconess who graduated from the Valparaiso training program in 1960.

It is interesting to note that, when the LDA Board next met, in March 1973, eight of the 15 individuals present at the meeting were deaconesses, two others were women, and only five were men.[80] The minutes of that Board meeting also show that, in addition to being concerned about the role of women in the church, the LDA took a proactive attitude toward the increase of female Theology instructors at Valpo. LDA Vice-President Rev. Curtis Peters reported concerning the LDA Education Committee, that it "continues to work with the Theology Department at Valparaiso University to up-grade the Theology Courses and to include women as teachers in the Theology Department."[81]

---

[77] "Report 5-04," in LCMS, *Convention Workbook (Reports and Overtures)*, 1975, 217-18.
[78] LCMS, *Proceedings*, 1975, 129.
[79] "Letter from Lucille Wassman and LDA Plenary Board to All Deaconesses," February 1973, 1.
[80] Deaconesses: Norma Jean Everist, Janice Orluske, Evelyn Middelstadt, Burnette Kunz, Eileen Peterson, Jackie Haug, Jean (nee Hoover) Schneider, Vanette Kashmer; other women: Lucille Wassman, Helen Albers; clergy: Curtis Harold Peters (b. 1942), Edward Schroeder, Arthur John Spomer (b. 1938); laymen: Paul Liebmann, Donald Mundinger. Evelyn Middelstadt, "Minutes of the Lutheran Deaconess Association Plenary Board Meeting, March 9, 1973, Deaconess Hall, Valparaiso, Indiana," Box: Board for Professional Education Services Box 5: Deaconess Materials and BHE Materials, found loose at front of box, CHI, St. Louis, Missouri, 1.
[81] Middelstadt, "Minutes of the Lutheran Deaconess Association Plenary Board Meeting, March 9, 1973," 1.

The LDA Plenary Board minutes for January 24, 1974, briefly stated, "Norma Jean Everist's resignation was announced."[82] The minutes provided no explanation for her action. The Board elected Curtis Peters to the Presidency, and he served the Association in that office until 1977.[83]

By May of 1973, the LDA Board invited student representatives to its Board meetings, and other students presented reports on topics such as the dorm's "House Council," the activities of Pi Delta Chi, and the new methods of selecting intern placements and graduate calls.[84] Two years later, in April 1975, the LDA tried to increase communication between its leadership and active deaconesses in the field by initiating joint annual meetings of the LDA and Deaconess Conference Boards.[85] These actions reflected the sincere desire on the part of the LDA to include deaconesses and future deaconesses in any decision-making on behalf of the diaconate.

The *NEWS Bulletin* sent to all "Contributors and Supporters of Deaconess Ministry" in fall 1974 announced the addition of a new LDA staff member:

> Deaconess Louise Williams has been added to our Deaconess Association staff. The Association extended a call to her in June and she began her work with us on August 22, 1974. Her title is: Director of Deaconess Services. Her responsibilities include the following: advisor to Pi Delta Chi, the students' professional sorority; coordinator of worship life; advisor to House Council and Kitchen Stewards; director of counseling arrangements; teaching the course "Deaconess Work;" director of interns; and working with Deaconesses in the Field.

> The areas of graduate placement, student recruitment, fund raising, public relations, academic counseling, development of new ministries and a vast amount of correspondence continue to be among the responsibilities of the Association's Executive Director, Dr. Lucille Wassman.[86]

---

[82] Jacqueline J. Haug, "Minutes of the Plenary Board Meeting of the Lutheran Deaconess Association," Deaconess Hall, Valparaiso, Indiana, January 24, 1974, Box: Board for Professional Education Services Box 5: Deaconess Materials and BHE Materials, found loose at front of box, CHI, St. Louis, Missouri, 1.

[83] Haug, "Minutes of the Plenary Board Meeting," January 24, 1974, 3.

[84] Middelstadt, "Minutes of the Lutheran Deaconess Association Plenary Board Meeting, May 4, 1973," 1.

[85] Sue Wendorf, "Minutes of the Lutheran Deaconess Association Plenary Board Meeting, April 11, 1975, Deaconess Hall, Valparaiso, Indiana," Box: Board for Professional Education Services Box 5: Deaconess Materials and BHE Materials, found loose at front of box, CHI, St. Louis, Missouri, 7.

[86] Williams completed her deaconess training at Valparaiso in 1967 and was placed at St. Peter's Lutheran Church in Edmonton, Alberta, Canada. Louise Williams, "A Deaconess

Table 1[87]
Enrollments in Deaconess Training, Social Worker Training,
Lay Training and Parish Worker Programs
at LCMS Synodical Colleges, 1967-1972

	1967	1968	1969	1970	1971	1972
Deac. Training	90	59	58	44	38	56
Social Worker	119	140	123	107	107	153
Lay Training	39	29	22	24	26	11
Parish Worker	81	85	54	59	56	54
TOTAL	329	313	257	234	227	274

The combined enrollments in the deaconess, social worker, lay training, and parish worker programs reached their highest level in 1967 when there were 329 students in these programs, representing five percent of the college enrollment at that time. As seen in Table 1, the social worker and deaconess training enrollments both showed sharp increases this past year. The decrease in the lay training enrollment this year is the result of the program being incorporated into the total operation of the college at Milwaukee, as recommended by the Board for Higher Education.

While Wassman and Williams worked full-time, Deaconess Vanette Kashmer had served the LDA as Field Work Advisor on a part-time basis since 1972. The NEWS Bulletin reported,

. . . Deaconess Vanette Kashmer is responsible for our students' field work experiences in churches and institutions of northwest Indiana. Each student is required to take a minimum of two semesters of field work. At present there are 38 of our young women involved. The field work or Practicum in Ministry is a two-credit course and includes required readings, lesson plans, reaction papers, rap sessions and weekly periods "in the field." Currently our students are involved in confirmation

Goes Forth," TLD 44, no. 2 (Summer 1967), 2. Letter from Lucille Wassman to "Our Contributors and Supporters of Deaconess Ministry." See also: Letter from Lucille Wassman to "All Deaconesses," September 1974.
[87] "Report of Board for Higher Education," in LCMS, Convention Workbook (Reports and Overtures), 1973, 243.

teaching, choir direction, hospital and shut-in calling, youth work, organ playing, evangelism calling, institutional ministry.[88]

On December 20, 1974, less than four months after Williams joined the LDA staff, Wassman wrote a letter to the Board of Directors informing them "that she had for some time been planning to return to full-time teaching and that she thought the roles of Executive Director too many and too diverse in nature."[89] Wassman held the Executive Director's post for only three and a half years, but during that time she increased student enrollment and made it possible for the LDA to achieve a balanced budget.[90]

When Wassman resigned, Williams became *Acting Executive Director*, and Kashmer agreed to take on new responsibilities and work full-time for an interim period. In April 1975, the LDA Board designated Kashmer as the *Associate Director* and officially installed her into that position during a service of Vespers on May 22, 1975.[91] Now the LDA needed to decide how to move forward in staffing decisions. And such an important decision, that would undoubtedly affect the future of the deaconess movement within the Missouri Synod, was felt to need the input of the diaconate itself.

THE DEACONESS CONVOCATION

In a letter sent to all deaconesses in March 1975, Williams explained that the Executive Committee of the LDA resolved to assemble a "Convocation of Deaconesses" in order to discuss staffing and other crucial issues facing the diaconate. The Convocation was to take place at Deaconess Hall on

---

[88] Vanette (nee Peter) Kashmer completed the Valparaiso deaconess program in 1971 and was placed at Trinity Lutheran Church, Evansville, Ind. "Spring Placements," *TLD* 49, no. 2 (Summer 1971): 6-7; Letter from Lucille Wassman to "Our Contributors and Supporters of Deaconess Ministry."

[89] Upon resigning the LDA post, Wassman left the LCMS to join the LCA. She taught at Birmingham Southern College, Birmingham, Alabama, for two years and then at Newberry College, Newberry, South Carolina, until her retirement in 1985. Wassman, telephone interview by CDN. Letter from Curtis H. Peters to "Friends of the Lutheran Deaconess Association," January 31, 1975, Box: Board for Professional Education Services Box 5: Deaconess Materials and BHE Materials, found loose at front of box, CHI, St. Louis, Mo.

[90] "Dr. Lucille Wassman Resigns as LDA Executive Director," News Release, LDA, Deaconess Hall, Valparaiso, Indiana, February 10, 1975, Box: Board for Professional Education Services Box 5: Deaconess Materials and BHE Materials, found loose at front of box, CHI, St. Louis, Mo.

[91] The Association also had good help in the form of a cook, bookkeeper, secretary, and maintenance man. Letter from Curtis H. Peters to "Friends of the Lutheran Deaconess Association," January 31, 1975.

May 21-23, 1975.[92] Every deaconess would receive topics and study materials to be discussed at their local area deaconess conferences. One representative from each area would attend the Convocation, to voice the opinions and perspectives of the deaconesses from her area.

The Convocation agenda included three topics:

1. The relationship of the LDA to the Missouri Synod and other organized church structures.

2. Questions pertaining to the identity and work of deaconesses, particularly secular-versus-church vocations and community-versus-job orientation.

3. Staffing of the LDA.[93]

When the women assembled in Valparaiso, the group included representatives from 13 of the 17 Area Conferences; five members of the LDC Board; six members of the LDA Board; plus Williams and Kashmer. The Convocation opened with a "celebration of the Holy Eucharist," in which LDA President Rev. Curtis Peters served as the celebrant and Louise Williams was the "homilist." The deaconess representatives from Wisconsin and Indiana North did not appreciate the fact that Williams preached at the worship service, and that the text of her homily appeared as the first item in the Convocation Minutes.[94]

The women who attended the gathering worked diligently for two and a half days. The vast majority of participants accepted the working position papers written on the first two topics. The third working paper, on staffing,

---

[92] Letter from Louise Williams to "Sisters," March 21, 1975, priv. col. of Nancy (nee Nicol) Nemoyer, Carlisle, Pa.

[93] "Convocation of Deaconesses—May 21-23, 1975, Deaconess Hall, Valparaiso, Indiana," pink sheet attached to letter from Louise Williams to "Sisters," March 21, 1975, priv. col. of Nancy (nee Nicol) Nemoyer, Carlisle, Pa.

[94] Area representatives listed on the last page of the Convocation Minutes included: Jocelyn Sproule (California-Hawaii-Japan); Karen Bakewicz (Illinois); Betty Mulholland (Indiana North); Phyllis Pleuss (Indiana South); Evelyn Middelstadt (Kansas-Oklahoma-New Guinea); Brenda Kasten (Michigan); Karen Melang (Missouri-Nigeria); Diane Greve (Nebraska-South Dakota-Wyoming); Hertha Fischer (Northeast); Debbie Nebel (Ohio-India); Phyllis Saathoff (Southeast); Claire Visser (Texas); Clara Strehlow (Wisconsin). The four Area Conferences that did not send representatives were: Northwest, Colorado, Illinois South, and Minnesota-Iowa-North Dakota-Manitoba. Betty Mulholland, notes from telephone interview by CDN, June 14, 2006, priv. col. of CDN, Pittsburgh, Pa.; Letter from Vanette Kashmer to "Deaconess Convocation Representatives, LDA Board and LDC Board," May 9, 1975, priv. col. of Betty Mulholland, Munster, Ind.

was finished after the Convocation and then mailed to the deaconesses with an invitation to provide feedback to the LDA staff.[95]

RELATIONSHIP TO OTHER SYNODS

The working position paper titled "Relationship of the Lutheran Deaconess Association to Organized Church Structures" adopted by the Convocation was particularly significant—not only because it helped define the relationship between the LCMS and the LDA that needed attention for so many years—but because when all was said and done, the paper revealed that the LDA was already on a path that, unless altered, could only take the diaconate further away from the Missouri Synod.

> Relationship of the Lutheran Deaconess Association to Organized Church Structures - Working Position Paper, May 23, 1975
>
> The LDA has had a tradition of autonomy since its very birth. From 1911, when the wheels of LCMS deaconess ministry first began to roll, to the present year of 1975, our diaconate has grown and sometimes groaned under a structure which was at best an auxiliary arm of the Missouri Synod. The LDA has been an organization seeking to train women for ministry. The Association is incorporated as a non-profit organization under the laws of the State of Indiana. It has sought to provide suitable education, guidelines, structures, and funds for the development and furtherance of the ministry of deaconesses. Although it has periodically sought closer affiliation and dialogue with the LCMS, and has traditionally seen the bulk of its activities in reference to that specific church body, the response of the Synod to our overtures has been tentative and ambiguous. Nevertheless, recognizing this history and appreciating both the challenges and the tensions which accompany such a relationship, the Convocation of Deaconesses, meeting in Valparaiso May 21-23, has elected to recommend that at this time we neither link ourselves more closely with the Synod nor terminate our affiliation with it.
>
> However, to "concentrate neither on linking nor leaving, but (to) affirm our joyful intention to get on with the Church's mission as Lutheran Deaconesses whenever and however that mission may encounter us and wherever it may lead us" we see as difficult if not impossible without clarifying, defining, and honestly stating where we are now and where we see ourselves going, with particular reference to 1) placement; 2) our relationship to the ALC and LCA diaconates and 3) our recruitment, training, and funding.

---

[95] Letter from Louise Williams to "Sisters," May 29, 1975, priv. col. of Betty Mulholland, Munster, Indiana, and priv. col. of Nancy (nee Nicol) Nemoyer, Carlisle, Pa.

I. Placement

At the present time, all intern and first graduate placements within the LCMS are channeled through LCMS structure via the Board of Placements. In recent years some of our sisters have received internship and graduate assignments in non-Missouri Synod parishes or institutions. The problem we have isolated is one of inconsistency, in that only deaconesses seeking LCMS positions need to be certified as placeable [sic] by the Board of Placements.

The Convocation therefore recommends that all intern and graduate calls be handled by the appropriate Lutheran church body. That is, those sisters receiving calls to the ministry within the ALC or LCA would follow procedures established by that church; those receiving calls to ministry within the LCMS would continue to go through the Board of Placements for their assignments. In any case, it is the LDA which certifies a woman as qualified to serve as a deaconess; it is also the LDA which facilitates and completes the calling process.

II. Relationship to ALC and LCA Diaconates

The placement of some of our deaconesses in ALC and LCA ministries within the last few years has raised the question of our relationship with the diaconates of those church bodies. In order to maintain a climate of openness, honesty, and mutual understanding among the three Lutheran diaconates with regard to these situations, the Convocation recommends that the ALC or LCA diaconate be informed of all ALC or LCA calls received by members of our diaconate. Furthermore, we recommend that the parish or agency extending the call be appraised of this procedure. Should the opposite situation occur, we request that the same procedure be followed by the appropriate ALC or LCA diaconate.

Note: We discussed the potential for one pan-Lutheran diaconate. However, structural differences and relationships between the other diaconates and their respective church bodies would seem to preclude such a development in the near future. The Convocation recommends, however, that this possibility be open to further discussion and investigation. We feel that because our diaconates are so dissimilar in terms of education and training, yet similar in concepts of Diakonia, that we have much to learn from each other.

With regard to those of our sisters who do accept positions in ALC or LCA ministries, the Convocation recommends that transferring their church memberships to those church bodies where they are serving will not exclude them from membership in the Lutheran Deaconess Conference or the Lutheran Deaconess Association. In those cases, the

Lutheran Deaconess Conference sees itself as maintaining an active relationship and support system with and for these sisters.

III. Recruitment, Training, Funding

The Convocation recommends that the LDA and the LDC continue to work towards establishing better rapport with district presidents, local clergy, and other LCMS agencies, organizations, and institutions for the purpose of recruitment possibilities. The importance of personal contact by deaconesses should not be underestimated. Furthermore, we affirm the current practice of accepting students from the ALC and LCA, although we do not actively recruit from their ranks.

The possibility of developing deaconess training/education centers at synodical college campuses was discussed at length and rejected for the following reasons:

1) at this time such a move could be seen as a political move with implications we do not intend to give;

2) another deaconess training center could be potentially devisive [sic] of the community as we now experience it;

3) plans for implementing such an additional center could conceivably require 3–5 years' work to complete. Therefore, the Convocation recommends that we affirm our good working relationship with Valparaiso University, that we recognize and appreciate the autonomy which we enjoy as an independent Association adjoined to this campus, and that we continue to maintain a single training/education center at this location.

The perennial need for financial support has not abated.

As a result of this entire discussion and the ensuing recommendation to neither link more closely with nor terminate our affiliation with the Synod at this point in time, the Convocation recognizes that there are inherent dangers in seeking to reap the benefits without shouldering the responsibilities of a closer association with the LCMS. We also are aware of the risks involved in leaving the Synod entirely, until and if we ever reach the point where our identity as a Lutheran diaconate is firmly established in American Lutheranism. We need to restate our felt need for honesty in declaring to the church who we are and where we see ourselves going. We need to keep a finger on the pulse of the Missouri Synod in order to continually reassess the nature of our relationship to the Synod. We need to be aware of and sensitive to the diversity of attitudes and outlooks within our sisterhood, and to be bold enough to step out in the directions indicated by our evaluation of contemporary situations. We need to be ready to take positive and affirmative action which is based not on our reaction to situations and events, but on our concept of our own identity and call to ministry.[96]

Not every Missouri Synod deaconess agreed with the conclusions in the above study paper. Indeed, the first sentence of the last paragraph reads as if it might have been inserted in recognition of dissenting views, or at least as an attempt to acknowledge the desire to *have one's cake and eat it too*. At least two deaconesses at the Convocation, and several others not at the Convocation, desired a closer relationship with the Missouri Synod, and expressed their dissatisfaction that the LDA was the sole authority that "certifies a woman as qualified to serve as a deaconess," without any input from the primary church body that it professed to serve.[97]

Certainly all Convocation attendees would have known that training LCA workers for LCMS church-worker positions, and training LCMS women to work in LCA (and even ALC) churches, would have been unacceptable in most circles of the Missouri Synod. And yet, the Association already had its foot in the door with some of this practice, since the LDA Board of Directors had decided about two years previous, "to treat LCMS, ALC and LCA parishes alike in filling intern positions," and as early as the 1973–74 school year, Executive Director Wassman informed the Board that there were "several interns serving in LCA parishes."[98] Of course, the LCMS was not in fellowship with the LCA, a church body that had authorized the ordination of women in 1970. Furthermore, many members of the LCMS were becoming increasingly dissatisfied with the Synod's state of fellowship with the ALC, and were campaigning for an alteration or dissolution of that fellowship.[99]

---

[96] The text includes corrections and additions made in pen in an identical manner on two different copies of the document. "Relationship of the Lutheran Deaconess Association to Organized Church Structures, Working Position Paper, May 23, 1975," priv. col. of Betty Mulholland, Munster, Indiana, and priv. col. of Nancy (nee Nicol) Nemoyer, Carlisle, Pa.

[97] Mulholland, notes from telephone interview by CDN, June 14, 2006.

[98] "Minutes of the Plenary Board Meeting of the Lutheran Deaconess Association," January 24, 1974, Box: Board for Professional Education Services Box 5: Deaconess Materials and BHE Materials, found loose at front of box, CHI, St. Louis, Missouri, 4.

[99] "The American Lutheran Church," five mimeographed pages, stamped "Confidential," Council of Presidents, April 25-30, 1981, Ft. Wayne, IN and St. Louis, MO, binder: Minutes Council of Presidents St. Louis, Mo. Feb. 27—March 3, 1981, Box: Council of Presidents Minutes May 1977—April 1981 Box #7, archive location: 111.1C.17, CHI, St. Louis, Mo.; Suelflow, August R., ed., *Heritage in Motion: Readings in the History of the Lutheran Church--Missouri Synod, 1962-1995*, St. Louis: Concordia, 1998, chapter 2; See also, "To Declare a State of 'Fellowship in Protest' with the ALC," Resolution 3-02A, in LCMS, *Proceedings*, 1977, 125-26.

STAFFING NEEDS

Everyone at the Convocation concurred that the LDA needed to fill the staffing gap created by the departure of Lucille Wassman. The majority of the discussion on this subject centered on whether or not a male should be added to the staff, and what type of administrative model should be used in the workplace. The Convocation concluded that a third deaconess should be added to the staff, and that the three deaconesses should work together in a sort of co-equal team ministry.[100]

At the annual LDC meeting held about six weeks after the Deaconess Convocation, the LDA Board stated that, "it was not wise to implement the Convocation recommendation regarding hiring three full-time staff people."[101] In her report to the 1976 Deaconess Conference, Williams explained that the LDA Board rearranged staff responsibilities, so that Kashmer held the new title of *Director of Student Services* and had charge of all student affairs, while Williams continued to be the *Director of Deaconess Services,* working with consecrated deaconesses, public relations, funding, and general administration of the LDA.[102] This new division of duties in the context of a team-ministry model would be used by the Association for several years to come.

---

[100] "Staffing, Working Position Paper, May 23, 1975," priv. col. of Betty Mulholland, Munster, Indiana, and priv. col. of Nancy (nee Nicol) Nemoyer, Carlisle, Pa.
[101] Louise Williams, "Director of Deaconess Services Report—Annual Deaconess Conference, July 11-14, 1976," Box: CDC, File: LDC 11-14 July 1976, CHI, St. Louis, Mo.
[102] *Ibid.*

Illustrations for Chapter Ten may be viewed at www.deaconesshistory.org.

CHAPTER 11

A HOUSE DIVIDED

Students of history who have the time to scan through Missouri Synod *Convention Workbooks* and *Proceedings* from the 1940s onward will note an increase in overtures and resolutions dealing with doctrinal disputes. Risking oversimplification, it can be stated that those divisions of opinion touched on issues of church fellowship; the doctrine of the ministry and nature of the mission of all believers; and most particularly, the doctrine of the Word.

As the LCMS moved into the late 1960s and early 1970s, tension within the church body was coming to a head. It affected pastors, vicars, teachers, deaconesses, and other church workers in the field; laity in the parishes; those who studied for full-time church professions; Lutheran students and professors in the LCMS Concordia system; and of course, Lutheran students and professors at Valparaiso University or other non-synodical colleges. Interestingly, the divisions of opinion became somewhat predictable. Concerned and informed laity, extremely loyal to their Synod, tended to voice agreement with the traditional or conservative views on issues, while many of the Synod's academics and pastors trained since 1950 leaned toward a more moderate or liberal understanding of the same issues. Naturally, there were many exceptions to these generalizations, and often, wherever the exceptions existed, friction in the Synod became the most intense.

It is not the purpose of this book to educate the reader about the history of the internal struggles borne by the Missouri Synod during the twentieth century. However, some knowledge of that turmoil is requisite to an understanding of how the LDA and its diaconate related to synodical controversy during the 1970s. For that purpose, the following quotation from *Heritage in Motion: Readings in the History of the Lutheran Church—Missouri Synod, 1962–1995,* by August R. Suelflow, provides a pertinent summary.[1]

---

[1] Further accounts and explanations can be read in volumes listed under *Secondary Sources* in the *Bibliography* of this book. For example: *Seminary in Crisis: The Inside Story of the Preus Fact Finding Committee,* by Paul A. Zimmerman and *Anatomy of an Explosion: Missouri in Lutheran Perspective,* by Kurt E. Marquart.

In the late 1960s there was a movement in the Missouri Synod to resist what some saw as liberalizing tendencies. The response of the conservatives was to rally behind the support of Dr. J. A. O. Preus II for President of Synod in 1969. This set the stage for the crisis that prevailed during much of the 1970s as Synod sought to reaffirm its belief in the verbal inspiration and inerrancy of Scripture and to condemn the aberrant use of higher criticism in the interpretation of Scripture. While the theological issues were an issue at other schools, such as the colleges at River Forest and Seward and the seminary at Springfield, Concordia Seminary under Dr. John H. Tietjen became the focal point of the controversy. ...

The crisis had its roots already in the early 1950s when a memorial was submitted to Synod requesting an investigation of the seminary faculty in St. Louis. Similar requests were sent to subsequent conventions and with increasing frequency. The presidencies of Drs. John W. Behnken and Oliver Harms were troubled by the theological problems that were developing within Synod, but primarily at Concordia Seminary. During the 1960s the Board of Control of Concordia Seminary in St. Louis spent considerable time discussing problems of Biblical interpretation, such as the Genesis accounts of creation and the Fall, the nature of Old Testament prophecies, the proper understanding of the book of Jonah, and principles of hermeneutics and exegesis.

The situation became more serious in late 1969 when it became apparent in a meeting of the Council of Presidents and the faculties of both seminaries that there was considerable disagreement in the proper understanding of the authority and interpretation of Scripture. A few months later, in early 1970, three members of the St. Louis faculty formed a Committee for Openness and Trust which issued the document "Call to Openness and Trust." This document advocated open Communion on the basis of a new understanding of the Lord's Supper and attacked Synod's position on the inerrancy of Scripture. It was repudiated at the 1971 Milwaukee convention. These and similar events motivated the synodical President to appoint a Fact-Finding Committee.

The Fact-Finding Committee submitted its report to the synodical President on June 15, 1971. After interviewing 45 men, studying their writings and course syllabi, and visiting classes and chapel, members of the committee concluded that there was considerable diversity in theological positions within the faculty and that there clearly was divergence from the established doctrinal position of Synod. As a result of these findings, President Preus asked the Board of Control to direct the faculty during the 1972-73 school year to refrain from using any avenue, such as class lectures, student consultations, and pastoral conferences, to cast doubt on the divine authority of Scripture, the historicity and factuality of Biblical events, the reality of Jesus' miracles, and the Gospel message.

In March of 1972, Dr. Preus, in consultation with the Vice-Presidents, issued *A Statement of Scriptural and Confessional Principles* as a guideline for the Board of Control to use in fulfilling its responsibilities. On September 1, 1972, Preus issued his "Report of the Synodical President" to inform the church of the results of the Fact-Finding Committee's work. One week later the seminary's president, Dr. John H. Tietjen, responded with his *Fact Finding or Fault Finding?* in which he rejected the validity of Preus' report. Late in 1972 the faculty majority responded to the Council of Presidents' recommendation that "each of the professors of Concordia Seminary, St. Louis, … assure the Church of his Biblical and confessional stance" with *Faithful to our Calling, Faithful to our Lord.* Each faculty member also prepared a statement of faith. …

At the 1973 Convention, Synod passed Resolution 3-09, which declared that the majority of the faculty at the St. Louis Seminary was in violation of Article II of the synodical Constitution, which requires unequivocal acceptance of the Old and New Testaments and all the symbolical books of the Evangelical Lutheran Church. The Preamble restates the three primary errors of the faculty majority, namely, rejection of the *sola scriptura* principle, Gospel reductionism, and setting aside of the third use of the law in the manner of neo-Lutheranism.

On July 24, 1973, the faculty majority protested Resolution 3-09 of the 1973 synodical convention which condemned several positions of the faculty as false doctrine and directed that these matters be turned over to the seminary's Board of Control. This protest electrified the seminary community during the 1973-74 school year. The seminary community was encouraged to take a "strong and concerted action" by way of posters, campus newspapers, and the activities of special committees. The situation became more tense after the board in its November 19, 1973 meeting refused to renew the contract of one professor, resolved to implement synod's retirement policy for faculty members 65 years of age, and resolved to review the doctrinal content of course syllabi. On December 13 over 400 students protested the board's action and hinted that they might leave the seminary.

When the Board of Control suspended President Tietjen on January 20, 1974, the students declared a moratorium on all classes until the board would identify which faculty members it considered false teachers. Later that same day the faculty went on strike. In a letter of January 22 to President Preus, the faculty blamed the Board of Control for bringing the seminary to a standstill. The faculty understood Dr. Tietjen's suspension as condemnation. On January 28 Dr. Preus urged the faculty to return to class and adjudicate the differences through channels provided by Synod. On February 12, the faculty gave the board an ultimatum: for classes to resume on February 19, the board would have to reverse the suspension of Dr. Tietjen and the department heads, renew the contract of one professor, reverse implementation of the retirement policy, and acknowledge the faculty's teaching as being in harmony with synod's position. The board did not yield and on February 17 asked the faculty to indicate by noon on February 18 whether or not they would resume teaching on the 19th. If they should refuse to return to the classroom, they would be held in breach of contract.

On February 18, 1974, the majority of the faculty and students exited the campus and on February 19, as promised, founded Concordia Seminary in Exile (Seminex) with over 400 students and all but five members of the faculty. On October 12, 1974, the Board of Control officially removed Dr. Tietjen from office.

Concordia Seminary continued to function with 100 students and five professors. Rebuilding the seminary was an intense and demanding process, but it succeeded beyond many people's expectations. The 1974-75 school year began with nearly 200 students and a faculty and executive staff of almost 25. Within a few years the seminary had fully recovered, and its reputation as a solidly conservative Lutheran seminary faithful to Scripture and the Confessions was restored.[2]

To say that the LCMS synodical controversy had a profound effect on members of the diaconate might be viewed as an understatement by deaconesses who remember the tension of those turbulent years. The following extracts, taken from a letter written by LDA President Norma Everist after her attendance at the 1973 Synodical Convention, reflect the anxiety and uncertainty felt by many deaconesses as the controversy unfolded.

Anyone not attending the 50th Regular Convention of the LC-MS in New Orleans July 6–13, 1973 will have a difficult time comprehending the emotionally charged atmosphere, indeed the historical significance of the proceedings. Those in attendance will vary in their impressions of the happenings. Some saw the convention as a series of political maneuverings by two sides, both of which showed lack of love. . . .

And the basic question arises, "Are we at the point of scism?" [sic] What effect will the passage of "A Statement" have on professional

2 Suelflow, August R., ed., Heritage in Motion: Readings in the History of the Lutheran Church--Missouri Synod, 1962-1995, St. Louis: Concordia, 1998, 423-26.

deaconesses? How much division exists in the church? Will subsequent calls request a deaconess of a particular doctrinal view? Will the concentration of power as evidenced by the elections effect [*sic*] our pre-deaconess programs at the junior colleges? Only time will tell us the answers. . . . The diaconate is a composite of many ways of expressing the Word of God. We dare not let division divide us, but through our unity we can radiate the unity which is possible in Jesus Christ.[3]

PULLED INTO THE BATTLE

Appeals for action, usually received from other professional church workers, drew deaconesses into the synodical battle. Many of these appeals used emotional or exaggerated language and did not accurately represent the events that transpired. The following letter from the St. Louis Area Deaconess Conference, sent to all LDA deaconesses on December 1, 1973, is a good example of one of these well-intentioned but inaccurate appeals.

Sister,

The political situation at Concordia Seminary, St. Louis, continues to deteriorate daily; the "end" is coming much sooner and with much greater force than had been anticipated. The faculty have been declared heretical and to be outlawed, not only from the Missouri Synod, but from the entire church universal. Persecution for the sake of Christ has become a reality for those brothers in Christ.

This struggle also touches our diaconate very personally, for one of the men under fire is [name], who has been a friend of deaconesses for many years and who has given of his talents for the sake of the ministry. As we officially noted at our Conference this summer, [name] is our friend and will continue to receive our support. With the advent of the Purge, there perhaps isn't a whole lot that can be done in a material way for our brothers. However, now more than ever, these men need to hear from us that we still support them, that they are in our prayers, that our concern extends through and beyond the mini-crucifixions which they're experiencing. Since this month also commemorates the Advent of God's son, our Area Conference wants to share with you one small thing we can <u>all</u> do to show our support for our friend [name] in these days of political trial and of Christmas celebration. We ask that each of you TODAY take five minutes to address a Christmas card to [name], a card in which you assure him that he and the rest of the faculty are daily in your prayers.

[3] Letter from Norma Everist to "LDA Board and LDC," July 1973, Box: Board for Professional Education Services Box 5: Deaconess Materials and BHE Materials, found loose at front of box, CHI, St. Louis, Mo.

And, since finances are also under pressure these days, we suggest that if possible you include a $5 or $2 or $10 check as yet another visible manifestation of our support.

DEACONESSES DON'T FORGET THEIR FRIENDS; a friend of ours needs our support. You can personally help in this ministry, sharing the Good News with our brother. It makes no difference if you know him personally; write as a sister of our community. Take time TODAY![4]

Rather than examining the theological issues involved or acknowledging the Missouri Synod's responsibility to maintain correct teaching and doctrine, the women who wrote the above letter focused only on friendship and an alleged injustice to friends. This emphasis was common among the supporters of those who eventually walked away from the Concordia Seminary Campus to become the first professors and student body of Seminex.[5]

VALPARAISO VOICES

Since the formation and education of deaconesses who wanted to serve in the Missouri Synod took place at Deaconess Hall and in the classrooms of Valparaiso University, it should be noted that many members of the university community involved themselves in the on-going discussion of synodical issues. Already in June 1972, Rev. Walter Erich Keller (b. 1929), Chairman of the VU Department of Theology and hence, academic advisor to all deaconess students, wrote an article in *The Cresset*, titled "A Scrutiny of a Statement on Scripture," in which he critiqued the theological position of

---

[4] Letter from St. Louis Area Deaconess Conference to "Sister," December 1, 1973, priv. col. of Betty Mulholland, Munster, Indiana.

[5] The St. Louis deaconesses may have taken their lead from seminary students. Concerning Concordia Seminary, the Board of Control later wrote, "The faculty majority cancelled classes for the announced purpose that the students might study the issues of the synodical controversy. But the students were exposed only to the faculty majority's position as supported by the student leaders; no one was invited to speak for the Board of Control or the Synod. It was apparent that the issues had become muddied and confused. Instead of considering the Synod's judgment (New Orleans Resolution 3-09) against the faculty majority's theological position, the students responded emotionally to what they believed was their professors' sincere Christian witness. The Synod's resolution had condemned a position, but many students apparently understood this as a condemnation of **persons**." The Board of Control, Concordia Seminary, *Exodus from Concordia: a Report on the 1974 Walkout*, St. Louis, 1977, 88.

"A Statement of Scriptural and Confessional Principles."[6] When Keller sent a copy of his article to the LCMS President on June 28, he wrote,

Dear Dr. Preus,

I am sending you the enclosed copy of the June,1972 issue of our Cresset, . . . not because it in any way represents a definitive refutation or a comprehensive alternative, but because it offers a necessary and valid perspective upon the theological problem you have raised. It is conceived as a contribution to what must necessarily be a frank and fraternal public discussion of the important issue. . . . [7]

This assumption that all interested individuals should engage in *public* conversation about the church's affairs permeated the educational culture of Valparaiso University. *The Cresset* featured more articles about "A Statement" and the doctrine of Scripture, but the most substantial contribution to continued discussion of the issues was probably "A Review Essay of A Statement of Scriptural and Confessional Principles," co-authored by four of Valpo's Theology professors: Department Chairman Keller, Kenneth F. Korby (editor of *The Cresset*), Robert C. Schultz (b. 1928), and David George Truemper (1939–2004).[8] The 33-page review essay appeared in two parts, the first in May 1973, and the second in October of the same year. Delegates at the 1973 LCMS convention in New Orleans officially adopted "A Statement of Scriptural and Confessional Principles" in the interval between the two publications.[9]

---

[6] Walter E. Keller, "A Scrutiny of a Statement on Scripture," *The Cresset* 35, no. 8 (June 1972): 6-9.
[7] Letter from Walter E. Keller to J.A.O. Preus, June 28, 1972, File: Valparaiso University *Cresset*, Box: JAO Preus Supplement Box 12 of 53, CHI, St. Louis, Mo.
[8] Walter E. Keller, Kenneth F. Korby, Robert C. Schultz, David G. Truemper, "A Review Essay of A Statement of Scriptural and Confessional Principles," *The Cresset* 36, no. 7 (May 1973): 6-20; Walter E. Keller, Kenneth F. Korby, Robert C. Schultz, David G. Truemper, "A Review Essay (Part II) of A Statement of Scriptural and Confessional Principles," *The Cresset* 36, no. 10 (October 1973): 21-38. See also, Robert C. Schultz, "Reflections on the Current Controversy in the Lutheran Church—Missouri Synod: An Attempt to Express Pastoral Concern," *The Cresset* 35, no. 10 (October 1972): 7-12; Steven A. Hein, "'A Scrutiny' Scrutinized," *The Cresset* 36, no. 3 (January 1973): 21-23.
[9] In January 1974, Korby used *The Cresset* letterhead to write to Rev. Elwood Zimmermann, President of the Indiana District of the LCMS, and the members of the Commission on Theology and Church Relations of the LCMS, to register his dissent from "A Statement" and to "ask my doctrinal supervisor and the Commission on Theology and Church Relations to recommend the withdrawal of A Statement." The May 1975 issue of *The Cresset* included an unsigned article titled, "The LCMS Convention Ought to Retract A Statement." Letter from Kenneth F. Korby to President Elwood Zimmermann and members of the CTCR of the LCMS, Box: Valparaiso University Box 1, CHI, St. Louis, Missouri; "The LCMS

On February 3, 1974—two weeks before the "walkout" from Concordia Seminary—304 Valparaiso University students signed a petition addressed to LCMS President Preus. The signatories declared "support (of) the actions of the 'faculty majority,' the staff, and the students of Concordia Seminary," and urged President Preus and the Concordia Seminary Board of Control "to retract their statements and actions on this issue, and pray for the restoration of peace in the LCMS."[10] Two days later, on February 5, many of the university's faculty and staff also sent a letter to the Board of Control, in protest of John Tietjen's suspension. On February 6, VU President Huegli gathered his faculty together in the Neils Science Center for an open meeting. After an introductory report from Keller, highlighting what had recently taken place in St. Louis, Huegli explained:

> . . . It is not our role as a University to sit in judgment on all of the events that have caused the difficulties which have engulfed the Church and its Seminary. Individuals among us have our own opinions about the matters of controversy, and are encouraged to express them. Our calling as a University is to serve as a marketplace to which all may freely bring ideas, and each has the right to speak his mind. This is in the very nature of a University. It is also a corollary of our freedom as a Christian people. The University as such is not partisan in matters of controversy, whether they be doctrinal or political, but it opens its doors to wide-ranging discussion in the search for solutions and for truth. . . . [11]

It was actually Valpo's Board of Directors that made the decision that the university would not take sides on the matters of controversy within the LCMS, and the Board's ruling "applied to the theology department as a collective entity as well."[12] However, this fact did not prevent individual professors from expressing their viewpoints, both inside and outside of the classroom, and a significant amount of discussion took place on the campus. John Tietjen addressed a large contingent of Valparaiso professors and students in the university Chapel in spring 1974; the Department of Theology hosted a series of lectures by three LCMS District Presidents representing the moderate, conservative, and middle-of-the-road positions;

Convention Ought to Retract A Statement," *The Cresset* 38, no. 7 (May 1975): 3-4; "To Adopt 'A Statement'—Resolution 3-01," in LCMS, *Proceedings*, 1973, 127-28.

[10] "A Statement by the Students of Valparaiso University," 19 reproductions of the "Statement," each page with various numbers of original signatures, Box: Valparaiso University Box #1, CHI, St. Louis, Mo.

[11] A.G. Huegli, "The University and the Crisis in the Church," February 5, 1974, Box: Valparaiso University Box #1, CHI, St. Louis, Mo.

[12] Richard Baepler, *Flame of Faith, Lamp of Learning: A History of Valparaiso University* (St. Louis: Concordia, 2001), 335.

and in April 1975, Dr. Robert Bertram, Chairman of the Systematics Department at Seminex, came to Valparaiso to speak to "students, professors, friends . . . and people from off campus" on the topic "SEMINEX, Valpo, and You."[13]

VU FACULTY MEMBERS RESPOND

The VU faculty's concern and involvement in debate about Missouri Synod issues was well known to the student body. The February 18, 1975, issue of *The Torch*, Valpo's bi-weekly campus newspaper written by students, included several articles on the subject including the full text of a faculty petition entitled, "In Response to the Dismissal of President John Tietjen," which defended the "publicly confessed doctrinal position" of John Tietjen, and stated that, "If, on the basis of this public confession, President Tietjen is guilty of holding, defending, allowing, and fostering false doctrine, then we too are guilty."[14] Regarding the faculty "Response," the student paper reported,

> In Oct. 1974, John Tietjen was dismissed as President of Concordia Seminary by its Board of Control, ... In response to the dismissal, three Valparaiso University professors from the Department of Theology, Frederick Niedner, Gwendolyn Sayler and Robert Weinhold, drafted a statement in protest to the Board's action.
>
> After the statement was drafted, it was circulated to the entire VU faculty for their consideration. Eventually 42 members signed this statement and last November the final statement was sent to Dr. Jacob A. O. Preus, president of the Missouri Synod, the Board of Control of Concordia

---

[13] The three District Presidents included Rev. Harold L. Hecht (1923-1990) of the English District; Rev. Karl Barth of the South Wisconsin District; Rev. Wilbert Griesse of the Missouri Mid-South District. Pat Camarena, "LCMS Controversy: Synod Stirs Again," *The Torch* (October 29, 1974): 1; Edna Mather, "Right, Left Vie in Missouri Synod Debate," *The Torch* (November 5, 1974): 1; Steven Krenz, "Bertram Outlines LCMS Issues, *The Torch* (April 11, 1975): 5.

[14] The petition was signed by (* indicates ordained): *James Albers, Gertrude Bluemel, *Richard Caemmerer, Robert Colyer, William Dallmann, Melvin Doering, *Thomas Droege, Philip Gehring, Veru Hahn, Thomas Hall, Arthur Hallerberg, Katherine Hallerberg, John Helms, Elmer Hess, Leonard Kochendorfer, William Kowitz, *Carl Krekeler, Van Kussrow, *Dale Lasky, Richard Lee, William Leoschke, *Herbert Lindemann, Sigrid Lindemann, *Theodore Ludwig, Anita Manning, Marvin Mundt, *Frederick Niedner, Mel Piehl, *Walter Rast, Alice Rechlin, Frederick Rechlin, (Deaconess) Gwendolyn Sayler, Martin Schaefer, *Philip Schroeder, Albert Scribner, William Seeber, *Edgar Senne, James Startt, Robert Stoltz, *Karl Thiele, *Robert Weinhold, and Normand Widiger. "In Response to the Dismissal of President John Tietjen," *The Torch* (February 18, 1975): 1, 5.

Seminary, the district presidents of the Missouri Synod and the **Missouri in Perspective**, the official publication of Evangelical Lutherans in Mission (ELIM).[15]

It should be stressed that this statement was issued by individual members of the VU faculty and should not be interpreted as an official statement of Valparaiso University, according to Dr. Weinhold and re-emphasized by the VU Board of Directors in their most recent meeting earlier this month. . . . The statement has also been sent to individual faculty members of other Missouri Synod affiliated institutions in hopes that more people will sign this document, according to Niedner.[16]

Another article in the same issue of *The Torch* noted,

Current problems and dissentions within the Lutheran Church—Missouri Synod, and their effect upon Valparaiso University, was discussed by the University's Board of Directors at its meeting in Chicago, Feb. 7 and 8. VU is related to the LCMS, though not under its direct jurisdiction. President Huegli reported that the University has received numerous inquiries relative to a private document signed by members of the VU faculty and staff, along with some others not associated with the University.. . . . [17]

Valparaiso University received a great deal of criticism from both clergy and laity in the wake of the "private" faculty petition. One of the primary complaints was that the university's policy to allow all opinions to be heard, unchecked, resulted in the vast majority of campus opinion moving further away from traditional Missouri Synod thinking, particularly in relation to the understanding of Holy Scripture. But the university also had other long-term problems. Valparaiso Emeritus Professor Baepler wrote:

---

[15] ELIM formed as a moderate caucus within the LCMS, following the 1973 synodical convention in New Orleans. After Seminex formed, ELIM dedicated a large portion of its resources to supporting that institution, and for several years, published *Missouri in Perspective*, a newspaper that provided moderate-to-liberal commentary on synodical affairs. Many of the leaders, ministers, and congregations that supported ELIM eventually left the LCMS in 1976 to form the Association of Evangelical Lutheran Churches (AELC), one of the three church bodies that came together to create the Evangelical Lutheran Church in America (ELCA) on January 1, 1988.

[16] David Hibbs, "Crisis in the LCMS . . . the Situation," *The Torch* (February 18, 1975): 5.

[17] The article is almost a word-for-word rendering of a Valparaiso University News Release from February 1975. Norman Temme, "Board Reaffirms University's Position Regarding Lutheran Church—Missouri Synod Tensions," NEWS: Valparaiso University, Valparaiso, Indiana, February 14, 1975, File: Valpo Univ., Box: JAO Preus Box 14, CHI, St. Louis, Missouri; "Board Reaffirms VU's Position Concerning the LCMS Tensions," *The Torch* (February 18, 1975): 1.

More practically, the synodical crisis added to VU's troubles in the 1970s. Forward to the Eighties[18] was just getting under way, and its outcome was uncertain. Budgets were pinching. Lutheran enrollment was dropping, and the new, more diverse student body challenged deeply rooted outlooks and practices. Furthermore, the Missouri Synod split seriously depleted the academic pipeline that had long furnished Valparaiso with many of its best faculty. For some on campus, the earlier dreams of building a unique Lutheran institution seemed threatened, and many wondered what kind of a university would emerge from an increasingly attenuated relationship to a church body, or bodies, with which VU was no longer as well connected. For the first time, the prospect of becoming a vaguely Christian university, sliding down the "slippery slope" to becoming just another private U.S. college, began disturbing those who had worked hard to make Valparaiso a strong Lutheran representative of the United States' religiously pluralistic higher education.[19]

THE DEACONESS PETITION

About a week after Concordia Seminary President John Tietjen was removed from office (October 1974), several deaconesses worked together to collect signatures for a petition titled, "A Statement of Concern to the Church." The full text of the original petition read:

STATEMENT OF CONCERN TO THE CHURCH

As Lutheran Deaconesses we can no longer remain silent in the present Synodical crisis; we are called by our Lord Jesus Christ to give our witness to the Church. We represent a variety of theological positions—some of us are "conservatives" and some are "moderates", some of us are members of ELIM and some consider ELIM devisive [sic] but together we proclaim our unity in the midst of our diversity, together we proclaim that there is room for all of us in the Church, and together, in the conviction that the Church is Christ-connected forgiven sinners who love each other in Christ, who deal openly and honestly with each other

WE PAINFULLY PROTEST TO THE CHURCH THAT THE BOARD OF CONTROL, CONCORDIA SEMINARY, ST LOUIS, IN CONVICTING JOHN TIETJEN OF "HOLDING, DEFENDING, ALLOWING, FOSTERING FALSE DOCTRINE, CONTRARY TO

---

[18] In his inaugural address delivered on October 7, 1978, VU President Robert V. Schnabel noted, "It was in the 'Huegli years' that the $28-million 'Forward to the Eighties' program, now over 90 percent completed, was begun, through which, in large measure, the University has been judged by higher education authorities as financially 'strong and gaining.'" www.valpo.edu/library/archives/presidents/schnabel.html

[19] Baepler, *Flame of Faith, Lamp of Learning*, 337.

ARTICLE 2" HAS, IN ITS <u>REFUSAL TO DEFINE IN ANY WAY</u>
<u>THE SPECIFIC CONTENT OF THAT FALSE DOCTRINE</u>, DEALT
DISHONESTLY AND UNLOVINGLY WITH A BROTHER IN THE
FAITH.

We do not agree on every possible theological issue with John Tietjen, but
we are convinced that the handling of his conviction was carried out in an
unChristian, and unloving manner. We call to the Church to join with us
in assuming responsibility to halt this unlovingness, to cry out loudly and
firmly for an atmosphere of openness, honesty, and trust, to petition the
Board of Control, Concordia Seminary, St. Louis, either to demonstrate
that John Tietjen is indeed guilty of the false doctrine of which he is
convicted or, if this is impossible, to retract the conviction and publicly
affirm John Tietjen's innocence.

Again, John Tietjen's theological position is not necessarily in every
respect ours. But in the midst of our diversity, we together hurt for John
Tietjen, his family, our own congregations, and the entire Church.

May God have mercy on us all.[20]

The collection of signatures for "Statement of Concern to the Church"
was highly orchestrated. The bottom half of the mimeographed sheet that
contained the original petition was titled "PERSONS ASKED TO MAKE
THE CALLS FOR SIGNATURES," and contained a list of twenty-five
deaconesses assigned to telephone all other deaconesses and interns that
lived in six "Zones" divided into twenty-two sections. It can be assumed
that at least seven of the twenty-five deaconesses on that list either declined
to make calls or were unable to do so, since their own names never
appeared with the petition.

According to a note of instruction to the women making calls, the
names of all deaconesses who consented to have their signatures added to
the petition were to be given, via telephone, to Deaconess Susan Wendorf
on October 23.[21] Wendorf would then attach the women's names to the
petition, and on October 24, mail the document to LCMS President J. A. O.
Preus, John Tietjen, The Board of Control of Concordia Seminary, LCMS
District Presidents, *The Lutheran Witness*, *Missouri In Perspective (MIP)*, and

---

[20] "Statement of Concern to the Church," October 1974, top half of mimeographed page,
priv. col. of Joyce Ostermann, Fort Wayne, Ind.
[21] Susan Wendorf graduated from the Valparaiso deaconess training program in 1969. She
served as Secretary of the LDA Board of Directors from 1975 to 1978, and was ordained as
a pastor in 1979.

Christian News.[22] A copy of "Statement of Concern to the Church" was also pinned to the notice board near the drinking fountain on the ground floor of Deaconess Hall, and signed by many of the students who lived in the Hall during the 1974-75 academic year.[23]

On November 4, 1974, *MIP* printed the petition under the headline, "We Can No Longer Remain Silent, Say 91 Deaconesses, 41 Students."[24] The words of the petition had been slightly polished before going to print, and as indicated by the headline, there were ninety-one names preceded by the title "Deaconess," and another 41 names listed under the heading, "Deaconess Students at Valparaiso University."[25]

The fact that ninety-one deaconesses signed the petition seems very impressive at first glance. If any members of the Missouri Synod had whipped out their 1974 copy of *The Lutheran Annual,* they would have noted that a total of 126 women were listed as LDA deaconesses, and 91 out of 126 is an impressive (72 percent) majority. However, closer scrutiny of the specific names printed with the petition provides a very different picture. Nine of the signatories were identified with the prefix *Deaconess Intern* rather than Deaconess. Since deaconess interns were still students in training, in order to be correct, the *MIP* headline should have read, "82 Deaconesses, 50 Students." Furthermore, when a comparison is made between the eighty-two "deaconess signatures," and the names of women included in the official directory of LDA deaconesses found in the 1974 *Annual,* only fifty-one of the eighty-two women who signed the petition as deaconesses are listed in the *Annual.*[26]

So where did the other thirty-one names come from? The answer is two-fold. Eight of the deaconesses had just graduated from Valparaiso University in 1974, and hence, *The Lutheran Annual* did not yet list their names. The other twenty-three women had been consecrated as deaconesses, but no longer fit into any of the four categories that would

---

[22] "Persons Asked to Make the Calls for Signatures," bottom half of mimeographed page (the top half contains the petition), priv. col. of Joyce Ostermann, Fort Wayne, Ind.
[23] The author saw this petition on the notice board at Deaconess Hall.
[24] "We Can No Longer Remain Silent, Say 91 Deaconesses, 41 Students," *Missouri in Perspective,* November 4, 1974, ELIM, St. Louis, 3. On November 11, 1974, *Christian News* reprinted all of page three of *Missouri in Perspective.* "We Can No Longer Remain Silent, Say 91 Deaconesses, 41 Students," *Christian News,* November 11, 1974, Lutheran News Inc., New Haven, 8.
[25] There appears to have been no effort made to contact students enrolled in the pre-deaconess programs at LCMS colleges to invite them to add their names to the petition.
[26] "Lutheran Deaconess Association," *The Lutheran Annual* (St. Louis: Concordia, 1973), 354-56; "We Can No Longer Remain Silent, Say 91 Deaconesses, 41 Students," 3.

have caused the LDA to list them as deaconesses in the *Annual*. In other words, the LDA considered none of the twenty-three women to be (1) a deaconess with a call, (2) a deaconess candidate available for a call, (3) a deaconess in graduate study, or (4) an emeritus deaconess.[27]

At this point some conclusions may be drawn. First, since only 51 of the 126 deaconesses (40 percent) listed in the 1974 *Annual* "signed" the deaconess petition, in spite of an aggressive campaign to affix all possible names to the document, there is reason to believe that support for John Tietjen *among working LCMS deaconesses* was not as strong as the petition writers or *MIP* headline writer would have liked the public to believe.

Furthermore, a strong link existed between the theological culture and influence of Valparaiso University and the majority of the signatories. As explained above, fifty students and eight women who had just graduated from Valparaiso "signed" the petition. Of the remaining seventy-four women whose names appeared with the petition, sixty-four graduated from Valparaiso University during the previous fourteen years, from 1960 to 1973.[28] It must also be noted that four of the deaconesses who signed the petition were closely associated with the deaconess training program at Valparaiso: Janice Orluske was a member of the LDA Board of Directors; Louise Williams and Vanette Kashmer had offices in Deaconess Hall and served the LDA as Director of Deaconess Services and Field Work Advisor, respectively; and Gwendolyn Sayler was a professor of Theology at Valparaiso University.

DISQUIET IN THE RANKS . . .

The LDA received several letters in reaction to the *MIP* article.[29] Both clergy and laity, loyal to the Missouri Synod and desirous of an end to the moderate influence in their Synod, asked questions about the LDA and its training program. Of course, some Valparaiso students made a deliberate

---

[27] "Listing of Deaconesses in Lutheran Annual," Resolution number 28 in *Lutheran Deaconess Conference Major Resolutions from 1970ff Printed in Chronological Order*, 15 mimeographed pages, priv. col. of Ruth (nee Broermann) Stallmann, St. Louis, Missouri, 6.

[28] The remaining ten signatories graduated between 1952 and 1959. None of the deaconesses in the *Annual* who had graduated between 1924 and 1951 signed the petition. (Graduation years are indicated in the *Annual*. For women who were not listed in the *Annual*, graduation years were confirmed by comparing names from the petition to a list of deaconesses (See Appendices 1.E. and 1.F.) provided by the LDA.

[29] Jacqueline Haug, "Minutes of the Executive Committee Meeting of the Lutheran Deaconess Association December 5, 1974," Box: Board for Professional Education Services Box 5: Deaconess Materials and BHE Materials, found loose at front of box, CHI, St. Louis, Missouri, 2.

decision not to sign the petition. And there were deaconesses in the field who refused to allow their names to be added to it. Some of those deaconesses already felt uneasy about the way that their sisters in Christ embraced tenets of the Women's Liberation Movement, pursued pan-Lutheran or ecumenical activities, and adopted principles of Biblical interpretation in line with the *Historical-Critical Method* infiltrating the Synod.[30] Over a period of about ten years, these women tried to temper what they saw as a gradual move away from traditional Missouri Synod doctrine and practice among their sisters at annual LDC Conferences as well as the smaller area deaconess conferences. In August 1971, five of the deaconesses invited Executive Director Lucille Wassman to meet with them over a turkey dinner in Munster, Indiana. Wassman listened politely to the women, asked many questions and appeared to be sympathetic, but nothing concrete ever came of the meeting.[31]

In the wake of the 1974 deaconess petition, one of the concerned deaconesses wrote to her District President, who was also responsible for ecclesiastical supervision of the LCMS clergy in Valparaiso. In early spring 1975, Indiana District President Elwood Henry "Woody" Zimmermann (1919–2006) and Rev. Carl Willard Baringer (1921–1981), Executive Secretary of Missions and Church Extensions for the Indiana District, met together with LDA President Peters, LDA Acting Executive Director Williams, and VU Department of Theology Chairman Keller, regarding issues related to deaconess training and formation. Though cordial and

---

[30] The phrase Historical-Critical Method refers to "a professional type of Scripture study which involves work with the Biblical text in it original languages and the use of the investigative procedures termed textual criticism, literary criticism, historical criticism, form criticism, redaction criticism, and content criticism. While the various 'criticisms' may be considered separately and selectively employed, faithful practitioners of the historical-critical method normally employ these investigative techniques in conjunction, as they work with the text of the Bible." Walter A. Maier, *Form Criticism Reexamined*, Contemporary Theology Series, St. Louis, Concordia, 1973, 7. Johann Salomo Semler is usually named as the father of the historical-critical approach to the Bible, ". . . the technique which not only handles the Bible as an object for historical scrutiny and criticism, but also as a book little different from and no more holy than any other, and surely not to be equated with the Word of God." Gerhard Maier, *The End of the Historical-Critical Method*, St. Louis, Concordia, 1974, 8.

[31] Most notably, the deaconesses who spoke up at LDC annual conferences included Clara Strehlow (graduate of Watertown, 1927), Martha Boss (Fort Wayne, 1938), Martha Eber (Fort Wayne, 1929), and Betty Mulholland (VU, 1955). Julia Hennig (VU, 1955), Ruth Broermann (VU, 1955), Mildred Brillinger (VU, 1956), and Luella Mickley (VU, 1959) also shared their common concerns at meetings of the Chicago Area Deaconess Conference. It was the latter five women who met with Wassman. "Meeting of Concordia Deaconess Conference founding members," July 28—August 1, 2003, Fort Wayne, Indiana, tape recordings, priv. col. of CDN, Pittsburgh, Pa.

"non-confrontational," the meeting gave the LDA Plenary Board some serious food for thought.[32] Following the meeting, Zimmermann replied to the concerned deaconess:

> Dear Betty,
>
> Thanks for your letter. You may have heard that we spent a little time with Professor Peters, Professor Keller, and Deaconess Louise Williams, and discussed the deaconess program with them.
>
> I think it would be very well for the Deaconess Association to determine what kind of relationship it wants with Synod. Presently Synod supports the Deaconess program in word, if not always with hard cash. Much of the solicitation for funds, however, is carried on within The Lutheran Church—Missouri Synod, and the Placement Committee of Synod promotes calls for Deaconesses.
>
> I think that the bond could be strengthened measurably if the Deaconess Association were wholly supportive of the Synod. I also believe that a move to divorce the Deaconess Association from the Lutheran Church—Missouri Synod, or to expand into a Pan-Lutheran association, would hurt the program and perhaps cause Synod to establish a counter-program in one of the present system schools. This, of course, is said off the record and reflects only my thinking.
>
> I really appreciate your wonderful support and fine spirit of cooperation. May the Lord continue to bless you in your ministry and enrich the lives of many through you.
>
> Cordial greetings in Christ,
>
> E. H. Zimmermann[33]

---

[32] Elwood Zimmermann, notes from telephone interview by CDN, July 12, 2006, priv. col. of CDN, Pittsburgh, Pa. The LDA Plenary Board minutes for April 10, 1975, recorded: "Meeting with Zimmermann and Baringer: . . . Curt stated that after the LDA representatives re-affirmed our faith in the theology department at Valparaiso the issue was dropped. Curt and Louise both felt that these issues will probably not be brought up again in their present form, and also reported that the letter from the deaconess community regarding the dismissal of John Tietjen or the intern at Beatty Hospital were not discussed at the meeting. It was hinted that the Synod, if displeased, could do something about it, such as discourage congregations from having deaconesses, make placement difficult, establish administrative control over the LDA, or establish a competing program. It was reported that a memorial is being presented at Anaheim to expand Ann Arbor's deaconess program from two years to four years." Sue Wendorf, "Minutes of the Plenary Board Meeting of the Lutheran Deaconess Association, Deaconess Hall, Valparaiso, Indiana, April 10, 1975," Box: Board for Professional Education Services Box 5: Deaconess Materials and BHE Materials, found loose at front of box, CHI, St. Louis, Missouri, 1.

. . . AND AMONG THE STUDENTS

Like several deaconesses in the field, some deaconess and pre-deaconess students at Valparaiso University did not agree with the moderate theological position embraced by the majority of their peers and professors. The minutes of the LDA Board of Directors meeting held in October 1975, for example, record the dissention of one of the women who served her internship during the 1975–76 school year.

> A letter from a deaconess intern was read, in which it was suggested that this Board seriously consider an alternative to Valparaiso University for deaconess education, specifically at Ann Arbor. Gwen Sayler responded on behalf of the Theology Department to charges that there is undue pressure from some members of the Department to conform to the "moderate" position within the Synod. It was felt that although this may happen on rare occasions, the Department is generally very conscious of not applying pressure for any position, particularly in the classroom. It was suggested that open discussions of the Synodical situation be held in the dorm so that all sides may receive a fair hearing. The suggestion for a Concordia-Ann Arbor alternative was discussed by the Board and respectfully declined at this time for a number of reasons. It was suggested that the letter be shared with the Theology Department without revealing the author of the letter.[34]

Under "Staff Reports" in the same set of minutes, the LDA secretary recorded "questions and comments" arising from the two-page written report submitted by Acting Executive Director Williams. These comments expose some interesting developments in the thinking of Board members.

> - A question was raised whether the LDA Board should act or react in articulating our identity. The point was made that we are first of all servants of God to His Church, and that our precedence of sisterhood in ministry is long-standing.
>
> - There is a strong job-orientation among present students; we are caught in the middle between wanting students to take responsibility in searching out job situations and providing them with enough job choices from

---

[33] Letter from President E. H. Zimmermann to Deaconess Betty Mulholland, April 21, 1975, priv. col. of Betty Mulholland, Munster, Ind.

[34] The minutes show that (Professor/Deaconess) Gwen Sayler attended the meeting in the stead of Theology Department Chairman Keller, an advisory member of the Board. Sue Wendorf, "The President's Report, Minutes of the Board of Directors Meeting of the Lutheran Deaconess Assoc. October 3-4, 1975," Box: Board for Professional Education Services Box 5: Deaconess Materials and BHE Materials, found loose at front of box, CHI, St. Louis, Missouri, 2.

which to choose. This job-orientation in students is often regarded by them as being in opposition to a sense of vocation.

- Is it mutually exclusive to define our identity in terms of either community or tasks? It was felt that both approaches contribute to our sense of identity and ministry.

- Is the church ready to receive our ministries? We in many ways prepare women for a ministry which is not readily accepted for the most part by the church.

- We need to think ahead to the 21st century, only 25 years away. The diaconate has been the only option open to women with a desire to minister within the church, but the ordination of women opens new avenues. How, if at all, are we preparing for this situation?

- Jan pointed out that we struggle in all these things often without the church's blessing, and we do not fully realize how profoundly we miss that blessing.[35]

Sadly, there were women who wanted to remain within the blessing of the church, but feared that they might not if they followed their dream of becoming deaconesses. As it became widely known that members of the diaconate and other individuals associated with VU supported John Tietjen, ELIM, and Seminex, many pre-deaconess students on LCMS college campuses chose to transfer to other church-worker programs rather than finish their education at Valparaiso. Other women, though warned by their conservative professors about the "bad theology" that they would be subjected to at Valpo, decided that their dream was worth the risk. One of these women—a senior in Deaconess Hall during the 1975–76 academic year—described her personal experience to the author.

I transferred from Ann Arbor to Valparaiso because becoming a deaconess was the only career path open to a woman in the church who was interested in studying theology. But I became rather disenchanted with the whole thing by the end of my internship. Theology was not the "path to God" I had hoped, Valpo was not the faith-enriching place I had sought, and the deaconess program would not lead me to find my vocation. During my internship year, I realized my gifts lay more in the area of teaching, so decided to pursue a teaching certificate instead of being consecrated as a deaconess.

The incident that best sums up my disenchantment with the deaconess program at Valpo occurred during my senior year. We were required to

---

[35] Wendorf, "The President's Report, Minutes of the Board of Directors Meeting of the Lutheran Deaconess Assoc. October 3-4, 1975," 1.

write a sermon and deliver it in the Deaconess Hall chapel. I wrote something based on a text in Matthew. As soon as I got up to preach, the ludicrous nature of the event just struck me. Five words weren't out of my mouth when I started laughing and couldn't stop. I must have laughed for five minutes straight. I tried to look at my notes and just read, but as soon as I looked up at the congregation of five suffering souls before me, I'd start laughing again. I just wanted to yell, "This is absurd." Perhaps it was at that point I realized I'd never be a deaconess. To me, a deaconess is a humble servant, not a pretender to the role of preacher or pastor, which is what we were being groomed for at Deaconess Hall.

I wanted to find out what it means to be a woman of God, to find my vocation. I loved the motto of the deaconess program, "Faith and Service in Christ," but felt betrayed when I came to see that there being a deaconess really had nothing to do with faith or service to Christ, but that it was about service to women and promoting women's causes. I didn't see that anything we were asked to do was in any way focused on true service. It was all about "what's in it for women?" It was Christian feminism—which, it seems to me, is an oxymoron. If I had to sum up my experience with the LDA, I would say that I felt betrayed. I was led to believe that being a deaconess was something that it was not. I came sincerely, wanting to serve. Instead, I was given feminism. And that's a serious betrayal.[36]

In addition to the feminism prevalent within the walls of Deaconess Hall, students needed to cope with the new ways of examining Scripture that they encountered in VU classrooms. Many theology professors believed that the Historical-Critical Method offered a valid approach to the study of Scripture and assigned students to write and do exegesis using that method. The third use of the law, as explained in Martin Luther's *Small Catechism*, was often discredited and replaced with a moderate formula for behavior. Students who grew up in conservative Christian homes and parishes were seldom indifferent to these new ideas, but found them either refreshing or completely repugnant. For the latter, it was still necessary to follow the maxim: *cooperate and graduate.*

DISTRICT CONVENTIONS

In summer 1976, when the Missouri Synod's biennial district conventions convened, the South Wisconsin District and Iowa District West both

---

[36] Interview of Kathryn (nee Baehr) McDonald by CDN and Nancy E. Nemoyer, June 16, 2006, Bedford, Pa., transcript, priv. col. of CDN, Pittsburgh, Pa.

adopted resolutions related to the training of deaconesses. The Wisconsin
resolution read:

> WHEREAS, Through the years many congregations and other ministries
> have been blessed by the faithful service of Lutheran Deaconesses, and
>
> WHEREAS, At the present time The Lutheran Deaconess Assn. is in
> need of leadership in order to take a meaningful place in the ministry of
> the LCMS; therefore be it
>
> RESOLVED, That the South Wisconsin District petition the Synod at its
> Dallas Convention to direct the President of Synod to appoint a
> committee to evaluate the Lutheran Deaconess Training Program at
> Valparaiso University, and to explore the possibility of establishing a
> deaconess program in one of our Synodical institutions; and be it further
>
> RESOLVED, That this committee report its findings to the 1979
> Synodical Convention.[37]

And the resolution passed at the Iowa convention read:

> WHEREAS, There is concern about the training of deaconesses on the
> campus of Valparaiso University where they are influenced by the
> theology being taught; and
>
> WHEREAS, There is no synodical control over Valparaiso University;
> and
>
> WHEREAS, There is ample evidence that the theology taught at
> Valparaiso University is not in accord with the official doctrine of the
> LCMS; therefore, be it
>
> RESOLVED, That the Iowa District West in convention express its
> concern with the deaconess program in our Synod; and be it finally
>
> RESOLVED, That we petition Synod's Board for Higher Education to
> look into this matter and resolve this problem either by moving the
> program to one of our Synodical campuses or by being assured by
> Valparaiso University that it will conform to our Synodical teaching.[38]

As inferred by both of the above resolutions, the church began to take
a look at whether or not the training of deaconesses as workers within the
LCMS should continue to take place at an institution of higher learning that
was neither supervised by nor answerable to the Synod. No evidence
suggests that the LDA made any public response to the action taken by the

---

[37] "Resolution 15-01: To Evaluate the Lutheran Deaconess Program (Overture 15-1, CW
p.85; Overture 15-8, CW p.100)," in South Wisconsin District LCMS, *Proceedings*, 1976, 93.
[38] "Deaconess Program," in Iowa District West LCMS, *Proceedings*, 1976, 89-90.

two Missouri Synod districts. However, Director of Deaconess Services Louise Williams did mention the district resolutions when addressing the LDC conference three weeks later.

> Church Relations. Of concern to all of us has been the Anaheim Convention and its aftermath—the dismissal of the district presidents, the formation of the AELC and English Synod, and the increasing tension and fragmentation within the LCMS. It is not always easy to discern the implications of all of this for us. Certainly *the position of the LDA has been to seek to serve as much of the Lutheran Church as possible* and to be agents of reconciliation and renewal in our ministry to all God's people. This will be increasingly difficult as the institutional church fragments and as there is increased emphasis in some circles upon control and proper certification. This summer at their conventions both the South Wisconsin and the Iowa West districts passed resolutions raising concerns about the training of deaconesses taking place outside LCMS control. All of this has potential implications for funding, recruitment, placement, and deaconess status. The next month (perhaps even couple of years) will be crucial for us. . . .[39]

CHANGES IN THE DEACONESS DIPLOMA

Although it makes sense to assume that the LDA always issued some sort of a deaconess diploma to women who finished their training, the first evidence of a diploma is found in a photograph of the 1934 Watertown graduating class, where all of the women are holding the diplomas that had just been presented to them.[40] Since the author has not found any deaconess diplomas awarded to women who attended the schools in Hot Springs, Beaver Dam, Watertown, or Fort Wayne, no comment can be made about the content of those documents. However, several diplomas issued to women who graduated from Valparaiso University have been found. The earliest of these, dated June 10, 1952, reads:[41]

---

[39] Louise Williams, "Director of Deaconess Services Report—Annual Deaconess Conference, July 11-14, 1976," Box: CDC, File: LDC 11-14 July 1976, CHI, St. Louis, Missouri, 3.

[40] Photograph, *TLD* 11, no. 3 (July 1934): 2.

[41] The picture of Christ, placed between the two sentences on the third line, showed only the head of Christ on the cross, wearing a crown of thorns. Dolores Jean Hackwelder, Oakmont, Pa., showed this diploma to the author; Hackwelder donated her diploma to Concordia Historical Institute, St. Louis, in 2005.

DIPLOMA

Lutheran Deaconess Association

Within the Synodical Conference

This I did for thee. (picture of Christ) What wilt thou do for me?

To all whom these presents concern, greeting!

Be it known by these presents that

Miss *Dolores Jean Hackwelder*

has satisfactorily completed the course of study prescribed by the Lutheran Training-school for Deaconesses at Valparaiso University and is hereby declared competent to render faithful service as a Lutheran deaconess.

May the Lord richly bless her labors of love!

(signatures of four LDA officers and Superintendent)

June 10, 1952

Sometime before 1969, the text of the deaconess diploma changed to the following wording:

In the Name of the Father

And of the Son

And of the Holy Ghost

_____[name]_____

has fulfilled the requirements established by

The Lutheran Deaconess Association

And Valparaiso University

And is awarded this diploma to signify

That she is eligible to serve as a Deaconess in

The Lutheran Church-Missouri Synod

(date; signatures of LDA President and LDA Executive Director)

"Faith and Service in Christ"

Two changes in the wording are noteworthy. The former diploma indicated that a woman satisfactorily completed the training course as set out by the Lutheran Training-school for Deaconesses *at* Valparaiso University, whereas, the latter diploma attested that a woman had fulfilled the requirements set out by the LDA *and* Valparaiso University. Also, in keeping with the shift in language explained in chapter six of this book, the latter diploma style no longer mentioned the Synodical Conference, and specified that a woman could serve *in The Lutheran Church—Missouri Synod.*

Interestingly, in the summer of 1975, very shortly after the Deaconess Convocation adopted the working position paper called "Relationship of the Lutheran Deaconess Association to Organized Church Structures,"[42] the annual LDC conference passed a resolution asking the LDA to remove reference to the Missouri Synod from the diploma.

1975—DEACONESS DIPLOMA

WHEREAS some of our sisters serve in institutions, agencies, and parished [*sic*] which are not connected to the LC-MS and

WHEREAS the current diploma to graduates uses the language "The LDA certifies Deaconesses to serve in LC-MS" therefore be it

RESOLVED, That we recommend to the LDA Board that action be initiated to change the wording of the Diploma to make it more inclusive as to be in line with the recent changes of the LDA constitution."[43]

At the following LDC conference held in July 1976, Deaconess Williams indicated that she and the LDA Board of Directors listened to the concerns of deaconesses in the field, and acted in harmony with the wishes of those women and the LDC as much as possible. Williams reported,

The Deaconess Services and Renewal (DS&R) Committee of the LDA has begun to work on some of the issues that have been raised by and about deaconesses. What is consecration? How does it relate to other rites of the church such as ordination, commissioning, etc? Should deaconess candidates be consecrated without a "call"? What is the relationship between certification, consecration, and placement and how do we relate to official church structures (Council of Presidents, etc.) here? May deaconesses be ordained to the pastoral office and remain deaconesses? What is and what should be the status of deaconesses who are not members of Lutheran congregations? Again the committee members will

---

[42] See section titled "Relationship to Other Synods" in Chapter 10.
[43] "Deaconess Diploma," Resolution number 59 in *Lutheran Deaconess Conference Major Resolutions from 1970ff Printed in Chronological Order,* 15 mimeographed pages, priv. col. of Ruth (nee Broermann) Stallmann, St. Louis, Missouri, 15.

be listening to you during this conference and will welcome your comments on these issues. I know that many of you have been thinking about these things and perhaps have been discussing them with others. Your written comments will be of special value to the committee in its deliberations.

Last year's [LDC] conference referred several items to the LDA. 1. The wording of the Deaconess Diploma has been revised to read as follows: "In the Name of the Father and of the Son and of the Holy Spirit. _____ has fulfilled the requirements established by the Lutheran Deaconess Association and is awarded this diploma to signify that she has been consecrated as a Lutheran deaconess and is eligible to serve as a deaconess in the Lutheran Church." 2. The DS&R Committee will recommend to the LDA Board the following regarding the status of non-Lutheran deaconesses: "Generally, women who are not members of a Lutheran parish cannot be members of our diaconate. Exceptions might be made in some cases, but the burden of justifying the exception would be on the deaconess making the request to remain in our diaconate.[44]

It is fascinating to see how the LDA acquiesced to the LDC, eliminating references to the Missouri Synod (and also to Valparaiso University) in the text of the deaconess diploma. But updating the diploma really only brought it in line with current practice. Several women already worked in ALC congregations, and some served the LCA. Copies of *The Lutheran Annual* published in 1973 and 1974 note "ALC" next to the workplace of one of the deaconesses, which would not have been considered unusual, given that the Missouri Synod entered into Pulpit and Altar Fellowship with the ALC in 1969. More interestingly, the 1975 *Annual* also included the information that two 1974 graduates served three "LCA" congregations.[45] A few years later, while deaconesses included in the *Annual* served LCA congregations, their entry details did not indicate that they served outside of the Missouri Synod.[46] How was this possible? Unlike the

---

[44] Williams, "Director of Deaconess Services Report—Annual Deaconess Conference, July 1976," 2.
[45] "Lutheran Deaconess Association," *The Lutheran Annual* (1973), 355; "Lutheran Deaconess Association," *The Lutheran Annual* (1974), 356; "Lutheran Deaconess Association," *The Lutheran Annual* (1975), 360, 362.
[46] Starting in 1978, "Deaconess Assignments" documents found in the minutes of the LCMS Council of Presidents indicate which deaconesses the LDA assigned to serve in ALC or LCA parishes. The Council of Presidents "Deaconess Assignments, 1977-78" shows two "Deferred Placements" (1976 graduates) going to LCA congregations, and "Deaconess Assignments, 1978-79" shows that the LDA placed five deaconesses in LCA congregations. These LCA congregations noted in the Council of Presidents documents are also listed in the *Annual* just like LCMS congregations, without being designated as LCA. "Deaconess

data for pastors and teachers, collected according to a particular format through the offices of LCMS District Presidents, the information about deaconesses published in *The Lutheran Annual* was submitted by the LDA and went to print without any editing.[47]

THE DISSENTERS MOBILIZE

Attending the 1976 Deaconess Conference in Valparaiso proved to be a disappointing experience for those attendees who did not appreciate worship led by clowns or the passing of resolutions that deliberately countered the doctrine and churchly practices of the Missouri Synod. One deaconess tried to speak to the Conference organizers about the worship, but was essentially brushed off, and then ignored. When she returned home, Betty Mulholland knew that she had to do something more. Her husband, Glenn, encouraged her to follow her heart and take action rather than just stewing about the problems. Betty telephoned another Chicago area deaconess, Ruth Broermann, and the women met to discuss and pray about the situation.[48]

Broermann and Mulholland decided that they should go to the LDA Board of Directors, to explain their dismay at the increasingly moderate nature of the diaconate and the training program, and to plead with the Board to take action to correct the problems. The deaconesses arranged to

---

Assignments, 1977-1978," binder: Official Copy Council of Presidents Minutes of 4/21-27/1978 Meeting 1) Agenda & Minutes 2) Inserts, Box: Council of Presidents Minutes May 1977—April 1981 Box #7, archive location: 111.1C.17, CHI, St. Louis, Missouri; "Deaconess Assignments, 1978-79," binder: Minutes—Council of Presidents Minutes, Minneapolis, Minnesota, March 6-8, 1979 & Minutes—Council of Presidents Fort Wayne, Indiana April 23-26, 1979, Box: Council of Presidents Minutes May 1977—April 1981 Box #7, archive location: 111.1C.17, CHI, St. Louis, Mo. See also *The Lutheran Annual* (1979 and 1980).

[47] Starting in 1975, every issue of *The Lutheran Annual* that included a section titled "Lutheran Deaconess Association," also included a note that read: "Please direct all changes in your listing to Lutheran Deaconess Association at the address above." In 1981, the format for the roster of deaconesses changed, omitting any mention of the LDA. In 1982, still with no mention of the LDA, a note was added: "Please address any changes in your listing to River Forest or Valparaiso." Starting in 1984, the note was altered to say that all changes should be forwarded to "your District President." Orville W. Richter, "Procedures for District Presidents," Department of Personnel and Statistics, The Lutheran Church—Missouri Synod, St. Louis, September 1978, Folder: Procedures for District Presidents, Department of Personnel and Statistics, September 1978, Box: Council of Presidents Minutes May 1977—April 1981 Box #7, archive location: 111.1C.17, CHI, St. Louis, Mo.

[48] Ruth (nee Broermann) Stallmann, Interview by CDN, transcript, St. Louis, Missouri, July 10, 2005, priv. col. of CDN, Pittsburgh, Pa.

meet with the Board early in fall 1976, but when the two women arrived at Deaconess Hall, they were told that LDA President Curtis Peters and Director of Deaconess Services Williams would listen to them over dinner at the Ponderosa Steakhouse in Valparaiso. Though disappointed that they would not be speaking to the whole Board, and that there would be no opportunity to answer questions from Board members, the deaconesses attended dinner with Peters and Williams.[49] Deaconess Emeritus (nee Broermann) Stallmann recalled:

> The two of them were cordial. I don't think I ate too much of anything. Betty did most of the talking and said that we had become aware of the trend of the deaconess conference toward ecumenicity; and also that, at that time, it was pretty well understood that becoming a deaconess might be the next step toward going for ordination. So we told them, since we were aware of it, that we thought this was contrary to Biblical principles. They didn't seem to be shocked by what we said, but they didn't go along with it either. Their responses indicated that they didn't believe there was anything wrong with what had happened at the deaconess conference. Again, they told us that we could not go to the Board meeting but that they would take what we had said to the Board.

> Betty and I had taken a lot of time—a number of hours on consecutive Saturdays—to prepare accurate documentation that would serve as evidence for what we saw happening in both the LDA and the LDC. The first part of that was looking through our files, and asking others for any papers that we didn't have, to put together a full set of minutes from previous years. Then we studied those minutes, decisions and resolutions, and traced the problems. We didn't want to use our own words to make any accusations. We simply quoted their own official papers, literally cutting and pasting from the minutes and resolutions that were typed on their own typewriters, so that we ended up with a collection of sequential evidence. When we finished, the documentation showed beyond a shadow of a doubt how things in the LDA and the LDC were moving further and further away from what we believed as Missouri Synod Lutherans. At the dinner in Valparaiso, we didn't hide anything. We told them how we had created the documentation and that we were planning to give each deaconess a copy. And so, when we got home, we mailed the documentation to every deaconess in LDC.[50]

---

[49] Stallmann, Interview by CDN.; Betty (nee Schmidt) Mulholland, Interview by CDN, July 25, 2005, priv. col. of CDN, Pittsburgh, Pa.

[50] Stallmann, Interview by CDN. See also, Letter from Betty Mulholland to Rev. Curtis Peters, October 6, 1976, priv. col. of Betty (nee Schmidt) Mulholland, Munster, Ind.

On September 18, 1976, before the women posted letters to every deaconess, Mulholland sent the documentation, along with a letter and a petition, to the LCMS BHE. She also mailed courtesy copies to LDA staff members; presidents of the LDA and LDC; the president of the Indiana District; and the president of the Missouri Synod.[51] Mulholland's cover letter explained,

> Gentlemen,
>
> This letter is being written as an introduction to the status of the deaconess program—both in the past and currently—and its relationship to the LC-MS.
>
> Historically, the diaconate within the LC-MS has always been synodically supportive and theologically conservative. Within the past twenty years it has become more and more moderate and now evidences a pan-Lutheran and ecumenical posture.
>
> The changes—some of them insidious—have horrified some of us who are under the umbrella of the diaconate.
>
> Enclosed are the following items:
>
> 1. A petition signed by active LC-MS deaconesses, asking the BHE to take the deaconess training program under its umbrella.
>
> 2. A resume of officially approved statements/resolutions of the Lutheran Deaconess Association and the Lutheran Deaconess Conference that show the gradual transitional status of being totally Missouri to the current posture of being all things to all men.
>
> 3. The documentation for the resume.

---

[51] Mulholland sent a separate letter to her district president ten days before the others, in which she implied that she was concerned that the LDA might remove her from the diaconate. She wrote, ". . . President Zimmerman, this is a plea that you study the various documents. If you feel our request is justified, we would like to be assured that Synod will find a place for those of us who have tasted and found that serving the Lord as a deaconess is a delightful experience. Perhaps our continuing to serve Him and providing an avenue for training others to share in the joy of serving Him as deaconesses can best be done thru a newly developed diaconate program by the L.C.M.S." Letter from Betty Mulholland to Rev. E. H. Zimmerman, September 8, 1976, priv. col. of Betty (nee Schmidt) Mulholland, Munster, Ind.

... Copies of the petition, resume and documentation are being sent with a cover letter to all active LC-MS deaconesses, asking them to react pro/con directly to the BHE. ...[52]

Five deaconesses signed the petition Mulholland referred to in her cover letter, which asked the BHE "to assume responsibility for the development and ongoing support of a deaconess training program," to facilitate changes in the synodical bylaws in order to place deaconesses under the supervision of district presidents, to choose one of the centrally located LCMS colleges to house a training program, and to consider providing separate housing for student deaconesses in some sort of a "deaconess house/dorm/hall."[53]

On September 22, 1976, the papers sent to the BHE were mailed to every Missouri Synod deaconess. The short accompanying letter read:

Dear Sister Deaconesses,

Enclosed is the material which we have sent to the BHE. If you are in agreement with the petition and wish to join us, please sign your copy and forward it to the BHE.

If, on the other hand, you feel strongly about it and care to share your feelings with the BHE or us, please jot down your thoughts and send them.

The future of the diaconate program lies solely in the Lord's hands. Our prayer is that our petition is to the glory of God and for furtherance of His kingdom.[54]

The importance of the materials meticulously compiled by Broermann and Mulholland cannot be underestimated. Known simply as the *Documentation* and *Resume of the Documentation*, they sparked reaction and discussion among deaconesses, and provided added incentive for the BHE to re-open discussion on the education of deaconesses for the Missouri Synod. In the future, the *Documentation* would be given to convention floor committees, and to any pastor or layman who requested a copy, particularly in the months preceding the 1977 and 1979 synodical conventions. The

---

[52] Letter from Betty Mulholland to BHE, September 18, 1976, priv. col. of Mildred (nee Evenson) Brillinger, Noblesville, Ind.

[53] Petition to BHE, from Deaconesses Betty Mulholland, Ruth Broermann, Luella Mickley, Julia Hennig, and Mildred Brillinger, attached to: Letter from Betty Mulholland to BHE, September 18, 1976, priv. col. of Mildred (nee Evenson) Brillinger, Noblesville, Ind.

[54] Letter from Betty Mulholland to Sister Deaconesses, September 22, 1976, priv. col. of Luella Mickley, Chicago, Illinois.

complete text of both documents can be read in Appendices 1.I and 1.J of this book.

Back in the BHE's Court

Deaconess Mulholland accumulated three large black bags of mail in response to the *Documentation* mailed to all LCMS Deaconesses. It is unknown how many letters the BHE received, but Item 20 in the Board's minutes for November 1976 began with the statement: "Several interested persons have addressed the Board for Higher Education concerning the Lutheran Deaconess Program."[55] The minutes also indicated that the Board received the resolution adopted at the 1976 Iowa District West convention, as well as correspondence from Deaconess Betty Mulholland and President Zimmermann of the Indiana District. The record of discussion and action noted:

> The Lutheran Deaconess Association is an authorized auxiliary program of the Lutheran Church—Missouri Synod. As such it is an individually chartered organization and has a direct relationship with the synodical Board of Directors. The Board for Higher Education has no direct line of responsibility or authority with the Lutheran Deaconess Association.
>
> The Board for Higher Education resolved the following:
>
> a) That the board inform the various inquiring parties that the Board for Higher Education has neither responsibility nor authority in the operation of the Lutheran Deaconess Association.
>
> b) Concerns are to be addressed either to the synodical Board of Directors or to the 1977 synodical convention through overtures.
>
> c) That the inquiring parties be encouraged to submit overtures to the 1977 convention expressing their wishes and concerns about the Deaconess Association program.[56]

---

[55] BHE correspondence was rarely included with the record of the Board minutes. It appears that correspondence belonging to the BHE is no longer extant, unless it can be found among the boxes at CHI that still need to be catalogued. *BHE Minutes,* November 18-20, 1976, item 20, CHI, St. Louis, Missouri, 14.

[56] BHE Executive Secretary Arthur M. Ahlschwede wrote to Deaconess Betty Mulholland, informing her of the three points resolved by the BHE, using the identical words that appear in the minutes. *BHE Minutes,* November 18-20, 1976, item 20, CHI, St. Louis, Missouri, 14; Letter from Arthur M. Ahlschwede to Betty Mulholland, November 22, 1976, Box: CDC, File: Pre-CDC Correspondence, CHI, St. Louis, Mo.

It was now November 1976. The BHE had not taken any action in regard to the LDA since November 1968, and in the intervening eight years, all of the men who once sat on the Board had been replaced.[57] Whether the BHE consistently believed that nothing could be done to resolve the long-standing issues between the Missouri Synod and the LDA for all of those years, or whether it simply did not occur to the men to discuss the subject, is difficult to determine. At any rate, after a long respite from the deaconess question, the Board took the resolution from Iowa to heart, and BHE Chairman, Rev. Lewis Charles Niemoeller (1911–1999), appointed Rev. Philip C. Gehlhar (b. 1931) "to prepare a report and recommendations relative to the training of deaconesses for the church."[58]

GEHLHAR'S REPORT TO THE BHE

Gehlhar put a great deal of effort into carrying out his assignment, writing and/or speaking to the LDA, Valparaiso University, the LCMS Statistical Department, all of the deaconesses who had previously corresponded with the BHE,[59] and former LDA Executive Director Walter Gerken. His report included several exhibits: a comparison of course requirements at various

---

[57] Members of the BHE in 1968 were Albert Huegli (Chairman), Elmer August Neitzel (1912-1998), Elmer Pflieger, Arthur Lorenz Grumm (b. 1924), Richard H. Engebrecht (b. 1926), Adolph Rittmueller, and Martin E. Strieter. In 1976 they were Lewis Niemoeler (Chairman), Philip C. Gehlhar, Ronald W. Irsch, Arthur P. Brackebusch, Walter F. Brunn, Alvin W. Czanderna, and Ray D. Halm. Arthur M. Ahlschwede served as the BHE Executive Secretary from 1962 to 1980, but the BHE minutes for Nov. 1968 and Nov. 1976 do not show one way or the other whether he was present at the meetings. See *The Lutheran Annual* (St. Louis: Concordia) for 1969 and 1977.

[58] The appointment of Gehlhar took place at the November BHE meeting, but was not included in the minutes for that meeting. The November minutes were corrected regarding this point at the subsequent BHE meeting in January 1977. See *BHE Minutes,* January 28-30, 1977, item 3, CHI, St. Louis, Missouri, 2110. "Report on Deaconess Proposals," to Esteemed Collegues [*sic*] from Pastor Philip C. Gehlhar, January 14, 1977, filed with BHE minutes for March 10-12, 1977, CHI, St. Louis, Mo.

[59] Although there may have been additional letters, it is known that Gehlhar wrote to Deaconesses Mildred Brillinger, Ruth Broermann, Julia Hennig, Luella Mickley, and Betty Mulholland; and to a former Deaconess, Mrs. Barbara (nee Amt) Manske (VU, 1961). In each of these cases, the letters included the following request: "We would appreciate any help and information you can give us. Specifically, what are your ideas about the deaconess ministry; the types of program and training, the fields of service, any information you feel would be helpful. Could you make specific proposals as to what the program should be, where it should be and the goals to be reached? Your personal comments are very much in order and will be appreciated." Letter from (Mrs.) Barbara S. Ness, Secretary, to "Deaconess," December 8, 1976, Box: CDC, File: Pre-CDC Correspondence, CHI, St. Louis, Mo.

LCMS colleges; the latest published information on the LDA and deaconesses carried on the roster (written by Lucille Wassman in February 1973); and correspondence from concerned deaconesses.

The following section of Gehlhar's "Report on Deaconess Proposal," dated January 14, 1977, includes a statistical summary of the deaconess workforce, and helps the modern reader to see the issues and conclusions that were presented to the Board.

Since the LDA began in 1919, 457 women have been consecrated as deaconesses in the LC-MS. Times of service vary from one to fifty years; although minimum expected service is three years, most serve considerably longer. The 1977 Lutheran Annual lists 122 deaconesses serving in parishes, institutions, and missions, 41 Junior, Senior and special students are at Valpo, 32 interns are in the field, and 50 are in the pre-deaconess programs in the (LCMS) colleges. Many who were consecrated as deaconesses have married pastors or are serving in the church though not on the active deaconess roster today.

The number of women being consecrated in recent years is reported to have been declining, however specific statistics could not be obtained by this writing. The statistical yearbook has not included reports since 1972 (see Exhibit B).

The LDA set the following requirements for deaconesses:

1. A major in theology with a minimum of 36 hours of credit.

2. Two semesters of supervised field work which provide the opportunity for practical experience in ministry in parish and institutional settings in the Valparaiso area.

3. Twelve months of internship experience in which the student can learn about deaconess ministry as she translates theology into service. Since she is still a student, she is under special guidance from her supervisor and is in a reporting relationship with the director of Student Services of the LDA.

4. Residency in Deaconess Hall while matriculating at VU.

The pre-deaconess program at our Junior Colleges was approved by the San Francisco Convention in 1959. Comparing college catalogs of the Pre-Deaconess Program Requirements we found some variation. This variation does not concern the LDA but a student coming from a secular school may be required to take special courses in religion, usually in a summer session. The Valpo program offers no special courses just for deaconesses.

The proposal to place the training of deaconesses under the auspices and direction of the Synod through the BHE was proposed in 1962 by Rev. Walter Gerken. Pastor Gerken served as Executive Director of the Lutheran Deaconess Association from 1960 to 67. When frustrated over the trends in the LDA and his inability to bring it under the Synod's control, he accepted a call into a parish.

The information and proposals from Deaconesses Betty Mulholland, Mildred Brillinger, Julia Hennig, and Luella Mickley are included as Exhibit C.[60]

Possible reasons for the decline of the program and concerns raised throughout the Synod are:

1. Valparaiso and the LDA are not officially part of the Lutheran Church—Missouri Synod

2. The moderate theological position expressed by the Valpo faculty that has caused distrust

3. Radical positions on women's equal rights and liberation

4. Pre-deaconess students switch programs to remain in the system or in the same college

5. More radical among women's ministry devotees now have the option of ordination to pastoral office by going to ALC seminaries or to Seminex.[61]...

---

[60] The information touched on the various types of positions in which deaconesses could serve in the LCMS or in LCMS-related church agencies; the administration of a deaconess program; synodical schools; a professional deaconess organization; and consecration. Letter from Deaconesses Mildred Brillinger, Julia Hennig, Luella Mickley, and Betty Mulholland to Pastor Philip C. Gehlhar, January 11, 1977, four pages typed, priv. col. of Betty (nee Schmidt) Mulholland, Munster, Ind.

[61] It was commonly known that, upon graduation from VU, or even after having served as a deaconess, some women attended Seminex or other seminaries, many of them with a view toward becoming ordained pastors. The "Report of Director of Deaconess Services/Acting Executive Director" presented to the April 1975 meeting of the LDA Plenary Board stated: "Of the 14 women completing the field and academic requirements this spring and summer, 7 wish placement." Thereafter followed a list of 14 names, with future plans for each woman noted. One said, "plans to go to Seminex," another two, "graduate study," and "C.P.E." (Clinical Pastoral Education). At the same meeting, the LDA Plenary Board "accepted" a list of nine "Recommended Assignments for Further Discussion of Topics" for use at "LDA/LDC Joint Boards Meeting." The second topic included on the list was "Relationship of Rite of Consecration to Rite of Ordination." Sue Wendorf, "Minutes of the Plenary Board Meeting of the Lutheran Deaconess Association, Deaconess Hall, Valparaiso, Indiana, April 11, 1975," Box: Board for Professional Education Services Box 5: Deaconess Materials and BHE Materials, found loose at front of box, CHI, St. Louis, Missouri, 8, 11.

Conclusions:

1. There is a need for the type of ministry in the church that only a deaconess can perform. Many women feel a call to serve the Lord other than as a teacher or a parish worker. Offering an exciting deaconess ministry will reduce the pressure for women's ordination.

2. Responsibility for training of professional church workers should be the concern of the BHE. Unless the BHE accepts this responsibility for deaconess training, the program will remain a foster child. If present trends continue, the future of the program does not look bright.

3. There is no need to add special courses at any school to accommodate a Deaconess training program on the upper level of college. Present courses in theology, psychology, science, etc., can be taken by students in a deaconess program.

4. Supervision of deaconess work in the field is not the responsibility of the BHE. A deaconess should work under the authority of a pastor and of the District President. I see no need for a deaconess board other than officers to arrange for an annual conference.[62]

After finishing his report, Pastor Gehlhar presented his fellow board members with an overture that he felt would be appropriate for the BHE to send to the 1977 Missouri Synod convention:

Suggested Overture for the Dallas Convention

Whereas, The Scripture allows for and encourages Christian women in active service of the Lord when such service does not involve authority over men (Rom 16:1, I Cor 14:33-35, I Tim 2:11-15, Tit 2:3), and

Whereas, A number of young women continue to desire to serve the Lord in His Church in positions other than teacher or parish worker, and

Whereas, The Lutheran Deaconess program has offered an important service to the church in the past through consecration of 457 deaconesses, 211 [sic][63] of whom are serving in parishes, institutions and missions of the church, and

Whereas, The Board for Higher Education is responsible for training of professional workers of the Church through the colleges and seminaries, be it therefore

---

[62] "Report on Deaconess Proposals," to Esteemed Collegues [sic] from Pastor Philip C. Gehlhar, January 14, 1977, filed with BHE minutes for March 10-12, 1977, CHI, St. Louis, Mo.

[63] 211 should have been 122. See statistics in Gehlhar report above, or *The Lutheran Annual* (St. Louis: 1977), 353-355.

Resolved, That the Lutheran Church—Missouri Synod offer four years of deaconess training plus one year of internship through its four year colleges at Bronxville, St. Paul, and Irvine, and be it further

Resolved, That the Board for Higher Education establish and supervise the curriculum for such a program.[64]

The conclusions in Gehlhar's report and his overture would have been heartily applauded by the deaconesses who had been corresponding with the Board, if only those women could have seen those materials! Instead, because the BHE directed them to do so, the women—ignorant of the fact that they had at least one strong ally sitting on the BHE—began to investigate the manner by which overtures could be submitted to a synodical convention.[65]

MARKET RESEARCH

In March 1977, the BHE decided that a marketing study should be carried out to determine whether the LCMS truly needed deaconesses or diaconal ministry. Since only one hundred and four deaconesses had been placed during the previous eleven years, and the market for deaconesses was apparently shrinking in the Missouri Synod as well as in other denominations, the Board resolved "to table consideration of the desirability of proposing that a deaconess program be added to the list of approved professional church work programs."[66] When the Board examined the marketing research two months later, its tentative conclusion was not positive.

The following considerations continue to enter into the total situation:

a) At the recent placement 24 deaconesses were available; only five requests were submitted for deaconesses.

b) Few requests come from the congregations. The requests are submitted by retirement homes, schools for the deaf, etc.

c) These requests could be easily handled by teacher education graduates or parish workers.

---

[64] "Suggested Overture for the Dallas Convention," attached to "Report on Deaconess Proposals," to Esteemed Collegues [sic] from Pastor Philip C. Gehlhar, January 14, 1977, filed with BHE minutes for March 10-12, 1977, CHI, St. Louis, Mo.
[65] "Meeting of Concordia Deaconess Conference founding members," July 28—August 1, 2003.
[66] BHE Minutes, March 10-12, 1977, item 32; CHI, St. Louis, Mo.

d) It is possible that the day of the deaconess is past.

The consideration continues under study.[67]

It was just as well that the conservative deaconesses never received feedback from the BHE as to that Board's progression of thought—or this story may have finished right here! As it was, in spite of their ignorance of Gehlhar's report and the subsequent market study commissioned by the BHE, the women had moved full steam ahead into another course of action.

A Second Letter to the Diaconate

On January 16, 1977, Deaconesses Brillinger, Hennig, Mickley, and Mulholland sent a second packet to all active LCMS deaconesses. This time the envelope included a three-page overture adopted by St. Paul's Lutheran Church, Hammond, Indiana, and submitted to the 1977 LCMS Synodical convention, along with a copy of all materials sent to the BHE. In their cover letter the women noted,

> . . . Many of our sisters are happy and content with the present mood and desires of the diaconate. Some of our sisters are indifferent. And some of our sisters are of the same mind as we are. We ask only that all of you keep the Diaconate in your prayers and pray His will be accomplished. If you have the time, please respond to any of us, for we are interested in your thoughts. . . . [68]

The second letter again drew a plethora of responses touching on both sides of the issue. Some writers were angry and talked about betrayal of the sisterhood. Others agreed with the "Whereas" phrases of the overture but could not bring themselves to risk their membership or friendships in the diaconate.[69] And of course, some women wanted to get back to consistently

---

[67] According to the Council of Presidents document, "Deaconess Placement, 1976-1977," three women received assignments to congregations, one to Lutheran Social Services, and one to Lutheran Council for Community Action. Another 19 women were listed as "Awaiting Placement." Of the six women receiving "Deferred Placement" (from 1975-76), one was placed in a congregation and five were assigned to institutions. "Deaconess Placement, 1976-1977," *Minutes - Council of Presidents*. Box: Council of Presidents Minutes 1951- April 1977 Box #9, archive location 111.1C.17, CHI, St. Louis, Missouri; *BHE Minutes,* May 5-7, 1977, item 31; CHI, St. Louis, Mo.

[68] Letter from Deaconesses Brillinger, Hennig, Mickley, and Mulholland to Sister Deaconesses, January 16, 1977, priv. col. of Mildred Brillinger, Noblesville, Ind.

[69] Some of the milder letters are in the CHI archives; Glenn Mulholland insisted that his wife, Betty, destroy the more strongly worded letters addressed to her.

correct Biblical teaching and practice, even if it meant severing ties with the LDC and LDA. As always, one of the most encouraging letters came from Deaconess Emeritus Clara Strehlow, of Oshkosh, Wisconsin, who had become a real mentor to the women. On the same day that she received the second letter, Strehlow wrote:

> Dear Betty,
>
> My, o my, you are to be commended for the thought and effort put forth as evidenced by these papers, regarding a change in the training of deaconesses. The various points are covered in such a professional manner. "Well done."
>
> Your plan to meet personally with the chairman of the floor committee is very good. We know at each Synodical Convention numerous overtures are not brought to the floor for discussion. True some for lack of time, nevertheless, others for lack of understanding by the committee. . . . Our congregation has sent in an overture, to the Dallas Convention, nevertheless I want to share your papers with the doctrinal concerns committee of Trinity. These men are responsible for the overture from here. . . .
>
> Becoming involved makes one realize what is meant by "The Church Militant." I pray God may also call forth men/women to take up the torch to lead Valparaiso University back to the straight and narrow way.
>
> God grant you grace and wisdom, and guard you from becoming weary in well doing.
>
> In His service and love,
>
> Clara E. Strehlow[70]

When all congregations and members of Synod received the 1977 LCMS *Convention Workbook* in the first week of May, Overture 6-92A, "To Request the Synod to Assume Full Responsibility for the Office of Deaconess," was identical to the overture distributed in the deaconess mailing.[71] The *Workbook* cited a total of 13 congregations that submitted "identical or similar" overtures.[72] The ten "Whereas" paragraphs in

---

[70] See Chapters 5 and 6 for more information about Strehlow. Letter from Clara E. Strehlow to Betty Mulholland, January 19, 1977, priv. col. of Betty (nee Schmidt) Mulholland, Munster, Ind.

[71] In 1977, LCMS by-laws set the deadline for receiving overtures to be included in the *Convention Workbook* as 16 weeks before the convention, which would have been March 25, 1977; and the *Workbook* had to be mailed out by ten weeks prior to the convention, which was May 6, 1977. Pearl Houghten, office of the Secretary of Synod, notes from telephone interview by CDN, July 25, 2006, priv. col. of CDN, Pittsburgh, Pa.

[72] The 13 congregations included St. Paul Lutheran Church, East Chicago, Ind.; Trinity, Westville, Ind.; Good Shepherd, Gary, Ind.; St. Paul's, Hammond, Ind.; Grace, Muncie, Ind.; Faith, Green Bay, Wis.; Trinity, Hobart, Ind.; St. John, Calument City, Ill.; St. John's,

Overture 6-92A quoted heavily from the Broermann and Mulholland *Documentation*, and the six "Resolved" statements read:

> *Resolved,* That the Synod assume responsibility for the complete education of women preparing for the office of the deaconess; and be it further
>
> *Resolved,* That the location of such education be at one or more of the Synod's existing senior colleges; and be it further
>
> *Resolved,* That the Lutheran Deaconess Association be invited to maintain its past and historic close affiliation with The Lutheran Church—Missouri Synod, thus reversing its apparent drift toward pan-Lutheranism; and be it further
>
> *Resolved,* That the Synod invite the Lutheran Deaconess Association to identify with, support, and relate to the synodical education of deaconesses in an advisory capacity; and be it further
>
> *Resolved,* That in the event that the Lutheran Deaconess Association does not agree with the Synod's assuming responsibility for this important ministry of the church, the Synod shall nevertheless recruit, support, educate, and place in its congregations and agencies the young women who graduate from its colleges as Lutheran deaconesses; and be it finally
>
> *Resolved,* That the women serving The Lutheran Church—Missouri Synod and its affiliated synods and agencies be organized throughout the Districts of the Synod in conferences following the pattern of pastors and teachers.[73]

It should be noted that the congregations and deaconesses who submitted the above resolution desired to see the LDA return to its original relationship with the LCMS (as in the third *Resolved*). Furthermore, the fourth *Resolved* was only a mirror image of what the Missouri Synod already did for the LDA. For fifty-eight years, the LCMS had been expected to "identify with, support, and relate to" the LDA deaconess training program, with very little opportunity for input, since the LDA was an independent and autonomous auxiliary organization. It was a reasonable request that the LDA should now do the same for the LCMS, that is, to "identify with, support, and relate to" a synodical training program, "in an advisory capacity."

Geneva, Ohio; Guardian, Dearborn, Mich.; St. John, Bingen, Decatur, Ind.; St. Paul, Chesterton, Ind.; Memorial, Bremerton, Wash.

[73] "To Request the Synod to Assume Full Responsibility for the Office of Deaconess," Overture 6-92A, in LCMS, *Convention Workbook (Reports and Overtures),* 1977, 259.

OTHER RELATED OVERTURES

In addition to Overture 6-92 A (and 6-92B-6-92M), the 1977 *Workbook* also contained four other resolutions touching on the topic of deaconess training:

1. "To Evaluate the Lutheran Deaconess Program (6-93)," as adopted by the South Wisconsin District at its 1976 convention;

2. "To Study Deaconess Training Program (6-94)," from Christ Lutheran Church in Troy, N.H., which asked the BHE to seriously consider "the possibility of *moving* the deaconess training program from Valparaiso University" to a "synodical school;"

3. "To Introduce Deaconess Program at Ann Arbor (6-95)," submitted by the Board of Control and Faculty of Concordia College, Ann Arbor, Michigan, believing that their campus was ideally suited for a *completely new* synodical Deaconess Program; and

4. "To Discontinue Colloquy Program for Deaconess Ministry (6-96)," from the BOD Iowa District West. This last overture directed that the Council of Presidents no longer "place the applicants for the deaconess ministry," that the deaconess colloquy program be discontinued, and that the Synodical *Handbook* be changed accordingly.[74]

SPEAKING BEFORE FLOOR COMMITTEES

Once an LCMS *Convention Workbook* has been published prior to a convention, a number of synodical "floor committees" meet in St. Louis to study the submitted overtures and finalize the resolutions to be considered by convention delegates. These floor committee meetings are, therefore, punctuated by presentations from individuals or groups who desire to speak to the issues of a particular overture.

In May 1977, Deaconesses Millie Brillinger, Ruth Broermann, Julia Hennig, Betty Mulholland, and Clara Strehlow came from three different states to appear before Floor Committee Six. After a brief introduction, the women drew attention to half a dozen items in the *Documentation* and then answered questions.[75] LDA Director of Deaconess Services, Deaconess Louise Williams, also appeared before the same committee on a previous

---

[74] LCMS, *Convention Workbook (Reports and Overtures)*, 1977, 259-60.

[75] Millie Brillinger, Ruth Broermann, Julia Hennig, Betty Mulholland, Clara Strehlow, "Presentation to Floor Committee in Spring (May 1977) prior to Dallas Con.," hand-written presentation script, two pages, priv. col. of Betty (nee Schmidt) Mulholland, Munster, Ind.

day. In an account of her pre-convention and convention experiences, Williams wrote:

> As the official representative of the Lutheran Deaconess Association, I was granted one-half hour's time before Floor Committee #6 which had been delegated responsibility for the memorials concerning the Deaconess Program. For approximately 15 minutes I highlighted parts of my written report and then entertained questions. Several members of the committee asked information questions about the required course work and the appointment of professors to teach Theology at VU. President Karl Barth of the South Wisconsin District asked about the Deaconess Conference's "consistently passing resolutions contrary to the Synodical position." President Emil Jaech of the Northwest District made some lauditory [*sic*] remarks regarding the involvement of deaconesses in his district. (LDA Board Member Florence Montz and Dr. Walter Keller were also present while I appeared before the committee.) . . . Florence Montz also had an opportunity to talk with members of the sub-committee after they had met with these (opposing) deaconesses.

Apparently there was some sentiment within the committee to recommend that a program be started immediately at Ann Arbor or River Forest, but the committee's final recommendation was that the matter be studied by the Board for Higher Education and that a report be given to the 1979 convention.

At the beginning of the meetings of the floor committees, President Preus gave the first part of his presidental [*sic*] address. It included the following paragraph:

> "The overtures pertaining to the Deaconess program ought to be approached with great care. There are many, many serious questions regarding the whole matter of the Deaconess program, and before undertaking to remove it from Valparaiso and make it a fully synodical program, we need to consider very seriously exactly what the whole Deaconess program is seeking to accomplish. We need to know how much it will cost us in the situation where we don't have enough money even to support what we have. We need to decide whether it should continue to be a recognized church profession with Board of Assignment involvement and colloquy procedures. Therefore, I believe that this whole matter ought to receive further study throughout the whole church before being acted upon by the convention."[76]

---

[76] Louise Williams, "Report on the Resolution 'To Study Deaconess Training Program' (6-12)," August 1977, one page mimeographed on legal-sized paper, priv. col. of CDN, Pittsburgh, Pa.

Floor Committee Six submitted only one resolution to the Dallas convention as a result of the 17 overtures received from different quarters. Convention delegates adopted that resolution, designated 6-12, with a few minor changes. The convention *Proceedings* for 1977 recorded:

> WHEREAS, The ministry of deaconess is an important one in our Synod; and
>
> WHEREAS, The deaconess should have the best possible training; and
>
> WHEREAS, Concerns have been raised with the various aspects of the program; therefore be it
>
> *Resolved,* That the Board for Higher Education be directed to conduct a study to determine the best situation for the future training, colloquy, and placement of deaconesses; and be it further
>
> *Resolved,* That the Board for Higher Education report to the 1979 synodical convention with concrete recommendations.
>
> **Action:** *Adopted as amended (14).*
>
> (This action was taken after declining to consider a substitute motion to establish a deaconess program at Ann Arbor or River Forest. The committee added "placement" and the convention "colloquy" by amendment.)[77]

LDA Positions Confirmed

There is no evidence to show that LDA leaders ever tried to refute accusations that the Association (or the LDC) participated in pan-Lutheran and ecumenical activities. On the contrary, at the 1977 LDC meeting held in Kansas City, Missouri, a month after the Missouri Synod convention, LDA officials indicated that the organization was still moving steadily in the direction of becoming a pan-Lutheran organization. LDA President Phyllis Kersten told the conference:

> In response to the LDC Conference resolution passed last year, the LDA has sought to continue its autonomous, free-standing character. Conversations initiated with Missouri Synod leaders and Louise's presentation before the Dallas Convention Floor Committee emphasized the past and present service of deaconesses to the church at home and abroad, and expressed the LDA's hope and desire that the present synodical relationship could be maintained—with students educated in the

---

[77] "To Study Deaconess Training program, Resolution 6-12," in LCMS, *Proceedings,* 1977, 176.

deaconess training program at Valpo and receiving calls into LCMS parishes and institutions for placement through Synod's Board of Assignments. Communication at the same time is being initiated with other Lutheran diaconates and with the ALC, LCA, and AELC and its constituent synods—to explore possibilities of educating and placing deaconess students in their church bodies, and more importantly, of finding ways to highlight—and keep from getting lost in the shuffle of Lutheran organizational change—the ministry of diakonia.[78]

On the same day that Kersten addressed the conference, LDA Director of Deaconess Services Williams gave her report. Commenting on "Relations with Church Structures," she stated,

I did not personally attend any organizational meetings of the AELC,[79] but I asked several deaconesses to attend and to report pertinent information to us. In the spring I met with AELC president, Dr. William Kohn,[80] to discuss possible areas of cooperation. I also informed several synod presidents of the availability of deaconess candidates who wished to work within the AELC.

During the past year I have talked with leaders of the ALC and LCA diaconates and I have initiated contacts with the persons in those church bodies responsible for educating and placing church workers. To this point the contacts have been primarily to share information and to begin to isolate areas, if any, in which we might work together.[81]

Later in her report, touching on the work of the LDA Deaconess Services and Renewal Committee, Williams announced,

Using last summer's (LDC) conference resolution, the (LDA) Board (of Directors) adopted the following general statement of deaconess identity with the understanding that certain undefined elements of it are becoming more defined by the policy and usage of the LDA and LDC:

A deaconess is a Lutheran woman who after special Lutheran theological and practical training is consecrated to serve, which service is manifested in leadership roles and/or professional positions within the Lutheran

---

[78] Phyllis N. Kersten, "Report of the LDA President," 1977 Lutheran Deaconess Conference, August 17, 1977, mimeographed pages, Box: CDC, File: LDC 15-18 Aug. 1977, CHI, St. Louis, Missouri, 1.

[79] See footnote 15 in this chapter.

[80] Rev. William H. Kohn (1915-1992).

[81] Louise Williams, "Report of the Director of Deaconess Services to the Annual Deaconess Conference 8-17-77," mimeographed sheets, Box: CDC, File: LDC 15-18 Aug. 1977, CHI, St. Louis, Missouri, 2.

Church and/or society, *and who is in community with the Lutheran Deaconess Conference.*[82]

Affirming the work of the LDA on this point, the women in attendance at the 1977 annual Lutheran Deaconess Conference adopted this definition of a deaconess, adding a further *Resolved:* "That expressed concerns such as 'exit' policies, dues requirements, etc., be left for determination by the Lutheran Deaconess Conference Board with ratification by the membership."[83]

This was a milestone in both LDA and LDC history. The deaconess identity statement had many implications for the *LDA diaconate,* which, from this point onward, would be considered to be *exactly the same as the membership of the LDC.* A woman could be considered a deaconess *if* she was in community with the LDC, whether she served in one of the many Lutheran church bodies or in society. But she was not a deaconess if she was not "in community" with the LDC. In that regard, the statement or definition of deaconess identity sent a huge message to any dissenters: Wake up girls!—Even if you are working as LCMS deaconesses, if you leave the LDC, we will no longer recognize you to be deaconesses!

BHE Study Gets Underway

In keeping with Resolution 6-12 passed at the Missouri Synod convention in Dallas, the BHE made plans to "conduct a study to determine the best situation for the future training, colloquy, and placement of deaconesses." The Board's minutes for January 1978 record:

> Deaconess Betty Mulholland submitted a request to meet with the Board for Higher Education concerning the Lutheran Deaconess program. Concordia Teachers College, River Forest, directed a request for the program. Long ago, Concordia College, Ann Arbor, also asked for the program.
>
> The board resolved that both Deaconess Betty Mulholland and Deaconess Louise Williams be asked to make presentations at the March meeting which will be held at Saint Paul's College, Concordia, Missouri.

---

[82] Emphasis added. The first premise of a "Deaconess Study Paper" presented to the 1974 LDC meeting stated, "Consecration and Commitment to the Community Qualify a Woman to be a Deaconess." Northwest Area Deaconess Conference, "Deaconess Study Paper," mimeographed pages, priv. col. of CDN, Pittsburgh, Pa., 2. Williams, "Report of the Director of Deaconess Services to the Annual Deaconess Conference 8-17-77," 3.
[83] "Proposal for Membership Designation for the Lutheran Deaconess Conference," mimeographed pages, Box: CDC, File: LDC 15-18 Aug. 1977, CHI, St. Louis, Missouri, 1-2.

They are to state their vision for the deaconess program along with potential revisions. It was also indicated that the two should be scheduled on separate days for presentation.[84]

On March 16, 1978, Betty Mulholland and Julia Hennig appeared before the BHE to make a case for a deaconess program to be established at one LCMS college, under the complete supervision of the Synod. The following day, Louise Williams and LDA President Kersten spoke to the Board in favor of retaining the current arrangement, outlining the history of the LDA, and explaining the new LDA Study Project launched in fall 1977 to "determine future directions for the LDA and diaconal ministry."[85]

During their appointed time with the Board, Hennig and Mulholland jotted down 13 questions that they could not answer due to the time constraints of the Board's meeting agenda. Somewhat discouraged and frustrated, the women returned home. Mulholland requested more time at a future BHE meeting in order to answer questions, but her request was denied. Over the next several months, in consultation with other like-minded deaconesses, the women formulated answers to the questions posed by the Board and created a ten-page document titled *A Missouri Synod Deaconess Program*, which they sent to the BHE before its September 1978 meeting. The "Prologue" of the document mentioned the hope that the BHE would "recommend the development of a LCMS Diaconate at the St. Louis Synodical Convention in 1979," and was signed by Deaconesses Brillinger, Hennig, Mickley, Mulholland, and a younger graduate, Joyce Ostermann.[86]

---

[84] *BHE Minutes,* January 19-21, 1978, item 20; CHI, St. Louis, Mo. Regarding the request from River Forest, see: *BHE Minutes,* November 16-19, 1977, item 17; CHI, St. Louis, Mo.
[85] *BHE Minutes,* March 16-18, 1978, items 2, 3, CHI, St. Louis, Missouri; "Missouri Synod's B.H.E. Pressured on Deaconess Study," *LDC News,* mimeographed newsletter, Box: CDC, File: LDC News 1978-1979, CHI, St. Louis, Missouri, 2; Letter from Louise Williams to all deaconesses on "LDA Study," January 10, 1978, mimeographed copy, priv. col. of Nancy (nee Nicol) Nemoyer, Carlisle, Pa.
[86] Mildred Brillinger, Julia Hennig, Luella Mickley, Betty Mulholland, Joyce Ostermann, *A Missouri Synod Deaconess Program,* September 7, 1978, mimeographed pages, priv. col. of Joyce Ostermann, Fort Wayne, Indiana; Letter from Betty Mulholland to Members of the BHE, September 8, 1978, priv. col. of Joyce Ostermann, Fort Wayne, Indiana; Letter from Clara Strehlow to Betty Mulholland, April 19, 1978, priv. col. of Betty Mulholland, Munster, Indiana; Clara E. Strehlow, "Answers to Questions Asked by Members of BHE, March 1978," original typed page, priv. col. of Betty Mulholland, Munster, Indiana; Clara Strehlow, "Additions to or Explanation of 'Answers to BHE' Mar. 1978," original typed page, priv. col. of Betty Mulholland, Munster, Ind.

RECENT DEVELOPMENTS

Section four of *A Missouri Synod Deaconess Program*, titled "Recent Developments," focused on significant events that took place between March and September 1978. One of the items that the women chose to include in this section was a rundown of current activities related to the LDA self-study project that Director of Deaconess Services Williams mentioned in her March address to the BHE.

> At the present time, the Lutheran Deaconess Association continues with its study project. Scheduled for the summer and fall of 1978 are the following plans:
>
> "Specified goals:
>
> To determine what deaconesses are now doing
>
> To assess attitudes about the diaconate
>
> To solicit ideas about the future
>
> People involved:
>
> All LDA deaconesses, pastors of the LCMS and AELC, Church leaders and selected 'cutting edge' people.
>
> Methods:
>
> Survey of all deaconesses, a random sample of LCMS and AELC pastors and 100 interested 'cutting edge' people suggested by LDA Board and deaconesses.
>
> Scheduled interview of LCMS District presidents, AELC Synod presidents, top leaders of the 4 major Lutheran bodies, Valpo leaders and LCUSA.
>
> Consultation with identified thinkers in the Church. Groups of 10 or 12 key people will be invited for dinner and conversation about the diaconate in New York, Chicago, St. Louis, Minneapolis-St. Paul and San Francisco."
>
> The August 1978 newsletter of the LDA reports that Dr. Martin E. Marty met with the LDA Board of Directors in January 1978 to explore the question of what kind of diaconal ministry will the church of the future need.[87]

The above outline of study project plans was a direct quotation from a four-page document "The Annual LDC Conference Committee" sent to all

---

[87] Brillinger, Hennig, Mickley, Mulholland, Ostermann, *A Missouri Synod Deaconess Program*, 3.

deaconesses registered to attend the 1978 annual Deaconess Conference. The full document actually covered every step of the study process from "Fall '77" to "Fall '79," and included consultation with "cutting edge" thinkers known to hold opinions contrary to the official LCMS position on subjects like Seminex, ELIM, and the interpretation of Scripture.[88]

LDA leaders and members of the diaconate placed a great deal of confidence in the highly structured study project, but exactly how the results would be used in the shaping of diaconal ministry for the future was yet to been determined.[89]

Conflict at the 1978 Deaconess Conference

The other item mentioned under "Recent Developments" in *A Missouri Synod Deaconess Program* was an incident related to the June 25–28 LDC gathering in Valparaiso, where conflict ensued when deaconesses began to notice that the conference "Worship Folder" listed a woman as celebrant for the Wednesday morning Eucharist.[90]

> The Rev. Norma Jean Everist, ordained pastor of the American Lutheran Church and a deaconess of the Lutheran Church—Missouri Synod (page 369 of the 1978 <u>Lutheran Annual</u>), was scheduled to celebrate Holy Eucharist during the conference. However, due to unresolved tensions within the former purely Missouri Synod organization, The Rev. Everist

---

[88] The goals for the study project were also listed at the outset of the document: "1. To explore present and future unmet needs in the church and world as possible targets for <u>diakonia.</u> 2. To develop a contemporary theology of <u>diakonia</u> drawing from the Scriptural and historical roots. 3. To assess present and future resources (financial, human, institutional) for the diaconal task of the church. 4. To involve the church in the process, to inform it of the outcome, and to inspire it to greater commitment to <u>diakonia.</u> 5. To make the organizational decisions necessary to facilitate continued <u>diakonia</u> which responds to the contemporary wounds of the church and world. 6. To celebrate the 60th Anniversary of the LDA." The Annual LDC Conference Committee, "Restatement of Goals for the LDA Study Project;" "Timeline and Outline of Steps Completed or in Progress;" "Timeline and Outline of Future Steps;" mimeographed pages, priv. col. of Nancy (nee Nicol) Nemoyer, Carlisle, Pa.

[89] In a group of notes provided below the "Timetable and Outline of Future Steps," notes three and four read: "Specific plans still need to be developed for adequate use of the materials generated by futurists; Specific plans need to be refined for the on-going Theological study and discussion in which we want to involve both scholars and practitioners." Annual LDC Conference Committee, "Restatement of Goals for the LDA Study Project," 4.

[90] "Worship Folder, Lutheran Deaconess Conference June 25-28, 1978," mimeographed pages, Box: CDC, File: Luth. Deac. Conf. 25-28 June 1978, CHI, St. Louis, Missouri, 6.

was substituted by The Rev. Keith Klockau, a Missouri Synod pastor and a member of the Board of Directors of the L.D.A.[91]

On August 1, 1978, Lutheran Deaconess Conference President, Deaconess Evelyn Middelstadt, wrote to every member of the LDC to clarify why the conference committee chose to have a male celebrant at the 1978 conference Eucharist, even though the women in conference voted to proceed with a female celebrant. Middelstadt explained,

> . . . If the committee had decided on a majority based on numbers, the service would have proceeded as planned. Looking at the whole picture, however, made us reach the conclusion that the group wanted it possible for the greatest number of persons present to commune. The picture indicated a significant number of votes for a male celebrant. The idea of two celebrants was discussed extensively by the committee as a viable option, but was ruled out partly because it was a new and unclear concept, partly because very few voted for it and parly [sic] because it would not help the concern about the public relations issue. Incidentally, option number seven (to have only a Missouri Synod service) received no favorable votes and a number of strong negative votes.[92]

The August 1978 LDA Newsletter declared that the LDC gathering had been the largest ever summer deaconess conference at Valparaiso, with ninety-two deaconesses and guests in attendance, and that Deaconess Evelyn Middelstadt had been re-elected as president of the LDC.[93] The same newsletter also carried the news that Director of Student Services, Deaconess Vanette Kashmer, had resigned her post in order to "pursue educational and personal interests which have been impossible to handle while working as Director of Deaconess Services."[94] The LDA called Deaconess Middelstadt to be the Association's new Director of Student Services, and in December Middelstadt announced that she was "resigning the Presidency of the Conference" in order to take up the position.[95]

---

[91] Rev. Keith Wessel Klockau (b. 1929). Brillinger, Hennig, Mickley, Mulholland, Ostermann, *A Missouri Synod Deaconess Program.*

[92] No reference was ever made to receiving input from a pastoral advisor in relation to this decision. Middelstadt noted, "Committee members besides myself were Bev Grage, Karen Bakewicz, Mary-Anne Jungst and Kathy Borgman." "Letter from Evelyn Middelstadt to Lutheran Deaconess Conference," August 1, 1978, priv. col. of Nancy (nee Nicol) Nemoyer, Carlisle, Pa.

[93] "Conference," Lutheran Deaconess Association News (August 1978), 3.

[94] "Resignation," Lutheran Deaconess Association News (August 1978), 2.

[95] "New Director Called," *LDC News,* November 1978, mimeographed newsletter, Box: CDC, File: LDC News 1978-1979, CHI, St. Louis, Missouri, 4; "President's Notes," *LDC*

In fall 1978, sentiment about the LDC Eucharist incident still remained high, and the September issue of *LDC News* printed the following unsigned comments.

On Conflict

The conflict at conference over the Rev./Deaconess Norma Jean Everist's presiding over the conference eucharist [*sic*] was painful. It was personally painful to Norma Jean. It was painful to those sisters who are preparing for and seeking ordination. It was painful to the St. Louis area who had struggled with this question and thought they had made a wise decision. It was painful to those in our community who felt we had reached some consensus already on this matter. And it was painful to those in our community who felt a woman celebrant, however rightfully ordained was not appropriate.

It is important to note that most of the participants at conference voted to hold the Eucharist as planned with Norma Jean as celebrant. But as is often true in groups, individuals move much faster to change than a community. So the committee chose not to, at this time, affirm Norma Jean's right and privilege to serve as pastor.

Perhaps now, what we need more than anything is patience. Patience to realize that new concepts take time to be recognized and lived out, even among sisters. And patience, too, to wait on God's healing for all those who were hurt or disillusioned through this incident.[96]

A comparison between the above passage and others found in the early chapters of this book will reveal just how far the LDA diaconate had wandered from its historical moorings![97] Rather than patience, an increasing number of individuals believed that what the LDC and the LDA really needed was to return to a simple acceptance and understanding of Scripture as the true and inerrant Word of God, the rule and norm for Christian living. This would be a difficult task, given the influences that were continually brought to bear on deaconesses who understood themselves to be living "in community;" in a "sisterhood" that took precedence over Scriptural or doctrinal truth.

The subtle peer pressure that permeated the deaconess community played a large role in producing loyalty to the sisterhood and a commitment

---

News, December 1978, mimeographed newsletter, Box: CDC, File: LDC News 1978-1979, CHI, St. Louis, Missouri, 1.

[96] "On Conflict," *LDC News,* September 1978, mimeographed newsletter, Box: CDC, File: LDC News 1978-1979, CHI, St. Louis, Missouri, 8.

[97] See for example, the 1929 sermon on Psalm 119:105 by Rev. Wm. Naumann in Chapter 4.

to the concepts of tolerance and of diversity in unity, particularly in the area of theology. It is interesting to note, for example, that on August 1, 1978, not many weeks after the tumultuous LDC meeting, the following paragraph was included at the end of a letter sent to all deaconesses from LDA staff member Williams.

> Dear Theology Department Alumni:
>
> Your undergraduate major department is working to provide a special Homecoming for you this year before the general Homecoming festivities begin. For Friday the 13ᵗʰ of October, beginning at 1:30 p.m. in the Christ College Refectory, we have planned a program which includes a discussion on the pros and cons of women's ordination to the pastoral office led by Dr. Ted Jungkuntz[98] and me, followed by a panel and open forum. We are also planning a picnic supper for fun and sociability, . . . Please plan to come and experience a close encounter of the departmental kind.
>
> Your friendly neighborhood theology department chairman.
>
> Walter Keller[99]

A similar but briefer invitation also appeared in the September issue of the *LDC News.*[100]

How were deaconesses, as well as others associated with the Department of Theology, to respond to such invitations? Should they be pleased and interested in an opportunity to be brought up-to-date with the different strains of theological thought at their alma mater? Indeed, was it so necessary to be on the "cutting edge" of issues in order to be a good deaconess out in the field? However deaconesses might have answered these questions for themselves, an objective appraisal of the theological culture, teaching, and practice at VU and within the LDA diaconate, at that point in history, revealed something significantly different from the traditional theological climate and doctrines of the Missouri Synod. Acknowledging that fact brought many individuals to the same conclusion: In order to have a Missouri Synod diaconate, the Missouri Synod needed to be in control of its own deaconess training program.

---

[98] Rev. Theodore R. Jungkuntz (b. 1932).

[99] The communication from Keller did not come on a separate sheet of paper, but was typed right at the end of Louise William's letter. Letter from Louise Williams to "Sister," August 1, 1978, priv. col. of CDN, Pittsburgh, Pa., 2.

[100] "Announcement," *LDC News,* September 1978, mimeographed newsletter, Box: CDC, File: LDC News 1978-1979, CHI, St. Louis, Missouri, 7.

Illustrations for Chapter Eleven may be viewed at www.deaconesshistory.org.

CHAPTER 12

GOD OPENS DOORS

When the next Missouri Synod *Convention Workbook* came out in spring 1979, it showed that eighteen memorials regarding deaconess training had been received and condensed into six resolutions.[1] In every case—with the exception of a proposal from the BHE—every overture addressed the desire for a *Missouri Synod* deaconess training program. The methods of establishing such a program varied in the resolutions, but they all called for expansion of an existing pre-deaconess program or the creation of a new program at Ann Arbor, River Forest, or both of the synodical seminaries.

The content of the BHE recommendation stood in stark contrast to the other resolutions and surprised those who had been providing information to the Board because it included both the relocation and renaming of the deaconess program. The full text of the BHE resolution read:

> WHEREAS, Dallas Res. 6-12 asked the Board for Higher Education (BHE) to study the deaconess training program; and
>
> WHEREAS, Representatives from the Lutheran Deaconess Association (LDA) appeared before the BHE to provide their perspectives of the program; and
>
> WHEREAS, Representatives of the BHE have studied the program and reported to the Board; and
>
> WHEREAS, Two synodical schools have expressed interest in having the program transferred to their campus; and
>
> WHEREAS, The primary function of the deaconess can be carried out satisfactorily by other church workers now being prepared on one of the synodical campuses; and
>
> WHEREAS, The LDA now conducts its activity on a nonsynodical campus (Valparaiso University), where there is no opportunity for supervision as outlined in Bylaw 6.05; and

---

[1] LCMS, *Convention Workbook (Reports and Overtures)*, 1979, 195-97.

WHEREAS, The Synod accepts responsibility for placement by the Council of Presidents and the Board of Assignments (4.97) and has a tenuous line of input as described in 4.91-4.96; and

WHEREAS, A deaconess program is exclusively reserved for women, but a parish assistant post may be filled by either a man or a woman; therefore be it

Resolved, That the Board for Higher Education invite the Lutheran Deaconess Association to relocate the training of its students to a synodical campus selected by the BHE; and be it further

Resolved, That the BHE invite the LDA to rename their graduates as parish assistants, who would be placed in the normal fashion described in Bylaws 6.163 and 6.169; and be it further

Resolved, That if the LDA accepts the invitations in the first two resolves, the BHE will work in harmony with the LDA to implement a parish assistant program with the LDA serving in an advisory capacity; and be it finally

Resolved, That if the LDA declines to accept the invitation extended in the first two resolves, they be advised that, effective January 1980, the deaconess programs will be eliminated as approved programs at all synodical schools by the BHE and that, effective in May 1980, the Synod will no longer assist in placing deaconesses as church workers as outlined in Bylaw 4.97.[2]

If the BHE resolution passed, and the LDA decided not to accept the invitations in the first two resolves, everything that the 1959 LCMS Convention in San Francisco established for the LDA would be reversed. The pre-deaconess programs operating at LCMS colleges for twenty years would disappear and the Council of Presidents would cease to place deaconess candidates.[3] On the other hand, if the resolution passed and the LDA agreed to accept the directives laid out by the BHE, the Valparaiso program would be re-located at a Missouri Synod college (chosen by the BHE); the LDA would partner with the Synod in an advisory capacity only; and deaconesses would henceforth be known as parish assistants. Needless to say, this resolution was unpopular with both the LDA and the growing band of conservative deaconesses that prayed for a new LCMS *deaconess* program.

---

[2] LCMS, *Convention Workbook (Reports and Overtures)*, 1979, 195-96.
[3] See Chapter 6. LCMS, *Proceedings*, 1959, 143.

PREPARING FOR THE CONVENTION

On May 4, 1979, the Executive Committee of the LDA Board of Directors met to formulate a response to the six resolutions printed in the LCMS *Convention Workbook*. Ten days later, Deaconess Louise Williams sent a letter to all deaconesses, summarizing the *Workbook* resolutions and explaining, "that we would <u>favor no change</u> in the present structuring of the deaconess program at this time."[4] Williams also announced that she and LDA President Kersten would be speaking to floor committee meetings at the end of May, and again just before the convention commenced in July, to defend the Association's position.[5]

While the LDA planned its convention strategy, Deaconess Mulholland and her associates did the same. These women were hopeful of success, if only the floor committee, and then as many delegates as possible, would read and understand the *Documentation*. It was during these crucial months of preparation for floor committee meetings that several younger women— most notably Kay Pritzlaff (VU, 1977), Nancy Nicol (VU, 1977), and Cheryl D. Naumann (VU, 1979)—began to bring their ideas and energies to the campaign.[6]

On May 26, dressed in their navy blue deaconess uniforms, Clara Strehlow, Betty Mulholland, Joyce Ostermann, Nicol, and Naumann appeared before "Floor Committee Six" to present their unified thoughts on the future of the diaconate in the Missouri Synod. The women thanked and commended the BHE for its resolution; stated their belief that the LDA would not agree to "relocate or rename" the deaconess program; and asked the committee to consider combining the resolution from the BHE with one of the other resolutions, such as 6-47A "To Request Synod to Assume Full Responsibility for Office of Deaconess,"[7] so that the LCMS

---

[4] Letter from Louise Williams to "Sister," May 14, 1979, mimeographed pages on Lutheran Deaconess Association, Inc. letterhead, priv. col. of Nancy (nee Nicol) Nemoyer, 1.

[5] *Ibid.*, 2.

[6] Kay Pritzlaff served her deaconess internship at Lutheran Homes, Inc. in Fort Wayne, Indiana, under the supervision of Deaconesses Mildred Brillinger and Joyce Ostermann (1976-77), and upon her consecration in 1977, returned to Lutheran Home as part of the Deaconess Corps. In February 1978, after Mildred Brillinger moved to another state, Nancy Nicol joined the Deaconess Corps at Fort Wayne. In 1979, Cheryl D. Naumann was placed at Lutheran Homes, Inc. in Kendallville, Indiana, a satellite of the Fort Wayne Home, 30 miles north of the city. Joyce Ostermann was the Supervisor of the Deaconess Corps for both the Fort Wayne and Kendallville locations.

[7] LCMS, *Convention Workbook (Reports and Overtures)*, 1979, 196.

would continue to recognize and train women specifically for the office of deaconess.[8]

THE FINAL RESOLUTION

When the subcommittee responsible for writing the deaconess resolution completed its work, the six overtures contained in the *Convention Workbook* had been meshed into one resolution, designated Resolution 6-05. Appearing on page 125 of *Today's Business,* the resolution read:

WHEREAS, The varied ministry of the church can well use the services of dedicated deaconesses; and

WHEREAS, The schools of the Synod have long prepared deaconesses at the freshman and sophomore college level; and

WHEREAS, The full deaconess program can be offered at Concordia College, River Forest, Ill., without adding curriculum or academic staff; and

WHEREAS, The Chicago metropolitan area offers an ideal setting for fieldwork and internship training; and

WHEREAS, The Board for Education has encouraged schools of the Synod to broaden their areas of service; therefore be it

Resolved, That the Synod authorize the BHE to direct Concordia College, River Forest, Ill., to establish a full deaconess training program on its campus by the fall of 1980.[9]

Short and crisp, Resolution 6-05 made no reference to moving or renaming an existing deaconess program, and no mention of the LDA or Valparaiso University. This was everything that the small group of conservative deaconesses hoped and prayed for—a simple directive for the Missouri Synod to establish its own deaconess training program on the campus of one of its own synodical colleges.

---

[8] The meetings for Floor Committee Six were held at Concordia Seminary in St. Louis, Mo. Betty Mulholland, Cheryl D. Naumann, Nancy Nicol, Joyce Ostermann, Clara Strehlow, Hand written presentation, five pages, May 26, 1979, Box: CDC, File: Pre-CDC Correspondence, CHI, St. Louis, Mo.

[9] "Subject: To Expand Deaconess Program, RESOLUTION 6-05," *Today's Business* Section B (Concordia: St. Louis, July 1979), 125.

GOD OPENS DOORS

Missouri Synod President J. A. O. Preus based his opening devotion for the "53rd Regular Convention" on Acts 14:27. Alluding to the convention theme, Preus remarked:

> *God Opens Doors* should be etched indelibly on the hearts, minds, intentions, and desires of the delegates. The process began when man closed the door through his sin and closed it so effectively that it could not be climbed over or broken through in any way. Nevertheless, through Christ God has made a door which no man can close. It is the single purpose of the church that through Christian testimony and lives of love its members are to say to the world, "The door is open. Come with us and enter into the opportunities which God has placed before us."[10]

The Convention was now underway. Two days earlier, Deaconesses Millie Brillinger, Mulholland, Naumann, Nicol, and Ostermann spoke briefly to Floor Committee Six, where they were followed by a presentation from LDA President Kersten and Deaconess Williams.[11] The wait was almost over. Resolution 6-05 would be addressed during "Session 2" in the afternoon, on that first day of the convention.[12]

ON THE CONVENTION FLOOR

The entire discussion on Resolution 6-05: "To Expand Deaconess Program" finished in about 13 minutes. However, delegates shared many thoughts and opinions on the subject in the space of that time. In order to give the reader a good feel for the volley of the debate, the following section comprises a literal transcript of the convention proceedings.

> [John C. Zimmermann[13]] Mr. Chairman and members of the convention, will you now turn to page one twenty-five, Resolution 6 dash 05, the subject, to expand deaconess program. And I will call upon . . . Pastor Eldor Meyer, the subcommittee chairman, . . . to read this resolution.

---

[10] LCMS, *Proceedings*, 1979, 21.

[11] Mildred Brillinger, Betty Mulholland, Cheryl D. Naumann, Nancy Nicol, Joyce Ostermann, "Topic Prepared for the Floor Committee, July 5, 1979," Hand written presentation, four pages, Box: CDC, File: Pre-CDC Correspondence, CHI, St. Louis, Missouri; "Meeting of Concordia Deaconess Conference founding members," July 28—August 1, 2003, Fort Wayne, Indiana, tape recordings, priv. col. of CDN, Pittsburgh, Pa.

[12] "Convention Schedule," *Today's Business* Section A (Concordia: St. Louis, July 1979), 41; LCMS, *Proceedings*, 1979, 25.

[13] Rev. John C. Zimmermann (b. 1914). Iowa East District President; Chairman of Floor Committee 6—Higher Education.

[Eldor Meyer[14]] Whereas the very ministry of the church can well use the services of dedicated deaconesses, and whereas the schools of the Synod have long prepared deaconesses at the freshman and sophomore college level, and whereas the full deaconess program can be offered at Concordia College, River Forest, Illinois, without adding curriculum or academic staff, and whereas, the Chicago metropolitan area offers an ideal setting for field work and internship training, and whereas the Board for Higher Education has encouraged schools of the Synod to broaden their areas of service, therefore be it resolved, that the Synod authorize the BHE to direct Concordia College, River Forest, Illinois, to establish a full deaconess training program on its campus by the fall of 1980.

[Herbert Israel[15]] Mr. Chairman, Herbert Israel, Eastern District. I move adoption of Resolution 6-05.

[J.A.O. Preus] The Resolution is now before you. Microphone Three.

[Arthur W. Freitag[16]] Mr. chairman, Art Freitag, lay delegate, Bremerton, Washington. I speak in favor of the resolution. Teachers graduating from Valparaiso University must be colloquized in order to be able to be placed in Lutheran Church Missouri Synod schools. The deaconess program is not under the control of the Lutheran Church Missouri Synod. And now I would like to speak to the convention as a father, of a girl who graduated as a deaconess from Valparaiso this May. I asked her to write to me, and what she thought of the resolution because I was concerned about it. I read you her letter.

"Dear dad, I am very happy to see that the committee for Higher Education has included the deaconess resolution 6-05. There are many reasons why it would be wise for the convention to pass this resolution. You remember how distraught I was at not being able to attend a synodical school to complete my deaconess training. You will also remember that I petitioned the Lutheran Deaconess Association to graduate from a synodical school and still be certified as a deaconess, but my request was unequivocally denied. I am sad when I recall the other four girls in my class at Ann Arbor, who would have made excellent deaconesses, but did not continue their education because they did not wish to go to a school whose theology department was not supervised by The Lutheran Church—Missouri Synod. All of our pastors, teachers, and

---

14 Rev. Eldor William Meyer (b. 1929). Nebraska District President.
15 Mr. Herbert Israel. Voting layman from Ithaca, New York.
16 Mr. Arthur Walter Freitag (b. 1927). Voting layman from Bremerton, Washington; father of Cheryl (nee Freitag) Naumann; elected member of Northwest District Board of Directors for 42 consecutive years (1964-2006). See also: Dwaine Brandt, gen. ed., *God Opens Doors: A Centennial Celebration of the Northwest District of the Lutheran Church—Missouri Synod*, Portland: Premier Press, 2000.

other church workers are trained, supervised, and placed by the Missouri Synod. At present, deaconess placements are approved by the Council of Presidents, but this is the end of the official involvement of the Synod in terms of any supervision with the deaconesses. As a 1979 graduate of the Lutheran Deaconess Program, I can only wholeheartedly endorse this resolution. Love, Cheryl. P.S. You may show this letter, and you have my permission to share this letter, with anyone you wish."

I also asked another deaconess who I know to write something about her theological training at Valpo, and this girl gave me a note that I have permission to read. And I asked her to say something about the Historical-Critical Method taught in her classes.

"Example in regards to the theological training at Valparaiso University. As a deaconess student at Valparaiso University in 1975, one of the course requirements for my training, taught by the chairman of the Theology Department, involved learning and writing an exegesis by the principles of the Historical-Critical Method. Verbal inspiration was not considered a valid point of reference, but was instead subtly ridiculed in front of the class as an unscholarly and childish opinion. Signed Nancy Nicol, deaconess."[17] Mr. Chairman, I support this resolution wholeheartedly. Thank you.

[J.A.O. Preus] Chairman of the Committee.

[John C. Zimmermann] Mr. Chairman, I would like, on behalf of the Committee, to give some background to you with regard to our thinking that led to this proposal. First of all, there is a matter of principle. All our other assigned church workers, those assigned by our Council of Presidents, are trained, or at least are certified, by a process over which the Synod itself has control. And our committee felt that the Synod in convention ought to have the opportunity to decide, whether they wanted to have a deaconess program which was also under the full control and aegis of The Lutheran Church–Missouri Synod. We pointed no finger at anybody. The deaconess program has—as we have known it—has graduated a lot of fine workers. I know a lot of them, very very personally. And they have been a blessing to the church, and we don't want to put those people down. They are not second rate people in the church. But the question is, do we want a deaconess program in the Synod, which is under the full control, the training, and finally the certification of these girls, for work in the church.

The second matter that really, our committee thought about, was the fact that we ought to provide an option for those girls who want that kind of

[17] Deaconess Nancy Eileen Nicol (later Nemoyer) graduated from VU in 1977 and was serving at Lutheran Homes, Inc., Fort Wayne, Ind.

program. We had letters. We had people appear before us personally, saying, "We want the Synod to provide for us a program - that is fully under the control of the Synod. We have two places where men can go to study for the ministry. We have at least four places where DCEs can be trained. We have six or eight choices that people have for the teaching ministry, but for the deaconess program we have just one choice. You either go there or they don't get into the program."

And that brings up the third point, this word *expand* the deaconess program. For quite a few years, a number of our institutions have trained deaconesses for the first two years. I know Concordia St. Paul does, I know that Seward does, I know that Winfield does, I know that there have been some at River Forest. And all that we are doing is giving one of these schools an opportunity to add the other two years. They already have the first two years. Now those are the considerations, which led our committee to place this proposal before you, so that the Synod in convention would have opportunity to decide: do we want also a deaconess program that is fully under the aegis of The Lutheran Church–Missouri Synod.

[J.A.O. Preus] Thank you. Microphone one.

[Paul Rummelmann[18]] Mr. President. Paul Rummelmann. Kouts, Indiana. Indiana District. I would like to submit a substitute resolution.

[J.A.O. Preus] That is in order. That comes under the so-called Behnken Rule that's on page eight of part one of the *Today's Business*. Would you please make your substitute motion?

[Paul Rummelmann] Yes, sir. Whereas the Lutheran Deaconess Association is not mentioned in Resolution 6 dash 05, but is affected by that resolution, and whereas for 60 years the LDA has been responsible for educating and supporting deaconesses who have served in Synod, and has educated over 500 deaconesses during that 60 year history, and whereas there has been no prior consultation by the Synod with the deaconess association regarding beginning a new deaconess program at Concordia College, River Forest, and whereas the Lutheran Deaconess Association is in the midst of a study to determine directions for the future of the deaconess program, therefore be it resolved that the Synod refer the resolution to the BHE for further study and consultation with the LDA, and report to the next convention.

[J.A.O. Preus] That is the substitute motion. Is it seconded?

It is seconded. Under the Behnken Rule on page eight, this is an undebatable motion. We will now vote immediately whether we wish to

---

[18] Mr. Paul Rummelmann. Voting layman from Kouts, Ind.

consider the substitute motion. It passes by a simple majority. So what you are going to do now is vote, do you wish to consider that. If you vote to, if the motion passes, that you wish to consider it, then we will discuss it. If you vote not to consider it, we go back to the pending original motion. Would the mover please bring that forward to the secretary?

All in favor of considering the substitute motion, please raise your hands. All opposed to considering it, please raise your hands. The ayes have it, and the motion is before us for consideration. [Immediate murmuring and booing of disapproval.]

[A voice from the convention floor] Division of the house. The no's had it.

[J.A.O. Preus] All in favor of considering the substitute motion—that is, do you want to talk about it? All in favor of considering it, please raise your hands. All opposed please raise your hands. Well then, either I said it wrong or you heard it wrong, but anyway it looks as if the motion to consider is defeated. So we have before us the original motion. All right, we now go to microphone two.

[John S. Cassidy[19]] John Cassidy, Pastoral delegate, Southern California District. On the basis of the strength of the present Lutheran Deaconess Association program with its 60 years of faithful service in training deaconesses, on the basis of their own self study, in which they are very much involved, looking at the theological historical roots of the diaconate and considering the options for service that they are looking at, and on the basis of the weakness in the resolution itself regarding the costs involved, the BHE studies, availability of River Forest for this particular situation which the resolution is proposing, the duplication involved, and the possible division of the diaconate which has struggled to be held together through recent tensions in the church and has come through this, I therefore move that we table this resolution.

[J.A.O. Preus] All right. It is moved to table the resolution. That is an undebatable motion, and it takes place immediately and it passes by a simple majority. All in favor of tabling this resolution please raise your hands. All opposed to tabling.

I believe there is not much question on that one. It is not tabled and it is before us. Please continue with discussion. Mike four.

[Gerald Garrett[20]] Gerry Garrett, Northern Illinois, pastor of Jehovah Lutheran Church in Chicago. I speak in favor of the motion from three basic reasons. First of all, in regard to a theological stance, I think we're

[19] Rev. John Smith Cassidy (b. 1944). Voting pastor from Los Angeles, California.
[20] Rev. Gerald Gene Garrett (b. 1933). Voting pastor from Chicago, Illinois.

aware that there are some differences between ourselves and Valparaiso University. Unfortunate as they may be, we keep being barraged by, by documents, by statements of essays, and clearly challenging that the Scriptures themselves are the Word of God. And this is something that would reflect in the teaching of the deaconess program regardless of what we say. And as I look, I look straight into the face of a man who was my mentor in school, in which, that I had to submit to, and to reflect my ideas in such a way, so that he could say that this man is qualified to be a member of the ministry of the Missouri Synod. And I think this is needed in regard to all of our church workers. And that's the first point.

The second point is, as a father of two children at Concordia, River Forest, in speaking of the beautiful relationship that I have had with that school, and knowing that they are fully equipped to handle all of the training for this work there in a single location. And the third point, to speak in favor of the area, in that we have any number of churches nearby, which are currently being used as student teaching locations, and which could easily be used to give the in-service training that would be so valuable for a deaconess program. And so I speak in favor of the motion.

[J.A.O. Preus] We will now invoke the pro con. Someone raised the question, is the two minute limit being enforced? And it is. The timekeeper, however, does not include in the two minutes or in the passage of the half hour, the time used by the floor committee, because we don't want them to be taking your time. Is there someone who wishes to speak against Resolution 6-05? Microphone four.

[William J. Meyer[21]] Mr. Chairman, Bill Meyer, Atlantic District. I'd like to speak against this resolution, primarily on the basis of understandings that I have with regard to the BHE and the LDA. One of the previous speakers indicated that the deaconess association has been operative, of service to the church for the past 60 years. It is my understanding that during that time there has always been an, an understood invitation to the Board of Higher Education to have representation come and meet with LDA, during its planning, during the processes whereby their program was being studied and implemented, and that during the years of its history there has not been a very great interest shown by Synod in the deaconess program, except for the last several years. And so my understanding, I guess one question that I would have, would be, to what degree has the Board of Higher Education worked with, in conjunction with, the Lutheran Deaconess Association, as it pertains to its current program and the problems which obviously exist within the church. And then secondly, and related to this, has the Board for Higher Education at any time sat down with Dr. Schnabel, the new President of Valparaiso,

---

[21] Rev. William John Meyer (b. 1937). Voting pastor from Patchogue, New York.

and spelled out some of the concerns which the people in Synod have, to try to work out a God-pleasing solution. My understanding is that neither of these have taken place. And in the light of this, this is why I oppose this resolution in its present form.

[J.A.O. Preus] BHE wish to respond?

[John C. Zimmermann] May we point out that this resolution does nothing with the deaconess program at Valpo. It is not suggesting that program be discontinued at all. So I don't know how pertinent that discussion is. But BHE may answer.

[J.A.O. Preus] Dr. Ahlschwede?

[Arthur M. Ahlschwede[22]] Mr. Chairman, only to substantiate the fact that there has not been the closest connection in the recent past. I would take the responsibility of that, because there seems to be an uncanny ability to schedule meetings that, when I probably should have been at the Lutheran Deaconess Association meeting, if the Board for Education or the Board of Directors were meeting, and I knew which one paid my pay check. The other thing too, that there has not been the opportunity to sit down with Dr. Schnabel. So that is correct, that there has not been any particular communication since he has taken office.

[J.A.O. Preus:] Next is microphone five. Are you speaking in favor of the resolution?

[Voice at microphone five:] Yes.

[J.A.O. Preus] You are speaking in favor. Then you have the floor.

[Voice at microphone five] No, against, sir.

[J.A.O. Preus] Oh, against. Alright, microphone six. In favor?

[Voice at microphone six] No, against.

[J.A.O. Preus] Mike three. In favor? He has the floor.

[James Nickel[23]] Pastor Nickel, from Indiana. This has not been a *recent* concern of mine, and I am sure of many other people. Practically ever since I've been a pastor I've been bothered by the fact that the Synod did not control the training of our deaconesses and their certification and so on. I had a deaconess in my parish at one point and there was a strong desire on her part to kind of be an associate pastor or something, and I found that same tendency with a lot of other deaconesses, and I think that comes from the training and the background. Many of us sitting here have

---

[22] Mr. Arthur M. Alschwede. Executive Secretary of the BHE.
[23] Rev. James T. Nickel (b. 1936). Voting pastor from Elkhart, Ind.

raised objections to this kind of orientation and training for years. It's not something that's coming up in 1979. And I think those people who say no attempts have been made to try to change this are in error. Many of us have raised our voices and tried to talk with Dr. Schnabel and many other people at Valpo, and have really, I think not been heard or at least not been effective. I speak very strongly in favor of this resolution to provide an alternative for those people who want it. Why should they be denied?

[J.A.O. Preus] Thank you. Microphone five.

[Max Bierwagen[24]] Max Bierwagen, Eastern District. Most of my concerns have been addressed in one manner or another, howbeit not to my satisfaction, so I would relinquish my time to Mr. Ed Lowitzer of the Eastern District, with permission of the chair.

[J.A.O. Preus] Is he ready to speak?

[Max Bierwagen] Yes.

[J.A.O. Preus] Alright.

[Edwin Lowitzer[25]] Mr. Chairman, Ed Lowitzer, Eastern District. I was also given a letter by one of the Valparaiso deaconess students which I would request privilege to read at this time.

She says, "I have completed my third year of training and will go out for a year of internship as a deaconess. I received my first two years of education at Concordia College, Bronxville, New York. I am concerned about the various resolutions listed in the *Workbook* concerning the deaconess program. One. While the deaconess may fill the role of a parish assistant, the concept of a deaconess is different. We form a community of sisters with other deaconesses of the Lutheran churches. At Valparaiso we begin to build that community, and a separate program would limit that community and support system. And two. While I support the synodical schools, I do feel along with my other sisters that the quality of education could not be duplicated at a synodical school. Among the sixteen required courses, we must take Deaconess Work, Clinical Deaconess Education, and two semesters of Field Work. I am concerned that these could not be duplicated, along with the excellent foundational theology courses. Three. I can understand the Board of Higher Education's concern about the theology taught at Valparaiso and their desire for more control. I would like to recommend further study and increased communication with the Lutheran Deaconess Association and

---

[24] Mr. Max Bierwagen. Voting layman from Dewitt, New York.
[25] Mr. Edwin Lowitzer. Voting layman from Rochester, New York.

Valparaiso University. In Christ's name, Kristine M. Zobel."[26] Thank you, Mr. Chairman.

[J.A.O. Preus] Thank you. Mike two. Are you opposed to the resolution?

[Voice at microphone two] Yes.

[J.A.O. Preus] Then I want someone who speaks for it. . . .

[Voice at microphone seven] Seven.

[J.A.O Preus] Seven.

[Inaudible voice[27]] I heartily endorse the resolution which we have before us here, and I feel that, in regard to the comments that have been made by the Chairman of the committee, as to reasons why they drew up this resolution, that if I am in order Mr. Chairman, I would like to call the question.

[J.A.O. Preus] The chair will recognize you and your right to do it, except he should have cautioned you before, that whether it's a calling for the question or calling to table, you are not to give an endorsement for your particular view, but you're simply to call the question. In this case the chair will recognize you since it's the first occasion.

[Inaudible voice] Call the question.

[J.A.O. Preus] A motion has been made to call the question. I heard a second over here. This means we terminate debate and we proceed immediately to vote if the vote to call the question passes. At this point in the debate it takes a two-thirds majority to pass. All in favor of terminating debate, please raise your hands. All opposed please raise your hands. The chair rules that the vote has the necessary two-thirds, and we have terminated debate. All then in favor of Resolution 6-05, please raise your hands. All opposed please raise your hands. The motion carries.[28] [Eruption of clapping.] Thank you. Next the committee chairman again, Dr. Zimmermann. . . .[29]

---

[26] Kristine Marie Zobel (later Blackwell) never finished her deaconess training at Valparaiso. She transferred to Concordia College, River Forest, and graduated with a BA in Theology in 1983. See Chapter 15 and Appendix 3.D. Zobel came from Rochester, New York.
[27] Inaudible voice when name is given. From the Nebraska District.
[28] "The vote to approve the new program passed by roughly a 65-35 percentage margin." "LCMS 'Begins' Deaconess Program," *Missouri in Perspective* July 20, 1979, ELIM, St. Louis.
[29] Cheryl D. Naumann, "Transcript of LCMS Convention Proceedings, Session Two, July 7, 1979." The author has agreed to preserve the anonymity of the individual who recorded this convention session and allowed use of the recording to create a transcript. The official LCMS reel-to-reel recording of the 53rd Synodical Convention is located in the LCMS

And the convention carried on to the next item of business.

The deaconesses at the convention—most of them sitting in the bleachers—were either extremely disappointed or exceedingly happy. The convention delegates did not asked the LDA to move or rename its deaconess program. The LDA would continue its work in the same manner of independence that it had always enjoyed, and the Association's graduates would be recognized and placed by the Council of Presidents for another seven years.[30] But at last, the Missouri Synod would have a deaconess training program of its own.

LOOKING TO THE FUTURE

The passing of Resolution 6-05 meant that women who desired to serve their Lord as deaconesses within the LCMS could now choose to receive their education at a Missouri Synod college. Concordia College, River Forest, Illinois—today called Concordia University Chicago—had been chosen as the provider of that educational option. Concordia's President, Rev. Dr. Paul Albert Zimmerman (b. 1918), enthused about the new venture. In September 1979, Zimmerman wrote:

> The Deaconess Program—An Expansion of Concordia's Mission
>
> The St. Louis Convention of The Lutheran Church—Missouri Synod in July authorized the Board for Higher Education "to direct Concordia College, River Forest, Illinois to establish a full deaconess training program on its campus by the fall of 1980." By taking this action the Synod expanded the mission of Concordia to educate professional church workers. Long known for its training of teachers of Christian schools, directors of Christian Education, and church musicians, Concordia recently added a pre-seminary program, as well as a social work program. Thus, the deaconess program comes as a logical addition to the mission of the college. . . .
>
> The Synod did not in its action speak negatively of the Lutheran Deaconess Association or of its program at Valparaiso University. It did provide an option for those women who desire to prepare for the deaconess office in Synod's schools. This is consistent with the manner of educating Synod's other workers. It is to be hoped that this new emphasis on the importance of an ancient office will result in renewed interest. The office of deaconess has much to offer to our church today. Concordia will

---

archives at CHI, and may be used by researchers who have received permission from the Secretary of Synod.

[30] See Chapter 15.

work hard to fulfill this sacred responsibility. We believe this expanded mission of Concordia will be a blessing upon all concerned. Please join us in praying for its success.[31]

After the River Forest deaconess program was established, it made sense that the women who graduated from the Concordia Deaconess Program—along with the Valpo graduates who no longer wished to be part of the LDC—should meet together regularly for spiritual, personal, and professional growth. Hence, in January 1980, deaconesses who campaigned for an LCMS deaconess program also established the *Concordia Deaconess Conference—Lutheran Church-Missouri Synod* (CDC).

The remaining chapters of this book document the history of CDC, the training of deaconesses *in the LCMS* for more than twenty-eight years, and the continuing growth of the deaconess movement within the Missouri Synod.

---

[31] Paul A. Zimmerman, "The Deaconess Program—An Expansion of Concordia's Mission," *The Forester* 4, no. 1 (September 1979): 2.

Illustrations for Chapter Twelve may be viewed at www.deaconesshistory.org.

PART II

OUR BATTLE FOR MISSOURI

Concordia Deaconess Conference—Lutheran Church-Missouri Synod (CDC) was organized by nine deaconesses who had worked individually and collectively toward the goal of establishing a deaconess training program within the Missouri Synod. Nearly 25 years later, these same nine women, minus one sainted sister, met together to share memories and resources, with the intent of recording their story for the posterity of the church. I write as one of these women, and on their behalf.

So many times—throughout our lives—we have been asked to explain the problems and events that preceded the 1979 LCMS convention, and how the CDC was born. And so it was obvious to us that the time had come to put oral narrations into an accurate written account, or the opportunity to do so might be lost forever.

We were women who desired to remain faithful to the Bible as the true and inerrant Word of God, and who wished to serve our Lord as Lutheran deaconesses under the umbrella of the Missouri Synod. Part II, written to the best of our collective memories, demonstrates some of the struggles we lived through while hoping and praying that the dream would be realized.

Soli Deo Gloria

Cheryl D. Naumann

In consultation with my sisters in the faith: Mildred Brillinger, Kay Gudgeon, Luella Mickley, Betty Mulholland, Nancy Nemoyer, Joyce Ostermann, and Ruth Stallmann.

CHAPTER 13

VIGNETTES FROM THE FOUNDERS
OF CDC

The first time I heard the word "Seminex" was the day that I arrived in Valparaiso. A Lutheran Layman's League acquaintance of my dad's, Dr. Al Looman, collected me from the Valparaiso bus station and took me to his home, where two or three other students and myself enjoyed a lovely dinner. One of the other students began talking, in a very animated way, about something called Seminex. I listened intently. I was interested in theology and had already decided to register in the pre-deaconess program at the University. When dessert was finished, I was taken to my room in Lankenau Hall, and became occupied with all of the things that a normal freshman does when arriving at college for the first time. Little did I know that our dinner conversation was the beginning of something that would deeply concern me in the weeks, months, and years to come.

* * *

Theology 101 was the first theology course taken by every student that attended Valpo, and I was excited to be going to the first class. I had all of my books, fresh paper, and was poised to take notes. About twenty of us sat in the classroom, waiting for the professor to arrive. She walked into the room and placed her briefcase on the front desk, broadside facing the class, so that a large *Seminex* bumper sticker was visible to everyone in the room. Without speaking, she continued to the blackboard and wrote her name, preceded by the title "Deaconess." This is amazing, I thought. Not only am I in the pre-deaconess program, but I have the privilege of having a deaconess for a theology professor.

The course syllabus revealed a basic introduction to Christianity, using *Mere Christianity* by C. S. Lewis as the primary textbook. In one of her first lectures, the professor asked us the simple question, "What is the Bible?" A lot of hands went up, and as each answer was given, the professor wrote it on the board—the story of Jesus, a book of morals, and so forth. There must have been six to eight responses when no more hands were raised. I thought to myself, there's something big missing on that list. So I raised my hand and said, "The Bible is the inspired and inerrant Word of God." Until that point every response had been written on the board with no comment from the professor. But this time she didn't turn to the board. She faced me squarely and said, "If you really believe that, you're going to have a hard time defending your faith for the rest of your life." I was pretty stunned by her statement, since it went against everything that my parents had taught me. But she wasn't finished. For what seemed like an eternity, the professor dissected and belittled my answer in front of the whole class. I wanted to crawl under my desk to escape the torrent of words and the sense of shame that I felt was being inflicted on me. I knew she wasn't right, but who was I to contradict, or even stand up to, the professor? I left that classroom profoundly affected, wondering why the foundation of my world was being shaken, of all places, at a Lutheran university.

* * *

Sometime early in that fall of 1974, I joined several students in the foyer of Deaconess Hall, where we waited for a "fieldwork" meeting to begin. The LDA Director of Student Services was going to hand out fieldwork placements for the semester, and though only a pre-deaconess student, I had asked to be allowed to do fieldwork, too. I sat on one of the couches and decided to start a conversation with the redhead on my left.

"So what do you think about all of this Seminex nonsense?" I offered.

"Shhh . . . later," came her whispered reply, with finger on her lips.

I paused for a moment and then started over by asking her name. She was Nancy Nicol, a junior transfer student from Concordia, Ann Arbor. The two of us were assigned to teach the sixth and seventh grade confirmation classes at Hope Lutheran Church in Cedar Lake. For several months we spent Saturday mornings traveling together to the fieldwork site. It was fun to share the teaching experience, but we each appreciated the opportunity for contact with another "conservative" Lutheran.

Nancy told me about her alma mater and invited me to visit the campus with her during homecoming weekend. While we were there, she spoke to President (Rev.) Merlin S. Pohl (1918–2003) about the possibility of starting a full deaconess training program at Ann Arbor. Two other alumni supported Nancy in her plea. President Pohl stated, and later confirmed in writing, "Concordia, Ann Arbor would be eager and ready to add the Deaconess program to its offerings."[1] This was the answer, I thought. I decided to transfer to Concordia, Ann Arbor for my sophomore year. If the Missouri Synod started a deaconess program on that campus, I would stay there to finish my training. If not, I would transfer my credits back to Valparaiso and finish the program there.

---

[1] Letter from Rev. M. S. Pohl to Miss Nancy L. [*sic*] Nicol, December 4, 1974, priv. col. of Nancy (nee Nicol) Nemoyer, Carlisle, Pa.

* * *

Nancy Nicol learned about the Synod's problems before she arrived at Deaconess Hall in the fall of 1974. She wanted to be a deaconess, but had reservations about attending Valparaiso. On October 12, 1973, at the beginning of her sophomore year of college, Nancy sent a letter to Dr. Arthur M. Ahlschwede, Executive Secretary of the LCMS BHE. She wrote,

> ". . . In looking ahead I find that to complete my training as a deaconess in the junior and senior levels that I am compelled to go to Valparaiso University, Ind. I am a bit dissatisfied with this lack of choice. Perhaps you could help me answer some questions: Why isn't the continuation of the deaconess program kept within Synod's system of schools? I fail to see how in attending Valpo I am supposed to be equally equipped as those church workers attending synodical schools, schools specifically functioning for the purpose of training church workers. It seems as though many of the courses offered at schools such as Concordia Senior College [CSC], Fort Wayne, would coincide with deaconess requirements. Is there any possibility that the furtherance of the deaconess program could involve a transfer to CSC or some other Missouri Synod school in the future? . . ."[2]

Dr. Ahlschwede's reply explained,

> ". . . The deaconess ministry in our church, although officially recognized, has since its beginning been sponsored by an autonomous organization, called the Lutheran Deaconess Association, with its own members, officers, and boards. It is that association which has chosen Valparaiso University as its 'training base.' The Synod has never seen fit either to press for changes in this system or to establish a parallel system, which it feels would represent unnecessary duplication of programs and effort. That is the reason why, at the present time, it is necessary to go to Valparaiso in order to become an actual <u>deaconess</u>. It is possible, of course, to attend our synodical schools, CSC or one of the teachers colleges, and to undertake a <u>similar</u> program . . ."[3]

Becoming a teacher, social worker, or Director of Christian Education didn't appeal to Nancy. Her heart was inclined to serve the Lord as a deaconess. Before finishing her Associate of Arts degree at Ann Arbor, she wrote to Rev. Milford C. Brelje (b. 1925) at Concordia Senior College, Fort

---

[2] Letter from Nancy Nicol to Dr. Arthur M. Ahlschwede, October 12, 1973, priv. col. of Nancy (nee Nicol) Nemoyer, Carlisle, Pa.

[3] Letter from Arthur M. Ahlschwede to Miss Nancy Nicol, October 16, 1973, priv. col. of Nancy (nee Nicol) Nemoyer, Carlisle, Pa.

Wayne, posing the same questions about the possibility of a deaconess program at CSC.

* * *

Nancy and I found the October 1974 "deaconess petition" in support of John Tietjen disturbing.[4] As the list of student names on the petition got longer, we realized that few of the other deaconess students shared our opinion of Seminex or our view of Scripture. No pressure was put on us to sign that paper. However, in order to avoid tension that might arise from confrontation, we found ourselves avoiding individuals that we thought might try to talk us into signing.

We decided, independently, to take action during the Thanksgiving vacation. I had plans to spend the break in St. Louis. Being young and naïve, I thought the best place to start was at the top, so I picked up the telephone in my dormitory room and called the office of LCMS President J. A. O. Preus. Strangely enough, Preus' secretary put me through to him, I asked for an appointment, and he agreed to see me. On November 29, Dr. Preus and I spent about two hours alone in his office. Preus was attentive and sympathetic as I presented the need for a synodical deaconess program. He provided fatherly encouragement but made no promises. Near the end of our meeting he invited me to his home for lunch. Mrs. Preus served a spread of Thanksgiving Day leftovers while the three of us talked about synodical issues and how they affected the diaconate.

* * *

Nancy spent Thanksgiving vacation with her parents in Ohio. She outlined her thoughts on paper, and on November 27, mailed letters to President Pohl (Concordia College, Ann Arbor), Arthur Ahlschwede (BHE Executive Secretary), and President J. A. O. Preus. Each of her letters included similar paragraphs:

> . . . I am sure that you are aware of a recent statement responding to the action of the Board of Control taken in regard to Dr. Tietjen, which was signed by a group of deaconesses and deaconess students. I did not sign the statement. Withholding my signature was not a passive, but was a definitive action. . . .
>
> My first concern is the effects of "bad" publicity on students, particularly those who, like myself, did not sign the statement and do not subscribe to the opinions expressed in the statement. There is a problem with being branded as a theological "liberal" by reason of the statement and by mere attendance at Valparaiso University. In the light of this publicity I am

---

[4] See section titled "The Deaconess Petition" in chapter 11.

quite concerned about the chances for a graduate call in a conservative environment. I feel that the system is weak in the fact that every aspiring Deaconess has no choice concerning at least two years of her education, which forces her into a stereotyped image.

Therefore I would like to offer a suggestion. Perhaps there is the possibility that Synod could adopt the Deaconess program into its synodical school system. This would not necessarily have to involve a complete transplant of the program. I would like to see a synodical school offer the program as another option. . . .

So I come to you. I am discouraged and disgusted with conditions as they are. I come to you in need of assurance and advice. The concerns expressed thus far are so very real to me that I am, reluctantly, considering leaving the Deaconess program. The situation is almost unbearable for me, not only in the present, but also in the future implications that will stay with me throughout a career as a Deaconess. I am seeking some response as to what is being done and what I can do to change the situation. . . .[5]

All three dignitaries sent cordial responses to Nancy.[6] The letter from Dr. Preus brought the most encouragement.

Dear Miss Nicol,

Thank you so much for your letter of November 27. By now you probably have heard that your co-worker, Cheryl Freitag, was in to see me and we had a long and I think very fruitful discussion.

I am grateful to you for not signing the Statement. It certainly was a definitive action.

Cheryl and I talked over the problems that beset a conservative deaconess. I would certainly suggest that you keep on with the program. There are many areas and conservative congregations where you can be placed. This can be handled through the Council of District Presidents, who actually do the placement. I have already talked to some district

---

[5] Letter from Nancy E. Nicol to President J. A. O. Preus, November 27, 1974; Letter from Nancy E. Nicol to President Merlin Pohl, November 27, 1974; Letter from Nancy E. Nicol to Arthur Ahlschwede, November 27, 1974; priv. col. of Nancy (nee Nicol) Nemoyer, Carlisle, Pa.

[6] Samuel I. Goltermann, Assistant Executive Secretary of the BHE, responded on behalf of Arthur Ahlschwede. Letter from Samuel I. Goltermann to Miss Nancy E. Nicol, December 6, 1974; Letter from J. A. O. Preus to Miss Nancy E. Nicol, December 9, 1974; Letter from Rev. M. S. Pohl to Miss Nancy L. [sic] Nicol, December 4, 1974; priv. col. of Nancy (nee Nicol) Nemoyer, Carlisle, Pa.

presidents regarding the matter of getting the right deaconesses into the right kind of congregations, and if you will let me know shortly before the time of your graduation I think this matter can be arranged for you personally.

Your letter, together with Cheryl's conversation, together with other information that comes my way, will serve as the basis for a discussion of the whole matter of the future of the Deaconess Program. It's too early to tell what might be done, but certainly we will give the matter very serious consideration. I don't want to commit myself to any definite program or plan at this time because there are so many factors to be considered.

. . . Keep your chin up and don't lose courage. Things are going very well in the Synod and you have to remember that it sometimes is darkest just before the dawn. I appreciate your writing and very much appreciate your attitude. Please feel free to write me at any time. Blessings and best wishes to you.

Sincerely,

J. A. O. Preus, President [7]

* * *

Nancy's vacation activity wasn't restricted to letter writing. On November 29, 1974, she and her dad, (later Rev.) Lloyd Ernest Fred Nicol (b. 1927), traveled for three hours to meet with Ohio District President Arthur Ziegler. In addition to the points she penned to other church leaders, Nancy told Ziegler of her distress at the liberal theology that was foisted on her and other deaconess students. She reasoned that, since deaconesses play such a vital role in the theological education of the people they serve, the Missouri Synod should be concerned about the theological indoctrination of its deaconesses.

Ziegler repeatedly reassured Nancy that the LDA placement committee considered the views of deaconess candidates in conjunction with the view of prospective churches. This was helpful. However, knowing that some congregations had already withdrawn financial support from the LDA over theological issues, Nancy wondered if any conservative congregation would be interested in applying for a deaconess by the time that she graduated. Closing the meeting with the words of Joshua 1:9, Ziegler told Nancy that the church needed deaconesses like her, and that he hoped she wouldn't

---

[7] Letter from J. A. O. Preus to Miss Nancy E. Nicol, December 9, 1974, priv. col. of Nancy (nee Nicol) Nemoyer, Carlisle, Pa.

drop out of the program. Between Ziegler's words, the support of her parents, and Preus' letter, Nancy decided to stick with the training.[8]

* * *

Those who lived through the events leading to the "walkout," the formation of Seminex, and the ensuing synodical battles will also recall the intense emotions that accompanied the discussion of theology or church politics at that time in our Synod's history. As a freshman at Valpo I remember thinking: these issues permeate our world; there is no rest or escape from them; we eat, sleep and shower theology.

At some point during the first semester, Nancy told me that two other women in Deaconess Hall, Wilma Kucharek and Kathy Baehr, shared the same theological stand that we did. For the rest of the year the four of us met together every afternoon from 4:30 to 5:00 p.m. This was our support group. We talked about what went on in our theology classes; cried and laughed together; consulted the Lutheran Confessions; read passages from Scripture; and always finished with prayer. We jokingly called ourselves "the faithful four." Fearing public rebuke from other students, we kept our meetings secret, sometimes using code words in case we were overheard.

On February 2, 1975, the four of us drove to St. Peter Lutheran Church in Arlington Heights, Illinois, to hear President J. A. O. Preus speak on "Lutheran Church—Missouri Synod—Yesterday, Today, Tomorrow." After the program we went to the church hall for coffee and cookies and the "Informal Meeting with Dr. Preus."[9] Preus seemed delighted to see the four of us and we reminded him briefly of our hopes for a Missouri Synod deaconess program. Three weeks later, I received a letter from Dr. Preus with an enclosure he called "a copy of the material having to do with the future of the Deaconess Association."[10] We were disappointed. The material consisted of the report of the "Ad Hoc Committee Concerning the Relationship of Deaconesses to the Synod" that Preus had appointed in

---

[8] It was over 30 years later when Nancy discovered that Rev. Ziegler served as President of the LDA from 1969–1971. See sections titled "Business As Usual, But Only in Valparaiso" in Chapter 9 and "More Discussion" in Chapter 10.

[9] The program included *Opening Prayer* by Rev. Robert Otto Bartz Sr. (1925-83), *Address* by Dr. J. A. O. Preus, and *Closing Prayer* by Rev. Theodore Frederick August Nickel (1904-96). "Group of Northwest Suburban Lay People, LC-MS, Sponsoring Dr. J. A. O. Preus, President Lutheran Church Missouri Synod," one-page flyer, priv. col. of Nancy (nee Nicol) Nemoyer, Carlisle, Pa.

[10] Letter from J. A. O. Preus to Miss Cheryl D. Freitag, February 19, 1975, Box: JAO Preus Supplement II, Box 9 of 53, File: Freitag letters, CHI, St. Louis, Mo.

1971. That report included a resolution initially written by the LDA, and if it was adopted, we knew that it would only confirm the status quo.[11]

The end of the 1974–75 school year meant the end of our foursome. I transferred to Concordia College, Ann Arbor. Wilma and Kathy opted for "delayed internships," and would return to Valpo in 1975–76 to finish their senior year. Nancy was going to serve her internship at a congregation in Mt. Olive, Illinois.

* * *

Before Nancy could go to her internship site she needed to attend summer school at Valpo to take a class called Principles and Practices of Biblical Interpretation. An avid writer, she recorded the reason in her personal journal.

> In late April I made an appointment for three of us with Dr. Walter Keller, head of the Valparaiso Theology department. The three of us were all Ann Arbor grads. Our proposal was that we should not have to take the required course (for deaconesses) "Principles and Practices of Biblical Interpretation" because we had all taken EBT [Elements of Biblical Theology]. To the appointment we took one syllabus from the EBT class. The appointment was on a Monday. We went into his inner office, sat around a small coffee table; he pulled up a fourth chair and confronted us. Kathy B. did the part of spokesman. He looked at the syllabus. Quizzed us on a few terms, . . . We weren't prepared for a quiz. He admitted, too, after he had us all shook up, that that wasn't fair. Keller pulled out a Bible then, and I can't remember too clearly, but I think the question was "pick a passage and then tell by what criteria you would interpret it." We stammered through that. He asked us to give him a few days to make the decision. We were to see him in morning chapel on Wednesday . . .

> Pam and I found each other after chapel on Wednesday. Together we found Dr. Keller. He said one sentence. "Girls, I would like to see you all in Principles and Practices of Bible Interpretation" . . . I would need to take it in the summer session, but the other two were returning for their senior year and could take it during the fall semester.

> Daily Dr. Keller ridiculed an image of conservatives. He was unaccepting of any differing points of view to the degree that the class just agreed because he appeared so obviously correct. I was isolated as a conservative. Dr. Keller never specifically called me one, but he was very pointed in some questions and comments. None of the old faithful four were around for support. It was good, I guess, that I did have some time like this alone there. I had to struggle through—just me and my God. In this

---

[11] See sections titled "The 1971 Milwaukee Convention" and "Success and Disappointment" in Chapter 10.

independence and isolation I learned much. I learned that I could be bold in expressing my opinions.

But in class I was not so bold. I decided that it would have done no good to catch Keller on his erroneous ideas. He probably would have been upset by constant interruptions; by what he might have considered my naivety, maybe closed-mindedness and I was truly afraid that it might affect my grade. I did speak several times, unveiling my colors, and he either passed off my comments, or completely ignored or destroyed my points.

At the end of the session, after grades were in, I turned in a class evaluation. Basically the main points of my evaluation dealt with: our departure from the topic to "what's wrong with Synod;" a class in speculation and questions with no answers, "us/they" contrast as divisive; that I was very sorry that I had to take it; and a few compliments on our class Bible study.[12]

* * *

In June 1975, Nancy expressed her thoughts about the Valpo-based deaconess program to Deaconess Vanette Kashmer, LDA Director of Student Services. Kashmer encouraged Nancy to contact Deaconess Jean Schneider, Vice President of the LDA. Deaconess Schneider met with Nancy to talk through her concerns about Valpo and her ideas for the future. On September 17, Nancy wrote to Schneider, enclosing a letter to LDA President Curt Peters and a proposal to be presented to the LDA Board of Directors, both of which Schneider forwarded to Peters.[13] Nancy's courageous letter to the Board read:

> With humility, prayer, and a great love for the Deaconess profession and life, I would like to present the following proposal to the Lutheran Deaconess Association Board.
>
> As a theology major at Valparaiso University, I found the theology classes in general (with some exception) to be outspokenly one-sided concerning the current synodical controversy and the theological issues involved.
>
> As a resident of Deaconess Hall I found the atmosphere in general to be unaccepting of diverse opinions, specifically again in relation to the current Synodical controversy and the theological issues involved. The

[12] Nancy E. Nicol, Book Two, personal journal, 1975, priv. col. of Nancy (nee Nicol) Nemoyer, Carlisle, Pa.

[13] Letter from Nancy Nicol to Jean Schneider, September 6, 1975, Letter from Nancy Nicol to Jean Schneider, September 17, 1975; Letter from Jean Schneider to Nancy Nicol, September 22, 1975, priv. col. of Nancy (nee Nicol) Nemoyer, Carlisle, Pa.

atmosphere thus tended to sway the viewpoints of some students due to peer pressure.

Neither of these situations at the University nor the dormitory were conducive to a good learning environment, nor to community relationships.

As a pre-Deaconess student I was acquainted with other pre-Deaconesses, bright and brilliant young ladies, who opted out of the Deaconess program for other professions. Their reason was that the Junior and Senior Deaconess students are compelled to attend Valparaiso University. It saddens me much to consider this potential drain (even as the Lord uses these bright and brilliant young ladies in other avenues of His work.)

Also, it might be noted that a single location of the Deaconess training program provides no option for the student in regard to geographical considerations.

Therefore in the light of my own experiences during the school year of 1974–75 as a student Deaconess at Valparaiso and a resident of Deaconess Hall, as a pre-deaconess, and in regard to geographical concerns, I propose that in addition to the Deaconess Program as established at Valparaiso University the LDA set up an alternative location for the training of prospective Deaconesses. I would further suggest that one alternative location to consider be Concordia Lutheran College, Ann Arbor, Michigan. Concordia's growth process from a Junior College to a four year school could quite naturally incorporate a curriculum for Deaconess students in its expansion.

May our Lord guide you as you consider this proposal.[14]

Nancy received a polite reply from President Peters, stating that the Board discussed her concerns and ideas at several meetings. However, regarding a second training program he wrote:

The possibility of developing an upper level deaconess program at another school has been explored in the past. It has generally been set aside because of cost factors and because of the desire for a unity among deaconesses which, it was thought, preparation at a single center might help to provide. Those factors are still important, but we are giving and will continue to give serious consideration to expanding our program to another school, although it does not appear that we will at this time."[15]

---

[14] Letter from Nancy E. Nicol to LDA Board of Directors, September 17, 1975, priv. col. of Nancy (nee Nicol) Nemoyer, Carlisle, Pa.
[15] Letter from Curtis H. Peters to Nancy E. Nicol, December 4, 1975, priv. col. of Nancy (nee Nicol) Nemoyer, Carlisle, Pa.

* * *

Joyce Ostermann earned an Associate of Arts degree from St. Paul's College, Concordia, Missouri and started at Valparaiso University in the fall of 1971. Joyce's academic advisor at St. Paul's tried to persuade her to transfer to Seward rather than Valpo, but she wasn't interested in being a teacher. Since eighth grade, Joyce had had her heart set on being a deaconess; on living out her confirmation verse: "Seek ye first the kingdom of God and His righteousness, and all these things shall be added unto you."[16]

However, from the time that Joyce began her deaconess training, she realized that something was wrong.

> I thought it was strange that Catholic priests and nuns partook of Holy Communion at the Liturgical Conferences held at Valparaiso. I also wondered about the validity of different things that we were taught in theology classes, for example, the "JEDP" theory.[17] There were a lot of questions in my head, but that's where they stayed because I had no one to talk to about them. I don't remember any other deaconess students questioning what we were taught. I was alone in my thinking.

> When I served my internship at Lutheran Home in Fort Wayne my supervisor was a deaconess. She was caught up in the women's liberation movement that was so popular in American culture at that time. I remember that when all the other interns and I returned to Deaconess Hall, almost everyone moaned things like, "I was oppressed" or "I didn't get to preach." It was almost as if something was wrong with you if you didn't have a bad male supervisor on internship. The general theme of dorm conversation was that deaconesses should be equal to pastors. We even discussed *The Feminine Mystique* at one Pi Delta Chi meeting.

> While living at Deaconess Hall, I was the student manager of the dorm food service. So in the summer of 1973, I managed the catering for the Lutheran Deaconess Conference meeting held at Valparaiso. There was a real uproar of excitement at the conference when one of the deaconesses announced she was going to attend seminary to become a pastor. Many negative comments were made about our Synod. At that point I definitely remember thinking, "I'm going to be a deaconess, but I am *never* going to be a member of this organization!"

---

[16] Matthew 6:33 from the Authorized King James Version.

[17] The JEDP theory states that the first five books of the Bible were not written entirely by Moses, but also by different authors after the time of Moses. The letters J, E, D, and P represent four supposed authors: one who uses Jehovah for God's name, another who uses Elohim for God's name, the author of Deuteronomy, and an assumed Priestly author of Leviticus. See Chapter 11, footnote 30, regarding the Historical-Critical Method.

In June of 1974, right after graduating from Valpo, I returned to Lutheran Home to work as a deaconess. During my absence, Lutheran Home hired Deaconess Mildred Brillinger. The two of us shared an office. A few days after being there, I said to Millie, "I'm sure glad to be away from that place!"—meaning Deaconess Hall, Valparaiso University, and deaconesses in general. Millie confided that she and several other deaconesses in the Chicago area shared serious concerns about the LDC and the LDA. I *finally* found someone else who thought the same way that I did about the issues. *(Joyce)*

* * *

In the summer of 1974, Betty Mulholland attended the annual LDC conference at Sheboygan, Wisconsin.

The theme of the LDC conference in Sheboygan was the synodical controversy.[18] When I had heard about all that I could swallow, I noticed that Dr. Paul Zimmerman walked into the room. He had been invited, along with others, to participate in a panel discussion on the synodical issues.[19] I had never met Dr. Zimmerman before, but I scooted up to him and said, "President Zimmerman, are you staying in Sheboygan over night, or are you going home tonight?"

He answered, "I'm leaving as soon as the presentation is finished and I close my briefcase."

I said to him, "Well, Dr. Zimmerman, please, may I ride with you to Forest Park? I'd like to go home to my mother-in-law's house."

"If you're ready, yes, otherwise I don't want to wait," he replied.

I said, "thank you;" ran up to my room; wrote my roommate a note saying, "I'm going home;" and phoned my husband to say, "Call your mother and tell her I'm coming tonight. The president of River Forest is bringing me home." I grabbed my suitcase, ran back downstairs, and sat down next to a lady by the door. I turned to the lady and said, "And you are?"

She answered, "I'm Genevieve Zimmerman. President Zimmerman is my husband."

---

[18] LDC conference attendees received and discussed the controversial pamphlet, "A Call to Openness and Trust," produced by Lutherans for Openness and Trust, c/o 1 Selma, St. Louis, Mo. 63119. Betty Mulholland, notes from telephone interview by CDN, September 1, 2005, priv. col of CDN, Pittsburgh, Pa.

[19] Panelists included Rev. Martin W. Bangert (b. 1932), Rev. John H. Baumgaertner (1909–91), Rev. Horst Wilhelm Jordan (b. 1941), Rev. Grant Carl Johann Quill (1922–2004), Rev. Mark C. Wegner (1916–99), and Rev. Paul Zimmerman. "Resolutions—Annual Deaconess Conference 1974," mimeographed pages, priv. col. of Luella Mickley, Chicago, Illinois, 5.

And I said, "Wonderful, I'm going home with you tonight."

Her eyes got as big as dinner plates and she said, "You are?"

The panel discussion began and emotions ran high in that room. In fact, they were so intense that you could almost say they were on fire. The panelists presented the pros and cons of the walkout. Now, there was one deaconess, who wore a gold-colored T-shirt that had "Seminex" written on the back of it. She stood at the back of the room. Every time President Zimmerman got up to speak she would face the back wall and spread eagle herself against the wall, so that all Dr. Zimmerman would see straight ahead of him was "Seminex." When I think of that scene to this day, and the rude manner in which he was treated, it still brings tears to my eyes. The women were very cruel to him, trying to entrap him with their questions, while on the other hand, clapping for the pro-Seminex speaker.

As soon as the panel discussion was over, Dr. and Mrs. Zimmerman left. I was right on their heels. We got in the car, he started down the expressway, and I leaned forward from the back seat and said, "Excuse me, President and Mrs. Zimmerman, please forgive my deaconess sisters. They don't know what they're saying."

I thought President Zimmerman was going to wreck the car because he turned and looked back at me and said, "What did you say?" I repeated the apology, because I hurt so badly for how terribly he was treated. Well, that opened the door, and we chatted all the way from Sheboygan to my mother-in-law's home in Forest Park, Illinois. I don't know how long that ride was, but it wasn't long enough, because we talked and talked. We cried and we laughed together.

When Dr. Zimmerman carried my suitcase into my mother-in-law's kitchen, he said to me, "Betty, any time you need any help you call my secretary, Charlotte, and tell her that you want to see me." *(Betty)*

* * *

The Chicago Area Deaconess Conference was quite active in the late 1960s and early 1970s. Millie Brillinger, Ruth Broermann, Luella Mickley, and Betty Mulholland attended that regional conference with about a dozen other women who worked in greater Chicago.

One of the exciting things that we did as deaconesses, in addition to attending the annual conference, was to attend area conferences. We would try to get together at least monthly, and would include some of the deaconesses that were on leave as mothers, or not working for other reasons, and this was good. But things changed during that turbulent time. It was obvious to several of us that liberal teachings were being permitted in the LDC and we became increasingly dissatisfied with the topics that were discussed at the area conferences. Controversial issues made it very difficult for us. We all loved each other. We had a great camaraderie stemming back to our days at Valpo, and the conference strengthened that great bond that originated at Valpo. But we also recognized that our bond needed to be in the Word and in Christ. *(Millie)*

I'll never forget one of the area conferences. It was during the time of the racial uprisings in Chicago. One of the other deaconesses and I got into an argument because she thought that everyone should go out and throw bricks at the police. I said, "I can't see Jesus out there throwing bricks." And she said, "Well, I do see Jesus throwing bricks, and I would do so too." Just like the current trends in society, a lack of respect for legitimate authority was prevalent among the deaconesses at the area conferences, whether we were talking about political issues, feminism, or Holy Scripture. *(Ruth)*

I served as the LDC treasurer for many years and enjoyed the fellowship of the other deaconesses at annual conference and at the area conference. I was always the type of person who wanted to go with the flow. But when I saw this polarization on issues, even though I wasn't as disillusioned as Betty and Ruth at first, I came to see that it was important for women to have another option for deaconess education. There were other deaconesses in the Chicago area that agreed with us. Some didn't want to get embroiled in any controversy. They were faithful to their work and just wanted to be left alone to continue serving the Lord like they had always done.[20] *(Luella)*

After a while several of us were so disturbed by what went on at the area conferences that we began to meet together apart from the conference. Sometimes we met at Luella's house and her mother would cook dinner for us; sometimes we met at Millie's; other times everyone would come to my home; and we also got together at the River Forest campus where Julia [Hennig] worked. We weren't thinking about the possibility of a new deaconess program. We struggled with the theological wanderings of our sister deaconesses. We studied Scripture and prayed that they would return to the doctrine of the Lutheran Confessions. We took our concerns to them at the annual conference and area conferences but they laughed at us, ignored us, and even suggested that we go and do our own thing.

When five of us met with Dr. Wassman in 1971, we hoped that she would join us in trying to deter deaconesses from pursuing the pastoral office,

---

[20] Deaconesses like Frieda Bremermann and Lulu Noess repeatedly shared their conservative viewpoints with individual members of the Chicago area conference, but never spoke out at LDC meetings.

and that she would stand with us in speaking out against LDC resolutions that were contrary to Missouri Synod teaching and practice. We believed that it was still possible to turn the LDC around from the direction that it was heading. *(Betty)*

* * *

Millie continued to meet with the conservative Chicago area deaconesses after moving to Decatur, Indiana, in 1972. In the summer of 1975, she was the only deaconess in that group to travel to southern California for the annual LDC meeting.

The first annual conferences I attended were real highlights for me. Then, as the years went on, problems crept into the LDC. Liberal speakers addressed the conference; anti-synodical sentiments increased; the topic discussions and resolutions moved further away from Missouri Synod teaching and thinking.

At the California conference in 1975, I was upset by how the women disregarded clear Biblical teaching and the doctrine of our church. I didn't go to California to try to change my sister deaconesses, but I shared my thoughts with some of them. Just like previous occasions when I'd expressed my misgivings, they responded in a patronizing manner, trying to reassure me with words like, "Oh Millie, don't worry about these things. They're not important."

But Scripture and doctrine *were* important to me. I started crying and a few of the women that I'd known for several years asked me what was wrong. I explained that I just couldn't attend the closing Communion service with them. I loved these women. I loved being a deaconess. And I loved the work that they were doing, too. So I was very torn. I thought, "This is it. The group is not going to change. These women are completely satisfied with where they are going." With that realization, I was very sad. I went out and cried.

That was a decisive point in my life. It's not something that I wanted to happen. I didn't want to break anything up. I was overwhelmed with a terrible feeling of loss, and began to go through what can only be described as a mourning process. I had come to the conclusion that the LDC was not going to change. I would need to move forward somehow with the other conservative deaconesses. *(Millie)*

* * *

The 1976 LDC conference took place at Valparaiso University. Millie wasn't present for the conference, but Betty Mulholland and Clara Strehlow were there and roomed together.

I was having a real hard time at that conference. The resolutions that had been adopted at the business meeting were heartbreaking. One of them was a "deaconess identity statement" that defined a deaconess to be someone who was "in community with the Lutheran Deaconess Conference." Another resolution asked the LDA Board of Directors to build relationships with the ALC, the LCA, and other "emerging Lutheran bodies," which of course, included many who left the Missouri Synod after the formation of Seminex.

On one of the evenings a Communion service was scheduled to take place in the Great Hall. Clara and I sat together in the back. There was a flip chart at the front, but I couldn't read it because of glare from the lights. After the opening hymn, two clowns mimed a disagreement and then made up with each other. I thought, "What on earth is this?" During the fight one of the clowns bumped the flip chart. When it was put back in place at a slightly different angle, I could read the words: "Confession and Absolution." That was the last straw for me. I couldn't believe that anybody who took Christ's atoning sacrifice seriously would mock our Lord by substituting that fiasco for confession and absolution. I went outside and sat on the bench and wept. After the service was over I went back to our room in Deaconess Hall and told Clara, "I cannot stay. I have to leave. I cannot handle this." Clara understood. I called my husband and he came to pick me up.

On our way home my husband said, "This is it! Every time I pick you up from area conference or annual conference you're so upset it takes you a month to settle down. Now, you either do something about it or stop attending the conferences!" *(Betty)*

* * *

Betty decided that she wasn't a quitter. But what could she *do*? She phoned Ruth and the two of them spent the next several Saturdays thinking, praying, and then putting together the *Documentation*.

We were sure that many deaconesses were simply unsuspecting victims of the bad theology they had been taught by people they trusted—people who were influential and very sincere in their teaching. We hoped and prayed that our sisters would take a good hard look at the evidence, see the error of their ways, and help us rectify the situation. It wasn't until Ruth and I had dinner with Curt Peters and Louise Williams in Valparaiso, that we really realized it was no longer possible to change either the LDC or the LDA. On that sad day I thought, "It's time to contact President [Paul] Zimmerman."

None of us knew anything about how decisions were made in the Missouri Synod.

True to his word, Dr. Zimmerman helped us as much as his schedule would allow. He taught us how Synod worked; how to write petitions and resolutions; how to make appointments for floor committee meetings; and the etiquette that should be observed while speaking to boards and committees. He also told us up front, "Ladies, if I had my way, we would have the deaconess training program at River Forest, but I want you to know that I do not intend to influence the Board for Higher Education." *(Betty)*

* * *

Once Betty, Ruth, Luella, Millie, and Julia finished writing the petition to the BHE, the women felt that it was only fair that the LDA should be informed about what they were doing. Betty agreed to serve as spokesman for the group, so before the petition was mailed, she and one of the other Chicago deaconesses visited the LDA office in Valparaiso.

> I don't remember which office we went to at Deaconess Hall, but both Louise Williams and Vanette Kashmer were there, as well as two other deaconesses. I explained that several of us believed the Missouri Synod should assume responsibility for the training of its deaconesses; that we would be sending every deaconess the *Documentation* and a copy of our petition to the BHE, in the hope that others would join our campaign; and that we were there to inform them of our actions, because we felt that it was only proper that they should receive first-hand knowledge from us about what we were doing and why.

> I handed a copy of the petition to Louise. She read it and passed it on to the next deaconess, who then read it and again passed it on. There was no discussion while the women were reading. When all four had finished reading the petition, Louise passed it back over the desk to me and simply said, "If you think the men of Missouri are going to listen to you, then go ahead and try." *(Betty)*

* * *

The staff of Lutheran Home in Fort Wayne included a *Deaconess Corps* of four to six women who processed admissions; coordinated volunteers; served as liaison between the Home and families; visited, prayed, and had individual devotions with the residents. During the 1970s, this unique model of team ministry also provided the training ground for several deaconess interns. When the LDA placed two interns at Lutheran Home for the 1976–77 year, Millie Brillinger and Joyce Ostermann were designated as internship supervisors for the students.

> I didn't sign the petition asking the BHE to establish a Missouri Synod deaconess program, but around the time that the petition was sent out I

started to accompany Millie to informal meetings with other conservative deaconesses. Since Millie and I were internship supervisors for the Valpo program, we thought it was important to be upfront with the LDA about our involvement in the movement for a Missouri Synod training program. So we drove to Valparaiso to speak with Louise Williams and Vanette Kashmer. We explained our position and volunteered to withdraw as deaconess intern supervisors, because we perceived that there could be a conflict of interest if we were working against a program that utilized us as supervisors. *(Joyce)*

Our meeting at Deaconess Hall was very cordial. We just wanted everything out in the open. We weren't there to flaunt what we were doing or to rub it in. We were struggling and experiencing grief over what we knew had to be done. Louise and Vanette knew that I signed the petition to the BHE and I wanted them to know that I would continue to pursue a Missouri Synod deaconess program. Their response was twofold, that Joyce and I should continue as internship supervisors and that they were confident we wouldn't have any undue influence on the interns. Louise said something like, "You aren't going to get that far with the BHE, so it's really not going to matter." *(Millie)*

* * *

Kay Pritzlaff was a deaconess intern at Lutheran Home during the 1976–77 school year. At the end of her internship, she was consecrated as a deaconess and continued to serve as part of the Deaconess Corps at the Home.

It was wonderful to be a part of the Deaconess Corps; to work with godly women who were dedicated to their vocation. I learned so much from Joyce and Millie. They never put any pressure on me to adopt their opinions, but as we worked together, they shared concerns about the LDA or LDC.

I only spent one year at Valparaiso because I had a Bachelor's degree from the Senior College and just needed to pick up the required Theology courses. So I wasn't exposed to as many problems as those women who spent two or more years there. Thinking back on it, I realized there were differences of opinion related to the synodical controversy at Valpo, but I never got involved in those debates. Some of the other students thought that becoming a deaconess was a stepping-stone to becoming a pastor. Later, at Lutheran Home, and too, when talking with people at the Fort Wayne seminary where I sang in the choir, I became more aware of the issues and decided to join ranks with the women who were campaigning for a Missouri Synod deaconess program. I never talked to committees or traveled to conventions. I supported the campaign with friendship and prayer." *(Kay)*

* * *

Sometime during the last half of my sophomore year at Concordia, Ann Arbor (1975–76), I stopped at President Pohl's office to ask him how things were progressing for establishing a deaconess program at the college. I still hoped that a program might be put in place so that I could stay at Ann Arbor to finish my deaconess training. The President explained that Ann Arbor would soon become a four-year college. However, with the closing of the Fort Wayne Senior College, building a pre-seminary program was the college's first priority, and there weren't enough resources—either financial or human—to take on the deaconess program.[21]

In the fall of 1976 I returned to Valparaiso as a junior. Nancy had finished her deaconess internship and was spending the first semester of her senior year at Valpo's foreign studies program in Reutlingen, Germany. Nancy and I roomed together in Deaconess Hall when she came back to Valpo for the second semester. At the end of the school year I got married, attended summer school, and went to my internship in Michigan; Nancy graduated, was consecrated, and started serving as a deaconess in Illinois. Neither of us knew that there were other deaconesses who shared our dream for a Missouri Synod deaconess program.

* * *

Ruth was the principal writer of the 1976 petition to the BHE. She also helped the group compose concise and winsome presentations for the 1977 floor committee meetings.

> I was the only one in the group that took business classes in college. I knew how to take shorthand and read it back, and the gals wanted to utilize that skill. On our trip down to St. Louis I sat in the middle of the back seat. Everyone made sure I had a pad of paper and a pen that could write. Once we were on the road I said, "OK, start." Everyone in the car would agree on some ideas and then I'd write a paragraph. I would read it back to them and ask, "Do you all agree?" Everyone had a vote and could cancel what was written if they thought it wasn't quite right. If there was a single objection to any word, we would pull out the word, go over the section, and insert something different. We worked this way during the entire journey to St. Louis and even continued after checking into the motel.

---

[21] As a result of this conversation with President Pohl, I was very surprised to see him at the BHE floor committee meeting in July 1979, stating that if River Forest started a deaconess program, it was only fair that Ann Arbor be allowed to do so at the same time. I later discovered that the 1977 *Convention Workbook* contained a resolution "To Introduce Deaconess Program at Ann Arbor (6-95)," submitted by the Board of Control and Faculty of Concordia College.

The floor committee chairman told us that we could speak for 15 minutes. However, we wanted to keep it shorter so that the committee would have time to ask questions. So when we finished the presentation it had to be cut, polished, cut again, polished, and finally, just as it was time to make our way to the meeting room, I made sure that Betty had a finished copy that she could read without any trouble, because she was our spokesman. *(Ruth)*

* * *

Already in her latter years as housemother of Deaconess Hall (1958–63), Clara Strehlow noted the theological differences that existed between herself and the LDA Director of Training. She was deeply concerned about the direction in which the LDA and the LDC were moving and articulated the "Missouri Synod position" whenever she could. As the conservative Chicago (and Fort Wayne) deaconesses met and worked on letters or presentations, they often spoke to Clara on the phone or wrote letters seeking her advice. The following letter, dated April 19, 1978, shows how Clara encouraged her sisters to be rooted in Scripture, to remain loyal to the Missouri Synod, and to continue in their course of action.

Dear Betty,

Thank you for your letter of April 3rd and special thanks to both you and Julia for your efforts to save our L.D.A. program for LCMS. I do ponder a great deal on the issues and pray the Lord will arouse the necessary help, confident He hears and will answer our prayers in due time, in His own way. Pastors Herzberger and Wambsganss labored long to bring the LDA into being. It may take more time than we hoped to bring order out of chaos again.

Here is the result of my considering the questions you sent. . . .

. . . None of the early deaconesses desired the preaching ministry. Much or all depends on the training. This is one reason why we seek separation from V.U. where profs teach the liberal "New theology."

In the past we deaconesses have accepted the words of our constitution that we are within and under Synod. Sisterhood and community is now being stressed by those deaconesses with the breakaway group of Synod (Seminex). Like other ELIM members, they want separation and yet retain the blessings of fellowship.

. . . Unless a new LDA within LCMS is formed, ties to the present association are not important.

. . . Ordination of deaconesses in other denominations, even the Catholic nuns, is the result of "New" theology and modern women's liberation.

This has no place in the thinking of those who adhere to the pure Word, as our LCMS upholds. Since the AELC group is opening in that direction I feel those deaconesses desiring ordination will remain with that group. I realize though that in these latter days it is difficult to predict what will be. Jesus warned us of the latter days.

Gratefully and cordially,

Clara[22]

* * *

Though my internship finished in the summer of 1978, I waited until January 1979 to go back to Valpo because I only needed one semester of classes to graduate. That last semester seemed like an endless one. My husband was still at college in Ann Arbor, so I lived in Deaconess Hall during the week and commuted the four hours to be with him on weekends. I truly wanted to serve the Lord as a deaconess, and it seemed that this was the only way to reach that goal.

When I returned to Valpo I needed to deal with new issues. Deaconess students were now required to preach a homily in the University Chapel. I went to Louise Williams to explain my belief that Scripture did not allow women to preach and that I couldn't go against my conscience, and she agreed to waive that requirement for me. I also heard that all returning interns were expected to take Clinical Pastoral Education (CPE), which met on Saturday mornings. I explained to Vanette Kashmer that I didn't think the class was necessary and I didn't want to spend another day away from my husband. She acknowledged that I couldn't be forced to take CPE, since I started deaconess training under a catalog that didn't require it, but lectured me about my attitude and commitment to the deaconess community, which she said were important factors in determining whether or not a student would be consecrated as a deaconess.

With such a shaky start to my last semester I was wary of doing anything to upset the LDA staff. When Louise consecrated the elements at a Eucharist service in the Deaconess Hall chapel, I spoke to no one about it but took comfort from reading the words of Luther's *Large Catechism*.[23] I stopped challenging theological statements made by professors or classmates and told myself, "Just cooperate and graduate."

---

[22] The questions that Clara answered in this letter were the 13 questions that the BHE asked Betty Mulholland and Julia Hennig at the March 1978 meeting in Concordia, Missouri. See section titled "BHE Study Gets Underway" in Chapter 11. Letter from Clara E. Strehlow to Betty Mulholland, April 19, 1978, priv. col. of Betty (nee Schmidt) Mulholland, Munster, Ind.

[23] Theodore G. Tappert, ed., *The Book of Concord* (Philadelphia: Fortress Press, 1959), 448.

* * *

In February 1978, Nancy joined the Deaconess Corps at Lutheran Home in Fort Wayne, where she worked with Joyce and Kay. About a year later, I visited the Home with a group of deaconess students who were interested in the possibility of serving at an institution. When we had a few minutes alone, Nancy mentioned that Joyce knew some deaconesses who were trying to establish a Missouri Synod training program and suggested that I might want to contact one of them named Betty. I wasn't sure what good it could do, but when I got back to Deaconess Hall I made the phone call.

A couple of weekends later, Joyce came to Valparaiso to pick me up and take me to Betty's house. I was nervous and cautious, but soon felt at home. "So how about it, Cheryl? Will you join us in the quest for a Missouri Synod diaconate?" Betty asked.

"Yes, I will," I answered. "It might be too late for me, but if I can do something to help other Missouri Synod gals that still want to be deaconesses, then count me in." My answer really only echoed something that I'd once heard Nancy say. As she wrote letters to synodical officials and the LDA, she often thought of a friend who had gone through the pre-deaconess program with her at Ann Arbor and then couldn't bring herself to transfer to Valpo to complete her training. This crusade was for women like Nancy's friend—and for those whom we felt certain would desire deaconess training in the future.

* * *

Whenever two or more of our group were on the road, in a motel, at the St. Louis seminary for floor committee meetings, or at a convention site, we spent a large amount of time in prayer together. In fact, the first and last order of business was always prayer. In public buildings our "meeting room" was usually the ladies' powder room, but we once used a large unlocked closet, and at the 1979 convention we met in a long narrow storage closet surrounded by shelves of paper.

As I recall, Betty or someone she designated would lead us in prayer. Our thoughts were simple: "Dear Lord, we thank you for this opportunity. Please give us strength and courage. Guide our thoughts and words. Bless our church leaders and give wisdom to all who make decisions for our Synod. Please bring our erring brothers and sisters back to the truth of Your Word. And if it is Your will, Lord, move the hearts of our Synod delegates to establish a Missouri Synod deaconess program, so that the women in our church who want to be deaconesses will be taught correct doctrine and practice, and will honor You with service that is faithful to Your Word. May Your will be done, in Jesus' Name."

CHAPTER 14

ANOTHER DEACONESS CONFERENCE

None of us who became the founding members of *Concordia Deaconess Conference—Lutheran Church-Missouri Synod* actually set out to create a new deaconess conference. Our one and only goal was to convince the Missouri Synod to establish its own deaconess program so that future students could have a choice about where they wanted to be educated and trained.

After our presentation to Floor Committee Six on May 26, 1979, Clara, Betty, Joyce, Nancy, and I made a beeline for the ladies' bathroom. We felt optimistic about the outcome of our meeting with the committee. As we used the facilities, someone said, "If Synod does establish its own deaconess program, we're going to need a deaconess conference for the graduates of that program."

There was a short pause in conversation while we pondered the idea. "What would we call it?" asked a different voice.

"How about Missouri Deaconess Association?"

"Or Missouri Deaconess Conference?"

"Or maybe Lutheran Deaconess Society?"

"Then we'd be LDS, just like the Latter Day Saints!" There was laughter and another pause.

"What about *Concordia* Deaconess Conference?" I offered.

"Well . . . we have so many Concordias already. Concordia seminaries, Concordia colleges, Concordia Historical Institute and . . ."

"Precisely!" came Betty's excited voice. "And the one thing that they all have in common is that they're Missouri Synod. *Concordia* equals Missouri."

By this time we were all standing by the sinks. Clara smiled and her whole face lit up. "I like it," she said. "*Concordia* means harmony, and we are in harmony with Synod."

"All right, then," we agreed in unison. By the time everyone had washed their hands, the CDC was born!

Corresponding with the LDC

The idea of a second deaconess conference was either brave or stupid, but we had come this far and there was really no turning back. The big question for us was whether or not the Missouri Synod would continue to recognize us as deaconesses if the LDA did not. Furthermore, would the Synod assume that graduates from its deaconess program would automatically join the Valparaiso-based Lutheran Deaconess Conference? All pastors in a given circuit went to the same circuit meetings regardless of the seminary that they attended. But we knew that such an arrangement might not work for women who were so completely different in their understanding and application of theology.

A week after LCMS convention delegates passed "Resolution 6-05: To Expand Deaconess Program," the five of us who attended the St. Louis convention drafted a letter to the LDC. We had heard that other deaconesses present at the St. Louis convention were angry and accusing us of trying to shut down the Valparaiso program. Of course, nothing could have been further from the truth. Our goal was a Missouri Synod program for Missouri Synod women. We expected the LDA to continue and even expand its pan-Lutheran program. Our letter intended to put the story straight. It read:

Dear Sisters of the Lutheran Deaconess Conference,

We are sure that by now you are aware of the action taken by the 53rd convention of the Lutheran Church—Missouri Synod regarding the establishment of a full deaconess training program at Concordia College, River Forest. We are also sure that you know we were supportive of the passing of this resolution. We are also sure that there are many opinions as to why we took this course of action. So to avoid gross misunderstandings of our actions, we wish to make the following statements:

During the 1970s we have observed the Lutheran Deaconess Conference taking a position on issues which reflects a theology inconsistent with doctrines held by The Lutheran Church—Missouri Synod. Examples of this are:

- resolutions supporting sisters preparing for the ministry

- members of the LDC holding membership in other Lutheran bodies than LCMS

- scheduling of Norma Jeanne Everist to celebrate Holy Eucharist at the 1978 annual deaconess Conference in Valparaiso, Indiana

- LDC membership in North American Diaconia

In light of the changing positions on doctrine and practice of the Lutheran Deaconess Conference, those of us who wish to remain true to the Missouri Synod can find little identity within this sisterhood. After long and prayerful consideration, we turned to our church and asked for recognition. We rejoice and thank God for the passing of resolution 6-05 establishing a training program at River Forest, for this is the first step in establishing a Missouri Synod identity.

We trust that this communication with the Lutheran Deaconess Conference will give you an understanding of our actions. We pray that as Christians we have not personally offended you, but if we have, we ask your forgiveness. We pray for each of you as you carry out your ministries. May the Lutheran Deaconess Conference continue to be a blessing to many.[1]

On July 26, LDC President Kathy Borgman read our letter to the deaconesses assembled for their annual meeting, after which Louise Williams "began a discussion on the actions taken at The Lutheran Church—Missouri Synod Convention."[2] The Key Note Address delivered by Williams the next morning contained references to us as well as the Synod. For example:

. . . Our inter-Lutheran character has raised questions for some about our worshipping and communing together and has raised more than eyebrows in the Missouri Synod. That was a contributing factor in causing some of our sisters to work hard for a purely Missouri Synod diaconate. And, it appears, it will cause some of our sisters to leave us. . . . Ordination of women as pastors is an issue to be reckoned with in any inter-Lutheran group today where some believe that it is wrong to have women serve as pastors and some believe it is right—even essential. For some of our sisters continued involvement of our ordained sisters is *a natural outgrowth of the direction of our recent past and of the identity statement.* . . . [3]

Both LDA and LDC leaders applauded the deaconess community's "unity in diversity" and "diversity in unity." Membership in the

---

[1] Letter from Deaconesses Betty Mulholland, Mildred Brillinger, Joyce Ostermann, Nancy Nicol, and Cheryl D. Naumann to Sisters of the Lutheran Deaconess Conference, July 19, 1979, priv. col. of Joyce Ostermann, Fort Wayne, Ind.

[2] Jeanette Rebeck, "Minutes Lutheran Deaconess Conference—Annual Meeting, July 26–30, 1979, Concordia College—Portland, Oregon," priv. col. of Nancy (nee Nicol) Nemoyer, Carlisle, Pa, 1.

[3] Emphasis added by author. Louise Williams, "Diaconate: Past, Present, and Possibilities," Key Note Address, Lutheran Deaconess Conference, Portland, Oregon, July 26–30, 1979, priv. col. of Nancy (nee Nicol) Nemoyer, Carlisle, Pa.

sisterhood—synonymous with membership in the LDC—now took the place of doctrine and churchly practice as the basis for diaconal unity and identity. The 1979 Deaconess Conference sought to solidify this position by passing the "Resolution—Reaffirmation and Communication" as follows:

> ... RESOLVED, that the Lutheran Deaconess Conference commend the Lutheran Deaconess Association Board and Staff for their faithful defense of diaconal ministry; and be it further
>
> RESOLVED, that the Lutheran Deaconess Conference at this time reaffirm the deaconess identity statement adopted in 1976 as follows: "A deaconess is a Lutheran woman who through special Lutheran theological and practical training is consecrated to serve, which service is manifested in leadership roles and /or professional positions within the Lutheran Church and/or society, and who is in community with the Lutheran Deaconess Conference," and be it further
>
> RESOLVED, we request the LDA Board in consultation with the LDC Board to communicate this reaffirmation to our own community, to all Lutheran judicatories in which we serve and to the Lutheran Church of America diaconate; and to reaffirm previous commitments to develop and maintain avenues for dialogue with appropriate officials of the LCMS, the ALC, the AELC, and the LCA; and that special attention be given to the LCA deaconess community; and be it finally
>
> RESOLVED, that we seize the moment created by the Missouri Synod convention to utilize the church's media to communicate information concerning deaconess ministry.[4]

After the LDC adopted the above resolution, conference attendees gave permission to the LDC Board to send a response to our letter (and a copy of that response to the chairman of every area conference).[5] At the end of September, the five of us received an identical letter, in which we were all addressed as "Deaconess." The body of the letter read:

> ... The members attending the conference this summer asked us to respond in two ways to your communication. First, you asked that you may be forgiven if you had personally offended any of us. We do forgive you.
>
> Second, we continue to adhere to our identity statement which was adopted in 1976. Part of that identity statement states that a deaconess is

[4] Jeanette Rebeck, "Minutes Lutheran Deaconess Conference—Annual Meeting, July 26–30, 1979, 5.
[5] Ibid., 3.

one who is in community with the Lutheran Deaconess Conference. We ask that you address yourselves to this statement and communicate with us as to where you presently see yourselves in relationship to the Lutheran Deaconess Conference.[6]

The women of the LDC were our peers. It hurt to know that our sisters who embraced the LDC identity statement would no longer consider us to be deaconesses if we parted company with the conference. The older ladies in our group realized, too, that since the LDA Board of Directors adopted the LDC identity statement in 1977, the association might inform the LCMS that we were no longer deaconesses.[7] At the very least, we were certain that the LDA would remove us from what was assumed to be the Synod's official roster of deaconesses, namely, the list of deaconesses that the LDA submitted for publication in the *Lutheran Annual* every year.

Although we didn't reply immediately to the LDC, primarily because we were busy with the formation of CDC, we didn't stop to count the cost before answering the letter. We refused to be bullied or blackmailed into membership in an organization that ignored clear Scriptural teaching and displayed disrespect for the Synod. In February, we wrote:

> Dear Kathy and LDC Board,
>
> Thank you for responding to our letter of last summer and for reading it to the Conference.
>
> You have requested our response to the LDC identity statement which reads "A deaconess is a Lutheran woman who is ... . . in community with the LDC."
>
> According to the <u>Handbook</u> of the LC-MS we meet the requirements for certification of eligibility as Lutheran Deaconesses. Community with the LDC is not specified in the <u>Handbook.</u> As LC-MS Deaconesses we wish to abide by LC-MS policies.
>
> May our heavenly Father continue to bless each of you.[8]

---

[6] Letter from Kathy Borgman to Deaconess Betty Mulholland, cc to Mildred Brillinger, Joyce Ostermann, Nancy Nicol, Cheryl D. Naumann, September 19, 1979, priv. col. of Betty Mulholland, Munster, Ind.

[7] Louise Williams, "Report of the Director of Deaconess Services to the Annual Deaconess Conference 8–17–77," mimeographed sheets, Box: CDC, File: LDC 15–18 Aug. 1977, CHI, St. Louis, Missouri, 3.

[8] Letter from Deaconesses Betty Mulholland, Mildred Brillinger, Joyce Ostermann, Nancy Nicol, and Cheryl D. Naumann to Kathy (Borgman) and LDC Board, February 26, 1980, priv. col. of Betty Mulholland, Munster, Ind.

Our letter addressed the core issue raised by the LDC. We had other concerns with the deaconess identity statement beyond its insistence on membership in the LDC. We believed that an open-ended interpretation of deaconess service "in leadership roles and/or professional positions within the Lutheran Church and/or society" encouraged unscriptural practices. For example, we knew that the LDA Director of Deaconess Services accepted invitations to preach, and that the LDA and LDC both understood "Lutheran Church" to include synods that were not in fellowship with the LCMS.[9] But the time for theological debate had ceased. We answered the question by appealing to what we firmly believed was the over-arching authority of the Synod to which we belonged. A few months later another letter came from the LDC:

> We received your letter in which you gave a response to the LDC identity statement.
>
> In your response you did not indicate how you see yourselves in relationship to the Lutheran Deaconess Conference. We would still appreciate your response.[10]

This short epistle sparked quite a bit of discussion among our group members. We felt that the last paragraph of our letter clearly showed our intention to continue to work as LCMS deaconesses, but without membership in LDC since the LCMS did not require us to be in "Community with the LDC." Now we were being asked for further clarification, which we interpreted as a request for an explicit resignation from the LDC.

Joyce and I never paid LDC dues, never attended a Deaconess Conference, and never considered ourselves to be members of the LDC. We felt that it was wrong to resign from an organization that we didn't belong to; and that if we did, we would be supporting the false notion that all LDA deaconesses became (and had to remain) members of the LDC. Clara assisted Superintendent Kohlmeier in organizing the Deaconess

---

[9] When we were in St. Louis, a convention delegate handed us the June 3, 1979, bulletin from Immanuel Lutheran Church, Kansas City, Missouri. An announcement in the bulletin read: "Deaconess Louise Williams, Immanuel's former parish deaconess and now an executive with the Lutheran Deaconess Association in Valparaiso, Indiana, will preach next Sunday morning at Overland Park Lutheran Church, 79th & Lowell, on the occasion of the 60th anniversary celebration of the LDA . . ." "Deaconess Louise Preaches Locally," Printed bulletin Vol. 60 No. 21, June 3, 1979, Immanuel Lutheran Church, 42nd and Tracy, Kansas City, Missouri, The LCMS, priv. col. of Betty Mulholland, Munster, Ind.

[10] Letter from Kathy Borgman to Betty (Mulholland), April 16, 1980, priv. col. of Betty Mulholland, Munster, Ind.

Conference in 1933, served as its first president, and remained an active member for 46 years.[11] Ruth, Luella, Millie, Betty, Kay, and Nancy also paid their LDC dues and attended conferences with varying degrees of regularity. Confident in our mutual resolve to remain loyal to the LCMS rather than the LDC, the latter seven women sent individual letters of resignation to the LDC. When the LDC replied to these letters of resignation from the deaconess conference, the replies had one significant thing in common: they were addressed to "Miss" or "Mrs" instead of being addressed to "Deaconess."[12]

MOVING FORWARD

Those of us who were employed as deaconesses continued with our jobs—working for the LCMS Northern Illinois District Office, at Lutheran homes for the elderly, and in LCMS congregations and schools. We used the title "Deaconess" just as we had done from the time of our consecrations, or from the time that we received our first placements and the LCMS Council of Presidents recognized us as deaconesses.[13] As the months went by and we received counsel and guidance from various synodical authorities, it became obvious that the Missouri Synod still viewed us as deaconesses, even if the LDC and LDA did not.[14]

The real turning point for us, in terms of morale and the courage to move forward in creating a new deaconess conference, came on November 10, 1979, during a meeting with President Paul Zimmerman in River Forest. Dr. Zimmerman assured us:

> I take the position that you are deaconesses. You've been consecrated and you have deaconess status. And you're serving in the Lutheran Church Missouri Synod. . . . I don't see under the *Handbook,* and under your status, particularly in view of the fact that Synod now has its own deaconess program, that you have to be members of the LDC to be considered a certified deaconess. You have to be placed by the Synod. That's all that you need. Membership in the LDA or LDC does not

---

[11] See chapter 5.

[12] See for example, letter from Louise Williams to Mrs. Betty Mulholland, August 22, 1980, priv. col. of Betty Mulholland, Munster, Ind.

[13] Some in our group became deaconesses before the LCMS Council of Presidents began acting as a placement board for deaconesses.

[14] See for example, letter from J.A.O. Preus (President LCMS) to Ruth Broermann (President CDC), March 11, 1980, priv. col. of Ruth (nee Broermann) Stallmann, St. Louis, Mo.

confer on you—in fact, I don't believe it ever did—the fact that you are a Missouri Synod Deaconess. It's the placement that does.

Now, if you're asking the other question, of listing in the *Annual* . . . I think what I need to do, as President of Concordia, is approach whoever puts out the *Lutheran Annual,* and simply point out to them that the next time they put out an *Annual*—it's not going to be 1980 obviously, I'm sure that's already on the press—that the 1981 *Annual* will need to carry a separate item for those deaconesses who are not members of the LDC, but who are certified deaconesses, placed by the Synod, and serving LCMS congregations or agencies, or for that matter, who are presently not in service but who hold the status of deaconess.[15]

Dr. Zimmerman spoke to LCMS Secretary, Dr. Herbert A. Mueller (1914-99), and later reported to CDC President Ruth Broermann: "Dr. Mueller fully agrees there should be no problem in getting the ladies listed in the *Lutheran Annual.* He could not find his notes, but he is sure that is already taken care of in the 1981 *Lutheran Annual.*"[16]

The section labeled "Deaconesses" in the 1981 *Annual* listed both CDC and LDC deaconesses together with no mention of either organization.[17] This seemed to be a good solution, since women belonging to both deaconess conferences served Missouri Synod congregations and institutions. However, the following year, we were very disappointed to see that the names and information for active CDC deaconesses did not appear in the 1982 *Lutheran Annual.* Deaconess Nancy Nicol telephoned the LCMS secretary to request that he investigate the matter. Dr. Mueller replied:

. . . what happened was essentially this: When the list of deaconesses arrived from Valparaiso University it was noticed that certain names were crossed out. On the assumption that this meant that these deaconesses were no longer active, their names were removed from the master list which was submitted for printing. The department working on these matters has been apprised of the fact that there will be two lists that will need to be correlated for the next <u>Annual</u>. So I am sure that this will not

---

[15] "Paul A. Zimmerman meeting with Ruth Broermann, Luella Mickley, Betty Mulholland, Cheryl D. Naumann, Nancy Nicol, and Clara Strehlow," transcript, November 10, 1979, priv. col. of CDN, Pittsburgh, Pa.

[16] Memo from Paul A. Zimmerman to Deaconess Ruth Broermann, copied to Deaconess Nancy Nicol, December 9, 1980, priv. col. of Nancy (nee Nicol) Nemoyer, Carlisle, Pa.; see also: Letter from Paul A. Zimmerman to Dr. Mueller, July 24, 1980, priv. col. of Nancy (nee Nicol) Nemoyer, Carlisle, Pa. and Letter from Herbert Mueller to Paul Zimmerman, August 5, 1980, priv. col. of Nancy (nee Nicol) Nemoyer, Carlisle, Pa.

[17] Through 1980, all deaconesses were listed in the *Annual* under the section heading, "Lutheran Deaconess Association."

happen again. Please convey the Synod's regrets to those who have been adversely affected.[18]

Two months later, under "official notices" in the LCMS *Reporter*, Mueller included a special article titled "Deaconess Listing." The article included a list of all deaconesses that should have been included in the *Annual* with the explanation: "The following have resigned from the Lutheran Deaconess Conference but not from the roster of LCMS Deaconesses listed on page 393 ff. of *The Lutheran Annual 1982*."[19] At last it was confirmed—in print for all to see—that the Missouri Synod did not endorse the LDA assertion that a deaconess "is one who is in community with the Lutheran Deaconess Conference." What a tremendous relief it was for us to know that this issue was now settled, forever.

One of our co-campaigners, Dr. Julia Hennig, did resign from the diaconate shortly before the 1979 LCMS convention for personal reasons. Though she no longer considered herself a deaconess, Julia supported the River Forest program by helping to write the deaconess curriculum and afterward served for many years on the "Admissions Review Committee" for deaconess students.[20]

After the 1979 convention, the remaining nine of us met together as often as possible, at Lutheran Home in Fort Wayne, at the Mulholland home in Munster, and at Concordia College in River Forest. We praised God for the priviledge of being used by Him, individually and collectively, to help bring about a Missouri Synod deaconess training program. We thanked God for the miracle of finding each other; that we no longer needed to be lone or lonely voices in a diaconate that valued sisterhood above correct doctrine and practice. We rejoiced in the new challenge before us: to establish a Missouri Synod deaconess conference that would allow and encourage deaconesses to remain faithful to the Scriptures and faithful to their calling in teaching, leadership, and service.

---

[18] Letter from Herbert Mueller to Miss Nicol, January 13, 1982, priv. col. of Nancy (nee Nicol) Nemoyer, Carlisle, Pa.

[19] Herbert Mueller, "Deaconess Listing," *Reporter* 8, no. 11 (March 22, 1982). See also: Letter from Nancy Nicol to Mr. Mueller, January 26, 1982, priv. col. of Nancy (nee Nicol) Nemoyer, Carlisle, Pa.; Memo from Paul A. Zimmerman to Deaconess Nancy Nicol, January 28, 1982, priv. col. of Nancy (nee Nicol) Nemoyer, Carlisle, Pa.

[20] "3D: A Decade of Deaconess Dedication, 1980–1990," mimeographed pages bound in folder, no pagination, River Forest, 1990.

PART III

IN THE MISSOURI SYNOD: 1980–2008

The 1979 decision to establish a deaconess training program *within* the LCMS brought a flurry of activity at Concordia College and among conservative deaconesses. Much work needed to be done to implement the Synod's resolution and to form a new deaconess conference for its graduates.

Part III traces the journey of the *Missouri Synod* deaconess movement for the last 28-plus years. It documents the growth and activities of the Concordia Deaconess Conference and the first synodical deaconess program; traces the chain of synodical legislation impacting deaconesses; and finally, witnesses to the great blessing given to the church through the many women who serve their Lord in this vocation.

CHAPTER 15

CONCORDIA DEACONESS
CONFERENCE

As the women who campaigned for a Missouri Synod deaconess training program continued to meet together in fall 1979, they pondered the idea of founding a new deaconess conference. The informal agendas for their "pre-organizational meetings" included Bible Study, discussion of issues related to the new training program and the synodical handbook, plus a great deal of brainstorming. The first guest speaker to attend one of these sessions, Dr. Elmer E. Foelber, presented an anecdotal lecture on the early days of deaconess training within the Synodical Conference.[1]

The deaconesses felt certain that a formalized conference would be needed for graduates of the River Forest program. Like pastors and teachers, deaconesses benefited from ongoing educational opportunities and dialogue with those who shared the same vocation. More than that, the church was also richer when its workers took time to grow in Christ and develop professional collegiality.

The first question that the women needed to answer was: If we are going to establish a Missouri Synod deaconess conference, *when* should it be organized? The 1979 LCMS convention mandated a full deaconess training program at Concordia College by fall 1980. If any students entered the River Forest program as juniors, then the first deaconess graduates would be placed in spring 1983. When the deaconesses consulted President Zimmerman on this question, he encouraged them to proceed as soon as they could, to "get a gang together and draw up a proposed constitution."[2] There were two benefits to achieving this sooner than later. First, those "deaconesses without a conference" would be able to join together with like-minded sisters in Christ; and second, the conference would be a well-oiled, solid organization by the time the first River Forest graduates were ready to join.

---

[1] See chapters 2 and following for more about Foelber.
[2] "Paul A. Zimmerman meeting with Ruth Broermann, Luella Mickley, Betty Mulholland, Cheryl D. Naumann, Nancy Nicol, and Clara Strehlow," transcript, November 10, 1979, priv. col. of CDN, Pittsburgh, Pa.

A CONSTITUTION

Before their November meeting with Dr. Zimmerman adjourned, the deaconesses agreed that they would convene again on January 12 for the express purpose of organizing a conference. They also appointed a Constitution Committee—consisting of the four Fort Wayne deaconesses, with Joyce Ostermann as chairman—to write a constitution that could be adopted at the January meeting.[3]

The Constitution Committee took great care to formulate a document that reflected a clear identity with the Missouri Synod. Hence, the name of the conference was not just "Concordia Deaconess Conference," but "Concordia Deaconess Conference—Lutheran Church-Missouri Synod." Furthermore, when composing "The objectives of Concordia Deaconess Conference," while incorporating ideas from group brainstorming sessions, the committee tried to draw as many parallels as possible between the official objectives of the LCMS and those to be adopted by the new organization.[4]

The objectives of Concordia Deaconess Conference

1. To give all glory to God.

2. To extend the Kingdom of God.

3. To aid the Synod, specifically in upholding and promoting the Deaconess ministry within the Synod.

4. To provide opportunity for spiritual, personal, and professional growth and fellowship for those who are Deaconesses in the LCMS.

Since the conference founders felt that deaconesses should never be forced to join CDC, Article III of the Constitution defined the conference as a "free association" of deaconesses "who hold membership in a congregation of the Lutheran Church-Missouri Synod and who subscribe to and live by the confessional position of the Lutheran Church-Missouri

---

[3] The Fort Wayne deaconesses on the Constitution Committee were Cheryl D. Naumann, Nancy Nicol, Joyce Ostermann, and Kay Pritzlaff. "Paul A. Zimmerman meeting," Nov. 10, 1979

[4] The "Objectives" of the LCMS had been a topic of study and discussion prior to the 1979 LCMS Convention, where delegates adopted a resolution that revised Article III of the Synod's Constitution. "Resolution 2-03," in LCMS, *Proceedings*, 1979, 104.

Synod."[5] The women hoped, and even assumed, that a graduate of the River Forest program would want to join the strictly Missouri Synod conference, but the choice to do so would be made by the deaconess herself. Therefore, deaconesses who graduated from the LCMS training program would not automatically become members of the CDC when they received their first placement, but would each need to make an individual application for membership in the conference.

January 12, 1980 was an incredibly happy day for the founders of CDC. The conference organizational meeting took place at Concordia College, River Forest, in the boardroom adjacent to President Zimmerman's office. Those gathered for the historic occasion began with prayer and the reading of God's Word. Business included discussion and adoption of the "initial draft" constitution and the election of officers: Deaconess Ruth Broermann, President; Deaconess Joyce Ostermann, Vice President; Deaconess Nancy Nicol, Secretary; and Deaconess Luella Mickley, Treasurer.[6] Dr. Paul A. Zimmerman was elected as first Spiritual Counselor for the conference and graciously accepted the position.[7]

The deaconesses met again on February 9, March 15, and April 26 for Bible study and mutual support and encouragement. They also applied for federal tax-exempt status, made minor adjustments to the constitution, and wrote by-laws for the constitution. President Zimmerman and an attorney from the Law Offices of Keck, Mahin & Cate reviewed the *Concordia Deaconess Conference—Lutheran Church-Missouri Synod Constitution and By-Laws*, reporting that the document was in good legal order.[8] With all of this groundwork complete, in June of 1980, the nine founding members adopted and signed the polished *Constitution*.[9]

---

[5] The full text of the original CDC "Constitution and By-Laws" is printed in Appendix 2.B.
[6] The names of all CDC officers (1980–2008) are listed in Appendix 3.A. "Concordia Deaconess Conference Organized," *The Forester* 4, no. 4 (February 1980): 2, 5.
[7] Zimmerman served as Spiritual Counselor until his retirement. The names of all CDC Spiritual Counselors (1980-2006) are listed in Appendix 3.B.
[8] Letter from Paul A. Zimmerman to Deaconess Ruth Broermann, March 18, 1980, priv. col. of Ruth (nee Broermann) Stallmann, St. Louis, Mo; Letter from Wesley S. Walton, Law Offices Keck, Mahin & Cate, to Dr. Paul A. Zimmerman, March 31, 1980, priv. col. of Ruth (nee Broermann) Stallmann, St. Louis, Mo.
[9] Appendix 2.A contains short biographies of the CDC founding members. On June 7, 1980, Clara Strehlow, Ruth Broermann, Luella Mickley, Betty Mulholland, Joyce Ostermann, Kay Pritzlaff, Nancy Nicol, and Cheryl D. Naumann signed the *CDC LCMS Constitution and By-Laws* (in the order listed). Since Mildred Brillinger could not be present for the signing in River Forest, the document was mailed to her to sign in Texas. Three copies of the constitution were signed: one for Concordia Historical Institute, a second for Dr.

THE CONFERENCE MOTTO

The women who formed the CDC intended to base every aspect of the new organization on the Word of God. They considered several Bible passages, particularly from the epistles of St. Paul, as possible mottos or sources from which to create a conference motto. Rather than choosing between a Bible verse and a shorter paraphrase of a Bible verse, the group finally settled on using 1 Thessalonians 1:2–3:

> We give thanks to God always for you all, constantly mentioning you in our prayers, remembering before our God and Father your work of faith and labor of love and steadfastness of hope in our Lord Jesus Christ.[10]

. . . *and* a paraphrase of the same passage:

> Working in faith
>
> Laboring in Love
>
> Remaining steadfast in the hope
>
> of our Lord Jesus Christ.

. . . as interchangeable mottos. The idea was that the paraphrase might be used for letterhead or display in small spaces, while the entire Scripture passage might be used where more space was available.[11]

UNIFORM, INSIGNIA, AND CROSS

Depending upon their length of service as deaconesses, the women who formed CDC had worn a variety of deaconess uniforms and one or more of the LDA cross pins. The group discussed the possibility of changing the color of the CDC deaconess uniform to light blue or red, but finally decided to stick to the navy blue that had been used by Synodical Conference deaconesses since 1948.[12]

By 1980, many LDA deaconesses no longer wore navy blue garb because it was understood within the diaconate that wearing the deaconess cross—pinned to any type of clothing, or even worn on a chain around the

---

Zimmerman's files at Concordia, and a third for the CDC archives, which to date have been held in trust by the appointed CDC Historian.

[10] Taken from the Revised Standard Version.

[11] Although 1 Thessalonians 1:2-3 and a paraphrase of this verse were chosen as interchangeable mottos for CDC, over a period of years this fact was forgotten, resulting in the practice of referring solely to the paraphrase as the conference motto.

[12] See chapter 8.

neck—was the same as being in uniform. Members of the CDC preferred to wear a full deaconess uniform, which they believed set deaconesses apart as professional women and reminded them of their consecration and service to the Lord. But in order to make the navy blue Concordia Deaconess Conference uniform distinctive, the women knew that a different deaconess cross and arm insignia had to be worn. They wanted a unique design that would identify the wearer as a Missouri Synod deaconess who was loyal to Scripture and the Lutheran Confessions.

In fall 1979, seminarian (later Rev. Dr.) Jonathan Charles Naumann (b. 1957), husband of Cheryl D. Naumann, often accompanied his wife to CDC pre-organizational meetings. Naumann was a student of art who enjoyed oil painting in his spare time. As early as October, when the deaconesses first began to share their ideas for a CDC insignia, Naumann assisted the women by sketching their designs. Some of these drawings incorporated doves and others featured symbols for the fruits of the Spirit, but every design included a cross at its center. Though many of their designs were beautiful and intriguing, the women felt that they were too complicated or cluttered for a logo. Out of ideas, the deaconesses asked Naumann to try creating a design of his own. He recalls,

> The women had some definite thoughts about what they wanted in an emblem. They asked me to draw a cross and maybe some serving hands that depicted love and generosity to people in need. One of the deaconesses made a gesture with her hands, lifting them up in an attitude of service so that I could visualize what they were trying to get across.[13]

The deaconesses were delighted with Naumann's drawing, which showed a pair of female hands lifted up in service, one on either side of an elegant cross. But how would the design look when translated onto a cloth insignia? Ruth Broermann took the design home and embroidered it on navy blue material, with the cross in gold and the hands in a "flesh" color. The women still liked the design, but decided that they preferred the cross on its own. Naumann put a few finishing touches on the cross, making sure that the style was sufficiently feminine as well as rich in symbolism. When he finished, Betty Mulholland said, in good Lutheran fashion, "OK, you're the artist. What does this mean?" Naumann grabbed a used envelope from the table and wrote on the back of it:

> The cross, the most widely known Christian symbol, is also the symbol for deaconess service.

---

[13] Jonathan C. Naumann, interviewed by CDN, September 1, 2006, priv. col. of CDN, Pittsburgh, Pa.

Concordia Deaconess Conference has adopted this cross design for use on its pin and patch.[14]

The arms of this cross stretch out to the four directions of the compass inscribed with the ichthus, the symbol for Jesus Christ. This symbolizes the worldwide scope of deaconess service in the name of Jesus.

The arms of the cross also flare into the shapes of Easter Lily blossoms, symbolizing the radiant joy of the resurrection of Christ; the source of Christian hope.[15]

At the same time that the CDC was officially established, the founding members adopted Naumann's cross design as the official conference cross, creating a gold cross lapel pin and a gold cross arm insignia from the same pattern. Once there were deaconess students at Concordia College, the CDC also approved a *student* insignia, with an identically shaped light blue cross in place of the gold one. Deaconess students enrolled in LCMS training programs may wear the CDC *student* insignia, however, the cross pin is never worn by a woman until she is commissioned as a deaconess. In 1986, the CDC passed the following resolution regarding the uniform worn by its members:

The official deaconess uniform of the Concordia Deaconess Conference is a two-piece navy blue business suit worn with a white blouse or a professional business-looking solid navy blue dress. The insignia is worn on the left shoulder approximately two to three inches below the shoulder seam. The cross pin is worn on the left lapel. This pin should be worn on the uniform only and should never be used as a utilitarian piece of jewelry. The deaconess uniform is to be worn by active and emeritus deaconesses, and may be worn by associate members, to all official functions of Concordia Deaconess Conference or when representing Concordia Deaconess Conference."[16]

In May 2005, during a formal banquet celebrating its 25th anniversary, the Concordia Deaconess Conference presented its eight living founding members with a special gift: a CDC cross pin with a sapphire set in the

---

[14] While LDC deaconesses referred to the "patch" worn on their uniform, Deaconess Nancy E. Nicol (first director of the Concordia Deaconess Program) preferred to called the logo an "insignia," and taught her students to use the latter terminology.

[15] Jonathan C. Naumann, Line drawing of cross and hand-written explanation, File: Concordia Deaconess Conference Originals of Official Materials, Box: CDC, Concordia Historical Institute, St. Louis, Mo.

[16] "Resolution #4—Establishing a Deaconess Uniform," Concordia Deaconess Conference, April 17–19, 1986, Black Binder called "CDC Resolutions," CDC Historian Archive Boxes, held in trust by appointed CDC Historian.

middle of the cross arms.[17] Only eight of these crosses were made in order to honor these special women.

The Concordia Deaconess Conference—Lutheran Church-Missouri Synod encourages its members to wear their deaconess uniform when "on duty," but has never suggested that a uniform should be mandatory for deaconesses. Members of the CDC are proud of their conference uniform, which identifies them as deaconesses who value faithfulness to Scripture and the Lutheran Confessions in their teaching, leadership, and service.[18]

THE FIRST CONFERENCE

The charter members of the Concordia Deaconess Conference had no intention of recruiting other consecrated deaconesses to join their society. However, they felt that they owed all LCMS deaconesses an opportunity to understand and ask questions about the CDC's existence as a "free conference" of deaconesses who adhered to the traditional doctrinal positions of the Missouri Synod. Toward that end, on September 8, 1980, CDC Secretary Kay Pritzlaff sent the following letter to all Missouri Synod deaconesses:

Dear Sister in Christ,

Greetings! This letter is written to invite you to the open meeting of the Concordia Deaconess Conference to be held October 3, 1980, on the campus of Concordia Theological Seminary, Fort Wayne, Indiana.

On the blue sheet enclosed, you will find an outline of the program for the day. We have an exciting program planned and pray that you will be so able to arrange your schedule so that you may join us.

Housing for Thursday or Friday night will be made available in our homes for anyone wishing to stay one of these nights. Please return the enclosed response card indicating your ability to be with us, and whether or not you

---

[17] The CDC anniversary committee commissioned Graduate Gemologist Karla Lewis, a member of St. Paul's Lutheran Church, downtown Chicago, to handcraft the cross pins.
[18] Only deaconesses who are members of the Concordia Deaconess Conference wear the CDC uniform. Other deaconesses who serve within the Missouri Synod, who are either members of the Valparaiso-based LDC or do not belong to any deaconess conference, are not entitled to wear the CDC pin or insignia. Designs for the CDC cross pin and insignia belong to the conference. Organizations that desire to feature or incorporate the CDC designs in a printed publication, web site, or other public display must first seek permission through the CDC Executive Committee. Contact information for the President of the Concordia Deaconess Conference may be found in the *Lutheran Annual*.

will need housing. For those staying over Thursday night, we'll have an informal gathering at Joyce Osterrmann's house.

We hope to see you then! God's blessings![19]

The September 15, 2008, issue of *Reporter* also featured an article inviting all "deaconesses employed by Missouri Synod congregations or Synod-affiliated agencies" to the open meeting.[20] Publicity photos for the event showed Deaconess Kay Pritzlaff reviewing the upcoming meeting schedule with Deaconess Susan Meyer.[21] Unfortunately, there appear to be no extant minutes from the open meeting, but in an early summary of CDC history, Nancy (nee Nicol) Nemoyer wrote:

> The fall meeting of the CDC was held October 3rd in Fort Wayne, IN on the campus of Concordia Theological Seminary. Rev. Robert Koch of Redeemer Lutheran Church, Warsaw, IN presented a paper on "Gender and Roles in Holy Scripture." Business highlights included listing in the *Lutheran Annual*, the deaconess uniform, use and sale of the official pin and insignia of the CDC, and membership. Deaconess Claire Krans was elected as Board member.[22]

While the October 3 gathering was indeed an "open" meeting, one very private event did not appear on the conference agenda. At 1 p.m., the Concordia Deaconess Conference founding members met in Kramer Chapel, at the foot of the steps before the altar. Dr. Paul Zimmerman led the women in a short rite of rededication to deaconess ministry, and presented each of them with their first CDC cross pin.[23] Deaconess Emeritus Betty Mulholland remembers the occasion well:

> When Dr. Zimmerman handed me my pin the tears just rolled down my face, because this was the final severance from the LDA and LDC. It was a culmination of all of the blessings that the Lord had showered on us. I felt He had brought us so far already, so much further than we ever

---

[19] Letter from Kay Pritzlaff to "Sister in Christ," September 8, 1980, File: Concordia Deaconess Conference, Old Notes, priv. col. of Nancy (nee Nicol) Nemoyer, Carlisle, Pa.
[20] "Concordia Deaconesses to Study Women's Roles," *Reporter* 6, no. 36 (September 15, 1980).
[21] Letter and photos from Fort Wayne Deaconesses to George Lange, Public Relations Department, Concordia College River Forest, no date, File: Concordia Deaconess Conference, Old Notes, priv. col. of Nancy (nee Nicol) Nemoyer, Carlisle, Pa.
[22] "3D: A Decade of Deaconess Dedication, 1980-1990," mimeographed pages bound in folder, no pagination, River Forest, 1990.
[23] See handwritten notes made by Nancy Nicol on printed agenda for "Concordia Deaconess Conference Friday October 3, 1980," File: Concordia Deaconess Conference, Old Notes, priv. col. of Nancy (nee Nicol) Nemoyer, Carlisle, Pa.

expected to be brought. It was as if the church itself had finally recognized us and was saying, "Go, my child, and complete your work."[24]

The publicity photos and Nemoyer's conference summary indicate that at least two other LCMS deaconesses joined CDC by October 1980. Before Concordia College, River Forest, certified its first group of deaconess candidates in 1983, ten "active" LCMS deaconesses had joined the CDC, more than doubling the conference's original charter membership number.[25]

THANKING GOD FOR THE FAITHFUL

During an early morning business meeting on April 9, 1983, CDC members surprised Deaconess Emeritus Clara Strehlow by presenting a resolution to create a scholarship endowment fund in her honor. The resolution read:

WHEREAS God's servant and servant of the church, Deaconess Clara Strehlow, has served for more than 50 years as a deaconess in The Lutheran Church—Missouri Synod,

AND WHEREAS she has been an inspiration in her dedication of faith, loyalty to the Word of God and commitment to the Synod,

AND WHEREAS she has been a charter member of the Conference and as the eldest is highly honored and respected,

THEREFORE BE IT RESOLVED that in thanksgiving to God for this loyal servant a Deaconess Clara Strehlow Endowment Fund be established at Concordia College, River Forest, Illinois, the benefits of which will be applied to Concordia's Deaconess Program,

AND BE IT FURTHER RESOLVED that the Concordia Deaconess Conference begin this fund with an initial gift of $200 from its treasury,

AND BE IT FURTHER RESOLVED that five or more of the members of the Concordia Deaconess Conference commit themselves to a gift each of $20 per month and/or ten of the members commit themselves to a gift each of $10 per month for no less than four years toward this fund,

---

[24] Betty Mulholland, telephone interview by CDN, summer 2006, priv. col. of CDN, Pittsburgh, Pa.

[25] The ten deaconesses who joined CDC (bringing the membership total from nine to nineteen) were Ruth Ann Endicott, Janice (nee Mattson) Grothe, Jane Hegg, Martha Hocket, Nancy Lingenfelter, Susan Meyer, Claire (nee Krans) Neagley, Karen Owens, Rhonda Silberstein, and Janice Weaver. See "Membership Lists" and conference minutes for the years 1981–83, three-ring navy blue binder, Concordia Deaconess Conference archives, held in trust by appointed CDC historian.

AND BE IT FINALLY RESOLVED that a prayer of thanksgiving be offered up at this time for the witness of Deaconess Clara Strehlow among us.[26]

On passing the resolution, the conference members stood. A heartfelt prayer of thanksgiving, led by Concordia Deaconess Program Director Nancy Nicol, moved everyone present. Strehlow was so stunned by the conference action that it took a few minutes for her to gain composure. When she finally did, she pointed her index finger upward, rolled her eyes toward heaven, and said, "To God be the glory; to God be the glory."

When her sisters initiated this tangible way to thank God for Strehlow, she was 87 years old and still leading Bible classes. Strehlow insisted on having the privilege of being the first deaconess in CDC to give a gift to the endowment fund. Since that time, The Deaconess Clara Strehlow Endowment Fund has provided assistance to dozens of young women aspiring to the vocation of deaconess.[27]

RECOGNITION OF SERVICE TO GOD

On its fifth anniversary in 1985, the CDC established the *Phoebe Award* to provide an opportunity to thank God for "deaconesses who have unselfishly and lovingly dedicated their lives to our Lord Jesus Christ" and who "exemplified the motto of our conference through their labors of deaconess service."[28] Deaconesses who have received the *Phoebe Award* to date are: Nancy Nicol (1985), Ruth Stallmann (1990), Betty Mulholland (1995), Christie Nelson (2000), and Joyce Ostermann (2005).

In 1990, the conference voted to create the *Dr. Paul A. Zimmerman Award* to acknowledge that, "the Lord has blessed Concordia Deaconess

---

[26] "Resolution #1: Deaconess Clara Strehlow Endowment Fund," CDC April 8-9, 1983, conference minutes in navy blue three-ring binders, Concordia Deaconess Conference archives, held in trust by appointed CDC historian. See also, untitled paragraph in news about people, *The Lutheran Witness* 103, no. 7 (July 1983); "The Deaconess Clara Strehlow Endowment Fund," three-panel tract (River Forest: Concordia College, 1986); "Proposal to the Concordia Deaconess Conference for the Scholarship Distribution from the Deaconess Clara Strehlow Endowment Fund," two mimeographed pages, April 19, 1986, priv. col. of Nancy (nee Nicol) Nemoyer, Carlisle, Pa.

[27] The Guidelines for distribution of the Deaconess Clara Strehlow Endowment Fund, as passed by the CDC on April 19, 1986, are in Appendix 3.C. Anyone desiring information on how to contribute to the fund may contact the Director of the Deaconess Program at Concordia University Chicago.

[28] "Resolution #1: Phoebe Award," CDC October 4–5, 1985, conference minutes in navy blue three-ring binders, Concordia Deaconess Conference archives, held in trust by appointed CDC historian.

Conference and Program with servants in Christ outside Deaconess Ministry who have worked in faith, labored in love, and remained steadfast in the hope of our Lord Jesus Christ."[29] The award was named for Zimmerman in recognition of his zealous work in support of the CDC since its inception. The first recipient of the *Dr. Paul A Zimmerman Award* was President Zimmerman himself (1990). Other individuals who have received the award are: Rev. Dr. Gary Leonard Bertels Sr. (1995), Rev. Dr. Steven A. Hein (2000), and Dr. Beverly Kay (nee Habeck) Yahnke (2005).

When the founders of the CDC think of Dr. Zimmerman, they also remember his wife, Genevieve Emmaline (nee Bahls) Zimmerman. Mrs. Zimmerman welcomed and graciously hosted deaconesses in her home as they met with her husband. She also often sat with conservative deaconesses in the "gallery" bleachers at LCMS synodical conventions, bolstering their morale with cheerful and encouraging words.

MISSION MINDED

From its founding, the Concordia Deaconess Conference has taken an active interest in learning about current mission endeavors. Those who organize annual conferences make it a point to include at least one presentation that centers on mission work carried out by deaconesses, other Missouri Synod missionaries, or our partner churches across the world. Every year the CDC chooses a different mission project for receipt of Conference worship offerings.

Sharing tools for the extension of God's Kingdom is a popular element of CDC conferences. Sessions on witnessing, "Prayer boxes," daily devotions, grief counseling, prison visits, listening skills, and ministry to individuals with special needs show the diversity of topics that have been considered by the conference.

In 1993, the CDC Spiritual and Professional Growth Committee printed "Devotional Insights," a collection of short devotions written by Deaconesses Kate Behm, Jeanne Dicke, Nancy Lingenfelter, Jeana Moe, Nancy Nemoyer, Angie Reitmeier, Theresa Rupholdt, Linda Smith, and Ro Williams. The *Introduction* to the booklet explained:

> The following pages, arranged according to their sequence in the Bible, contain devotional material that was submitted by women of the Concordia Deaconess Conference. It is hoped the messages will give

---

[29] "Resolution 1990-06: Resolution to Establish Dr. Paul A. Zimmerman Award," CDC April 25–28, 1990 conference minutes in navy blue three-ring binders, Concordia Deaconess Conference archives, held in trust by appointed CDC historian.

meaning and inspiration from God's Word and promote a better understanding of who we are and what we do as "sisters in Christ"—serving in our respective roles and places in His Kingdom. All praise and glory to God, Who called us to be His own in Christ Jesus![30]

Communication with Members

As the membership of CDC grew larger and included women from every region of the United States (and a few who lived abroad), it became important for the conference to find ways of increasing communication among members, especially when they were unable to attend national conferences.[31]

Early in 1987, Deaconess Pamela Nielsen, who was serving as the appointed Public Relations Coordinator for CDC, volunteered to do the legwork for launching a conference newsletter. Nielsen's research showed that CDC members believed the newsletter "should contain inspirational and news items, be uplifting, give a student update, and share area news."[32] The newsletter was to be published quarterly, with postage paid by the conference. On August 10, 1987, Nielsen mailed out the first CDC newsletter under the heading, "Light Reading: News, Views & Who's Who."[33]

The conference liked the prototype, and when Deaconess Sara Nordling was assigned the PR post after Nielsen, she became editor of the paper. In December 1987, Nordling published "Vol. I No. 2" with the new title: *Blues News*. She took responsibility for the compilation and distribution of *Blues News* through the end of 1991.[34] Since that time, *Blues News* has seen several different editors and publication formats. Issues have included messages from the conference's Spiritual Counselor and President, discussion of synodical resolutions, an exploration of theological questions, information about conferences, poetry, news from individual deaconesses, devotional pieces, articles about missions, and book reviews.

---

[30] "Introduction," *Devotional Insights* (River Forest: CDC, 1993), CDC Archives, held in trust by appointed CDC historian.
[31] CDC conferences took place bi-annually through 1988 and annually every year thereafter.
[32] "Concordia Deaconess Conference Business Meeting Minutes, Concordia College, Ann Arbor, MI, April 23–25, 1987," conference minutes in navy blue three-ring binders, Concordia Deaconess Conference archives, held in trust by appointed CDC historian.
[33] "Light Reading: News, Views & Who's Who," File: *Blues News* 1987–2001, plastic archive boxes, Concordia Deaconess Conference archives, held in trust by appointed CDC historian.
[34] File: *Blues News* 1987–2001, plastic archive boxes, Concordia Deaconess Conference archives, held in trust by appointed CDC historian.

In step with the 21st century explosion of technology, CDC members frequently use email to communicate with one another. A weekly "Call to Prayer" email presents a series of prayers with regular petitions that name individual members of CDC (on a rotating basis), the three LCMS deaconess training programs, the mercy agencies of the Church, LCMS World Relief and Human Care, and other synodical missions, congregations, and institutions. CDC Executive Committee members utilize both email and on-line "conference calls" to address urgent business between regular face-to-face meetings.[35] In 2008, the CDC Public Relations Committee, under the leadership of PR Coordinator Deaconess Jennifer Phillips, developed and launched the conference's first website at www.concordiadeaconessconference.org.[36]

PROMOTING DEACONESS SERVICE IN SYNOD

Discussion and decisions regarding "Public Relations" comprised the largest part of the CDC's first business meeting in October 1980. The conference officers made plans to attend the LCMS Great Commission Convocation in St. Louis from November 7–9, 1980, where they would staff a display booth about deaconess ministry. In preparation for that event, the CDC created a slide presentation and funded the printing of information pamphlets. These women were seasoned "convention goers," having already accomplished the same sort of public relations work at LWML conventions and district LCMS conventions throughout the previous summer.[37] Deaconess Nancy Nicol (later Nemoyer), recalls the

---

[35] See for example: "Email minutes for the Executive Committee of the CDC July 20-21, 2008" or "Email minutes for the Executive Committee of the CDC October 15-20, 2008," File: Executive Committee Meetings, CDC Historian Archive Boxes, held in trust by appointed CDC Historian.

[36] Other members of the PR Committee included Deaconesses Rogene Lis, Ruth McDonnell, and Kim Schave. Phillips publicly thanked Schave and her husband, Rev. Steve Schave, for constructing a temporary CDC website while a professional graphic artist, Steve Blakey, worked on a more permanent site. Other world wide web domain addresses owned by CDC include www.concordiadeaconess.org and www.concordiadeaconess.org. Using either of these web addresses will take one to the home page for www.concordiadeaconessconference.org. "Minutes of the Annual Business Meeting of the CDC, First Session: Thursday June 26, 2008," File: Annual Meeting 2008 – Mequon, CDC Historian Archive Boxes, held in trust by appointed CDC Historian.

[37] Expenses for travel and registration were always borne by the deaconesses who actually attended the conventions. The fees for setting up a booth or display table were paid by CDC. "Concordia Deaconess Conference Meeting, Concordia Seminary—Fort Wayne, Indiana, October 3, 1980," Box: CDC, File: CDC correspondence 1983–1984 (also meetings 1980–86 and Newsletters), CHI, St. Louis, Mo.

valuable assistance that CDC members gave during her tenure as Director of the Concordia Deaconess Program.

> The Concordia Deaconess Conference put the Program Director on the agenda of every meeting. The women listened intently to my reports and asked if there were any ways they could help. In some cases they served as fieldwork supervisors. Members of CDC came in to speak from time to time about their special expertise and some even taught a class. They "mentored" students, kind of like big sisters, and became pen pals to them.
>
> In the early days, the CDC funded the first couple of brochures about the River Forest training program. With the Phoebe and Zimmerman awards, the conference recognized individuals who contributed to the spread of the program and deaconess ministry. Good public relations articles resulted—in papers like the *Reporter* or the *Forester*—and I often told the students that their own commendable witness and work, as also the good work carried out by the CDC, reflected well on our training program.[38]

In April 1987, the CDC formed a committee, with Deaconess Karen Aumick as Chairman, for the purpose of pursuing the production of a public relations video.[39] The committee outlined the need and objectives for a "visual aid in promoting deaconess ministry," applied for grant funds from the AAL, and interviewed production companies. After the committee reported in 1988, the conference voted to move forward with the video production as recommended by the committee. CDC also resolved to accept responsibility for the cost of reproducing the video and helping to promote its use when production was complete.[40] By fall 1988, several Fort Wayne and Chicago area deaconesses had been filmed for the video. *Deaconess: Privileged to Serve* premiered at the next CDC meeting in St. Louis on April 7, 1989.[41] The video provided a modern component to the

---

[38] Nancy (nee Nicol) Nemoyer, interview by CDN, summer 2006, priv. col. of CDN, Pittsburgh, Pa.

[39] The full committee included Deaconesses Karen Aumick, Kristen Hannenberg, Pamela Nielsen, and Lori Wilbert. As the video production progressed, Deaconesses Cathy Fanslau and Laura Herman played significant roles in executing the project.

[40] "Deaconess Video Resolution: Concordia Deaconess Conference Business Meeting Minutes, Concordia Theological Seminary, Fort Wayne, Indiana, April 13–16, 1988," conference minutes in navy blue three-ring binders, Concordia Deaconess Conference archives, held in trust by appointed CDC historian.

[41] *Deaconess: Privileged to Serve* can be viewed in the library at Concordia University Chicago. CDC Conference agenda, April 5-8, 1989, File: Spring CDC—St. Louis, Mo. '89, plastic file box, Concordia Deaconess Conference archives, held in trust by appointed CDC historian; "Concordia Deaconess Conference Business Meeting Minutes, Elburn, Il, October 27–28,

CDC deaconess booth at the 1989 LCMS Convention in Wichita, Kansas, and continued to be utilized as a popular public relations tool for deaconess ministry and the LCMS training program well into the 1990s.

Just as the members of CDC campaigned for a Missouri Synod deaconess training program, the conference continued to work for the passing of other resolutions supporting deaconesses and deaconess ministry within the Synod. Such resolutions dealt with diverse issues such as colloquy, nomenclature, and membership in Synod.[42] More recently, the CDC has cooperated with Synod-wide initiatives to promote deaconess ministry throughout the Synod. For example, the President of CDC was a member of the *Deaconess Task Force* set up by the LCMS Department of World Relief and Human Care in 2002.[43]

A PROFESSIONAL CODE OF ETHICS

At its first meeting after the 1986 LCMS Synodical convention, the CDC established a Constitutional Review Committee in order to review and update its constitution in line with developments in the Missouri Synod.[44] When the new committee met, its members discussed the possibility of introducing a Code of Ethics as an attachment to the constitution. The CDC decided to "table this issue" at its October 1987 meeting, but in April 1988, the conference voted to "appoint an adjudication committee whose responsibility will be to form a code of ethics."[45]

In April 1990, the conference went one step further, by resolving "to establish a Code of Ethics and Adjudication Guidelines," in keeping with Article 5 of the newly revised CDC constitution which stated, "The CDC shall adopt a Code of Ethics, adopt Guidelines for Adjudication, and elect a

---

1988," File: 1988 Fall CDC—Deaconry—Elburn, Il., plastic archive boxes, Concordia Deaconess Conference archives, held in trust by appointed CDC historian.

[42] See chapter 16.

[43] See chapter 16 for more information on the Deaconess Task Force.

[44] See chapter 16 for more information on resolutions related to deaconesses passed at the 1986 LCMS Convention. "Concordia Deaconess Conference Business Meeting Minutes, Concordia College, Mequon, WI, October 11, 1986," File: Fall '86, plastic file box, Concordia Deaconess Conference archives, held in trust by appointed CDC historian.

[45] Concordia Deaconess Conference Business Meeting Minutes, Concordia College, Ann Arbor, MI, October 8, 1987, conference minutes in navy blue three-ring binders, Concordia Deaconess Conference archives, held in trust by appointed CDC historian; Concordia Deaconess Conference Business Meeting Minutes, Elburn, Illinois, April 14, 1988, conference minutes in navy blue three-ring binders, Concordia Deaconess Conference archives, held in trust by appointed CDC historian.

Board of Adjudication."[46] However, when the next revision of the CDC constitution was adopted in 1993, Article 5 was eliminated and a new Article 12 read, "The CDC will refer to the Constitution and By-Laws of Synod for procedural direction when an issue arises that is not addressed in the Constitution and By-laws of the CDC."[47] These latter changes provided guidance for the CDC in matters that might include adjudication, but did not really touch on the question of a written code of ethics.

For several years, and particularly when the CDC applied for Articles of Incorporation in the state of Illinois, conference members dealt with a great deal of legal paperwork, including revisions to the constitution.[48] Conference leaders needed to focus on these pressing matters, with little time for thought about a code of ethics. Finally, in her 2002 President's Address, Deaconess Joyce Ostermann brought the discussion full circle:

> . . . I want to spend the next 14 months discussing with CDC members, "What does it mean to uphold the Scriptures and the Lutheran Confessions?" All members. Not just a few who are on the deaconess chat line and not just a few who easily engage in email discussion. . . . I would like to see such discussion develop into a document called "The Standard of Practice for Members of Concordia Deaconess Conference." The LCMS has not undertaken the task of writing a document outlining the proper role of deaconess service. We must do this ourselves and in consultation with proper LCMS officials. . . . we need to begin with the age-old question: What is a deaconess? . . . We need to begin dialogue on issues of practice. . . . It is my goal that by next year we will come to the annual conference with ideas discussed and will be ready to adopt an updated uniform policy, amend our constitution if necessary, and develop a first draft of a CDC standard of practice. This conference began the theme, "Serving under the Scriptures and Confessions." We will select our presenters for next year's conference (2003) based on their ability to assist us as we develop our standards of practice. . . .

> Probably many of you have not thought through this issue as thoroughly as I have. Since I was one of the charter members of CDC, I can tell you

---

[46] Concordia Deaconess Conference Business Meeting Minutes, Concordia University, River Forest, Illinois, April 26, 1990," File: CDC D3—Conference—C.U. River Forest, April 25–28, '90, plastic file box, Concordia Deaconess Conference archives, held in trust by appointed CDC historian.

[47] 1993 Constitution, conference minutes in navy blue three-ring binders, Concordia Deaconess Conference archives, held in trust by appointed CDC historian.

[48] Concordia Deaconess Conference—Lutheran Church-Missouri Synod is registered with the County Clerk's Office, Greene County, Illinois. The original documents of Incorporation, awarded on February 5, 1996, are filed in the offices of McDonald, Strickland, and Clough, Attorneys at Law, Carrollton, Illinois.

that we purposefully put into our constitution that we would uphold Scripture and the Lutheran Confessions . . . We formed CDC largely to identify ourselves as deaconesses who practice *under* the Scriptures and *under* the Confessions. Some of us have been members of the other deaconess organization. We know that they accepted a wide variety of practices, causing them to lose their identity as Missouri Synod deaconesses. I do not want that to happen to us. We must keep our identity by establishing a standard of practice for our members.[49]

For three years in a row—2002, 2003, and 2004—the annual CDC conference focused on the theme: "Deaconess Service Under the Confessions." In 2003, the women studied *The Augsburg Confession* and "Scriptural Foundations for Diaconal Service." They also spent many sessions brainstorming about the *purpose* of a code of ethics, a *preamble* for a code of ethics, and numerous ethical code *categories*. In 2004, conference time included discussion and review of the final draft of the code, and "trying out" the new code to ensure that it could provide "sound and sufficient guidance for the daily service of Deaconesses."[50] At last, at its 25th anniversary conference in 2005, after a little more tweaking and polishing, the CDC unanimously adopted its first *Code of Ethics*![51] The full text of the *Code*, which embodies both theological and professional ethics informing the conduct of a Missouri Synod deaconess, can be found in Appendix 3.D.

Concordia Deaconess Conference members have expressed relief that the *Code of Ethics* is finally complete. In one deaconess's words,

"We are tired of being asked by the church to define ourselves; tired of repeating the same battles; tired of being pestered about the possibility of going for women's ordination. We hope we have learned from history. When the church reads our Constitution and *Code of Ethics*, it will know where we stand. Even after twenty-five years of existence as a conference, we have moved forward, wiser and better informed about our vocation as deaconesses. With the *Code of Ethics* we are better equipped to remain

---

[49] Joyce A. Ostermann, The President's Address to the Conference, April 2002, File: 2002, plastic file box, Concordia Deaconess Conference archives, held in trust by appointed CDC historian.

[50] Case studies for "trying out" the *Code of Ethics* were based on actual ethical dilemmas posed by CDC members at the close of the 2003 conference. "Deaconess Service Under the Confessions, Schedule of Events and Goals of the Conference," File: May 2004 Conference, plastic file box, Concordia Deaconess Conference archives, held in trust by appointed CDC historian.

[51] See also: "Deaconesses Adopt First Code of Ethics," *Reporter* (July 2005).

faithful to the Scriptures as we carry out a ministry of mercy in the name of Jesus Christ."[52]

AN APPRECIATION OF HISTORY

The very first Constitution and By-Laws signed by the CDC founding members included provision for three *Appointed Officers,* namely a Public Relations Coordinator, a Parliamentarian, and an Historian.[53] Conference Historians have maintained the official archives of the conference, kept a photographic record of members, and submitted appropriate documents and memorabilia to Concordia Historical Institute in St. Louis. Many of the CDC archives for 1980-2000 are stored in the deaconess office at Concordia University Chicago.[54] All other archive boxes and files are "held in trust" by the current conference Historian.

After the 2008 annual business meeting, CDC Historian Cheryl D. Naumann compiled a "working reference book" that includes all Resolutions and motions passed by the conference from 1980 through 2008. This document is updated each year and copies are given to all deaconesses who join the conference.

DIFFERENT ISSUES FOR DIFFERENT ERAS

At various stages in the life and development of the Concordia Deaconess Conference, the organization has been described as being in the throws of "growing pains." Such comments have usually accompanied—and still accompany—other observations related to a growth in membership or a necessary shift in the primary focus of the conference.

When CDC started in 1980, the conference was preoccupied with raising the profile of deaconess ministry and LCMS deaconess training, as well as doing whatever it could financially and otherwise to support the LCMS training Program. Once it was obvious that the Concordia Deaconess Program was moving from strength to strength on its own steam, the CDC turned its attention to other issues that affected deaconess

---

[52] Words spoken to the author by a CDC member the evening after the Code of Ethics was adopted.

[53] See Appendix 2.C. for entire text of the June 7, 1980 Constitution and By-Laws.

[54] In April 2008 the Historian noted that archived items at CUC were beginning to deteriorate due to old age. The Executive Committee subsequently authorized expenditure of up to $450 for acid-proof files, boxes, and photo containers to preserve those materials. "April 5-19, 2008 meeting via email correspondence," in navy blue three-ring binders, Concordia Deaconess Conference archives, held in trust by appointed CDC historian.

ministry within the Synod. After the 1989 LCMS convention voted to change the Synod's constitution to accept deaconesses into membership, the conference began to devote more time to the spiritual and professional nurturing of its members. As the new millennium approached, members of CDC held differing opinions about topics like chaplaincy and whether or not there should be additional deaconess programs in the Synod. In the midst of so many changes, the conference leadership from every era can be commended for efforts to maintain a loving and open conference, where members could find common ground in their faithfulness to Scripture and the Lutheran Confessions.

In June 2008, CDC members unanimously passed a motion "to direct the Executive Committee to apply for Recognized Service Organization (RSO) status with the LCMS."[55] This initiative reflects the CDC's desire to continue to be identified with the Missouri Synod, particularly as one of the "service organizations that extend the mission and ministry of the Synod but are not part of the Synod as defined by its Constitution and By-Laws."[56]

Today, CDC membership is growing quickly as the Missouri Synod certifies deaconesses from three training programs: at Concordia University Chicago; Concordia Seminary, St. Louis; and Concordia Theological Seminary, Fort Wayne. The CDC plays an important role in bringing deaconesses from these three different schools together in a mutual understanding, camaraderie, and celebration of what it means to live the vocation of deaconess and deliver a ministry of mercy through teaching the faith, providing spiritual care, and carrying out acts of love.

In its entire history—and no doubt in the future, as opportunities for deaconess service broaden within the Missouri Synod and among LCMS partner churches around the world—one thing about the conference has remained constant: the CDC is committed to its identity as a free association of orthodox Lutheran deaconesses.

TWENTY-EIGHT YEARS OF CONFERENCES

The fourth objective of the Concordia Deaconess Conference, "to provide opportunity for spiritual, personal, and professional growth and fellowship

---

[55] "Motion 2008-14," CDC June 27, 2008 conference minutes in navy blue three-ring binders, Concordia Deaconess Conference archives, held in trust by appointed CDC historian.

[56] "Granting of RSO Status by Agencies of the Synod," 5.8.12 Agency Policies, LCMS Board of Directors Policy Manual, July 7, 2004. See also: "Fresh Start for RSO Process," *Reporter* 2, no. 5 (April 2008).

for those Deaconesses in the Lutheran Church Missouri Synod," has been accomplished through the convening of regular conferences. Not only are deaconess conferences usually fun, they provide restful opportunities for learning, meditation, sharing ideas, renewing and finding friendships, developing a support system, ministry networking, and rejoicing together in the privilege of being a deaconess.

For many years, the CDC deliberately chose conference locations with a view to promoting the deaconess movement within the Missouri Synod. As conferences met at LCMS seminaries and colleges, the CDC created opportunities for faculty and students to learn more about deaconess training and service. Occasionally a school would invite the Director of the Concordia Deaconess Program to speak to the student body at an open forum on deaconess ministry. When these talks took place, particularly at the seminaries, future pastors received a good idea of how a deaconess might work with them some day in their congregations.

This chapter finishes with an overview of CDC conferences for 28 years.[57] God has truly blessed these gatherings for the betterment of the church, for the benefit of deaconesses, and for the comfort of those whom they serve. To God be the glory!

CDC CONFERENCES: 1981–2013

March 7, 1981—Concordia College, River Forest

Dr. Lyle Mueller, Northern Illinois District Executive for Evangelism and Missions, spoke on "Witnessing in One's Daily Life." The CDC committed itself to working closely with the Concordia College deaconess program, particularly in the areas of promotion, public relations, and fund raising.

May 1, 1981—Concordia College, River Forest

Deaconess Joyce Ostermann led a devotion titled "The Master Carpenter." The conference voted to print 5,000 "Deaconess brochures" and 1,000 P.R. stickers for distribution at summer conventions. Each deaconess intern was assigned a CDC pen pal.

Feb. 22, 1982—Concordia Seminary, St. Louis

Samuel Nafzger, Executive Secretary of the Commission on Theology and Church Relations, addressed the conference on "Ministry." Nafzger's

---

[57] Information in the "overview" is taken from conference minutes and anniversary booklets housed in the Concordia Deaconess Conference archive, held in trust by appointed CDC historian.

words, that "the office of deaconess would seem to qualify for the church to consider as an auxiliary office," encouraged the women.[58]

Sept. 30-Oct. 2, 1982—home of Joyce Ostermann, Fort Wayne

Seminarians Richard Gudgeon and Joe Barbour presented lectures on "The Dynamics of Anxiety" and "Communications and Problem Solving." Grant monies awarded to the CDC from Aid Association for Lutherans (AAL) covered: 1) production of the filmstrip, "A Loving Presence"[59] (50 copies); 2) A new brochure, "For She Has Been a Helper of Many. . ." (20,000 copies); and 3) a new convention display board.[60]

April 8-9, 1983—Concordia College, River Forest

Dr. Paul Zimmerman led devotions on Matthew's account of the resurrection. Professors Steven Hein and Nancy Nicol co-presented "The Role of Women in the Church." The conference honored its oldest member by establishing the *Deaconess Clara Strehlow Endowment Fund.*

Oct. 7-8, 1983—Lutheran Homes, Inc., Fort Wayne

Dr. George Kraus, Concordia Seminary Professor of Ministry to the Deaf and Handicapped, discussed his devotional book for pastors and his wife's devotional book for wives of professional church workers. Yearly dues started at $30 per member.

May 4-5, 1984—NID LWML Deaconess Seminar Room, River Forest

Professor Steven Hein spoke on the "Sanctity of Life." The conference resolved that members should "take a pro-life approach in all counseling opportunities." Members treated seven senior deaconess students to lunch and invited them to join CDC following their placements.

Oct. 12-13, 1984—Concordia Theological Seminary, Fort Wayne

Rev. John Saleska instructed the conference on "Law/Gospel Counseling" and Mrs. Helen Kraus led a Bible study titled "Six Steps to Walking in the Way of the Lord." A large number of Seminary students attended the "Convocation Hour" with CDC, to hear how deaconesses

---

[58] See also: "Deaconesses Hear Nafzger on Ministry," *Reporter* 8, no. 8 (March 1, 1982): 4.
[59] Rev. Merlin Petersen suggested the creation of a filmstrip, wrote the script, and took photographs for it. One copy of "A Loving Presence" is in the CDC Archives, held in trust by appointed CDC historian.
[60] See also: "Handle Anxiety by Calling on God Speaker Tells Deaconess Conference," *Reporter* 8, no. 40 (October 11, 1982).

might be of assistance to pastors in their parishes. The conference purchased a marker board and three coffee servers for the Concordia College Deaconess Seminar room.

April 19-20, 1985—St. Paul's Lutheran Church, Munster, Indiana

Speakers included Rev. A. O. Gebauer on "Heaven," Rev. Alan Barber on "Bio-ethics," and Rev. John Sattler with a Bible study on "Life." Area conference meetings were to commence wherever possible.

Oct. 4-5, 1985—St. John's Lutheran Church, Lombard, Illinois

Topic presentations were given by NID President Theodore Laesch on "Jonah and His Stress," Deaconess Joyce Ostermann on "Stress and Relationships," and Dr. Harold Brockberg on "Stress Burnout." Mr. Harold Burrow demonstrated the AAL "Stress Kit."

April 17-19, 1986—LCMS International Center, St. Louis

LCMS President Ralph Bohlmann opened the conference with a devotion. Speakers included Rev. Chris Hinkle on "Using Computers in the Congregation," Rev. John Johnson on the CTCR report: "Women in the Church," and Dr. Louis Brighton on "Revelation." Attendees toured the International Center, the LLL building, CHI, CPH, and Concordia Seminary, where they hosted a gathering for seminary students.

Oct. 9-11, 1986—Concordia College, Mequon

Nurse Carol Meier spoke about "Nutrition" and Dr. Timothy Maschke explained "Spiritual Gifts." Deaconesses provided sectional presentations on ministry relating to the deaf, mentally retarded, mentally ill, marriage counseling, aging, and prison work. A constitutional review committee was appointed.

April 23-25, 1987—Concordia College, Ann Arbor

Dr. Warren Wilbert presented "Teaching: An Adult Ministry" and Rev. Randall Shields gave a "Learning Plan Workshop." Deaconess Cheryl D. Naumann spoke on "Missions in the United Kingdom." The CDC purchased pew Bibles for St. Columba Lutheran Church, East Kilbride, Scotland; a map for the Deaconess Seminar room; and pens to distribute at the LWML convention. "Fun Night" featured pizza and bowling.

Oct. 8-10, 1987—Walcamp, Kingston, Illinois

Dr. Walter A. Maier III led a Bible Study on "Christian Growth" and Dr. Gerald Schalk discussed "Growing Spiritually Through Prayer." Chicago, St. Louis, and Northeastern Indiana deaconess reported on their active area conferences.

April 13-16, 1988—Concordia Theological Seminary, Fort Wayne

Conference sessions included the study of John 21, "Hymnology and Practice" and "The New Age Movement." Early riser "prayer walks" were part of the agenda. CDC ordered 2,500 buttons to be handed out at LCMS youth gatherings.

Oct. 27-28, 1988—Fellowship Deaconry, Elburn, Illinois

Several Bible studies focused on the theme: "Where Two or Three are Gathered Together." The conference resolved to fund the reproduction of a new video produced by Bill Cvala, titled, "Deaconess: Privileged to Serve." CDC membership consists of 46 deaconesses (25 active, 20 associate, and one emeritus).

April 5-8, 1989—Concordia Seminary, St. Louis

Several changes to the CDC constitution were discussed. Since most LCMS churches and agencies cover expenses for only one professional conference per year, the CDC decided to hold one annual conference and encourage more area conferences for further support and spiritual refreshment.

April 25-28, 1990—Concordia University, River Forest

A joint celebration of the tenth anniversary of CDC and the Concordia Deaconess Program took place under the theme: "3D: A Decade of Deaconess Dedication." Retiring Concordia Deaconess Program Director, Nancy Nicol, presented "A Vision for the Future." Since deaconesses can now hold membership in Synod, the CDC constitution was altered to parallel that of Synod.

April 11-13, 1991—Marion Conference Center, Catholic University, Washington D.C.

Conference sessions featured an in-depth study of the book of Colossians and focused on the theme of "Building Sisterhood." New Concordia Deaconess Program Director Kristin Wassilak gave her first report to the conference. Participants visited Mount Vernon, Arlington

Cemetery, and Capitol Hill, and several enjoyed an optional night tour of the monuments.

April 29-May 2, 1992—Archbishop Cousins Center, Milwaukee
Dr. Gary Bertels presented the keynote address: "Whatever You Do As a Leader . . . A Servant . . . A Single . . . A Wife . . . A Mother." Dr. Paul Dietz and Rev. Eugene Visser led Bibles studies on Nehemiah and Jonah. The Professional and Spiritual Growth Committee requested that each deaconess write and submit devotions to be included in a CDC devotional booklet. Individual deaconesses signed a "Prayer Covenant" to pray for one another during the duration of the conference.

April 21-24, 1993—Concordia Theological Seminary, Fort Wayne
Seminary professors lectured on "Pastoral Care;" "Hymnody," "The Entanglement of Sacred and Secular Music;" "Missions and Deaconesses;" and "Loehe and Neuendettlesau." President Lauren Morgan used her annual Report to stimulate ideas for achieving conference objectives, asking: (1) How are we accomplishing this objective? (2) What things could we be doing? (3) What hinders us from keeping this objective? Plans were made for a CDC booth at the Great Commission Convocation.

April 27-30, 1994—Concordia University, River Forest
Conference Bible study and plenary sessions centered on I Thessalonians 5:11, "Build One Another Up." Rev. Robert Nemoyer and Rev. Jeff Meyers served as facilitators for "Book Sharing: *Christ Esteem.*" Workshop electives included "Budgeting and Debt Management," "Medical Ethics and End of Life Issues," "Adult Education Methods," and "The Post-Abortive Woman." An optional fun day incorporated lunch in downtown Chicago with window-shopping on the Magnificent Mile and visits to the John Hancock Building and Water Tower Place.

April 19-22, 1995—Concordia Seminary, St. Louis
Seminary professors presented exegetical studies on different aspects of the Aaronic blessing found in Numbers 6:24–26. Seminary President Johnson and his wife hosted a reception for CDC in their home. A tour of the International Center included meeting LCMS President Barry and participating in a Question and Answer period with the LCMS Council of Presidents. The "Schedule for Husbands" featured sessions called "Communication" and "Romancing Your Deaconess," trips to the gymnasium, and a tour of Anheuser-Busch Brewery.

April 24-27, 1996—Concordia University, F.G. and Embassy Suites Hotel, Lombard, Illinois

Deaconess Kristin Wassilak shared the content of her Master's Thesis. Sectionals focused on different aspects of "Defense of the Christian Faith." The conference agreed to support a Deaconess Student Mentor Program. A NO-Talent Show, "White Elephant" gift exchange, and conversation with students rounded off the entertainment.

April 23-26, 1997—St. Paul Lutheran Church and Concordia University, Austin

Dr. Norb Firnhaber led an exegetical study of John 8:1–11 and Dr. Leonard E. Stahlke presented a Bible study on "The Diaconate" based on 1 Corinthians 12:4–6. An Open Forum for Church Professionals featured speakers on parish nursing, parish education, and grief ministry in prison. The conference voted to spend $4,400 on promotional materials for the Concordia University Deaconess Program.

March 11-14, 1998—Concordia Theological Seminary, Fort Wayne

Dr. Roger Pittelko, English District President, spoke on "Deaconess Service in the LCMS" and "Deaconess Issues and Church Polity." Dr. Kenneth Korby taught four plenary sessions titled (1) The Diaconate; (2) Loehe; (3) Prayer Life; (4) Devotional Life.[61] Deaconesses challenged seminarians to a game of volleyball.

April 23-25, 1999—Cedar Valley Center, West Bend, Wisconsin

Dr. Richard Eyer led a seminar based on his book, "Pastoral Care Under the Cross." "Reconnection" sessions gave all deaconesses the opportunity to "show and tell" about their own ministry. Sunrise worship services took place before breakfast. A mission offering of $560 was earmarked for the work of Lutheran Heritage Foundation in Sudan.

March 15-18, 2000—Concordia University, River Forest

An evening cruise on "Spirit of Chicago" provided the setting for a banquet celebrating the 20th anniversary of CDC and the Concordia Deaconess Program. Rev. Ted Kober presented eight hours of instruction in "Responding to Conflict Confessionally." A memorial service for

---

[61] Korby's four lectures were video-recorded. Kenneth F. Korby, "Concordia Deaconess Conference 1998: Lectures by Rev. Dr. Kenneth Korby," Four Sessions on Four Video Tapes: (1) The Diaconate; (2) Loehe; (3) Prayer Life; (4) Devotional Life, held in trust by appointed CDC historian.

Deaconess Darcy Ewald took place in the University chapel. The conference voted to pay a year's educational expenses for five girls at House of Living Water, Thailand.

April 25-28, 2001—Pioneer Camp and Retreat Center, Angola, New York

Rev. Bob Myers led five sessions related to the theme, "Be Still and Know That I Am God." Other discussions centered on a study of Psalm 46 and "Finding a Balance for Effective Ministry." Deaconess students shared creative ideas for helping the CDC assimilate new graduates. Recreation time included hiking, a trip to Niagara Falls, and canoeing on Lake Erie.

April 15-17, 2002—St. Paul's Lutheran Church, Munster, Indiana

Dr. Michael Eschelbach explored the topic of "Confessional Deaconess Service in Light of the New Testament." Dr. Beverly Yahnke presented "Psychology and Theology in Service of Hurting Christians." Dr. Detlev Schulz lectured on "The Feminism of the LCMS." The conference expressed a desire to support its second objective, "To extend the Kingdom of God," by means of servant events.

June 9-11, 2003—Concordia Theological Seminary, Fort Wayne

Professor Harold L. Senkbeil addressed the subject of "The Doctrine of the Ministry and its Relationship to the Service of Deaconesses." Dr. Beverly Yahnke spoke on "Christian Ethics." These two speakers helped the conference lay groundwork for developing a "Deaconess Code of Ethics." A picnic and evening fireside chats brought variety to the agenda.

May 10-12, 2004—Concordia Theological Seminary, Fort Wayne

Reports were received from the Directors of the three Deaconess Programs at River Forest, St. Louis, and Fort Wayne. Rev Steven Briel conducted Bibles studies titled "She Shall be Called Woman" and "The Service of Women in the New Testament Church." The conference pondered its draft Code of Ethics and discussed possible improvements.

May 16-18, 2005—Concordia University, River Forest

Special events celebrating the 25th Anniversary of the CDC included a panel presentation by CDC charter members and Dr. and Mrs. Paul A. Zimmerman on the "History of CDC." Dr. Lawrence Rast informed the conference about "Deaconess History Pre-CDC" and Rev. Matthew Harrison presented his visionary answer to "Where Are We Going From

Here?" The "Concordia Deaconess Conference Code of Ethics" was unanimously adopted. Thanks and tribute were given Deaconess Kristin Wassilak, retiring Director of the River Forest deaconess training program.

June 25-28, 2006—Pallottine Renewal Center, Florissant, Missouri

Dr. Paul Maier, Rev. Daniel Preus, and Rev. Todd Wilken led Bible Studies and presentations related to the theme: "Modern Heresies: An Attempt to Deceive." Several conference attendees provided table displays explaining their work as LCMS deaconesses or deaconess interns.

June 10-13, 2007—Concordia University, Ann Arbor

Bible studies by Pastor John Berg and plenary presentations by Dr. David Ludwig focused on the general theme of "Resting in the Lord; Renewed by His Strength." Activities included a Health Fair, photographs by "LifeTouch" for a CDC photo directory, and a dessert buffet with Intern Display Board and games. Conference offerings supported two LCMS mission projects in Kenya.

June 25-28, 2008—Concordia University Wisconsin

Presentations were given by Rev. Kenneth Wieting on "The Blessings of Weekly Communion" and Rev. Martino Sanders on "1 Peter 1:3-8 – Born Again to a Living Hope." The conference created a permanent Public Relations Committee and restructured the CDC Executive Committee to include a Member-at-Large for Annual Conference Logistics, Member-at-Large for Membership, and Member-at-Large for Spiritual and Professional Growth. During the 2008 CDC business meeting, it was resolved that the next five annual conferences should be held at the following venues:

June 3-6, 2009—Concordia Theological Seminary, Fort Wayne

2010—Concordia University Chicago

30th Anniversary of CDC and the Concordia Deaconess Program in Chicago

2011—Concordia University Nebraska

2012—Concordia Seminary, St. Louis

10th Anniversary of St. Louis Deaconess Program

2013—Concordia Theological Seminary, Fort Wayne

10th Anniversary of Fort Wayne Deaconess Program[62]

---

[62] Illustrations for Chapter Fifteen may be viewed at www.deaconesshistory.org.

CHAPTER 16

CONCORDIA DEACONESS PROGRAM

As soon as the LCMS decided to train deaconesses at River Forest, President Zimmerman appointed a Deaconess Advisory Council and a Faculty Task Force Committee to prepare for the inauguration of the program in the fall of 1980. The advisory group provided the college with "grass roots advice from deaconesses in the field, as well as from administrators and pastors who represent institutions and congregations to which deaconesses are called to serve."[1] The task force wrote the deaconess curriculum and progressed it through Concordia's Academic Policies Committee, the Faculty Senate, and the college's Board of Control.[2]

THE DEACONESS CURRICULUM

In March 1980, the LCMS BHE approved the new deaconess program curriculum.[3] Students enrolled in the Deaconess Program would receive a Bachelor of Arts degree with a major in theology; a minor in church music, psychology, or sociology; a concentration in education, youth work, counseling, music, Hispanic American ministry, urban ministry, or foreign languages; and four specialized courses dealing with the specifics of

---

[1] Mr. Fred Nieno, Administrator of Lutheran Homes, Inc., Fort Wayne, served on the advisory council for several years, along with Chicago area pastors and CDC deaconesses. Letters from Paul A. Zimmerman to Deaconesses Joyce Ostermann, Nancy Nicol, Luella Mickley, Cheryl D. Naumann, Ruth Broermann, Kay Pritzlaff, and Betty Mulholland, Box: CDC, File: CDC Correspondence 1983–1984 (also meetings 1980–86 and newsletters), CHI, St. Louis, Mo.

[2] The Faculty Task Force consisted of Norman Young (Chairman), Donald Gnewuch (Secretary), Julia Hennig, Rev. Roy Rinehard, Rudolph Block, and Betty Mulholland (representing the Deaconess Advisory Council). The Task Force met on Sept. 7, Sept. 25, Oct. 2, and Oct. 9, 1979. "Historical List," single typed page, priv. col. of Nancy (nee Nicol) Nemoyer, Carlisle, Pa.

[3] *BHE Minutes*, March 21–22, 1980, item 10; CHI, St. Louis.

diaconal ministry. A year of internship between the junior and senior year meant that it would take five years to complete the training.[4]

General studies courses required for the bachelor's degree matched the liberal arts curriculum in place at River Forest and other LCMS colleges. This made it easy for LCMS colleges to continue to offer the pre-deaconess program (freshman and sophomore years). In fact, though many deaconess students would attend Concordia for four years of academic study, just as many would transfer to River Forest for their junior year, from both synodical and nonsynodical schools.[5]

Concordia College already offered all courses mandated by the deaconess program, with the exception of the deaconess work classes. The Faculty Task Force suggested that the college call a deaconess to serve as the Director of the new program. Her duties would include developing and teaching the four professional courses, as well as supervising the internship and field work experiences.[6]

In January 1980, the BHE authorized Concordia to appoint Miss Claire Ellen Krans as "instructor in Deaconess Service subjects."[7] A 1975 graduate of Valparaiso, Deaconess Krans served at St. Paul Lutheran Church, Flint, Michigan, and had expressed her support for a synodical deaconess program in an encouraging letter to convention campaigners in 1977.[8] However, Krans declined the call.[9]

Two months later, Concordia College issued another call, to Miss Nancy Eileen Nicol (b. 1954), admissions coordinator in the Deaconess Corps at Lutheran Home, Fort Wayne. Nicol became a deaconess in 1977. She campaigned for a Missouri Synod deaconess program both before and after her graduation from Valpo, and had just become a founding member of CDC. After much prayer and deliberation, 25-year-old Nicol accepted the challenge to be the first Director of the Concordia Deaconess Program

---

[4] "Deaconess Program," mimeographed outline of courses taken by deaconess students, 1980, priv. col. of Nancy (Nicol) Nemoyer, Carlisle, Pa.
[5] Letter from Rudolph C. Block, Academic Dean, to Dr. Arthur M. Ahlschwede, BHE, February 26, 1980, priv. col. of Ruth (Broermann) Stallmann, St. Louis, Mo., 5.
[6] Ibid., 2.
[7] BHE Minutes, January 17–19, 1980, item 40; CHI, St. Louis.
[8] Letter from Deaconess Claire E. Krans to Deaconess Betty Mulholland, March 22, 1977, Box: CDC, File: Correspondence, CHI, St. Louis, Mo.
[9] Krans came to the conclusion that she was not geographically mobile due to a budding relationship with Rev. Richard Neagley, whom she married in June 1981. Claire (nee Krans) Neagley, notes from telephone interview by CDN, Sept. 1, 2006, priv. col. of CDN, Pittsburgh, Pa.

and Resident Deaconess on Concordia's college campus.[10] Nicol's role as Director would grow to include a broad range of activities in areas such as public relations, fund raising, recruitment and admissions, and academic counseling.[11]

CONCORDIA COLLEGE, RIVER FOREST, ILLINOIS

Concordia College, now called Concordia University Chicago, is the oldest institution in the LCMS Concordia University System.[12] In 1855, Rev. Friedrich Johann Carl Lochner (1822–1902) and Rev. Philipp Fleischmann (1815–78) founded a "teachers' seminary" in Milwaukee, Wisconsin, to educate teachers for Lutheran day schools. In 1857, the Missouri Synod assumed responsibility for the school, moved it to Fort Wayne, and combined it with the theological seminary there.[13] The college moved two more times: to Addison, Illinois, in 1864, and finally to the 40-acre River Forest campus in 1913.

The Deaconess Program Proposal sent to the BHE from Concordia's Task Force explained the benefit of the River Forest site for deaconess training.

> The excellent location of Concordia in a large metropolitan area, surrounded by many Lutheran congregations and several large Lutheran agencies such as Lutherbrook in Addison, Lutheran Family Services, and the Lutheran Home for the Aged in Park Ridge, provides many opportunities for field work experiences in different settings. Guest lecturers for class meetings and for evening meetings should be relatively easy to find for the same reason.[14]

Concordia's campus ethos placed a major emphasis on preparing professional church workers for service within the Missouri Synod. Along

---

[10] Appendix 2.A. includes a list of places Nicol served before accepting the post at Concordia. She resigned her position as the first elected secretary of CDC when she accepted the call to Concordia College. Letter from Paul A. Zimmerman to Nancy Nicol, March 28, 1980, priv. col. of Nancy (nee Nicol) Nemoyer, Carlisle, Pa.

[11] Nancy (nee Nicol) Nemoyer, interview by CDN, audio recording, June 16, 2006, Bedford, Pa., priv. col. of CDN, Pittsburgh, Pa.

[12] The institution has had several names: Concordia Teachers' College (1864-1979); Concordia College (1979-90); Concordia University, River Forest (CURF) (1990-2006); Concordia University Chicago (CUC) (2006-).

[13] In 1861, the LCMS moved its Fort Wayne seminary to St. Louis, and later moved it to Springfield, Illinois, and then back to Fort Wayne, where it remains today.

[14] Letter from Rudolph C. Block, Academic Dean, to Dr. Arthur M. Ahlschwede, BHE, February 26, 1980, priv. col. of Ruth (Broermann) Stallmann, St. Louis, Mo., 4.

with strong teacher education programs, the college offered Director of Christian Education (DCE) and Social Work Programs, as well as the recently launched pre-seminary program. It seemed natural to introduce another parallel venture.

> The Deaconess Program will be a welcome addition to the complexity of church professional programs already operating on the campus. While the college envisions some expansion in general education programs, such as computer science and business, it believes its main mission and future commitment to be in continuing to educate students for various ministries.[15]

Program Objectives

Not surprisingly, the "Deaconess Program Objectives" developed by Director Nicol reflected the close relationship between the LCMS and Concordia College. The objectives read:

1. to be responsible to the LCMS in the training of women to serve as Deaconesses.

2. to maintain a high standard of academic preparation in Deaconess training.

3. to aid parishes and agencies of the LCMS in an understanding of the role of the Deaconess in the church today.

4. to provide students with opportunities for practical experience in Deaconess work within the diversity of a multi-ethnic society.

5. to identify and cultivate students' personal qualities for ministry.

6. to stimulate an appreciation for and consecration toward the ministry of the Deaconess within the context of the church's ministry in proclamation of the gospel.[16]

To be "responsible to the LCMS" acknowledges accountability to the Synod. To assist parishes and agencies in "understanding the role of the deaconess" suggests a further responsibility to the entities that might someday employ deaconesses. To promote "the ministry of the Deaconess *within the context of the church's ministry* in proclamation of the gospel" deliberately melds diaconal ministry—a ministry of mercy—to the very core of the church's evangelical mission. With such objectives in place, the Concordia Deaconess Program set out to determine the future direction of

---

[15] *Ibid.*

[16] Nancy Nicol, "Deaconess Program Objectives," typed sheet, June 11, 1981, priv. col. of Nancy (nee Nicol) Nemoyer, Carlisle, Pa.

deaconess ministry in the Missouri Synod; endeavoring to provide the Synod with workers that would remain faithful to Scripture in their teaching, leadership and service.

THE FIRST STUDENTS

Concordia received several dozen inquiries about the deaconess program from prospective students even before the BHE approved the curriculum. By the fall of 1980, 18 students—five freshmen, five sophomores, seven juniors, and one special student—enrolled in the program. The students hailed from eleven states, including three from Illinois; two each from California, Indiana, Michigan, Minnesota, and Missouri; and one each from Iowa, Ohio, New Mexico, and New York. Five of the deaconess students transferred to Concordia, River Forest from other LCMS colleges, and another four transferred from nonsynodical colleges and universities, including Valparaiso.[17] Before the end of the year, five more River Forest students joined the program, for a total of 23 deaconess students during 1980–81.[18]

Interestingly, if the college had been able to offer all five years of deaconess training in 1980–81, the initial enrollment would have been even higher. In April 1980, Concordia's Academic Dean wrote to CDC President Ruth Broermann:

> . . . I am sending you a complete copy of the Deaconess Program Proposal submitted to the BHE. . . . If you look at pages 8 and 9 of the proposal you will see the deaconess specialization of 28 hours. What we are talking about is the course <u>Deaconess Work II</u> for 4 hours and the Seminars . . . You should find them interesting as you consider the possibility of developing these courses for us and possibly teaching them this coming year. Frankly, I feel uncomfortable about rushing into this instead of sequencing the program in as we have done with all other programs initiated at Concordia. However, there are several Valparaiso interns who have insisted on coming to Concordia to try and complete their work and we are trying to accommodate them. Therefore, please

---

[17] Nancy E. Nicol, "CDC Report, October 3, 1980," green box, priv. col. of Nancy (nee Nicol) Nemoyer, Carlisle, Pa.

[18] Nancy E. Nicol, "A Year End Report to the President, the Deaconess Program, Concordia College, River Forest, Illinois, June 9, 1981," Deaconess Office Archives, Concordia University, RF, Illinois.

look this material over and let us know whether or not you will be able to help us out.[19]

In the end, timing and class size issues resulted in the college first providing deaconess internships in 1981–82 and the senior year of academic study in 1982–83. Because of this "sequencing" of the new program, only two of the returning Valparaiso interns, Kristine Marie (nee Zobel) Blackwell and Cheryl Ann (nee Johnson) Gruenwald, waited to complete their training in River Forest.[20]

HOUSING DEACONESS STUDENTS

Concordia's administration knew that if the Concordia Deaconess Program was to be successful, it would need to deal with that age-old question, "What is a deaconess?" and now, particularly, "What is a Missouri Synod deaconess?" Certainly a Missouri Synod deaconess subscribed wholeheartedly to the doctrinal position of the Synod. But what did one of these women look like and how did she act in real life?

As one step toward forming an answer to this question, the college housed its "Resident Deaconess" and deaconess students together on the ground floor of Brohm Hall, on an inside hallway facing the center of campus. While redheaded "Deaconess Nancy" lived in a small apartment normally occupied by residence hall directors, her responsibility lay in being a model deaconess for her students. Once a week Nicol led the women in evening devotions in her apartment. The rest of the time, when not teaching or traveling to internship and field work sites, her door was open for discussion and counseling.[21] In a memo to the college's President, Dean of Students, and Housing Director, Deaconess Nicol wrote:

The principles for such a concentration [of deaconess students] are:

1. So that the limited number of students in this new program not be lost among other more established programs.

---

[19] Letter from Rudolph C. Block to Deaconess Ruth Broermann, Box: CDC, File: CDC Correspondence 1983–1984 (also meetings 1980–86 and newsletters), CHI, St. Louis.
[20] Blackwell married and had a baby before graduating with Concordia's first deaconess class in 1983. Gruenwald also married, and because she waited for her husband's seminary education to finish before resuming her deaconess training, she graduated with the second deaconess class in 1984. Kris Blackwell, interview by CDN, audio recording, October 4, 2005, Pittsburgh, Pa., priv. col. of CDN, Pittsburgh, Pa.; Cheryl Gruenwald, notes from telephone interview by CDN, December 11, 2006, priv. col. of CDN, Pittsburgh, Pa.
[21] Nemoyer, interview by CDN, audio recording, June 16, 2006.

2. To help establish a clear identity of what a Deaconess is in the interplay of student discussion and life in the dorm.

3. To encourage a positive feeling of "sisterhood"—an historic value of Deaconesses.

4. To facilitate attendance at the Deaconess student meetings.

The rationale for not making common housing a mandatory requirement is:

1. To avoid an attitude of superiority or exclusivity.

2. To allow some freedom of choice, recognizing roommate preferences.[22]

As implied by the last two points, if deaconess students made specific requests to live in a different dormitory, the college honored their requests as much as possible. After two years of this Brohm Hall arrangement, the college stopped assigning deaconess students to live together and the Program Director moved to another campus apartment in Krauss Hall.[23] A year later she moved off campus. Nicol's renewed employment agreement referred to her as "Instructor, Director of Deaconess Program" and then as "Assistant Professor," with no further reference to being the "Resident Deaconess."[24] During the first two months that she lived on campus, Nicol's office was in her personal residence. Later, the College provided her with an office in Kretzmann Hall, which is still the Director's office today.

THE DEACONESS SEMINAR ROOM

Director Nicol continued to host weekly evening devotions, but it was difficult for the growing number of deaconess students to sit comfortably in her small living room. Sometime during the 1980–81 academic year, the college designated an empty basement storage room in Krauss Hall as a future "Deaconess Seminar room." The room needed some substantial renovation before it could be used. In April 1983, Nicol reported to the CDC:

---

[22] Memo to Dr. Paul Zimmerman, Dean A. Wingfield (Dean of Students), and Colette Cheramie (Housing Director) from Deaconess Nancy Nicol, Folder: Program Ideas, Deaconess Office Archives, Concordia University Chicago, 3.

[23] Before the fall of 1983 the Director moved again, to an Oak Park apartment owned by the college, about four blocks from campus. Nemoyer, interview by CDN, audio recording, June 16, 2006.

[24] "Concordia College, River Forest, Illinois, Employment Agreement," December 13, 1983, and December 3, 1985, priv. col. of Nancy (nee Nicol) Nemoyer, Carlisle, Pa.

The Northern Illinois District LWML gave significant monies toward the renovation and furnishing of a Deaconess Seminar room. A detailed dream sheet has been drawn up, submitted, and priced. This space will be invaluable in fostering a closeness between students as it becomes a familiar meeting place as well as a practical space for community outreach, and for other uses such as district LWML committee meetings and CDC meetings in the future.[25]

On October 21, 1983, Concordia College's campus pastor, Rev. Thomas R. Acton, led LWML officers, faculty members, deaconesses, and students in a service of dedication for the "NID LWML Deaconess Seminar Room."[26] The finished room sported new carpet, cabinets, bookshelves, chairs, couches, loveseats, and original paintings.[27] From that time onward, the Deaconess Seminar room provided a warm and inviting venue for the specialized Deaconess Seminar courses, Bible Study, prayer, and fellowship among the students.[28]

A HIGHER PROFILE

Missouri Synod proceedings from the 1980s reflected a renewed desire to find ways for women to actively participate in carrying out the church's mission, while remaining loyal to the Synod's understanding of God's Word and the role of women in His church. In his report to the 1983 synodical convention in St. Louis, LCMS President Ralph Arthur Bohlmann (b. 1932) declared, "We especially need to involve more women with their fantastic gifts in the service of congregations and our church body."[29] In a *Lutheran Witness* article published two months later Bohlmann wrote:

At all levels of our synodical life, we need to make it clear that we value and want to expand the role of women in service to our Lord and His

---

[25] Nancy Nicol, "Report to the Concordia Deaconess Conference, meeting at Concordia College, River Forest," April 8, 1983, File: Reports from CDC: Director, 1983– , CDC Historian Archive Boxes, held in trust by appointed CDC Historian, 4.
[26] Nicol was an elected Vice-President of the Northern Illinois District LWML and also served on the International LWML Christian Growth Committee (1983–87). Dedication service bulletin, October 21, 1983, 9:00 p.m., white scrapbook titled "The Deaconess Program, Concordia College, River Forest, Illinois," Deaconess Office Archives, Concordia University, RF, Illinois.
[27] Annette Heimke, "New Deaconess Seminar Room Gift of Northern Illinois Women," *The Forester* (November 1983): 2.
[28] Nemoyer, interview by CDN, audio recording, June 16, 2006.
[29] Ralph A. Bohlmann, "7. Human Care," in LCMS, *Proceedings*, 1983, 69.

Church. Not only should we support the central role of women in Christian families but also encourage other service and leadership roles.[30]

In January 1984, Bohlmann appointed nine women to serve as members of a President's Commission on Women (PCW). Two of the women—Concordia Deaconess Program Director Nancy Nicol and Mrs. Marie L. Meyer—had trained as deaconesses.[31] The six tasks assigned to the PCW included the directive "to recommend appropriate service and ministry opportunities for women at all levels of church life."[32] In addition to presenting new ideas for service, the PCW's published report (1988) suggested several areas in which the Synod might enhance and increase the involvement of LCMS women in *existing* ministries. Regarding the diaconate, the PCW wrote:

> The deaconess program equips women with theological competence and skills for relating faith to life. These skills allow a deaconess to serve full-time in a variety of settings: congregations, institutions, church or state facilities for the aged and mentally retarded, hospital chaplaincies, prisons, campus ministries and social service agencies.

> COULD the church provide for deaconess staff representation at synodical headquarters so that issues affecting, or being affected by, deaconess service might interface with the decision-making structure of the Synod?

> COULD continuing theological training for deaconesses be encouraged at the seminaries and other institutions of the Synod in order to better equip these women to carry out their functions?

> COULD a "clearing house" of deaconesses who are available for service be coordinated through the synodical structure?

> COULD the Synod provide resource material for deaconess ministry similar to that available to teachers and DCEs?

> COULD the Synod reconsider its 1983 decision not to include deaconesses in the category of Ministers of Religion?[33]

---

[30] Ralph A. Bohlmann, "From the President," *The Lutheran Witness* 102, no. 9 (September 1983), 34.
[31] The other seven women appointed by Bohlmann were: Alberta Barnes, Jean Garton (Chairman), Elsie A. Gerhardt, Maricarol Kolster, Emily Moore, Candace Mueller, and Louise M. Mueller.
[32] The President's Commission on Women, "God's Woman for all Generations," 91-page report (St. Louis: LCMS Board for Communication Services, 1988), 4.
[33] *Ibid.*, 70.

482 IN THE FOOTSTEPS OF PHOEBE

The PWC report created fresh interest in the possibilities for diaconal ministry within the Synod. Though some of the above challenges took longer than others to investigate, almost all of them led to positive action on the part of LCMS committees, the Concordia Deaconess Program, or the CDC. However, one question that is still being asked today, more than twenty years after publication of the PWC report, is whether or not the LCMS could establish an official "clearing house" to facilitate the flow of information between LCMS certified (and rostered) deaconesses and the churches, institutions, and mission fields that may be interested in acquiring their services.[34]

JUST THE BEGINNING

The Missouri Synod's creation of a deaconess training program necessitated a chain of other changes that could only be realized through additional synodical legislation. The River Forest faculty submitted an overture to the 1981 LCMS convention to revise "regulations for certification by colloquy to the deaconess ministry" as they appeared in Bylaws 4.91 through 4.98 of the synodical *Handbook*.[35] When convention delegates adopted the resolution, it was clear that the Synod intended to take responsibility for every aspect of deaconess education and certification. The following excerpts from the three-page resolution demonstrate the overarching changes:

4.91 Colloquy Board for the Deaconess Ministry

[Former wording:] The Colloquy Board for the Deaconess Ministry shall consist of a Vice-President of the Synod appointed by the President of the Synod, the Director of Training and the Executive Director of the Lutheran Deaconess Association (LDA). . . .

[New wording:] The Colloquy Board for the Deaconess Ministry shall consist of a Vice-President of the Synod appointed by the President of the Synod, and one representative from each of the entities preparing deaconesses for the LCMS. . . .

---

[34] At their annual meeting in 2008, the members of Concordia Deaconess Conference moved to "direct the President to secure an appointment to meet with the LCMS Council of Presidents, not only to promote deaconess ministry in the LCMS, but to particularly encourage the Presidents to look for possible places of service for deaconesses in their districts." CDC, *Minutes*, June 27, 2008, 14.

[35] "Overture 6-49: To Revise By-laws re Deaconess Programs," in LCMS, *Reports and Overtures*, 1981, 266–68.

4.92 Functions

[Former wording:] The Colloquy Board for the Deaconess Ministry shall—a. direct the synodical activity in matters of colloquies for the deaconess ministry in keeping with standards set by the LDA . . .

[New wording:] The Colloquy Board for the Deaconess Ministry shall—a. direct the synodical activity in matters of colloquies for the deaconess ministry according to regulations adopted by the Synod; . . .

4.93 and 4.94 Application for Admission

[Former wording:] Applications of candidates for the deaconess ministry shall be directed to the Executive Director of the LDA. Only such applicants shall be considered as meet the entrance requirements of the colloquy program of the LDA. . . . The District President shall assure the Colloquy Board of his endorsement of the applicant. The LDA shall approve the applicant before the Colloquy Board can act favorably on the application. . . .

[New wording:] Application for admission into the colloquy program shall be directed to one of the entities preparing deaconesses for the Synod. . . . The preparatory entity shall submit for publication in an official periodical of the Synod the request for colloquies of all persons whose applications have been approved by the District President and the Colloquy Board for the Deaconess ministry. If no valid objection is filed within four weeks after the publication of such notice, the colloquy procedure may continue. . . .[36]

Once Resolution 6-16 passed, Concordia College, River Forest, could certify deaconess candidates by colloquy and the LCMS had defined its authority and responsibility for every aspect of the colloquy process. Again, this convention action was only the beginning of much more to come. In particular, the recent proliferation of church work careers, coupled with a general confusion about the tax status of those who pursued those careers, would precipitate a serious study of the classification of synodical workers.

CLASSIFICATION

At the same time that the Concordia Deaconess Program started, the BHE coincidentally adopted two documents "establishing criteria to be applied in determining 'church work program' and 'church work student' status."[37] The latter document noted that the BHE utilized three categories for

---

[36] "Resolution 6-16, in LCMS, *Proceedings,* 1981, 189–91.
[37] *BHE Minutes,* September 11–13, 1980, Section H. item 1; CHI, St. Louis.

classification of "ordained or licensed church workers": (1) Pastor (parish pastor, missionary, campus pastor, institutional chaplain, armed forces chaplain); (2) Teacher (LCMS elementary, high school, college, seminary); and (3) Parish Assistant (deaconess, DCE, parish worker, minister of education, minister of music, director of evangelism, youth director, administration, guidance and counseling, stewardship). The document also stated,

> In the future the Board for Higher Education may expand or reduce the number of ministries under each category in consultation with the Council of Presidents. Faculties at institutions with approved programs will certify the candidates. The graduates of all recognized church worker programs will be placed into the professional ministry of the church by the Council of Presidents in accordance with Handbook regulations. All candidates placed from any of the [three] categories above will hold status as ministers of the gospel.[38]

The September 1980 BHE minutes explained that while the BHE adopted the document, it expressed concern about use of the phrase "ministers of the gospel." Noting "a special concern about the status of such workers with the I.R.S.," the Board directed the BHE Executive Secretary to send copies of the document to presidents of LCMS colleges and seminaries, the Commission on Theology and Church Relations, the Council of Presidents, the LCMS Board of Directors, and the Synod's legal counsel, for their feedback.[39]

The Synod's Board of Directors responded by writing a resolution, subsequently presented to the 1981 LCMS convention as Resolution 5-08, with only one *Resolved*:

> . . . that only those duly ordained pastors and duly commissioned male teachers who are listed on the Synod's official membership rosters shall be regarded by the Synod as qualifying as "ministers of the Gospel," "ministers of religion," "ministers of the church" or similar titles for purposes of United States income taxes, social security, unemployment taxes, and selective service.[40]

Rather than pass this resolution, the 1981 convention delegates chose to refer it back to the BOD for further study.[41]

---

[38] *BHE Minutes*, September 11–13, 1980, Section H. item 1; CHI, St. Louis.
[39] *Ibid.*
[40] Resolution 5-08, in LCMS, *Proceedings,* 1981, 176.
[41] The BOD held extensive consultations with "theologians, historians, legal counsel, executives dealing with our elementary and secondary schools, constitutionalists, faculty

In 1983, a refined overture (5-38) appeared in the next *Convention Workbook*, defining three "Classifications of Positions in the Synod": (1) Minister of Religion, Ordained; (2) Minister of Religion, Commissioned; and (3) Certified Professional Church Worker, Lay. The resolution mandated that the Synod declare individuals in categories one and two be "regarded fully by Synod as ministers of religion . . . required to be members on their own of the LCMS together with congregations which hold membership in the Synod."[42] The big surprise, however, was that deaconesses were listed in category three, while category two included male *and female* elementary, secondary, and college teachers; plus male *and female* DCEs. This classification puzzled deaconesses, particularly in light of a 1981 CTCR document which designated commissioning as "restricted for placing a person into an office clearly auxiliary to the central functions of the pastoral ministry," and then stated, "This would include male and female teachers, deaconesses, directors of Christian Education, etc."[43]

On May 28, 1983, CDC President Joyce Ostermann, accompanied by CDC Board Member Betty Mulholland and Concordia Deaconess Program Director Nancy Nicol, appealed to convention Floor Committee Five to create another classification titled "Minister of Religion, Consecrated," especially for deaconesses. Ostermann reasoned that deaconesses received specialized training and consecration in a manner parallel to the training and commissioning of female teachers. Furthermore, the Council of Presidents placed deaconesses in their first call, just like female teachers (and not like any of the other certified lay workers).[44] In spite of these efforts, Resolution 5-09A remained unchanged and was passed at the 1983 convention.[45]

---

members of our teacher colleges, District Presidents, and others." "To Classify Ministers of Religion: Background," in LCMS, *Proceedings*, 1983, 178.

[42] "Resolution 5-38: To Classify Ministers of Religion," in LCMS, *Reports and Overtures*, 1983, 221.

[43] Commission on Theology and Church Relations, "The Ministry: Offices, Procedures, and Nomenclature" (St. Louis: Concordia, 1981), 34.

[44] Letter from Joyce Ostermann to Rev. Wilbert Griesse, May 18, 1983, priv. col. of Joyce Ostermann, Fort Wayne, Indiana; "Presentation to Floor Committee #5—Structure and Constitution, by members of Concordia Deaconess Conference," May 28, 1983, Box: CDC, File: 1983/1986 Synodical Presentations on the Status of Deaconess as the Third Category Church Worker, CHI, St. Louis, Mo.

[45] In response to a request from the convention floor, "the Chair" ordered that answers given to delegate questions concerning this resolution be included in the official minutes of the convention "so that no misunderstanding can come about at a future time." "Resolution 5-09A: To Classify Ministers of Religion," in LCMS, *Proceedings*, 1983, 178–80.

FURTHER STUDY

Almost three years later, in April 1986, LCMS President Bohlmann and First Vice President Robert Charles Sauer (b. 1921) invited the Concordia Deaconess Conference (assembled in St. Louis) to "evaluate the ranking" of deaconesses in the third category.[46]

At its April 19 business meeting, the CDC unanimously passed a resolution asking the LCMS "to reconsider the classification of deaconess from 'church worker-lay' to another classification which would include deaconesses on the roster of Synod."[47] CDC members believed that if they were rostered, like pastors and teachers, deaconesses would have advocates on the Board for Professional Education Service, would be included in *Handbook* procedures holding them accountable to Synod, would be given more professional growth opportunities, and would benefit from new avenues for calling deaconesses from the field.[48]

Upon receiving the CDC Resolution, President Bohlmann forwarded it to two synodical committees and wrote to Deaconess Ostermann, "I believe an excellent case can be made for reconsidering the current classification status of deaconesses."[49]

NEW BY-LAWS

In the meantime, the newly released 1986 LCMS *Convention Workbook* included a proposal for new by-laws for "Certified Professional Church Workers, Lay," which sparked a great deal of debate.[50] Professor Kurt Marquart of Concordia Theological Seminary, Fort Wayne, indicated his

---

[46] Cecil Angel, "Deaconesses Want Respect in Church Hierarchy," *Fort Wayne News-Sentinel*, June 7, 1986, Fort Wayne, Ind. See also: "Deaconesses Want to Change Classification," *Reporter* 12, no. 19 (May 19, 1986): 1.

[47] Letter from Deaconess Joyce Ostermann to Dr. Ralph Bohlmann, April 23, 1986, Box: CDC, File: 1983/1986 Synodical Presentations on the Status of Deaconess as the Third Category Church Worker, CHI, St. Louis, Mo.

[48] "Requesting the LCMS to Reclassify Deaconesses from 'Certified Church Worker—Lay' to Other Category," Concordia Deaconess Conference, April 17–19, 1986, Box: CDC, File: 1983/1986 Synodical Presentations on the Status of Deaconess as the Third Category Church Worker, CHI, St. Louis, Mo.

[49] Letter from Ralph A. Bohlmann to Miss Ostermann, May 7, 1986, Box: CDC, File: 1983/1986 Synodical Presentations on the Status of Deaconess as the Third Category Church Worker, CHI, St. Louis, Mo.

[50] Much debate centered around the phrase "ministers of religion" in the By-laws, since it was a secular and legal term rather than a theological category. LCMS, *Reports and Overtures*, 1986, 261–63.

deep concern about the wording and effect of the proposed Bylaws in a letter to LCMS Secretary Walter Rosin. Marquart wrote:

> In addition to "ordained" and "commissioned" ministers the proposed new By-Laws suggest yet another category, "Certified Professional Church Workers, Lay," including deaconesses and "lay ministers," among others. This is misleading because it suggests that "commissioned ministers," that is, school teachers and "DCEs" are not laymen. . . .
>
> The classification of deaconesses among "church workers, lay," while school teachers are "commissioned ministers" is particularly unfortunate. We have it on the highest authority that Phoebe was a "minister of the church in Cenchrea" (Rom. 16:1). The very word "deacon" or "deaconess" means "minister" (in the generic sense). Deacons and deaconesses (Acts 6, though the term is not used there) represent in fact the first auxiliary office established by the church, still in apostolic times. This ancient office should not be made to appear subordinate to the school teacher's office.
>
> Since it seems desirable to relate our churchly offices to the IRS's category of "minister of religion," there could be a brief appendix somewhere to the effect that "the following" (certainly including deaconesses), as determined by the Synod from time to time, are regarded as "ministers of religion" in the sense and for the purposes of Federal laws and regulations.[51]

Once again, CDC members rallied to the May convention floor committee meetings in St. Louis. Speaking to the Floor Committee for Leadership and Organization, the women argued that the proposed *Handbook* change which assigned supervision of deaconesses "solely with the congregations and other entities which have employed them," was out of step with four LCMS Constitution objectives that specified responsibility for "Pastors, teachers, *and other church workers.*"[52] The CDC deaconesses eagerly desired procedures that would "call Deaconesses to be accountable

---

[51] Letter from Kurt Marquart to Walter Rosin, May 25, 1986, Box: CDC, File: 1983/1986 Synodical Presentations on the Status of Deaconess as the Third Category Church Worker, CHI, St. Louis, Mo.

[52] Those present included Concordia Deaconess Program Director, Deaconess Nancy Nicol; Deaconesses Joyce Ostermann, Betty Mulholland, and Ruth Stallmann; and Deaconess Candidate Kristin Hannenberg. "Presentation to the Floor Committee for Leadership and Organization, Re: Resolution 5-163 'To Amend By-laws of Synod,'" May 31, 1986, Box: CDC, File: 1983/1986 Synodical Presentations on the Status of Deaconess as the Third Category Church Worker, CHI, St. Louis, Mo., 1–2.

to Synod and Synod to be responsible for Deaconesses."[53] The women suggested that, since the Synod assumed direct supervision of *members* of Synod, "Perhaps Deaconesses should become members of Synod."[54]

In the end, delegates at the 1986 LCMS convention in Indianapolis adopted the "New Chapter 7 By-Laws for Certified Professional Church Workers, Lay" with all of their controversial nomenclature.[55] Interestingly, some of the by-laws created an anomaly that would need to be remedied by another resolution.

THE GRANDFATHER RESOLUTION

The classification of "consecrated lay workers" applied to deaconesses, lay ministers, parish workers, parish assistants, directors of evangelism, and lay teachers (who opted not to join the Synod). However, the Synod's new by-laws restricted "eligibility" for placement in this third category to "men and women who have completed courses of study prescribed or approved by the Board for Professional Education Services *and* offered by one of the Synod's colleges." In addition, one of the four prerequisites for consecration or installation as a lay worker stated that the individual needed to receive a degree, diploma, or certificate from a Missouri Synod college.[56]

The only deaconesses that could meet this stipulation were the 28 women who completed the LCMS deaconess program and graduated from Concordia College, River Forest, between 1983 and 1986. Technically, all other deaconesses trained by the LDA at Fort Wayne, Beaver Dam, Watertown, Hot Springs, or Valparaiso (including the Director of the LCMS Deaconess Program!) could no longer be classified as Missouri Synod "Certified Professional Church Workers, Lay."

Fortunately, the LCMS Commission on Structure, chaired by Mr. John Daniel, anticipated and prepared a solution for this irregularity, which the 1986 convention adopted in Resolution 5-24, "To 'Grandfather' Certified Lay Workers." The resolution read:

---

[53] "Presentation to the Floor Committee for Leadership and Organization, Re: Resolution 5-163", 3.
[54] *Ibid.*,
[55] "To Provide New Chapter 7, By-Laws for 'Certified Professional Church Workers, Lay,'" in LCMS, *Proceedings*, 1986, 169–70.
[56] *Ibid.*

Whereas, . . . Lay professional church workers will be certified by the Synod only under conditions set forth in proposed [and adopted] Bylaws designated as sections 7.01-7.43; and

Whereas, There are now serving dedicated lay workers who have previously been certified as lay workers and who would find it difficult or impossible to meet the [new Bylaw] requirements for certification; therefore be it

Resolved, That (1) all "certified professional church workers—lay," as reflected in the records of the districts of the Synod on July 24, 1986, and (2) those certified and assigned at any time prior to September 1, 1986, will continue to be eligible to be regarded as certified professional church workers—lay for as long as they are regularly performing the duties of the office (e.g. deaconess, lay minister) . . .[57]

The "Grandfathering" of consecrated lay workers preserved the status quo of the men and women already working in the field. However, deaconess students who intended to graduate from Valparaiso University or other non-synodical institutions after September 1, 1986, would need to complete a synodical colloquy program to be certified and placed as professional church workers in the Missouri Synod.[58]

MEMBERSHIP IN SYNOD

Following the 1986 synodical convention, Deaconess Program Director Nicol made it known that she would continue to pursue the re-classification of deaconesses in conjunction with efforts made by the CDC.[59] Throughout 1987 and 1988, the CDC sent sample resolutions to interested pastors and synodical officials, with the result that several congregations and district conventions adopted resolutions encouraging the Synod "to study the feasibility of reclassifying deaconesses as 'Ministers of Religion—Commissioned.'"[60]

---

[57] "To 'Grandfather' Certified Lay Workers, Resolution 5-24," in LCMS, *Proceedings*, 1986, 183.

[58] Appendices 1.E and 1.F include the names of all LDA graduates eligible for placement in the LCMS (1922–86), as determined by the Grandfather Resolution. If a woman graduated from VU after 1986 and subsequently completed the LCMS colloquy program for deaconess, her name appears in Appendix 3.F.

[59] Letter from Deaconess Nancy E. Nicol to Dr. W. J. Sohns, Chairman, Council of Presidents, December 18, 1986, Box: CDC, File: 1983/1986 Synodical Presentations on the Status of Deaconess as the Third Category Church Worker, CHI, St. Louis, Mo.

[60] See for example, "New Jersey District Convention Re-elects Sandmann President," *Reporter* 14, no. 19 (May 23, 1988): 1; Letter from CDC President Kristin Hannenberg to all

The women's persistence paid off. Delegates to the 1989 LCMS convention in Wichita, Kansas, passed Resolution 3-11A: "To Declare Deaconesses Eligible for Synodical Membership."[61] Ironically, neither Deaconess Nancy nor any of the other founding members of the CDC witnessed the monumental adoption of the resolution. Two weeks later, the Director wrote:

> Almost every day in *Today's Business* there was a revision—a more carefully worded version [of the resolution]—it was so exciting—we could tell they were planning for it to pass and wanted it to be in proper form. Then I had to leave on Wednesday. . . I went home to pray for it. On Thursday at 10 p.m. I got an excited phone call from Kristin, Lauren, and Sara. They gave me a blow-by-blow account of each speaker, each argument, and how each of the three (one resolution blossomed to three as they fleshed out the details) passed!!![62]

Resolution 3-11A mandated changes to Articles V and VI of the LCMS Constitution, making it necessary for LCMS congregations to ratify the decision via separate ballot sheets, to be sent to Synod's Secretary by January 30, 1990.[63] *The Northern Light* reported,

> Deaconesses in the LCMS can become "commissioned ministers of religion" following a change in the Constitution which took effect February 1 [1990]. By a synodwide vote of 2,300 to 207, congregations ratified the constitutional amendment adopted at last summer's convention in Wichita. . . .
>
> "It's not a status thing," said Deaconess Nancy Nicol Nemoyer, of the effort for the change which was launched in the early 1980s. "It was a matter of some very practical concerns. There has been no call system for

---

CDC members, November 30, 1987, Deaconess Office Archives, Concordia University, RF. The Concordia College Faculty also joined the campaign by adopting an overture which later appeared verbatim in the 1989 LCMS *Convention Workbook.* "Agenda, Meeting of the Plenary Faculty, November 21, 1988," mimeographed sheet, numbered page 11, priv. col. of Nancy (nee Nicol) Nemoyer, Carlisle, Pa.; "To Classify Deaconesses in Category Other Than Certified Professional Church Workers, Lay," in LCMS, *Convention Workbook (Reports and Overtures),* 1989, 175.

[61] "To Declare Deaconesses Eligible for Synodical Membership Resolution 3-11A," in LCMS, *Proceedings,* 1989, 116–17.

[62] Sara [nee Bauman] Nordling (RF 1985); Kristin Hannenberg (RF 1986); Lauren Morgan (RF 1987). The speech delivered by lay delegate Deaconess Sara Nordling in favor of the resolution can be found in *Blues News* Vol. 3, No. 2, CDC Archives, held in trust by appointed CDC historian. Letter from Nancy Nemoyer to Betty Mulholland, August 4, 1989, priv. col. of Betty Mulholland, Munster, Ind.

[63] "Ballot, Proposed Constitutional Amendment," regarding Articles V and VI, priv. col. of Nancy (nee Brandt) Lingenfelter, Morrisdale, Pa.

deaconesses; no structured responsibility or accountability relationship with the district (and thereby Synod) where the deaconess was serving."

... A two-step process is underway to reclassify deaconesses serving in the LCMS. By March 15, papers were to have been filed by individuals to take advantage of a "one-time window of opportunity" for certification. Those eligible were any graduates of past approved (and Concordia's) deaconess program who are members of LCMS congregations. The second step is for certified deaconesses who are serving under a call to apply for membership in the Synod as a Minister of Religion—Commissioned. . . .[64]

Once active deaconesses received certification for membership in the LCMS as Ministers of Religion—Commissioned, the Synod stipulated that congregations or institutions employing the deaconesses needed to go through the formality of commissioning and installing the women at their current location of service.[65] This process felt awkward to seasoned deaconesses—to be commissioned and installed in the places where they were already serving—but such occasions provided opportunities for education about diaconal ministry.[66] The rite for "Commissioning and Installation of One Called to the Ministry of Deaconess in the Church," distributed by LCMS District Presidents for this purpose, can be read in Appendix 3.G.

Though the deadline for submitting certification papers closed in March 1990, the Council of Presidents later received a few women "by exception" onto the LCMS Deaconess roster after reading appeals from their District Presidents.[67] At this point in time, there was no other way for a non-synodically trained woman to officially *rejoin* the LCMS diaconate, since the action of the 1983 convention in classifying deaconesses as lay workers eliminated the deaconess colloquy program.[68]

---

[64] Jackie Bussert, "Deaconesses Welcome Change in Synodical Classification," *The Northern Light* 4, no. 8 (April 1990), 1.

[65] Letter from Arnold E. Kromphardt, LCMS Eastern District President, to Nancy L. Lingenfelter, June 4, 1990, priv. col. of Nancy (nee Brandt) Lingenfelter, Morrisdale, Pa.

[66] "Background Information About Today's Installation," Bulletin from St. John's Lutheran Church, Morrisdale, Pa., November 18, 1990, priv. col. of Nancy (nee Brandt) Lingenfelter, Morrisdale, Pa.

[67] Helen (nee Haase) Tesch, interview by CDN, transcript, Coon Rapids, Minnesota, March 25, 2006, priv. col. of CDN, Pittsburgh, Pa.; Letter from Rev. David D. Buegler, President Ohio District LCMS to Dr. John Heins, President Michigan District LCMS, March 30, 1993, Deaconess Office Records, Concordia University, RF.

[68] The LCMS Council of Presidents, Board for Professional Education Services, and Committee on Concern for the Church and its Workers all agreed that colloquy programs should be used for alternate admission into the "professional" ministry of the Church. This

Becoming a part of the "Ministers of Religion—Commissioned" category meant that deaconesses would be required to attend an annual conference provided by their LCMS district. In areas where there are larger numbers of deaconesses, a few districts have tried to provide deaconess conferences. In most districts, deaconesses are invited to attend an annual gathering that includes all "Commissioned" workers.[69]

A NEW PROGRAM DIRECTOR

Throughout the 1980s, the Concordia Deaconess Program in River Forest grew at a steady pace. As her responsibilities multiplied, Deaconess Nicol acquired student assistants, fieldwork coordinators, internship coordinators, and supplemental instructors where needed.[70] In December 1986, Nicol married Rev. Robert Jay Nemoyer Jr. (b. 1952). When the Nemoyers' first child was born in 1988, "Deaconess Nancy" dropped to three-quarters of her work time and Concordia hired Deaconess Lauren Morgan to serve as Assistant Director of the Deaconess Program (while also serving at Messiah Lutheran Church, Chicago). This arrangement continued until 1990, when Nemoyer withdrew from deaconess work to be a full-time homemaker.

On her retirement, coinciding with celebrations marking the tenth anniversary of the Concordia Deaconess Program and the CDC, Nemoyer gave inspirational speeches on God's blessings to the deaconess program and "A Vision for the Future." The Director's closing words typified her model of servanthood, and the way that she habitually pointed glory and acclaim away from herself to others:

> When I accepted the call to be director of the deaconess program, I was nervous about many things, one of which was my lack of knowledge about teaching. I met one evening with Prof. Warren Wilbert, husband of a co-worker (at that time) and professor at the Fort Wayne Seminary in the area of teaching and parish administration. He gave me some guidelines and charts but finally concluded: "You may have all or none of the techniques but in the end what will matter most is that you give yourself to each student, that on graduation day you will hate to see them

---

designation no longer applied to deaconesses when Synod placed them in the lay worker category in 1983.
[69] Kristin Wassilak, interview by CDN, transcript, February 7, 2005, River Forest, IL., priv. col. of CDN, Pittsburgh, Pa.
[70] See Appendix 3.E for lists of individuals who worked as student assistants, field work coordinators, internship coordinators, and supplemental instructors. Nancy Nicol, "Report to the Concordia Deaconess Conference, The Deaconess Program, Concordia College—River Forest," October 4, 1985, CDC Archives, held in trust by appointed CDC historian.

go for they take a part of you, but that will also be your joy for you have touched a life for the Kingdom." More than that has happened; you have given yourself to me in exchange for very little. We will always be a part of each other in this great body of Christ. Let us recall Clara Strehlow's focus—"To Him be the glory."[71]

The Director's successor would be one of her own students—Deaconess Kristin Renee (nee Hannenberg) Wassilak (b. 1963). A capable and intelligent woman, 27-year-old Wassilak worked as Nemoyer's student assistant (1985–86); was President of CDC (1987–90); and an advisory member of the LCMS Lay Ministry Study Committee (1988–89).[72] From the time of her placement in 1986, Wassilak had been a parish deaconess at Good Shepherd Lutheran Church in Des Plaines, Illinois, It would be her joy to take the Concordia Deaconess Program through its next 15 years.

A DEACONESS COLLOQUY PROGRAM

The same convention delegates who declared deaconesses eligible for membership in the LCMS as "Ministers of Religion—Commissioned" also recognized the need for a procedure to allow deaconesses from training programs other than Concordia College to be certified for such membership. Hence, the 1989 LCMS convention adopted Resolution 3-19, which not only requested a formal process for deaconesses already serving the LCMS to be classified in the second category, but also resolved:

That the Board for Higher Education Services, in consultation with the Board of Regents of Concordia College, River Forest, develop a colloquy program or other procedure or vehicle whereby women trained as deaconesses at non-synodically approved schools or programs may be certified for membership in the LCMS as Ministers of Religion, Commissioned; . . . [73]

Concordia Deaconess Program Director Wassilak became the primary author of a draft Deaconess Colloquy proposal that, after input from interested parties and minor alterations, was adopted in the form of

---

[71] Nancy Nemoyer, "NN Reflects—From the Director's Chair," 1990, priv. col. of Nancy (nee Nicol) Nemoyer, Carlisle, Pa. See also, Nancy Nemoyer, "A Vision for the Future," 1990, priv. col. of Nancy (nee Nicol) Nemoyer, Carlisle, Pa.
[72] Kristin Hannenberg was born on July 2, 1963, at Lutheran Deaconess Hospital in Chicago. She married Robert Fredrick Wassilak on May 28, 1988. "Mennicke Chairs—Lay Ministry Committee Begins Work," *Reporter* 14, no. 4 (February 1, 1988).
[73] "To Establish Procedures for Certification of Deaconesses, Resolution 3-19," in LCMS, *Proceedings*, 1989, 120.

Resolution 6-07 at the 1992 LCMS Convention in Pittsburgh.[74] In her presentation to Convention Floor Committee Six (Higher Education) in St. Louis on May 30, 1992, Wassilak explained:

> This colloquy process is similar in intent, purpose, and wording to our pastoral and teacher colloquies. . . . The women desiring deaconess certification who will be served by this colloquy are:
>
> 1. the mature woman seeking a second career who has volunteered for many years in the church.
>
> 2. a deaconess not certified by the LCMS (such as LDA graduates since 1986 and ELCA deaconesses).
>
> 3. a woman from a special ethnic or linguistic group (such as the woman graduates of the LCMS Hispanic Institute [TEE] program).
>
> 4. a woman who is already an LCMS certified church worker (teacher, DCE, lay minister).
>
> Among prospective deaconess students are women from each of these four categories. There is a substantial need for the Deaconess Colloquy![75]

Indeed, soon after the LCMS adopted Resolution 6-07, a number of women applied for entrance to the colloquy program, including three women who completed the LCMS Hispanic Institute program, two LDA deaconesses serving in LCMS congregations, and several other non-traditional students.[76] The resolution authorized Concordia's colloquy examining committee to outline an appropriate course of study for each

---

[74] Regarding various input, see: Letter from Louise Williams to Rudy Block, Director of Curriculum Services, June 17, 1991; Memo from Deaconess Kristin Wassilak to President E. Krentz, Dr. Elaine Sipe, and Dr. Gary Bertels, July 11, 1991; Memo from Deaconess Kristin Wassilak to Dr. Michael Stelmachowicz and Dr. Rudy Block, July 25, 1991; Memo from Dr. Rudy Block to President Eugene Krentz, Deaconess Kristin Wassilak, Dr. Elaine Sipe, and Dr. Gary Bertels, August 6, 1991; Letter from Rudy Block to Deaconess Louise Williams, October 3, 1991; Memo to Theology Department from Kristin Wassilak, October 11, 1991; Memo to University Faculty from Steve Wente, Faculty Forum, January 22, 1992; all located in File: Colloquy 1991–94, Concordia University Archives, Concordia University, RF, Ill. "To Establish Deaconess Colloquy Program, Resolution 6-07," in LCMS, *Proceedings*, 1992, 162–63.
[75] Kristin Wassilak, "Presentation to Floor Committee 6—HIGHER EDUCATION, Subject: Deaconess Colloquy; Resolution 6-31, 6-32; *Workbook* pages 277-78 and the resolution from the Concordia University Faculty," May 30, 1992, File: Colloquy 1991–94, Concordia University Archives, Concordia University, RF, Ill., 1.
[76] Memo from Deaconess Kristin Wassilak to Dr. Eugene Krentz and Dr. Elaine Sipe, Re: Deaconess Colloquy, April 16, 1993, File: Colloquy 1991–94, Concordia University Archives, Concordia University, RF, Ill., 2.

colloquy student "on the basis of her needs and ecclesiastical background, determined by the student's application materials and an oral interview."[77] Thus the new Deaconess Colloquy procedures created a flexible alternate route to deaconess certification in the LCMS.

In April 1993, Concordia President Eugene L. Krentz named Deaconess Wassilak as Director of Deaconess Colloquy for the university. LCMS President Alvin L. Barry (1931–2001) appointed First Vice-President August T. Mennicke (1932–2002) to chair the synodical Deaconess Colloquy Committee, with President Krentz as the second of only two voting committee members.[78] On August 21, 1993, Wassilak addressed the LCMS Council of Presidents, bringing the men up to date "on the Deaconess Colloquy situation as well as the whole Deaconess Program in general."[79]

THE COLLOQUY PROGRAM MATURES

The real benefit of Deaconess Colloquy to the Church is reflected in the fact that from the time the first colloquy students completed their work in 1995, exactly fifty percent of Concordia's deaconess students have received certification through colloquy. This means that for thirteen years, Deaconess Colloquy made it possible for twice the number of women to become eligible for deaconess service in the Missouri Synod. Deaconess Wassilak vigorously promoted the colloquy program alongside the normal educational route offered at Concordia University. In spring 2001, Wassilak wrote in an "Admission and Recruitment" newssheet published by Concordia Seminary, St. Louis:

> . . . Deaconess students study at Concordia University, River Forest, Ill., and may complete deaconess certification at the undergraduate or graduate level. Students who already hold a bachelor's degree apply to the personally tailored Deaconess Colloquy Program, which allows for some distance education.
>
> Wives of seminary students may wish to consider enrolling in the deaconess program. Deaconess education requires at least 34 semester hours in theology, which can be taken during your stay at Concordia

---

[77] "To Establish Deaconess Colloquy Program, Resolution 6-07," 162–63.

[78] Letter from Dr. Al Barry to Dr. Augie Mennicke, Re: Deaconess Colloquy Program, August 2, 1993, File: Mennicke Correspondence, Concordia University Archives, Concordia University, River Forest, IL.

[79] Letter from Rev. Paul T. McCain to Mrs. Kristin Wassilak, August 5, 1993, File: Colloquy 1991–94, Concordia University Archives, Concordia University, River Forest, Ill.

Seminary. The 34 hours of theology can be fulfilled through the M.A. degree offered through Concordia Seminary's Graduate School. . . .[80]

Since the Deaconess Colloquy process required women to possess or obtain a bachelor's degree, it inevitably excluded women who found a college degree in the English language to be prohibitive.[81] Deaconess Wassilak regretted the loss of these women to the church's workforce and resolved to find a solution. Her proposal, backed by Concordia University and the synodical Colloquy Committee for Deaconess Ministry, was adopted by the 2001 LCMS convention via "Resolution 5-05: To Amend Bylaws re Deaconess Colloquy."[82] The "Rationale" for the resolution argued:

> . . . The LCMS has historically recognized that church workers need not be identically educated for a particular church office. At simultaneous points in our history, some pastors did not earn a degree, others earned bachelors degrees, and others completed masters degrees. In exceptional cases, the degree requirement can be waived.
>
> Some Lutheran women who desire to become deaconesses but are not fluent in academic English find that they cannot obtain collegiate general education in their own language. Over 50% of the more than 30 Spanish-speaking women who desire to pursue deaconess education are over the age of 40. To learn English well and to then complete a general education would place them into their 50s and 60s. During those years they could have been actively serving in the church as called deaconesses.
>
> Rigorous theological and diaconal education is currently available in Spanish. Spanish-speaking women in the deaconess colloquy are currently required to take the following college-level courses offered through Concordia Seminary, St. Louis, Hispanic Institute of Theology and Concordia University. . . .
>
> New standards may include courses to ensure professional expectations (in communication skills, for example), *but without the requirement of a degree.*[83]

---

[80] Kristin R. Wassilak, "Complementing Offices: Pastor and Deaconess," *The Servant* 8, no. 4 (Easter 2001): 4.

[81] Synodical *Handbook* By-Law 6.129 allowed a "two year renewable approval for deaconess ministry" for women working toward a bachelor's degree, however, since many diaconal placements required full deaconess certification, this provision proved to be insufficient.

[82] "To Amend By-laws re Deaconess Colloquy: Resolution 5-05," in LCMS, *Proceedings,* 2001, 151–52.

[83] *Ibid.*

Interestingly, in 2004, the LCMS standardized all church worker colloquy programs for the "Minister of Religion—Commissioned" category, so that deaconess colloquy procedures only apply to women who have completed non-synodical deaconess training programs and wish to receive LCMS certification.[84] Administration of this Deaconess Colloquy is handled solely at Concordia University Chicago, in compliance with the LCMS *Handbook* (containing the Synod's Constitution and By-Laws), which states:

Deaconess Colloquy Admission and Curriculum

3.8.3.5.7 Before submitting an application to the deaconess colloquy program, each prospective applicant shall have been a communicant member in good standing of a congregation of the Synod for at least the past two years and shall possess a bachelor's degree from an accredited institution.

(a) Each applicant shall have already received training to do the work of a deaconess and shall have served at least three years in a recognized ministry of their previous church body.

(b) Applicants who do not meet these requirements are to be directed to a Synod institution that offers a deaconess program for enrollment in an undergraduate or alternate-route program.

(c) Additional admission requirements may be established by the Board for University Education … Students shall complete eight courses in biblical interpretation, church history, the Lutheran Confessions, doctrine, the beliefs of other religious bodies, and the ministry of the deaconess.

(a) The courses shall be taken in a traditional classroom setting from a Synod college/university, with faculty of a Synod college/university teaching via CUEnet, or in another setting with the prior approval of the Board for University Education.

(b) Students shall complete an internship under the supervision of a Synod institution offering a bachelor's degree leading to deaconess certification or one year of successful deaconess ministry in an LCMS congregation or an agency recognized by the Synod.[85]

The Synod's narrower definition of colloquy, as applying only to women who "have already received [non-synodical] training to do the work of a deaconess" and have "served in their previous church body," made it

---

[84] "Resolution 5-12A: To Amend Commissioned Ministry Colloquy Bylaws," in LCMS, *Proceedings*, 2004, 143–46.

[85] *2007 Handbook*, The Lutheran Church-Missouri Synod. St. Louis: LCMS, 2007, 146.

necessary for additional training opportunities to be created for the LCMS woman who already had a bachelor's degree but was seeking a second career as a deaconess. In order to answer this need, in April 2005, Concordia University Chicago began offering a "Post-Baccalaureate Deaconess Certification Program," which can be completed with or without a Master of Arts in Religion degree. Students are able to enter this certification program with a bachelor's degree in any subject.[86]

A woman who wishes to serve as a deaconess in the LCMS but does not have a bachelor's degree–regardless of her age–is encouraged to enroll in the undergraduate deaconess program at River Forest. Spanish-speaking women are now accommodated through the Center for Hispanic Studies located at Concordia Seminary, St. Louis.[87]

A FEW HICCUPS

In August 2002, Concordia's administration informed its faculty that the university was experiencing economic difficulties that would require budget cuts and implementation of the institution's Reduction in Force (RIF) Policy.[88] Concordia's Board of Regents resolved to apply the RIF policy to the position of Director of the Deaconess Program, and imposed a "Moratorium," or ban, on accepting new admissions for deaconess training.[89] This action troubled the deaconess community and prompted a plethora of correspondence from congregations, pastors, and laity in every quarter of the Synod. Many individuals noted that elimination of the Director's post would eventually kill the Deaconess and Deaconess

---

[86] Krissé L. Paulson, "Concordia University's Deaconess Program Celebrates 27 Years," *Forester Magazine* 1, no. 1, (2006): 10; "Post-Baccalaureate Deaconess Certification Program, Approved, University College Policies Committee, April 18, 2005," Deaconess Office Archives, Concordia University Chicago, RF, Illinois.

[87] Hispanic students studied under the Hispanic Institute of Theology in Chicago until it moved to St. Louis in 2006. Email from Gloria DeCuir to CDN, October 20, 2008, priv. col. of CDN, Pittsburgh, Pa.

[88] The RIF policy was designed as "a process for removing from the university competent faculty whose position must be eliminated due to budgetary constraints or programmatic changes." "2.221 Reduction in Force Policy," *Faculty Handbook*, January 2000, Concordia University, River Forest, IL., 22–28; Letter from "The undersigned concerned CURF faculty members" to University President George Heider, District President William Ameiss, The Concordia University Board of Regents, The LCMS Board of Higher Education, February 9, 2003, File: Reduction in Force, Concordia University Archives, Concordia University, RF, Illinois, 1.

[89] Letter from George C. Heider to Prof. Kristin Wassilak, February 17, 2003, File: Reduction in Force, Concordia University Archives, Concordia University, RF, Ill.; "RF Board Put Moratorium on Deaconess Admissions," *Reporter* (June 2003): 5, 7.

Colloquy Programs, and some questioned the Board's authority to euthanize a church worker program that had been established by synodical resolution.[90]

The LCMS Board of Directors resolved to ask the BHE "to encourage the River Forest regents to reconsider eliminating Wassilak's position."[91] On April 14, 2003, Deaconess Wassilak appeared before the Faculty Welfare Committee to appeal the elimination of her position, but lost the appeal.[92] Finally, in October 2003, the Board of Regents reinstated the Deaconess Program, and two months later reinstated the Director's position.[93] *The Northern Light* reported:

> The Board of Regents of Concordia University, River Forest, with the encouragement of the Board of Higher Education of the Lutheran Church Missouri Synod has concluded that it is in the best interest of the mission of the Synod, and the university, to reinstate the deaconess training program at the River Forest campus.
>
> Concordia University, River Forest, is currently the only institution in the Concordia University System to offer an undergraduate deaconess program. . . . "The Board of Regents felt that a strong expression of support from around the Synod merited a renewed effort to promote deaconess training, both within the Synod and here at River Forest," said Dr. Ralph Reinke, chief executive and chief operating officer of the university. . . .
>
> The Northern Illinois District convention this summer was among others in the Synod urging that the deaconess program be reinstated at the River Forest school. The resolution urges direct, ongoing financial support for the program, both from congregations and from individual donors. The program was originally cut for fiscal reasons. . . .
>
> Rev. Bill Ameiss, NID president and chairman of the university Board of Regents, commented, "With cost cutting measures fully in place and fiscal stability well under way, it was both a joy and a relief for the regents to be able to reinstate the deaconess program. The university's number one

---

[90] Emails and letters, File: Deaconess Program 2003, The President's Files, Concordia University, RF, Ill.

[91] "RF Board Put Moratorium on Deaconess Admissions," *Reporter* (June 2003), 5.

[92] Kristin Wassilak, "Hearing: Faculty Welfare Committee," April 14, 2003, priv. col. of Kristin Wassilak, Forest Park, Ill.; See also: "Wassilak Narrative for Appeal," March 19, 2003, priv. col. of Kristin Wassilak, Forest Park, Ill.

[93] Kristin Wassilak, notes from telephone interview by CDN, December 30, 2006, priv. col. of CDN, Pittsburgh, Pa.

priority is, and remains, the training and preparation of church workers for the Missouri Synod."[94]

At the time that Concordia's Board of Regents restored the Deaconess Program, the university had 52 deaconess students: 37 enrolled in courses at the River Forest campus and 15 colloquy students working with distance learning and other LCMS institutions.[95] Since that time enrollment has remained healthy, and if the renewed interest in diaconal ministry within the LCMS is any indicator, Concordia should have a flourishing deaconess program for many years to come.

TWENTY-FIVE YEARS OF BLESSING

In May 2005, the Concordia University Deaconess Program and Concordia Deaconess Conference celebrated 25 years of God's blessings. Since their inception these two entities have worked hand-in-hand: the Program Director acting as an advisor to the CDC Executive Committee, and the CDC encouraging and supporting the confessional training of deaconesses. Together these entities have endeavored to ensure that Missouri Synod deaconesses remain faithful to Scripture in their teaching, leadership, and service.

The women that have rubbed shoulders for 25 years in the Concordia Deaconess Program and the CDC are all about service to Christ within the context of the mission of the Church: a ministry of mercy that complements the ministry of Word and Sacraments. Deaconess Kristin Wassilak provided a beautiful summary of this diaconal ministry in an Easter 2001 issue of *The Servant*:

> The roles of deaconesses include spiritual care, instruction in the faith and human care. A deaconess serves people with a variety of needs, but the primary focus is the first area—spiritual care. Spiritual care involves listening to the concerns of the heart, accompanying people who are suffering, and bringing God's Word of Law and Gospel to them as they struggle. A deaconess teaches the faith in Bible class, in confirmation class, in devotions and in the private care of souls. The needs of the church and community in each setting provide the context for human care. . . .

---

[94] "Concordia Reinstates Deaconess Program," *The Northern Light* 18, no. 3 (December 2003): 1, 3.
[95] "River Forest Regents Reinstate Deaconess-Training Program," *Reporter* (November 2003): 4.

The offices of pastor and deaconess are connected and complementary, not competitive. The pastor and deaconess work as partners for the benefit of the church. A good example of this partnership is the "Choosing of the Seven" in Acts 6. The needs of people can be intense and overwhelming.

If the pastor tries to fill all the needs himself, he neglects his primary ministry of the Word. The deaconess prepares the way for the Word and sacraments and watches over the souls who have experienced the means of grace. The deaconess encourages the priesthood of all believers in deeds of love towards their neighbor so service is multiplied. Even in an institutional setting, the goal of a deaconess is not to become the patient's primary spiritual caregiver. But she points the patient to a community of faith—a local congregation and the pastor.[96]

A THIRD DIRECTOR

On February 1, 2005, Deaconess Wassilak sent an email to the "RF Deaconess ListServ" announcing: ". . . the Lord is opening up doors for me to serve elsewhere, primarily to our family. Therefore, I have submitted notice that this is my last academic year at CURF in a full-time capacity."[97]

Similar to the tenth anniversary celebrations when Director Nemoyer bade her farewell, the silver anniversary included tributes to "Deaconess Kristin" from friends and colleagues. CDC President Grace Rao noted that Wassilak had been her "teacher, mentor, and role model"; a dear sister in Christ, who "listens with her heart and helps us with her hands."[98]

Again, following the pattern from when she became Director, one of Wassilak's students would be her successor. In May 2005, Concordia's Board of Regents chose Deaconess Jennie Joleen Waters (b. 1961) to serve as the third Director of the Concordia Deaconess Program.

Waters received a Certificate of Advanced Studies in Theology and deaconess certification from Concordia in 1993; served as Deaf Ministry Facilitator for the LCMS New England District (1993-97); and worked as a parish deaconess at Zion Lutheran Church, Marshall, Michigan (2002-05). "Deaconess Jennie" brought new skills and experience to the Directorship, with advanced degrees in elementary education and special education,

---

[96] Kristin R. Wassilak, "Complementing Offices: Pastor and Deaconess," *The Servant* 8, no. 4 (Easter 2001): 4.

[97] Email from Kristin Wassilak to CRFDEAC Listserv members, February 1, 2005, priv. col. of CDN, Pittsburgh, Pa.

[98] Deaconess Grace Rao, CDC President, hand-written speech, May 16, 2005, priv. col. of CDN, Pittsburgh, Pa.

which she utilized in public school teaching from 1983-90 and 1997-2002. She served on the CDC public relations committee and, from 2002 onward, was already an active member of the LCMS Deaconess Task Force and Deaconess Council.[99]

MISSION WORK – AT HOME AND ABROAD

A member of the LCMS Board for Mission Services for six years (2001-07), Deaconess Waters has a passion for missions which spills over into her work as Director of the Deaconess Program. In December 2005, Waters took a group of deaconess students to New Orleans for a week to help the survivors of hurricane Katrina. She also accompanied students on a 13-day "mercy mission expedition" to Latvia in May 2006[100] and led a ten-day visit to Panama in summer 2008. Convinced of the value of mission experiences for deaconess formation, Waters explained:

> I encourage all of the deaconess students to participate in at least one week of cross-cultural mission work that takes them outside of their personal comfort zone. This kind of experience contributes to the development of a servant heart, which is fundamental to a ministry of mercy. I enjoy observing the students in these settings, where events and reactions can be processed together and right away. Though mission work is not part of the official curriculum of the deaconess program, some students have arranged to receive academic credit for their experiences by combining them with readings on the Theology of Mercy and participating in other "academic" exercises like writing evaluation, synthesis, and reflection papers.

> Another one of the neat things about going on mission trips with a group of people is that these experiences are community building. They tend to tighten the bonds between deaconess students and also build new relationships with the people who are being served. One of the goals of going abroad is to connect our students with other deaconesses or deaconess students throughout the world, so that there is a better understanding of the big picture of world Lutheranism and the diaconal work that is being carried out across the globe. As a result of the trip to Panama, we now have a "sister-to-sister program" where our students and

[99] See Chapter 18 for information on these two entities sponsored by LCMS World Relief/Human Care.
[100] See Heidi Bishop and Jennie Waters, "The Evangelical Lutheran Church of Latvia: a Church of Mercy," *Mercy Works* 2, no. 1/2 (summer/fall 2007): 24-26.

the Panama deaconess students are matched as pen pals for encouragement and collaboration.[101]

During the time that Waters has directed the deaconess program, five students have had extended foreign experience through being assigned to deaconess internships in England, Macau, Paraguay, and Thailand. Former program director Wassilak also placed deaconess interns in England, Germany, Guatemala, Venezuela, and Taiwan.

Many opportunities for cross-cultural mission work exist in the United States, particularly among Hispanic people. In 2007, Concordia University Chicago added the choice of a minor in Spanish to complement the major in Theology required of women in the undergraduate deaconess training program. In addition to Spanish, students can still choose to minor in Biblical languages, Psychology, Social Work, Sociology, or other disciplines appropriate to a woman's unique skills and talents that will help prepare her for service as a deaconess.[102]

DIAKONIA DAYS

One of the challenges for the deaconess movement within the LCMS is a lack of knowledge about the deaconess vocation. And though Lutheran women understand that God comes to them with His mercy through Word and Sacraments, many have never had an opportunity to consider how they might become professional church workers and servants of mercy to others.

In 2006, Deaconess Waters initiated an annual Diakonia Days Summer Camp for young women of high school age, confirmed in the LCMS, to explore the vocation of deaconess. These popular week-long camps have included a variety of activities, including daily devotions and chapel services; classes led by Theology professors and deaconesses; volunteering in a soup kitchen; visiting a nursing home and a home for persons with developmental disabilities; working with underprivileged children; taking part in community service projects; and enjoying Chicago-style pizza and other unique features of the city.[103]

Waters has reported that during their time at Diakonia Days, participants have grown in their personal faith and in their desire to serve

---

[101] Jennie J. Waters, interview by CDN, notes, River Forest, Illinois, September 2008, priv. col. of CDN, Pittsburgh, Pa.

[102] For example, minors in Communications and Business Management.

[103] "Diakonia Days," www.cuchicago.edu/departments/deaconess/diakonia_days.asp.

the Lord and His people.[104] Not surprisingly, some of the women who have attended the camps have matriculated into the undergraduate deaconess training program in River Forest.

POISED FOR THE FUTURE

Almost thirty years have elapsed since delegates at the 1979 LCMS Synodical convention in St. Louis voted to "authorize the BHE to direct Concordia College, River Forest, Ill., to establish a full deaconess training program on its campus by the fall of 1980."[105]

Starting with its first graduating class in 1983, the Concordia Deaconess Program has trained and certified 167 women to serve as deaconesses in The Lutheran Church-Missouri Synod. It is appropriate to thank and praise God for this gift to the Church, and to ask Him to continue to bless those who train the next generation of His servants in diaconal ministry.

Today, Concordia University Chicago, the Director of the Deaconess Program, the Theology Department and all other supporting faculty and staff, continue to be committed to the provision of a quality deaconess education which equips graduates to be faithful to the Scriptures in their teaching, leadership, and service.

---

[104] Jennie Waters, "Domestic Grant Program Report Form," August 13, 2007-July 31, 2008, Deaconess Office Archives, RF, Illinois.

[105] See Chapter 12. "Subject: To Expand Deaconess Program, RESOLUTION 6-05," *Today's Business* Section B (Concordia: St. Louis, July 1979), 125.

Illustrations for Chapter Sixteen may be viewed at www.deaconesshistory.org.

CHAPTER 17

TWENTY-FIRST-CENTURY EXPANSION

The last eight years (2001–09) have seen more advancement of the deaconess movement in the Missouri Synod than any other comparable period in the Synod's history. The main thrust of this activity has been in increasing options for deaconess training and raising the profile of current work, emerging opportunities, and future potential for LCMS diaconal ministry in the United States and around the world.

ADDITIONAL POST-GRADUATE TRAINING

Though Concordia University Chicago provided deaconess training for post-graduate students as well as undergraduate students, many individuals within the church felt the importance of adding more training choices for students already holding bachelor's degrees. The proponents of this view believed that additional training programs in new geographical locations could bolster overall enrollment. They further argued that the LCMS had two seminaries for training pastors and ten locations for training teachers, setting precedent for the creation of more centers for deaconess training. Since the additional sites would need master's level theology courses, the Synod's seminaries seemed the obvious choice.

Quiet consideration of seminary-based deaconess training took place very early in the history of the *Missouri Synod* deaconess movement. On September 30, 1980—only 15 months after the LCMS resolved to establish a deaconess program at River Forest—Concordia's Dean of Students (later Rev.) Albert Berton Wingfield, Education Professor Anne Driessnack, and Deaconess Program Director Nancy Nicol met with Seminary President Robert David Preus (1924–95).[1] Former Director (Nicol) Nemoyer recalls:

> We went to Fort Wayne at the invitation of Dr. Preus to brainstorm about future possibilities for deaconess training at the seminary. Preus was so happy that the program was in the Synod. He really liked deaconesses and

---

[1] Nancy E. Nicol (Nemoyer), Entry for September 30, 1980, CPH Calendar Diaries 1980–1990, priv. col. of Nancy (nee Nicol) Nemoyer, Carlisle, Pa.

had a good feeling for what diaconal work was all about. He envisioned a second program at the seminary as the next logical step. We sat down and hand-sketched what a curriculum at the seminary level might look like. There was no talk about personnel—just curriculum. Except for Dr. Zimmerman, no one knew about the meeting because we thought it might look disloyal to Concordia College. We understood that it was necessary to give the River Forest program some years to mature—to really set the standards—and then we could move toward creating other training opportunities in the Synod.[2]

When President Preus met CDC deaconesses, he often greeted them with phrases like, "Hi, ladies. When are we going to start working to get a deaconess program in Fort Wayne?"[3] In the summer of 1987, CDC President Joyce Ostermann and Deaconess Betty Mulholland met with Preus to discuss issues related to deaconess training, wherever that might be carried out.[4] The minutes of the CDC Executive Committee meeting for February 25, 1989, marked "CONFIDENTIAL," consisted entirely of a detailed outline titled, "For Discussion: Deaconess training at a seminary?"[5]

When Dr. Dean Orrin Wenthe became President of Concordia Theological Seminary, Fort Wayne, he made it clear that he was just as interested in diaconal ministry as his predecessor.[6] This fact encouraged two members of the seminary staff, Deaconesses Joyce Ostermann and Pamela Nielsen, to meet together over lunch on a weekly basis to ponder how deaconess formation might take place in the seminary environment. Nielsen explained to the author:

Discussion about the possibility of training deaconesses at Fort Wayne had been going on for some time, and Dr. Wenthe appeared to be eager

---

[2] Nancy (nee Nicol) Nemoyer, interview by CDN, audio recording, June 16, 2006, Bedford, Pa., priv. col. of CDN, Pittsburgh, Pa.

[3] Joyce Ostermann, in conversation with other CDC founding members, August 21, 2004, audio recording, Fort Wayne, Ind., priv. col. of CDN, Pittsburgh, Pa.

[4] Letter from Robert Preus to Deaconess Joyce Ostermann, August 10, 1987, Box: CDC, File: 1983/1986 Synodical Presentations on the Status of Deaconess as the Third Category Church Worker, CHI, St. Louis, Mo.

[5] The outline included three sections: A. The pros and cons of the River Forest Environment for Deaconess Training; B. The pros and cons of a Seminary Environment for Deaconess Training; C. Stages for Exploring Feasibility. The latter section included the statement: "At some points a 'no support' sign post halts the exploration (e.g. if CDC would not support such a move, it should not be pursued)." "CDC Executive Committee, February 25, 1989," untitled file in green archive box, priv. col. of Nancy (nee Nicol) Nemoyer, Carlisle, Pa.

[6] Joyce Ostermann, in conversation with other CDC founding members, August 21, 2004 audio recording.

for it to happen. As Confessional Lutheran deaconesses we struggled with whether or not it was a good idea. Our fear was that bringing women to the seminary to train them might be perceived as a step toward the ordination of women, or worse, that it might actually pave the way for women's ordination if the seminary ever fell into the wrong hands. That kept us from taking action for several years. But we could see the benefits of women getting rich theological instruction alongside future pastors, with whom they would someday work. Joyce and I shared our thoughts with Betty Mulholland and the three of us composed a letter, which we sent to over a hundred pastors, asking them to petition Synod to allow the two seminaries to offer deaconess training.[7]

The 2001 LCMS *Convention Workbook* revealed that nine congregations memorialized Synod to authorize graduate level deaconess education at either one or both of its seminaries.[8] In the end, by a vote of 984 to 86, convention delegates passed a composite resolution that read:

To Provide Deaconess Training at the Seminary Level – Resolution 5-06B

Whereas, The church follows the teaching and example of Jesus Christ to engage the service of women in various forms of discipleship; and

Whereas, The church has many women who have been gifted by God who seek additional forms of service; and . . .

Whereas, Our Synod at present has only one location, River Forest, for all deaconess training . . . and

Whereas, The Board of Regents of Concordia Theological Seminary, Fort Wayne, invited the Synod to add the training of deaconesses on a graduate level in addition to their current academic offerings in response to various constituencies of the church, and

Whereas, The faculties of both of our seminaries are well equipped for the education of deaconesses; . . . therefore be it

Resolved, That The Lutheran Church—Missouri Synod in convention encourage the continued training of deaconesses at Concordia University, River Forest, and permit Concordia Theological Seminary, Fort Wayne, and Concordia Seminary, St. Louis, to offer graduate level deaconess training, directing all three schools to work with the Board for Higher

---

7 Pamela Nielsen, interview by CDN, May 21–22, 2006, transcript, priv. col. of CDC, Pittsburgh, Pa.

8 Angelica, Allen Park, MI; St. John, Maryville, IL; Grace, Versailles, MO; Shepherd by the Lakes, Syracuse, IN; Concordia, Mound City, MO; St. Peter, Craig, MO; St. John, Corning, MO; Zion, Corunna, IN; Grace, Grand Island, NE. LCMS, *Convention Workbook,* 2001, 218.

Education to establish standards of deaconess education, practice and placement.[9]

In contrast to the Synod's 1979 *mandate* to establish a deaconess program at Concordia, River Forest, the 2001 resolution simply *permitted* both seminaries "to offer graduate level deaconess training." Significantly, the resolution also undergirded the Synod's commitment to "continued training of deaconesses at Concordia University, River Forest (Chicago)."

UP AND RUNNING!

In fall 2002, Concordia Seminary, St. Louis (CSL), launched the Missouri Synod's second deaconess program with an enrollment of nine students. When the program started, women could choose to pursue an *MA in Spiritual Care and Deaconess Studies* or an *MA in Exegetical Theology and Deaconess Studies*. In 2004, the seminary added an *MA in Deaconess Studies* as the first professional graduate degree with no major or minor. As of 2005, while the new MA degree remained unchanged, deaconess students also have the option of majoring in Exegetical, Practical, or Systematic Theology (and minoring in one of the areas different from their major).[10]

Until 2005, CSL administered the Deaconess Program through its graduate school, and in 2005, appointed Dr. Bruce M. Hartung as the Faculty Director of Deaconess Studies.[11] The primary instructors responsible for specialized deaconess courses have been Deaconess Theresa Jo List (2002–04) and Deaconess Gloria May DeCuir (2004–). These talented women served as Assistant to the Dean of the Graduate School for Deaconess Studies for three years and one year respectively, administering the day-to-day needs of their students and the program. When List retired due to health issues in 2005, DeCuir's title was changed to Assistant Director of Deaconess Studies.

In August 2006, Concordia Seminary released its first publication of *Deaconess*. The seminary's PR department reported:

> The newsletter highlights deaconess education and offers insight into the lives of current deaconess students and graduates. . . . *Deaconess* will be published three times per year and is sent free of charge to all pastors and deaconesses in the LCMS. . . . Articles in the first issue of *Deaconess*

---

[9] "To Provide Deaconess Training at the Seminary Level: Resolution 5-06B," in LCMS, *Proceedings*, 2001, 152.

[10] "Information on St. Louis," email attachment from Deaconess Gloria DeCuir to CDN, June 1, 2006.

[11] See Appendices 3.H and 3.I.

include "Deaconess Serves in Alaska," "Deaconess Intern Reaches Hispanics," "Serving as a Deaconess," and "From the President."[12]

AND YET ANOTHER!

The Missouri Synod's third deaconess program opened at Concordia Theological Seminary, Fort Wayne (CTS), in September 2003, with twelve students. An official "Inauguration of the Deaconess Program" took place during a beautiful Order of Vespers in Kramer Chapel on January 19, 2004, with many LCMS deaconesses and pastors in attendance.[13] Single women in the CTS program live on the seminary campus in Phoebe House, a modern-day version of the traditional deaconess motherhouse.

Dr. Arthur Albert Just Jr. has been the sole Director of Deaconess Studies for CTS since the program started in 2003. In 2007, an additional position of Associate Director of Deaconess Studies was created. Deaconess Rose E. (nee Gilbert) Adle occupied this position from 2007-08, followed by Deaconess Rachel D. Thompson starting in fall 2008.

CTS designed its Deaconess Studies curriculum to satisfy academic requirements for the Master of Arts in Religion degree, with a dual focus on theological studies *and* human care. The seminary's most recent tract on Deaconess Studies notes:

> A rigorous program of theological study provides the foundation for the charitable life. . . . Jesus calls us to a life of charity when He tells us to "Be merciful, even as your Father is merciful" (Luke 6:36). Deaconess Studies is a portal through which women may enter into consecrated service of Christ and His Church, providing acts of mercy through various vocations and tasks that serve the needy in our midst.[14]

WORKING TOGETHER FOR GOD'S KINGDOM

Before the new post-graduate programs could be launched, some cooperative groundwork had to be laid. Representatives from the seminaries, Concordia University Chicago, and the BHE met together (in Dec. 2001 and Feb. 2002) to discuss topics such as common procedures

---

[12] "Seminary Releases New Seminary Publication," distributed via email from CSL to CSLNEWS listserv, August 1, 2006.
[13] Bulletin for "Order of Vespers on the occasion of the Inauguration of the Deaconess Program, Week of Epiphany II, 19 January, 3:45 p.m.," priv. col. of CDN, Pittsburgh, Pa.
[14] "Be merciful, even as your Father is merciful." Deaconess Studies, Concordia Theological Seminary, Fort Wayne, Ind., trifold tract, June 2006, 3.

and the future direction(s) of diaconal education.[15] In November 2002, the BHE announced an agreed process for certification and placement of seminary-trained deaconesses:

> The BHE staff and the seminary presidents (on 8 November 2002) agreed that the seminary faculty that teaches the deaconess student will certify the deaconess student for service in the church, and placement of a certified deaconess student should be by way of the ordinary route (procedure) of commissioned ministers. The program director at the seminary will be responsible for calls and placement at the institutional level.[16]

Dr. Just and Deaconess List have both expressed particular appreciation for the valuable advice and counsel received from Deaconess Kristin Wassilak while setting up the seminary deaconess programs.[17] At the celebration of the Inauguration of the deaconess program at CTS, Wassilak spoke on "The Deaconess as Expression of the Church's Care." The concluding portion of her presentation outlined four challenges and visions for the future of the deaconess movement in the Missouri Synod.

> **1. It is a challenge for three LCMS deaconess training programs to work in respectful cooperation with one another.** ... My vision for the future is that the three Programs will freely share resources, exchange faculty and staff, and join in cooperative ventures like retreats, public relations and projects for the good of students and the Church. As we exercise Christ's mercy and care towards one another, God is glorified.

> **2. It is a challenge to effectively communicate the necessity for the deaconess role to the Church.** ... We need consistent flow of communication about deaconesses through a variety of means, broad and narrow, media blitz and one-on-one, reaching people and pastors where they are. The deaconess programs at the seminaries will be extraordinarily helpful to influence tomorrow's pastors. LCMS WR/HC has also given very helpful PR in their publications. But I believe there is a more fundamental challenge – I'll come back to this issue in my fourth point.

---

[15] Kristin Wassilak, interview by CDN, River Forest, IL., February 7, 2005, transcript, priv. col. of CDN, Pittsburgh, Pa.

[16] Memorandum from L. Dean Hempelmann to Deaconesses Kristin Wassilak, Theresa List; Drs. Bruce Schuchard, Daniel Gard, Andrew Bartelt, William Weinrich, Peter Scaer, November 26, 2002, File: Seminary Education, Deaconess Office Archives, Concordia University, River Forest, IL.

[17] Arthur A. Just, "Tribute to Deaconess Kristin Wassilak," delivered Concordia University Chicago, May 16, 2005, CDC Archives, held in trust by appointed CDC historian; Theresa List, notes from telephone interview by CDN, September 16, 2006, priv. col. of CDN, Pittsburgh, Pa.

3. It is a challenge for deaconesses to faithfully fulfill their calling.
… On an individual basis, our chief challenge is obedience to the 1st commandment. Selfishness, pride and self-deprecation are our chief obstacles to faithful service. In other words, we get in the way. But thanks be to God who does not leave us in this state. As we receive the nourishment of our souls from His Word and Sacraments, we are free to live new lives in Him! …

4. It is a challenge to become a Church with a mission of mercy and care. … Educating present and future pastors and leaders about the deaconess vocation is a secondary issue. Before diaconal works will be welcome, the Church must first know that mercy is an essential mission. … It won't be easy to educate and inspire the Church for mercy and care. In all of us there is a certain level of denial about the depth of pain and suffering in our own lives and in our communities. Once we know about suffering, apathy is defenseless.

The future of the deaconess movement is not in what it has been, not in traditions, but it is in the reality of what God has for us to do now. The actual ministry of deaconess is as fluid as the needs of the Church. The exact form, exact structure, is not necessarily important. It is only important that the structure serve the Church's needs for mercy and care. …[18]

Communication and cooperation continues to take place among the three LCMS training institutions. For example, joint fall retreats provide opportunities for fellowship and intellectual exchange among students. Commissioned deaconesses also have the opportunity to meet together regularly at Concordia Deaconess Conference gatherings for the mutual sharing in personal, spiritual, and professional growth. The greatest challenge that still remains is in educating the Church to the deep need for a ministry of mercy, which both supplements and points people back to the ministry of Word and Sacraments.

SUPPORT FROM THE LWML

The one auxiliary organization that can without a doubt be said to have always understood and supported the deaconess movement in the Missouri Synod is the Lutheran Women's Missionary League. In fact, from the time of the League's inception in 1942, to its $60,000 contribution for the

---

[18] Kristin R. Wassilak, "The Deaconess as Expression of the Church's Care," presentation on the occasion of Day of Celebration for the Inauguration of the Deaconess Program, Concordia Theological Seminary, Fort Wayne, Indiana, January 19, 2004.

Deaconess Chapter House in 1955, provision of a deaconess seminar room at Concordia University Chicago in 1983, and so forth, the LWML has consistently voted to provide funds for the next stage of the "vision" of diaconal ministry in the Synod.[19]

LWML mission grants for the 2005-2007 biennium included $100,000 for Deaconess Training via the Ethnic Immigrant Institute of Theology (EIIT).[20] Sponsored jointly by Concordia Seminary, St. Louis and LCMS World Mission, EIIT is a distance-education training program for immigrants to the United States who desire to serve as pastors or deaconesses in the Missouri Synod. Regarding EIIT students, the LCMS World Mission website explains:

> Many students work full-time secular jobs and serve in their individual pastoral and diaconal ministries while enrolled in the program. They are mentored by their local pastor and were recommended for the program through their districts. Students spend one week together each year on the seminary campus in intensive classes and seminars. EIIT is one leadership training tool through which LCMS church planting is made possible. ...[21]

In summer 2007, LWML convention delegates voted to give $50,000 for the work of "Deaf Lay and Clergy Training – Concordia Seminary, St. Louis."[22] Education of the deaf through this program includes a deaconess track parallel to courses provided by EIIT, with video-taped "signed" lectures.[23]

Pre-Deaconess Programs

None of the three institution-based LCMS Deaconess Programs require prospective students to attend a pre-deaconess program before entering their deaconess training programs. Undergraduate women may apply to the deaconess program at Concordia University Chicago during their sophomore year at Concordia or at any other university. Women who

---

[19] "LWML Mission Grants Listed by Biennium," www.lwml.org. See also Chapters Four and Sixteen.

[20] "LWML Mission Grants 2005-2007," *Lutheran Woman's Quarterly* 65, no. 2 (Summer 2007): 27.

[21] www.lcms.org/pages/internal.asp?NavID=8084.

[22] "LWML Mission Grants 2007-2009 Biennium," *Lutheran Woman's Quarterly* 65, no.3 (Fall 2007): 22.

[23] Andrew Hugh Bartelt, notes from telephone interview by CDN, November 24, 2008, priv. col. of CDN, Pittsburgh, Pa.

already hold an undergraduate degree in any subject can apply to any of the three LCMS Graduate Deaconess Programs.[24]

However, as this book goes to print, six LCMS universities have begun to offer courses that they refer to as "pre-deaconess" in the sense that they provide preparation for, or an introduction to, subjects related to the curriculum of the three official LCMS deaconess training programs.[25] In November 2008, an "Articulation Agreement" was established between Concordia University Chicago and Concordia University Ann Arbor, listing classes that women could take at Ann Arbor that would seamlessly transfer to Chicago when starting the undergraduate deaconess program in their junior year.[26] This type of arrangement provides some flexibility for women who desire to spend their first two years of university a bit closer to home.

Some women – who already know that they would like to pursue a master's degree – choose to complete a bachelor's degree before beginning deaconess training at a master's degree level at Concordia University Chicago; Concordia Seminary, St. Louis; or Concordia Theological Seminary, Fort Wayne.

It is important for these educational choices to be weighed carefully by women who desire the vocation of deaconess. They need to think about their God-given gifts, talents, and interests, and then determine which educational model is best for them. The twenty-first century woman can be a deaconess in the LCMS after five years of undergraduate deaconess training (including the one-year internship), or she can choose to do a bachelor's degree in any subject followed by deaconess training in conjunction with a three-year master's degree (again, including an internship).

The Deaconess Task Force

In 2002, Rev. Matthew Harrison, Executive Director of LCMS World Relief and Human Care (WR/HC), secured funds to create a Deaconess Task Force for the purpose of promoting diaconal ministry in the Missouri Synod. The Task Force reviewed current ideas and literature on the

---

[24] This paragraph was originally written by the author for inclusion on the LCMS World Relief and Human Care web page: www.lcms.org/pages/internal.asp?NavID=9095.

[25] The six universities include those located in Ann Arbor, Michigan; Irvine, California; Bronxville, New York; St. Paul, Minnesota; Mequon, Wisconsin; and Seward, Nebraska.

[26] Jennie J. Waters, interview by CDN, notes, River Forest, Illinois, September 2008, priv. col. of CDN, Pittsburgh, Pa.

diaconate, pursued ideas for student financial aid, produced PR materials on deaconess ministry, and promoted deaconess professional care.[27]

When the task force finished its work, WR/HC established a Deaconess Council under the guidance of Rev. John Fale. This council concentrated most of its efforts toward the production of a DVD designed to help the LCMS understand deaconesses and diaconal ministry.[28] The department explained its desire to be involved with projects like the Deaconess Council "because of the strong historic and ongoing human care component in deaconess ministry."[29]

In April 2006, WR/HC started publishing *Mercy Works,* with an initial circulation of 45,000 copies.[30] A showcase for diaconal work within the Missouri Synod and her partner churches, the journal's mission statement reads:

Mercy Works

Lift up the place of mercy in the life of the church, grounded in the Lutheran theology of faith, active in embodied love, that recognizes and serves Christ, who hides Himself in the suffering of the neighbor.[31]

The department of WR/HC continues to be a prime mover in advancing deaconess education in the US and abroad, printing devotional studies about mercy, and providing various grants for deaconess internships, student "mercy mission expeditions," and other LCMS diaconal activities. Six of the WR/HC department web pages (on the official LCMS website) are dedicated to information about diaconal ministry, deaconess education, and the Concordia Deaconess Conference.[32]

---

[27] Deaconess Task Force Minutes, Sept. 25, 2002; Jan. 22, 2003; May 7, 2003; Aug. 4, 2003; Jan. 20, 2004; Jan. 18, 2005, LCMS WR/HC, St. Louis.
[28] "In Service to Our Lord: A Presentation of the Deaconess Ministry" is a 25-minute DVD hosted by Deaconess Kristin Wassilak, with an Introduction by LCMS President Gerald B. Kieschnick. "Deaconess Council Notes," email from Deanna Cheadle to Arthur A. Just, Kristin Wassilak, Sara Bielby, and Gloria DeCuir, March 2, 2005, LCMS WR/HC, St. Louis.
[29] www.lcms.org/pages/internal.asp?NavID=9093.
[30] *Mercy Works* managing editors are Rev. John Fale and Deaconess Grace Rao; Advisory and Contributing Editors: Deaconess Pamela Nielsen, Rev. John Pless, Rev. Mark Sell, and Dr. Beverly Yahnke.
[31] "Contents," *Mercy Works* 1, no. 1 (Spring 2006): 3.
[32] See for example: www.lcms.org/pages/internal.asp?NavID=9093.

A HOUSEHOLD WORD

During the twenty-first century, the subject of deaconess work has been prevalent in other LCMS media. For example, the Spring 2005 *Issues in Christian Education* published by Concordia University, Nebraska, focused entirely on the history, education, and roles of deaconesses in the Synod. Also, in May 2005, Dr. Arthur A. Just spoke about the deaconess office on the national radio program, *Issues, Etc.* In his March 16, 2006, "Pastoral Letter to Pastors of the Lutheran Church—Missouri Synod," LCMS President Gerald B. Kieschnick wrote:

> As congregations strive to meet their needs and those of their communities, I remind you that there are theologically trained deaconesses available for calls. Deaconesses are equipped to work with people in all age groups, lead Bible studies, assist with visiting shut-ins, make hospital calls, lead evangelism and outreach events, and more. Please consider calling a deaconess, if appropriate to your situation, when reviewing your staff needs.[33]

Thanks to these types of communication, the work of WR/HC, the expansion of deaconess education sites in the LCMS, and last but not least, the example of dedicated deaconesses serving in the field, the once unfamiliar name of "deaconess" is becoming a household word in Missouri Synod homes.

The LCMS needed to train its own deaconesses to ensure faithfulness in their teaching, leadership, and service. When the Synod embraced this challenge, the dream became a reality that has borne much fruit for the propagation of the Gospel of Jesus Christ. By the grace of God, Missouri Synod deaconesses will continue to dedicate their lives to a ministry of mercy, at institutions, in congregations and schools, on Synodical boards and committees, and in the home and foreign mission fields of our Synod.

SOLI DEO GLORIA

---

[33] Gerald B. Kieschnick, "A Pastoral Letter to Pastors of the Lutheran Church Missouri Synod From President Jerry Kieschnick," March 16, 2006.

Illustrations for Chapter Seventeen may be viewed at www.deaconesshistory.org.

APPENDICES FOR PART I

CHAPTERS 1–12

APPENDIX 1.A.: BOOKS LISTED AS "REFERENCES" FOR THE 240 LESSONS IN *A HANDBOOK OF OUTLINES FOR THE TRAINING OF LUTHERAN DEACONESSES* BY PAUL E. KRETZMANN

APPENDIX 1.B.: A FORM OF INSTALLATION OF DEACONESSES, AS FOUND IN THE APPENDIX OF *A HANDBOOK OF OUTLINES FOR THE TRAINING OF LUTHERAN DEACONESSES* BY PAUL E. KRETZMANN

APPENDIX 1.C.: DIRECTORS OF THE LDA DEACONESS TRAINING PROGRAM

APPENDIX 1.D.: PRESIDENTS OF THE LUTHERAN DEACONESS ASSOCIATION

APPENDIX 1.E.: GRADUATES OF THE LDA DEACONESS TRAINING PROGRAMS IN FORT WAYNE (INDIANA), BEAVER DAM (WISCONSIN), WATERTOWN (WISCONSIN), AND HOT SPRINGS (SOUTH DAKOTA) FROM 1922-1942

APPENDIX 1.F.: GRADUATES OF THE LDA DEACONESS TRAINING PROGRAM IN VALPARAISO, INDIANA FROM 1944 TO 1986

APPENDIX 1.G.: "BACKGROUND DISCUSSION GUIDE" MAILED BEFORE MEETING TO ALL PARTICIPANTS IN THE DEACONESS DISCUSSION MEETING, JANUARY 24, 1968, CHICAGO

APPENDIX 1.H.: REPORT BY ARNE P. KRISTO ON THE DEACONESS DISCUSSION MEETING HELD JANUARY 24, 1968, CHICAGO

APPENDIX 1.I.: *DOCUMENTATION*, COMPILED BY DEACONESS RUTH BROERMANN AND DEACONESS BETTY MULHOLLAND, 1976

APPENDIX 1.J.: *RESUME OF DOCUMENTATION*, WRITTEN BY DEACONESS RUTH BROERMANN AND DEACONESS BETTY MULHOLLAND, 1976

APPENDIX 1.K.: *A LITANY FOR DEACONESSES*, WRITTEN BY KENNETH F. KORBY

APPENDIX 1.A.: BOOKS LISTED AS "REFERENCES" FOR THE 240 LESSONS IN *A HANDBOOK OF OUTLINES FOR THE TRAINING OF LUTHERAN DEACONESSES* BY PAUL E. KRETZMANN

Ohl, *The Inner Mission*

Wacker, *The Deaconess Calling*

Mergner-Spaeth, *The Deaconess and Her Work*

Dennis, *Christian Missions and Social Progress*

Brace, *Gesta Christi*

Pierson, *The Modern Mission Century*

M.E. Sangster, *Women of the Bible*

Wheeler, *Deaconesses Ancient and Modern*

Bancroft, *Deaconesses in Europe*

Potter, *Sisterhoods and Deaconesses*

Golder, *History of the Deaconess Movement*

Bliss, *Encyclopedia of Missions*

Laurie, *Women in Persia*

Rudolph, *Women in India*

Jens, *Principles of Deaconess Work*

"Woman in the Church", *Theol. Quart.*, 1920, Jan. and April

Haddock, *Power of Will*

Keyser, *A System of General Ethics*

Schaller, *The Book of Books*

Concordia Bible Class

Popular Commentary

Kretzmann, *Psychology and the Christian Day-school*

Kretzmann, *Psychology*

McMurry, *How to Study*

Starch, *Educational Psychology*

Annuals and Calendars of various Lutheran bodies

Hunt, *Lutheran Home Missions*

Works on American Lutheran church history, such as Graebner, Finck, Fritschel, Jacobs, and Neve

Bente [no title given]

Annual, Kalender, Synodical Reports

Missionsvortraege

Fritz, *The Practical Missionary*

Gardner, *Winners of the World*

Smith, *Short History of Christian Missions*

Our Colored Mission

Singmaster, *The Story of Lutheran Mission*

Dein Reich komme; Vanji Bhumi, and other pamphlets

Stock, *Story of the Bible*

Popular Commentary, New Testament

Christian Art

Hurlbut, *Bible Atlas*

Lindemann, *Scholia*

Hunton, *Favorite Hymns*

Concordia Triglotta

Graul, *Distinctive Doctrines*

Luecke, *Distinctive Characteristics of the Lutheran Church*

Huffcut, *The Elements of Business Law*

Borden-Hooper-McVey [no title given], and others

Kretzmann, *The Teaching of English*

Sheatsley, *The Lord Thy Healer*

Schuette, *The Devotional Life of the Church Worker*

Beck, *Evangelische Paramentik*

Some titles are used multiple times throughout the outline of eight courses. Publishers and dates of publication for the textbooks are not included in *A Handbook*.

APPENDIX 1.B.: A FORM OF INSTALLATION OF DEACONESSES, AS FOUND IN THE APPENDIX OF *A HANDBOOK OF OUTLINES FOR THE TRAINING OF LUTHERAN DEACONESSES* BY PAUL E. KRETZMANN

(The form here offered is the simplest ceremony of its kind, eliminating everything that savors of Romanism and false asceticism.)

The installation of deaconesses at the end of their probation period may take place either in the regular communion services, the rite being inserted at the close of the General Prayer, or a special service may be arranged for the ceremony. The following order may be observed:

A Hymn of Invocation to the Holy Spirit may be sung. Then may follow antiphonal chanting, with appropriate versicles, and the following Collect:

O Lord God, heavenly Father, who by the blessed light of Thy divine Word hast led us to the knowledge of Thy Son; we most heartily beseech Thee so to replenish us with the grace of Thy Holy Spirit, that we may ever walk in the light of Thy truth and, rejoicing with sure confidence in Christ our Savior, may in the end be brought unto everlasting salvation; through the same, Thy Son, our Lord, who liveth and reigneth with Thee and the Holy Ghost, ever one God, world without end. Amen.

Then may follow the reading of appropriate Scripture passages, such as 1 Timothy 3, 8–11 or 1 Pet. 3, 3–5.

After a hymn pertaining to the subject of the sermon there shall follow the Sermon.

Officiating Clergyman: In the name of the Father, and of the Son, and of the Holy Ghost, Amen. Dear sisters in Christ the Lord: Whereas you, of your own free will and inspired with a commendable zeal to be of direct service to the Lord in the external work of His kingdom, have declared your willingness to work in the office of a Christian deaconess and have, to that end, served for the customary probationary period and been found adequately prepared to undertake the labors of this office, I beseech and admonish you in the Lord that in this your office you show all good fidelity, willingness, obedience, and faithfulness flowing from a childlike faith in Jesus Christ, to the glory of His holy name and the edification of the Church, so that due to your labors the name of God may also in our midst be hallowed more and more, that His kingdom may be furthered, and that thus His good and gracious will may be done.

In order, then, that the believers here present, as representatives of the Church, may know your willingness to take upon you the duties of Lutheran deaconesses, I ask you before God and in the presence of this His congregation:

Will you diligently and faithfully perform the duties of your office in conformity with the Word of God, according to the ability which God giveth? If so, declare it by saying:

(Here shall the probationers answer): Yes, with the help of God.

(Then the installing clergyman, taking each of the probationers by the hand, shall say): May God, our dear and faithful heavenly Father, grant you strength, and with His grace fulfil [*sic*] what we are unable to do. May He richly bless you according to His infinite grace. Amen.

Let us pray.

O Almighty God, who didst call Phoebe and Dorcas and other holy women to be servants of Thy Church, and didst enable them to succor Thine apostles, and others also; behold these Thy servants who have given themselves to a like ministration. Grant unto them, we pray Thee, the fulness [*sic*] of Thy grace and strength, replenish them with all Christian womanly virtues, and adorn them with innocency of life that, by their labors and good examples, they may faithfully serve Thee, to the glory of Thy name, and to the benefit of Thy holy Church, through Jesus Christ, our Lord. Amen.—Depart in peace. Amen.

Collect: O God, who through the grace of Thy Holy Spirit dost pour the gift of charity into the hearts of Thy faithful people; grant unto Thy servants health both of mind and body, that they may love Thee with their whole strength, and with their whole heart perform those things which are pleasing unto Thee; through Jesus Christ our Lord. Amen.

Then shall follow the Aaronic Benediction and a closing Doxology.

APPENDIX 1.C.: DIRECTORS OF THE LDA DEACONESS TRAINING PROGRAM

Rev. Philipp Wambsganss Jr., Director, 1919–1923

Rev. Bruno Poch, Superintendent, 1923–32

Rev. Herman Bernard Kohlmeier, Superintendent, 1932–41

Rev. Arnold Fred Krentz, Superintendent and Executive Director, 1941–61

Rev. Walter Carl Gerken, Executive Director, 1961–67

Rev. Arne Pellervo Kristo, Executive Director, 1968–71

Dr. Lucille Emily Wassman, Executive Director, 1971–75

Deaconess E. (Emma) Louise Williams, Director of Deaconess Services and Executive Director, 1976–2007

Deaconess Lisa Polito, Executive Director, 2008–

APPENDIX 1.D.: PRESIDENTS OF THE LUTHERAN DEACONESS ASSOCIATION

Rev. Philipp Wambsganss Jr., 1919–33

Rev. Walter A. Klausing, 1933–55

Rev. Edgar H. Albers, 1955– 69

Rev. Arthur Ziegler, 1969–71

Rev. Herbert Steinbauer, 1971–73

Deaconess (later Rev.) Norma Jean Cook Everist, 1973–1974

Rev. Curtis H. Peters, 1974–77

Ms. (later Rev.) Phyllis Kersten, 1977–81

Deaconess Judy Hoshek, 1981–82

Ms. Susan Thompson, 1982–86

Deaconess Deborah Nebel, 1986–89

Deaconess Elaine Plackner, 1989–92
Ms. Lynn Bahls, 1992–98
Deaconess Carolyn Becker, 1998–99
Rev. Paul Thielo, 1999–2000
Deaconess Sheryl Andreasen, 2000–04
Deaconess Deborah Matern Graf, 2004–08
Deaconess Cherryll Irene Hoffman, 2008–

APPENDIX 1.E.: GRADUATES OF THE LDA DEACONESS TRAINING PROGRAMS IN
FORT WAYNE (INDIANA), BEAVER DAM (WISCONSIN), WATERTOWN
(WISCONSIN), AND HOT SPRINGS (SOUTH DAKOTA) FROM 1922 TO 1942[1]

Fort Wayne, 1922
Ina Kempff
Fort Wayne, 1923
Clara Dienst, Bessie Stenke, Muriel Watson, Clara Wiebke
Fort Wayne, 1924
Martha Eber, Elsie Mohr, Esther Tassinari
Fort Wayne, 1925
Hulda Buegel, Beata Randt , Ruth Trettin
Beaver Dam, 1925
Martha Koehler, Pauline Meyer, Louise Rathke , Louise Wegner
Fort Wayne, 1926
Amelia Doctor, Lydia Hass, Amanda Kaiser, Alma Miller, Meta Schrader
Beaver Dam, 1926
Martha Breitenfeld, Adeline Harms
Fort Wayne, 1927
Rosina Bremer, Martha Buchholz, Elsie Mahler, Clara Mueller
Hot Springs, 1927
Esther Larsen, Lulu Noess
Watertown, 1927
Louise Gieschen, Erna Heck, Thelma Mattil, Louise Moehlenbrock, Henrietta
Nanke, Johanna Schmidt, Clara Strehlow, Ida Stolte
Fort Wayne, 1928
Gertrude Oberheau, Minnie Spurgat, Louise Stillmann
Beaver Dam, 1928
Selma Vogel
Watertown, 1928
Cora Leader, Margaret Leader, Anna Schrader
Fort Wayne, 1929
Pauline Barthel, Elsbeth Buchholz, Minerva Klockziem, Rena Ruppenthal, Esther
Schabacher, Margaret Spencer

---

[1] The Lutheran Deaconess Association, Valparaiso, Indiana, provided the names for
Appendices 1.E. and 1.F.

Beaver Dam, 1929
Wilhelmine Boerger, Martha Herzberg, Dorothea Koenig, Margaret Lauterbach, Frieda Poetter
Watertown, 1929
Minnie Hecht, Lydia Lutz, Martha Schmidt, Martha Theilmann
Fort Wayne, 1930
Gestina Nordmann
Beaver Dam, 1930
Dorothea Langhoff, Bertha Schimke, Alma Schumann
Watertown, 1930
Margaret Gieschen, Marie Labrenz, Anna Marty
Fort Wayne, 1931
Ida Henry, Clara Rodenbeck
Watertown, 1931
Joann Bahr, Viola Haag, Martha Naumann, Leone Rixe, Oneida Witte
Fort Wayne, 1932
Edith Cornelius, Ida Schillinger
Fort Wayne, 1933
Amelia Erdelbrock, Gertrude Hogan, Margaret Lutz, Henrietta Sanders
Beaver Dam, 1933
Alverda Johnson
Watertown, 1933
Margaret Bliefnick, Marie Bliefnick, Katherine Laesch, Gertrude Mueller, Christine Seckel, Ida Trinklein, Annchen Vierck
Fort Wayne, 1934
Helen Kluck, Margaret Schillinger
Beaver Dam, 1934
Nellie Bender, Alice Dey, Irma Gallmeyer, Irene Neuendorf, Bertha Pohlmann, Talke Renken, Dorothea Redner, Dona Werling, Emma Wolshky
Watertown, 1934
Clara Bekemeier, Concordia Krueger, Frieda Martin, Ruth Nichols
Fort Wayne, 1935
Esther Fuchs, Alice Klitzing, Dorothy Leuenhagen, Helen Richter, Clara Schaller
Beaver Dam, 1935
Gladys Connolly, Esther Haeger, Clara Hilken, Mathilde Pfund, Edna Stuebs
Fort Wayne (Central Training School) 1936
Erna Bartsch, Mathilda Johnson, Henrietta Thorsness
Fort Wayne, 1937
Elisabeth Behlke, Florence Storck
Chicago, 1938
Frieda Bremermann
Fort Wayne, 1938
Thelma Bemarkt, Martha Boss, Anita Heidmann

Fort Wayne, 1939
Ruth Beach, Margaret Fish, Marie Hartos, Salome Mueller, Christine Rapier, Marie Twenhafel, Emma Wehrenbrecht
Fort Wayne, 1940
Margaret Fiene, Adeline Rink, Gertrude Simon
1941
No graduates
Fort Wayne, February 1942
Frieda Marth, Rose Ziemke
Fort Wayne, July 1942
Esther Matz
1943
No graduates

APPENDIX 1.F.: GRADUATES OF THE LDA DEACONESS TRAINING PROGRAM IN VALPARAISO, INDIANA FROM 1944 TO 1986

1944
Jessie Bowers*, Irma Gade*, Malinda Stuckwisch*
1945
Clara Gade*
*Women who started their training in Fort Wayne and finished in Valparaiso.
1946
Muriel James, Nettye Kimberley
1947
No graduates
1948
Mary Elaine Kluge, Aileen Resner
1949
Betty Gallion, Lois Jank
1950
Grace Braeger, Dorothy Gohr, Grace Pomerenke, Lois Roepke, Kathleen Rubow, Marian Speckhard
1951
Mary Arbeiter, Ruth Berg, Elaine Davis, Clara Hermes, Elizabeth Kujawski
1952
Dolores Hackwelder, Evelyn Middelstadt, Anita Rentz, Dorothy Stanke
1953
Betty Buss, June Finger, Shirley Groh, Gloria Guetzke, Rose Marie Harms, Barbara Looman, Shirley Marks, Dorothy Murphy, Naomi Schubkegel, Irma Thoele, Joan Wagner, Eleanor Weidner, Elaine Yoreo, Lucille Zimmerman
1954
Mary Bohrer, Ada Mundinger, Verne Scheiderer, Marilyn Schultz, Esther Siller, Marian Wehe, Eunice Weidner

1955

Beth Andert, Ruth Broermann, Hertha Fischer, Julia Hennig, Jean Hoover, Mary Jungemann, Bonnie Long, Marilyn Meier, Irma Pflueger, Eunice Riemer, Rita Sadosky, Betty Schmidt, Joan Stengel, Joyce Wendorf

1956

Catherine Bewie, Val Dierks, Mildred Evenson, Dorothy Folkers, Louise Fox, Gloria Jungemann, Diane Markussen, Ruth Mueller, Nadene Tresemer

1957

Ilene Behlmaier, Jane Godwise, Lorraine Ehmann, Rhoda Gilmer, Lois Graesser, Esther Kusch

1958

Doris Awe, Marilyn Brammeier, Geraldine Eubanks, Della Henning, Joan Jensen, Shirley Miller, Gladys Noreen, Janice Orluske, Marilyn Siewert, Mertice Spaude, Germaine Vaag

1959

Lorraine Mae Behling, Marlene Birkholz, Kathleen Blaine, Edith Casson, Laverne Cottet, Ruth Jacobsen, June Julius, Luella Mickley, Sylvia Miller, Maris Mummert, Evonne Pfaff, Janet Severence, Jane Sielaff

1960

Grace Anderson, Cherryll Cook, Norma Jean Cook, Carolyn Gresens, Merrlyn Gudim, Nina Kohls, Rachel Kriefall, Marie Otten, Lois M. Petersen, Anna Elizabeth Schroeder

1961

Barbara Amt, Patricia Astalos, Betty Bader, Joan Cole, Patricia Downey, Dolores Frederking, Gretchen Gaver, Laurie Gruenbeck, Jacqueline Haug, Margaret Heine, Edith Hovey, Winifred Messner, Beverly Reardon, Dolores Seyfert, Maureen Smith, Sharon Thompson, Lucille Wiese, Lila Zingerline

1962

Connie Allen, Helen Beckman, Beverly Berner, Joyce Coryell, Leona Irsch, Karna Kohtz, Nancy Leland, Maralyn Marske, Patricia Martin, Mary Ann Mejdrick, Katherine Miller, Sharon Rahn, Nobuko Sasaki, Susan Werner

1963

Sally Brandt, Hedda Carlson, Janice Hartman, Carol Jungermann, Geraldine Leistico, Jeannie Louie, Judith Nelson, Rhoda Rasmusson, Meta Roth, Jean Sanfilippo, Arletta Schramm, Audrey Vanderbles, Elaine Warinsky, Alberta Weames, Pamela Zimmermann

1964

Elaine Albers, Betty Beckmann, Lorna Bender, Judith Calkin, Kathleen Ehlert, Carole Garwood, Grace Henneman, Audrey Hohenstein, Ona Klema, Shirley Moeller, Carol Schewe, Corinne Siebel, Deloris Thieme

1965

Nancy Brandt, Ruth Anne Abbott, Carol Heinemann, Gretchen Kirsch, Jeanne Lowe, Janet Maynard, Rebecca McGrew, Mary Taylor, Rosemary Wehking

1966

Janet Arnold, Linda Bachoritch, Charlene Hanusch, Shirley Heine, Ruth Helmkamp, Beverly Herwig, Suzanne Krueger, Justine Miller, Virginia Noller, Loraine Rathman, Velma Roth, Barbara Savo, Charlotte Schulze, Janice Yung

1967

Edythe Bauer, Janice Hochradel, Diane Jawort, Burnette Kunz, Diane Melang, Mary Strohschein, Alice Vossler, E. Louise Williams

1968

Marlys Abley, Darlene Kirchhof, Carol Krieger, Caroline Munger, Sarah Nelson, Carol Peterson, Faith Reiner, Miriam Rueger, Anne Marie Sargent, Carol Sokofski, Janet Thompson, Judith Worst

1969

Linda Beery, Bonnie Belasic, Kathryn Bickel, Elizabeth Bloomfield, Lois Braham, Shirley Geyer, Helen Haase, Phyllis McIntire, Corinne Mott, Eileen Peterson, Jane Richter, Peggy Shea, Carole Stockwell, Susan Wallich, Donna Warren, Susan Wendorf, Dianna Werlinger, Kaylyn Zerbst

1970

Linda Bickel, Margaret Cannon, Carole Corniels, Lynne Dorlon, Berneal Hobratschk, Carol Ives, Jeanette Kothe, Janet Lautanen, Karen Fluegge Melang, Sheryl Olson, Barbara Schroeder, Janice Siemers, Janet Umpleby, Joann Underwood

1971

Diane Anderson, Sara Doolen, Mary-Anne Flohr, Judith Hoshek, Dorothy Kruse, Vanette Peter, Gwendolyn Sayler, Janet Sprecher, Adrienne Washburn

1972

Janice Barnes, Catherine Bierlein, Kathryn Borgman, Meridel Christianson, Dianna Fenske, Beverly Grage, Diane Greve, Anita Mohr Grunow, Mary Gunderson, Gayle Heinzelman, Karen Hentsch, Joan Jacobsen, Janice Holtmeier Janzow, Barbara Kloehn, Katherine Linder, Deborah Kolke Nebel, Arlene Maffit, Diane Marten, Eunice Miller, Ruth Nickodemus, Phyllis Saathoff, Eileen Semelka, Carol Steficek, Susan Webb, Patricia Winecke, Karen Zimmerman

1973

Emma Alunen, Mary Baumann, Barbara Hitt, Margaret Hutton, Brenda Kasten, Carol Kodweis, Karen Kraetzner, Suzanne Nagel, Mary Raabe

1974

Jeanette Barber, Betty Boyer, Stella Brown, Kathryn Jergemeyer, Grace Jewett, Joyce Ostermann, Margee Page, Carol Peterson, Diane Remer, Jocelyn Sproule, Vivian Steinbrenner, Claire Visser

1975

Jamie Alden, Laura Anderson, Dorothy Boettcher, Diane Everson, Ruth Hanusa, Betty Havey, Marlene Hedrich, Martha Kaempfe, Claire Krans, Ann Kuch, Carol Peters, Rhonda Silberstein, Rhonda Wieck

1976

Lorraine Beltz, Mary Doversberger, Eva Fanslau, Sally Franz, Tracy Grennrich, Jane Hinze, Joan Jenzen, Edith Krieger, Melissa Kyle, Suzanne Larson, Marilyn Mayberry, Sally Meyer, Deanna Ochs, Susan Schulze, Barbara Smith, Ruth Ann Waetzig

1977

Carolyn Appel, Kathy Bykonen, Margaret Claus, Diana Dickhardt, Cathleen Dornon, Nancy Eaton, Faith Feltz, Jane Galko, Dawn Gerike, Darlene Grega, Rhoda Grever, Donna King, Wilma Kucharek, Linda Morath, Patricia Muehrer, Nancy Nicol, Anne Nuechterlein, Kay Pritzlaff, Linda Reinemer, Kathleen Reitz, Judy Robinson, Verna Schroeder, Jan Voges, Dianna Waterworth, Joanne Wehrmeister, Christine Witt, Nancy Wright

1978

Phyllis Baltimore, Candace Baltzelle, Gwenn Bazajou, Kathy Delventhal, Brenda Gold, Janet Hall, Cindy Hartman, Ruth Ann Heffelfinger, Denise Hegemann, Nancy Houser, Terry Kleeman, Miriam Kling, Linda Kyd, Suzanne Landmann, Debra Lucht, Lindysue Luster-Bartz, Janice Mattson, Cathy Neeb, Joanne Neugebauer, Mary Robish, Jill Schmidt, Janelle Schudde, Kay Svalberg, Mary Carol Thomas, Susan Wacker, Pat Young

1979

Sheryl Andreasen, Jeanne Dicke, Ruth Dyer, Paula Fredrickson, Maggie Harris, Kathleen Herzberg, Betty Knapp, Deborah Larson, Beverly Lipscomb, Cheryl D. Naumann, Darlene Nelson, Christine Raess, Andrea Schultz, Pamela Siemers, Ramelle Timm

1980

Susan Albers, Susan Bergeson, Susan Bergquist, Janet Sue Conrady, Marilyn Feldhaus, Cheryl Huntley, Kay Johnson, Vivian Jones, Erika Mittelstaedt, Susan Raney, Dawn Riske, Roberta Sauer, Luanne Veale, Karen Waschkies, Debra Ann Wehking, Susan Wiese

1981

Cheryl Adkins, Christine Bauer, Linda Beckstrand, Marilyn Buse, Kay Marlene Cassel, Michelle Coon, Ann Hintz, Elizabeth Kerr, Evelyn Kilgas, Cindy Lou Martin, Brenda Mensing, Brenda Neitzke, Debra Peters, Pamela Smith, Raeleen Steinwand, Bonnie Zimmerman

1982

Marcia Bernthal, Cynthia Donnell, Carole Ford, Betsy Green, Kathryn Grosswein, Gloria Ann Klawiter, Rebekah Lehman, Cynthia Kay Luft, Lois Martin [Diebel], Darlene Elaine Mortimer, Ellen Rodenbeck

1983

Paula Nadine Anderson, Sandra Milkan Eacret, Susan Gunderson, Nanette Howard, Nancy Jean Mecham, Kathy Vanderhoof, Karen Lynn Westbrooks

1984

Leah Hafemeister, Christine Lintala, Karen McClendon, Nona Pankonein, Pamela Preuss

1985
Patricia Diener, Hilary Hefferlin, Paula Hepola, Lorna Hill, Vickie Hoover, Brenda Jaffe, Mary Ruth Lange, Heidi Michelsen
1986
Laura Buchinger, Claire D'Aoust, Mari Lynn Maxwell, Lorinda Schwarz, Kris Zierke

APPENDIX 1.G.: "BACKGROUND DISCUSSION GUIDE" MAILED BEFORE MEETING TO ALL PARTICIPANTS IN THE DEACONESS DISCUSSION MEETING, JANUARY 24, 1968, CHICAGO, ILLINOIS[2]

DEACONESS PROGRAM 1–24–68

I. What to do about the third profession

In considering the future of the Deaconess Program, there are several clear alternatives we might take. We are listing these alternatives below. Not all of them are inconsistent with the others. The differences will become apparent as you read on.

A. Leave the program unchanged

The first logical alternative would be to do nothing; i.e., to move forward with the structure left as is.

The new feature of this choice would be that it would, first, be a deliberate choice. It would be a re-affirmation of the fact that the Deaconess Program in our church is a cooperative venture involving the Deaconess Association, Valparaiso University, and the BHE.

The second element in this alternative is that it would need to involve a frank recognition to all concerned that the Deaconess Program is an exception to other programs preparing workers for Synod. Synod has always, according to our understanding, insisted that if a worker is placed by Synod, that worker must also have been educated directly by Synod. To re-affirm our present situation, then, would mean that we would openly state in the case of the Deaconess Program we have a program that prepares workers for Synodical placement but that their education is "franchised" to the Lutheran Deaconess Association and Valparaiso University.

B. Leave the program unchanged except for returning to direct placement of deaconesses instead of Synodical placement

Another option would be to change nothing except the procedure for initial placement for graduating deaconesses. The Deaconess Association, in years past, was always responsible for both initial and subsequent placement of deaconesses. One could argue that this is still the best way for the program to develop its own strengths. One of the inevitable consequences of Synodical placement has been a certain loss of the ability on the part of the program to chart its own course.

---

[2] "Background Discussion Guide: Deaconess Program," Box: Board for Professional Education Services Box 5: Deaconess Materials and BHE Materials, found loose at front of box, CHI, St. Louis, Missouri. See Chapter Nine.

An advantage involved in Synodical placement consists of the status factor. Also, Synodical placement may simplify the securing of initial positions.

C. Turn the program over entirely to the Lutheran Deaconess Association

This option would presumably involve the Association in returning to its original circumstances; i.e., operating its own school.

D. Turn the program over entirely to Valparaiso University

This, too, is a logical possibility. There is at least some precedent for this in that the University now operates the Youth Leadership Program.

This alternative would also provide the Deaconess Program with a solid institutional backing as well as theological undergirding.

Alternatively, however, the question must be raised as to whether (other than in finances) this arrangement would provide the deaconess program with anything that it does not already have either actually or potentially. In addition, the University would be obligated to raise an even higher budget in order to do the work currently being done by the LDA.

E. Turn the program over entirely to Synod.

This choice would immediately force several decisions:

Should the main center for deaconess education remain at Valparaiso University, or should it be moved to a Synodical campus?

If the program is moved to a Synodical campus, which campus should it be, or should it be a new one?

Would it be possible to operate the program as a Synodical program and yet have it located on the campus of Valparaiso University through some special arrangement?

If the program were turned over to the Synod entirely, then it would presumably need to pay off any remaining indebtedness currently held by the Deaconess Association, in addition to adding to its annual operating budget an estimated $150,000.

F. Change the Deaconess Association to an Association of persons concerned with promoting deaconess ministry but without involvement on the student level.

This option would remove the Deaconess Association from student affairs. Furthermore, this option would not solve the educational questions.

With this choice, a decision would have to be made as to whether the executives of the Deaconess Association would be carried in the Synodical budget or whether the Association itself would still finance itself through voluntary fund-raising.

Under this option the precise ministry of the Deaconess Association would need to be more clearly defined than we have done above. In a general way, however, its purposes would be to secure positions for deaconesses, counsel them, support their annual conference, and interpret their work to the church at large.

G. We could make the deaconess program Pan-Lutheran.

If the program represents a valid ministry, would it not be possible to utilize the ecumenical possibilities of Valparaiso University by enlarging the program from being a specifically Missouri Synod program to being an all-Lutheran program?

This alternative is not inconsistent with all of the preceding options.

As a matter of fact, the Lutheran Deaconess Association was originally established for the Synodical Conference. Therefore, there is precedent for more than Missouri Synod involvement.

Valparaiso University and the Lutheran Deaconess Association could promote the program on a Pan-Lutheran basis by themselves. However, another possibility would be to involve the Lutheran Council of the U.S.A. If it were deemed advisable, we could initiate contact with the Lutheran Council for discussion as to whether it would be interested in a new and all-Lutheran training program.

H. Finally, another option (which is not inconsistent with the preceding options) is to establish a separate college for deaconesses at Valparaiso University.

This option has not, to our knowledge, been seriously considered in the past. It has so many ramifications that even now it could not be thoroughly considered. It is only mentioned as a possibility in connection with our total discussion.

The value of such a college would be in the clearer planning of curriculum in terms of the requirements of the deaconess program. It would have precedent on the campus of Valparaiso in the form of both Christ College and the new School of Nursing.

On the other side of the ledger, it must be admitted that there is a real question as to whether or not the supposed advantages of such a college might not be attainable under the present management; i.e., in fact, whether they are not already being attained under the present arrangement.

Perhaps one could say that if we went for a Pan-Lutheran Deaconess Program the idea of a separate college for deaconesses might become more worth looking at.

II. A theology for Deaconess Work

How does the deaconess program fit into the totality of the concept of ministry? How can the deaconess program help the church to break through the barrier of seeing professional ministry confined largely to the role of the ordained clergyman? How can we help both pastor and deaconess (as well as other professional workers) to see that each has a valid role to play in the total ministry of the church and that neither is a threat to the other? We need to probe the question of multiple ministry.

How can we keep alive the connection between the dynamic of ministry and the possibilities for deaconess ministry? That is to say, are there underlying principles by means of which we can keep ourselves open to new possibilities as they arise without necessarily feeling that we must change merely for the sake of change? In other words, is there any principle which, if built into the deaconess program, will keep the program responsive to new valid forms of ministry and cause us to promote possibilities?

III. The BHE and the sub-committee of the LDA have suggested that the LDA immediately engage an outsider to conduct a study of the program

The purpose for this study would be to have him gather all possible information about out program, a well as other deaconess programs, and then to make recommendations.

APPENDIX 1.H.: REPORT BY ARNE P. KRISTO ON THE DEACONESS DISCUSSION MEETING HELD JANUARY 24, 1968, CHICAGO

Deaconess Discussion Meeting
January 24, 1968
Chicago, Illinois

Persons present for the meeting: Dr. Oliver Harms, Dr. O. P. Kretzmann, Dr. A.G. Huegli, Dr. Samuel Goltermann, Messrs. Adolph Rittmueller and Harold Hollmann, and Pastors E.H. Albers, Hartwig Schwehn, and Arne Kristo.

The meeting was called to order at 12:55 p.m. by the Chairman, Pastor Albers. The chairman read "A Statement and a Proposal," a copy of which was distributed to each participant at the meeting. After this, the meeting continued with general discussion.

The following represent some of the questions and comments made during the discussion:

1. Is the training deaconesses received adequate for the character of the work assignment given to them after graduation?

2. Can the LDA finance itself under the present circumstances, i.e. during a vacancy in the office of Executive Chairman?

3. Would it be preferable to have students interested in the deaconess program attend Valparaiso University for all four years of the program?

4. The deaconess program must be viewed in the context of multiple ministry.

5. One of the factors contributing to the strength of The Missouri Synod has been that it does many things through "independent" groups.

6. There should be consultation between those persons responsible for the deaconess program and the Synodical BHE on curriculum matters, but without total amalgamation of the program into the Synodical structure.

7. There would be great value in having an outside person do an impartial study of the program to see if it is reflecting today's circumstances adequately.

8. A study ought to be made to determine what happens to the deaconess after graduation.

9. There ought to be a study made of the relationship of the deaconess to other ministries of the church.

10. Even if a study is undertaken, it was stated that this does not mean that "everything stops."

11. Can we do anything on a Pan-Lutheran basis?

12. Many questions ought to be kept open at the present time, including even the question of the existence of the deaconess program.

Dr. Harms stated that he would be personally willing to support the following propositions:

1. That in a General Way, the structure of the deaconess program be continued in the immediate future as it has been in the past. (This statement refers to Item Roman 1, Capital A, on the Background Discussion Guide which had been mailed earlier to the participants.)

2. That the present system of giving students the option of attending one of the Synodical Junior Colleges for the first two years be kept open.

3. That the LDA conduct a vigorous campaign for financial support but not in a "wholesale" manner and that the campaign should be pinpointed and directed to specific targets.

4. That the Deaconess Association set itself the goal of securing enough income to take over the 50% tuition remission currently granted by the University. If the Association finds it impossible to do this, the President said he would be willing to support an annual Synodical subsidy toward the program of an amount up to $60,000 with the view toward making it possible for the LDA not only to carry out its program but also to permit it to take over the 50% tuition remission hitherto granted by the University.

5. That the Deaconess Association do all in its power to project a favorable public image. The President stated that he would be willing to contribute to the creation of this image by suggesting to the Synodical Board of Directors and/or the Board of Higher Education that they issue a favorable statement about the program.

The group reached a general consensus on the following items:

1. The deaconess program is to continue under the general stipulations of item Roman 1, Capital A, of the agenda (see above).

2. An outside researcher is to be hired by the Deaconess Association for the purpose of conducting a study of the total program and to offer suggestions to the Board of the LDA. During the study, the BHE is to be kept informed.

3. Dr. Harms should issue a statement of encouragement and support for the program.

4. Some type of Synodical Advisory Committee should exist. The question of whether this should be a new committee or whether the presently existing Synodical Advisory Committee would fill this need was not determined. Dr. Harms suggested that liaison with Synod would best be maintained through the BHE.

Respectfully submitted,
Arne Kristo[3]

APPENDIX 1.I.: *DOCUMENTATION*, COMPILED BY DEACONESS RUTH BROERMANN AND DEACONESS BETTY MULHOLLAND, 1976

DOCUMENTATION

No. 1 ARTICLES OF ASSOCIATION OF THE LUTHERAN DEACONESS ASSOCIATION OF THE EVANGELICAL—LUTHERAN SYNODICAL CONFERENCE OF NORTH AMERICA

January 31, 1920

---

[3] Arne Kristo, "Deaconess Discussion Meeting, January 24, 1968, Chicago, Illinois," Box: Board for Professional Education Services Box 5: Deaconess Materials and BHE Materials, found loose at front of box, CHI, St. Louis, Missouri.

Article One—Name

The name of the Association shall be THE LUTHERAN DEACONESS

ASSOCIATION OF THE EVANGELCIAL—LUTHERAN
SYNODICAL CONFERENCE OF NORTH AMERICA.

Article Three—Object

The object of this Association shall be to educate and train Lutheran
Deaconesses for the care of the sick and the poor in the congregations of
the Evangelical—Lutheran Synodical Conference, and for the
administering of charity and mercy in the charitable institutions and in the
home and foreign mission work of said Synodical Conference; and to
erect and maintain Lutheran Deaconess Schools, Motherhouses and other
Institutions of like character likely to promote the purposes of the Society;
and for that purpose to own, hold and sell real estate.

No. 2 CONSTITUION OF LUTHERAN DEACONESS ASSOCIATION,
March 1, 1957

No. 2. The purpose or purposes for which it is formed are as follows:

A. To recruit, encourage, select, educate and train young women of the
Lutheran Church, Missouri Synod and affiliated Synods.

    a.   To serve said church bodies and their various parishes and mission
stations at home and abroad;

    b.   To assist the various agencies of said church bodies in teaching,
nursing, and caring for the physically and mentally handicapped;

    c.   To minister to those who are emotionally distressed in the parishes of
said church bodies;

    d.   To direct youth work in the parishes of said church bodies.

No. 7.   Membership: Any communicant member of the Lutheran Church,
Missouri Synod, or Synods affiliated with said Lutheran Church, Missouri Synod,
pledging himself or herself to an annual contribution of at least $1.00 may become
a member of this corporation. There shall be only one class of membership and
each member in good standing shall be entitled to one vote.

No. 3 ARTICLES OF INCORPORATION OF THE LUTHERAN
DEACONESS ASSOCIATION, INC. as amended May, 1975

Article 2. The purpose or purposes for which it is formed are as follows:

A. To <u>foster, encourage and support the maintenance of a female Lutheran Diaconate.</u>

    a. to recruit women and prepare them by education and formation for entry into the diaconal ministry;

    b. to erect and maintain Deaconess Schools, residences, and other buildings of similar character needed to promote the purposes and attain the goals of said Corporation;

    c. to engage professional staff that will guide the formation of Deaconess Students, provide services to members of the Diaconate in the name of the Lutheran Deaconess Association, Inc., and promote the aims of the Diaconate in the church and world;

    d. to provide an ongoing ministry of encouragement, support, and necessary services to members of the Diaconate.

B. To serve the church, with <u>primary reference</u> to the Lutheran Church - Missouri Synod, its parish congregations, missions, institutions and agencies.

C. To assist the church in the creation of new ministries and in the support of existing ministries.

D. To assist the members of the Diaconate in creating new ministries where human needs are not presently being met by the church or secular agencies.

E. To exercise the general powers authorized by Indiana Code, sections 23-7-1.1-1 Through 23-7-1.1-65, as amended in 1971.[4]

Article 7. <u>Membership: Any person who supports the aims of the Lutheran Deaconess Association,</u> Inc., and evidences this support with a contribution of $10.00 or more, may become a member of this Corporation for a year from the date of receipt of the contribution. There shall be only one class of membership and each member in good standing shall be entitled to one vote.

---

[4] The LDA Constitution is the same as the LDA Articles of Incorporation. "Constitution— ... the 1955 Indiana Law referred to in the present Articles of Incorporation was very specific and detailed, and was repealed and a new section added in 1971 which has no tie to the LC-MS included in it." Sue Wendorf, "Minutes of the Plenary Board Meeting of the Lutheran Deaconess Association, Deaconess Hall, Valparaiso, Indiana, April 11, 1975," Box: Board for Professional Education Services Box 5: Deaconess Materials and BHE Materials, found loose at front of box, CHI, St. Louis, Missouri, 6; Sue Wendorf, "Minutes of the Plenary Board Meeting of the Lutheran Deaconess Association, Deaconess Hall, Valparaiso, Indiana, January 24, 1975, Box: Board for Professional Education Services Box 5: Deaconess Materials and BHE Materials, found loose at front of box, CHI, St. Louis, Missouri, 2.

No. 4 Resolution of the Lutheran Deaconess Conference No. 12 taken from MAJOR RESOLUTIONS FROM 1970ff. [1970 and following] PRINTED IN CHRONOLOGICAL ORDER.

12. 1972—RELATIONSHIP TO OTHER DIACONATES

WHEREAS we have been and are excited about our relationship to and with other diaconates and religious orders, and

WHEREAS the conferences of this year and the past two years have not only afforded us opportunity for growth in relationships with our own sisters, but also the sisters of the Daughters of Divine Charity, and of the North American Deaconess and of Diakonia, and

WHEREAS the new wind blowing is invigorating, be it

RESOLVED, That we personally thank the Lord of the Church for these opportunities and these people, and be it further,

RESOLVED, That the secretary of this conference be requested to pen a note to the outgoing president and the newly elected president of Diakonia assuring them of our continued prayers on their behalf.

No. 5 Resolution of the LDC No. 14

14. 1972—DEACONESS SERVICE

WHEREAS the Church today more than ever needs the service and leadership of theologically astute women on its circuit, district, and Synodical boards and committees, be it RESOLVED, that LDC vigorously publicize the total list of names of deaconesses together with an area contact person and that individual deaconesses unabashedly and in true humility seek out new contacts and opportunities to preach and teach the Word publicly, to participate in the decision –making process of the Church structure, to give guidance and serve as a resource person and counselor to the agencies and organizations of the Church at large, in order that deaconesses may have broader avenues of theological service open to them in synodical structure, publications, seminaries, and prepatory schools.

No. 6 Resolution of the LDC No. 28

28. 1973 LISTING OF DEACONESSES IN LUTHERAN ANNUAL

WHEREAS all consecrated deaconesses have for almost two years been considered active deaconesses in whatever their specific activities of service, and

WHEREAS a person's identity is greatly enhanced and her service thereby enlived [sic] when she is recognized as a whole professional person,

WHEREAS some deaconesses are in a process of growth in identity, inquiry about possible forms of salaried and non-salaried service and continuing education and thereby not at a good point of "decision" as to their official role as deaconesses, and

WHEREAS The <u>Lutheran Annual</u> holds that it is the responsibility of deaconesses and the Lutheran Deaconess Association and its Executive Director to designate who is and who is not a deaconess and who should and who should not be listed in the Annual, and

WHEREAS The amount of compensation (tax questions, etc.,) is considered less important by the Department of Research and Statistics than the possession of a "call", therefore be it, RESOLVED, That all consecrated deaconesses "with call" be listed in the 1974 <u>Lutheran Annual</u> (together with year and place of graduation and home or office address as preferred), and be it

RESOLVED, That deaconesses available for call be listed as candidates, and be it

RESOLVED, That deaconesses in graduate study be listed as such, and be it

RESOLVED, That emeritus deaconesses be listed as such, and be it

RESOLVED, That due to the September deadline for the 1974 Annual, private consultation here at conference and any necessary long distance phone calls be made to make our list to be submitted to the Annual be as complete as possible by August 15 and that an additional reforming of the publicized list of "Deaconesses with Call" be an ongoing process during the year, and be it,

RESOLVED, That a statement be placed in the Annual: "The following is a list of deaconesses with call. For a complete list of consecrated deaconesses of the Lutheran Deaconess Association write to....." and be it further,

RESOLVED, To have a study on <u>non-salaried deaconesses and deaconesses who are in no-church related positions</u>, and be it finally

RESOLVED, To list in the Annual those who are listed and those who want to be added, and that these names be added by the deadline.

No. 7 Resolution of the LDC No. 32

32. <u>1973—COMMUNITY SUPPORT</u>

WHEREAS it appears that the Synod in convention has taken a stand which may jeopardize the ministry of some of our sisters, and

WHEREAS we have taken upon ourselves the responsibility for the support of one another through our community, and

WHEREAS the expression of our concern and support should be in specific forms, therefore be it

RESOLVED, That we ask the LDC Board to inform all of us as to relationships and procedures to be followed if specific stands are demanded of us, and be it further,

RESOLVED, That we, as a community, commit ourselves to the support of one another through our prayers, our community, and our treasures, and be it further,

RESOLVED, That our area conferences be responsible for being informed about each deaconess in their area, and that they keep all of us informed of specific persons we should be remembering in our prayers, and be it further,

RESOLVED, That we individually offer of our homes and sustenance to those deaconesses in need, and finally be it

RESOLVED, That we make a sacrificial offering to our contingency fund, so that we may realistically support one another.

No. 8 Resolution of the LDC No. 43 (1974)

43. RECOGNITION OF DEACONESSES WITHIN SYNODICAL DISTRICTS—NOT PASSED, TABLED FOR COMMITTEE

WHEREAS Deaconesses receive regular calls to serve the church within districts, and

WHEREAS Deaconesses now serve their districts in whatever ways they can and are interested in serving more fully through boards, committees, and offices with their special talents, and

WHEREAS the professional life of deaconesses would be enhanced by receiving communications concerning pastoral workshops, training sessions, and educational opportunities, and

WHEREAS districts function with the categories of Pastor, Teacher, and lay person and

WHEREAS Deaconesses and other professional church workers (excluding pastors and teachers) are considered to be "lay persons", and

WHEREAS we feel that "lay person" is an inadequate term to describe the talents and responsibilities of deaconesses and other professional church workers, therefore be it RESOLVED, That the Lutheran Deaconess Conference encourage individual deaconesses and/or area conferences through local congregations to memorialize Synod in Convention in 1975 to request Synod to direct districts to create a fourth category to include Deaconesses and other trained professional church workers for all district communications and representation on boards and committees, and be it further,

RESOLVED, That LDC have representation at the open hearing of the appropriate resolution committee of the 1975 Synodical Convention to explain this resolution.

No. 9 Resolution of the LDC No. 44. (1974)

44. ATTENDANCE AT NORTH AMERICAN DIAKONIA AND INTERNATIONAL DIAKONIA MEETINGS

RESOLVED, That the boards of the Lutheran Deaconess Conference and Lutheran Deaconess Association be encouraged to jointly explore outside funding possibilities to facilitate the attendance of deaconesses at North American Diakonia and International Diakonia meetings. Such explorations should be undertaken immediately.

Reasons:

1.   LDA membership in International Diakonia and LDC membership in NAD is a vital part of our growth and nurture as a diaconate.

2.   Funding from large organizations (e.g. AAL. Lutheran Brotherhood) may be available from professional growth of deaconesses and the furthering of ecumenical ventures among diaconates.

3.   Cooperative efforts and well-prepared proposals for funding stand a better chance of consideration by sources of funding, than might those which may be submitted separately.

4.   Cost of attendance by more than a few of our community at North American Diakonia and International Diakonia meetings, often exceeds funds available to the LDA, LDC, and/or individual deaconesses.

5.   The next triennial conference of International Diakonia will be held in Germany in July 1975. The possibility of a study tour of deaconess establishments and communities in Europe is being explored by the Central Committee of the NAD.

No. 10 Resolution of the LDC No. 46 (1974)

46. STATUS OF DEACONESSES IN RELATION TO SYNOD

WHEREAS it was decided in 1973 that deaconesses maintain their independent status in relation to Synod, and

WHEREAS the current situation in Synod may cause problems for deaconesses, be it, RESOLVED, That every deaconess receive a copy of and an explanation of the decision concerning the status of deaconesses in Synod.

No. 11 Resolution of the LDC No. 47. (1974)

47.   ASSISTANCE TO SISTERS IN NEED

WHEREAS it appears that the Synod in convention has taken a stand which may jeopardize the ministry of some of our sisters, and

WHEREAS we have taken upon ourselves the responsibility for the support of one another through our community, and

WHEREAS the expression of our concern and support should be in specific forms, therefore be it,

RESOLVED, That we ask the LDC Board to inform all of us as to relationships and procedures to be followed if specific stands are demanded of us, and be it further

RESOLVED, That we, as a community, commit ourselves to the support of one another through our prayers, our community, and our treasures, and be it further

RESOLVED, That our area conferences be responsible for being informed about each deaconess in their area, and that they keep all of us informed of specific persons we should be remembering in our prayers, and be it further

RESOLVED, That we individually offer of our homes and sustenance to those deaconesses in need, and finally be it

RESOLVED, That we make a sacrificial offering to our contingency fund, so that we may realistically support one another.

No. 12 Resolution of the LDC No. 55

55. 1975—MEMBERSHIP IN LDC

WHEREAS we have been called by God, trained in Lutheran theology and consecrated as servants,

WHEREAS we have much to be joyful about in our diversities and commonalities, and WHEREAS the LDC Constitution states that all consecrated deaconesses who have completed the educational or colloquy requirements of the LDA are members, therefore be it RESOLVED, That sisters holding membership in any Lutheran church remain a part of the Lutheran Deaconess Conference and be it further

RESOLVED, That the LDA and LDC Boards be requested to study and deal with the status of our sisters who no longer hold membership in any Lutheran church.

No. 13 Resolution of the LDC No. 58

58. 1975—MEMBERSHIP IN ASSOCIATED ORGANIZATIONS

WHEREAS membership in the LDC is determined only by the LDA and LDC

WHEREAS our community has maintained an openness to and acceptance of sisters of a variety of theological views within the framework of our basic subscription to the Holy Scriptures and the Lutheran Confessions as well as a diversity of positions relative to church politics and

WHEREAS some of our sisters are associated with, Balance, Inc.: Doctrinal Concerns Program (DCP); Evangelical Lutherans in Mission (ELIM), Federation of Authentic Lutherans (FAL); Lutheran Church in Mission (LCM); and/or Seminary in Exile (Seminex); and others are associated with none of the above,

WHEREAS termination of membership in the community has been a personal decision, and not a conference initiated decision, be it

RESOLVED, That the LDC continue to affirm membership of all sisters in our community in the same manner as we have in the past.

No. 14 Resolution of the LDC No. 59

59. 1975—DEACONESS DIPLOMA

WHEREAS some of our sisters serve in institutions, agencies, and parishes which are not connected to the LC-MS and

WHEREAS the current diploma to graduates uses the language "The LDA certifies Deaconesses to serve in LC-MS" therefore be it

RESOLVED, That we recommend to the LDA Board that action be initiated to change the wording of the Diploma to make it more inclusive and to be in line with the recent changes of the LDA constitution.

No. 15 Resolution of the LDC No. 60

60. 1975—ADVANCED THEOLOGICAL TRAINING

WHEREAS we affirm our uniformity of theological training as an education basis for our diaconal ministry and affirm our diversity of talents with which we work out this ministry and

WHEREAS we have for many years encouraged our sisters who wished to continue their education beyond the basic Bachelor's Degree to seek advanced degrees and professional skills in such areas as music, social work, education, theology and

WHEREAS some of our sisters, in reflection with their sisters in area conference have determined their unique gifts lie in the area of public proclamation of the Word and celebration of the Sacraments, be it therefore,

RESOLVED, that we recognize, although we may not understand those of our sisters who are now seeking and/or holding a Master of Divinity Degree.

No. 16. Resolution of the LDC No. 9 1976

#9—Re: Deaconess Identity

WHEREAS, a statement on deaconess identity is vital to give direction to the future shaping of our ministry, and

WHEREAS, the issue has been extensively discussed to allow for adequate input, Therefore be it

RESOLVED That the Conference adopt the following statement on Deaconess identity and recommend it to the Lutheran Deaconess Association Board:

> A deaconess is a Lutheran woman who through special Lutheran theological and practical training is consecrated to serve, which service is manifested in leadership roles and/or professional positions within the Lutheran Church and/or society, and who is in community with the Lutheran Deaconess Conference.

And further be it

RESOLVED, That expressed concerns such as "exit" policies, dues requirements, etc. be left for determination by the Lutheran Deaconess Conference board with ratification by the membership.

No. 17. Resolution of the LDC No. 12 1976

#12—Re: Relationships with Church Structures

WHEREAS, members of the Lutheran Deaconess Conference currently serve and/or hold membership within several Lutheran church bodies, and

WHEREAS, emerging Lutheran structures indicate potential areas of service, and

WHEREAS, we remain concerned to maintain relations with the LCMS to facilitate continued service within that synod by deaconesses who choose to minister within the LCMS, and

WHEREAS, we also see our ministry as being open to the wider Lutheran church family, and

WHEREAS, we carry out our service in a variety of Lutheran judicatories without having developed formal procedures and statements of policy and commitment regarding service in the wider Lutheran family,

THEREFORE BE IT RESOLVED, That we request the LDA Board in consultation with the LDC Board:

-seek to fully realize our structural autonomy within the Lutheran family by zealously and prayerfully seeking to develop new sources of income in order to broaden our base of financial support.

-arrange for representation of their boards at the constituting conventions of emerging Lutheran bodies.

-approach the administration of new Lutheran Church structures and encourage the development of formal relationships for cooperative ministry as follows:

1. by calling our interns, graduates and other consecrated deaconesses.

2. by suggesting and identifying needs for ministry within their membership which might be met by deaconesses.

3. by allowing and encouraging us to recruit women from their membership.

4. by urging their congregations to support us financially

5. by inviting their leadership to meet jointly with the LDC and LDA Boards to discuss full implementation of the above.

-share with the LC-MS administration our decision to affirm our diaconate's autonomy, our unity in diversity, our commitment to the Scriptures and the Lutheran Confessions and our commitment to serve within the entire Lutheran family.

-Invite the LC-MS to continue to accept our ministry and that we request the LDA board to take appropriate steps to assure ongoing avenues for calls within the LC-MS for those sisters who wish to serve in the LC-MS.

-Discuss current placement procedures with the LC-MS Council of Presidents Board of Assignments in order to promote continuing graduate placements of deaconesses who choose to serve within the LC-MS

-Share our position with the LCA and ALC diaconates.

-Communicate with the ALC and LCA administrations in order to inform them of our position.

-Continue to place LDC deaconesses in positions within the LC-MS, ALC and LCA as opportunities arise.

Finally, we request that this resolution be fully implemented by the time of the Annual Conference of the Lutheran Deaconess Conference in 1977.

APPENDIX 1.J.: RESUME OF THE DOCUMENTATION, WRITTEN BY DEACONESS
RUTH BROERMANN AND DEACONESS BETTY MULHOLLAND, 1976.

RESUME OF DOCUMENTATION

(to be read in conjunction with the *Documentation*)

No. 1 Articles of Association of LDA, January 31, 1920

> Note: defining phrase "Synodical Conference" in Art. I & III

No. 2 Constitution of LDA, March 1, 1957

> Note: No. 2 "Lutheran Church, Missouri Synod and affiliated Synods"
>
> No. 7 Membership—same as above

No. 3 Articles of Incorporation of LDA May 1975

> Note: Art. 2-B "primary reference"

> In March '57 identity and membership was LCMS & affiliated
> Synods. In May '75 the wording is "primary reference" to
> LCMS, showing the shift away from exclusive LCMS
> attachment.

Art. 7 Membership: "<u>Any</u> person"

> In March -57 membership was communicant member of LCMS.
> In May '75 membership is any person who supports LDA - not
> necessarily even Lutheran.

No. 4 Resolution of Lutheran Deaconess Conference No. 12. 1972—Relationship
to other Diaconates

> Note: Relationship to and with other diaconates & religious orders.

> These are affiliated with a variety of church bodies, not especially
> Lutheran.

No. 5 Resolution of LDC No. 14. 1972—DEACONESS SERVICE

> Note: "preach and teach the Word publicly"

No. 6 Resolution of LDC No. 28. 1973—LISTING OF DEACONESSES IN
LUTHERAN ANNUAL

> Note: deaconesses to be "considered active in whatever their specific
> activities of service"

"non-salaried deaconesses and deaconesses who are in non-church related positions"

> Anyone who has been consecrated is a "deaconess" regardless of whatever activity she is doing, whether church or secular.

No. 7 Resolution of LDC No. 32. 1973—COMMUNITY SUPPORT

> Note: "Synod in convention has taken a stand which may jeopardize the ministry of some of our sisters"

No. 8 Resolution of LDC No. 43. (1974)—RECOGNITION OF DEACONESSES WITHIN SYNODICAL DISTRICTS Not Passed, Tabled for Committee

> Note: "memorialize Synod in convention …to create a fourth category to include Deaconesses"

> Even this resolution asking for a voice in district affairs was rejected. This did <u>not</u> include placing deaconesses under the supervision of the district presidents.

No. 9 Resolution of LDC No. 44. (1974)—ATTENDANCE AT NORTH AMERICAN DIAKONIA AND INTERNATIONAL DIAKONIA MEETINGS

> Note: No. 1 "membership…vital part of our growth and nurture"

> No. 2 "furthering of ecumenical ventures among diaconates"

> This Resolution ignores LCMS stand on ecumenical affiliation by considering other diaconates as necessary.

No. 10 Resolution of LDC No. 46 (1974)—STATUS OF DEACONESSES IN RELATION TO SYNOD

> Note: "deaconesses maintain their independent status in relation to Synod"

No. 11 Resolution of LDC No. 47. (1974)—ASSISTANCE TO SISTERS IN NEED

> Note: "Synod in convention has taken a stand which may jeopardize the ministry of some of our sisters"

No. 12 Resolution of LDC No. 55. 1975—MEMBERHSIP IN LDC

> Note: "sisters holding membership in <u>any</u> Lutheran Church"

> Membership in the LDC continues through the name of "Lutheran" regardless of Synodical affiliation.

No. 13 Resolution of LDC No. 58. 1975 - MEMBERSHIP IN ASSOCIATED ORGANIZATIONS

Note: "our community has maintained an openness to and acceptance of sisters of a variety of theological views….as well as a diversity of positions relative to church politics"

"affirm membership of all sisters in our community"

No. 14 Resolution of LDC No. 59. 1975—DEACONESS DIPLOMA

Note: "sisters serve in institutions, agencies, and parishes which are not connected to the LCMS…change the wording of the Diploma to make it more inclusive and to be in line with the recent changes of the LDA constitution"

No. 15 Resolution of LDC No. 60. 1975—ADVANCED THEOLOGICAL TRAINING

Note: "public proclamation of the Word and celebration of the Sacraments"

No. 16 Resolution of LDC No. 9. 1976—DEACONESS IDENTITY

Note in definition: "leadership roles and/or professional positions within the Lutheran Church and/or society"

This puts into writing the policy of opening deaconess positions to include anything in the secular world.

No. 17 Resolution of LDC No. 12. 1976—RELATIONSHIPS WITHIN CHURCH STRUCTURES

Note: a. "currently serve and/or hold membership within several Lutheran Church bodies"

b. "emerging Lutheran structures indicate potential areas of service"

c. "concerned to maintain relations within LCMS"

d. "representation of their boards at the constituting conventions of emerging Lutheran bodies"

e. "administrations of new Lutheran Church structures"

f. "our decision to affirm our diaconate's autonomy...to serve within the entire Lutheran family"

g. "continue to place LDC deaconesses in positions within the LCMS, ALC and LCA as opportunities arise"

h. "this resolution be fully implemented...in 1977" This climaxes the departure from a definition of "Synodical Conference Diaconate" to a completely pan-Lutheran organization with ecumenical ties to other diaconates.

R/ Lord, have mercy upon us; Christ, have mercy upon us; Lord, have mercy upon us.

V/ O God, our dear Father in heaven:

R/ Make us bold to trust You as beloved children.

V/ Lord Jesus, our precious Savior and Brother, Who for joy didst become our Servant:

R/ Lead us to joyful service of the needy.

V/ Holy Spirit, Giver of Life to the Church

R/ Nourish our life on the Courage of Christ.

V/ Holy, Blessed Trinity, Author and Executor of the Mystery of our salvation:

R/ Unite our hearts to praise Your Name.

V/ Father, after Whom the whole family in heaven and on earth is named:

R/ Make us grateful for the companionship of other people, receiving them as gifts of Your grace;

Shape us into companions for those who have not learned to live in community; And satisfy with Your own gracious gifts those of our sisters who work in isolated places.

V/ Jesus, Suffering Redeemer and Praying Priest:

R/ Assist us by patient bearing of injuries to spread the peace of Your Cross;

by steadfast endurance without envy or resentment to demonstrate Your victory;

by steady and faithful prayer to carry our brother into Your gracious presence.

V/ Jesus: Friend of sinners, Companion of the outcast, Associate of the needy:

R/ Enlighten our eyes to see You in our needy brother.

V/ Holy Spirit, Purifier of sinners, make us sharers in the holiness of God:

R/ Bestow upon us the Mind of Christ that we neither think more highly of ourselves than we ought to think, nor deprecate ourselves in unbelief, calling common what you have called clean.

V/ Holy Spirit, Fire of God, coming down from heaven, filling the Church:

R/ Warm our hearts to love God and our neighbor with our whole beings.

V/ Holy Spirit, Guide into all Truth:

R/ Assist us in our teaching that we may joyfully bear the burden of the unlearned and ignorant; Help us share our insight without putting on airs; Cause us to learn without envy and recrimination; Endow us with patience and skill to communicate Your Truth.

V/ Father of pity, Son of compassionate suffering, Spirit of consolation and courage:

R/ Remember in mercy the sick and dying, the suffering and persecuted, the fearful and distraught, the bored and despairing, By Your goodness relieve each according to his need and fortify them to trust You as Father.

V/ God of Righteousness:

R/ Convert to Yourself those who hate You; Arouse those who have become dull towards You; Enlighten those who have blinded their eyes to You; Strengthen those who trust You; Guide those who seek You.

V/ I believe that God has made me and all creatures:

R/ Teach me, O my Maker, to look upon my person and my abilities as Your gifts, so that I may trust Your care for me, so that I may be delivered from jealousy and envy, so that I may see You hidden in my neighbor and there serve You with gladness.

To You, generous Father, I offer thanks and praise, honor and glory.

V/ I believe that Jesus Christ is my Lord:

R/ By Your Cross, gracious Lord, crucify in me all evil desires and unbelief;

By Your unspotted righteousness, gracious Lord, bedeck me in Your own Self that I may be delivered to God forever; By Your service to fallen mankind, gracious Lord, lead me to serve You among the fallen of the earth;

By Your glorious resurrection from the dead, gracious Lord, raise me to live with You forever.

V/ I believe in the Holy Spirit, Lord and Giver of life:

R/ Creator Spirit, raise me up anew by confidence in Your daily and rich forgiveness of my sins;

Creator Spirit, bind me in the unity of love with Your saintly community;

Creator Spirit, enlighten my eyes to see the saints You have made in Your congregation;

Creator Spirit, quicken in me the lively anticipation of my resurrection from the dead.

V/ Blessed Lord, Who has caused the Holy Scriptures to be written for our learning:

R/ Speak to us; we are listening; Strengthen us in our need.

V/ Blessed Lord, Who has taken us into the death and resurrection of Your Son in our Baptism:

R/ Make our lives a living from and returning to that holy Font.

V/ Blessed Lord, Who, nourishing us on the Body and Blood of Christ, creates us into a new fellowship:

R/ Make us to be indeed the Body of Christ and the vehicle of love and joy in this world, until we offer the full and perfect praise forever.   Amen.

APPENDICES FOR PART II

CHAPTERS 13–14

APPENDIX 2.A.: SHORT BIOGRAPHIES OF THE NINE FOUNDING MEMBERS OF CONCORDIA DEACONESS CONFERENCE—LUTHERAN CHURCH-MISSOURI SYNOD

APPENDIX 2.B.: CONCORDIA DEACONESS CONFERENCE—LUTHERAN CHURCH-MISSOURI SYNOD INITIAL DRAFT CONSTITUTION ADOPTED JANUARY 12, 1980

APPENDIX 2.C.: CONSTITUTION AND BY-LAWS ADOPTED AND SIGNED BY FOUNDING MEMBERS ON JUNE 7, 1980

APPENDIX 2.D.: "A CHRONOLOGICAL ACCOUNT OF THE SEQUENCE OF EVENTS OF THE INVESTIGATION OF CONCORDIA SEMINARY, SAINT LOUIS," AS FOUND WITH THE "MINUTES OF THE LCMS BHE," MAY 4–5, 1973

MILDRED LORETTA (EVENSON) BRILLINGER

July 30, 1933–

Deaconess Training: Valparaiso (1954–56)

Consecration: June 24, 1956 at St. Peter's Lutheran Church, Easton, Minnesota

Fields of service:

St. Mark's Lutheran Church and Lutheran Home for Girls, Detroit, Michigan (Internship—1955); St. Matthew's Lutheran Church, Worthington, Minnesota (1956–60); Lutheran Homes, Inc., Ft. Wayne, Indiana (1974–78); St. John's Lutheran School, Lincoln, Texas (1983–86); Lutheran Child and Family Service, Detroit, Michigan (1987).

On August 6, 1960 "Millie" married Otto Arnold Brillinger. They have been blessed with three children: Catherine (1962), Carol (1963), and Daniel (1965).

Millie taught grades 1–4 at St. Peter's Lutheran School in Gibbon, Minnesota before becoming a deaconess. In the 1960s, she was employed as a Social Worker for the State Department of Child Welfare in Springfield, Illinois, and later as a Family Counselor for the city of Calgary, Alberta, Canada. Millie recalls that she has been interested in missions since the day of her confirmation and was motivated to become a deaconess in order to do mission work. When her husband, Otto, retired from the pastoral ministry, Millie and he became volunteer missionaries in Nigeria (1993), Kazakhstan (1994 to present), and Lithuania (1995 to present).

"It is my prayer that deaconesses may continue to be trained, dedicated and noble servants of our Lord. May we do all things to His glory, now and forever"! Millie

* * *

KAY LORRAINE (PRITZLAFF) GUDGEON

August 25, 1953–

Deaconess Training: Valparaiso (1975–76)

Consecration: August 7, 1977 at St. John's Lutheran Church, Plymouth, Wisconsin

Fields of service:

Lutheran Homes, Inc., Ft. Wayne, Indiana (Internship—1976–77); Lutheran Homes, Inc., Ft. Wayne, Indiana (1977–84).

CDC leadership positions: Secretary (1980–84); Membership Committee; Nominations Committee

On May 28, 1983 Kay married Richard Gene Gudgeon. They have been blessed with two children: Michael (1984) and Sarah (1987).

As part of the "Deaconess Corps" at Lutheran Homes, Kay worked with an assigned caseload of residents and also served as Coordinator of Volunteer Services. A talented musician, she directed the Lutheran Homes Choir, played the organ for the Homes' Chapel Services, and sang in choirs at Concordia Theological Seminary and St. Paul's Lutheran Church in Ft. Wayne. She also coordinated the Sunday School music program at Redeemer Lutheran Church, Ft. Wayne.

Kay unofficially retired from full-time deaconess work to stay at home with her children. She did occasional work as a home typist and then secured a position as a home-based medical transcriptionist. When the children went to school, Kay's job evolved into an administrative assistant position with a multi-physician ophthalmology practice, where she is still employed.

"It was my privilege to serve with the Deaconess Corps for eight years. I value my years of involvement with CDC and the deaconess program." Kay

* * *

LUELLA ELOISE MICKLEY

September 18, 1922–2007

Deaconess Training: Valparaiso (1956–59)

Consecration: March 1, 1959 at Golgotha Lutheran Church, Chicago, Illinois

Fields of service:

Golgotha Lutheran Church, Chicago, Illinois (1959–87); Golgotha Lutheran School, Chicago, Illinois (1961–87); Northern Illinois District LCMS (1978–87); Retired: 1987. Grace Lutheran School, Chicago, Illinois (1987–91).

CDC leadership positions: Treasurer (1980–86)

Luella has always been passionately involved in caring for the welfare of the children and youth of the church. She spent many summers working at Arcadia Lutheran Camp in Michigan and instigated the founding of "Koinonia," a youth group for young adults. In the parish, Luella taught junior confirmation classes, instructed the Sunday School teachers, and was in charge of the Walther League.

A professionally trained teacher, Luella started a Kindergarten at Golgotha Lutheran School, where she subsequently taught Kindergarten or pre-Kindergarten classes for twenty-five years. Her students loved their cheerful and caring teacher, and many were delighted to see their own children go into her classroom over the years. At the same time, Luella visited individuals at nursing homes on behalf of the Northern Illinois District's Project Compassion program.

"I was baptized and confirmed at Golgotha and always felt at home there. When the congregation called me to be a deaconess I had a lot to be thankful for. It meant so much to me to be able to serve." Luella

* * *

BETTY RUTH (SCHMIDT) MULHOLLAND

December 13, 1933–

Deaconess Training: Valparaiso (1951–55)

Consecration: May 22, 1955 at Trinity Lutheran Church, St. Joseph, Michigan

Fields of service:

Bethesda Lutheran Home, Watertown, Wisconsin (Internship—1952); Bethesda Lutheran Home, Watertown, Wisconsin (1955); St. Paul's Lutheran Church, Munster, Indiana (1968–98). Retired: January 1, 1998.

CDC leadership positions: Executive Committee member (1981–84; 1996–98); Nominations Committee; Children's Committee; Award Committee; Parliamentarian

On June 18, 1955 Betty married Glenn Austen Mulholland. They were blessed with four children: Daniel (1956), Mark (1957), Julia (1958), and Stephen (1960–1997).

Once the Missouri's Synod's first deaconess training program was established at Concordia College, River Forest, Betty became a member of the adjunct faculty and taught the "Senior Specialization Courses" for 1982-83. Since then she has been a frequent guest lecturer in River Forest and Ft. Wayne, sharing her insights and expertise regarding the role and duties of a deaconess. Betty served the Indiana District Board of Social Ministry (1970–90) and was secretary of the Lutheran Home of Northwest Indiana Endowment Corp. for 25 years. After retiring from 30 years of parish ministry, she was appointed to the LCMS Nomenclature Study Committee and the New Hymnal subcommittee on Pastoral Rites.

"God's timing is not our timing. If the Lord means it to be, it will be. We are in the hands of our loving heavenly Father." Betty

* * *

CHERYL DOROTHY (FREITAG) NAUMANN

June 23, 1956–

Deaconess Training: Valparaiso (1974–75, 76–77, 79)

Consecration: May 20, 1979 at Memorial Lutheran Church, Bremerton, Washington

Fields of service:

St. Paul's Lutheran Church, Ann Arbor, Michigan (Internship—1977–78); St. Paul's Lutheran Church, Ann Arbor, Michigan (1978); Lutheran Home for the Aged, Kendallville, Indiana (1979–80); Redeemer Lutheran Church and School, Oakmont, Pennsylvania (2004–present).

CDC leadership positions: Constitution Committee; Historian; Secretary (2006–)

On June 4, 1977 Cheryl married Jonathan Charles Naumann. They were blessed with six children: Brian (1980), David (1981), Edward (1982), Gordon (1984), Nigel (1986), and Dorothy (1990).

For 21 years Cheryl lived in the United Kingdom, assisting her pastor husband in mission work at St. Columba Lutheran Church, East Kilbride, Scotland (1982–88) and St. Andrew's Lutheran Church, Ruislip, England (1988–2003). In 1991, with a research thesis entitled *Martin Luther's Use of the Church Fathers in His lectures on Genesis 1.1–11.26*, she received a Master of Theology degree (in Theology and Church History) from Glasgow University. Staying at home to care for her children, Cheryl managed a London branch of CPH and developed a career as a free-lance corporate writer and editor. From 1996–99 she served as editor of *British Lutheran*, the official organ of the Evangelical Lutheran Church of England.

"Be strong and courageous. Do not be terrified; do not be discouraged, for the Lord your God will be with you wherever you go (Joshua 1:9)." Cheryl

* * *

NANCY EILEEN (NICOL) NEMOYER

August 2, 1954–

Deaconess Training: Valparaiso (1974–75, 76–77)

Consecration: June 12, 1977 at St. John's Lutheran Church, Marysville, Ohio

Fields of service:

Immanuel Lutheran Church, Mt. Olive, Illinois (Internship—1975–76); Lutherbrook Child Care Center, Addison, Illinois (1977–78); Lutheran Homes, Inc., Ft. Wayne, Indiana (1978–80); Concordia College, River Forest, Illinois (1980–90).

CDC leadership positions: Secretary (1980)

On December 27, 1986 Nancy married Robert Jay Nemoyer Jr. They have been blessed with three sons: Aaron (1988), Nathan (1990), and Joel (1992).

Nancy served as the first Director of the LCMS Deaconess Training program at Concordia College, River Forest, Illinois. Her responsibilities included recruitment, interviewing students, planning each new Deaconess course syllabus and seeing it through the approval process, teaching the three professional deaconess courses, securing field work and internship sites, supervision of field workers and interns, developing brochures, academic and personal counseling, coordinating with the Admissions Office and the candidate placement officer, and fund raising. She received an MA degree in Theology and Education in 1985. Nancy has held offices or leadership roles at every level of the LWML and served on the LCMS President's Commission on Women from 1983–89.

In 1990, Nancy left deaconess ministry for the vocation of full time homemaker and pastor's wife, and still enjoys the challenge of home-schooling her sons.

"Nothing in my hands I bring, Simply to Thy cross I cling." Nancy

* * *

JOYCE ANN OSTERMANN

August 20, 1951–

Deaconess Training: Valparaiso (1971–72, 73–74)

Consecration: June 5, 1974 at Zion Lutheran Church, Litchfield, Illinois

Fields of service:

Lutheran Homes, Inc., Ft. Wayne, Indiana (Internship—1972–73); Lutheran Homes, Inc., Ft. Wayne, Indiana (1974–84); Lutheran Retirement Village, Crown Point, Indiana (1984–87); Lutheran Homes, Inc., Kendallville, Indiana (1987–90); Concordia Theological Seminary, Ft. Wayne, Indiana (1997–present).

CDC leadership positions: Vice President (1980–82); President (1982–87; 2000–2004); Executive Board member (1987–89); Secretary (1998–2000); Constitution Committee

Joyce's administrative and organizational skills have been a blessing to the CDC, especially during the many years that she held executive offices. From 1985–87 Joyce assisted the LCMS deaconess program by serving as internship supervisor.

Joyce supervised the Deaconess Corp. and social workers at Lutheran Homes, and later served as a Director of Social Services and then as Home Administrator. She holds an Indiana Social Worker's License and Indiana Health Facilities Administrator's License, and earned a Public Administrator Master's degree. Joyce was Executive Assistant to the Director of Financial Aid at Concordia Theological Seminary for ten years and is currently the Data Base Manager for the Office of Institutional Advancement at CTS. Since 2002, Joyce has been a member of the LCMS Deaconess Task Force.

"My hope is that someday we won't need the CDC; that the LCMS will have so many deaconesses that each district will provide professional deaconess conferences just like the pastor and teacher conferences that are in place now." Joyce

* * *

RUTH SUZANNAH (BROERMANN) STALLMANN

April 8, 1918–

Deaconess Training: Valparaiso (1954–55)

Consecration: January 23, 1955 at Redeemer Lutheran Church, Evansville, Indiana

Fields of service:

Concordia Lutheran Church, Berwyn, Illinois (Internship—1954); Lutheran Action Council, Washington D.C. (1955–56); Trinity Lutheran Church, New Hyde Park, New York (1958–59); St. Matthew's Lutheran Church, Chicago, Illinois (1959–61); LCMS Campus Ministry Office, Chicago, Illinois (1963–68); Northern Illinois District LCMS (1968–81). Retired: May 15, 1981. St. Stephen's Lutheran Church, St. Louis, Missouri (1981–82).

CDC leadership positions: President (1980–82); Vice President (1982–83)

On June 6, 1981 Ruth married a widower, Reinhold Otto Stallmann, and became stepmother to four children: Carl (1952), Carol (1953), Mark (1958), and Marcia (1961).

Before training to be a deaconess, Ruth held a Doctor of Chiropractor degree and was employed as a college professor. Part of her job for the Northern Illinois District was to instruct congregations in the implementation of "Project Compassion." In the 1980s, she sat on the LCMS Task Force on Aging and the LCMS Social Ministries Task Force. Ruth's leadership skills and experience made her a natural choice for first president of CDC. Since 2004 she has been a volunteer at Laclede Oaks Campus, administered by Lutheran Social Services of St. Louis.

"A great joy and a thrill emanated from my daily experiences as a deaconess, especially in the spiritual realm." Ruth

* * *

CLARA ELSA FLORA STREHLOW

November 28, 1895–December 12, 1985

Deaconess Training: Bethesda Lutheran Home, Watertown, Wisconsin (1925–27)

Consecration: May 1, 1927 at St. John's Lutheran Church, Watertown, Wisconsin

Fields of service:

The Kinderheim, Addison, Illinois (1927–40); Institute for the Deaf, Detroit, Michigan (1941); Grace Lutheran Church, St. Louis, Missouri (1941–57); Deaconess Hall, Valparaiso, Indiana (1958–63). Retired: June 30, 1963.

Throughout Clara's 36 years of active deaconess service and 22 years as Deaconess Emeritus she was known as a pioneer in the Lutheran deaconess movement. A frequent speaker at Associated Lutheran Charities Conferences, Clara wrote articles in many publications, outlining the work that Deaconesses could do for their Lord "in His wretched ones and His poor." In 1934, Clara was a founding member of the Conference for Deaconesses and served as its president from 1934–38. When Deaconess Hall was completed in Valparaiso, she became the first live-in House Director (1958–63).

Clara was a cherished and respected advisor to the Concordia Deaconess Conference from the time of its inception. Her sage advice always pointed to God's Word, where she found joy and strength for every challenge in life. An example of genuine servanthood, humble and dedicated to her Lord, Clara's life was an inspiration to all who knew her.

"What I have done is not important. It's what He has done through me that counts." Clara.

APPENDIX 2.B.: CONCORDIA DEACONESS CONFERENCE—LUTHERAN CHURCH-MISSOURI SYNOD DRAFT CONSTITUTION ADOPTED JANUARY 12, 1980

CONCORDIA DEACOENSS CONFERENCE CONSTITUTION

Article 1 The name of the organization is Concordia Deaconess Conference—Lutheran Church-Missouri Synod. The organization is an ecclesiastical organization operating for church purposes only and not for profit.

Article 2 The objectives of Concordia Deaconess Conference are:

1. To give all glory to God.

2. To extend the Kingdom of God.

3. To aid the Synod, specifically in upholding and promoting the Deaconess ministry within the Synod.

4. To provide opportunity for spiritual, personal, and professional growth and fellowship for those who are Deaconesses in the LCMS.

Article 3 The Conference is a free association of consecrated Deaconesses who hold membership in a congregation of the Lutheran Church-Missouri Synod and who subscribe to and live by the confessional position of the LC-MS. Membership into the Conference is contingent upon holding membership in no other Deaconess conference.

1. Voting Membership

Voting Membership is held by those who are consecrated Deaconesses, regularly called or appointed to serve in a parish or agency of the LC-MS, and whose first position ordinarily was obtained by placement by the Council of Presidents of the Lutheran Church-Missouri Synod.

2. Associate Membership

Associate Membership is held by those who meet the criteria of Paragraph #1, but are not presently employed as a Deaconess in an LC-MS parish or agency. Associate members do not have the privileges of voting or holding office.

3. Retired Membership

Retired Membership is held by consecrated Deaconesses who meet the criteria of Paragraph #1, but have retired from active service in an LC-MS parish or agency. Retired members have voting privileges but cannot hold office.

Article 4 The Conference has the following officers.

1. President 2. Vice-President 3. Secretary 4. Treasurer

Article 5 The Spiritual Counselor will be a pastor of the LC-MS and will be selected by the Conference annually.

Article 6 The Conference has the following committees.

1. Executive Committee

2. Membership Committee

3. Spiritual and Professional Growth Committee

Article 7 The conference will meet annually and at other times as called by the membership.

Article 8 Amendments to the constitution will be made only at the annual meeting and must be published and circulated to the membership at least 60 days prior to that meeting. Amendments will be passed by a 2/3 majority of those present.

APPENDIX 2.C.: CONSTITUTION AND BY-LAWS ADOPTED AND SIGNED BY CDC FOUNDING MEMBERS ON JUNE 7, 1980

Concordia Deaconess Conference—Lutheran Church-Missouri Synod
CONSTITUTION

Article 1 The name of the organization is Concordia Deaconess Conference— Lutheran Church-Missouri Synod. The organization is an ecclesiastical organization operating for church purposes only and not-for-profit.

Article 2 The objectives of Concordia Deaconess Conference are:

    1. To give all glory to God.

    2. To extend the Kingdom of God.

    3. To aid the Synod, specifically in upholding and promoting deaconess service within the Synod.

    4. To provide opportunity for spiritual, professional and personal growth and fellowship for those who are deaconesses in the Lutheran Church-Missouri Synod.

Article 3 The Conference is a free association of consecrated deaconesses who hold membership in a congregation of the Lutheran Church-Missouri Synod and who subscribe to and live by the confessional position of the Lutheran Church-Missouri Synod. Membership in the Conference is contingent upon holding membership in no other deaconess conference.

    1. Voting Membership is held by those who are consecrated deaconesses, regularly called or appointed to serve in a parish or agency of the Lutheran Church-Missouri Synod, and whose first position ordinarily was obtained by placement by the Council of Presidents of the Lutheran Church-Missouri Synod.

    2. Associate Membership is held by those who meet the criteria of voting membership, but are not presently employed as a deaconess in a Lutheran Church-Missouri Synod parish or agency. Associate members do not have the privileges of voting or holding office.

    3. Emeritus Membership is held by consecrated deaconesses who meet the criteria of voting membership but have retired from active service in the Lutheran Church-Missouri Synod parish or agency. Retired members have voting privileges but cannot hold office.

Article 4 The Conference has the following officers.

    1. President

    2. Vice-President

3. Secretary

4. Treasurer

Article 5 The Spiritual Counselor will be a pastor of the Lutheran Church-Missouri Synod and will be elected by the conference annually.

Article 6 The Conference has the following regular committees.

1. Executive Committee

2. Membership Committee

3. Spiritual and Professional Growth Committee

Article 7 The conference will hold regular meetings of the membership. The conference will meet at least once a year.

Article 8 Amendments to the constitution will be presented to the membership at a regular meeting of the membership. Notice of the meeting and proposed constitutional changes shall be sent to the membership sixty days prior to the scheduled meeting. A two-thirds majority vote of those present will amend the constitution.

Concordia Deaconess Conference - Lutheran Church-Missouri Synod

BY-LAWS

I. Duties of the Officers

A. President

1. Shall preside at all meetings of the conference and executive committee.

2. Shall appoint members of committees and appointed officers.

3. Shall be ex-officio member of all committees except nominating.

4. Shall receive and approve all expense vouchers.

5. Shall assume leadership of the conference and represent the conference in matters of synodical status.

6. Shall report to the conference and executive committee.

B. Vice-President

1. Shall serve as assistant to the president and perform the duties of the office in absence of the president.

2. Shall serve as chairman of the Spiritual and Professional Growth Committee.

3. Shall edit the conference newsletter.

C. Secretary

1. Shall keep a report of the proceedings of all meetings of the conference and executive committee.

2. Shall serve as chairman of the Membership Committee.

3. Shall keep a current membership list and mailing list.

4. Shall notify members of meetings and other information necessary.

5. Shall conduct correspondence on behalf of the conference.

D. Treasurer

1. Shall receive and deposit all monies received by the conference.

2. Shall keep itemized accounts of all receipts and disbursements.

3. Shall make all authorized payments.

4. Shall submit all financial reports.

5. Shall submit records for annual audit.

II Appointed Officers

A. Historian

B. Parliamentarian

C. Public Relations Coordinator

III Elections

A. Terms of office shall be two years with president and secretary elected in the odd years and vice-president and treasurer elected in the even years.

B. Each officer shall serve until her successor is elected. She may succeed herself to the same office for one additional term.

C. Elections will be held at a regular meeting of the membership. Notice of the meeting and a slate of candidates shall be sent to the membership sixty days prior to the scheduled election.

D. A majority vote of those present shall constitute an election.

IV Committees

A. Executive Committee

1. Shall consist of elected officers and two executive committee members. The Spiritual Counselor and Director of the Deaconess Program shall serve on the executive committee as advisory members.

2. Executive Committee members shall be elected for two-year terms, one elected in the odd year and the other in the even. They shall not be eligible for re-election.

3. Shall meet at the call of the president.

4. Shall have the responsibility to carry out all valid resolutions passed by the conference.

5. Shall accept new members and yearly review eligibility status of all members.

B. Membership Committee

    1. Shall review credentials of prospective members and recommend applicants to the executive committee.

    2. Shall review the status of members yearly and give a report to the executive committee.

    3. Shall contact members who have not been active and encourage their participation.

    4. Shall be made up of three members, one being the secretary of the conference who will serve as chairman of this committee.

C. Spiritual and Professional Growth Committee

    1. Shall arrange for spiritual and professional growth programs at the request of the executive committee.

    2. Shall assist the vice-president in preparing the conference newsletter.

    3. Shall be made up of three members, one being the vice-president of the conference who will serve as Chairman of this committee.

V. Conference Activities

    A. Shall elect officers as required by the Constitution.

    B. Shall amend the constitution and by-laws of the conference.

    C. Shall adopt official deaconess conference pin, patch, motto and other logo to identify the conference.

    D. Shall pass resolutions designed to further the expansion of the objectives of the conference.

    E. Shall adopt an annual budget and set dues.

VI. Amendments

Amendments to the By-laws will be presented to the membership at a regular meeting of the membership. A majority vote of those present shall constitute a change in by-laws.

Appendix 2.D.: "A Chronological Account of the Sequence of Events of the Investigation of Concordia Seminary, Saint Louis," as found with the "Minutes of the LCMS BHE," May 4–5, 1973. (CHI, St. Louis) April 20, 1970

In a letter to the Board of Control of Concordia Seminary, Saint Louis, Doctor J. A. O. Preus announced that he had decided to appoint a Fact Finding Committee.

April 29, 1970

Commission on Constitutional Matters agreed that the Synodical president was acting within his constitutional rights and responsibilities in appointing a Fact Finding Committee.

May 14, 1970

Doctor Tietjen released the public statement that he welcomed the inquiry on two grounds: a) "First, it will demonstrate how truly Lutheran we are, and b) "It will help our church clarify what it really means to be Lutheran." Doctor Tietjen also stated on May 14, 1970: "I regret that Doctor Preus has chosen to dignify the accusations of the Seminary by conducting an investigation. The Constitution and Bylaws of our church body provide adequate procedures for those who have questions to raise or charges to make. An inquiry by the President of the Synod is not at all necessary."

May 15, 1970

As a result of a conversation with Doctor John H. Tietjen, President Preus stated that he would attempt to carry out the contemplated interviews, not through a fact finding committee, but personally with the help of the vice-president and other resource people.

July 6, 1970

President Preus met with the president and vice-president of the seminary, President Scherer of the Missouri District, the Secretary of the Synod, and five professors serving as department chairmen of the Seminary. The purpose was to discuss the ground rules for the planned inquiry.

September 9, 1970

President Preus wrote the Board of Control of Concordia Seminary that he was abandoning the plan to carry out the investigation personally and that "in the interest of objectivity and fairness he was reverting to the procedure he had originally proposed, namely, appointing a committee to handle the work."

September 22, 1970

The Board of Control of Concordia Seminary concurred with the decision of the Synodical president that there should be a fact-finding investigation of Concordia Seminary. However, it was the board's opinion that the Board of Control itself should conduct the investigation for the Synodical president. An invitation was extended to President Preus to meet with the Board of Control on October 19, 1970.

October 2, 1970

The Fact Finding Committee itself had its initial meeting with President Tietjen at which time it discussed ground rules for the interviews with the faculty members.

October 19, 1970

President Preus met with the Board of Control of Concordia Seminary to discuss the proposed inquiry. As a result of this meeting the board resolved: "In response to the decision by President Preus that the Fact Finding Committee inquire into the doctrine and life of Concordia Seminary, the board of control stand ready to cooperate with the special committee which the president of the Synod has appointed to function in his behalf. The board then added five concerns which it had relative to the fact-finding process and the manner in which it should be carried out.

October 23, 1970

President Preus addressed a letter to the Board of Control agreeing with the greater part of its recommendations relative to the manner in which the Fact Finding Committee should function.

November 3, 1970

The faculty of Concordia Seminary published a DECLARATION reaffirming their ordination vows and seeking to "reassure the members of the Synod concerning the confessional position of the faculty." This was accompanied by a minority statement of explanation signed by five faculty members: "We are convinced that there are basic theological differences within the faculty including matters pertaining both to the interpretation of Holy Scriptures and to the meaning of confessional subscription in the Lutheran Church. In the present context we believe that the DECLARATION, by its failure to call attention to the existences of such differences, will be seriously misunderstood by our Synod."

November 12, 1970

The Fact Finding Committee met with President Tietjen and three faculty representatives to continue the discussion of the procedures. It was agreed to interview professors for a period of approximately one hour and 45 minutes to two hours with the interview to be taped and a transcript to be furnished to the president of the Seminary (who was to be present at all interviews), the professor interviewed, and the members of the committee. The president of the Seminary also recorded the interviews and furnished the professor a tape recording. It was furthermore agreed that each professor could bring along a friend or counsel as he desired.

December 11, 1970-March 6, 1971

The Fact Finding Committee interviewed faculty members.

November 19-20, 1971

Interviews were held with four professors who were on leave at the time of the Fact Finding Committee activity.

June 15, 1971

The Fact Finding Committee submitted its report to the Synodical president.

June, 1971

"Upon receipt of the Fact Finding Committee report in 1971, the Synodical president immediately transmitted it to President Tietjen and to the members of the Board of Control."

July 9-16, 1971

At the Milwaukee Convention there was considerable discussion in the floor committee on theological matters and in the convention sessions concerning the timing of the release of the Fact Finding Committee report to the Synod. It was agreed, however, that it was necessary to give the Board of Control opportunity to review the report and to take action if that seemed desirable. Accordingly, the Synod adopted Resolution 2-28:

Whereas, The president of the Synod has submitted the report of the Fact Finding Committee to the Board of Control of Concordia Seminary, Saint Louis, and

Whereas, the Synod is desirous that a conclusion be brought about by the Holy Spirit under the Word of God, therefore be it;

Resolved, That the Synod direct the Board of Control to take appropriate action on the basis of the report, commending or correcting where necessary, and be it further:

Resolved, That the Board of Control report progress directly to the President of the Synod and the Board for Higher Education; and be it finally

Resolved, That the president of the Synod report to the Synod on the progress of the Board of Control within one year.

September 29, 1971

The synodical president and the chairman of the Fact Finding Committee met with the Board of Control and gave them an opportunity to ask questions concerning the report.

October, 1971

The Board of Control began its interviews with the faculty members of Concordia Seminary.

March 3, 1972

President Preus issued a pastoral letter to the members of the Lutheran Church-Missouri Synod: congregations, pastors, and teachers. This dealt with the situation involving the reappointment of professor Arlis Ehlen. In the same letter Doctor Preus explained his reasons for issuing A STATEMENT OF SCRIPTURAL AND CONFESSIONAL PRINCIPLES. He noted that the document was not intended to be "a new standard of orthodoxy," but rather a set of guidelines for the Board of Control and for the Synod to use to identify theological and doctrinal issues which the Synod needs to consider and resolve.

May 17, 1972

The synodical president met with the faculty of Concordia Seminary, Saint Louis, to present to them a list of thirteen theological and doctrinal concerns which issued from the data given in the Fact Finding Committee report.

June 22, 1972

The Board of Control submitted its report concerning the Fact Finding Committee report and its activities relative to it: "Progress Report of the Board of Control of Concordia Seminary, Saint Louis, Missouri, to the President of the Synod and to the Board for Higher Education in Response to the Directive of the Synod in Milwaukee Convention Resolution 2-28."

September 1, 1972

Upon receipt of the above mentioned report Doctor Preus issued his "Report of the Synodical President to The Lutheran Church-Missouri Synod."

September 8, 1972

Doctor Tietjen issued a report: "Fact Finding or Fault Finding? An Analysis of President J. A. O. Preus' Investigation of Concordia Seminary."

September 16, 1972

President Preus met with the Board for Higher Education and discussed the recently distributed "Report of the Synodical President to The Lutheran Church-Missouri Synod in Compliance with Resolution 2-28." At the invitation of the Board for Higher Education President Tietjen met with the board and responded to the invitation to speak as he saw the situation at Concordia Seminary, Saint Louis, and in The Lutheran Church-Missouri Synod.

November 11, 1972

Prior to the meeting the chairman and the executive secretary discussed the feasibility of inviting a knowledgeable individual to attend the Board for Higher Education meeting and to summarize for the board the following documents: a) Report of the synodical president b) Fact Finding or Fault Finding. Doctor John W. Klotz, Academic Dean, Concordia Senior College, Fort Wayne, accepted the invitation and responsibility for such a presentation. A period of two and one-half hours was devoted to this summarization.

February 19, 1973

The Board of Control of Concordia Seminary, Saint Louis, adopted a "Report of the Board of Control to the Lutheran Church-Missouri Synod, the President of the Synod, and the Board for Higher Education on Action Taken in Response to the Directive of the Synod in Milwaukee Convention." The Board of Control also submitted this report to the Synod as part of the board's report to the New Orleans synodical convention.

March 9, 1973

Doctor Preus met with the Board for Higher Education and orally discussed the February 20, 1973 "Report of the Board of Control of Concordia Seminary, Saint Louis, re: Resolution 2-28."

March 23, 1973

Doctor Preus mailed the outline and documentation for the material which he presented at the March 9 meeting in Chicago. He requested, "For the time being I am requesting that you keep this matter entirely confidential and among yourselves."

March 31, 1973

The executive committee of the Board for Higher Education augmented by board member Neitzel, and the executive secretary met to formulate procedure plans for the next board meeting.

APPENDICES FOR PART III

CHAPTERS 15–17

APPENDIX 3.A.: OFFICERS OF THE CONCORDIA DEACONESS CONFERENCE—LUTHERAN CHURCH-MISSOURI SYNOD FROM 1980—2009.

APPENDIX 3.B.: SPIRITUAL COUNSELORS FOR CONCORDIA DEACONESS CONFERENCE—LUTHERAN CHURCH-MISSOURI SYNOD FROM 1980–2009

APPENDIX 3.C.: GUIDELINES FOR DISTRIBUTION OF THE DEACONESS CLARA STREHLOW ENDOWMENT FUND, PASSED BY CONCORDIA DEACONESS CONFERENCE—LUTHERAN CHURCH-MISSOURI SYNOD ON APRIL 19, 1986

APPENDIX 3.D.: CONCORDIA DEACONESS CONFERENCE—LUTHERAN CHURCH-MISSOURI SYNOD CODE OF ETHICS

APPENDIX 3.E.: DIRECTORS OF THE LCMS DEACONESS TRAINING PROGRAM AT CONCORDIA COLLEGE, RIVER FOREST, ILLINOIS, AND THEIR ASSISTANTS

APPENDIX 3.F.: GRADUATES OF THE LCMS DEACONESS TRAINING PROGRAM AT CONCORDIA COLLEGE/UNIVERSITY IN RIVER FOREST, ILLINOIS, 1983–2008

APPENDIX 3.G.: RITE FOR "COMMISSIONING AND INSTALLATION OF ONE CALLED TO THE MINISTRY OF DEACONESS IN THE CHURCH."

APPENDIX 3.H.: DIRECTORS OF THE LCMS DEACONESS TRAINING PROGRAM AT CONCORDIA SEMINARY, ST. LOUIS, MISSOURI, AND THEIR ASSISTANTS

APPENDIX 3.I.: GRADUATES OF THE LCMS DEACONESS TRAINING PROGRAM AT CONCORDIA SEMINARY IN ST. LOUIS, MISSOURI, 2004–2008

APPENDIX 3.J.: DIRECTORS OF THE LCMS DEACONESS TRAINING PROGRAM AT CONCORDIA THEOLOGICAL SEMINARY, FORT WAYNE, AND THEIR ASSISTANTS

APPENDIX 3.K.: GRADUATES OF THE LCMS DEACONESS TRAINING PROGRAM AT CONCORDIA THEOLOGICAL SEMINARY IN FORT WAYNE, INDIANA, 2006–2008

APPENDIX 3.A.: OFFICERS OF THE CONCORDIA DEACONESS CONFERENCE—
LUTHERAN CHURCH-MISSOURI SYNOD FROM 1980—2009.

Presidents
Deaconess Ruth (nee Broermann) Stallmann, 1980–82
Deaconess Joyce Ostermann, 1982–87
Deaconess Kristin (nee Hannenberg) Wassilak, 1987–90
Deaconess Karen Kosberg (Aumick), 1990–92[1]
Deaconess Cathy Fanslau, 1992–93
Deaconess Lauren (nee Morgan) Olsen, 1993–94
Deaconess Sara (nee Bauman) Nordling, 1994–96
Deaconess Jeanne Dicke, 1996–2000
Deaconess Joyce Ostermann, 2000–04
Deaconess Grace Rao, 2004–06
Deaconess Pamela (nee Reagin) Nielsen, 2006–

Vice–Presidents
Deaconess Joyce Ostermann, 1980–82
Deaconess Ruth (nee Broermann) Stallmann, 1982–83
Deaconess Jennifer Haney, 1984–87
Deaconess Karen Aumick, 1987–90
Deaconess Lauren (nee Morgan) Olsen, 1990-93
Deaconess Crystal van Dyke, 1993–97
Deaconess Faith (nee Feltz) Marburger, 1997–2001
Deaconess Angie Reitmeier, 2001–03
Deaconess Linda Meyer, 2003–2005
Deaconess Linda Nobili, 2005–2007
Deaconess Deborah Rockrohr, 2007–

Secretaries
Deaconess Nancy Nicol (Nemoyer), 1980[2]
Deaconess Kay Pritzlaff (Gudgeon), 1980–84
Deaconess Faith (nee Feltz) Marburger, 1984–88
Deaconess Susanne (nee Hanke) Smith, 1988–90
Deaconess Darla Schmidt, 1990–92
Deaconess Susanne (nee Hanke) Smith, 1992–94
Deaconess Julie Hadler, 1994–96
Deaconess Sarah Gaffney, 1996–98
Deaconess Joyce Ostermann, 1998–2000
Deaconess Jeanna Moe, 2000–02
Deaconess Julie Heck, 2002–06
Deaconess Lauren (nee Morgan) Olsen, 2006
Deaconess Cheryl D. Naumann, 2006–

Treasurers
Deaconess Luella Mickley, 1980–86

---

[1] Kristin Wassilak resigned as President of CDC when she became Director of the River Forest Deaconess Program in 1990. Vice President Karen Kosberg (Aumick) served as Acting President from 1990 to 1992.

[2] Nancy Nicol resigned as Secretary of CDC when she became Director of the River Forest Deaconess Program in 1980.

Deaconess Laura Budzynski, 1986
Deaconess Jeanna Moe, 1986–95
Deaconess Linda Meyer, 1995–97
Deaconess Angie Reitmeier, 1997–99
Deaconess Laura Budzynski, 1999–2001
Deaconess Jeanne Dicke, 2001–2003
Deaconess Jenny Wendling, 2003–2005
Deaconess Linda Meyer, 2005
Deaconess Suzanne Fingerle, 2005–2007
Deaconess Carol (nee Olday) Schroeder, 2007–

Other "Members-at-Large" Board Members between 1980–2009

Deaconesses Claire (nee Krans) Neagley, Betty Mulholland, Jean Bright, Cathy Fanslau, Joyce Ostermann, Sara Nordling, Cathi Wurster, Jeanne Dicke, Rosemary Williams, Sarah Gaffney, Margaret Christiansen, Michelle Gallmeier, Beth Niermann, Pamela Nielsen, Ruth Drum, Grace Rao, Brenna Nunes, Patty Kristofic, Cheryl D. Naumann, Lauren Olsen, Ruth McDonnell, Renée Young, Linda Cosgrove.

APPENDIX 3.B.: SPIRITUAL COUNSELORS FOR CONCORDIA DEACONESS CONFERENCE—LUTHERAN CHURCH-MISSOURI SYNOD FROM 1980–2009

Rev. Dr. Paul A. Zimmerman, 1980–84
Rev. Osmar Otto Lehenbauer, 1985–86
Position vacant, 1987
Rev. Paul B. Dancy, 1988–93
Rev. Jeffrey Todd Meyers, 1993–99
Rev. Mark Hill, 1999–2002
Rev. Dr. Michael Eschelbach, 2002–06
Rev. John M. Berg, 2007–

APPENDIX 3.C.: GUIDELINES FOR DISTRIBUTION OF THE DEACONESS CLARA STREHLOW ENDOWMENT FUND, PASSED BY CONCORDIA DEACONESS CONFERENCE—LUTHERAN CHURCH-MISSOURI SYNOD ON APRIL 19, 1986

I. Restrictions

    A. To deaconess students, Concordia College, River Forest, only.

    B. Must have a 2.5 in Theology.

    C. Distribution first to all colloquy students enrolled in the deaconess program (not applicable during internship).

    D.   Distribution secondly based on need in this order of priority

        1. Senior

        2. Junior

II. Disbursement

    A.   Awarded in the fall of each year

B. From the interest only. Principal continues to grow from contributions.

C. In the amount of $200 each (that amount to be re-evaluated by the Concordia Deaconess Conference every 3 years, 1989, 1992, 1995, 1998, etc.)

Summary: The Deaconess Clara Strehlow Endowment Fund, established by the Concordia Deaconess Conference, encourages education for faithful deaconess service to the Church. The principal amount will continue to grow through the contributions of those who support this goal. The interest only will be awarded each fall as scholarship grants of $200 to each deaconess colloquy student, then as available to senior and then junior deaconess students according to need. Only deaconess students with a GPA of 2.5 or higher in Theology are eligible. This will be administered through the financial aid office, Concordia College, River Forest.

APPENDIX 3.D.: CONCORDIA DEACONESS CONFERENCE—LUTHERAN CHURCH-MISSOURI SYNOD *CODE OF ETHICS*

Purpose

The Concordia Deaconess Conference (CDC), affirming its desire to glorify the Triune God—Father, Son, and Holy Spirit—and to reflect His love and grace in Christ, establishes this Code of Ethics. The Code, rooted in Holy Scripture and the Confessions, is intended to establish clear standards and definitions for the professional behavior and practices of its members. This Code of Ethics expresses the Concordia Deaconess Conference's unity of belief and outlines members' responsibilities and obligations to God, to the church, to colleagues and to each individual who is to be served. The Code serves the conference as a mirror, rule and curb, and is intended to teach, strengthen and affirm its members.

Preamble to the Code of Ethics

The primary mission of the CDC is to support deaconesses as they bring Christ's caring presence, love, and perspective to others. A deaconess points to Christ, who is present in Word and Sacrament, provided by the Office of the Public Ministry.

Biblical history and the tradition of the LC-MS have shaped CDC's Code of Ethics. Diaconal service is mentioned in the New Testament, as in the case of Phoebe, a deaconess of the church at Cenchrea (Romans 16:1). Throughout subsequent centuries, interest in formal diaconates flourished and waned. Following a revival of diaconal ministry in nineteenth-century Europe, German Lutherans brought their vision of diaconal service to the United States. In 1919, the Lutheran Deaconess Association within the Synodical Conference was established, and in 1934, the Lutheran Deaconess Conference was founded. Changes within these two groups prompted nine deaconesses to establish the CDC in 1980, after the LC-MS voted to establish its own deaconess training program in 1979.

Members of the CDC support the Office of the Public Ministry and serve in an auxiliary office. Commissioned by the church, a deaconess provides diaconal service with emphasis on spiritual care, teaching the youth, and works of mercy. In this way Christ's own peace, hope and mercy are conveyed to those in need. A Deaconess may be called to serve in the parish, in institutional settings, or in foreign and domestic missions.

The following statements are an expression of these principles regarding the professional conduct of a deaconess.

Theological Ethics

In her promises made at commissioning, a deaconess commits herself to serve in accordance with the Word of God, the Ecumenical Creeds, and the Confessions of the Church. Therefore, a deaconess of the CDC is a woman who:

1. Believes, teaches, and confesses the Scriptures as the infallible and inerrant Word of God and the Lutheran Confessions as a true exposition of that Word.

2. Points others to Word and Sacrament provided by the Office of the Public Ministry.

A. Upholds the deaconess office as auxiliary to the Office of the Public Ministry which it supports and assists.

B. Refrains from performing the distinctive roles of the Office of the Public Ministry: public preaching of the Word, administering the Sacraments, and exercising the Office of the Keys.

3. Maintains a life rooted in Word and Sacrament through worship, confession and absolution, study and prayer.

4. Is a communicant member in good standing in an LC-MS congregation or partner church.

Professional Ethics

By the grace of God a deaconess is committed to grow in love for those she serves, to strive for excellence in her skills, and to adorn the Gospel with a godly life (John 13). In accord with the promises made at her commissioning, a deaconess of the CDC shall strive to:

1. Aptly express the faith in word and deed.

2. Properly apply the distinction between Law and Gospel in her caregiving and teaching.

3. Continue education in the Scriptures and theology.

4. Continue education that is necessary to provide excellent service in her setting.

5. Demonstrate a servant attitude, e.g., loving, compassionate, hospitable, selfless, sincere, humble, respectful, approachable, encouraging, nurturing.

6. Maintain standards of professional integrity, e.g., uses appropriate language, speaks the truth in love, is trustworthy, manages time well, fulfills responsibilities, works diligently, and resolves conflict according to Biblical principles. A deaconess respects the work of her colleagues, speaks the truth in love, and uses appropriate channels to express differences.

7. Maintain confidentiality, except in cases where immediate danger is perceived or safety becomes an issue.

8. Maintain government standards as they apply to her position; i.e., mandatory reporting, privacy and confidentiality laws.

9. Seek opportunities to extend the Church's hand of mercy to the household of faith and the community.

10. Exercise servant leadership without prejudice or favoritism.

11. Uphold the sanctity of human life from conception to death.

12. Demonstrate competency in her areas of responsibility; i.e., youth, music, education, care-giving, developmental disabilities.

13. Make use of allotted time for vacation and time off, maintaining healthy limits and boundaries for personal and family life.

14. Be devoted to the well-being of others: physically, spiritually, and emotionally.

15. Remain within her competence in counseling situations and refer to other professionals when needed.

16. Strive to avoid overlapping relationships that result in the impairment of professional discretion and impartial judgment.

17. Maintain appropriate sexual boundaries.

18. Limit sexual intimacy to heterosexual marriage as instituted by God.

19. Neither accept nor offer gifts that involve expectations that would extend, curtail or alter the service offered.

20. Encourage and uplift sister deaconesses.

21. Demonstrate commitment to her professional organizations, including the CDC.

22. Be aware of warning signs in her own behavior and mood and seek help to address these needs.

APPENDIX 3.E.: DIRECTORS OF THE LCMS DEACONESS TRAINING PROGRAM AT CONCORDIA COLLEGE, RIVER FOREST AND THEIR ASSISTANTS

Directors of the Deaconess Program
Deaconess Nancy Eileen (nee Nicol) Nemoyer, 1980–1990
Deaconess Kristin Renee (nee Hannenberg) Wassilak, 1990–2005
Deaconess Jennie Joleen Waters, 2005–

Assistant Director of the Deaconess Program
Deaconess Lauren Morgan, 1988–90

Student Assistant to the Director of the Deaconess Program
Miss (later Deaconess) Darla Schmidt, 1983–85[3]

Senior (Student) Assistants
Kristin Hannenberg (Wassilak) 1985–86; Carol Olday 1986–87; Meg Montagne 1987–88; Linda Heintz 1988–89; Kathy Bjorklund 1989–90, Mary Bartel 1990–91; Joy Sievers and Kari Olson 1991–92; Kari Olson 1992–93; Krista Noack 1993–94; Renee Wunder 1994–95; Claudia Loehrke and Natalie Watt 1995–96; Sally Kloppe 1996–97; Jenny Wendling 1997–98; Heidi Weirich 1998–99; Melissa Owens 1999–2000; Chandlebray Hein 2000–01; Kelli Lange 2001–02; Marta Kukal 2002–04; Kristen Cecil (Graduate Assistant) 1999–2000; Deanna Cheadle (Graduate Assistant) 2001–04; Sarah Schultz (Graduate Assistant) 2006-07; Carrie Gregory (Graduate Assistant) (2007-08); Deaconess Intern Sarah Schultz (2007-08).

Field Work Coordinators
Deaconess Lori Wilbert, 1985–87
Deaconess Cathy Fanslau, 1987–88
Deaconess Margaret Christiansen, 1993–94

Internship Coordinators
Deaconess Joyce Ostermann, 1985–87
Deaconess Pamela Nielsen, 1987–88
Deaconess Karen (Aumick) Kosberg, 1988–93
Deaconess Linda Meyer, 1993–2003
Deaconess Gloria Roggow, 2003–2004
Deaconess Kristin Wassilak, assisted by Deaconesses Rachel Kennell, Patricia Kristofic, Rogene Lis, Cheryl D. Naumann, and Erna Schmid, 2004–2005
Deaconess Kristin Wassilak, 2005–

Supplemental Instructors for Deaconess Work classes 1980–2008
Deaconesses Carol Goldfish, Betty Mulholland, Nancy Nemoyer, Pamela (nee Reagin) Nielsen, Jennie Waters, Theresa List, Gloria Roggow, Kristin Wassilak

APPENDIX 3.F.: GRADUATES OF THE LCMS DEACONESS TRAINING PROGRAM AT CONCORDIA COLLEGE/UNIVERSITY IN RIVER FOREST, FROM 1983–2008

1983
Irene Campbell, Cathy Collins, Darcy Ewald, Bonnie Niermann, Carolyn Ranker, Kris Blackwell

1984

---

[3] Darla Schmidt agreed to a proposal from Director Nicol, to spread her senior over two years in order to work part time for the program.

Karen Aumick, Jean Bright, Cheryl Gruenwald, Jennifer Haney, Brenda Heling, Pamela Kruse, Myrna Larsen, Jeana Moe, Lydia Scharnitzke, Lori Wilbert
1985
Sara Bauman, Laura Herman, Stephanie Madson, Pamela Reagin, Deborah Roth, Darla Schmidt
1986
Cathy Fanslau, Susanne Hanke, Kristin Hannenberg, Eunice Jaech, Carole King, Sue Lunog
1987
Monica Eickmeyer, Lori Burton, Annette Surak, Donna Gage, Michelle Gentzen, Lauren Morgan, Kathie Oakes
1988
Jane (nee Cole) Loza, Margaret Montagne
1989
Gail Fountain, Judith Hoehne, Linda Heintz, Carol Olday, Esther Venske, Cathi Wurster
1990
Peggy Backs, Julie (nee Mayer) Hadler, Linda Meyer, Christie Nelson, Elizabeth Niermann, Crystal van Dyke
1991
Julie (nee Hilligoss) Ruecker, Carla Olbeter, Elena Joy Sasieta, Rosemary Williams
1992
Kate Behm, Kathy Bjorklund, Erna (nee Baehr) Schmid, Doris (nee Wilaby) Timmer
1993
Margaret Christiansen, Sarah (nee Utecht) Gaffney, Michelle Gallmeier, Kathleen (nee Ringler) Lock, Sarah Nack, Jennie Waters
1994
Mary (nee Bartel) Laesch, Cathi Clark, Angeline Reitmeier, Theresa (nee Rupholdt) List, Bonnie Voss
1995
Martha Marquardt, Kari Olson, Jessie Perez (C),[4] Teresita Rodriguez (C), Irma Rojas (C), Renee Wunder
1996
Carol Goldfish (C), Judy Pfotenhauer (C), Diane Philipp (C)
1997
Mary Anne Casault (C), Mary Cesar, Ruth Drum (C), Judy Evangelista, Suzanne Fingerle (C), Patricia O'Dell, Elizabeth Posey (C), Karla Remmele
1998
Holly Flandermeyer, Julie Heck, Linda Hoke, Claudia Loehrke, Sharon Teague, Natalie Watt

---

[4] (C) indicates deaconess training via the synodically established Colloquy program. See Chapter Sixteen.

1999

Kimberly Barnett, Gianna (nee Hoem) Bessert, Rita Footh (C), Kristin (nee Geske) Meyer (C), Sunny Kan

2000

Margaret Anderson (C), Kelly Hardt (C), Barbara Herzinger (C), Sally Kloppe, Gretchen (nee Tolliver) Krueger, Cathy Meyer (C), Grace Rao (C), Gloria Roggow (C), Sue Simmons (C), Donna Vogt, Jennifer Wendling

2001

Mary Barney (C), Ruth Ann Endicott (C), Heidi (Weirich) Goehman, Cheryl Hart (C), Sylvia Johnson (C), Rachel Kennell, Patricia Kristofic (C), Kristen (Cecil) Lutjens (C), Linda Nobili (C), Brenna Nunes (C), Sara Perez-Arche (C), Nicole Tucker, Angelia (nee Wiley) Armstrong

2002

Marlene Anderson (C), Lauren (nee Dorr) Braaten, Kim Bueltmann, Grace Forsyth (C), Jeri Morrison, Norma Neuhart, Linda Seward (C), Genevieve (nee Tracy) Wagner, Tressa Weyer

2003

Emily Carder, Christina Cummings (C), Juanita Ebert (C), Katherine Lottes Einspahr (C), Loraine Rathman (C)

2004

Melissa (nee Owens) Amendt, Sarah (nee Palmer) Baughman, Mary Hess, Chandlebray (nee Hein) Hopfensperger, Kelli (Lange) Kramer, Rogene Lis (C), Cheryl D. Naumann (C)

2005

Deanna Cheadle (C), Mireya (nee Alvarez) Johnson (C), Katie Keller, Marta (nee Kukal) Naumann, , Doreen Scheuerman (C), Renée Young (C)

2006

April Bishop, Jana (nee Knight) Peters, Elizabeth Kestner, Susan Leistico, Rahel Musa (NC),[5] Sara Oxley (C), Jennifer Phillips (C), Angela Stangeland, Doris Snashall (C), Frances (nee Owen) Szeto (C), Barbara (nee Worthington) Coffin (C)

2007

Susan Ziegler (Reinhardt) (cert),[6] Heidi Bishop, Sara (nee Pollert) Lemon, Jane (nee Mason) Obersat (C), Elizabeth Borth (C), Nadine (DuBois) Grayl

2008

Erica Bluege, Heather (nee Broge) Orr, Karen Rubel

---

[5] (NC) designates completion of deaconess training under the "New Colloquy guidelines" established in 2004. Regarding deaconess education, this means that "Colloquy" applies only to those women who have completed a non-LCMS deaconess program and desire LCMS certification. Women in the above lists with (C) written after their names from 2004 onward were already part of the old Colloquy program when the new one came into effect.
[6] (cert) indicates completion of deaconess training via the "Post-Baccalaureate Deaconess Certification Program" approved by the University College Policies Committee on April 18, 2005.

APPENDIX 3.G.: RITE FOR "COMMISSIONING AND INSTALLATION OF ONE CALLED TO THE MINISTRY OF DEACONESS IN THE CHURCH." MARKED "FINAL VERSION: 2/20/90"

1. This rite is administered by those so authorized to commission and install, according to the Church's usual order, such candidates as have been certified by the Church to be ready and prepared for and regularly called to the ministry of deaconess.

2. The rite is set within the Divine Service before the Prayer of the Church, or The Prayers. The Propers are those of the Sunday or festival on which the commissioning and installation take place.

3. Ordinarily the pastor of the congregation is the presiding minister. It is appropriate that other pastors serve as assisting ministers, according to local custom and the direction of the presiding minister.

4. Before the service begins, the presiding minister gathers all who will take part in it in some convenient place for the Word of God and prayer. Than all enter the church together, the called going before the assisting ministers, and the presiding minister last of all. **Sit**

5. When the time for the commissioning and installation has come, the candidate presents herself before the altar. The presiding minister, standing before the altar, says:

P   In the name of the Father and of the + Son and of the Holy Spirit.

C   Amen.

6. The minister addresses the congregation:

P   Dear brothers and sisters in Christ, _____ has been called in the Church's usual order to the ministry of deaconess in the Church, a ministry established to strengthen and support the office of the public ministry and its work. She has prepared herself for this ministry by prayer and study. She has been examined and declared ready to undertake this sacred responsibility.

Hear the Word of God concerning this ministry.

7. One or more of the following portions of Holy Scripture are read.

A   I commend to you our sister Phoebe, a servant of the church in Cenchrea. I ask you to receive her in the Lord in a way worthy of the saints and to give her any help she may need from you, for she has been a great help to many people, including me. (Rom. 16:1-2) Above all, love each other deeply, because love covers over a multitude of sins. Offer hospitality to one another without grumbling. Each one should use whatever gift he has received to serve others, faithfully administering God's grace in its various forms. If anyone speaks, he should do it as one speaking the very words of God. If anyone serves, he should do it with the strength God provides, so that in all things God may be praised through Jesus Christ. To Him be the glory and the power for ever and ever. Amen. (I Peter 4:8-11) Jesus called the disciples together and said, "You know that the rulers of the Gentiles lord it over them, and their high officials exercise authority over them. Not so with you. Instead, whoever wants to become great among you must be your servant, and whoever wants to be first must be your slave—just as the Son of Man did not come to be served, but to serve, and to give His life as a ransom for many." (Matt. 20:25-28) Let the word of Christ dwell in you richly as you teach and admonish one another with all wisdom, and as you sing psalms, hymns and spiritual songs with gratitude in your hearts to God. And whatever you do, whether in word or deed, do it all in the name of the Lord Jesus, giving thanks to God the Father through Him. (Col. 3:16-17)

8. The minister asks the candidate:

P   Do you believe the canonical books of the Old and New Testaments to be the inspired Word of God and the only infallible rule of faith and practice?

R   I do.

P   Do you accept the three Ecumenical Creeds, namely, the Apostles', the Nicene, and the Athanasian Creeds, as faithful testimonies to the truth of the Holy Scriptures, and do you reject all errors which they condemn?

R   I do.

P   Do you believe that the Unaltered Augsburg Confession is a true exposition of the Word of God and a correct exhibition of the doctrine of the Evangelical Lutheran Church; that the Apology of the Augsburg Confession, the Small and Large Catechisms of Martin Luther, the Smalcald Articles, the Treatise on the Authority and Primacy of the Pope, and the Formula of Concord--as these are contained in the <u>Book of Concord</u>—are also in agreement with this one scriptural faith?

R   I do.

P   Do you solemnly promise faithfully to serve [continue in serving] God's people as a deaconess in accordance with the Word of God, the Ecumenical Creeds and the Confessions, or Symbols, of the Church?

R   I do.

P   Will you, trusting in God's care, seek to grow in love for those you serve, strive for excellence in your skills, and adorn the Gospel of Jesus Christ with a godly life?

R   I will with the help of God.

9. The minister addresses the congregation:

P   Brothers and sisters in Christ, you have heard the confession and solemn promise of _____ called to serve [continue in serving] the Church. I ask you now, in the presence of God: Will you receive her, show her fitting love and honor, and support her by your gifts and fervent prayer? If so, answer: We will with the help of God.

C   We will with the help of God.

P   The almighty and most merciful God strengthen and assist you always.

10. The minister asks the candidate:

P   Are you ready and willing to assume [continue] the work of this ministry?

R   I am.

11. The candidate kneels. The minister continues:

P   _____, I commission you to the office of deaconess and install you as <u>title of position</u> in [at] <u>place</u>, in the name of the Father and of the + Son and of the Holy Spirit.

R   Amen.

Stand

12. The following Prayers are said.

P   Let us pray.

Gracious and most merciful Lord, we thank You for providing faithful women in Your
Church to assist and support the office and work of the public ministry among us. Grant
Your blessing to those called to the office of deaconess that by their labors Your people may
be sustained and built up in the saving faith; through Jesus Christ, Your Son, our Lord.

C   Amen.

P   Almighty God, the fountain and source of all wisdom, we thank You for hearing
our prayers and leading _____ to accept our call. Grant to her Your Holy Spirit and
adorn her with wisdom and power from on high. Incline both young and old to godliness
and obedience, and let them so profit by instruction in Your holy Word that they may serve
You all their days and finally obtain eternal life; through Jesus Christ, our Lord, who lives
and reigns with You and the Holy Spirit, one God, now and forever.

C   Amen. Our Father who art in heaven, hallowed be Thy name ...

13. The minister dismisses and blesses the newly commissioned and installed.

P   Go then in peace and joy. The almighty and most merciful God, the Father, the +
Son, and the Holy Spirit, go with you, bless and strengthen you for faithful service in His
name.

C   Amen.

14. The newly commissioned and installed rises and is welcomed and greeted in the name of the Lord by the
minister and fellow workers:

         Peace be with you.

R   Peace be with you.

15. All return to their places. The service continues with the Prayer of the Church, or The Prayers.

NOTES: Preparation for the Rite

         A chair is provided near the chancel for the seating of the one to be commissioned and installed.

APPENDIX 3.H.: DIRECTORS OF THE LCMS DEACONESS TRAINING PROGRAM AT
CONCORDIA SEMINARY, ST. LOUIS, MISSOURI, AND THEIR ASSISTANTS

Dean of the Graduate School (including Diaconal Studies)
Dr. James W. Voelz, 2002
Dr. Bruce G. Schuchard, 2002–05
Faculty Director of Deaconess Studies
Dr. Bruce M. Hartung, 2005–
Assistant to the Dean of the Graduate School, for Diaconal Studies
Deaconess Theresa Jo (nee Rupholdt) List, 2002–05
Deaconess Gloria May (nee Saggars) DeCuir, 2004– [7]
Assistant Director of Deaconess Studies
Deaconess Gloria DeCuir, 2004–

---

[7] Working through the Director of Residential Field Education, Dr. William Utech.

Field Work Coordinators
Deaconess Theresa List, 2002–04
Deaconess Gloria DeCuir, 2004–
Internship Coordinators
Deaconess Theresa List, 2002–04
Deaconess Gloria DeCuir, 2004–05
Dr. Glenn Nielson, 2005–
Supplemental Instructors for Deaconess Work Classes 2002–2008
Doctors Charles P. Arand, Joel D. Biermann, Gerhard H. Bode, Kent Burreson, Louis A. Brighton, Anthony Cook, Timothy P. Dost, Jeffery A. Gibbs, Arthur F. Graudin, Bruce M. Hartung, Jeffrey J. Kloha, Robert A. Kolb, Reed R. Lessing, David M. Lewis, Thomas E. Manteufel, Richard W. Marrs, David R. Maxwell, Glenn A Nielsen, Norman E. Nagel, Joel P. Okamoto, A.R. Victor Raj, Robert Rosin, Henry L. Rowald, Timothy E. Saleska, Leopoldo A. Sanchez, William W. Schumacher, Bryan R. Salminen, James W. Voelz; Quentin F. Wesselschmidt; Professor William W. Carr; Deaconess Candidate Sarah Day; Deaconesses Gloria M. DeCuir, Theresa Jo List, Kristin R. Wassilak, Karen Westbrooks; Kathryn R. Riesmeyer.

APPENDIX 3.I.: GRADUATES OF THE LCMS DEACONESS TRAINING PROGRAM AT CONCORDIA SEMINARY IN ST. LOUIS, MISSOURI, 2004–2008

2004
Gloria M. DeCuir
2005
Sandra J. Bowers, Sarah R. Day
2006
Tonya L. Eza, Maricela Flamenco*, Melissa (nee Hahn) Sindlinger, Rose E. Gilbert (Adle), Tara R. (nee Kaspar) Korsch, Ruth E. McDonnell, Eva N. (nee Morlok) Rickman, Elly Sifuentes*, Gayle G. Truesdell [* training via the Hispanic Institute]
2007
Phaedra (nee Fisher) Serbus, Michele Lieske
2008
Elizabeth (nee Meckler) Ahlman, Luz Guerrero, Ashley (nee Stabb) Hesson, Rachel (nee Lingren) Merrill, Sarah (nee Pierce) Sacco

APPENDIX 3.J.: DIRECTORS OF THE LCMS DEACONESS TRAINING PROGRAM AT CONCORDIA THEOLOGICAL SEMINARY, FORT WAYNE, AND THEIR ASSISTANTS

Director of Deaconess Studies
Dr. Arthur Albert Just Jr., 2003–
Associate Director of Deaconess Studies
Deaconess Rose E. (nee Gilbert) Adle, 2007–2008
Deaconess Rachel D. Thompson, 2008–
Administrative Assistant
Cynthia V. Johnson, 2003–
Assistant Director for Counsel and Nurture
Deaconess Intern Sara M. Bielby, 2004–05

Admission Counselor
Deaconess Intern Deanna Cheadle, 2004–05
Cynthia V. Johnson, 2005–
Field Work Coordinators
Deaconess Intern Sara M. Bielby, 2004–05
Dr. Arthur A. Just Jr., 2003–04; 2005–
Internship Coordinator
Dr. Arthur A. Just Jr., 2003–
Supplemental Instructors for Deaconess Courses 2003–2008
Doctors Arthur Just, Beverly Yahnke, Roger Olsen, Stan Veit, Robert Roethemeyer, Carl Fickenscher, Harold Senkbeil; Deaconess Interns Sara Bielby, Deanna Cheadle; Deaconesses Kristen Wassilak, Betty Mulholland, Jennie Waters, Joyce Ostermann, Mireya Johnson, Cheryl D. Naumann, Pamela Nielson, Brenna Nunes, Grace Rao, Rose E. Gilbert, Rachel D. Thompson; Angie Moellering, Renae Ideboen, Lana Arnold, Carla Waterman, Amy Rast.

APPENDIX 3.K.: GRADUATES OF THE LCMS DEACONESS TRAINING PROGRAM AT CONCORDIA THEOLOGICAL SEMINARY IN FORT WAYNE, INDIANA, 2006–2008

2006
Sara M. Bielby, Linda Cosgrove, Angela Lubbesmeyer, Karoline Nee, Kim Schave
2007
Judith E. Anderson, Nicole Larsen-Mellot, Patricia Nuffer, Julie Ann Raffa
2008
Karen Blank, Nicole Boyle, Christine Buchinger, Melissa DeGroot, Deborah Hanson, Shaina Mitchell, Mary Moerbe, Megan Smith, Rachel D. Thompson

SELECTED BIBLIOGRAPHY

A COMPREHENSIVE BIBLIOGRAPHY AND PHOTOGRAPHS CAN

BE VIEWED AT WWW.DEACONESSHISTORY.ORG

PRIMARY SOURCES[1]

Albers, Edgar H. "Definitive Statements and Statistics, Prepared for The Board of Directors The Lutheran Church—Missouri Synod and Its Board of Higher Education." Fort Wayne: LDA, 1968.

———. *Newsletter.* (Fort Wayne: LDA, June 1968).

Angel, Cecil. "Deaconesses Want Respect in Church Hierarchy." *Fort Wayne News-Sentinel,* June 7, 1986.

"Articles of Association of the Lutheran Deaconess Association of the Evangelical-Lutheran Synodical Conference of North America." January 31, 1920.

Assignment of Calls File. Concordia Historical Institute, St. Louis, MO.

Associated Lutheran Charities File. Concordia Historical Institute, St. Louis, MO.

Baepler, Richard. *Flame of Faith, Lamp of Learning: A History of Valparaiso University.* St. Louis: Concordia, 2001.

———. "John Strietelmeier: Called to the 'Holy Laity.'" *Concordia Historical Institute Quarterly* Vol. 78, no. 4 (Winter 2005).

Baepler, Walter A. *A Century of Grace: A History of the Missouri Synod, 1847–1947.* St. Louis: Concordia, 1947.

"Be merciful, even as your Father is merciful." Deaconess Studies, Concordia Theological Seminary, Fort Wayne, IN. June 2006.

Bethesda Messenger 35, no. 2 (March 1944).

Board for Higher Education Minute Books. Concordia Historical Institute, St. Louis, MO.

Board for Professional Education Services File. Concordia Historical Institute, St. Louis, MO.

Board of Directors Collection. Concordia Historical Institute, St. Louis, MO.

---

[1] All bibliographic materials from the private collections of Ruth (nee Broemann) Stallmann, Betty Mulholland, Joyce Ostermann, Cheryl D. Naumann, and Nancy (nee Nicol) Nemoyer will be bequeathed to Concordia Historical Institute, St. Louis, MO, or the Concordia Deaconess Conference Archives. In November 1982, Clara Strehlow gave her private collection to Nancy Nicol for deposit in the Deaconess Office Archives, Concordia College, River Forest, Illinois (now Concordia University, Chicago).

Bohlmann, Ralph A. "From the President." *The Lutheran Witness* 102, no. 9 (September 1983).

Bradfield, Margaret. *The Good Samaritan: The Life and Work of Friedrich von Bodelschwingh.* London: Marshall, Morgan & Scott, 1960.

Braun, Mark E. *A Tale of Two Synods: Events That Led to the Split Between Wisconsin and Missouri.* Milwaukee: Northwestern, 2003.

Braun, Marcus R. "A Layman's Concern About His Church." Address before the Lutheran Laymen's League Zone Rally, St. John's Evangelical Lutheran Church, Clinton, Iowa, May 7, 1967.

Brillinger, Mildred (nee Evenson). Private collection. Noblesville, Indiana.

Buchheimer, L. B. "Highlights in the History of the Female Diaconate." *Concordia Theological Monthly* 21, no. 4 (April 1950).

Caemmerer, Richard R. "Lutheran Social Action." In *The Thirty-seventh Annual Convention of the Associated Lutheran Charities.* Watertown: Jansky Printing, 1938.

————. "The Application of Christian Ethics to Current Social Problems." In *The Forty-third Annual Convention of the Associated Lutheran Charities.* Watertown: Jansky Printing Co., 1946.

Camarena, Pat. "LCMS Controversy: Synod Stirs Again." *The Torch* (October 29, 1974).

Cayton, Andrew, Elisabeth Perry, Linda Reed, and Allan Winkler. "Americans on the Home Front." In *America: Pathways to the Present.* Upper Saddle River, NJ: Prentice Hall, 2005.

Christian News. "We Can No Longer Remain Silent, Say 91 Deaconesses, 41 Students." (November 11, 1974).

Christianson, Gerald, and David Crowner. *The Spirituality of the German Awakening: Texts by August Tholuck, Theodor Fliedner, Johann Hinrich Wichern, Friedrich von Bodelschwingh.* Mahwah, NJ: Paulist Press, 2003.

College of Presidents Files. Concordia Historical Institute, St. Louis, MO.

Commission on Theology and Church Relations, LCMS. *The Ministry: Offices, Procedures, and Nomenclature.* St. Louis: Concordia, 1981.

Concordia Deaconess Conference Archives. Held in trust by appointed CDC historian.

Concordia Deaconess Conference Collection. Concordia Historical Institute, St. Louis, MO.

Concordia Seminary, Board of Control. *Exodus from Concordia: A Report on the 1974 Walkout.* St. Louis: Concordia Seminary, 1977.

Concordia Theological Seminary: Evangelical Lutheran Synod of Missouri, Ohio and Other States, One Hundred and Third Year 1941–1942. St. Louis: Concordia, 1941.

Council of Presidents Collection. Concordia Historical Institute, St. Louis, MO.

Course Catalog for Valparaiso University College of Arts and Sciences. Archives, Valparaiso University Christopher Center, Valparaiso, IN. 1945–46; 1946–47; 1947–48; 1948–49; 1950–51.

Deaconess Hall Adds Dimensions to Your Deaconess Program, The Annual Meeting November 8, 1957 Holy Cross Church, Fort Wayne, Indiana. Mimeograph, no pagination.

"Deaconess Items." In *Proceedings Evangelical Lutheran Synodical Conference of North America.* Vol. 3. 1924–44. Translated by Jonathan C. Naumann.

Deaconess Office Archives, Concordia University, River Forest, IL.

Der Bote aus Bethesda 17, no. 4, no. 6 (July and November 1926).

————, "Historical Sketch of the Associated Lutheran Charities within the Synodical Conference." 17, no. 6 (November, 1926).

"Diaconissensache." Pages 189–90 in *Synodical Bericht, Ferhandlungern der Deutschen Evangelisch-Lutherishen Synode von Missouri, Ohio und anderen Staaten, versammelt als Driezehnte Delegatensynode* Anno Domini 1911 (St. Louis: Concordia, 1911). Translated by Otto A. Brillinger.

Diakonia of the Church in a New Age: A Colloquium to Celebrate 20 Years of Partnership between Valparaiso University and the Lutheran Deaconess Association in the Education of Deaconesses for The Lutheran Church—Missouri Synod. May 1–3, 1964, Wesemann Hall, Valparaiso University.

Dicke, Peter Heinrich, and Elanor Katherine Daib, trans. "Autobiography of Peter Heinrich Dicke: Pastor and Pioneer Missionary." *Concordia Historical Institute Quarterly* 78, no. 3 (Fall 2005).

Duemling, E. A. "Opening Address." In *Proceedings of the Twenty-ninth Annual Conference of the Associated Lutheran Charities.* Watertown: Jansky Printing Co., 1929.

Eggers, F. H. "Training of Practical Deaconesses." *Der Bote aus Bethesda* 17, no. 2 (1926).

Evangelical Lutheran Synod of Missouri, Ohio, and Other States. *Eingaben für die Achtzehnte Delegatensynode versammelt zu St. Louis, Mo., von 9. bis zum 18. Juni 1926.* St. Louis: Concordia, 1926.

————. *Proceedings of the Thirty-third Regular Convention of the Evangelical Lutheran Synod of Missouri, Ohio, and Other States, Assembled at Holy Cross Ev. Luth. Church, St. Louis, MO., June 9–18, 1926.* St. Louis: Concordia, 1926.

————. *Proceedings of the Thirty-fifth Regular Convention of the Evangelical Lutheran Synod of Missouri, Ohio, and Other States, Assembled at Milwaukee, Wisconsin June 15–24, 1932.* St. Louis: Concordia 1932.

————. *Proceedings of the Thirty-sixth Regular Convention of the Evangelical Lutheran Synod of Missouri, Ohio, and Other States, Assembled at Cleveland, Ohio June 19–28, 1935.* St. Louis: Concordia 1935.

————. *Proceedings of the Thirty-seventh Regular Convention of the Evangelical Lutheran Synod of Missouri, Ohio, and Other States, Assembled at St. Louis, Missouri June 15–24, 1938.* St. Louis: Concordia 1938.

————. *Proceedings of the Thirty-eighth Regular Convention of the Evangelical Lutheran Synod of Missouri, Ohio, and Other States, Assembled at Fort Wayne, Indiana June 18–27, 1941.* St. Louis: Concordia 1941.

Fort Wayne, Indiana: Lutheran Deaconess Association 1948–1960. Indiana LCMS District Archives, Fort Wayne, IN.

Fliedner, Theodore. *Journey of Emigrants to North America for the Emigration of Four Deaconesses and for the Establishment of a Deaconess Motherhouse in Pittsburgh in Pennsylvania, in June 1849/* Translated by Bertha Mueller.

For the Life of the World, "Deaconess Program Begins First Year." 7, no. 4 (October 2003).

Fritschel, Herman L. *A Story of One Hundred Years of Deaconess Service by The Institution of Protestant Deaconesses Pennsylvania, and the Lutheran Deaconess Motherhouse at Milwaukee, Wisconsin 1849 to 1949.* Milwaukee: Lutheran Deaconess Motherhouse, printed by North American Press, 1949.

The Forester, "Concordia Deaconess Conference Organized." 4, no. 4 (February 1980).

Gerberding, G. H. *The Life and Letters of W. A. Passavant, D.D.* Greenville, PA: Young Lutheran Co., 1906.

"God's Blessing with Us." In *Second Annual Report of the Lutheran Deaconess Association within the Ev. Luth. Synodical Conference of North America.* Fort Wayne, IN: Lutheran Deaconess Association, 1921.

Golder, C. *History of the Deaconess Movement in the Christian Church.* Cincinnati: Jennings & Pye, 1903.

Graebner, J. R. "Deaconesses." *The Lutheran Witness* 39, no. 15 (July 20, 1920).

Griffen, Dale E. "In memoriam: Deaconess Rose Ziemke." *Concordia Historical Institute Quarterly* 74, no. 4 (Winter 2001).

Groh, Shirley A. "The Role of Deaconess through the Ages." Fort Wayne: LDA, 1955.

Heimke, Annette. "New Deaconess Seminar Room Gift of Northern Illinois Women." *The Forester* (November 1983).

Heissenbuttel, Ernest G., and Roy H. Johnson. *Pittsburgh Synod History: Its Auxiliaries and Institutions 1845–1962.* Warren, OH: Pittsburgh Synod of the United Lutheran Church, 1963.

Herzberger, F. W. "Errichtung eines lutherischen Diaconissenheims." Pages 131–33 in *Eingaben fur die Delegatensynode 1911* zu St. Louis, Mo. St. Louis: Concordia, 1911. Translated by Otto A. Brillinger.

———. "The Lutheran Charities Association of the Synodical Conference." *The Lutheran Witness* 39, no. 15 (July 20, 1920).

Hibbs, David. "Crisis in the LCMS . . . the Situation." *The Torch* (February 18, 1975).

Holtman, Anna M. "Lutheran Nurses' League." In *Proceedings of the Twenty-fifth Annual Conference of the Associated Lutheran Charities, St. Louis, Mo. October 12–14, 1926.* Watertown: Jansky Printing Co., 1929.

Hot Springs Star 38, no. 50; 39, no. 1; 39, no. 8; 39, no. 23; 40, no. 15 (April 10, 1924; May 1, 1924; June 19, 1924; October 2, 1924; August 6, 1925).

Huegli, A. G. "The Church in the Great Society." *The Cresset* 28, no. 9 (September 1965).

Indiana LCMS District Archives, Fort Wayne, IN.

Kirsch, John Paul. "Deaconesses in the United States Since 1918: A Study of the Deaconess Work of the United Lutheran Church in America in Comparison with the Corresponding Programs of the Other Lutheran Churches and of the Evangelical and Reformed, Mennonite, Episcopal, and Methodist Churches." PhD thesis, New York University, 1961.

Kohlmeier, H. B. *1919–1944 25th Anniversary of the Lutheran Deaconess Association within the Synodical Conference.* Fort Wayne, IN: Nuoffer Print, 1944.

———. "New Developments in Deaconess Work." In *Proceedings of the Thirty-fifth Annual Conference of the Associated Lutheran Charities.* Watertown: Jansky Printing Co., 1935.

———. "Outlines of Course for the Deaconess School." In *Proceedings of the Thirty-fourth Annual Conference of the Associated Lutheran Charities.* Watertown: Jansky Printing Co., 1935.

———. "Requirements for a Parish Deaconess." In *Thirty-fourth Annual Convention Associated Lutheran Charities.* Watertown: Jansky Printing Co., 1935.

Korbitz. "Deaconess Work—Analyzed!" *American Lutheran* 14, no. 5 (May 1931): 16–17 (1,284–85).

Korby, Kenneth F. "A Litany for Deaconesses." *Nexus* (January 1961).

————. *Concordia Deaconess Conference 1998: Lectures by Rev. Dr. Kenneth Korby.* (1) *The Diaconate.* (2) *Loehe.* (3) *Prayer Life.* (4) *Devotional Life.* Contact CDC historian.

Krentz File. Concordia Historical Institute. St. Louis, MO.

Krentz File. Lutheran Deaconess Association Archives, Valparaiso, IN.

Krentz, Arnold F. "Deaconess Endeavors." *Lutheran Woman's Quarterly* (April 1945).

————. "Integration of the Lutheran Deaconess Movement with the Work of the Associated Charities." In *Fortieth Annual Convention Associated Lutheran Charities.* Watertown: Jansky Printing Co., 1941.

Krenz, Steven. "Bertram Outlines LCMS Issues." *The Torch* (April 11, 1975).

Kretzmann, O. P. "By the Way." *The Walther League Messenger* (September 1942 and April 1943).

Kretzmann, P. E. *A Handbook of Outlines for The Training of Lutheran Deaconesses.* St. Louis: Young Women's Lutheran Deaconess Association of St. Louis, Mo.

———— File. Concordia Historical Institute. St. Louis, MO.

————. "The Office of Deacon: I Timothy 3.8–13." *Popular Commentary: New Testament* 2. St. Louis: Concordia, 1922.

————. "Nurse, Deaconess, Social Worker." *Concordia Theological Monthly* 8, no. 12 (December 1937).

Lankenau, F. C. "Francis James Lankenau, D.D., A Biography." *Concordia Historical Institute Quarterly* 12, no. 3 (October 1939).

LCMS Bureau of Statistics. Personnel Records of Retired and Deceased

Leppien, Patsy A. and J. Kincaid Smith. *What's Going on Among the Lutherans?* Milwaukee: Northwestern, 1992.

Lindemann, Paul. "The Woman in the Church." *Theological Quarterly* 24 (January and April 1920).

Loehe, Wilhelm. *Wilhelm Loehe, Gessammelte Werke, Herausgegeben im Aufrage der Gesellschaft fur Innere un Ausere Mission im Sinne der lutherischen Kirche* Vol. IV. Edited by Klaus Ganzert. Translated by Holger Sonntag. Neuendettelsau: Freimund, 1954.

————. *Von der Barmherzigkeit.* 4th ed. Neuendettelsau: Buchhandlung der diakonissen=anstalt, 1927.

Lucking, F. Dean. *A Century of Caring: The Welfare Ministry Among Missouri Synod Lutherans 1868–1968.* St. Louis: LCMS Board of Social Ministry, 1968.

Lutheran Church—Missouri Synod, The. *Convention Workbook (Reports and Overtures) Forty-eighth Regular Convention, Denver, Colorado, July 11–18, 1969.* St. Louis: Concordia, 1969.

————. *Convention Workbook (Reports and Overtures) Forty-ninth Regular Convention, Milwaukee, Wisconsin, July 9–16, 1971.* St. Louis: Concordia, 1971.

————. *Convention Workbook (Reports and Overtures) Fifty-first Regular Convention, Anaheim, California, July 4–11, 1975.* St. Louis: Concordia, 1975.

————. *Convention Workbook (Reports and Overtures) Fifty-second Regular Convention, Dallas, Texas, July 15–22, 1977.* St. Louis: Concordia, 1977.

————. *Convention Workbook (Reports and Overtures) Fifty-third Regular Convention, St. Louis, Missouri, July 6–13, 1979.* St. Louis: Concordia, 1979.

———. *Convention Workbook (Reports and Overtures) Fifty-fourth Regular Convention, St. Louis, Missouri, July 3–10, 1981*. St. Louis: Concordia, 1981.

———. *Convention Workbook (Reports and Overtures) Fifty-fifth Regular Convention, St. Louis, Missouri, July 8–15, 1983*. St. Louis: Concordia 1983.

———. *Convention Workbook (Reports and Overtures) Fifty-sixth Regular Convention, Indianapolis, Indiana, July 18–25, 1986*. St. Louis: Concordia 1986.

———. *Convention Workbook (Reports and Overtures) Fifty-seventh Regular Convention, Wichita, Kansas, July 7–14, 1989*. St. Louis: Concordia 1989.

———. *Convention Workbook (Reports and Overtures) Sixty-first Regular Convention, St. Louis, Missouri, July 14–20, 2001*. St. Louis: Concordia 2001.

———. *Proceedings of the Forty-first Regular Convention of The Lutheran Church—Missouri Synod, Milwaukee, Wisconsin, June 21–30, 1950*. St. Louis: Concordia 1950.

———. *Proceedings of the Forty-second Regular Convention of The Lutheran Church—Missouri Synod, Houston, Texas, June 17–26, 1953*. St. Louis: Concordia 1953.

———. *Proceedings of the Forty-fifth Regular Convention of The Lutheran Church—Missouri Synod, Cleveland, Ohio, June 20–29, 1962*. St. Louis: Concordia, 1962.

———. *Proceedings of the Forty-eighth Regular Convention of The Lutheran Church—Missouri Synod, Denver, Colorado, July 11–18, 1969*. St. Louis: Concordia, 1969.

———. *Proceedings of the Forty-ninth Regular Convention of The Lutheran Church—Missouri Synod, Milwaukee, Wisconsin, July 9–16, 1971*. St. Louis: Concordia, 1971.

———. *Proceedings of the Fiftieth Regular Convention of The Lutheran Church—Missouri Synod, New Orleans, Louisiana, July 6–13, 1973*. St. Louis: Concordia, 1973.

———. *Proceedings of the Fifty-first Regular Convention of The Lutheran Church—Missouri Synod, Anaheim, California, July 4–11, 1975*. St. Louis: Concordia, 1975.

———. *Proceedings of the Fifty-second Regular Convention of The Lutheran Church—Missouri Synod, Dallas, Texas, July 15–22, 1977*. St. Louis: Concordia, 1977.

———. *Proceedings of the Fifty-third Regular Convention of The Lutheran Church—Missouri Synod, St. Louis, Missouri, July 6–12, 1979*. St. Louis: Concordia, 1979.

———. *Proceedings of the Fifty-fourth Regular Convention of The Lutheran Church—Missouri Synod, St. Louis, Missouri, July 3–10, 1981*. St. Louis: Concordia, 1981.

———. *Proceedings of the Fifty-fifth Regular Convention of The Lutheran Church—Missouri Synod, St. Louis, Missouri, July 8–15, 1983*. St. Louis: Concordia 1983.

———. *Proceedings of the Fifty-sixth Regular Convention of The Lutheran Church—Missouri Synod, Indianapolis, Indiana, July 18–25, 1986*. St. Louis: Concordia 1986.

———. *Proceedings of the Fifty-seventh Regular Convention of The Lutheran Church—Missouri Synod, Wichita, Kansas, July 7–14, 1989*. St. Louis: Concordia 1989.

———. *Proceedings of the Fifty-eighth Regular Convention of The Lutheran Church—Missouri Synod, Pittsburgh, PA, July 10–17, 1992*. St. Louis: Concordia 1992.

———. *Proceedings of the Sixty-first Regular Convention of The Lutheran Church—Missouri Synod, St. Louis, MO, July 14–20, 2001*. St. Louis: Concordia 2001.

———. *Proceedings of the Sixty-second Regular Convention of The Lutheran Church—Missouri Synod, St. Louis, MO, July 10–15, 2004*. St. Louis: Concordia 2004.

———. *Reports and Memorials, Forty-fourth Regular Convention, The Lutheran Church—Missouri Synod, Meeting as the Twenty-Ninth Delegate Synod, San Francisco, California, June 17–27, 1959*. St. Louis: Concordia, 1959.

———. *Reports and Memorials Forty-fifth Regular Convention The Lutheran Church—Missouri Synod, Cleveland, Ohio, June 20–30, 1962.* St. Louis: Concordia, 1962.

———. *Today's Business.* [Fifty-third Regular Convention of The Lutheran Church—Missouri Synod.] Sections A, B, and C. St. Louis: Concordia, 1979.

Lutheran Deaconess vols. 1–49 (1924–71).

Lutheran Deaconess Association Archives. Lutheran Deaconess Association, Valparaiso, IN.

Lutheran Deaconess Association Collection. Concordia Historical Institute, St. Louis, MO.

Lutheran Women's Missionary League Collection. Concordia Historical Institute, St. Louis, MO.

Der Lutheraner, "Wie sich ein Iowaisches Kirchenlicht uber das Diakonissenwesen anslagt." Translated by Arthur H. Baisch. 26, no. 5 (November 1, 1869): 35–36.

Maier, Gerhard. *The End of the Historical-Critical Method.* St. Louis: Concordia, 1974.

Maier, Walter A. *Form Criticism Reexamined.* Contemporary Theology Series. St. Louis, Concordia, 1973.

Marshall, Karen K. "Lutheran Missions: Advocates of People." *St. Louis Globe-Democrat* (September 21–22, 1974).

Mather, Edna "Right, Left Vie in Missouri Synod Debate." *The Torch* (November 5, 1974).

Mayer, Herbert T. "Editorial: The Task Ahead." *Concordia Theological Monthly* 40, no. 8 (September 1969).

Meyer, Carl S., ed. *Moving Frontiers: Readings in the History of The Lutheran Church—Missouri Synod, 1847–1962.* St. Louis: Concordia, 1964.

Meyer, Lawrence B. *Missouri in Motion.* New York: National Press, 1973.

Meyer, Ruth Fritz. *Women on a Mission: The Role of Women in the Church from Bible Times Up to and Including a History of The Lutheran Women's Missionary League during Its First Twenty-five Years.* St. Louis: Concordia, 1967.

"Mission School." In *The 1947 Vicar.* St. Louis: Concordia Seminary. In Concordia Seminary Library Archives.

Missouri in Perspective, "Deaconess Groups Establish Ties." (August 4, 1980).

———, "LCMS 'Begins' Deaconess Program." (July 20, 1979).

———. "We Can No Longer Remain Silent, Say 91 Deaconesses, 41 Students." (November 4, 1974).

Mueller, Herbert. "Deaconess Listing." *Reporter* 8, no. 11 (March 22, 1982).

Mulholland, Betty (nee Schmidt). Private collection. Munster, IN.

Naumann, Cheryl D. (nee Freitag). Private collection. Pittsburgh, PA.

Naumann, Wm. T. "Deaconess School at Watertown, Wis." *Der Bote aus Bethesda* 17, no. 6 (November 1926).

———. "Sermon Preached at the Installation of Lutheran Deaconesses at Watertown, Wis. May 5, 1929." *Der Bote aus Bethesda* 20, no. 3 (May 1929).

Nemoyer, Nancy (nee Nicol). Private collection. Carlisle, PA.

Neuhart, Norma D. *The Work of the Lutheran Church—Missouri Synod with People Who Are Mentally Retarded—Past, Present, and Future.* River Forest, IL: Concordia University, 2002.

1944 Bethany College Bulletin. Department of Archives and History, Evangelical Lutheran Synod, Mankato, MN.

"1919–1944 Silver Anniversary of Lutheran Deaconess Service within the Synodical Conference." Fort Wayne, IN: LDA, 1944.

Norpel, Mary Louise. "The Relevance of the Lutheran Deaconess Tradition in America for Post-Conciliar Religious Life Among Roman Catholic Women." Doctoral diss., Catholic University of America, Washington DC, 1971.

The Northern Light, "Concordia Reinstates Deaconess Program." 18, no. 3 (December 2003).

Nightingale, Florence. *The Institution of Kaiserswerth on the Rhine: For the Practical Training of Deaconesses, under the Direction of the Rev. Pastor Fliedner.* 2d ed. Düsseldorf-Kaiserswerth: Diakonissenanstalt, 1851.

Ohl, J. F. *The Inner Mission.* Philadelphia: United Lutheran Publication House, 1911.

Olson, Jeannine E. *One Ministry Many Roles: Deacons and Deaconesses through the Centuries.* St. Louis: Concordia, 1992.

Ostermann, Joyce Ann. Private collection. Fort Wayne, IN.

"Overture No. 5." In *Proceedings of the Fifty-fifth Convention of the Central District of the Evangelical Lutheran Synod of Missouri, Ohio and Other States Assembled at Fort Wayne, Ind., June 24–29, 1928.* St. Louis: Concordia, 1929.

Paulson, Krissé L. "Concordia University's Deaconess Program Celebrates 27 Years." *Forester Magazine* 1, no. 1 (2006).

Poch, B. "Report of Deaconess Association." In *Proceedings of the Twenty-eighth Annual Conference of the Associated Lutheran Charities, Watertown, Wisc. Sept. 17–19, 1929.* Watertown: Jansky Printing Co., 1929.

President's Commission on Women, the LCMS. "God's Woman for All Generations." St. Louis: LCMS Board for Communication Services, 1988.

Proceedings of the Fortieth Convention, South Wisconsin District, The Lutheran Church—Missouri Synod June 21–24, 1976, Concordia College, Milwaukee, Wisconsin. Milwaukee: Kremer Enterprises, 1976.

Proceedings of the Sixty-eighth Convention of The Lutheran Church—Missouri Synod Eastern District, Camp Pioneer, Angola New York, June 27–July 1, 1949.

Proceedings Twenty-fifth Convention and Fortieth Anniversary Iowa District West, The Lutheran Church—Missouri Synod, Lake Okoboji, Iowa, June 20–24, 1976. N.P.

"Programs of Study," and "Courses of Instruction." *Concordia Junior College Bronxville, New York, Announcements for 1956–57.*

Prokopy, Paul G, and Erwin Umbach, eds. *Convention Year-Book of the Thirty-Fifth International Convention of the Walther League.* St. Louis: Concordia, 1927.

Randt, Beata. "The Joy of Deaconess Work." *American Lutheran* 9, no. 3 (March 1926).

Red Wing Daily Republican (June 22, 1910).

"Report of the Executive Board." In *Thirty-sixth Annual Convention Associated Lutheran Charities.* Watertown: Jansky Printing Co., 1937.

Reporter, "Concordia Deaconesses to Study Women's Roles." 6, no. 36 (September 15, 1980).

———, "Deaconesses Hear Nafzger on Ministry." 8, no. 8 (March 1, 1982).

———, "LDA Concerned, Vows to Continue Despite Synod Deaconess Program." (November 26, 1979).

———, "River Forest Regents Reinstate Deaconess-Training Program." (November 2003).

———, "Synod Board Receives Proposal for Deaconess Training Program." (November 26, 1979).

Rodenbeck, Clara. "Our Missions." *The Lutheran Witness* 51 (March 15, 1932).

St. John's College Academic Information, "The Pre-Deaconess Program." 33, no. 8 (June–July 1955).

Saint Paulus Evangelische Lutherische Kirche UAC, Hammond, Indiana 1882–1907. 25th anniversary book published by congregation. Translated by Betty Mulholland.

See His Banner Forward Go. St. Louis: Concordia, 1947.

The Seminarian, "Campus Women Are Interesting, Active." 38, no. 8 (March 12, 1947).

Sieck, Louis J. "Attitude Lutherans Should Take Towards Woman's Suffrage." *Lutheran Witness* 38, nos. 10–12 (May 13, 1919; May 27, 1919; June 10, 1919).

Simon, Henry E. "A Galatians 2:20 Missionary." In *One Cup of Water.* St. Louis: LWML, 1996.

St. Paul's Evangelical Lutheran Church Records. Vol. 1, 1846–49; Vol. 1–2, 1849–53; Vol. 12, 1837–56, #9. St. Paul's Evangelical Lutheran Church, 1126 S. Barr St., Fort Wayne, IN.

Stallmann, Ruth (nee Broermann). Private collection. St. Louis, MO.

Stiemke, Frederick Adolf. *A History of the Ministry of the Lutheran Church—Missouri Synod with People Who Have Mental Retardation.* Edited by Thomas Heuer and Timothy Dittloff, Watertown: National Christian Resource Center, Bethesda Lutheran Homes and Services, Inc., 1997.

Strehlow, Clara. Papers. Deaconess Office Archives. Concordia University, River Forest, IL.

Suelflow, August R., ed. *Heritage in Motion: Readings in the History of The Lutheran Church—Missouri Synod, 1962–1995.* St. Louis: Concordia, 1998.

Taege. Marlys, *Why Are They So Happy? The Story of Bethesda Lutheran Homes and Services, Inc.* Watertown, WI: Bethesda Lutheran Homes and Services, Inc., 1996.

Tesch, Helen (nee Haase). Private collection. Coon Rapids, MN.

Thirty-sixth Annual Convention Associated Lutheran Charities. Watertown: Jansky Printing Co., 1937.

"This, That, and the Other Thing. No. 3." In *Second Annual Report of the Lutheran Deaconess Association within the Evangelical Lutheran Synodical Conference of North America.* Fort Wayne, IN: Lutheran Deaconess Association, 1921.

The Torch, "Board Reaffirms VU's Position Concerning the LCMS Tensions" (February 18, 1975).

———. "In Response to the Dismissal of President John Tietjen." (February 18, 1975).

"3D: A Decade of Deaconess Dedication, 1980–1990." Mimeographed pages bound in folder. River Forest, IL, 1990.

"Tuesday, September 17th." In *Proceedings of the Twenty-eighth Annual Conference of the Associated Lutheran Charities, Watertown, Wisc. Sept. 17–19, 1929.* Watertown: Jansky Printing Co., 1929.

U.S. News & World Report, "Violence Hits Schools, Colleges." (May 20, 1968).

Valparaiso University Collection. Concordia Historical Institute, St. Louis, MO.

Walther, C. F. W. *Walther Speaks to the Church, Selected Letters.* Edited by Carl. S. Meyer. St. Louis: Concordia, 1973.

———. "Dr. Walther's First Presidential Address." Translated by Paul F. Koehneke. *Concordia Historical Institute Quarterly* 33, no. 1 (April 1960).

———. *The Proper Form of an Evangelical Lutheran Congregation Independent of the State.* Translated by Th. Engelder. St. Louis: Concordia, 1938.

Walther League File. Concordia Historical Institute, St. Louis, MO.

Wambsganss, Elizabeth Hess. "Autobiographical Notes." Translated by Fred Wambsganss. *Concordia Historical Institute Quarterly* 28, no. 1 (Spring 1955).

Wambsganss, Fred Sr. "Five Decades of Pastoral Activity." *Concordia Historical Institute Quarterly* 30, no. 4 (Winter 1958): 145–53.

Wambsganss, Philipp [Jr.]. "An Appeal for Deaconesses." *Der Bote aus Bethesda* 14, no. 4 (July 1923).

———. "Lutherische Diaconissen-Gesellschaft." Translated by Jonathan C. Naumann. *Evangelisch-Lutherisches Gemeinde-Blatt* (December 7, 1919): 389–90.

Wassilak, Kristin. "Presentation to Floor Committee 6—HIGHER EDUCATION, Subject: Deaconess Colloquy; Resolution 6–31, 6–32; *Workbook* pages 277–78 and the resolution from the Concordia University Faculty." May 30, 1992. Colloquy 1991–94 File. Concordia University Archives, Concordia University, River Forest, IL.

Weiser, Frederick S. *Love's Response: A Story of Lutheran Deaconesses in America.* Introduction by F. Eppling Reinartz. Philadelphia: Board of Publication of the United Lutheran Church in America, 1962.

———. "Serving Love: Chapters in the Early History of the Diaconate in American Lutheranism." Bachelor's thesis, Lutheran Theological Seminary, Gettysburg, PA., 1960.

———. comp. *Pioneers of God's Future: A Directory of Deaconesses of the Evangelical Lutheran Church in America Who Have Served in the United States and Canada 1848–1991.* Gladwyne, PA: Lutheran Deaconess Community, 1991.

———. "Study of the Lutheran Deaconess Association Made for the Board of Directors The Lutheran Church—Missouri Synod and its Board for Higher Education," June 29, 1968, Box: Board for Professional Education Services Box 5: Deaconess Materials and BHE Materials, 111.1.0.09 Supp X, CHI, St. Louis. [Dawn, I would like to include this one as it is so pivotal to one of the chapters.]

———. *To Serve the Lord and His People: Celebrating the Heritage of a Century of Lutheran Deaconesses in America 1884–1984.* Introduction by Sister Frieda Gatzke. Gladwyne, PA: Deaconess Community of the Lutheran Church in America, 1984.

Zimmerman, Gloria. Private collection. Seattle, WA.

Zimmerman, Paul A. "The Deaconess Program—An Expansion of Concordia's Mission." *The Forester* 4, no. 1 (September 1979).

SECONDARY SOURCES

Affeldt, Don A. "Comment on Current Issues: Amen to Women's Liberation." *Cresset* 35, no. 3 (January 1972).

Affirm, "To Expand Deaconess Program." Convention Issue, no. 1 (July 7, 1979).

Anderson, Laura. "From the Editor's Mail Bag." *Missouri in Perspective* (October 8, 1979).

"Application to the LCMS Deaconess Colloquy." River Forest, IL: Concordia College, 1981.

Bertermann, Eugene R. "Report on 'Building for Christ.' " *The Lutheran Witness* 75, no. 14 (July 3, 1956).

Bielby, Sara M. "How Does the Deaconess Serve?" *For the Life of the World* 7, no. 4 (October 2004).

Block, Rudolph C., and Nancy E. Nemoyer. "Deaconesses: Ministries Among Us." *The Lutheran Witness* (December, 1988).

Bussert, Jackie. "Deaconesses Welcome Change in Synodical Classification." *The Northern Light* 4, no. 8 (April 1990).

Caring, "Deaconess Ministry: Helping Children with Disabilities." (Fall 2005).

———, "Deaconess Ministry: White House Officials Join Seminary for 'Historic Moment.' " (Spring 2004).

———, "Highlighting Diakonia Partnership Opportunities." (Spring 2004).

———, "One-on-One with a Human Care Leader: Instilling Every Student with a Caring Heart." (Winter 2006).

Clark, Stephen B. *Man and Woman in Christ: An Examination of the Roles of Men and Women in Light of Scripture and the Social Sciences*. Ann Arbor: Servant Books, 1980.

"Concordia College, River Forest, Illinois: Concordia Deaconess Program." River Forest, IL: Concordia College Office of Admissions, 1985–86.

Cottam, Joe. "Deaconess Explains New River Forest Program at Convocation Hour." *Called to Serve* (Spring 1983).

"Deaconess." River Forest, IL: Concordia Office of Undergraduate Admissions, 1996.

"Deaconess? What's That?" River Forest, IL: Concordia College Admissions Office, 1981.

Deaconess: A Newsletter for Deaconess Studies of Concordia Seminary, St. Louis, Missouri..

"The Deaconess Clara Strehlow Endowment Fund." River Forest, IL: Concordia College, 1986.

"Deaconess Ministry: Concordia University." River Forest, IL: Concordia University, 1998–99.

"Deaconess Service in the Lutheran Church—Missouri Synod." Fort Wayne: Concordia Deaconess Conference, 1980.

Deaconess Task Force Minutes. Sept. 25, 2002; Jan. 22, 2003; May 7, 2003; Aug. 4, 2003; Jan. 20, 2004; Jan. 18, 2005. St. Louis: LCMS World Relief and Human Care.

Faculty Handbook. River Forest, IL: Concordia University, 2000.

Focus, "160 Received Vicarage/Deaconess Assignments." 23, no. 4 (Summer 2006).

———, "248 Calls and Vicarages Issued." 21, no. 4 (Summer 2004).

———, "269 Calls and Vicarages Issued, 12 Deaconess Assignments Celebrated." 22, no. 4 (Summer 2005).

———, "Practical Service as a Deaconess Intern." 23, no. 3 (Spring 2006).

———, "Seminary's Deaconess Program Approved." 20, no. 1 (Fall 2002).

For the Life of the World, "Concordia Deaconess Conference Meets at CTS." 7, no. 3 (July 2003).

———, "CTS Deaconess Program Continues with Outstanding Growth." 9, no. 1 (January 2005).

———, "CTS Deaconess Program . . . Reaching Out with His Care." 8, no. 1 (January 2004).

———, "Deaconesses Participate in Mid-Winter Retreat." 9, no. 2 (April 2005).

———, "First Deaconesses Placed for Service." 10, no. 3 (July 2006).

———, "Internships April 26, 2005." 9, no. 3 (July 2005).

———, "Vicars, Deaconesses, Candidates Receive Assignments During April Services." 9, no. 3 (July 2005).

————, "2005 Marks 160th Academic Year" (photo of deaconess students with program director). 9, no. 4 (October 2005).

————, "Seminary Announces Calls, Vicarages, Deaconess Internships, and Deaconess Placements." 10, no. 3 (July 2006).

Forester, "Deaconess Director Announces First Synodical Intern Placement." 7, no. 1 (September 1981).

Gehres, Karen. "Sayler: From Student to Teacher." *The Torch* (October 25, 1974).

Gilbert, Rose. "Friends of Phoebe: The Deaconess as Missionary." *The Servant* 12, no. 3 (Trinity 2005).

"God's Woman For All Generations: A Report of the President's Commission on Women." St. Louis: LCMS Board for Communication Services, 1987.

Harrison, Matthew. "We Need Deaconesses." *Reporter* (August, 2003).

Hartman, T. H. "A Deaconess Learns How to Serve the Church." *AAL Correspondent* (Spring 1958).

Hein, Steven A. " 'A Scrutiny' Scrutinized." *The Cresset* 36, no. 3 (January 1973).

Hierseman, Judy. "Deaconess Secure in Her Faith, Work." Religion Section, *Green Bay Press-Gazette* (Nov. 1, 1980).

Impson, Beth. *Called to Womanhood*. Wheaton, IL: Crossway Books, 2001.

Janzow, Walter Theophil. "Secularization in an Orthodox Denomination." PhD diss., University of Nebraska, 1970.

Jepsen, Bee. *Women Beyond Equal Rights*. Waco, TX: Word Books, 1984.

Keller, Walter E. "A Scrutiny of a Statement on Scripture." *The Cresset* 35, no. 8 (June 1972).

Kersten, Phyllis. "Deaconesses: Consecrated as Servants." *The Lutheran Witness* 102, no. 5 (May 1983).

Kilbane, Kevin. "True Calling: Deaconess Program Gives Women Opportunity to Help." *The News-Sentinel* (February 13, 2004).

Krentz, Arnold F. "Deaconess Services." *The Lutheran Witness* 68, no. 15 (July 26, 1949).

————. "What Does a Deaconess Do?" *The Lutheran Witness* 76, no. 12 (July 4, 1957).

O.P. Kretzmann, "Campus Commentary," March 1974, File: Kretzmann, Box: JAO Preus II Box 5, CHI, St. Louis.

O.P. Kretzmann, "Our Greater War—'Sin and Grace,' 'Good and Evil,' 'Time and Eternity': Three addresses delivered at the meeting of the District Chairmen of Valparaiso University," August 24–26, 1943. Kretzmann, O.P. "The Idea of a University." *The Christian Scholar* 44, no. 4 (Winter 1961).

Krull, Kim Plummer "In God's 'Secret Service.' " *The Lutheran Witness* 121, no. 1 (January 2002).

Liefeld, Walter, and Ruth A. Tucker. *Daughters of the Church: Women and Ministry from New Testament Times to the Present*. Grand Rapids: Zondervan, 1987.

Long, Ralph H., ed. *The Lutheran World Almanac and Encyclopedia 1934–37*. Vol. 8. New York: National Lutheran Council, 1937.

Lutheran Witness, "Fort Wayne Deaconess Called to River Forest." 49, No. 9 (September 1980).

————, "Northern Indiana Deaconesses Share at Annual Conference." 49, no. 9 (September 1980).

Marquart, Kurt E. *Anatomy of an Explosion: Missouri in Lutheran Perspective.* Edited by David P. Scaer and Douglas Judisch. Fort Wayne, IN: Concordia Theological Seminary Press, 1977.

Missouri in Perspective, "Deaconess Board Retains Education Program at Valparaiso University." (December 3, 1979).

———, "Deaconess Education." (July 2, 1979).

Naumann, Cheryl D. "85 Years of Deaconess History: Starting in Fort Wayne." *For the Life of the World* 8, no. 2 (April 2004).

Newsweek, "A New Lutheran Spirit." (July 24, 1967).

———, "Old-Time Religion." (July 28, 1969).

Nicol, Nancy E. "For She Has Been a Helper of Many: Deaconess Program, Concordia College, River Forest, Illinois." River Forest, IL: Concordia Deaconess Conference, 1980–81.

———. "A Synopsis of Deaconess History." *Lutheran Woman's Quarterly* 44, , o. 3 (Summer 1986).

———. "The Deaconess Internship." River Forest, IL: Concordia College, 1982.

Preloger, Bob. "New Deaconess Program Outlined." *The Forester* 4, no. 2 (December 1979).

President's Files. Concordia University, River Forest, IL.

Preus, J. A. O. *A Statement of Scriptural and Confessional Principles.* St. Louis: Concordia, 19xx.

———. "With One Voice." St. Louis: LCMS Commission on Constitutional Matters, 1974.

Rast, Lawrence R. Jr. "Head-On Collision." *The Lutheran Witness* 116, no. 5 (May 1977).

Reardon, Bev, and Becky McGrew. "What Is a Deaconess? Paths of Faith; Fields of Service." *The Lutheran Witness* (April 16, 1963).

"Report of the Commission on the Comprehensive Study of the Doctrine of the Ministry and A Position Paper on The Role of Women in the Life of the Church for presentation to the Fifth Biennial Convention of the Lutheran Church in America, Minneapolis Minnesota, June 25–July 1, 1970." Board of Publication, Lutheran Church in America.

Reporter, "Council places almost 800 grads." 6, no. 16 (April 28, 1980).

———, "Deaconess Conference Celebrates Its Fifth Anniversary in Synod." 11, no. 40 (October 21, 1985).

———, "Deaconesses Form Group: Stress Ministry in Synod." 6, no. 2 (January 21, 1980).

———, "Deaconesses Adopt First Code of Ethics." (July 2005).

———, "Deaconess Program Authorized for Concordia, River Forest." 5, no. 27 (July 11, 1979).

———, "Deaconess Supply Is Largest in History." (February 21, 1977).

———, "Delegates Open Membership to Deaconesses." (August 14, 1989).

———, "First Deaconess Class Will Graduate in May." 9, no. 9 (March 7, 1983).

———, "Handle Anxiety by Calling on God Speaker Tells Deaconess Conference." 8, no. 40 (October 11, 1982).

———, "Mennicke Chairs—Lay Ministry Committee Begins Work." 14, no. 4 (February 1, 1988).

———, "New Jersey District Convention Re-elects Sandmann President." 14, no. 19 (May 23, 1988).

————, "New Synodical Deaconess Program Opens at Concordia, River Forest." 6, no. 38 (September 29, 1980).

————, "Nicol Becomes Director of Deaconess Program at Concordia, River Forest." 6, no. 26 (July 7, 1980).

————, "RF Board Put Moratorium on Deaconess Admissions." (June 2003).

————, "River Forest Regents Reinstate Deaconess-Training Program." (November 2003).

Schroeder, Annette. "Compassionate Ministry." *The Lutheran Witness* 116, no. 5 (May 1997).

Schultz, Robert C. "Reflections on the Current Controversy in The Lutheran Church—Missouri Synod: An Attempt to Express Pastoral Concern." *The Cresset* 35, no. 10 (October 1972).

The Servant, "Friends of Phoebe: Deaconesses in the Lutheran Church?" 11, no. 3 (Lent 2004).

————, "Friends of Phoebe: Serving as a Deaconess." 12, no. 1 (Church Militant 2004).

————, "Friends of Phoebe: Why a Deaconess?" 12, no. 2 (Lent 2005).

Simon, Henry E. "The Legacy of Gertrude Simon." *Lutheran Woman's Quarterly* (Spring 1980).

Spectator, "Phoebe's Memoirs—A Deaconess Student's Story." 65, no. 18 (April 18, 1986).

"10 Minutes with a Deaconess: A Candid Interview Reveals the Struggles, the Joys, and the Opportunities for Services That Are Part of the Job Description of a Deaconess." St. Louis: LCMS Office of Higher Education, 2001.

Tietjen, John H. *Memoirs in Exile: Confessional Hope and Institutional Conflict.* Minneapolis: Fortress, 1990.

Time, "Lutherans: A Move Toward Unity." (August 1, 1969).

Van Natta, Tim. "The Role and Function of the Deaconess in the Lutheran Church—Missouri Synod." Master's thesis, Concordia Theological Seminary, Fort Wayne, IN, 1978.

Wassilak, Kristin. "Complementing Offices: Pastor and Deaconess." *The Servant* 8, no. 4 (Easter 2001).

Wassilak, Kristin. Private collection. Forest Park, IL.

————. "Today's Deaconesses." *For the Life of the World* 8, no. 3 (July 2004).

Weiser, Frederick S. "The Origins of Lutheran Deaconesses in America." *Lutheran Quarterly* 8, no. 4 (1999).

Wiedenkeller, Judy. "Reaching Out in Guatemala City." *Lutheran Woman's Quarterly* 63, no. 3 (Fall 2005).

Williams, Louise. "Deaconesses Share in Education Ministry." *LEA News* 10, no. 1 (March 1977).

Zimmerman, Paul A. *Seminary in Crisis: The Inside Story of the Preus Fact Finding Committee.* St. Louis: Concordia, 2006.

INDEX

Pflieger, Elmer, 285, 376fn
Pfotenhauer, Johann Friedrich, 22, 33, 93, 157
Phillips, Jennifer, 457
Phoebe (Phebe), vii, 23, 32, 44, 81, 179-80, 180fn, 197, 200, 240, 242, 327fn, 487, 521, 568, 574
Phoebe Award, 454, 458
Pi Delta Chi, 196-198, 196fn, 232, 265, 337-38, 421
Pingel, Louis M., 54-55, 54fn, 120, 129, 254
Pittsburgh, Pennsylvania, 5-9, 12, 169, 241-42, 494
Poch, Bruno, 40, 43, 48-49, 53, 57-58, 67, 73, 81, 93-97, 104-9, 105fn, 112fn, 113-14, 117, 159-60, 229, 231, 521
Pohl, Merlin S., 412, 414, 429, 429fn
Pre-deaconess training, 118, 143, 181-86, 252, 265, 267-68, 271, 351, 363-64, 377, 395-96, 420, 432, 474, 512-13
President's Commission on Women, 481-82, 553
Preus II, Jacob Aall Otteson, 332, 335, 348-49, 353-55, 358, 385, 399-407, 414-15, 417, 560-64
Preus, Robert David, 505-6

R

Rao, Grace, 501, 514fn, 566-67, 578
Rast Jr., Lawrence R., 470
Rehwinkel, Alfred Martin, 143
Reitmeier, Angie, 455, 466-67
Resolution 3-09 – Re St. Louis Seminary Faculty (1973), 349, 352fn
Resolution 3-11 – To Declare Deaconesses Eligible for Synodical Membership (1989), 489-91
Resolution 5-06B – To Provide Deaconess Training at Seminary Level (2001), 507-8
Resolution 5-09A – To Classify Ministers of Religion (1983), 483-85
Resolution 5-24 – To "Grandfather" Certified Lay Workers (1986), 488-89
Resolution 6-05 – To Expand Deaconess Program (1979), 398-409
Resolution 6-16 – To Revise By-laws re Deaconess Programs (1981), 482-83

Resolution 35 – Deaconess Training Program (1959), 186-91
Resume of the Documentation, 373-74, 543-45; *see also Documentation*
Rinehard, Roy, 473fn
Rittmueller, Adolph, 287, 289, 376fn, 531
Romans 16:1-2, vii, 23, 32, 44, 79, 81, 180fn, 239, 240, 242, 255, 379, 487, 568, 574
Ruhland, Frederick, 16

S

Sauer, Robert Charles, 486
Sayler, Gwendolyn, 355, 360, 363
Scherer, Charles W., 29
Schlechte, August, 16
Schnabel, Robert Victor, 268-69, 269fn, 279fn, 357fn, 404-6
Schmidt, Otto Henry, 160, 213-16
Schmoe, Louis, 29, 30fn
Schmucker, Samuel, 7
Scholarships, 168-71, 184, 222, 226, 228, 243, 252, 256, 264, 266, 325, 453
Schroeder, Edward, 273, 317-18, 318fn
Schultz, Robert C., 353
Schwehn, Hartwig, 285, 289, 293, 531
Schweppe, William H., 213
Seminex, 245fn, 350-52, 355, 356fn, 364, 378, 378fn, 391, 411-12, 414, 417, 423, 426, 431, 540
Servanthood, 81-86, 237, 237fn, 242, 492; servant heart, 502; attitude, 570
Severson, William C., 180
Sihler, Wilhelm, 8-11
Sisterhood, 14, 122, 124, 197, 244, 299, 303, 320fn, 343, 363, 381, 393, 431, 437-38, 443, 467, 479
Smith, Linda, 455
Sponland, Ingeborg, 110, 247
St. John's College, Winfield, Kansas, 182-83, 270-71, 402
St. Paul's, Concordia, Missouri, 270
St. Paul's Lutheran Church, Fort Wayne, IN, 8-10, 27, 105, 112, 155, 162fn, 171, 550; St. Paul's School, 164
St. Paul's Lutheran Church, Hammond (Munster), IN, 17fn, 381, 382fn, 466, 470, 551

Printed in the United States
215896BV00003B/1/P

9 780758 608314